S0-AFO-097

Henry D. Thoreau

Dylan Thomas.

Countee Cullen

D.H. Lawrence

Charles Dickens

Jonathan Swift

Daniel DeFoe

G. Bernard Shaw

Phillis Wheatley

Stephen Crane

Langston

Langston Hughes

Bret Harte

Henry W. Longfellow

oscar wilde

Thornton Wilder

Edgar A Poe

Ernest Hemingway

J. Austen

Sinclair Lewis

Herman Melville

R Lee

Ivan Turgenev

A Bradstreet

T. S. Eliot

Jack London

Thomas Hardy

MACMILLAN LITERATURE SERIES

SIGNATURE EDITION

DISCOVERING LITERATURE

INTRODUCING LITERATURE

ENJOYING LITERATURE

UNDERSTANDING LITERATURE

APPRECIATING LITERATURE

AMERICAN LITERATURE

ENGLISH LITERATURE
WITH WORLD MASTERPIECES

WORLD LITERATURE

FRONT COVER, detail, and BACK COVER: *On the Trail,* 1892, watercolor over graphite, Winslow Homer, American (1836–1910).
National Gallery of Art, Washington, D.C. Gift of Ruth K. Henschel in memory of her husband, Charles R. Henschel.

GENERAL ADVISERS

READING AND INSTRUCTIONAL METHODS
Jack Cassidy
Professor of Education
Millersville University
Millersville, Pennsylvania

TEACHER'S PROFESSIONAL RESOURCES
Robert DiYanni
Professor of English
Pace University
Pleasantville, New York

CONSULTANTS

Stanlee Brimberg, Teacher, Bank Street School for Children, New York, New York

Mary Sue Douglass, Teacher, Fort King Middle School, Ocala, Florida

Katherine Duncan, Teacher, Franklin Middle School, Long Beach, California

Beverly Ellenport, Reading Supervisor, Deerfield School, Mountainside, New Jersey

Ann Ferrell, Middle School Reading-Language Arts Consultant, Fulton County, Georgia

Emily Flores, English Department Chair, Coke Stevenson Middle School, San Antonio, Texas

Charlotte Geyer, Coordinator Secondary Language Arts, Seminole County, Florida

Maureen Griffith, Teacher, Hampton Middle School, Allison Park, Pennsylvania

Nancy Guy, Teacher, West Hartsville Elementary School, Hartsville, South Carolina

Barbara Langer, Teacher, Circle Christian School, Orlando, Florida

Terry Leister, Language Arts Curriculum Director, Northshore School District, Bothell, Washington

Anita Moss, Professor of English and Editor of *Children's Literature in Education*, Department of English, University of North Carolina at Charlotte, Charlotte, North Carolina

Barbara Nellis, Teacher, Greenhills High School, Cincinnati, Ohio

Shirley Nichols, Secondary Supervisor of Language Arts and Reading, Marion County Schools, Ocala, Florida

Robert S. Ranta, Supervisor of English, The Public Schools of Edison Township, Edison, New Jersey

Jerry Reynolds, Implementation Associate, Rochester Public Schools, Rochester, Minnesota

Marie Rogers, Teacher, Independence High School, Matthews, North Carolina

Mary B. Sigmon, Teacher, Windsor Park Elementary School, Charlotte, North Carolina

Tina Wilson, Teacher, First Ward Elementary School, Charlotte, North Carolina

ART CONSULTANT
Jeffrey Rian

WRITERS
Camillo Cimis
Judith Farer
Nancy Ford
Jan C. Kraus
Lois Markham
Karen McAuley
David Pence, Jr.
Annemarie Sbaschnig
Duncan Searl
Diane Tacsa
Abigail Winograd

MACMILLAN LITERATURE SERIES

DISCOVERING LITERATURE

SIGNATURE EDITION

GLENCOE/McGRAW-HILL
A Macmillan/McGraw-Hill Company
Mission Hills, California

Copyright © 1991 by Glencoe/McGraw-Hill Educational Division.

All rights reserved. Printed in the United States of America. Except as permitted under the United States Copyright Act of 1976, no part of this publication may be reproduced or distributed in any form or by any means, or stored in a database or retrieval system, without prior permission of the publisher.

ACKNOWLEDGMENTS

Grateful acknowledgment is given authors, publishers, and agents for permission to reprint the following copyrighted material. Every effort has been made to determine copyright owners. In the case of any omissions, the Publisher will be pleased to make suitable acknowledgments in future editions.

Arizona Quarterly
FRANCISCO JIMÉNEZ: "The Circuit" from *The Arizona Quarterly*, Autumn 1973. Copyright by Arizona Board of Regents. Reprinted by permission of *The Arizona Quarterly* and the author.

Arte Público Press
PAT MORA: "Mi Madre" from *Chants*. Copyright © 1985 by Pat Mora.
GARY SOTO: "The Jacket" from *Small Faces*. Copyright © 1986 by Gary Soto. Both are reprinted by permission of Arte Público Press.

Isaac Asimov
ISAAC ASIMOV: "Sarah Tops" was first published under the title "Try Sarah Tops" in *Boy's Life*. Copyright © 1975 by Boy Scouts of America. Reprinted by permission of the author.

Astor-Honor, Inc.
CHINUA ACHEBE: "Why the Tortoise's Shell Is Not Smooth" from *Things Fall Apart*. Copyright © 1959. Reprinted by permission of Astor-Honor, Inc.

Brandt & Brandt Literary Agents, Inc.
JOAN AIKEN: "Lob's Girl" from *A Whisper in the Night*. © 1981, 1982, 1983, 1984 by Joan Aiken Enterprises, Ltd. Reprinted by permission of Brandt & Brandt Literary Agents, Inc.

Curtis Brown, Ltd.
ANTONIA FRASER: "A Narrow Escape" from *Robin Hood*. Copyright © 1971 by Antonia Fraser.
MAXINE KUMIN: "The Microscope" first published in *The Atlantic Monthly*. Copyright © 1963 by Maxine Kumin. Both are reprinted by permission of Curtis Brown, Ltd.

Send all inquiries to:
Glencoe/McGraw-Hill
15319 Chatsworth Street
P.O. Box 9509
Mission Hills, CA 91395-9509

Pupil's Edition ISBN 0-02-635031-9
Teacher's Annotated Edition ISBN 0-02-635032-7

1 2 3 4 5 6 7 8 9 97 96 95 94 93 92 91

Joseph Bruchac
JOSEPH BRUCHAC: "Birdfoot's Grampa" from *Entering Onondaga*. Copyright © 1975 by Joseph Bruchac. Reprinted by permission of the author.

Cambridge University Press
HOTTENTOT: "Song for the Sun that Disappeared Behind the Rainclouds" from *African Poetry*, edited by Ulli Beier. Reprinted by permission of Cambridge University Press.

Don Congdon Associates, Inc.
RAY BRADBURY: "The Flying Machine" from *The Golden Apples of the Sun*. Copyright © 1953, © renewed 1981 by Ray Bradbury. Reprinted by permission of Don Congdon Associates, Inc.

Dell Publishing Company
JOAN AIKEN: "Lob's Girl" from *A Whisper in the Night*. Copyright © 1981, 1982, 1983, 1984 by Joan Aiken Enterprises, Ltd.
GLORIA GONZÁLEZ: "The Boy with Yellow Eyes" from *Visions: Nineteen Short Stories by Outstanding Writers for Young Adults* edited by Donald R. Gallo. This story is copyright © 1987 by Gloria González. Both are reprinted by permission of Dell Publishing, a division of Bantam, Doubleday, Dell Publishing Group, Inc.

Doubleday & Company, Inc.
CHARLES FINGER: Excerpt from *Tales from Silver Lands*. Copyright 1924 by Doubleday, a division of Bantam, Doubleday, Dell Publishing Group, Inc.
DON MARQUIS: Excerpt from *Archy and Mehitabel*. Copyright 1927 by Doubleday, a division of Bantam, Doubleday, Dell Publishing Group, Inc.
THEODORE ROETHKE: "The Bat" copyright 1938 by Theodore Roethke. From *The Collected Poems of Theodore Roethke*.
NANCY WOOD: "Who Will Teach Me?" from *Many Winters*. Copyright © 1974 by Nancy Wood. All are reprinted by permission of Doubleday, a division of Bantam, Doubleday, Dell Publishing Group, Inc.

Dutton Children's Books
JEAN GEORGE: *My Side of the Mountain*. Copyright © 1959 by Jean George, renewed 1987 by Jean George. Reprinted by permission of the publisher, Dutton Children's Books, a division of Penguin Books, USA Inc.

Faber and Faber Ltd.
T. S. ELIOT: "Macavity: The Mystery Cat" from *Old Possum's Book of Practical Cats*. Reprinted by permission of Faber and Faber Ltd.

continued on page 651

CONTENTS

Mystery!

Literature that intrigues and delights—tales of mystery, problem solving, and imagination

Preview   1

Other Lands, Other Worlds

Literature that explores a variety of life experiences over a wide range of settings around and beyond our planet

Myths, Tales, and Fabulous Beasts

Literature that tells tales grown from the oral
traditions of many different countries

Heroes and Survivors

Literature of adventure, courage,
struggle, and victory

Disasters
Great and Small

Literature that tells the stories of both
natural and personal catastrophies

Preview   324

Science and Storytellers

Literature that focuses on the excitement
of scientific endeavor and discovery

Passages

Literature that highlights critical
moments of learning and growth

The Novel

Literature that combines all the elements of fiction to explore a variety of themes and carry the reader on a full-scale adventure

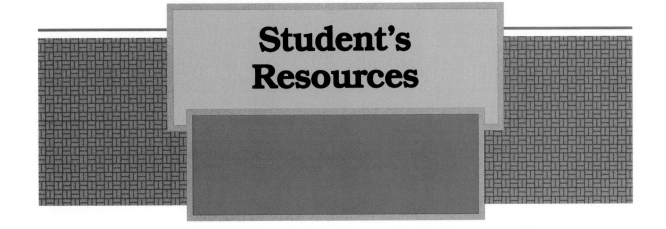

Student's Resources

Preview

Y ou know what a mystery is.

A mystery is a secret.

A mystery is a shadow on the wall—or in someone's eyes.

A mystery is a story that begins, "It was a dark and stormy night. . . ."

A mystery is anything that is secret or hidden or unknown. A mystery can be as bizarre as a visit from a ghost or as commonplace as the sound in a seashell. Some mysteries are puzzles waiting to be solved by keen-eyed detectives. Other mysteries lie hidden in objects you touch every day.

The literature that follows explores many different mysteries—each with a great or small secret at its heart. Within each mystery something waits to be discovered. What discoveries will *you* make as you read?

Starry Night, Vincent van Gogh, c. 1889.

A Model for Active Reading

As you read anything, you think about it. You wonder. You ask yourself questions, and you come up with some answers. You put both your feelings and your mind into what you read. When you do this, you are an active reader.

Here is an example of the kinds of reactions a reader can have to the beginning of a story. The comments show some of the thoughts that went through one reader's mind while reading the story for the first time.

On the following pages you will find the entire story. Make a point of thinking and reading actively as you enjoy the story. What ideas and questions occur to you as you read?

Isaac Asimov

Sarah Tops

> I guess this story is about a girl or woman named Sarah.

I came out of the Museum of Natural History[1] and was crossing the street on my way to the subway when I saw the crowd about halfway down the block; and the police cars, too. I could hear the whine of an ambulance.

> Sounds like there's been an accident.

For a minute, I hesitated, but then I walked on. The crowds of the curious just get in the way of officials trying to save lives. My Dad, who's a detective on the force, complains about that all the time.

> Who is telling the story?

I just kept my mind on the term paper I was going to have to write on air pollution for my 8th-grade class and mentally arranged the notes I had taken during the museum program on the subject.

> So the person telling the story is in eighth grade.

Of course, I knew I would read about it in the afternoon papers. Besides, I would ask Dad about it after dinner. He sometimes talked about cases without telling too much of the real security details.

> What is "it"? The accident, I suppose.

After I asked, Mom looked kind of funny and said, "He was in the museum at the very time."

> The person telling the story is a boy.

> What happened "at the very time"? an accident or a crime? Is this a mystery?

photograph ©1990 Jill Krementz

When he was three years old, Isaac Asimov (born 1920) came to the United States from Russia with his parents. At seven he was already teaching his younger sister how to read. He soon began reading the science-fiction magazines in his father's candy store. He has been busy reading and writing ever since. Asimov writes a book every six weeks on average. He has published over four hundred works—more than any other author in America. "It's not my fault," he says. "I like to write and people seem willing to let me."

I saw the crowd about halfway down the block; and the police cars, too. I could hear the whine of an ambulance.

Isaac Asimov

Sarah Tops

I came out of the Museum of Natural History[1] and was crossing the street on my way to the subway when I saw the crowd about halfway down the block; and the police cars, too. I could hear the whine of an ambulance.

For a minute, I hesitated, but then I walked on. The crowds of the curious just get in the way of officials trying to save lives. My Dad, who's a detective on the force, complains about that all the time.

I just kept my mind on the term paper I was going to have to write on air pollution for my 8th-grade class and mentally arranged the notes I had taken during the museum program on the subject.

Of course, I knew I would read about it in the afternoon papers. Besides, I would

ask Dad about it after dinner. He sometimes talked about cases without telling too much of the real security details.

After I asked, Mom looked kind of funny and said, "He was in the museum at the very time."

I said, "I was working on my term paper. I was there first thing in the morning."

Mom looked very worried. "There might have been shooting in the museum."

"Well, there wasn't," said Dad soothingly. "This man tried to lose himself in there and he didn't succeed."

"I would have," I said. "I know the museum, every inch."

Dad doesn't like me bragging, so he frowned a little and said, "They didn't let him get away entirely—caught up with him outside, knifed him, and got away. We'll catch them, though. We know who they are."

He nodded his head. "They're what's left of the gang that broke into that jewelry

---

1. **Museum of Natural History:** New York City museum housing one of the world's largest collections of natural science exhibits.

New York with Moon, Georgia O'Keeffe, 1925.

store two weeks ago. We managed to get the jewels back, but we didn't grab all the men. And not all the jewels either. One diamond was left. A big one—worth $30,000."

"Maybe that's what the killers were after," I said.

"Very likely. The dead man was probably trying to cross the other two and get away with that one stone for himself. They turned out his pockets, practically ripped off his clothes, after they knifed him."

"Did they get the diamond?" I asked.

"How can we tell? The woman who reported the killing came on him when he was just barely alive. She said he said three words to her, very slowly, 'Try—Sarah—Tops.' Then he died."

"Who is Sarah Tops?" asked Mom.

Dad shrugged. "I don't know. I don't even know if that's really what he said. The woman was pretty hysterical. If she's right and that's what he said then maybe the killers didn't get the diamond. Maybe the dead man left it with Sarah Tops, whoever she is. Maybe he knew he was dying and wanted to have it off his conscience."

"Is there a Sarah Tops in the phone book, Dad?" I asked.

Dad said, "Did you think we didn't look? No Sarah Tops, either one P or two P's. Nothing in the city directory. Nothing in our files. Nothing in the FBI files."

Mom said, "Maybe it's not a person. Maybe it's a firm. Sarah Tops Cakes or something."

"Could be," said Dad. "There's no Sarah Tops firm, but there are other kinds of Tops companies and they'll be checked for anyone working there named Sarah."

I got an idea suddenly and bubbled over. "Listen, Dad, maybe it isn't a firm either. Maybe it's a *thing*. Maybe the woman didn't hear 'Sarah Tops' but 'Sarah's top'; you know, a *top* that you spin. If the dead guy has a daughter named Sarah, maybe he gouged a bit out of her top and stashed the diamond inside and—"

Dad grinned. "Very good, Larry," he said. "But he doesn't have a daughter named Sarah. Or any relative by that name as far as we know. We've searched where he lived and there's nothing reported there that can be called a top."

"Well," I said, sort of let down and

disappointed, "I suppose that's not such a good idea anyway, because why should he say we ought to *try* it? He either hid it in Sarah's top or he didn't. He would know which. Why should he say we should *try* it?"

And then it hit me. What if—

I said, "Dad, can you get into the museum this late?"

"On police business? Sure."

"Dad," I said, kind of breathless, "I think we better go look. *Now.* Before the people start coming in again."

"Why?"

"I've got a silly idea. I—I—"

Dad didn't push me. He likes me to have my own ideas. He thinks maybe I'll be a detective too, someday. He said, "All right. Let's follow up your lead."

We got there just when the last purple bit of twilight was turning to black. We were let in by a guard.

I'd never been in the museum when it was dark. It looked like a huge, underground cave, with the guard's flashlight seeming to make things even darker and more mysterious.

We took the elevator up to the fourth floor, where the big shapes loomed in the bit of light that shone this way and that as the guard moved his flash. "Do you want me to put on the light in this room?" he asked.

"Yes, please," I said.

There they all were. Some in glass cases, but the big ones in the middle of the large room. Bones and teeth and spines of giants that ruled the earth, millions of years ago. I said, "I want to look close at that one. Is it all right if I climb over the railing?"

"Go ahead," said the guard. He helped me.

I leaned against the platform, looking at the grayish plaster material the skeleton was standing on.

"What's this?" I said. It didn't look much different in color from the plaster.

"Chewing gum," said the guard, frowning. "Those darn kids—"

"The guy was trying to get away and he saw his chance to throw this—hide it from the gang—"

Dad took the gum from me, squeezed it, and then pulled it apart. Inside, something caught the light and flashed. Dad put it in an envelope and said to me, "How did you know?"

I said, "Well, look at it."

It was a magnificent skeleton. It had a large skull with bone stretching back over the neck vertebrae.[2] It had two horns over the eyes, and a third one, just a bump, on the snout. The nameplate said: Triceratops.[3]

---

2. **vertebrae** [vur′tə brē′]: the small bones that make up the backbone.
3. **Triceratops** [trī ser′ə tops′]: plant-eating North American dinosaur with three horns, a snout, and a bony shield on the neck.

READER'S RESPONSE

When did *you* guess the solution to the mystery?

STUDY QUESTIONS

Recalling

1. What does Larry's father do for a living?
2. According to Larry's father, what happened outside the museum?
3. What does the woman who reported the killing say that she heard?
4. Describe the first two suggestions that Larry makes for solving the mystery.
5. Larry has a "silly idea." Where does he lead his father, and what do they find there?

Interpreting

6. Who or what is Sarah Tops?
7. Think about the various suggestions Larry makes to his father. What qualities that would be valuable in a detective does Larry show?

Extending

8. Is it more fun to guess the solution to a mystery before the end than it is to be surprised by the ending? Explain.

READING AND LITERARY FOCUS

The Short Story

A **short story** is a fictional account of events written in prose. Usually each event in a story leads logically to the next event. A character may face a problem, and the problem may grow more complicated as the story goes on. Then it is settled in some way before the story's end.

Think about a story that you already know—for example, *Alice's Adventures in Wonderland*. Alice becomes curious about a mysterious white rabbit. Her situation grows more complicated when she falls down a rabbit hole into the topsy-turvy world of Wonderland and cannot find her way home. Finally her problem is solved when she wakes up and realizes that she has been dreaming all along.

The events of a story usually occur in a particular time and place. The time and place may change as the story goes on. For example, *Alice's Adventures in Wonderland* begins on a lazy summer afternoon in England. The action moves to the bizarre world of Wonderland and then back to England. All the action takes place within a few hours, for Alice wakes up in time to have her afternoon tea.

Often authors create stories to illustrate their ideas about life. The author of *Alice's Adventures in Wonderland* wanted to express the idea that things are not always what they seem to be. Alice finds herself in a world that keeps changing—much as the scenes in a dream keep shifting.

Thinking About the Short Story

1. Who is the main character in "Sarah Tops," and what difficulty does this character face?
2. What does this character do to solve the problem by the end of the story?

VOCABULARY

Synonyms

A **synonym** is a word that has the same or nearly the same meaning as another word. *Run* and *dash* are synonyms. The italicized words below are from "Sarah Tops." Choose the word that is *nearest* the meaning of each *italicized* word, *as the word is used in the story*. Write the number of each item and the letter of your choice on a separate sheet.

1. *security* guards
   - (a) strong
   - (b) royal
   - (c) silent
   - (d) protective

2. spoke *soothingly*
   - (a) comfortingly
   - (b) intelligently
   - (c) lengthily
   - (d) briefly

3. the *hysterical* child
   - (a) immature
   - (b) injured
   - (c) frantic
   - (d) stubborn

4. an uneasy *conscience*
   - (a) awakening
   - (b) speaking ability
   - (c) moral sense
   - (d) situation

Gloria Gonzalez (born 1940) has been a newspaper reporter, television writer, novelist, short story writer, and playwright. Since turning her television play *Gaucho* into a novel, Gonzalez has devoted herself full time to writing for the theater because, as she says, "I require the excitement and challenge of an instant reaction from a friendly or hostile audience."

If Norman was slow motion, Willie was definitely fast forward. Which brings us to the stranger, who fit somewhere in between.

• •

Gloria Gonzalez

The Boy with Yellow Eyes

Only a handful of the residents of Preston Heights[1] recall the actual events. And even then, years and conflicting accounts have clouded the facts.

Still, in some quarters, and especially during the relentless winters unique to the hillside village, the incident is spoken of with pride and awe.

Till today, if you get a couple of old-timers in the same room, a heated debate will erupt over the mundane detail of whether Norman was ten or going on thirteen. They'll also argue whether he lost one shoe or both in the scuffle.

What the parties do agree on is that it happened in Preston Heights and it involved Norman and his next-door neighbor Willie, whose age for some reason is never questioned—thirteen.

And of course . . . the stranger.

Opinions are equally divided on whether the stranger's limp was caused by a deformed right or left leg. But everyone, to a man, can tell you exactly what the Vice President of the United States was wearing when he arrived and what he ordered for lunch. (In fact, his discarded gingham cloth napkin, since laundered, is part of the local exhibit, which includes his signature in the hotel's register.)

The only other point of total agreement is that Norman was the least likely of heroes. He had none of the qualities that could have foretold his sudden fame.

Norman was not the kind of kid who would cause you to break out in a grin if you saw him ride your way on a bike.

1. He couldn't ride a bike.
2. He rarely emerged from his house.
3. He was considered . . . well . . . weird.

This last opinion was based on the fact that Norman would only be seen heading toward or leaving the library, and always

---

1. **Preston Heights:** town near Chicago, Illinois.

hugging an armful of books. To the town-folk it seemed unhealthy for a young boy to read so much. They predicted a total loss of eyesight by the time he reached nineteen.

Willie, however, was a kid who, had there been a Normal Kid Pageant, would have won first and tied for second and third. A dynamic baseball player, daring bike rider, crackerjack newspaper delivery boy—he was the town's delight. Never mind that he was flunking all school subjects and had a reputation as a bully, he was, after all, "a real boy."

The differences did not escape the boys themselves. Though neighbors, separated only by splintery bushes, they never as much as shared a "Hi."

To Willie, Norman was simply the kid with the yellow eyes. Not that they were actually yellow—more of a brown-hazel—but often, the way the sunlight bounced off the thick eyeglasses, it seemed to create a yellow haze.

(Years later, in a rare interview, Norman was asked if he had missed having friends while growing up. He replied: "Not at all. I had Huck and Tom Sawyer."[2])

To Norman, Willie was exhausting. He talked fast, ran fast, walked fast, and, he suspected, even slept fast. (If such a thing could be measured.) It was tiring just to sit behind him in class and listen to his endless chatter.

If Norman was slow motion, Willie was definitely fast forward. Which brings us to the stranger, who fit somewhere in between.

Some say the stranger arrived one early summer day on foot. Others believe he came on the bus from Boulder.[3]

One fact is undisputed: he took a room on the second floor of McCory's hotel. Not that he had much of a choice; it was the only lodging in town. The hotel dated back to the construction of the first railroad. It had been hastily thrown together to house the army of laborers that would lay the train tracks. Unfortunately, the hilly terrain stymied the work force and the project was eventually abandoned, leaving behind three passenger and two freight cars.

George McCory, the town's undertaker, purchased the hotel and soon found he could make more money by housing the living.

The hotel parlor soon became the common milling ground. Here you could always get into a game of checkers, buy stamps, mail a letter, or receive news of neighboring towns via the traveling salesmen.

That's why when the stranger first arrived, his presence went almost unnoticed. It was only after he was still visible over a period of weeks that others became aware of him. A tall, muscular man in his thirties with a ready smile, he made a favorable impression. Maybe it was the limp. Many attributed it to the war then raging in Europe.[4] Too polite to inquire, the hotel regulars silently accepted his "wound."

Since the man was never seen during the day and rarely till after supper, his comings and goings drew much speculation. Local gossip had it that he was an artist

---

2. **Huck and Tom Sawyer:** Huck Finn, young hero of Mark Twain's novel *The Adventures of Huckleberry Finn* (1884), and Tom Sawyer, Huck's friend and the hero of Twain's *Adventures of Tom Sawyer* (1876).

3. **Boulder** [bōl′dər]: city in north-central Colorado, near Denver.
4. **attributed** [ə trib′ūt id] **. . . Europe:** thought the stranger was wounded fighting in World War II, an international conflict lasting from 1939 to 1945.

who'd come to Preston Heights to paint the unusual terrain. This theory was fueled by the sight of the man always carrying a dark satchel. Some held that the man was famous.

Perhaps that legend would have endured except for three insignificant, unrelated events:

1. The library decided to paint its reading room.

2. Willie's baseball coach had a tooth pulled.

3. The stranger overslept.

On the day of the "incident," Norman headed, as usual, to the library. Mrs. Brenner, the librarian, met him at the entrance and explained that due to the cleanup work the library was temporarily closed.

The thought of studying in his stuffy bedroom (no air could circulate because of all the books he ordered from Chicago and New York publishers) sent him instead to the railroad yards.

The discarded railroad cars—which had been painted a zippy burgundy when new—now bore the scars of merciless winters and oppressive summers. Vandalism and neglect had added to the toll. For too many years, kids had deemed it their own amusement park. In recent time, the decaying cars had even been abandoned by the vandals. Rumor had it that rats and raccoons openly roamed the burgundy cars.

Norman knew it wasn't true. At least once a month, when the weather was nice, he would head for the rail yard, lugging his books, to settle comfortably in a cushioned seat in car #7215, his head pressed against the wooden window frame (now paneless). When the day's shadow hit the bottom of the page, he knew to close the book and head home.

On this day, the high position of the sun assured him of at least four uninterrupted hours of reading.

Across town, in the school yard, Willie stood with friends swinging his baseball bat at air. He looked forward to practice almost as much as to the games. That's why when the coach appeared to say he had to cancel due to an impacted tooth, the teenager found himself at a loss as to what to do.

It was too early to start his newspaper money collection. Knowing it was best to strike when families were seated for dinner, he wandered aimlessly toward the rail yards with a mind to picking up some chunky rocks and using them as balls to swat about the empty field.

And so it was that he found himself in the proximity of car #7215.

The unusually warm weather had its effect on the stranger who now dozed in the freight car, an iron link away from #7215. The heat had caused him to discard his usual caution in return for a slight breeze. He had lifted the huge steel doors that slid upward, affording him a welcome breeze from the quiet countryside. The cool air had lulled his senses, stretching his customary nap long past its normal half hour.

Perhaps it was his two months of success, his feeling of invincibility, or his unconscious desire for danger that caused him to be careless this day. In any event, when he awoke, he did not bother to lower the steel door.

He opened his black satchel and removed the network of tubes, cylinders, wires, bolts, and antennas, which he expertly positioned in a matter of minutes. It was by now an automatic labor. His mind refreshed by sleep, he thought ahead to the coming week when he would be safely aboard the steamer that would carry him across the ocean. The lightness of his touch, as he twisted the spidery wires, reflected his carefree attitude.

Norman's first reaction was to ignore Willie's sudden entrance.

"You see my ball go by here?"

Norman didn't even look up from the book he was reading. "No."

"Not exactly a ball, more like a rock," Willie said, sitting on the armrest of a seat, with his legs blocking the aisle.

"No," Norman answered.

Normally, Willie would have stalked out, but it was cooler inside the car, and most appealing of all, Norman looked so relaxed and comfortable that he felt compelled to ruin it.

"What are you doing, anyway?"

"Reading."

"I figured that. That's all you ever do. Aren't you afraid you're going to lose your eyesight?"

Norman's lack of response did not still Willie.

"I think reading is dumb."

"I think hitting a rock with a stick is dumb."

"Oh, yeah? You ever try it?"

"No. You ever try reading?"

"When the teacher makes me. I'd rather hit a rock. It's fun."

"So is reading."

Willie didn't buy it. "When I hit a ball, I'm *doing* something. Reading is not doing."

Norman removed his glasses and closely regarded Willie with his full attention.

"Do you know what I was *doing* when you barged in here? I was running through a haunted castle being chased by a vampire who was very, very thirsty. If that isn't 'doing,' I don't know what is."

This led to Norman's explaining the plot of Bram Stoker's *Dracula*.[5] Willie, totally engrossed, sat on the floor listening to the tale of horror.

Norman was telling him about Renfield[6]—and his daily diet of spiders and insects—when a distant clicking sound averted his attention.

"Probably a woodpecker," Willie said, urging the other boy to get back to the story.

Norman stretched his neck closer to the sound.

"If it is, it's the smartest woodpecker in history," Norman said, straining to hear.

Something in Norman's expression caused Willie to whisper, "What are you talking about?"

Norman swiftly signaled him to be quiet and silently crept toward the source of the tapping.

Willie, suddenly frightened for reasons he could not explain, followed closely. "What is it?" he asked, gripping his baseball bat.

The tapping was louder now.

"It's coming from the freight car." Norman dropped to the floor, his body hunched against the steel door separating them from the other car. Willie fell alongside him. "What is it?" he half pleaded.

Norman took a pencil from his pocket and began scribbling furiously on the margins of the library book. Willie noticed that he wrote with the rhythm of the clicking sound. Whenever the tapping stopped for a moment, so did Norman's pencil.

Willie glanced at the jottings, but it was difficult to make out the words. He did make out one short phrase. "End is near."

---

5. **Bram Stoker's *Dracula*:** British author's horror novel (published in 1897) about the vampire Count Dracula.
6. **Renfield:** character in *Dracula*.

Freight Cars, Gloucester, Edward Hopper, 1928.

Norman and the clicking stopped at the same time.

"What does it mean?" Willie whispered, his fear growing. He had known fear once before, when a stray dog, foaming at the mouth, had cornered him behind the general store. But this was worse. Here the threat was unknown.

Norman quickly stashed the book under a seat and jumped to his feet. "We have to stop him!" he told Willie.

"Who?"

"The spy," Norman said as he slid open the heavy door and dashed outside.

A startled Willie sat frozen.

The bright sun slammed Norman in the face as he jumped from the train car and rolled underneath the freight compartment. He was silently happy to see Willie join him seconds later.

"What are we doing?" Willie asked, frightened of the answer.

"Waiting."

"For what?" he whispered.

"Him," Norman said, pointing to the underbelly of the rusted car.

Before Willie could reply, the stranger jumped from above their heads, clutching his dark suitcase. They watched as his limping form started to move away.

Norman sprung from under the car, raced after the man, and—to Willie's horror—tackled him from behind. The satchel went flying in the surprise attack.

"Grab it! Grab it!" Norman screamed.

The stranger clawed the ground and struggled to his feet, fighting like a wild man. His eyes were ablaze with hate. His arms, hands, and feet spun like a deranged windmill. His actions were swift but Norman was quicker. Try as he might to grab the boy, the man kept slashing at the air. He managed to clutch the boy's foot, but Norman quickly wiggled out of his shoe. The man grabbed him by his pants leg and pulled him to the ground.

"Do something!" Norman screamed at Willie, who stood paralyzed with fear. The man was now crouched over the boy's body and was gripping his neck.

Willie, seeing Norman's legs thrash helplessly in the air, swung his baseball bat with all his strength and caught the stranger—low and inside.

"About time," Norman coughed, massaging his throbbing neck.

Hours later, sitting in the hotel lobby with the chief of police, the boys watched wearily as swarms of people dashed up and down the stairs. They knew the man's room was being torn apart.

In the hotel kitchen the stranger was surrounded by FBI agents who had been summoned from the state capital, seventy-eight miles away. More were en route[7] from Washington, D.C.

By nightfall the hotel was completely isolated from the public and everyone heard of how Willie and Norman had caught themselves a real-life Nazi[8] spy.

It took weeks for the full story to emerge, and even then the citizens felt that the whole story would never be revealed. (Norman's *Dracula* book, for instance, had been whisked away by agents.) What was learned was that the man had been transmitting information to a colleague in Boulder. That man had managed to slip away and was now believed to be back in Berlin.[9] Two of the strangers' conspirators[10] in New York— one a woman—were arrested and being held in a federal prison outside of Virginia.

Three months later, in a highly publicized visit, the Vice President of the United States came to Preston Heights to thank the boys personally. Film crews shot footage[11] of the unlikely trio that would be shown in movie theaters throughout the country; Preston Heights would never be the same.

The cameras were there when Norman was asked how he had been able to understand the Morse code.[12] "I learned it from a book," he said.

Asked how he had been able to overpower the man, Willie grinned. "Easy. I'm batting .409 on the school team."

---

7. **en route** [än root']: on the way.

8. **Nazi** [nät'sē]: member or follower of the party that controlled Germany under the leadership of Adolf Hitler from 1933 to 1945.
9. **Berlin** [bər lin']: capital of Germany during World War II.
10. **conspirators** [kən spir'ə tərz]: group of two or more persons who secretly plan to perform an evil or criminal act.
11. **footage** [foot'ij]: material contained on motion-picture film, measured in feet.
12. **Morse code:** system of tapped signals invented by Samuel F. B. Morse (1791–1872), in which combinations of dots and dashes, or short and long sounds, are used to send messages.

Larimer Avenue Bridge, John Kane, 1932.

Preston Heights blossomed under the glare of national attention. Tourists visiting the state made it a point to spend the night at McCory's hotel and gawk at the corner table in the dining room where the Vice President ate lunch with the boys and their parents.

Willie did not go on to become a major league slugger. Instead, he left Preston Heights to join the navy and rose to the rank of chief petty officer upon retirement.

Norman attended Georgetown University and went on to serve as press secretary for a New Jersey senator.

Every Christmas they exchange cards and a list of books each has read during the previous year.

Norman is still ahead of Willie, two to one.

READER'S RESPONSE

Whom would you rather have as a friend, Norman or Willie? Why?

STUDY QUESTIONS

Recalling

1. What contrasting descriptions of Norman and Willie are given? List three for each boy.
2. What three "insignificant, unrelated events" lead to the "incident" that reveals the truth about the stranger?
3. When the boys are arguing in the railroad car, what is Norman's response to Willie's comment that "Reading is not doing"?
4. Describe the steps Norman and Willie take to capture the stranger.
5. How does Norman know what the stranger has been doing?

Interpreting

6. Why do Norman and Willie make a good team?
7. What does Willie learn about the value of reading?
8. We read that "Norman was the least likely of heroes." What truly heroic qualities does he show in this story?

Extending

9. Like this story, many works focus on the contrast between mental and physical abilities. What story, movie, or television show focuses on this subject? How does it turn out?

READING AND LITERARY FOCUS

Plot

The **plot** is the sequence of events in a story. Most plots hinge on a **conflict**, or a problem of some kind. For example, in the film *E. T.* a boy named Elliott finds a creature from outer space. Elliott's conflict, or problem, is the care and protection of his new friend, E. T.

In any good plot one event leads to another; for instance, the story of Elliott and E. T. grows more complicated. More people learn about E. T., who becomes ill and must return to his home.

Events in a plot gradually build up to a **climax**, the point of highest interest in the story. At that point we know how the story will end—how the conflicts will be worked out. The climax of *E. T.* occurs when Elliott and his friends rescue E. T. and return him to his spaceship. Then we know that E. T. will return home safely.

Thinking About Plot

1. What is the conflict between Norman and Willy? Between the boys and the stranger?
2. What is the climax of the story?

COMPOSITION

Writing About Plot

Write a short essay about the plot of "The Boy with Yellow Eyes." **Prewriting:** Make a chart in which you list the main conflicts and events and identify the climax of the story. **Writing:** First present the main conflicts in the story. Then pick from your prewriting chart the three or four most important events in the plot. Explain how these events are related to each other, and show how they lead to the story's climax. Then tell why this event is the peak of interest for the reader. End by explaining how the climax works out the various conflicts in the story. **Revising:** Review your essay to see that you have expressed your ideas clearly and logically. *For help with this assignment, see Lesson 1 in the Writing About Literature Handbook at the back of this book.*

Writing a Story

Imagine that Norman and Willy form a detective team. Write a story about another mystery that the boys solve together. Begin by briefly describing each boy in your own words. Make sure that the events of your plot are related to one another. You might create a situation in which Norman again uses his brains and Willy again uses his physical strength to solve the mystery. *For help with this assignment, see Lesson 4 in the Writing About Literature Handbook at the back of this book.*

Roald Dahl (born 1916) has been called a "master of horror," for his stories often focus on the bizarre. Dahl started out as a businessman but was sidetracked into writing. "Scribbling some notes" for a famous writer about his own experiences in World War II, Dahl found that he had written a short story. He went on to write a number of popular children's books, including *James and the Giant Peach* and *Charlie and the Chocolate Factory* (the basis for the film *Willy Wonka and the Chocolate Factory*). After his first few batches of fiction, he says, "the stories became less and less realistic and more fantastic. But becoming a writer was pure fluke."

'We have it *all* to ourselves, she said. . . . You see, it isn't very often I have the pleasure of taking a visitor into my little nest."

• •

Roald Dahl

The Landlady

Billy Weaver had traveled down from London on the slow afternoon train, with a change at Reading on the way, and by the time he got to Bath[1] it was about nine o'clock in the evening and the moon was coming up out of a clear starry sky over the houses opposite the station entrance. But the air was deadly cold and the wind was like a flat blade of ice on his cheeks.

"Excuse me," he said, "but is there a fairly cheap hotel not too far away from here?"

"Try The Bell and Dragon," the porter answered, pointing down the road. "They might take you in. It's about a quarter of a mile along on the other side."

Billy thanked him and picked up his suitcase and set out to walk the quarter-mile to The Bell and Dragon. He had never been to Bath before. He didn't know anyone who lived there. But Mr. Greenslade at the Head Office in London had told him it was a splendid town. "Find your own lodgings," he had said, "and then go along and report to the branch manager as soon as you've got yourself settled."

Billy was seventeen years old. He was wearing a new navy-blue overcoat, a new brown trilby hat,[2] and a new brown suit, and he was feeling fine. He walked briskly down the street. He was trying to do everything briskly these days. Briskness, he had decided, was *the* one common characteristic of all successful businessmen. The big shots up

---

1. **Bath:** a historic city in southwestern England.

2. **trilby hat:** a soft felt hat.

at Head Office were absolutely fantastically brisk all the time. They were amazing.

There were no shops on this wide street that he was walking along, only a line of tall houses on each side, all of them identical. They had porches and pillars and four or five steps going up to their front doors, and it was obvious that once upon a time they had been very swanky residences. But now, even in the darkness, he could see that the paint was peeling from the woodwork on their doors and windows, and that the handsome white façades[3] were cracked and blotchy from neglect.

Suddenly, in a downstairs window that was brilliantly illuminated by a street-lamp not six yards away, Billy caught sight of a printed notice propped up against the glass in one of the upper panels. It said BED AND BREAKFAST.[4] There was a vase of yellow chrysanthemums, tall and beautiful, standing just underneath the notice.

He stopped walking. He moved a bit closer. Green curtains (some sort of velvety material) were hanging down on either side of the window. The chrysanthemums looked wonderful beside them. He went right up and peered through the glass into the room, and the first thing he saw was a bright fire burning in the hearth. On the carpet in front of the fire, a pretty little dachshund[5] was curled up asleep with its nose tucked into its belly. The room itself, so far as he could see in the half-darkness, was filled with pleasant furniture. There was a baby-grand piano and a big sofa and several plump armchairs; and in one corner he spotted a large parrot in a cage. Animals were usually a good sign in a place like this, Billy told himself; and all in all, it looked to him as though it would be a pretty decent house to stay in. Certainly it would be more comfortable than The Bell and Dragon.

On the other hand, a pub[6] would be more congenial than a boardinghouse. There would be beer and darts in the evenings, and lots of people to talk to, and it would probably be a good bit cheaper, too. He had stayed a couple of nights in a pub once before and he had liked it. He had never stayed in any boardinghouses, and, to be perfectly honest, he was a tiny bit frightened of them. The name itself conjured up images of watery cabbage, rapacious[7] landladies, and a powerful smell of kippers[8] in the living-room.

After dithering about like this in the cold for two or three minutes, Billy decided that he would walk on and take a look at The Bell and Dragon before making up his mind. He turned to go.

And now a queer thing happened to him. He was in the act of stepping back and turning away from the window when all at once his eye was caught and held in the most peculiar manner by the small notice that was there. BED AND BREAKFAST, it said. BED AND BREAKFAST, BED AND BREAKFAST, BED AND BREAKFAST. Each word was like a large black eye staring at him through the glass, holding him, compelling him, forcing him to stay where he was and not to walk away from that house, and the next thing he knew, he was actually moving across

---

3. **façades** [fə sädz′]: the fronts of buildings.
4. **BED AND BREAKFAST:** boardinghouse offering breakfast and rooms for rent.
5. **dachshund** [däks′hoont′]: German breed of dog with a long body and short legs.

6. **pub:** tavern or inn.
7. **rapacious** [rə pā′shəs]: greedy; living on live prey.
8. **kippers:** salted and smoked fish, such as herring or salmon, often eaten for breakfast in Great Britain.

Hampstead, John Atkinson Grimshaw, 1881.

from the window to the front door of the house, climbing the steps that led up to it, and reaching for the bell.

He pressed the bell. Far away in a back room he heard it ringing, and then *at once*—it must have been at once because he hadn't even had time to take his finger from the bell-button—the door swung open and a woman was standing there.

Normally you ring the bell and you have at least a half-minute's wait before the door opens. But this dame was like a jack-in-the-box. He pressed the bell—and out she popped! It made him jump.

She was about forty-five or fifty years old, and the moment she saw him, she gave him a warm welcoming smile.

"*Please* come in," she said pleasantly.

She stepped aside, holding the door wide open, and Billy found himself automatically starting forward. The compulsion or, more accurately, the desire to follow after her into that house was extraordinarily strong.

"I saw the notice in the window," he said, holding himself back.

"Yes, I know."

"I was wondering about a room."

"It's *all* ready for you, my dear," she said. She had a round pink face and very gentle blue eyes.

"I was on my way to The Bell and Dragon," Billy told her. "But the notice in your window just happened to catch my eye."

"My dear boy," she said, "why don't you come in out of the cold?"

"How much do you charge?"

"Five and sixpence[9] a night, including breakfast."

It was fantastically cheap. It was less than half of what he had been willing to pay.

"If that is too much," she added, "then perhaps I can reduce it just a tiny bit. Do you desire an egg for breakfast? Eggs are expensive at the moment. It would be sixpence less without the egg."

"Five and sixpence is fine," he answered. "I should like very much to stay here."

"I knew you would. Do come in."

She seemed terribly nice. She looked exactly like the mother of one's best school-friend welcoming one into the house to stay for the Christmas holidays. Billy took off his hat, and stepped over the threshold.

"Just hang it there," she said, "and let me help you with your coat."

There were no other hats or coats in the hall. There were no umbrellas, no walking-sticks—nothing.

"We have it *all* to ourselves," she said, smiling at him over her shoulder as she led the way upstairs. "You see, it isn't very often I have the pleasure of taking a visitor into my little nest."

The old girl is slightly dotty,[10] Billy told himself. But at five and sixpence a night, who gives a hang about that? "I should've thought you'd be simply swamped with applicants," he said politely.

"Oh, I am, my dear, I am, of course I am. But the trouble is that I'm inclined to be just a teeny weeny bit choosy and particular—if you see what I mean."

"Ah, yes."

"But I'm always ready. Everything is always ready day and night in this house just on the off-chance that an acceptable young gentleman will come along. And it is such a pleasure, my dear, such a very great pleasure when now and again I open the door and I see someone standing there who is just *exactly* right." She was halfway up the stairs, and she paused with one hand on the stair-rail, turning her head and smiling down at him with pale lips. "Like you," she added, and her blue eyes traveled slowly all the way down the length of Billy's body, to his feet, and then up again.

On the second-floor landing she said to him, "This floor is mine."

They climbed up another flight. "And this one is *all* yours," she said. "Here's your room. I do hope you'll like it." She took him into a small but charming front bedroom, switching on the light as she went in.

"The morning sun comes right in the window, Mr. Perkins. It *is* Mr. Perkins, isn't it?"

"No," he said. "It's Weaver."

"Mr. Weaver. How nice. I've put a water-bottle between the sheets to air them out, Mr. Weaver. It's such a comfort to have a hot water-bottle in a strange bed with clean sheets, don't you agree? And you may light the gas fire at any time if you feel chilly."

"Thank you," Billy said. "Thank you ever so much." He noticed that the bedspread had been taken off the bed, and that the bedclothes had been neatly turned back on one side, all ready for someone to get in.

"I'm so glad you appeared," she said, looking earnestly into his face. "I was begin-ning to get worried."

"That's all right," Billy answered brightly. "You mustn't worry about me." He put his

---

9. **five and sixpence:** an amount of money worth, at the time of the story, less than one dollar.
10. **dotty:** crazy or peculiar.

suitcase on the chair and started to open it.

"And what about supper, my dear? Did you manage to get anything to eat before you came here?"

"I'm not a bit hungry, thank you," he said. "I think I'll just go to bed as soon as possible because tomorrow I've got to get up rather early and report to the office."

"Very well, then. I'll leave you now so that you can unpack. But before you go to bed, would you be kind enough to pop into the sitting-room on the ground floor and sign the book?[11] Everyone has to do that because it's the law of the land, and we don't want to go breaking any laws at *this* stage in the proceedings, do we?" She gave him a little wave of the hand and went quickly out of the room and closed the door.

Now, the fact that his landlady appeared to be slightly off her rocker didn't worry Billy in the least. After all, she not only was harmless—there was no question about that—but she was also quite obviously a kind and generous soul. He guessed that she had probably lost a son in the war, or something like that, and had never gotten over it.

So a few minutes later, after unpacking his suitcase and washing his hands, he trotted downstairs to the ground floor and entered the living-room. His landlady wasn't there, but the fire was glowing in the hearth, and the little dachshund was still sleeping soundly in front of it. The room was wonderfully warm and cozy. I'm a lucky fellow, he thought, rubbing his hands. This is a bit of all right.

He found the guest-book lying open on the piano, so he took out his pen and wrote down his name and address. There were only two other entries above his on the page, and, as one always does with guest-books, he started to read them. One was a Christopher Mulholland from Cardiff. The other was Gregory W. Temple from Bristol.

That's funny, he thought suddenly. Christopher Mulholland. It rings a bell.

Now where on earth had he heard that rather unusual name before?

Was it a boy at school? No. Was it one of his sister's numerous young men, perhaps, or a friend of his father's? No, no, it wasn't any of those. He glanced down again at the book.

Christopher Mulholland
    231 Cathedral Road, Cardiff
Gregory W. Temple
    27 Sycamore Drive, Bristol

As a matter of fact, now he came to think of it, he wasn't at all sure that the second name didn't have almost as much of a familiar ring about it as the first.

"Gregory Temple?" he said aloud, searching his memory. "Christopher Mulholland? . . ."

"Such charming boys," a voice behind him answered, and he turned and saw his landlady sailing into the room with a large silver tea-tray in her hands. She was holding it well out in front of her, and rather high up, as though the tray were a pair of reins on a frisky horse.

"They sound somehow familiar," he said.

"They do? How interesting."

"I'm almost positive I've heard those names before somewhere. Isn't that odd? Maybe it was in the newspapers. They

---

11. **sign the book:** register as a guest at a hotel or boardinghouse by signing a guest book.

weren't famous in any way, were they? I mean famous cricketers[12] or footballers or something like that?"

"Famous," she said, setting the tea-tray down on the low table in front of the sofa. "Oh no, I don't think they were famous. But they were incredibly handsome, both of them, I can promise you that. They were tall and young and handsome, my dear, just exactly like you."

Once more, Billy glanced down at the book. "Look here," he said, noticing the dates. "This last entry is over two years old."

"It is?"

"Yes, indeed. And Christopher Mulholland's is nearly a year before that—more than *three years* ago."

"Dear me," she said, shaking her head and heaving a dainty little sigh. "I would never have thought it. How time does fly away from us all, doesn't it, Mr. Wilkins?"

"It's Weaver," Billy said. "W-e-a-v-e-r."

"Oh, of course it is!" she cried, sitting down on the sofa. "How silly of me. I do apologize. In one ear and out the other, that's me, Mr. Weaver."

"You know something?" Billy said. "Something that's really quite extraordinary about all this?"

"No, dear, I don't."

"Well, you see, both of these names—Mulholland and Temple—I not only seem to remember each one of them separately, so to speak, but somehow or other, in some peculiar way, they both appear to be sort of connected together as well. As though they were both famous for the same sort of

thing, if you see what I mean—like . . . well . . . like Dempsey and Tunney, for example, or Churchill and Roosevelt."[13]

"How amusing," she said. "But come over here now, dear, and sit down beside me on the sofa and I'll give you a nice cup of tea and a ginger biscuit before you go to bed."

"You really shouldn't bother," Billy said. "I didn't mean you to do anything like that." He stood by the piano, watching her as she fussed about with the cups and saucers. He noticed that she had small, white, quickly moving hands, and red finger-nails.

"I'm almost positive it was in the newspapers I saw them," Billy said. "I'll think of it in a second. I'm sure I will."

There is nothing more tantalizing than a thing like this that lingers just outside the borders of one's memory. He hated to give up.

"Now wait a minute," he said. "Wait just a minute, Mulholland . . . Christopher Mulholland . . . wasn't *that* the name of the Eton[14] schoolboy who was on a walking-tour through the West Country, and then all of a sudden . . ."

"Milk?" she said. "And sugar?"

"Yes, please. And then all of a sudden . . ."

"Eton schoolboy?" she said. "Oh no, my dear, that can't possibly be right because

---

12. **cricketers:** players of cricket, popular British team sport played on a grass field with a ball, bats, and wickets.

---

13. **Dempsey . . . Roosevelt:** Jack Dempsey and Gene Tunney were American heavyweight boxing champions during the 1920s. Sir Winston Churchill (1874–1965), of Great Britain, and Franklin Delano Roosevelt (1882–1945), of the United States, were closely associated during World War II, when both men were the leaders of their respective countries.
14. **Eton:** England's largest and most famous school for boys, located at Eton, a town near London.

Detail, *Tea Leaves*, Anna Broadbridge, late nineteenth century.

my Mr. Mulholland was certainly not an Eton schoolboy when he came to me. He was a Cambridge[15] undergraduate. Come over here now and sit next to me and warm yourself in front of this lovely fire. Come on. Your tea's all ready for you." She patted the empty place beside her on the sofa, and she sat there smiling at Billy and waiting for him to come over.

He crossed the room slowly, and sat down on the edge of the sofa. She placed his teacup on the table in front of him.

"*There* we are," she said. "How nice and cozy this is, isn't it?"

Billy started sipping his tea. She did the same. For half a minute or so, neither of them spoke. But Billy knew that she was looking at him. Her body was half turned toward him, and he could feel her eyes

---

15. **Cambridge:** famous university in Cambridge, a city in eastern England.

resting on his face, watching him over the rim of her teacup. Now and again, he caught a whiff of a peculiar smell that seemed to emanate[16] directly from her person. It was not in the least unpleasant, and it reminded him—well, he wasn't quite sure what it reminded him of. Pickled walnuts? New leather? Or was it the corridors of a hospital?

At length, she said, "Mr. Mulholland was a great one for his tea. Never in my life have I seen anyone drink as much tea as dear, sweet Mr. Mulholland."

"I suppose he left fairly recently," Billy said. He was still puzzling his head about the two names. He was positive now that he had seen them in the newspapers—in the headlines.

"Left?" she said, arching her brows. "But my dear boy, he never left. He's still here. Mr. Temple is also here. They're on the fourth floor, both of them together."

Billy set his cup down slowly on the table and stared at his landlady. She smiled back at him, and then she put out one of her white hands and patted him comfortingly on the knee. "How old are you, my dear?" she asked.

"Seventeen."

"Seventeen!" she cried. "Oh, it's the perfect age! Mr. Mulholland was also seventeen. But I think he was a trifle shorter than you are; in fact I'm sure he was, and his teeth weren't *quite* so white. You have the most beautiful teeth, Mr. Weaver, did you know that?"

"They're not as good as they look," Billy said. "They've got simply masses of fillings in them at the back."

_____
16. **emanate** [em'ə nāt']: come forth or originate from.

"Mr. Temple, of course, was a little older," she said, ignoring his remark. "He was actually twenty-eight. And yet I never would have guessed it if he hadn't told me, never in my whole life. There wasn't a *blemish* on his body."

"A what?" Billy said.

"His skin was *just* like a baby's."

There was a pause. Billy picked up his teacup and took another sip of his tea, then he set it down again gently in its saucer. He waited for her to say something else, but she seemed to have lapsed into another of her silences. He sat there staring straight ahead of him into the far corner of the room, biting his lower lip.

"That parrot," he said at last. "You know something? It had me completely fooled when I first saw it through the window. I could have sworn it was alive."

"Alas, no longer."

"It's most terribly clever the way it's been done," he said. "It doesn't look in the least bit dead. Who did it?"

"I did."

"*You* did?"

"Of course," she said. "And have you met my little Basil as well?" She nodded toward the dachshund curled up so comfortably in front of the fire. Billy looked at it. And suddenly, he realized that this animal had all the time been just as silent and motionless as the parrot. He put out a hand and touched it gently on the top of its back. The back was hard and cold, and when he pushed the hair to one side with his fingers, he could see the skin underneath, grayish-black and dry and perfectly preserved.

"Good gracious me," he said. "How absolutely fascinating." He turned away from the dog and stared with deep admiration at the little woman beside him on the sofa. "It

Rooms for Tourists, Edward Hopper, 1945.

must be most awfully difficult to do a thing like that."

"Not in the least," she said. "I stuff *all* my little pets myself when they pass away. Will you have another cup of tea?"

"No, thank you," Billy said. The tea tasted faintly of bitter almonds,[17] and he didn't much care for it.

"You did sign the book, didn't you?"

"Oh, yes."

---

17. **bitter almonds:** a sign of the presence of potassium cyanide, an extremely poisonous substance known for a taste and smell similar to that of bitter almonds.

"That's good. Because later on, if I happen to forget what you were called, then I could always come down here and look it up. I still do that almost every day with Mr. Mulholland and Mr. . . . Mr. . . ."

"Temple," Billy said. "Gregory Temple. Excuse my asking, but haven't there been *any* other guests here except them in the last two or three years?"

Holding her teacup high in one hand, inclining her head slightly to the left, she looked up at him out of the corners of her eyes and gave him another gentle little smile.

"No, my dear," she said. "Only you."

READER'S RESPONSE

What do you think the landlady plans to do with Billy?

STUDY QUESTIONS

Recalling

1. Describe the landlady as she first appears to Billy. What is Billy's opinion of her state of mind?
2. What does Billy recall about Christopher Mulholland?
3. According to the landlady, where are her other guests?
4. What has the landlady done with the parrot and the dachshund?

Interpreting

5. What do you think happened to Christopher Mulholland and Gregory Temple? What might Billy see if he went to the fourth floor of the house?
6. Mention three danger signals that Billy ignores. Why do you think he ignores these signals?
7. Do you think that Billy will "catch on" to the landlady in time? Why or why not?

Extending

8. Why do you think people enjoy reading stories that describe frightening situations?

READING AND LITERARY FOCUS

Suspense

When you read a good story, you become caught up in the plot. You want to see what will happen next. You want to know how the conflict will be settled. This growing interest is called **suspense.**

Suspense builds as the events of the plot unfold. For example, in "The Landlady" Billy vaguely remembers reading something about the landlady's two previous tenants. We want to know what Billy remembers and whether it has anything to do with the landlady's odd behavior. As we learn more about the other young men, our suspense increases, and we begin to worry about what will happen to Billy.

Thinking About Suspense

1. Explain how the following sentences add to the story's suspense: "'But my dear boy, he never left. He's still here. Mr. Temple is also here.'"
2. Does the story's final sentence add to the suspense you felt? Why or why not?

Victorian Interior, Horace Pippin, 1958.

Marjorie Sharmat (born 1928) began her writing career at the age of eight, when she and a friend published *The Snooper's Gazette* in Portland, Maine. Since then she has written close to one hundred books for children, including the best-selling *Nate the Great* and the Maggie Marmelstein novels. Two recent books are *How to Meet a Gorgeous Guy* and *How to Meet a Gorgeous Girl*. Sharmat's son Craig, a guitarist, was the inspiration for "May I Have Your Autograph?"

If your favorite rock star were in town, how would you go about getting his or her autograph?

• •

Marjorie Sharmat

May I Have Your Autograph?

I am sitting in an overstuffed chair in the lobby of The Dominion Imperial International Hotel. So help me, that's really the name. I am surrounded by overgrown ferns, ugly but expensive floral carpeting, chandeliers[1] that make me think of *The Phantom of the Opera*,[2] stuck-up hotel employees in silly-looking uniforms who give me dirty looks—and nobody my age. Except my friend Wendy, who dragged me here.

Wendy is here to meet a guy, but he doesn't know it. In fact, he's never heard of Wendy. But that doesn't stop her from being in love with him. Well, maybe not in love. I think love is for people you've at least met. Wendy has never met Craig the Cat. That's

the name of the guy. At least that's his stage name. He's a rock star who's been famous for over six months. Even *my* parents have heard of him.

Wendy is here to get Craig the Cat's autograph on his latest album. On the album jacket, Craig is wearing a black cat costume and he's sitting on a garbage pail with a bottle of spilled milk beside him. He is holding his guitar in his long, furry arms.

Wendy constantly talks about Craig the Cat. But it was like discussing something that was going on in another time frame, on another continent. I didn't mind. It was nicely, safely unreal. Until Craig the Cat came to town today. He's giving a string of benefit performances across the country for some kind of animal group that's devoted to saving "the cats."

"That includes everything from alley cats to exotic tigers," Wendy told me.

"How do you know?"

"I know."

---

1. **chandeliers** [shand'əl ērz']: elaborately decorated lighting fixtures that hang from the ceiling.
2. ***The Phantom of the Opera:*** published in 1911, French writer Gaston Leroux's horror story about a mysterious man who lives in the passages underneath the Paris Opera House.

We used our allowance money to buy tickets. That landed us exactly five rows from the back of the auditorium.

"This is so frustrating," Wendy said as we stretched our necks. "I must get closer."

"How close?" I joked.

"I want his autograph," she answered. "I'm not joking."

"Lots of luck."

Wendy doesn't believe in luck. After the concert she dragged me here, to this hotel lobby where we are now sitting. We just sit.

"Are we waiting for him to come into the lobby?" I ask.

"No. He probably got spirited into the hotel through a back or side entrance." Wendy looks at her watch. "He's showered and is relaxing now. He's feeling rested, triumphant, and receptive."

"Receptive to what?"

"To meeting us. To autographing *my* album."

"How are you going to accomplish that? You don't actually know that he's staying at this hotel, and even if he is, you don't know his room number."

Wendy stands up. "Don't be so negative, Rosalind. Come," she says.

I follow her to one of those telephones that connect the caller to hotel rooms. She dials a number. She waits. Then she says, "Craig the Cat, please." She looks at me. "I found him! Listen!" She tilts the receiver so that I, too, can hear what's being said. It's a strain, but I can hear.

A woman is on the other end. "How did you find out where Craig the Cat is staying?" she asks. "The leak. I need to know where the leak is."

"There isn't any. I'm the only one with the information. Please be nice. I want his autograph."

"Who doesn't."

"Help me get it, please. What are my chances?"

"Poor to nonexistent."

"Oh."

"I'm his manager and, my dear, I'm his mother. I protect Craig from two vantage points. I keep a low profile. Now, how many other fans know where he's staying?"

"None that I know of."

"You mean you didn't peddle the information to the highest bidder?"

"I wouldn't do that."

"Maybe not, dear, but I'm tired of his fans. They tug at Craig's whiskers. They pull his tail. Leave him alone! I'm hanging up."

Click.

Wendy sighs. "We'll just have to wait until he goes into that place over there to eat."

"Haven't you ever heard of room service?"

"Craig doesn't like room service. He doesn't like dining rooms, either. He's a coffee shop person."

"How do you know?"

"I know."

"How did you know his room number?"

"I knew."

"And you knew his mother is his manager?"

"I knew."

We are sitting in the overstuffed chairs again. Wendy is watching and waiting. I see no human-size cat in the lobby. I feel like going to sleep.

Almost an hour goes by. Suddenly, Wendy pokes me. "It's him! It's him!"

I look up. A guy who seems to be about twenty or twenty-five is passing by with a woman who looks old enough to be his mother. He is lean. She is not. They are dressed normally.

I whisper to Wendy. "*That's* Craig the Cat? How do you know? He looks like an ordinary guy."

Wendy doesn't answer. She stands up and starts to follow the guy and the woman. They are heading for the hotel coffee shop. I follow all of them. I see the guy and the woman sit down. They are looking at menus.

Wendy rushes up to them, clutching her album. "May I have your autograph?" she asks the guy.

The woman glares at Wendy. "He doesn't give autographs," she says. "He's just a civilian. Can't you see he's just a civilian?"

"*You're Craig the Cat!*" Wendy says to the guy.

She says it too loudly.

"How do you know I'm Craig the Cat?" the guy asks. Also too loudly.

People in the coffee shop turn and stare. They repeat, "Craig the Cat!"

Suddenly somebody with a camera materializes and aims the camera at Craig. Wendy bends down and puts her face in front of Craig's. It happens so fast, I can't believe it. The photographer says, "Get out of the way, kid."

Craig's mother glares at the photographer. "Shoo!" she says, waving her hand. "Shoo immediately!"

The photographer leaves. So does Wendy. She runs back to me. I am hiding behind a fern.

Wendy has lost her cool. "Let's get out of here before we're kicked out or arrested," she says.

We rush toward a door.

"Wait!" Someone is yelling at us.

When I hear the word *wait*, it's a signal for me to move even faster. But Wendy stops. "It's *him*!" she says, without turning around.

I turn. It *is* Craig the Cat. He's alone. He rushes up to Wendy. "How did you know me?" he asks. "I didn't tell the media where I was staying. And I certainly didn't give out my room number. I wasn't wearing my cat costume. And I was with my mother. So *how*?"

Wendy looks at me. She's trying to decide if she should answer. Something in her wants to and something in her doesn't want to. She turns back to Craig. "I'm an expert on you," she says. "I know you like fancy, old hotels, and this is the oldest and the fanciest in town. I know your lucky number is twelve, so I figured you'd stay on the twelfth floor in room 1212. I know you always wear red socks when you're not performing. So tonight I watched ankles in the lobby. And I knew you'd be with your manager—your mother."

"What about the photographer?"

"I know you don't want to be photographed without your cat costume. In an interview of October eighth of this year, you said it would wreck your feline image. So when I saw the photographer trying to take your picture, I put my face in front of yours."

"You did that for me?"

"I'd do it for any special friend."

"But you don't know me."

"Yes, I do. When I read about someone, I get to know him. I don't believe everything I read, of course. I pick out certain parts. I

look for the reality behind the unreality. I went through seventy-one pages about Craig the Cat, in eleven different magazines, and I ended up thinking of you as my friend."

Craig the Cat is staring at Wendy as if *he's* the fan. He's in awe of *her*! It's nothing very earthshaking. It's not like there's a crowd roaring or it's a summit meeting of world leaders or a momentous change in the universe. It's just a small, nice moment in the lobby of The Dominion Imperial International Hotel, and it will never go away for Wendy.

We're back in the hotel coffee shop. Four of us are sitting around a table, eating. Craig's mother is beaming benevolently[3] like a contented mother cat presiding over her brood, which now includes Wendy and me in addition to Craig. After we finish eating, Wendy hands her record album to Craig. "Now may I have your autograph?" she asks.

Craig pulls out a pen and writes on the album jacket. I hope that Wendy will show me what he writes. Maybe she won't. Whatever she does will be okay, though. Maybe this will be the first private entry in her collection of reality and unreality about her new friend, Craig the Cat.

She's entitled.

As for me, I'm now sitting in a chair in a hotel coffee shop as a new and honored member of this Clan of the Cat. It has been a strange and kind of wonderful day, thanks to my friend, Wendy the Expert. I'm glad I'm here. If you take away some of the ferns and a few fat chairs and most of the carpeting, The Dominion Imperial International Hotel definitely has possibilities.

---

3. **benevolently** [bə nev'ə lənt lē]: with sympathy and feeling for others; kindly.

READER'S RESPONSE

What does Rosalind mean when she says of Wendy near the end of the story, "She's entitled"?

STUDY QUESTIONS

Recalling

1. Why has Wendy brought Rosalind with her to the Dominion Imperial International Hotel?
2. Describe what happens at the restaurant table.

3. What explanation does Wendy give for correctly guessing Craig's hotel and room number? How does she recognize Craig without his costume?
4. What special favor does Wendy do for Craig?

Interpreting

5. What sets Wendy apart from the typical fan of a celebrity?
6. Why might Craig be "in awe of" Wendy by the end of the story?

Extending

7. What do you think an individual gains from being a fan of a celebrity?

Thinking Skills: Problem Solving

DEFINITION

Problem solving is a way of thinking. A good problem solver starts with basic information about a problem and then thinks in an orderly fashion, following several clear steps.

STEPS

1. **State the goal.**
   What do you want to find out or accomplish?

2. **List the givens.**
   What information do you have?

3. **List the obstacles.**
   What is stopping you from solving the problem? What information do you need?

4. **Identify the methods.**
   What specific actions are you going to take to remove each obstacle?

5. **Carry out the plan.**

6. **Check the results.**
   Have you solved the problem?

EXAMPLE

Imagine that the great detective Sherlock Holmes is called in to solve a murder that has taken place in a remote English castle.

1. **State the goal.** Holmes must correctly identify the murderer.

2. **List the givens.** Holmes gathers every detail about the crime and the people in the castle when the crime was committed.

3. **List the obstacles.** Holmes is stumped because every person has a perfect alibi.

4. **Identify the methods.** Holmes decides that he must not assume anything. His method is to question everything unless it can be proved.

5. **Carry out the plan.** Holmes questions whether a *person* committed the crime. Then he questions whether there was a *crime* at all. Questioning the obvious opens up other possibilities: Maybe the "crime" was committed by an animal. Holmes reexamines the victim with this in mind and finds that a poisonous snake killed the victim.

6. **Check the results.** Holmes finds that a poisonous snake living in a wall of the castle slithers out each night into the particular room where the victim was killed.

ACTIVITY 1

Problem Solving in "May I Have Your Autograph?"
Follow the six steps of problem solving to describe what Wendy does in this story. Remember that Wendy, like Sherlock Holmes, "doesn't believe in luck."

ACTIVITY 2

Problem Solving in Literature
Follow the six steps of problem solving to describe what happens in another selection in this book. Remember that people are constantly solving problems in ordinary human relationships, in the process of growing up, in real-life adventures, in folk tales, and in science.

Eve Merriam (born 1916) feels that she is fortunate because "my work is my main pleasure." Besides her many volumes of poetry, Merriam has written song lyrics, essays, biographies, novels, and stories. She regards herself primarily as a poet, however: "While I find all forms of writing absorbing," she says, "I like poetry as the most immediate and richest form of communication." It is not surprising that one of her favorite poetic subjects is poetry itself.

Can you think of any poems that are fun to read?

Eve Merriam

How to Eat a Poem

Don't be polite.
Bite in.
Pick it up with your fingers and lick the juice that
   may run down your chin.
It is ready and ripe now, whenever you are.

5 You do not need a knife or fork or spoon
or plate or napkin or tablecloth.

For there is no core
or stem
or rind
10 or pit
or seed
or skin
to throw away.

Still Life with Apples and Bananas,
Charles Demuth, watercolor, 1925.

READER'S RESPONSE

Was reading this poem work or play?

STUDY QUESTIONS

Recalling

1. How are you supposed to hold the poem that you are eating? What runs down your chin?
2. What items don't you need? Why?

Interpreting

3. Merriam is talking about various ways of reading a poem. What would the "polite" way be? What does she mean when she tells us instead to "bite in"?
4. What might the "juice" of a poem be?
5. Why is there nothing of the poem left to throw away?

Extending

6. Create your own offbeat description of reading a poem (for example, how to wash a poem, how to wear a poem). Give one reason why *your* comparison makes sense.

READING AND LITERARY FOCUS

Poetry and Mystery

Poetry is imaginative writing that combines words, pictures, and sounds to create a special effect. A poem can be like a magic lantern that casts a special light on an ordinary object. Just how each poem casts its light is a small mystery. You can begin to solve that mystery if you know what the parts of a poem are and how they add to the poem as a whole.

Every poem has a **speaker**—the person or thing that "tells" the poem. Often the speaker is the poet, but sometimes the poet speaks in the voice of another person, an animal, or an object. The speaker of "How to Eat a Poem" is probably the poet, Eve Merriam.

You have probably noticed that poems look different on the page from stories and other works in prose. The sentences of a poem are broken up into lines, and these lines are usually shorter than prose lines. Each new line often begins with a capital letter. Some poets group the lines of a poem together into **stanzas.** Usually each stanza develops a single idea.

Poems often create special effects with sound. Some poems follow a regular **rhythm,** or beat, perhaps making you think of surging waves or tapping feet. Eve Merriam's poem does not have a regular rhythm; most of the lines are of different lengths. But did you notice that the short lines in the last stanza *do* have a similar rhythm? Many poems also contain **rhymes**, words that share similar sounds. Although Merriam's poem does not have many rhymes, the words *polite* and *bite* in the first stanza rhyme.

What you may remember most about a poem are the vivid images that it creates. For example, Merriam's poem makes you see the poem as a piece of ripe, juicy fruit.

Just like authors of stories, poets write in order to express their ideas and visions of life. Some poets present their ideas by telling stories in their poems. Other poets express their thoughts and feelings more directly. For example, Eve Merriam does not want you to tiptoe around poetry. Right from the start she tells you to tackle a poem with gusto. "Don't be polite," she says. "Bite in."

Thinking About Poetry

1. How many stanzas are in Merriam's poem? What idea does each stanza express?
2. What general impression of poetry does this poem create?
3. How can you tell from this poem that Merriam loves poetry and wants you to love it too?

Federico García Lorca (1899–1936) is regarded as Spain's greatest modern poet. During his short life he wrote four books of poetry and three plays. His poetry is known for its vivid images, which often reflect the lives of Spanish peasants. García Lorca spent a year in the United States; and one of his books is entitled *Poeta en Neuva York* (*A Poet in New York*). Shot during the Spanish civil war, García Lorca came to be regarded as a hero in the cause of freedom.

What do you hear when you listen to a seashell?

Federico García Lorca

Conch Shell

They have brought me a conch shell.[1]

  Within it sings
a map sized sea.
My heart
5 fills up with water
and little fish
of shadow and silver.

They have brought me a conch shell.

———————

1. **conch** [kongk] **shell:** a large, spiral-shaped shell.

READER'S RESPONSE

What might be mysterious about Lorca's conch shell?

STUDY QUESTIONS

Recalling

1. What "sings" inside the conch shell?
2. With what does the speaker's heart fill up?

Interpreting

3. Why does the speaker say there is a sea inside the conch shell? Why does the speaker call the sea "map-sized"?
4. How do you think the speaker feels about the conch shell that is given to him?

Extending

5. What is magical about the sound of the sea? What other sounds of nature do you find magical?

When Joan Aiken (born 1924) was five years old, she bought a huge pad of writing paper and began to jot down poems and stories. "I always intended to be a writer," she says. First published at seventeen, she has since written over sixty books. Most of her works have a touch of strangeness or enchantment about them. Aiken says that she writes "the sort of thing I should have liked to read myself when I was young, and am helped by comments and criticisms from my own children, who read each work as it goes along."

Have you ever been a dog's best friend?

• •

Joan Aiken

Lob's Girl

Some people choose their dogs, and some dogs choose their people. The Pengelly family had no say in the choosing of Lob; he came to them in the second way, and very decisively.

It began on the beach, the summer when Sandy was five, Don, her older brother, twelve, and the twins were three. Sandy was really Alexandra, because her grandmother had a beautiful picture of a queen in a diamond tiara[1] and high collar of pearls. It hung by Granny Pearce's kitchen sink and was as familiar as the doormat. When Sandy was born everyone agreed that she was the living spit[2] of the picture, and so she was called Alexandra and Sandy for short.

On this summer day she was lying peacefully reading a comic and not keeping an eye on the twins, who didn't need it because they were occupied in seeing which of them could wrap the most seaweed around the other one's legs. Father—Bert Pengelly—and Don were up on the Hard[3] painting the bottom boards of the boat in which Father went fishing for pilchards. And Mother—Jean Pengelly—was getting ahead with making the Christmas puddings because she never felt easy in her mind if they weren't made and safely put away by the end of August. As usual, each member of the family was happily getting on with his or her own affairs. Little did they guess how soon this state of things would be changed by the large new member who was going to erupt into their midst.

Sandy rolled onto her back to make sure that the twins were not climbing on slippery rocks or getting cut off by the tide. At the same moment a large body struck her

---

1. **tiara** [tē ar'ə]: a small crown worn by women.
2. **living spit:** exact image or likeness.

3. **Hard:** sheltered beach or stone roadway that slopes down to the water's edge.

forcibly in the midriff and she was covered by flying sand. Instinctively she shut her eyes and felt the sand being wiped off her face by something that seemed like a warm, rough, damp flannel. She opened her eyes and looked. It was a tongue. Its owner was a large and bouncy young Alsatian, or German shepherd, with topaz eyes, black-tipped prick ears, a thick, soft coat, and a bushy black-tipped tail.

"*Lob!*" shouted a man farther up the beach. "Lob, come here!"

But Lob, as if trying to atone[4] for the surprise he had given her, went on licking the sand off Sandy's face, wagging his tail so hard while he kept on knocking up more clouds of sand. His owner, a gray-haired man with a limp, walked over as quickly as he could and seized him by the collar.

"I hope he didn't give you a fright?" the man said to Sandy. "He meant it in play—he's only young."

"Oh, no, I think he's *beautiful*," said Sandy truly. She picked up a bit of drift-wood and threw it. Lob, whisking easily out of his master's grip, was after it like a sand-colored bullet. He came back with the stick, beaming, and gave it to Sandy. At the same time he gave himself, though no one else was aware of this at the time. But with Sandy, too, it was love at first sight, and when, after a lot more stick-throwing, she and the twins joined Father and Don to go home for tea, they cast many a backward glance at Lob being led firmly away by his master.

"I wish we could play with him every day," Tess sighed.

"Why can't we?" said Tim.

Sandy explained, "Because Mr. Dods-worth, who owns him, is from Liverpool, and he is only staying at the Fisherman's Arms till Saturday."

"Is Liverpool a long way off?"

"Right at the other end of England from Cornwall, I'm afraid."

It was a Cornish fishing village where the Pengelly family lived, with rocks and cliffs and a strip of beach and a little round harbor, and palm trees growing in the gardens of the little whitewashed stone houses. The village was approached by a narrow, steep, twisting hill-road, and guarded by a notice that said LOW GEAR FOR 1½ MILES, DANGEROUS TO CYCLISTS.

The Pengelly children went home to scones[5] with Cornish cream and jam, thinking they had seen the last of Lob. But they were much mistaken. The whole family was playing cards by the fire in the front room after supper when there was a loud thump and a crash of china in the kitchen.

"My Christmas puddings!" exclaimed Jean, and ran out.

"Did you put TNT[6] in them, then?" her husband said.

But it was Lob, who, finding the front door shut, had gone around to the back and bounced in through the open kitchen window, where the puddings were cooling on the sill. Luckily only the smallest was knocked down and broken.

Lob stood on his hind legs and plastered Sandy's face with licks. Then he did the same for the twins, who shrieked with joy.

"Where does this friend of yours come from?" inquired Mr. Pengelly.

"He's staying at the Fisherman's Arms—I mean his owner is."

---

4. **atone** [ə tōn′]: make up for.

5. **scones** [skōnz]: small biscuits, often round.
6. **TNT:** flammable compound used as an explosive.

Lynmouth, Devon, Albert Goodwin (1845–1932).

"Then he must go back there. Find a bit of string, Sandy, to tie to his collar."

"I wonder how he found his way here," Mrs. Pengelly said when the reluctant Lob had been led whining away and Sandy had explained about their afternoon's game on the beach. "Fisherman's Arms is right round the other side of the harbor."

Lob's owner scolded him and thanked Mr. Pengelly for bringing him back. Jean Pengelly warned the children that they had better not encourage Lob any more if they met him on the beach, or it would only lead to more trouble. So they dutifully took no notice of him the next day until he spoiled their good resolutions by dashing up to them with joyful barks, wagging his

tail so hard that he winded Tess and knocked Tim's legs from under him.

They had a happy day, playing on the sand.

The next day was Saturday. Sandy had found out that Mr. Dodsworth was to catch the half-past-nine train. She went out secretly, down to the station, nodded to Mr. Hoskins, the stationmaster, who wouldn't dream of charging any local for a platform ticket, and climbed up on the footbridge that led over the tracks. She didn't want to be seen, but she did want to see. She saw Mr. Dodsworth get on the train, accompanied by an unhappy-looking Lob with drooping ears and tail. Then she saw the train slide away out of sight around the next headland, with a melancholy wail that sounded like Lob's last good-bye.

Sandy wished she hadn't had the idea of coming to the station. She walked home miserably, with her shoulders hunched and her hands in her pockets. For the rest of the day she was so cross and unlike herself that Tess and Tim were quite surprised, and her mother gave her a dose of senna.[7]

A week passed. Then, one evening, Mrs. Pengelly and the younger children were in the front room playing snakes and ladders.[8] Mr. Pengelly and Don had gone fishing on the evening tide. If your father is a fisherman, he will never be home at the same time from one week to the next.

Suddenly, history repeating itself, there was a crash from the kitchen. Jean Pengelly leaped up, crying, "My blackberry jelly!" She and the children had spent the morning picking and the afternoon boiling fruit.

But Sandy was ahead of her mother. With flushed cheeks and eyes like stars she had darted into the kitchen, where she and Lob were hugging one another in a frenzy of joy. About a yard of his tongue was out, and he was licking every part of her that he could reach.

"Good heavens!" exclaimed Jean. "How in the world did *he* get here?"

"He must have walked," said Sandy. "Look at his feet."

They were worn, dusty, and tarry. One had a cut on the pad.

"They ought to be bathed," said Jean Pengelly. "Sandy, run a bowl of warm water while I get the disinfectant."

"What'll we do about him, Mother?" said Sandy anxiously.

Mrs. Pengelly looked at her daughter's pleading eyes and sighed.

"He must go back to his owner, of course," she said, making her voice firm. "Your dad can get the address from the Fisherman's tomorrow, and phone him or send a telegram. In the meantime he'd better have a long drink and a good meal."

Lob was very grateful for the drink and the meal, and made no objection to having his feet washed. Then he flopped down on the hearthrug and slept in front of the fire they had lit because it was a cold, wet evening, with his head on Sandy's feet. He was a very tired dog. He had walked all the way from Liverpool to Cornwall, which is more than four hundred miles.

The next day Mr. Pengelly phoned Lob's owner, and the following morning Mr. Dodsworth arrived off the night train, decidedly put out,[9] to take his pet home. That parting was worse than the first. Lob whined, Don walked out of the house, the twins burst out crying, and Sandy crept up to her bedroom afterward and lay with her face pressed into the quilt, feeling as if she were bruised all over.

Jean Pengelly took them all into Plymouth to see the circus on the next day and the twins cheered up a little, but even the hour's ride in the train each way and the Liberty horses and performing seals could not cure Sandy's sore heart.

She need not have bothered, though. In ten days' time Lob was back—limping this time, with a torn ear and a patch missing out of his furry coat, as if he had met and tangled with an enemy or two in the course of his four-hundred-mile walk.

Bert Pengelly rang up Liverpool again.

---

7. **senna** [sen′ə]: medicine made from the dried leaves of plants.
8. **snakes and ladders:** board game for children.

9. **put out:** annoyed or inconvenienced.

Mr. Dodsworth, when he answered, sounded weary. He said, "That dog has already cost me two days that I can't spare away from my work—plus endless time in police stations and drafting newspaper advertisements. I'm too old for these ups and downs. I think we'd better face the fact, Mr. Pengelly, that it's your family he wants to stay with—that is, if you want to have him."

Bert Pengelly gulped. He was not a rich man; and Lob was a pedigreed dog. He said cautiously, "How much would you be asking for him?"

"Good heavens, man, I'm not suggesting I'd sell him to you. You must have him as a gift. Think of the train fares I'll be saving. You'll be doing me a good turn."

"Is he a big eater?" Bert asked doubtfully.

By this time the children, breathless in the background listening to one side of this conversation, had realized what was in the wind and were dancing up and down with their hands clasped beseechingly.

"Oh, not for his size," Lob's owner assured Bert. "Two or three pounds of meat a day and some vegetables and gravy and biscuits—he does very well on that."

Alexandra's father looked over the telephone at his daughter's swimming eyes and trembling lips. He reached a decision. "Well, then, Mr. Dodsworth," he said briskly, "we'll accept your offer and thank you very much. The children will be overjoyed and you can be sure Lob has come to a good home. They'll look after him and see he gets enough exercise. But I can tell you," he ended firmly, "if he wants to settle in with us he'll have to learn to eat a lot of fish."

So that was how Lob came to live with the Pengelly family. Everybody loved him and he loved them all. But there was never any question who came first with him. He

A Clovely Cottage, Arthur Wilkinson, watercolor, late nineteenth century.

was Sandy's dog. He slept by her bed and followed her everywhere he was allowed.

Nine years went by, and each summer Mr. Dodsworth came back to stay at the Fisherman's Arms and call on his erstwhile[10] dog. Lob always met him with recognition and dignified pleasure, accompanied him for a walk or two—but showed no signs of wishing to return to Liverpool. His place, he intimated, was definitely with the Pengellys.

In the course of nine years Lob changed less than Sandy. As she went into her teens he became a little slower, a little stiffer, there was a touch of gray on his nose, but he was still a handsome dog. He and Sandy still loved one another devotedly.

One evening in October all the summer visitors had left, and the little fishing town looked empty and secretive. It was a wet, windy dusk. When the children came home from school—even the twins were at high school now, and Don was a full-fledged fisherman—Jean Pengelly said, "Sandy, your Aunt Rebecca says she's lonesome because

---

10. **erstwhile** [urst'hwīl']: former.

Uncle Will Hoskins has gone out trawling,[11] and she wants one of you to go and spend the evening with her. You go, dear; you can take your homework with you."

Sandy looked far from enthusiastic.

"Can I take Lob with me?"

"You know Aunt Becky doesn't really like dogs— Oh, very well." Mrs. Pengelly sighed. "I suppose she'll have to put up with him as well as you."

Reluctantly Sandy tidied herself, took her schoolbag, put on the damp raincoat she had just taken off, fastened Lob's lead[12] to his collar, and set off to walk through the dusk to Aunt Becky's cottage, which was five minutes' climb up the steep hill.

The wind was howling through the shrouds of boats drawn up on the Hard.

"Put some cheerful music on, do," said Jean Pengelly to the nearest twin. "Anything to drown that wretched sound while I make your dad's supper." So Don, who had just come in, put on some rock music, loud. Which was why the Pengellys did not hear the truck hurtle down the hill and crash against the post office wall a few minutes later.

Dr. Travers was driving through Cornwall with his wife, taking a late holiday before patients began coming down with winter colds and flu. He saw the sign that said STEEP HILL. LOW GEAR FOR 1½ MILES. Dutifully he changed into second gear.

"We must be nearly there," said his wife, looking out of her window. "I noticed a sign on the coast road that said the Fisherman's Arms was two miles. What a narrow, dangerous hill! But the cottages are very pretty— Oh, Frank, stop, *stop!* There's a child, I'm sure it's a child—by the wall over there!"

Dr. Travers jammed on his brakes and brought the car to a stop. A little stream ran down by the road in a shallow stone culvert, and half in the water lay something that looked, in the dusk, like a pile of clothes—or was it the body of a child? Mrs. Travers was out of the car in a flash, but her husband was quicker.

"Don't touch her, Emily!" he said sharply. "She's been hit. Can't be more than a few minutes. Remember that truck that overtook us half a mile back, speeding like the devil? Here, quick, go into that cottage and phone for an ambulance. The girl's in a bad way. I'll stay here and do what I can to stop the bleeding. Don't waste a minute."

Doctors are expert at stopping dangerous bleeding, for they know the right places to press. This Dr. Travers was able to do, but he didn't dare do more; the girl was lying in a queerly crumpled heap, and he guessed she had a number of bones broken and that it would be highly dangerous to move her. He watched her with great concentration, wondering where the truck had got to and what other damage it had done.

Mrs. Travers was very quick. She had seen plenty of accident cases and knew the importance of speed. The first cottage she tried had a phone; in four minutes she was back, and in six an ambulance was wailing down the hill.

Its attendants lifted the child onto a stretcher as carefully as if she were made of fine thistledown.[13] The ambulance sped

---

11. **trawling** [trôl'ing]: fishing with a trawl, a large net dragged over the ocean bottom to catch fish.
12. **lead** [lēd]: rope or leash used for walking a dog.

13. **thistledown** [this'əl doun']: silky fuzz on the flower of a thistle.

Landing the Catch, Hubert Coop, watercolor, early twentieth century.

off to Plymouth—for the local cottage hospital did not take serious accident cases—and Dr. Travers went down to the police station to report what he had done.

He found that the police already knew about the speeding truck—which had suffered from loss of brakes and ended up with its radiator halfway through the post office wall. The driver was concussed[14] and shocked, but the police thought he was the only person injured—until Dr. Travers told his tale.

At half-past nine that night Aunt Rebecca Hoskins was sitting by her fire thinking aggrieved[15] thoughts about the inconsiderateness of nieces who were asked to supper and never turned up when she was startled by a neighbor, who burst in exclaiming, "Have you heard about Sandy Pengelly, then, Mrs. Hoskins? Terrible thing, poor little soul, and they don't know if she's likely to live. Police have got the truck driver that hit her—ah, it didn't ought to be allowed, speeding through the

---

14. **concussed** [kən kust′]: injured by a blow to the brain.

15. **aggrieved** [ə grēvd′]: showing or expressing hurt feelings or injured pride.

place like that at umpty miles an hour, they ought to jail him for life—not that that'd be any comfort to poor Bert and Jean."

Horrified, Aunt Rebecca put on a coat and went down to her brother's house. She found the family with white shocked faces; Bert and Jean were about to drive off to the hospital where Sandy had been taken, and the twins were crying bitterly. Lob was nowhere to be seen. But Aunt Rebecca was not interested in dogs; she did not inquire about him.

"Thank the lord you've come, Beck," said her brother. "Will you stay the night with Don and the twins? Don's out looking for Lob and heaven knows when we'll be back; we may get a bed with Jean's mother in Plymouth."

"Oh, if only I'd never invited the poor child," wailed Mrs. Hoskins. But Bert and Jean hardly heard her.

That night seemed to last forever. The twins cried themselves to sleep. Don came home very late and grim-faced. Bert and Jean sat in a waiting room of the Western Counties Hospital, but Sandy was unconscious, they were told, and she remained so. All that could be done for her was done. She was given transfusions to replace all the blood she had lost. The broken bones were set and put in slings and cradles.[16]

"Is she a healthy girl? Has she a good constitution?" the emergency doctor asked.

"Aye, doctor, she is that," Bert said hoarsely. The lump in Jean's throat prevented her from answering; she merely nodded.

"Then she ought to have a chance. But I won't conceal from you that her condition is very serious, unless she shows signs of coming out from this coma."[17]

But as hour succeeded hour, Sandy showed no signs of recovering consciousness. Her parents sat in the waiting room with haggard faces; sometimes one of them would go to telephone the family at home, or to try to get a little sleep at the home of Granny Pearce, not far away.

At noon next day Dr. and Mrs. Travers went to the Pengelly cottage to inquire how Sandy was doing, but the report was gloomy: "Still in a very serious condition." The twins were miserably unhappy. They forgot that they had sometimes called their elder sister bossy and only remembered how often she had shared her pocket money with them, how she read to them and took them for picnics and helped with their homework. Now there was no Sandy, no Mother and Dad, Don went around with a gray, shuttered face, and worse still, there was no Lob.

The Western Counties Hospital is a large one, with dozens of different departments and five or six connected buildings, each with three or four entrances. By that afternoon it became noticeable that a dog seemed to have taken up position outside the hospital, with the fixed intention of getting in. Patiently he would try first one entrance and then another, all the way around, and then begin again. Sometimes he would get a little way inside, following a visitor, but animals were, of course, forbidden, and he was always kindly but firmly turned out again. Sometimes the guard at

---

16. **slings and cradles:** Slings are cloth loops hung from the neck to support an injured arm or hand; cradles are frames used to protect a broken leg.

17. **coma** [kō′mə]: unconscious state, caused by injury, from which a person cannot be aroused.

the main entrance gave him a pat or offered him a bit of sandwich—he looked so wet and beseeching and desperate. But he never ate the sandwich. No one seemed to own him or to know where he came from; Plymouth is a large city and he might have belonged to anybody.

At tea time Granny Pearce came through the pouring rain to bring a flask of hot tea with brandy in it to her daughter and son-in-law. Just as she reached the main entrance the guard was gently but forcibly shoving out a large, agitated, soaking-wet Alsatian dog.

"No, old fellow, you can *not* come in. Hospitals are for people, not for dogs."

"Why, bless me," exclaimed old Mrs. Pearce. "That's Lob! Here, Lob, Lobby boy!"

Lob ran to her, whining. Mrs. Pearce walked up to the desk.

"I'm sorry, madam, you can't bring that dog in here," the guard said.

Mrs. Pearce was a very determined old lady. She looked the porter in the eye.

"Now, see here, young man. That dog has walked twenty miles from St. Killan to get to my granddaughter. Heaven knows how he knew she was here, but it's plain he knows. And he ought to have his rights! He ought to get to see her! Do you know," she went on, bristling, "that dog has walked the length of England—*twice*—to be with that girl? And you think you can keep him out with your fiddling rules and regulations?"

"I'll have to ask the medical officer," the guard said weakly.

"You do that, young man." Granny Pearce sat down in a determined manner, shutting her umbrella, and Lob sat patiently dripping at her feet. Every now and then he shook his head, as if to dislodge something heavy that was tied around his neck.

Presently a tired, thin, intelligent-looking man in a white coat came downstairs, with an impressive, silver-haired man in a dark suit, and there was a low-voiced discussion. Granny Pearce eyed them, biding her time.

"Frankly . . . not much to lose," said the older man. The man in the white coat approached Granny Pearce.

"It's strictly against every rule, but as it's such a serious case we are making an exception," he said to her quietly. "But only *outside* her bedroom door—and only for a moment or two."

Without a word, Granny Pearce rose and stumped upstairs. Lob followed close to her skirts, as if he knew his hope lay with her.

They waited in the green-floored corridor outside Sandy's room. The door was half shut. Bert and Jean were inside. Everything was terribly quiet. A nurse came out. The white-coated man asked her something and she shook her head. She had left the door ajar, and through it could now be seen a high, narrow bed with a lot of gadgets around it. Sandy lay there, very flat under the covers, very still. Her head was turned away. All Lob's attention was riveted on the bed. He strained toward it, but Granny Pearce clasped his collar firmly.

"I've done a lot for you, my boy, now you behave yourself," she whispered grimly. Lob let out a faint whine, anxious and pleading.

At the sound of that whine Sandy stirred just a little. She sighed and moved her head the least fraction. Lob whined again. And then Sandy turned her head right over. Her eyes opened, looking at the door.

"Lob?" she murmured—no more than a breath of sound. "Lobby, boy?"

The doctor by Granny Pearce drew a quick, sharp breath. Sandy moved her left arm—the one that was not broken—from below the covers and let her hand dangle down, feeling, as she always did in the mornings, for Lob's furry head. The doctor nodded slowly.

"All right," he whispered. "Let him go to the bedside. But keep ahold of him."

Granny Pearce and Lob moved to the bedside. Now she could see Bert and Jean, white-faced and shocked, on the far side of the bed. But she didn't look at them. She looked at the smile on her granddaughter's face as the groping fingers found Lob's wet ears and gently pulled them. "Good boy," whispered Sandy, and fell asleep again.

Granny Pearce led Lob out into the passage again. There she let go of him and he ran off swiftly down the stairs. She would have followed him, but Bert and Jean had come out into the passage, and she spoke to Bert fiercely.

"*I* don't know why you were so foolish as not to bring the dog before! Leaving him to find the way here himself—"

"But, Mother!" said Jean Pengelly. "That can't have been Lob. What a chance to take! Suppose Sandy hadn't—" She stopped, with her handkerchief pressed to her mouth.

"Not Lob? I've known that dog nine years! I suppose I ought to know my own granddaughter's dog?"

"Listen, Mother," said Bert. "Lob was killed by the same truck that hit Sandy. Don found him—when he went to look for Sandy's schoolbag. He was—he was dead. Ribs all smashed. No question of that. Don told me on the phone—he and Will Hoskins rowed a half mile out to sea and sank the dog with a lump of concrete tied to his collar. Poor old boy. Still—he was getting on. Couldn't have lasted forever."

"*Sank him at sea?* Then what—?"

Slowly old Mrs. Pearce, and then the other two, turned to look at the trail of dripping-wet footprints that led down the hospital stairs.

In the Pengellys' garden they have a stone, under the palm tree. It says: "Lob. Sandy's dog. Buried at sea."

READER'S RESPONSE

What really happened in the hospital room?

STUDY QUESTIONS

Recalling

1. How far does Lob travel to reach the Pengelly family after his owner returns to Liverpool?
2. Why does Lob's owner give the dog away?
3. What happens to Sandy nine years later?
4. What does Granny Pearce see outside the hospital? What is Sandy's reaction to her visitor?
5. What does Granny Pearce learn about Lob?

Interpreting

6. How would you account for Lob's behavior after the accident?
7. Describe Sandy's and Lob's feelings for each other. What does the story's ending suggest about the power of these feelings?

Extending

8. What might be mysterious about a pet's attachment to an owner?

VOCABULARY

Using the Dictionary

A **dictionary** is a book that lists words in alphabetical order and presents meanings and other information about those words. See the following sample entry for the word *hospital:*

hos·pi·tal (hos′pit əl) *n.* **1.** institution providing medical, surgical, or psychiatric treatment for the sick or injured. **2.** place providing medical care for animals. **3.** repair shop for specified small items: *a watch hospital, a doll hospital.* [Old French *hospital* place to receive persons in need, from Medieval Latin *hospitale* place to receive guests, going back to *hospes* guest, host. . . .]

— *Macmillan Dictionary*

Each word that is listed is called an **entry word**. Entry words are divided into syllables by dots or spaces. For example, the entry here shows that *hospital* has three syllables. The dictionary shows you where to divide the word should you need to write it on two lines.

The **pronunciation** is the way a word is spoken. The dictionary gives an entry word's pronunciation in parentheses after its listing. The letters used in the pronunciation make up a **phonetic alphabet**. The dictionary's **pronunciation key** explains the sounds of these letters.

The **part of speech** is a label that tells how a word is used in a sentence. The abbreviation for an entry word's part of speech usually appears after the pronunciation. For example, the word *hospital* is marked *n.* for noun. Some words can be used as different parts of speech. The word *dog,* for example, can be used as a noun or as a verb.

The **definition**, or meaning, of a word follows the part of speech. Many words have more than one definition. Each definition is numbered, and the most common one is usually listed first.

Most dictionaries also give the entry word's **etymology** [et′ə mol′ə jē], or origin and history. The etymology is shown in brackets either before or after the definition. For example, the word *hospital* comes from an Old French word, *hospital,* which means "place to receive persons in need." This word in turn comes from a Medieval Latin word, *hospitale,* meaning "place to receive guests." This word comes from the Latin word *hospes,* which means both "guest" and "host."

To help you find a word, each dictionary has two guide words at the top of each page. These **guide words** are the first and last entry words on the page. All the other entry words on that page fall alphabetically between the two guide words.

The italicized words below are from "Lob's Girl." Use a dictionary to answer the questions.

1. What is the first meaning of *constitution*?
2. What is the pronunciation of *culvert*?
3. Where would you divide *shuttered* if you could not fit it on one line?
4. What is the origin of the word *agitated*?
5. What does *gadgets* mean? What is its origin?

Thinking Skills: Evaluating

DEFINITION

Evaluating is a way of thinking about something and making a judgment about it. When you evaluate, you apply criteria to make your judgment. Criteria are the standards, rules, or tests on which a judgment can be based.

STEPS

1. **State the reason or purpose for your evaluation.**
   What do you want to evaluate? Why do you want to evaluate it?

2. **Identify the criteria.**
   What specific rules, tests, or standards will you use to make your judgment?

3. **Apply the criteria.**
   Does the subject of your evaluation meet each specific criterion? Does it meet some criteria better than others?

4. **Draw a conclusion.**
   The conclusion is your evaluation of how well the subject meets the criteria.

EXAMPLE

Imagine that you have just heard a new song on the radio and a friend asks you, "Is it a good song?" Of course, you probably answer "yes" or "no" without talking about all your criteria for a good song. In your mind, however, you make your evaluation based on criteria.

1. **State the reason or purpose for your evalua-tion.** You want to evaluate the song in order to give your friend an accurate answer.

2. **Identify the criteria.** You choose to evaluate the song according to its rhythm, melody, lyrics, and performance.

3. **Apply the criteria.** You think that the song has a strong rhythm, a great melody, and is performed with real skill and excitement. You think the lyrics are terrible, however.

4. **Draw a conclusion.** You conclude that the song is good, but it could have been better.

ACTIVITY 1

Evaluating "Lob's Girl"

Follow the four steps of evaluating to answer the question "Is 'Lob's Girl' a good story?" Identify your criteria carefully, being very specific about what you think makes a good story. You may want to include one or more of the following criteria: an exciting plot, believable characters, characters you care about, interesting details about how other people live, parts that make you laugh, parts that make you cry, an effect on your own life.

ACTIVITY 2

Evaluating a Work of Literature

Evaluate another selection in this book or any other work of literature that you have read. Follow the four steps. Remember that different people may have different criteria for good literature. What is important is that you think about your criteria and they reflect what you believe.

Dan Lacy (born 1914) grew up in Virginia and was educated in North Carolina. Trained as a historian, he has been interested in the mystery of Roanoke for much of his professional life. Lacy worked for the State of North Carolina during the 1930s and in 1938 signed a birth certificate that the state created for Virginia Dare, the first child of the Roanoke colony, on the 350th anniversary of her birth. Lacy has written about the Roanoke settlement several times; his book *The Lost Colony* was published in 1972. The following selection about Roanoke is the first chapter of Lacy's work *The Colony of North Carolina.*

The first English settlement in America vanished without a trace. What happened to the 117 men, women, and children who settled Roanoke Island in 1587?

• •

Dan Lacy

Roanoke: The Lost Colony

Roanoke Island is small, flat, and sandy—about twelve miles long and three miles wide. It lies between Pamlico and Albemarle sounds,[1] hidden from the Atlantic Ocean by a long chain of narrow islands, really little more than sand dunes, known as the Outer Banks of North Carolina. Even today only very small ships can reach the sounds by threading their way through narrow inlets[2] in the Outer Banks, inlets that may change with every storm.

Hundreds of years ago, in the summer of 1587, a small band of men, women, and children landed on Roanoke Island and began to clear the trees and build huts. They had sailed from England in three tiny ships, a journey that had lasted for weeks. They came with food and tools and supplies to build homes and establish a permanent colony in the New World.

Englishmen had been on Roanoke Island before this group. Since Columbus's landing[3] in America nearly a century before, expeditions from Spain had conquered and settled Florida, Mexico, the Pacific coast of South America,[4] and most of the larger islands in the Caribbean.[5] Fortunes were

---

1. **Pamlico** [pam′li kō′] **and Albemarle** [al′bə märl′] **sounds:** narrow, shallow bodies of water on the North Carolina coast.
2. **inlets:** narrow channels of water between islands or leading inland from a larger body of water.

3. **Columbus's** [kə lum′bəs əz] **landing:** discovery of America in 1492 by Christopher Columbus (c. 1451–1506), Italian explorer sailing for Spain.
4. **Pacific coast of South America:** In the 1530s and 1540s Spanish explorers conquered the areas that are now Peru and Chile.
5. **Caribbean** [kar′ə bē′ən]: tropical sea bounded on the west by Central America, on the south by South America, and on the north and east by the islands of the West Indies.

made for Spain from the gold and silver mines in Mexico and Peru. An ocean current[6] called the Gulf Stream flows northward from Florida to North Carolina along the coast of what is now the United States. Every year fleets of large, slow Spanish galleons[7] made their way along the coast, following the Gulf Stream until they could strike out east across the Atlantic, laden with American treasure for the king of Spain.

England was then a relatively poor country, far less wealthy and powerful than Spain. But Englishmen were eager to share in the treasures of the New World. They wanted an English empire in America and they wanted a chance to capture Spanish treasure ships and seize their cargoes of gold and silver.

Roanoke Island gave them a chance to do both. It could be their first foothold[8] on the new continent. And light, swift English ships could slip out through the inlets and seize unsuspecting Spanish treasure ships, then retreat back through the same inlets, where large Spanish ships of war could not follow.

Sir Walter Raleigh, a wealthy knight and favorite of Queen Elizabeth I, was given the right to explore and settle the coast of what is now the southern United States. In 1584 he sent an expedition that picked Roanoke Island as the best place for a first colony. The following year a large group of soldiers was sent to the island to build a fort. They used up all their supplies. and before a relief ship came they abandoned the fort

and returned to England on ships commanded by Sir Francis Drake,[9] who by good fortune had stopped at Roanoke Island on his way back from the Caribbean.

When the English settlers landed in 1587 ready to found their colony, they expected to find more than a dozen men who had been left to hold the island over the winter of 1586–87. But all they found was one bare skeleton and the ruins of a destroyed fort. From friendly Indians they learned the story. A band of hostile Indians had attacked the little fort and killed most of the men. The rest had fled in a boat and had never been seen again.

In spite of this warning of the dangers around them, the colonists set out to make their new homes. The fort was restored. Dirt-floored huts were built to provide shelter. A palisade[10] of tree trunks sunk deep in the ground was erected as a wall around the little settlement. Fields were cleared to plant crops. The colonists knew, however, that they did not have sufficient supplies to last them until crops could be harvested the following year. They urged John White, governor of the colony, to return to England so that he could persuade Sir Walter Raleigh to send an immediate relief expedition with more supplies.

Before White left at the end of August 1587, two important things happened—the first children of English parents were born in America. One of the settlers was Governor White's daughter, Eleanor, who made the journey with her husband, Ananias Dare. She had left England knowing she

---

6. **ocean current:** portion of a body of water flowing continuously in a definite direction.
7. **galleons** [gal′ē ənz]: large sailing ships used from the fifteenth to the seventeenth centuries.
8. **foothold:** secure position that can be used as a firm base for further progress or advancement.

9. **Sir Francis Drake:** English admiral and explorer (c. 1540–1596), commander of the first English voyage around the world.
10. **palisade** [pal′i sād′]: fence of stakes set close together to provide protection or defense; here, a group of tree trunks that serve such a purpose.

Indian Village of Pomeiooc, John White, drawing and watercolor, 1585.

would bear a child in the New World. On August 18 the baby was born, a little girl who was christened Virginia. And before a week passed a second baby was born in the colony, a boy to Dyonis and Margery Harvey.

White sailed from a happy and hopeful colony. But when he reached England, he found the country full of preparations for war with Spain. It was too dangerous to try the stormy Atlantic in winter, and with the arrival of spring 1588, England's one thought was to defend itself against an enormous Spanish fleet that had been formed for an invasion. Neither ship nor man could be spared for any other purpose. The great battle with the Armada, as the Spanish fleet was called, took place in the summer of 1588. Helped by a violent storm, the smaller English fleet won a complete victory. But Raleigh was left without money or time to organize a relief expedition that

year, and in 1589 a relief ship was turned back by storms and a Spanish attack.

Not until 1590 did White have a chance to get back to Roanoke Island. His ship made it through the narrow inlet and anchored in the sound. White and a few sailors launched a small boat and rowed to the site of the colony but it was nighttime, and too dark to go on shore. The men played English tunes on a trumpet and loudly sang English songs, so that the colonists they hoped to find on shore would not think they were attacking Indians or Spaniards and fire at them.

There was no answer, but White felt sure that the colonists were safe, for he thought he saw a fire burning on shore. Next morning he eagerly hurried up the beach, hoping to see his daughter and granddaughter, who would have just turned three.

But when John White reached the palisade around the little village, his heart sank. The gate hung open, and on one of the gateposts were carved the letters C R O. Inside all was abandoned. The huts stood empty. Pumpkins grew on the dirt floors and vines twined through the windows. The only sound came from deer scampering away from the newcomers. A trench had been opened, in which trunks and boxes had been buried. Books, papers, and pieces of armor, some of them White's own that he had left, were scattered about, mildewed and rusted by the rain. The settlers were gone, leaving nothing of value except the buried chests and a few bars of iron and lead too heavy to carry.

They were gone, but where? On a tree was carved the full word CROATOAN. White had agreed with the colonists when he left three years before that if they moved, they would carve on a tree the name of the place to which they were going. If they were in serious trouble, they were to carve a cross above the name. There was no cross, and White was cheered by this. He knew of a friendly Indian village called Croatan near Cape Hatteras.[11] One of their chiefs, Manteo, had gone back to England with one of the earlier expeditions and had returned with White's colonists. He spoke English and had been very helpful. No doubt the colonists had sought shelter in his village when they ran short of food or were pressed[12] by the hostile Indians of the mainland. White was encouraged by the fact that there was no evidence of fighting on Roanoke Island.

He hoped to leave the next day for Croatan. But a severe storm arose that left the British ships battered and unable to sail to the village. The captain of the little fleet had to put out to sea and was not willing to bring his damaged ships back to the stormy Outer Banks. John White never got back to Roanoke, and no white man ever saw the settlers again. They had become the Lost Colony.

Nobody knows what happened to them. Apparently they stayed at Roanoke Island for a year or two and then left, but not because of an Indian attack. They probably ran out of food and went to Croatan, as their carving said, hoping to live on fish and oysters and such food as they could get from Manteo's friendly tribe. They may have built a ship or used a small pinnace[13] left with them in an effort to return to England, and may have been lost at sea. Twenty years later the English settled Jamestown in Virginia and sent out explorers to try to learn the fate of the lost colonists. They heard many rumors, but most of them said that Powhatan, the Indian ruler of the whole area, had wiped out the colony because it had become allied with other tribes that warred with Powhatan. Other rumors said that some of the settlers had survived and lived among the Indians, intermarrying with them but still speaking the English language and living in houses built in the English manner. But no such survivors, if there were any, were ever found. Whatever their fate, they live in memory as the first English men and women to cross the ocean intending to make their homes and their children's homes forever in the New World.

---

11. **Cape Hatteras** [hat′ər əs]: point of land extending out from an island off the eastern coast of North Carolina; site of many shipwrecks.
12. **pressed:** repeatedly attacked, harassed, or annoyed.

---

13. **pinnace** [pin′is]: a small boat.

READER'S RESPONSE

If you were John White, how would you feel about not being able to land on Croatan?

STUDY QUESTIONS

Recalling

1. What is Roanoke, and where is it located?
2. Why did England want to establish colonies in America?
3. Who was John White, and why did he sail to England in August 1587?
4. What did White find at Roanoke in 1590? What did he see on a gatepost? On a tree?
5. List two of the various explanations that have since been suggested for the mystery of Roanoke.

Interpreting

6. Which explanation for the disappearance of Roanoke do you find most likely? Why?
7. Mention four ways in which life was harder for the colonists than it is for us today.

READING AND LITERARY FOCUS

Nonfiction and Mystery

Nonfiction is factual prose writing. It focuses on actual events, people, and places. The writer of nonfiction allows us to see the real-life world in a new and memorable way.

There are many different types of nonfiction. A **biography** is the story of someone's life written by another person. An **autobiography** is the story of a person's life written by that person. Newspaper articles, personal essays, and informative books on any subject imaginable are other types of nonfiction. Dan Lacy's account of Roanoke is an example of informative historical writing.

One of the most gripping subjects for a nonfiction writer is a real-life mystery. The real world can be a mysterious and disorderly place. Often when the trail of facts ends, the nonfiction writer is left with an unsolved mystery. A fiction writer could invent a tidy solution to the mystery of Roanoke Island. A history writer like Dan Lacy, however, cannot depart from the facts: He must leave the loose ends dangling.

Thinking About Nonfiction and Mystery

1. The colonists arriving on Roanoke found a skeleton and a destroyed fort, yet they decided to remain on the island. What ideas about the colonists' inner strength does this suggest?
2. What idea about the Roanoke settlers is suggested by Lacy's final sentence?

COMPOSITION

Writing About Nonfiction

What main idea about the Roanoke colony does Dan Lacy express in this selection? **Prewriting:** Make a list of several possible main ideas. After reviewing the selection, choose the idea that seems most appropriate. Then make a chart, listing specific facts, details, and examples that the author uses to express this idea. **Writing:** First present the main idea. Then choose from your chart the items that relate most closely to the idea, and explain the relationship. **Revising:** Reread your work to make sure you have expressed your ideas clearly and logically. *For help with this assignment, see Lesson 6 in the Writing About Literature Handbook at the back of this book.*

Writing About a Real-Life Mystery

Write about a real-life mystery in which you played a part. The mystery may be ordinary or unusual. First briefly describe the mystery and how you became involved in it. Then explain how you (or someone else) solved it. End by explaining what the mystery has taught you about life in general.

T. S. (Thomas Stearns) Eliot (1888–1965) is one of the most important writers of this century. He was born in St. Louis, Missouri, and studied at Harvard University. After graduation he went to England and eventually made his home there. As a result, Eliot is regarded as both an American and an English author. Most of Eliot's poetry is serious and thoughtful. Besides his serious poetry, however, he wrote *Old Possum's Book of Practical Cats,* a series of playful, funny poems about cats. "Macavity: The Mystery Cat" comes from this book, which became the basis for the musical *Cats.*

**You may seek him in the basement, you may look up in the air—
But I tell you once and once again, *Macavity's not there!***

• •

T. S. Eliot

Macavity: The Mystery Cat

Macavity's a Mystery Cat: he's called the Hidden Paw—
For he's the master criminal who can defy the Law.
He's the bafflement of Scotland Yard, the Flying Squad's[1] despair:
For when they reach the scene of crime—*Macavity's not there*!

5　Macavity, Macavity, there's no one like Macavity,
He's broken every human law, he breaks the law of gravity.
His powers of levitation would make a fakir[2] stare,
And when you reach the scene of crime—*Macavity's not there*!
You may seek him in the basement, you may look up in the air—
10　But I tell you once and once again, *Macavity's not there*!

Macavity's a ginger cat, he's very tall and thin;
You would know him if you saw him, for his eyes are sunken in.
His brow is deeply lined with thought, his head is highly domed;
His coat is dusty from neglect, his whiskers are uncombed.
15　He sways his head from side to side, with movements like a snake;
And when you think he's half asleep, he's always wide awake.

---

1. **bafflement** [baf'əl mənt] **. . . Squad:** a cause of great puzzle or confusion
for Scotland Yard, the branch of the London police involved in solving crimes,
and for the Flying Squad, a police unit organized for rapid movement.
2. **fakir** [fə kēr']: member of a Moslem or Hindu religious group; here [fā'kər],
referring to someone who has unusual powers.

Macavity, Macavity, there's no one like Macavity,
For he's a fiend in feline shape, a monster of depravity.[3]
You may meet him in a by-street, you may see him in the square—
20 But when a crime's discovered, then *Macavity's not there!*

He's outwardly respectable. (They say he cheats at cards.)
And his footprints are not found in any file of Scotland Yard's.
And when the larder's looted, or the jewel-case is rifled,
Or when the milk is missing, or another Peke's[4] been stifled,
25 Or the greenhouse glass is broken, and the trellis[5] past repair—
Ay, there's the wonder of the thing! *Macavity's not there!*

And when the Foreign Office[6] find a Treaty's gone astray,
Or the Admiralty[7] lose some plans and drawings by the way,
There may be a scrap of paper in the hall or on the stair—
30 But it's useless to investigate—*Macavity's not there!*
And when the loss has been disclosed, the Secret Service[8] say:
"It *must* have been Macavity!"—but he's a mile away.
You'll be sure to find him resting, or a-licking of his thumbs,
Or engaged in doing complicated long division sums.

35 Macavity, Macavity, there's no one like Macavity,
There never was a Cat of such deceitfulness and suavity.[9]
He always has an alibi,[10] and one or two to spare:
At whatever time the deed took place—MACAVITY WASN'T THERE!
And they say that all the Cats whose wicked deeds are widely known
40 (I might mention Mungojerrie, I might mention Griddlebone)
Are nothing more than agents for the Cat who all the time
Just controls their operations: the Napoleon[11] of Crime!

---

3. **depravity** [di prav′ə tē]: state of being morally bad, or wicked.
4. **Peke:** Pekingese, a dog with a flat face and a long, silky coat.
5. **trellis** [trel′is]: structure made of crossed wooden or metal strips, used to support growing vines.
6. **Foreign Office:** government department that handles relations between countries.
7. **Admiralty** [ad′mər əl tē]: British government department in charge of naval affairs.
8. **Secret Service:** government department or bureau that performs secret operations such as spying.
9. **deceitfulness and suavity** [swäv′ə tē]: dishonesty and a smooth, sophisticated manner.
10. **alibi** [al′ə bī′]: claim or proof of having been elsewhere at the time a crime was committed.
11. **Napoleon** [nə pō′lē ən]: Napoleon Bonaparte (1769–1821), French military leader and conqueror, emperor of France from 1804 to 1815.

READER'S RESPONSE

What is your candidate for the funniest phrase or line in this poem?

STUDY QUESTIONS

Recalling

1. According to the first stanza, whom or what does Macavity baffle? What do people find when they reach the scene of the crime?
2. According to the third stanza, what does Macavity look like?
3. Mention three examples of Macavity's crimes, as described in the third and fourth stanzas.
4. What does the poem's last line call Macavity?

Interpreting

5. Find two examples of exaggeration in the poem. What do these examples add to the picture of Macavity?
6. Does the speaker disapprove of Macavity or admire him? How can you tell?

VOCABULARY

Antonyms

Antonyms are words that have opposite or nearly opposite meanings. *Noisy* and *quiet* are antonyms. The capitalized words in the following numbered items are from "Macavity: The Mystery Cat." Choose the word that is *most nearly opposite* the meaning of each capitalized word, *as the word is used in the selection.* Write the number of each item and the letter of your choice on a separate sheet.

1. DEFY: (a) resist (b) yield
   (c) improve (d) argue
2. FIEND: (a) angel (b) genius
   (c) animal (d) devil
3. DECEITFULNESS: (a) hope (b) despair
   (c) dishonesty (d) candor
4. STIFLED: (a) rescued (b) yawned
   (c) killed (d) frustrated
5. LEVITATION: (a) sense of humor
   (b) ability to float (c) silence
   (d) tendency to fall

Born in Tennessee, Henry Sydnor Harrison (1880–1930) spent his twenties as a newspaperman on the *Times-Dispatch* in Richmond, Virginia. He subsequently chose to devote himself to writing fiction and six months later finished his first novel, *Queed.* Based on Harrison's experiences as a newspaperman, *Queed* became a bestseller. In addition, Harrison wrote six more novels and numerous short stories.

"Oh, they'll never catch her, sir—never! She's too smart for 'em all, Miss Hinch is."

● ●

Henry Sydnor Harrison

Miss Hinch

In the bright light of the entrance to the 126th Street subway, two strangers came almost face to face. One was an old woman, white-haired, wrinkled, spectacled, and stooped. She was wearing an old black hat, wispy veil, and blue shawl. The other, a gentleman, was going more slowly down the drafty steps. He studied the woman from behind with a singular intentness.

An express train was just thundering in, which the man, slowed as he was by a lame foot and a stout cane, was barely in time to catch. He entered the same car with the woman and chanced to take a seat directly across from her. It must have been after half-past eleven, and the sleet and bitter cold were discouraging to travel. The car was almost deserted. Even in this underground retreat, the bitter breath of the night blew and bit, and the old woman shivered under her shawl. At last, her teeth chattering, she got up in an apologetic sort of way and moved toward the better-pro-

tected rear of the car, feeling the empty seats as she went in search of hot pipes. The man's eyes followed her, and he watched her sink down, presently, into a seat on his own side of the car. A young couple sat between them now; he could no longer see the woman, beyond occasional glimpses of her black knees and her ancient bonnet, skewered on with a long steel hatpin.

Nothing could have seemed more trivial than this change of seats on the part of a thin-blooded and half-frozen passenger. But it happened to be a time of mutual doubt and mistrust in the metropolis.[1] Through days of fruitless searching for a fugitive outlaw of extraordinary gifts, the nerve of the city had been slowly strained to the breaking point.

The man pondered; mechanically he

---

1. **metropolis** [mi trop′ə lis]: large city.

turned up his coat collar and fell to stamping his icy feet. He was a gentleman, by his garb—rather short, very full-bodied, bearded, and somewhat puffy-faced, with heavy cheeks cut by deep creases. Well-lined against the cold though he was, he, too, began to suffer visibly and presently was forced to retreat in his turn, seeking out a new place where the heating apparatus gave a better account of itself. He found one only two seats beyond the old woman, limped into it, and soon relapsed into his own thoughts.

The woman in the hat and shawl sat in a sad kind of silence, and the train hurled itself roaringly through the tunnel. After a time, she glanced timidly at the man, and her look fell swiftly from his face to the discarded "ten-o'clock-extra" lying by his side. She removed her dim gaze and let it travel casually about the car; but before long it returned again, pointedly, to the newspaper. Then, with some obvious hesitation, she bent forward and said, "Excuse me, but would you please let me look at your paper a minute, sir?"

The man came out of his reverie instantly and looked up with almost an eager smile. "Certainly. Keep it if you like; I am quite through with it."

The woman opened the paper with gloved fingers. The garish[2] headlines told the story at a glance:

EARTH OPENED AND SWALLOWED MISS HINCH—HEADQUARTERS VIRTUALLY ABANDONS CASE—EVEN JESSIE DARK SEEMS STUMPED.

Below the spread was the story, marked "by Jessie Dark." Jessie Dark, it was clear, was a most extraordinary journalist—a "crime expert." More than this, she was a crime expert to be taken seriously, it seemed—no mere office-desk sleuth,[3] but an actual performer with a formidable list of notches on her gun; and nearly every one of them involved the capture of a woman.

Nevertheless, it could not be pretended that the paragraphs in this evening's extra seemed to foreshadow a new triumph on the part of Jessie Dark at an early date; and the old woman in the car presently laid down the newspaper with an irrepressible[4] sigh.

The man glanced toward her kindly. The sigh was so audible that it seemed to be almost an invitation; besides, public interest in the great case was so tense that conversation between total strangers was the rule wherever two or three were gathered together.

"You were reading about this strange mystery, perhaps?"

The woman, with a sharp intake of breath, answered, "Yes, sir. Oh, sir, it seems as if I couldn't think of anything else."

"Ah?" he said, without surprise. "It certainly appears to be a remarkable affair."

Remarkable indeed the affair seemed. In a tiny little room within ten steps of Broadway,[5] at half-past nine o'clock on a fine evening, Miss Hinch had killed John Catherwood with the light sword she used in her well-known representation of the Father of his Country.[6] So far the tragedy

---

2. **garish** [gar′ish]: glaring.

3. **sleuth** [slōōth]: detective.
4. **irrepressible** [ir′i pres′ə bəl]: unable to be held back or controlled.
5. **Broadway:** street running through New York City, noted in one section as a theater district.
6. **Father of his Country:** George Washington (1732–1799), first President of the United States.

was commonplace enough. What had given it extraordinary interest was the amazing faculty of the woman, which had made her famous while she was still in her teens. She happened to be the most astonishing impersonator[7] of her time. Her brilliant act consisted of a series of character changes, many of them done in full sight of the audience with the assistance only of a small table of properties[8] half concealed under a net. Some of these transformations were so amazing as to be beyond belief, even after one had sat and watched them. Not her appearance only, but voice, speech, manner, carriage, all shifted incredibly to fit the new part; so that the woman appeared to have no permanent form or fashion of her own, but to be only so much plastic human material out of which her cunning could mold at will man, woman, or child.

Without her disguises, she was a tall, thin young woman with strongly marked features and considerable beauty of a bold sort. What she would look like at the present moment nobody could even venture a guess. Having stabbed John Catherwood in her dressing room at the theater, she had put on her hat and coat, dropped two wigs and her make-up kit into a handbag, said good night to the doorman, and walked out into Broadway. Within ten minutes the body of Catherwood was found and the chase begun. That had been two weeks ago. Since then, no one had seen her. The earth, indeed, seemed to have opened and swallowed her. Yet her features were almost as well known as a president's.

"A remarkable case," repeated the man, rather absently; and his neighbor respectfully agreed.

After that she hesitated a moment and then added with sudden bitterness, "Oh, they'll never catch her, sir—never! She's too smart for 'em all, Miss Hinch is."

Attracted by her tone, the man inquired if she was particularly interested in the case.

"Yes, sir—I got reason to be. Jack Catherwood's mother and me was at school together, and great friends all our life long. Oh, sir," she went on, as if in answer to his look of faint surprise, "Jack was a fine gentleman, with manners and looks and all. But he never grew away from his old mother, sir—no, sir, never! Maybe he done things he hadn't ought, as high-spirited lads will, but he was a good boy in his heart. And it does seem hard for him to die like that—and that woman free to go her way, ruinin' and killin'."

"My good woman," said the man presently, "compose yourself."

The woman dutifully lowered her handkerchief and tried to compose herself, as bidden.

"But oh, sir, she's that clever. Through poor Jack we of course heard much gossip about her, and they do say that her best trick was not done on the stage at all. They say, sir, that let her only step behind her screen for a minute—for she kept her secrets well, Miss Hinch did—and she's come walking out to you, and you could go right up to her in the full light and take her hand, and still you couldn't make yourself believe that it was her."

"Yes," said the man, "I have heard that she is remarkably clever—though, as a stranger in this part of the world, I never saw her act. It is all very interesting and strange."

---

7. **impersonator** [im pur′sə nāt′ər]: person who takes on the appearance, voice, or behavior of another.
8. **properties:** movable items used on the set of a play.

He turned his head and stared through the rear door at the dark, flying walls. At the same moment the woman turned her head and stared full at the man. When he turned back, her gaze had gone off toward the front of the car, and he picked up the paper thoughtfully.

"I'm a visitor in the city, from Denver, Colorado," he said presently, "and knew nothing about the case until an evening or two ago, when I attended a meeting here. Upon my word, the people talked of nothing else. I confess they got me quite interested in their gossip. So tonight I bought this paper to see what this extraordinary woman detective it employs had to say about it. I must say I was disappointed, after all the talk about her."

"Yes, sir, indeed, and no wonder, for she's told Mrs. Catherwood herself that she's never made such a failure as this, so far. It seemed like she could always catch women, sir, up to this. It seemed like she knew in her own mind just what a woman would do, where she'd try to hide and all; and so she could find them time and time when the men detectives didn't know where to look. But, oh, sir, she's never had to hunt for such a woman as Miss Hinch before!"

The subway was slowing down, and the few other passengers on the car rose for their station.

"Grand Central!"[9] cried the guard.

The door rolled shut behind the departing passengers, and the train flung itself on its way. Within the car, a lengthy silence ensued. The man stared thoughtfully at the floor, and the old woman fell back upon her borrowed paper. She appeared to be rereading the observations of Jessie Dark with considerable care. Presently she lowered the paper and began a quiet search for something under the folds of her shawl; at length, her hands emerging empty, she broke the silence with a timid request.

"Oh, sir—have you a pencil you could lend me, please? I'd like to mark something in the piece to send to Mrs. Catherwood. It's what she says here about the disguises, sir."

The kindly man felt in his pockets, and after some hunting produced a pencil—a fat white one with blue lead. She thanked him gratefully.

"How is Mrs. Catherwood bearing all this strain and anxiety?" he asked suddenly. "Have you seen her today?"

"Oh, yes. I've been spending the evening with her since seven o'clock and am just back from there now. Oh, she's very much broke up, sir."

She looked at him hesitatingly. He stared straight in front of him, saying nothing, though he knew, in common with the rest of the reading world, that Jack Catherwood's mother lived, not on 126th Street, but on East Tenth. Presently he wondered if his silence had not been an error of judgment. Perhaps that misstatement had not been a slip, but something cleverer.

The woman went on with a certain eagerness: "Oh, sir, it does look to Mrs. Catherwood, and me too, that if Jessie Dark was going to catch her at all, she'd have done it before now. Look at those big, bold blue eyes Miss Hinch had, sir, with lashes an inch long, they say, and that terrible long chin. They do say she can change the color of her eyes, not forever of course, but put a few of her drops into them and make them look entirely different for a time. But that chin, sir, ye'd say—"

9. **Grand Central:** major New York City railroad terminal and subway station.

Nighthawks, Edward Hopper, 1942.

She broke off; for the man had suddenly picked up his heavy stick and risen. "Here we are at Fourteenth Street," he said, nodding pleasantly. "I must change here. Good night. Success to Jessie Dark, I say!"

He was watching the woman's faded face intently, and he saw just that look of respectful surprise break into it that he had expected. "Fourteenth Street, sir! I'd no notion at all we'd come so far. It's where I get out too, sir, the expresses not stopping at my station."

"Ah?" said the man, with the utmost dryness.

He led the way, limping and leaning on his stick. They emerged upon the chill and cheerless platform. The man, after a few steps, stopped and turned. The woman had halted. Over the intervening space their eyes met.

"Come," said the man gently. "Come, let us walk about a little to keep warm."

"Oh, sir—it's too kind of you, sir," said the woman, coming forward.

From other cars two or three blue-nosed people had got off to make the change; one or two came straggling in from the street; but, scattered over the bleak concrete expanse, they detracted[10] little from the isolation that seemed to surround the woman and the man. Step for step, the odd pair made their way to the extreme northern end of the platform.

"By the way," said the man, halting abruptly, "may I see that paper again for a moment?"

"Oh, yes, sir—of course," said the

_____

10. **detracted** [di trakt'id]: lessened or took away from.

woman, producing it from beneath her shawl. "If you want it back, sir—"

He said that he wanted only to glance at it for a moment; but he fell to looking through it page by page, with considerable care. The woman glanced at him several times with timid respect. Finally she said hesitatingly, "I think, sir, I'll ask the ticket-chopper[11] how long before the next train. I'm very late as it is, sir; and I still must stop to get something to eat before I go to bed."

"An excellent idea," said the man.

He explained that he, too, was already an hour behind time and was spending the night with cousins in Newark, to boot. Side by side, they retraced their steps down the platform, got the schedule from the sleepy chopper, and started slowly back again. But, before they had gone very far, the woman all at once stopped short and, with a white face, leaned against the wall.

"Oh, sir, I'm afraid I'll just have to stop and get a bite somewhere before I go on. You'll think me foolish, sir; but I missed my supper entirely tonight, and there is quite a faint feeling coming over me."

The man looked at her with apparent concern. "Do you know, my friend, you seem to anticipate all my own wants: Your mentioning something to eat just now reminded me that I myself was all but famishing." He glanced at his watch, appearing to deliberate. "Yes, there is still time before my train. Come, we will find a modest eating place together."

They ascended the stairs together and, coming out into Fourteenth Street, started west. In the first block they came to a brilliantly-lit eating place. But the woman timidly preferred not to stop there, saying that the glare was very bad for her old eyes. There was an unpretentious restaurant two blocks farther on, called Miller's Restaurant, if the gentleman didn't mind stopping there. He did not.

They entered by the front door and sat down at a table facing each other. The woman read the menu through and finally ordered poached eggs on toast. The man ordered the same. Just as they were finishing the simple meal, the woman said apologetically, "If you'll excuse me, sir—could I see the bill of fare[12] a minute? I think I'd best take a little pot of tea to warm me up, if they do not charge too high."

"I haven't the bill of fare," said the man.

They looked diligently for the cardboard strip, but it was nowhere to be seen. The waiter drew near.

"Yes, Ma'am! I certainly left it there on the table when I took the order."

"I'm sure I can't imagine what's become of it," repeated the man, rather insistently.

He looked hard at the woman and found that she was looking hard at him. Both pairs of eyes fell instantly.

The waiter brought another bill of fare; the woman ordered tea; the waiter came back with it. The man paid for both orders with a dollar bill that looked hard-earned.

The tea proved to be very hot; it could not be drunk down at a gulp. The man, watching the woman intently as she sipped, seemed to grow more and more restless. His fingers drummed the tablecloth; he could hardly sit still. All at once he said, "What is that calling in the street? It sounds like newsboys."

---

11. **ticket-chopper:** official responsible for collecting and canceling tickets.

12. **bill of fare:** menu.

The City from Greenwich Village, John Sloan, 1922.

The woman put her old head on one side and listened. "Yes, sir. There seems to be an extra edition out."

"Upon my word," he said after a pause, "I believe I'll go get one."

He rose slowly, took down his hat from the hanger near him, and grasping his heavy stick, limped to the door. Leaving it open behind him, much to the annoyance of the proprietor in the cashier's cage, he stood a moment in the little vestibule,[13]

_____
13. **vestibule** [ves′tə būl′]: lobby or entrance hall.

looking up and down the street. Then he took a few slow steps eastward, beckoning with his hand as he went, and so passed out of sight of the woman at the table.

The restaurant was on the corner, and outside the man paused for half a breath. He turned the corner into the darker cross street and began to walk, continually looking about him. Presently his pace quickened, quickened so that he no longer even used his stout cane. A newsboy thrust an extra under his very nose, and he did not even see it.

Far down the street, nearly two blocks away, a tall figure in a blue coat stood under a street light, stamping his feet in the freezing sleet; and the hurrying man sped straight toward him. But he did not get very far. As he passed the side entrance at the extreme rear of the restaurant, a departing guest dashed out so recklessly as to run full into him, stopping him dead.

Without looking, he knew who it was. In fact, he did not look at her at all, but turned his head hurriedly east and west, sweeping the cross street with a swift eye. But the old woman, having drawn back with a sharp exclamation as they collided, rushed breathlessly into apologies.

"Oh, sir—excuse me, sir! A newsboy popped his head into the side door just after you went out, sir, and I ran to him to get you the paper. But he got away too quick for me, sir; and so I—"

"Exactly," said the man in his quiet, deep voice. "That must have been the very boy I myself was after."

On the other side, two men had just turned into the street, well muffled against the night, talking cheerfully as they trudged along. Now the man looked full at the woman, and she saw that there was a smile on his face.

"As he seems to have eluded us both, suppose we return to the subway?"

"Yes, sir; it's full time I—"

"The sidewalk is so slippery," he went on gently, "perhaps you had better take my arm."

The woman did as she was bidden.

Behind the pair, in the restaurant, the waiter came forward to shut the door and lingered to discuss with the proprietor the sudden departure of his two patrons. However, the bill had been paid in full, with a liberal tip for service; and so there was no special complaint to make. After listening to some markedly unfavorable comments on the ways of customers, the waiter returned to his table to set it in order.

On the floor in the carpeted aisle between tables lay a white rectangle of cardboard, which he readily recognized as one of their bills of fare, face downward. He stopped and picked it up. On the back of it was some scribbling, made with a blue lead pencil. The handwriting was very loose and irregular, as if the writer had had his eyes elsewhere while he wrote; and it was with some difficulty that the waiter deciphered this message:

> *Miss Hinch 14th St. subway.*
> *Get police quick.*

The waiter carried this curious document to the proprietor, who read it over a number of times. He was a dull man and had a dull man's suspiciousness of a practical joke. However, after a good deal of discussion, he put on his overcoat and went out for a police officer. He turned west, and halfway up the block met an elderly bluecoat[14] sauntering east. The officer looked at the scribbling and dismissed it as a wag's foolishness of the sort that was bothering the life out of him a dozen times a day. He walked along with the proprietor; and as they drew near to the latter's place of business, both became aware at the same moment of footsteps thudding nearer up the cross street from the south. As they looked up, two young police officers, accompanied by a man in a uniform like a streetcar conductor's, swept around the corner and dashed straight into the restaurant.

---

14. **bluecoat:** policeman.

Night Shadows, Edward Hopper, etching, 1921.

The first officer and the proprietor ran in after them and found them staring about rather vacantly. One of the breathless arms of the law demanded if any suspicious characters had been seen about the place, and the proprietor said no. The officers, looking rather flat, explained their errand. It seemed that a few moments before, the third man, who was a ticket-chopper at the subway station, had found a mysterious message lying on the floor by his box. When it had come, how long it had lain there, he had not the slightest idea. However, there

it was. One officer exhibited a crumpled white scrap torn from a newspaper, on which was scrawled in blue pencil:

Miss Hinch Miller's Restaurant.
Get police quick.

The first police officer produced the message on the bill of fare, so utterly at odds with this. The proprietor, now reminding himself, mentioned the man and the old woman who had taken poached eggs and tea together, called for a second bill of fare, and departed so unexpectedly by different doors. The ticket-chopper recalled that he had seen the same pair at his station; they had come up, he remembered, and questioned him closely about trains. The three officers were momentarily puzzled by this testimony. But it was soon plain to them that if either the woman or the man really had any information about Miss Hinch—which was highly unlikely—they would never have stopped with peppering the neighborhood with silly little contradictory[15] messages.

"They're a pair of old fools trying to have sport with the police, and I'd like to run them in for it," growled the older officer; and this was the general verdict.

The little conference broke up. The proprietor returned to his cage, the waiter to his table; the subway man departed on the run for his chopping-box; the three officers passed out into the bitter night. They walked together, grumbling, and their feet, perhaps by some subconscious impulse, turned eastward toward the subway. In the middle of the next block a man came running up to them.

"Officer, look what I found on the sidewalk a minute ago. Read that scribble!"

He held up a white slab, which proved to be a bill of fare from Miller's Restaurant. On the back of it the three peering officers saw, almost illegibly[16] scrawled in blue pencil:

Police!
Miss Hinch 14th St. subw—

The hand trailed off on the *w* as though the writer had been suddenly interrupted.

The older officer threatened arrests. But the second officer raised his head from the bill of fare and said suddenly, "Tim, I believe there's something in this. Suppose, now, the old woman was Miss Hinch herself, for instance, and the man was shadowing her while pretending he never suspicioned her, and Miss Hinch not daring to cut and run for it till she was sure she had a clean getaway. Well, now, Tim, what better could he do—"

"That's right!" exclaimed the third police officer. "Specially when you think that Hinch carries a gun, and will use it too! Why not have a look in at the subway station anyway, the three of us?"

This proposal carried the day. The three officers started for the subway, the citizen following. Unconsciously their pace quickened until all three broke into an open run.

However, the man and the woman had five minutes' start and that, as it happened, was all that the occasion required. On Fourteenth Street, as they made their way arm in arm to the station, they were seen, and remembered, by a number of pedestrians. It was observed by more than one that the old woman lagged as if she were tired, while the man, supporting her on his arm, steadily kept her up to his own brisk gait.

So walking, the pair descended the subway steps, came out upon the bare platform again, and presently stood once more at the extreme uptown end of it, just where they had waited half an hour before. Nearby a careless porter had overturned a bucket of water, and a splotch of thin ice ran out and over the edge of the concrete. Two young men distinctly heard the man warn the woman to look out for this ice. Far away to the north was to be heard the faint roar of an approaching train.

---

15. **contradictory** [kon'trə dik'tər ē]: contrary or in opposition to one another; not consistent.
16. **illegibly** [i lej'ə blē]: in a manner that is difficult to read.

The woman stood nearest the track, and the man stood in front of her. In the vague light their looks met, and each was struck by the pallor[17] of the other's face. In addition, the woman was breathing hard, and her hands and feet betrayed some nervousness. It was difficult now to ignore the fact that for an hour they had been clinging desperately to each other, at all costs; but the man made a creditable[18] effort to do so. He talked ramblingly, in a kind voice, for the most part of the deplorable weather and his train to Newark, for which he was now so late. And all the time both of them were incessantly turning their heads toward the station entrance, as if expecting some arrival.

As he talked, the man kept his hands unobtrusively busy. From the edge of his black coat he drew a pin and stuck it deep into the ball of his middle finger. He took out his handkerchief to dust the hard sleet from his broad hat, and under his overcoat he pressed the handkerchief against his bleeding finger. While making these small arrangements, he held the woman's eyes with his own, chatting kindly; and, still holding them, he suddenly broke off his random talk and peered at her cheek with concern.

"My good woman, you've scratched your cheek somehow! Why, bless me, it's bleeding quite badly."

"Never mind," said the woman, and looked hurriedly toward the entrance.

"But, good gracious, I must mind! The blood will fall on your shawl. If you will permit me—ah!"

Too quick for her, he leaned forward and, through the thin veil, swept her cheek hard with his handkerchief; and, removing it, held it up so that she might see the blood for herself. But she did not glance at the handkerchief, and neither did he. His gaze was riveted upon her cheek, which looked smooth and clear where he had smudged the clever wrinkles away.

Down the steps and upon the platform pounded the feet of three flying police officers. But it was quite evident now that the express would thunder in just ahead of them. The man, standing close in front of the woman, took a firmer grip on his heavy stick and smiled full into her face.

"Miss Hinch, you are not so terribly clever, after all!"

The woman sprang back from him with an exclamation, and in that moment her eye fell upon the police. Unluckily, her foot slipped upon the treacherous ice—or it may have tripped on the stout cane when the man suddenly shifted its position. In the next breath the express train roared past.

The body of the woman was not mangled or mutilated in the least. There was a deep blue bruise on the left temple, and apparently that was all; even the ancient hat remained on her head, skewered fast by the long pin. It was the man who found the body, huddled at the side of the track where the train had flung it—he who covered the still face and superintended the removal to the platform. Two eyewitnesses of the tragedy pointed out the ice on which the unfortunate woman had slipped, and described their horror as they saw her companion spring forward—just too late to save her.

Not wishing to bring on a delirium of excitement among the half-dozen chance bystanders, two police officers drew the man

---

17. **pallor** [pal'ər]: paleness.
18. **creditable** [kred'i tə bəl]: worthy of approval or praise.

quietly aside and showed him the three mysterious messages. Apparently much affected by the woman's shocking end, he readily owned to having written them. He briefly recounted how the woman's movements had arrested his attention, and how, watching her closely on the car, he had finally detected that she wore a wig. Unfortunately, however, her suspicions appeared to have been aroused by his interest in her; and thereafter a long battle of wits had ensued between them—he trying to call the police without her knowledge, she dogging him close to prevent that, and at the same time watching her chance to give him the slip. He recalled how, in the restaurant, when he had invented an excuse to leave her for an instant, she had made a bolt and narrowly missed getting away; and finally how, having brought her back to the subway and seeing the police at last near, he had exposed her make-up and had spoken her name, with unexpectedly shocking results.

"And now," he concluded in a shaken voice, "I am naturally most anxious to know whether I am right—or have made some terrible mistake. Will you look at her, officer, and tell me if it is—she?"

But the older officer shook his head over the well-known ability of Miss Hinch to look like everybody else in the world but herself. "I'll leave it for headquarters," he said. "But, if it is her, she's gone to her reward, sir. Now, would you give me your name, sir. They may want you in the morning."

The man gave it: Mr. Theodore Shaler, of Denver; city address, 245 East 126th Street. Having thus discharged his duty in the affair, he started sadly to go away; but passing by the silent figure stretched on a bench under the ticket-chopper's overcoat, he bared his head and stopped for one last look at it.

The man's gentleness and efficiency had already won favorable comments from the bystanders, and of the first quality he now gave a final proof. The dead woman's wadded-up handkerchief, which somebody had recovered from the track and laid upon her breast, had slipped to the floor; and the man, observing it, stooped silently to restore it again. This last small service chanced to bring his head close to the head of the dead woman; and, as he straightened up again, her projecting hatpin struck his cheek and ripped a straight line down it. This in itself would have been a trifle, since scratches soon heal. But it happened that the point of the hatpin caught under the lining of the man's perfect beard and ripped it clean from him; so that, as he rose with a sudden shrill cry, he turned upon the astonished onlookers the bare, smooth chin of a woman, curiously long and pointed.

There was only one such chin in the world, and anyone in the street would have known it at a glance. Amid a sudden uproar, the police closed in on Miss Hinch and handcuffed her.

This much the police did. But it was quite distinctly understood that it was Jessie Dark who had really made the capture, and the papers next morning printed pictures of the unconquerable little woman and of the hatpin with which she had reached back from another world to bring her greatest adversary[19] to justice.

---

19. **adversary** [ad'vər ser'ē]: opponent; enemy.

READER'S RESPONSE

Did the ending take you by surprise? Why?

STUDY QUESTIONS

Recalling

1. Describe the man and woman in the subway car.
2. Why is Miss Hinch the talk of the town?
3. What are Miss Hinch's and Jessie Dark's special talents?
4. Describe the manner in which the man and the woman leave the restaurant.
5. What items are found by the restaurant owner, the ticket chopper, and the man in the street?
6. Explain how the identities of Jessie Dark and Miss Hinch are finally revealed.

Interpreting

7. At what point did you begin to suspect that one of the two old people was Miss Hinch?
8. What light does the ending shed on each of these events: (a) the woman's request for the newspaper, (b) the man's departure from the restaurant, and (c) the man's statement, "Miss Hinch, you are not so terribly clever, after all!"
9. Is Miss Hinch's capture the result of bad luck, or does she contribute to her own downfall?

READING AND LITERARY FOCUS

Clues: Predicting Outcomes

Mystery writers love to create puzzles for you to solve. They give some help in the form of **clues,** or hints about the story's outcome. One of the most enjoyable aspects of reading a mystery is noticing these clues. When you interpret clues correctly, you can predict how a story is going to end.

The author of "Miss Hinch" has prepared you for the possibility that the old man may be Miss Hinch. You know that Miss Hinch played the part of George Washington; therefore, she can make herself look like a man. This clue helps prepare you for the story's stunning outcome.

Thinking About Clues and Predicting Outcomes

While the couple is waiting on the subway platform, the woman is clearly more nervous than the man. Explain how this clue points to the story's outcome.

COMPOSITION

Answering an Essay Question

Write an essay that answers the following question: Why does Miss Hinch act as she does throughout the story? **Prewriting:** First write a general statement in answer to the question. **Writing:** Incorporate your statement into a paragraph in which you describe two examples of Miss Hinch's actions. Explain her reasons for each action. Finally tell what both actions reveal about Miss Hinch's character. **Revising:** Be sure that you have answered the question accurately and logically. Make sure that your final copy does not contain any errors in grammar, spelling, or punctuation. *For help with this assignment, see Lesson 2 in the Writing About Literature Handbook at the back of this book.*

Writing Dialogue

Imagine that Miss Hinch is being questioned by the police after her capture. Write the dialogue that she has with the police officers as they ask her about the death of Jessie Dark. Does Miss Hinch brag about her successful disguise? Is she furious that she has been caught at last? Are the police officers impressed with Miss Hinch or angry with her?

CHALLENGE

Staging a Scene

Working with other students, stage one section of "Miss Hinch" as a skit. You might choose the scene in the subway car at the beginning of the story, for example, or the scene in Miller's Restaurant. Find parts of costumes that will help the actors create the characters effectively. Use props that will make the scene vivid.

Mystery!

People love mysteries, and they love solving them. The desire to solve mysteries has resulted in great discoveries by the world's outstanding thinkers—explorers in many fields. In everyday life people follow mysteries in the news, at work, and at school.

1. **Oral Report** Numerous famous fictional detectives have kept their popularity with readers for generations. Many of the best known of these sleuths are heroes of whole series of mysteries. While most of them have some clearly defined weaknesses, their amazing ability to get to the truth every time gives them a special aura.

   Working with a group, plan an oral report on famous fictional detectives. Brainstorm with the group to pick three or four favorites with as wide an appeal as possible. Then go to the library, and research the author, the audience he or she had in mind, and the length of time it took for the work to become popular. In a group meeting identify and list the different personality traits of the various detectives. Identify the qualities that make each detective popular. Organize your group notes, and report to the class. If you wish, hand out to the rest of the class bibliographies of mysteries you recommend.

2. **Mystery Game** With a group research, plan, and design a mystery board game for presentation to a toy manufacturer. Brainstorm first about mystery games that you have played. Decide on a basic idea for your game, and create a set of rules involving suspects, motives, finding clues, and arriving at a solution. Design the board and playing pieces, and make a model for your presentation.

   At the presentation each part of the project—research, creation of rules, and artistic design—should be discussed by the person or persons responsible for that part. The rest of the class, acting as representatives of the toy company, should respond with comments and questions.

Collaborative Learning:
Across the Curriculum

Mystery!

1. **Literature and Art: Short Story** Many works of art have
   an air of mystery about them. For example, Leonardo da
   Vinci's Mona Lisa, painted in the early 1500s, has fascinated viewers for centuries. Who was this woman? Why
   is she smiling that strange, little smile?

   With a group, plan to write a short story that solves
   the mystery of the Mona Lisa. Find a large reproduction
   of the painting, and place it where everyone can see it.
   Then brainstorm about the qualities that make it seem
   mysterious. Go to the library, and research what is
   known about this woman.

   Then as a group look again at the painting. Each
   member should offer a theory about the mystery of the
   Mona Lisa. Write down the theories, and create a story
   outline. Then write the story. Read your story aloud,
   make final changes, and present it to the class.

2. **Literature and Science: Oral Report** Sometimes it is
   not the content of a painting that is the source of mystery. Instead, the question becomes whether you are
   seeing what the painter intended you to see. For example, in Rembrandt's magnificent painting *Nightwatch*,
   the brilliantly lighted foreground is in sharp contrast to
   the dark, rather gloomy background. In recent years,
   through sophisticated scientific techniques, we have
   learned that the painting was painted not as a night
   scene (the explanation for the blackness of the background) but as a day scene. Now the look as well as the
   tone and feeling of the painting is completely different.

   With a group research the amazing story of Rembrandt's *Nightwatch*, the result of art experts' and scientists' working together. Find pictures of the painting
   both before and after its cleaning, and pass them around
   during your report. If possible, find slides of the painting
   before and after the cleaning, and project them for the
   entire class to see together. Have a question-and-answer
   period at the end of the report.

Preview

A book can take you anywhere in this world or out of it. You can go to Mars and back in the time it takes to read a poem. You can read your way down a rabbit hole or through a magical tollbooth. It is fun to discover other worlds through reading. Sometimes you can discover new things about your own world as well.

In the literature that follows, you will travel to actual places you can find on a map—Mexico, China, Spain; you will also visit the uncharted, imaginary world of Dictionopolis. You will even see the everyday world in a strange new way, through the eyes of rabbits and through the eyes of tourists from outer space.

Your imagination can travel faster than the speed of light. It needs only some well-chosen words for wings.

Carnival of Harlequin, Joan Miró, 1924–1925.

A Model for Active Reading

Active reading means involving yourself in what you read. It means thinking as you read. Even when an exciting story pulls you in, take the time to ask yourself questions about it.

Here is an example of the kinds of thoughts and feelings an active reader might have at the beginning of a story.

On the following pages you will find the entire story. Remember that the more actively you read, the more you'll enjoy the story.

Elizabeth Borton de Treviño

from **El Güero**

Grass was high, and that helped us to leave the house and the barracks without any soldiers seeing us and stopping us. Besides, what could anyone see? Just the heads of two boys, Inditos[1] probably, boys with long hair and skin darkened by the sun. The coyote[2] skins were the same color as the waving grass.

We left about dusk, just after the guards had departed from our house for the barracks. I felt unhappy leaving Mamacita[3] and Tía[4] Vicky alone.

Then I thought, a guard is a guard, and if they are taking care that the women do nothing outside the house but wash and hang up clothes, they would probably guard against an attack by a wildcat or some wandering snake.

We walked until the stars rose high over our heads, and Coyote said it was the hour when the night begins its descent toward dawn. Then we looked about for a place to sleep.

"Better just here in the tall grass," decided Coyote. "Snakes live near the rocks, and anyhow, I wore my snake cord, to protect us."

Someone is escaping from soldiers. Is this a war story?

Why were guards in the house? What will happen to the boys if they are caught?

This is wild country!

Coyote can tell time by the stars. What time is it? Midnight?

There are two boys wearing coyote skins to hide in the grass.

Are these women members of his family? What danger are they in?

What is a snake cord? a weapon?

Elizabeth Borton de Treviño [trā vēn'yō] (born 1904) grew up in California and now lives in Cuernavaca, Mexico. Over the last forty years she has written several novels, her memoirs, a biography, and many books for children. *El Güero* [we'rō] the book from which the following excerpt comes, is based on the early adventures of the author's father-in-law, Porfirio Treviño Arreola, who was known as El Güero—the Fair-Haired One.

In the late 1870s El Güero moves with his family from Mexico City to the isolated town of Ensenada in Baja California, a peninsula just south of the United States border. There El Güero befriends El Coyote, a boy who has lived among the Indians on the harsh frontier. The ruthless Captain Alanis imprisons the boys' fathers because the two men oppose the captain's unlawful schemes. The boys embark on a dangerous mission to free their fathers. A kind sea merchant, Captain Forker, helps El Güero make his way toward the Mexican authorities to get help.

I went to get a drink. The water in the cask was about three-quarters down. That was when I got the idea that saved us.

• •

Elizabeth Borton de Treviño

from **El Güero**

Grass was high, and that helped us to leave the house and the barracks without any soldiers seeing us and stopping us. Besides, what could anyone see? Just the heads of two boys, Inditos[1] probably, boys with long hair and skin darkened by the sun. The coyote[2] skins were the same color as the waving grass.

We left about dusk, just after the guards had departed from our house for the barracks. I felt unhappy leaving Mamacita[3] and Tía Vicky alone.

Then I thought, a guard is a guard, and if they are taking care that the women do nothing outside the house but wash and hang up clothes, they would probably guard against an attack by a wildcat or some wandering snake.

---

1. **Inditos** [ēn dē'tōs]: Spanish for "Indian youths."
2. **coyote:** [kī' ō' tē, kī' ōt]

3. **Mamacita** [mä mä sē'tä]: Spanish for "dear little mother"; "mommy."

We walked until the stars rose high over our heads, and Coyote said it was the hour when the night begins its descent toward dawn. Then we looked about for a place to sleep.

"Better just here in the tall grass," decided Coyote. "Snakes live near the rocks, and anyhow, I wore my snake cord, to protect us."

"How? What is a snake cord?"

"See? Here. I have it wound around my waist. It is a rope woven of spiky fiber. When we lie down, we make a circle around us with this cord. Snakes will not cross it; they will go around. They don't attack, anyway. They only attack when they are scared, or startled. Mostly they run away."

So we lay down, and the grass kept out the little gusts of cold wind, and with our skins over us, we slept well enough.

In the morning we went down to the beach and dug some clams. Coyote made a small fire, with pulled dry grass, enough to boil our water, and we cooked the clams. They made a good breakfast, with a couple of the tortillas that Tía Vicky had made for us.

The beach there was long and flat, studded with boulders, and there seemed to be no settlers anywhere near. We walked on, but by nightfall we had not found any place that Coyote thought safe enough. The land was rocky, with sparse grass and occasional trees.

"We must find a good tree and sleep in it," he said, and studied them, until we came to one with thick branches and heavy leaves. He showed me how, and we each got into a crotch of the branches and hung there, with arms and legs down on each side.

"You'll get used to it," he told me. "It is the safest of all; you won't fall, even asleep. When the wild sheep are moving, the rams are very fierce. They can butt you and knock you down, and stamp on you."

"Is that why you want to sleep in a tree?" I asked. "Did you see any wild sheep?"

"I saw dark clouds of dust, and there are no people living around here. It must be a herd of something. And they are moving south; they will overtake us. But if we stay here, they will pass us by. We will wait, in the morning, until they have gone."

I was tired from the walking and the sun, and I fell asleep, clinging to my branch. I startled awake a time or two, but finally I got used to it, and when it was morning, I felt rested. There were strange sounds, a sort of uneasy rumbling and snapping, with the baaing of sheep in several tones, some lower, some higher, some trembly, as if baby sheep were crying. I saw what Coyote had feared, a large band of sheep, with several huge rams, heavy-horned. They were passing along where we had walked the day before, raising heavy dust. They took their time, pulling up grass to eat and loitering, but the big leaders seemed to be anxious for them to move forward and be on the march. We saw them butting the strays back into line and trying to hurry them along.

"They are frightened," commented Coyote. "Something has scared them. We must wait here awhile longer and perhaps we will find out what is after them."

We hadn't long to wait. Two men on horseback, carrying guns, came galloping along. Sheepskins, still bloody, were hanging across the horses behind the saddles.

"They are hunting the sheep, but only

for their skins," he told me. "They will turn back north soon; they cannot carry much more."

Later, when we went forward, we found where they had killed the beasts and skinned them, leaving the carcasses for the wild creatures to eat.

"Shall we cover this meat over?" I asked Coyote. "It will draw the mountain lions."

"No. They won't venture down. They have been frightened by the shots. The meat is fresh. We will eat some ourselves and leave the rest for the birds."

We made a fire and roasted some pieces we were able to hack off.

"If we had time, I would cut strips and dry them in the sun, to make jerky.[4] But we can't delay."

After we had eaten, and packed some of the fresh-roasted meat to take with us, we started walking north again. The land began to rise steeply. Looking down toward the sea, we found a place where cliffs surrounded a small cove which seemed to be free of boulders and rocks.

"This is a perfect place!" I cried. "We can signal from up here and we will be seen against the sky when they look up."

"Is there some way down?" asked Coyote, and he himself answered by searching carefully to find a break in the cliffside, or a gulley that we might scramble down to the beach. Coyote found one, half hidden by bushes, but they served for handholds along the steep way down. We returned to the top of the cliff to begin our watch.

"Now, if only they will see us! If only

Mesas in Shadow, Maynard Dixon, 1926.

Captain Forker, or one of the sailors, will look up," I said.

We sat down and kept our eyes on the sea. After a while, everything became blurry, and I felt very sleepy.

Coyote noticed and said, "The water and the light make magic! They force you to close your eyes!"

"It hypnotizes me. My father told me about hypnotism. You know what it is?"

"Anyone or anything that forces you to sleep, to yield your will. I know. You must not look all the time at the water. Every few seconds, look away, at something here close by."

We took turns and kept watch for the rest of the day, and then, wound in our coyote skins, we slept there on the clifftop, ready to wake with first light.

Two days went by. It was monotonous and I began to lose hope, to be uncertain and worried. Besides, we were hungry. The tortillas we had brought were gone, we had eaten our meat, and we had only some tea.

"You watch. I will snare something—a bird or a squirrel—and find water. The

---

4. **jerky** [jur′kē]: meat that has been cured by cutting into strips and drying, usually in the sun.

gulleys mean water has been here, water is near. I must go and find it." Coyote went and I was alone. When he came back, he had a squirrel, skinned and gutted, and we made a fire and roasted bits of it. And he had found some water in a little pool, which evidently filled and spilled over, running down toward the sea, whenever it rained. I was so hungry and so glad to be eating that I forgot to watch, but Coyote kept glancing toward the water.

It was Coyote who suddenly stood up, took off one of his skins, and waved it around over his head.

There it was, Captain Forker's boat! I knew it from the shape, and besides, it was quite near. I could almost see the *Emily* painted on its side.

I waved my coyote skin, too, and was shouting, though of course they couldn't hear us.

"I think they noticed us because of the fire," said Coyote.

Anyway, to my joy, I saw that they had put down a skiff and were rowing toward shore. We started down the cliffside at once, falling and hurtling along in our haste. When I landed on the beach of the little cove, I was all torn and scraped, but I was never so glad to see anyone as I was to see Captain Forker, who had come in the skiff with one sailor.

He grabbed me and gave me a great bear hug, and listened as I told him everything that had happened.

"And so we came to wait for you because you are the only one who can help us free our fathers," I finished.

He was silent, thinking. He looked very unhappy and worried.

Then he said, "But I am a foreigner; I have no rights in Mexico. Captain Alanis

wouldn't pay the slightest attention to me. He might take it into his head to jail me, too! He needs the supplies I am bringing in, so he will have to let me tie up at the pier to unload. But I'll wager he won't let me leave my boat. And he'll hustle me away."

I told him I had thought of a plan.

"I haven't the Amparo,"[5] I said. "But I am the son of a Judge, and I can tell the authorities what has happened and about the Amparo. They surely would know what to do!"

"But the closest Mexican authorities are all the way around the tip of Baja California[6] and up the other side, on the Bay of Cortés, at La Paz,"[7] he answered. "A long way."

"Would you take me?"

"Well, I have to, the way I see it" was his answer. "But what worries me now is how I am going to hide you when I dock at Ensenada,[8] to unload the cargo for Captain Alanis. What if they decide to come aboard, to search my boat? They may have noticed that you are not around."

"I will go back and be seen around the house," offered El Coyote, "and I can say you are sick."

"We'll have to risk it that way," said Captain Forker. "So, you come with me on the *Emily*, Güero. Say goodbye to your friend."

---

5. **Amparo** [äm päˊrō]: important Mexican legal document that protects citizens from being imprisoned or treated by authorities in an illegal manner.
6. **Baja** [bäˊhä] **California**: long narrow peninsula in northwestern Mexico, separating the Gulf of California from the Pacific Ocean.
7. **La Paz** [lä päzˊ]: city in southeast Baja California.
8. **Ensenada** [enˊsə näˊdä]: seaport in north Baja California.

But Coyote never said goodbye, and he was already starting to scramble up the cliffside. We waited until we saw that he had safely reached the top, and then I got into the skiff and we rowed back to the *Emily.*

When we climbed on deck, and the skiff had been tied on alongside, Captain Forker said, "Güero, it is not far to Ensenada now, by sea, so I think we should hold off until tomorrow evening so Coyote can get there. That way we can go in at night, unload in a hurry, and steam[9] out when it's still dark."

I was thirsty, and I remembered the water cask that was reserved for the captain and his crew, as their drinking water, and I went to get a drink. The water in the cask was about three-quarters down. That was when I got the idea that saved us.

The next day, as night was falling, Captain Forker tied up. Two soldiers were there, waiting for him. Sure enough, they pushed past Captain Forker and began a systematic search. But they didn't think to look into each water cask. And there I was, totally submerged in one, with just my nose and eyes above water, and the cover in place. They stamped around irritably, finally did the unloading, and left. I heard them quarreling on the beach about how to carry the heavy boxes of supplies up to the barracks. I kept still and did not move in the water cask.

Untitled, Frederic Remington (1861–1909).

Captain Alanis came down and, after some talk, irritably paid Captain Forker for the cargo, signed the papers, and departed. At last, with great thankfulness, I heard the sailors casting off,[10] and we began to slide out of the bay. I heard the boat's engine and felt the gentle heave and surge of the waters outside the bay. Even then, I waited and listened. At last Captain Forker bellowed, "Where in tarnation are you, Güero?"

I climbed out of the water cask, dripping, gooseflesh all over me, my teeth chattering.

"We're rid of them, and away!" he shouted and he grabbed me, all sopping as I was, even my coyote skin, and gave me a great bear hug.

---

9. **steam**: travel by power furnished by an engine using steam under pressure to supply energy.

10. **casting off**: freeing a boat from a dock by untying the ropes.

READER'S RESPONSE

Would you enjoy having an adventure like the one described by El Güero? Why or why not?

STUDY QUESTIONS

Recalling

1. Where do the boys spend their first and second nights away from home?
2. Why do they spend the next two nights on a cliff?
3. What does Captain Forker agree to do for El Güero? What concern does he express to the boy?
4. What does El Güero do to protect himself on the ship?

Interpreting

5. Give three examples of El Coyote's survival skills and resourcefulness.
6. What do you think El Güero learns from his experiences with El Coyote and on board the ship?

READING AND LITERARY FOCUS

Setting

The **setting** is the time and place in which a literary work unfolds. To create a clear, vivid setting, writers use precise and lifelike details that allow you to feel as though you are living in the world of the story.

El Güero is set in Mexico just below the border with the United States. The action takes place outside Ensenada, a town on the Pacific coast of Baja California. As El Güero and El Coyote make their way northward, El Güero describes the beach as "long and flat, studded with boulders." He notes that

"there seemed to be no settlers anywhere near." These details describe a harsh, unwelcoming landscape. They also help us sense the boys' weariness and loneliness.

Thinking About Setting

Mention two dangers that the boys face in the Baja wilderness, and explain how they adapt to them.

COMPOSITION

Writing About Setting

Write a composition about the descriptive details that enable you to picture the Baja countryside in *El Güero*. **Prewriting:** Look over the story, and list the details that you find especially striking. Note which senses they appeal to—sight, hearing, smell, taste, or touch. **Writing:** Begin by stating your general impression of the setting. Then support your ideas with details from the story. **Revising:** Review your composition to see that you have expressed your ideas clearly and logically.

Creating a Setting

Write a composition describing a particular street in your town. First take notes on the colors, textures, sounds, and other details of the setting, as if you were a reporter. Then write your description, guiding the reader from one spot to the next until the entire setting is described.

CHALLENGE

Illustration

Draw or paint a picture of El Güero and El Coyote on their adventure. Choose a particular scene—for example, the boys sleeping in the trees or waving their coyote skins at the *Emily*. After selecting your scene, reread the passage carefully so that you can include the descriptive details provided by the author.

The Hottentot people of South Africa call themselves Khoikhoi [koi koi'] (Men of Men). Before the arrival of the Dutch settlers in the 1600s, these people ruled much of the southern part of Africa. The Europeans called these Africans Hoïtentots, probably in imitation of the clicking sounds in their language. Once herders and hunters who roamed over vast areas, the Hottentot people now live largely in European communities.

What would you do if the sun disappeared forever?

Hottentot Traditional

Song for the Sun That Disappeared Behind the Rainclouds

The fire darkens, the wood turns black.
The flame extinguishes, misfortune upon us.
God sets out in search of the sun.
The rainbow sparkles in his hand,
5 The bow of the divine hunter.
He has heard the lamentations[1] of his children.
He walks along the milky way, he collects the stars.
With quick arms he piles them into a basket
Piles them up with quick arms
10 Like a woman who collects lizards
And piles them into her pot, piles them
Until the pot overflows with lizards
Until the basket overflows with light.

---

1. **lamentations** [läm′ ən tā′shənz]: mournful cries of great sorrow or grief.

READER'S RESPONSE

*A song can make you cry or cheer you up,
make you feel proud or angry. What do you
think* this *song is meant to do?*

●●

STUDY QUESTIONS

Recalling

1. What is happening, according to the first two
   lines?
2. What does God set out to do? What has he
   heard?
3. What does he collect? What is this action like?
4. With what does the basket finally overflow?

Interpreting

5. Why might the disappearance of the sun be
   especially frightening to the Hottentot people?
6. What feeling about God does the poem create
   by showing him as a hunter striding along the
   Milky Way?
7. What feeling does the poem create by comparing God to a woman collecting lizards in a pot?

Extending

8. Mention another harmless natural event that
   people might find frightening.

COMPOSITION

Writing About a Title

A title often provides a clue to the meaning of a
literary work. Explain how the title "Song for the Sun
That Disappeared Behind the Rainclouds" makes
the poem more meaningful. **Prewriting:** Cover the
title with your hand, and read through the poem as
if you did not know the title. Jot down your impressions. Then reread the poem while thinking about
the title, and make notes of how your understanding
of the poem has changed. **Writing:** Using your
prewriting notes, write a paragraph in which you
describe how the title increases your understanding
and appreciation of the entire poem. **Revising:**
Review your paragraph, checking to see that you
have expressed your ideas clearly and logically.
Review for effective word choice and organization.
Make sure that your final copy is free of errors in
grammar, spelling, and punctuation.

Writing a Poem About a Natural Event

Write a poem about a natural event that you once
found—or still find—frightening. Describe the event
—a storm, fog, nightfall—in fanciful terms. For
example, nightfall could be a giant wearing a dark
blue cape.

Richard Adams (born 1920) was raised in England's Berkshire countryside, the setting of the novel *Watership Down*. Adams remembers that as a boy he "imagined himself to be a King in an imaginary country." In *Watership Down* Adams creates an imaginary world in which the characters are rabbits. These rabbits have their own language and customs, and they face great dangers in order to find a better life. The novel began as a story Adams told his children, who encouraged him to put it down on paper. *Watership Down* is now popular with children and adults alike and has been made into a film. Adams has also written *Plague Dogs*, which protests cruelty to animals.

"There isn't any danger here, at this moment. But it's coming—it's coming. Oh, Hazel, look! The field! It's covered with blood!"

Richard Adams

from **Watership Down**

THE JOURNEY

1. The Notice Board

The primroses were over. Toward the edge of the wood, where the ground became open and sloped down to an old fence and a brambly ditch beyond, only a few fading patches of pale yellow still showed among the dog's mercury and oak-tree roots. On the other side of the fence, the upper part of the field was full of rabbit holes. In places the grass was gone altogether and everywhere there were clusters of dry droppings, through which nothing but the ragwort would grow. A hundred yards away, at the bottom of the slope, ran the brook, no more than three feet wide, half choked with kingcups, watercress and blue brooklime. The cart track crossed by a brick culvert and climbed the opposite slope to a five-barred gate in the thorn hedge. The gate led into the lane.

The May sunset was red in clouds, and there was still half an hour to twilight. The dry slope was dotted with rabbits—some nibbling at the thin grass near their holes, others pushing further down to look for dandelions or perhaps a cowslip that the rest had missed. Here and there one sat upright on an ant heap and looked about, with ears erect and nose in the wind. But a blackbird, singing undisturbed on the outskirts of the wood, showed that there was nothing alarming there, and in the other direction, along the brook, all was plain to be seen, empty and quiet. The warren[1] was at peace.

---

1. **warren**: area in which rabbits live.

At the top of the bank, close to the wild cherry where the blackbird sang, was a little group of holes almost hidden by brambles. In the green half-light, at the mouth of one of these holes, two rabbits were sitting together side by side. At length, the larger of the two came out, slipped along the bank under cover of the brambles and so down into the ditch and up into the field. A few moments later the other followed.

The first rabbit stopped in a sunny patch and scratched his ear with rapid movements of his hind leg. Although he was a yearling and still below full weight, he had not the harassed look of most "outskirters"—that is, the rank and file[2] of ordinary rabbits in their first year who, lacking either aristocratic parentage[3] or unusual size and strength, get sat on by their elders and live as best they can—often in the open—on the edge of their warren. He looked as though he knew how to take care of himself. There was a shrewd, buoyant air about him as he sat up, looked around and rubbed both front paws over his nose. As soon as he was satisfied that all was well, he laid back his ears and set to work on the grass.

His companion seemed less at ease. He was small, with wide, staring eyes and a way of raising and turning his head which suggested not so much caution as a kind of ceaseless, nervous tension. His nose moved continually, and when a bumblebee flew humming to a thistle bloom behind him, he jumped and spun round with a start that sent two nearby rabbits scurrying for holes before the nearest, a buck with black-tipped ears, recognized him and returned to feeding.

"Oh, it's only Fiver," said the black-tipped rabbit, "jumping at bluebottles[4] again. Come on, Buckthorn, what were you telling me?"

"Fiver?" said the other rabbit. "Why's he called that?"

"Five in the litter,[5] you know; he was the last—and the smallest. You'd wonder nothing had got him by now. I always say a man couldn't see him and a fox wouldn't want him. Still, I admit he seems to be able to keep out of harm's way."*

The small rabbit came closer to his companion, lolloping on long hind legs.

"Let's go a bit further, Hazel," he said. "You know, there's something queer about the warren this evening, although I can't tell exactly what it is. Shall we go down to the brook?"

"All right," answered Hazel, "and you can find me a cowslip. If you can't find one, no one can."

He led the way down the slope, his shadow stretching behind him on the grass. They reached the brook and began nibbling and searching close beside the wheel ruts of the track.

It was not long before Fiver found what

*Rabbits can count up to four. Any number above four is *hrair*—"a lot," or "a thousand." Thus they say *U Hrair*—"The Thousand"—to mean, collectively, all the enemies (or *elil*, as they call them) of rabbits—fox, stoat, weasel, cat, owl, man, etc. There were probably more than five rabbits in the litter when Fiver was born, but his name, *Hrairoo*, means "Little Thousand"—i.e., the little one of a lot or, as they say of pigs, "the runt." [Adams]

2. **rank and file**: members who make up the body of a group, as distinguished from the leaders.
3. **aristocratic parentage** [ə risʹtə kratʹik pārʹən tij]: born of parents who belong to the privileged upper class or nobility.

4. **bluebottles**: large flies with steel-blue bodies.
5. **litter**: young produced by an animal at one birth.

they were looking for. Cowslips are a delicacy among rabbits, and as a rule there are very few left by late May in the neighborhood of even a small warren. This one had not bloomed and its flat spread of leaves was almost hidden under the long grass. They were just starting on it when two larger rabbits came running across from the other side of the nearby cattle wade.[6]

"Cowslip?" said one. "All right—just leave it to us. Come on, hurry up," he added, as Fiver hesitated. "You heard me, didn't you?"

"Fiver found it, Toadflax," said Hazel.

"And we'll eat it," replied Toadflax. "Cowslips are for Owsla*—don't you know that? If you don't, we can easily teach you."

Fiver had already turned away. Hazel caught him up by the culvert.

"I'm sick and tired of it," he said. "It's the same all the time. 'These are my claws, so this is my cowslip.' 'These are my teeth, so this is my burrow.'[7] I'll tell you, if ever I get into the Owsla, I'll treat outskirters with a bit of decency."

"Well, you can at least expect to be in the Owsla one day," answered Fiver.

*Nearly all warrens have an *Owsla*, or group of strong or clever rabbits—second-year or older—surrounding the Chief Rabbit and his doe and exercising authority. Owslas vary. In one warren, the Owsla may be the band of a warlord; in another, it may consist largely of clever patrollers or garden-raiders. Sometimes a good storyteller may find a place, or a seer, or intuitive rabbit. In the Sandleford warren at this time, the Owsla was rather military in character (though, as will be seen later, not so military as some). [Adams]

6. **cattle wade**: shallow place in a body of water where cattle cross.
7. **burrow**: hole dug in the ground by an animal for shelter or refuge.

"You've got some weight coming and that's more than I shall ever have."

"You don't suppose I'll leave you to look after yourself, do you?" said Hazel. "But to tell you the truth, I sometimes feel like clearing out of this warren altogether. Still, let's forget it now and try to enjoy the evening. I tell you what—shall we go across the brook? There'll be fewer rabbits and we can have a bit of peace. Unless you feel it isn't safe?" he added.

The way in which he asked suggested that he did in fact think that Fiver was likely to know better than himself, and it was clear from Fiver's reply that this was accepted between them.

"No, it's safe enough," he answered. "If I start feeling there's anything dangerous I'll tell you. But it's not exactly danger that I seem to feel about the place. It's—oh, I don't know—something oppressive, like thunder: I can't tell what; but it worries me. All the same, I'll come across with you."

They ran over the culvert. The grass was wet and thick near the stream and they made their way up the opposite slope, looking for drier ground. Part of the slope was in shadow, for the sun was sinking ahead of them, and Hazel, who wanted a warm, sunny spot, went on until they were quite near the lane. As they approached the gate he stopped, staring.

"Fiver, what's that? Look!"

A little way in front of them, the ground had been freshly disturbed. Two piles of earth lay on the grass. Heavy posts, reeking of creosote[8] and paint, towered up as high as the holly trees in the

8. **creosote** [kre′ə sot′]: tarlike liquid used to preserve wood.

hedge, and the board they carried threw a long shadow across the top of the field. Near one of the posts, a hammer and a few nails had been left behind.

The two rabbits went up to the board at a hopping run and crouched in a patch of nettles on the far side, wrinkling their noses at the smell of a dead cigarette end somewhere in the grass. Suddenly Fiver shivered and cowered down.

"Oh, Hazel! This is where it comes from! I know now—something very bad! Some terrible thing—coming closer and closer."

He began to whimper with fear.

"What sort of thing—what do you mean? I thought you said there was no danger?"

"I don't know what it is," answered Fiver wretchedly. "There isn't any danger here, at this moment. But it's coming—it's coming. Oh, Hazel, look! The field! It's covered with blood!"

"Don't be silly, it's only the light of the sunset. Fiver, come on, don't talk like this, you're frightening me!"

Fiver sat trembling and crying among the nettles as Hazel tried to reassure him and to find out what it could be that had suddenly driven him beside himself. If he was terrified, why did he not run for safety, as any sensible rabbit would? But Fiver could not explain and only grew more and more distressed. At last Hazel said, "Fiver, you can't sit crying here. Anyway, it's getting dark. We'd better go back to the burrow."

"Back to the burrow?" whimpered Fiver. "It'll come there—don't think it won't! I tell you, the field's full of blood—"

"Now stop it," said Hazel firmly. "Just let me look after you for a bit. Whatever the trouble is, it's time we got back."

He ran down the field and over the brook to the cattle wade. Here there was a delay, for Fiver—surrounded on all sides by the quiet summer evening—became helpless and almost paralyzed with fear. When at last Hazel had got him back to the ditch, he refused at first to go underground and Hazel had almost to push him down the hole.

The sun set behind the opposite slope. The wind turned colder, with a scatter of rain, and in less than an hour it was dark. All color had faded from the sky: and although the big board by the gate creaked slightly in the night wind (as though to insist that it had not disappeared in the darkness, but was still firmly where it had been put), there was no passer-by to read the sharp, hard letters that cut straight as black knives across its white surface. They said:

> This ideally situated estate, comprising six acres of excellent building land, is to be developed with high class modern residences by Sutch and Martin, Limited, of Newbury, Berks.

2. The Chief Rabbit

In the darkness and warmth of the burrow Hazel suddenly woke, struggling and kicking with his back legs. Something was attacking him. There was no smell of ferret or weasel. No instinct told him to run. His head cleared and he realized that he was alone except for Fiver. It was Fiver who was clambering over him, clawing and grabbing like a rabbit trying to climb a wire fence in a panic.

"Fiver! Fiver, wake up, you silly fellow! It's Hazel. You'll hurt me in a moment. Wake up!"

He held him down. Fiver struggled and woke.

"Oh, Hazel! I was dreaming. It was dreadful. You were there. We were sitting on water, going down a great, deep stream, and then I realized we were on a board—like that board in the field—all white and covered with black lines. There were other rabbits there—bucks and does. But when I looked down, I saw the board was all made of bones and wire; and I screamed and you said, 'Swim—everybody swim'; and then I was looking for you everywhere and trying to drag you out of a hole in the bank. I found you, but you said, 'The Chief Rabbit must go alone,' and you floated away down a dark tunnel of water."

"Well, you've hurt my ribs, anyway. Tunnel of water indeed! What rubbish! Can we go back to sleep now?"

"Hazel—the danger, the bad thing. It hasn't gone away. It's here—all round us. Don't tell me to forget about it and go to sleep. We've got to go away before it's too late."

"Go away? From here, you mean? From the warren?"

"Yes. Very soon. It doesn't matter where."

"Just you and I?"

"No, everyone."

"The whole warren? Don't be silly. They won't come. They'll say you're out of your wits."

"Then they'll be here when the bad thing comes. You must listen to me, Hazel. Believe me, something very bad is close upon us and we ought to go away."

"Well, I suppose we'd better go and see the Chief Rabbit and you can tell *him* about it. Or I'll try to. But I don't expect he'll like the idea at all."

Hazel led the way down the slope of the run[9] and up toward the bramble curtain. He did not want to believe Fiver, and he was afraid not to.

It was a little after ni-Frith, or noon. The whole warren were underground, mostly asleep. Hazel and Fiver went a short way above ground and then into a wide, open hole in a sand patch and so down, by various runs, until they were thirty feet into the wood, among the roots of an oak. Here they were stopped by a large, heavily built rabbit—one of the Owsla. He had a curious, heavy growth of fur on the crown of his head, which gave him an odd appearance, as though he were wearing a kind of cap. This had given him his name, Thlayli, which means, literally, "Furhead" or, as we might say, "Bigwig."

"Hazel?" said Bigwig, sniffling at him in the deep twilight among the tree roots. "It is Hazel, isn't it? What are you doing here? And at this time of day?" He ignored Fiver, who was waiting further down the run.

"We want to see the Chief Rabbit," said Hazel. "It's important, Bigwig. Can you help us?"

"We?" said Bigwig. "Is *he* going to see him, too?"

"Yes, he must. Do trust me, Bigwig. I don't usually come and talk like this, do I? When did I ever ask to see the Chief Rabbit before?"

"Well, I'll do it for you, Hazel, although I'll probably get my head bitten off. I'll tell him I know you're a sensible fellow. He ought to know you himself, of course, but he's getting old. Wait here, will you?"

_____
9. **run**: track or path made or used frequently by animals.

Bigwig went a little way down the run and stopped at the entrance to a large burrow. After speaking a few words that Hazel could not catch, he was evidently called inside. The two rabbits waited in silence, broken only by the continual nervous fidgeting of Fiver.

The Chief Rabbit's name and style was Threarah, meaning "Lord Rowan Tree." For some reason he was always referred to as "*The* Threarah"—perhaps because there happened to be only one threar, or rowan, near the warren, from which he took his name. He had won his position not only by strength in his prime, but also by level-headedness and a certain self-contained detachment, quite unlike the impulsive behavior of most rabbits. It was well known that he never let himself become excited by rumor or danger. He had coolly—some even said coldly—stood firm during the terrible onslaught of the myxomatosis,[10] ruthlessly driving out every rabbit who seemed to be sickening. He had resisted all ideas of mass emigration and enforced complete isolation on the warren, thereby almost certainly saving it from extinction. It was he, too, who had once dealt with a particularly troublesome stoat by leading it down among the pheasant coops and so (at the risk of his own life) onto a keeper's gun. He was now, as Bigwig said, getting old, but his wits were still clear enough. When Hazel and Fiver were brought in, he greeted them politely. Owsla like Toadflax might threaten and bully. The Threarah had no need.

"Ah, Walnut. It is Walnut, isn't it?"

"Hazel," said Hazel.

"Hazel, of course. How very nice of you to come and see me. I knew your mother well. And your friend—"

"My brother."

"Your brother," said the Threarah, with the faintest suggestion of "Don't correct me anymore, will you?" in his voice. "Do make yourselves comfortable. Have some lettuce?"

The Chief Rabbit's lettuce was stolen by the Owsla from a garden half a mile away across the fields. Outskirters seldom or never saw lettuce. Hazel took a small leaf and nibbled politely. Fiver refused, and sat blinking and twitching miserably.

"Now, how are things with you?" said the Chief Rabbit. "Do tell me how I can help you."

"Well, sir," said Hazel rather hesitantly, "it's because of my brother—Fiver here. He can often tell when there's anything bad about, and I've found him right again and again. He knew the flood was coming last autumn and sometimes he can tell where a wire's been set. And now he says he can sense a bad danger coming upon the warren."

"A bad danger. Yes, I see. How very upsetting," said the Chief Rabbit, looking anything but upset. "Now, what sort of danger, I wonder?" He looked at Fiver.

"I don't know," said Fiver. "B-but it's bad. It's so b-bad that—it's very bad," he concluded miserably.

The Threarah waited politely for a few moments and then he said, "Well, now, and what ought we to do about it, I wonder?"

"Go away," said Fiver instantly. "Go away. All of us. Now. Threarah, sir, we must all go away."

The Threarah waited again. Then, in an extremely understanding voice, he said, "Well, I never did! That's rather a tall

10. **myxomatosis** [mik′sə mə tō′sis]: severe disease of rabbits that is spread by mosquitoes.

Young Hare, Albrecht Dürer, watercolor and gouache on paper, 1502.

order, isn't it? What do you think yourself?"

"Well, sir," said Hazel, "my brother doesn't really think about these feelings he gets. He just has the feelings, if you see what I mean. I'm sure you're the right person to decide what we ought to do."

"Well, that's very nice of you to say that. I hope I am. But now, my dear fellows, let's just think about this a moment, shall we? It's May, isn't it? Everyone's busy and most of the rabbits are enjoying themselves. No elil for miles, or so they tell me. No illness, good weather. And you want me to tell the warren that young—er—young—er—your brother here has got a hunch[11] and we must all go traipsing across country to goodness knows where and risk the consequences, eh? What do you think they'll say? All delighted, eh?"

"They'd take it from you," said Fiver suddenly.

"That's very nice of you," said the Threarah again. "Well, perhaps they would, perhaps they would. But I should have to consider it very carefully indeed. A most serious step, of course. And then—"

"But there's no time, Threarah, sir," blurted out Fiver. "I can feel the danger like a wire round my neck—like a wire— Hazel, help!" He squealed and rolled over in the sand, kicking frantically, as a rabbit does in a snare. Hazel held him down with both forepaws and he grew quieter.

"I'm awfully sorry, Chief Rabbit," said Hazel. "He gets like this sometimes. He'll be all right in a minute."

"What a shame! What a shame! Poor fellow, perhaps he ought to go home and rest. Yes, you'd better take him along now. Well, it's really been extremely good of you to come and see me, Walnut. I appreciate it very much indeed. And I shall think over all you've said most carefully, you can be quite sure of that. Bigwig, just wait a moment, will you?"

As Hazel and Fiver made their way dejectedly down the run outside the Threarah's burrow, they could just hear, from inside, the Chief Rabbit's voice assuming a rather sharper note, interspersed with an occasional "Yes, sir," "No, sir."

Bigwig, as he had predicted, was getting his head bitten off.

3. Hazel's Decision

"But, Hazel, you didn't really think the Chief Rabbit would act on your advice, did you? What were you expecting?"

It was evening once more and Hazel and Fiver were feeding outside the wood with two friends. Blackberry, the rabbit with tipped ears who had been startled by Fiver the night before, had listened carefully to Hazel's description of the notice board, remarking that he had always felt sure that men left these things about to act as signs or messages of some kind, in the same way that rabbits left marks on runs and gaps. It was another neighbor, Dandelion, who had now brought the talk back to the Threarah and his indifference to Fiver's fear.

"I don't know what I expected," said Hazel. "I'd never been near the Chief Rabbit before. But I thought, 'Well, even if he won't listen, at least no one can say

---

11. **has got a hunch**: has a strong feeling that something is going to happen.

afterward that we didn't do our best to warn him.'"

"You're sure, then, that there's really something to be afraid of?"

"I'm quite certain. I've always known Fiver, you see."

Blackberry was about to reply when another rabbit came noisily through the thick dog's mercury in the wood, blundered down into the brambles and pushed his way up from the ditch. It was Bigwig.

"Hello, Bigwig," said Hazel. "You're off duty?"

"Off duty," said Bigwig, "and likely to remain off duty."

"How do you mean?"

"I've left the Owsla, that's what I mean."

"Not on our account?"

"You could say that. The Threarah's rather good at making himself unpleasant when he's been woken up at ni-Frith for what he considers a piece of trivial nonsense. He certainly knows how to get under your skin. I dare say a good many rabbits would have kept quiet and thought about keeping on the right side of the Chief, but I'm afraid I'm not much good at that. I told him that the Owsla's privileges didn't mean all that much to me in any case and that a strong rabbit could always do just as well by leaving the warren. He told me not to be impulsive and think it over, but I shan't stay. Lettuce-stealing isn't my idea of a jolly life, nor sentry duty in the burrow. I'm in a fine temper, I can tell you."

"No one will steal lettuces soon," said Fiver quietly.

"Oh, that's you, Fiver, is it?" said Bigwig, noticing him for the first time. "Good, I was coming to look for you. I've

been thinking about what you said to the Chief Rabbit. Tell me, is it a sort of tremendous hoax to make yourself important, or is it true?"

"It *is* true," said Fiver. "I wish it weren't."

"Then you'll be leaving the warren?"

They were all startled by the bluntness with which Bigwig went to the point. Dandelion muttered, "Leave the warren, Frithrah!" while Blackberry twitched his ears and looked very intently, first at Bigwig and then at Hazel.

It was Hazel who replied. "Fiver and I will be leaving the warren tonight," he said deliberately. "I don't know exactly where we shall go, but we'll take anyone who's ready to come with us."

"Right," said Bigwig, "then you can take me."

The last thing Hazel had expected was the immediate support of a member of the Owsla. It crossed his mind that although Bigwig would certainly be a useful rabbit in a tight corner, he would also be a difficult one to get on with. He certainly would not want to do what he was told— or even asked—by an outskirter. "I don't care if he is in the Owsla," thought Hazel. "If we get away from the warren, I'm not going to let Bigwig run everything, or why bother to go?" But he answered only, "Good. We shall be glad to have you."

He looked round at the other rabbits, who were all staring either at Bigwig or at himself. It was Blackberry who spoke next.

"I think I'll come," he said. "I don't quite know whether it's you who've persuaded me, Fiver. But anyway, there are too many bucks in this warren, and it's pretty poor fun for any rabbit that's not in the Owsla. The funny thing is that you feel terrified to stay and I feel terrified to go. Foxes here, weasels there, Fiver in the middle, begone dull care!"

He pulled out a burnet leaf and ate it slowly, concealing his fear as best he could; for all his instincts were warning him of the dangers in the unknown country beyond the warren.

"If we believe Fiver," said Hazel, "it means that we think no rabbits at all ought to stay here. So between now and the time when we go, we ought to persuade as many as we can to join us."

"I think there are one or two in the Owsla who might be worth sounding,"[12] said Bigwig. "If I can talk them over, they'll be with me when I join you tonight. But they won't come because of Fiver. They'll be juniors, discontented fellows like me. You need to have heard Fiver yourself to be convinced by him. He's convinced me. It's obvious that he's been sent some kind of message, and I believe in these things. I can't think why he didn't convince the Threarah."

"Because the Threarah doesn't like anything he hasn't thought of for himself," answered Hazel. "But we can't bother with him any more now. We've got to try to collect some more rabbits and meet again here, fu Inlé. And we'll start fu Inlé, too: we can't wait longer. The danger's coming closer all the time—whatever it is—and, besides, the Threarah isn't going to like it if he finds out that you've been trying to get at rabbits in the Owsla, Bigwig. Neither is Captain Holly, I dare say. They won't mind odds and ends like us clearing off, but they won't want to lose you. If I

were in your place, I'd be careful whom I picked to talk to."

4. The Departure

Fu Inlé means "after moonrise." Rabbits, of course, have no idea of precise time or of punctuality. In this respect they are much the same as primitive people, who often take several days over assembling for some purpose and then several more to get started. Before such people can act together, a kind of telepathic feeling has to flow through them and ripen to the point when they all know that they are ready to begin. Anyone who has seen the martins and swallows in September, assembling on the telephone wires, twittering, making short flights singly and in groups over the open, stubbly fields, returning to form longer and even longer lines above the yellowing verges[13] of the lanes—the hundreds of individual birds merging and blending, in a mounting excitement, into swarms, and these swarms coming loosely and untidily together to create a great, unorganized flock, thick at the center and ragged at the edges, which breaks and re-forms continually like clouds or waves—until that moment when the greater part (but not all) of them know that the time has come: they are off, and have begun once more that great southward flight which many will not survive; anyone seeing this has seen at work the current that flows (among creatures who think of themselves primarily as part of a group and only secondarily, if at all, as individuals) to fuse them together and impel them into action without conscious thought or will: has seen at work the an-

---

12. **sounding**: finding out the feelings and opinions of.

13. **verges** [vurj′iz]: grass shoulders of roads.

gel which drove the First Crusade into Antioch[14] and drives the lemmings[15] into the sea.

It was actually about an hour after moonrise and a good while before midnight when Hazel and Fiver once more came out of their burrow behind the brambles and slipped quietly along the bottom of the ditch. With them was a third rabbit, Hlao—Pipkin—a friend of Fiver. (Hlao means any small concavity[16] in the grass where moisture may collect—e.g., the dimple formed by a dandelion or thistle cup.) He too was small, and inclined to be timid, and Hazel and Fiver had spent the greater part of their last evening in the warren in persuading him to join them. Pipkin had agreed rather hesitantly. He still felt extremely nervous about what might happen once they left the warren, and had decided that the best way to avoid trouble would be to keep close to Hazel and do exactly what he said.

The three were still in the ditch when Hazel heard a movement above. He looked up quickly.

"Who's there?" he said. "Dandelion?"

"No, I'm Hawkbit," said the rabbit who was peering over the edge. He jumped down among them, landing rather heavily. "Do you remember me, Hazel? We were in the same burrow during the snow last winter. Dandelion told me you were going to leave the warren tonight. If you are, I'll come with you."

Hazel could recall Hawkbit—a rather slow, stupid rabbit whose company for five snowbound days underground had been distinctly tedious. Still, he thought, this was no time to pick and choose. Although Bigwig might succeed in talking over one or two, most of the rabbits they could expect to join them would not come from the Owsla. They would be outskirters who were getting a thin time and wondering what to do about it. He was running over some of these in his mind when Dandelion appeared.

"The sooner we're off the better, I reckon," said Dandelion. "I don't much like the look of things. After I'd persuaded Hawkbit here to join us, I was just starting to talk to a few more when I found that Toadflax fellow had followed me down the run. 'I want to know what you're up to,' he said, and I don't think he believed me when I told him I was only trying to find out whether there were any rabbits who wanted to leave the warren. He asked me if I was sure I wasn't working up some kind of plot against the Threarah and he got awfully angry and suspicious. It put the wind up me, to tell you the truth, so I've just brought Hawkbit along and left it at that."

"I don't blame you," said Hazel. "Knowing Toadflax, I'm surprised he didn't knock you over first and ask questions afterward. All the same, let's wait a little longer. Blackberry ought to be here soon."

Time passed. They crouched in silence while the moon shadows moved northward in the grass. At last, just as Hazel was about to run down the slope to Blackberry's burrow, he saw him come out of

---

14. **First Crusade into Antioch** [an′tē ok′]: first of the military expeditions attempted by European Christians between 1096 and 1270 to recover the Holy Land from the Moslems; the city of Antioch is located in southern Turkey, near the Mediterranean Sea.

15. **lemmings**: micelike rodents that, during their search for food, often drown when they swim out to sea.

16. **concavity** [kon kav′ə tē]: surface that curves inward; hollow.

his hole, followed by no less than three rabbits. One of these, Buckthorn, Hazel knew well. He was glad to see him, for he knew him for a tough, sturdy fellow who was considered certain to get into the Owsla as soon as he reached full weight.

"But I dare say he's impatient," thought Hazel, "or he may have come off worst in some scuffle over a doe and taken it hard. Well, with him and Bigwig, at least we shan't be too badly off if we run into any fighting."

He did not recognize the other two rabbits and when Blackberry told him their names—Speedwell and Acorn—he was none the wiser. But this was not surprising, for they were typical outskirters— thin-looking six-monthers, with the strained, wary look of those who are only too well used to the thin end of the stick. They looked curiously at Fiver. From what Blackberry had told them, they had been almost expecting to find Fiver foretelling doom in a poetic torrent. Instead, he seemed more calm and normal than the rest. The certainty of going had lifted a weight from Fiver.

More time went slowly by. Blackberry scrambled up into the fern and then returned to the top of the bank, fidgeting nervously and half inclined to bolt at nothing. Hazel and Fiver remained in the ditch, nibbling halfheartedly at the dark grass. At last Hazel heard what he was listening for; a rabbit—or was it two?— approaching from the wood.

A few moments later Bigwig was in the ditch. Behind him came a hefty, brisk-looking rabbit something over twelve months old. He was well known by sight to all the warren, for his fur was entirely gray, with patches of near-white that now caught the moonlight as he sat scratching

himself without speaking. This was Silver, a nephew of the Threarah, who was serving his first month in the Owsla.

Hazel could not help feeling relieved that Bigwig had brought only Silver—a quiet, straightforward fellow who had not yet really found his feet among the veterans. When Bigwig had spoken earlier of sounding out the Owsla, Hazel had been in two minds. It was only too likely that they would encounter dangers beyond the warren and that they would stand in need of some good fighters. Again, if Fiver was right and the whole warren was in imminent peril, then of course they ought to welcome any rabbit who was ready to join them. On the other hand, there seemed no point in taking particular pains to get hold of rabbits who were going to behave like Toadflax.

"Wherever we settle down in the end," thought Hazel, "I'm determined to see that Pipkin and Fiver aren't sat on and cuffed around until they're ready to run any risk just to get away. But is Bigwig going to see it like that?"

"You know Silver, don't you?" asked Bigwig, breaking in on his thoughts. "Apparently some of the younger fellows in the Owsla have been giving him a thin time—teasing him about his fur, you know, and saying he only got his place because of the Threarah. I thought I was going to get some more, but I suppose nearly all the Owsla feel they're very well off as they are."

He looked about him. "I say, there aren't many here, are there? Do you think it's really worth going on with this idea?"

Silver seemed about to speak when suddenly there was a pattering in the undergrowth above and three more rabbits came over the bank from the wood. Their

Italian Landscape, Albrecht Dürer, watercolor, c. 1495.

movement was direct and purposeful, quite unlike the earlier, haphazard[17] approach of those who were now gathered in the ditch. The largest of the three newcomers was in front and the other two followed him, as though under orders. Hazel, sensing at once that they had nothing in common with himself and his companions, started and sat up tensely. Fiver muttered in his ear, "Oh, Hazel, they've come to—" but broke off short. Bigwig turned toward them and stared, his nose working rapidly. The three came straight up to him.

"Thlayli?" said the leader.

"You know me perfectly well," replied Bigwig, "and I know you, Holly. What do you want?"

"You're under arrest."

"Under arrest? What do you mean? What for?"

"Spreading dissension and inciting to mutiny.[18] Silver, you're under arrest too,

---

17. **haphazard** [hap'haz'ərd]: lacking order, direction, or planning.

18. **Spreading dissension** [di sen'shən] . . . **mutiny**: causing sharp differences of opinion and urging a revolt against authority.

for failing to report to Toadflax this evening and causing your duty to devolve [19] on a comrade. You're both to come with me."

Immediately Bigwig fell upon him, scratching and kicking. Holly fought back. His followers closed in, looking for an opening to join the fight and pin Bigwig down. Suddenly, from the top of the bank, Buckthorn flung himself headlong into the scuffle, knocked one of the guards flying with a kick from his back legs and then closed with the other. He was followed a moment later by Dandelion, who landed full on the rabbit whom Buckthorn had kicked. Both guards broke clear, looked round for a moment and then leaped up the bank into the wood. Holly struggled free of Bigwig and crouched on his haunches, scuffling his front paws and growling, as rabbits will when angry. He was about to speak when Hazel faced him.

"Go," said Hazel, firmly and quietly, "or we'll kill you."

"Do you know what this means?" replied Holly. "I am Captain of Owsla. You know that, don't you?"

"Go," repeated Hazel, "or you will be killed."

"It is you who will be killed," replied Holly. Without another word he, too, went back up the bank and vanished into the wood.

Dandelion was bleeding from the shoulder. He licked the wound for a few moments and then turned to Hazel.

"They won't be long coming back, you know, Hazel," he said. "They've gone to

turn out the Owsla, and then we'll be for it right enough."

"We ought to go at once," said Fiver.

"Yes, the time's come now, all right," replied Hazel. "Come on, down to the stream. Then we'll follow the bank—that'll help us to keep together."

"If you'll take my advice—" began Bigwig.

"If we stay here any longer I shan't be able to," answered Hazel.

With Fiver beside him, he led the way out of the ditch and down the slope. In less than a minute the little band of rabbits had disappeared into the dim, moonlit night.

5. In the Woods

It was getting on toward moonset when they left the fields and entered the wood. Straggling, catching up with one another, keeping more or less together, they had wandered over half a mile down the fields, always following the course of the brook. Although Hazel guessed that they must now have gone further from the warren than any rabbit he had ever talked to, he was not sure whether they were yet safely away: and it was while he was wondering—not for the first time—whether he could hear sounds of pursuit that he first noticed the dark masses of the trees and the brook disappearing among them.

Rabbits avoid close woodland, where the ground is shady, damp and grassless and they feel menaced by the undergrowth. Hazel did not care for the look of the trees. Still, he thought, Holly would no doubt think twice before following them into a place like that, and to keep beside the brook might well prove safer than wandering about the fields in one direction and another, with the risk of find-

---

19. **devolve** [di volv′]: be passed on to another person.

ing themselves, in the end, back at the warren. He decided to go straight into the wood without consulting Bigwig, and to trust that the rest would follow.

"If we don't run into any trouble and the brook takes us through the wood," he thought, "we really shall be clear of the warren and then we can look for somewhere to rest for a bit. Most of them still seem to be more or less all right, but Fiver and Pipkin will have had as much as they can stand before long."

From the moment he entered it, the wood seemed full of noises. There was a smell of damp leaves and moss, and everywhere the splash of water went whispering about. Just inside, the brook made a little fall into a pool, and the sound, enclosed among the trees, echoed as though in a cave. Roosting birds rustled overhead; the night breeze stirred the leaves; here and there a dead twig fell. And there were more sinister, unidentified sounds from further away; sounds of movement.

To rabbits, everything unknown is dangerous. The first reaction is to startle, the second to bolt. Again and again they startled, until they were close to exhaustion. But what did these sounds mean and where, in this wilderness, could they bolt to?

The rabbits crept closer together. Their progress grew slower. Before long they lost the course of the brook, slipping across the moonlit patches as fugitives and halting in the bushes with raised ears and staring eyes. The moon was low now and the light, wherever it slanted through the trees, seemed thicker, older and more yellow.

From a thick pile of dead leaves beneath a holly tree, Hazel looked down a narrow path lined on either side with fern and sprouting fireweed. The fern moved slightly in the breeze, but along the path there was nothing to be seen except a scatter of last year's fallen acorns under an oak. What was in the bracken? What lay round the further bend? And what would happen to a rabbit who left the shelter of the holly tree and ran down the path? He turned to Dandelion beside him.

"You'd better wait here," he said. "When I get to the bend I'll stamp. But if I run into trouble, get the others away."

Without waiting for an answer, he ran into the open and down the path. A few seconds brought him to the oak. He paused a moment, staring about him, and then ran on to the bend. Beyond, the path was the same—empty in the darkening moonlight and leading gently downhill into the deep shadow of a grove of ilex trees. Hazel stamped, and a few moments later Dandelion was beside him in the bracken. Even in the midst of his fear and strain it occurred to him that Dandelion must be very fast: he had covered the distance in a flash.

"Well done," whispered Dandelion. "Running our risks for us, are you—like El-ahrairah?"*

Hazel gave him a quick, friendly glance. It was warm praise and cheered him. What Robin Hood[20] is to the English and John Henry[21] to the American Negroes, Elil-Hrair-Rah, or El-ahrairah—The Prince

*The stresses are the same as in the phrase "Never say die." [Adams]

---

20. **Robin Hood**: according to English legend, twelfth-century outlaw who lived in Sherwood Forest with his band of followers and robbed the rich to give help to the poor.
21. **John Henry**: legendary black American celebrated in songs and stories for his great strength.

with a Thousand Enemies—is to rabbits. ... For that matter, Odysseus[22] himself might have borrowed a trick or two from the rabbit hero, for he is very old and was never at a loss for a trick to deceive his enemies. Once, so they say, he had to get home by swimming across a river in which there was a large and hungry pike.[23] El-ahrairah combed himself until he had enough fur to cover a clay rabbit, which he pushed into the water. The pike rushed at it, bit it and left it in disgust. After a little, it drifted to the bank and El-ahrairah dragged it out and waited awhile before pushing it in again. After an hour of this, the pike left it alone, and when it had done so for the fifth time, El-ahrairah swam across himself and went home. Some rabbits say he controls the weather, because the wind, the damp and the dew are friends and instruments to rabbits against their enemies.

"Hazel, we'll have to stop here," said Bigwig, coming up between the panting, crouching bodies of the others. "I know it's not a good place, but Fiver and this other half-sized fellow you've got here— they're pretty well all in. They won't be able to go on if we don't rest."

The truth was that every one of them was tired. Many rabbits spend all their lives in the same place and never run more than a hundred yards at a stretch. Even though they may live and sleep above ground for months at a time, they prefer not to be out of distance of some sort of refuge that will serve for a hole. They have two natural gaits—the gentle,

lolloping forward movement of the warren on a summer evening and the lightning dash for cover that every human has seen at some time or other. It is difficult to imagine a rabbit plodding steadily on: they are not built for it. It is true that young rabbits are great migrants and capable of journeying for miles, but they do not take to it readily.

Hazel and his companions had spent the night doing everything that came unnaturally to them, and this for the first time. They had been moving in a group, or trying to: actually, they had straggled widely at times. They had been trying to maintain a steady pace, between hopping and running, and it had come hard. Since entering the wood they had been in severe anxiety. Several were almost tharn— that is, in that state of staring, glazed paralysis that comes over terrified or exhausted rabbits, so that they sit and watch their enemies—weasels or humans— approach to take their lives. Pipkin sat trembling under a fern, his ears dropping on either side of his head. He held one paw forward in an awkward, unnatural way and kept licking it miserably. Fiver was little better off. He still looked cheerful, but very weary. Hazel realized that until they were rested they would all be safer where they were than stumbling along in the open with no strength left to run from an enemy. But if they lay brooding, unable to feed or go underground, all their troubles would come crowding into their hearts, their fears would mount and they might very likely scatter, or even try to return to the warren. He had an idea.

"Yes, all right, we'll rest here," he said. "Let's go in among this fern. Come on, Dandelion, tell us a story. I know you're

---

22. **Odysseus** [ō dis'ē əs]: in ancient Greek legend, king of Ithaca and one of the shrewdest Greek leaders in the Trojan War.
23. **pike** [pīk]: large, flesh-eating fish.

handy that way. Pipkin here can't wait to hear it."

Dandelion looked at Pipkin and realized what it was that Hazel was asking him to do. Choking back his own fear of the desolate, grassless woodland, the before-dawn-returning owls that they could hear some way off, and the extraordinary, rank animal smell that seemed to come from somewhere rather nearer, he began.

6. *The Story of the Blessing of El-ahrairah*

"Long ago, Frith made the world. He made all the stars, too, and the world is one of the stars. He made them by scattering his droppings over the sky and this is why the grass and the trees grow so thick on the world. Frith makes the rivers flow. They follow him as he goes through the sky, and when he leaves the sky they look for him all night. Frith made all the animals and birds, but when he first made them they were all the same. The sparrow and the kestrel[24] were friends and they both ate seeds and flies. And the fox and the rabbit were friends and they both ate grass. And there was plenty of grass and plenty of flies, because the world was new and Frith shone down bright and warm all day.

"Now, El-ahrairah was among the animals in those days and he had many wives. He had so many wives that there was no counting them, and the wives had so many young that even Frith could not count them, and they ate the grass and the dandelions and the lettuces and the clover, and El-ahrairah was the father of them all." (Bigwig growled appreciatively.) "And after a time," went on Dandelion, "after a time the grass began to grow thin and the rabbits wandered everywhere, multiplying and eating as they went.

"Then Frith said to El-ahrairah, 'Prince Rabbit, if you cannot control your people, I shall find ways to control them. So mark what I say.' But El-ahrairah would not listen and he said to Frith, 'My people are the strongest in the world, for they breed faster and eat more than any of the other people. And this shows how much they love Lord Frith, for of all the animals they are the most responsive to his warmth and brightness. You must realize, my lord, how important they are and not hinder them in their beautiful lives.'

"Frith could have killed El-ahrairah at once, but he had a mind to keep him in the world, because he needed him to sport and jest and play tricks. So he determined to get the better of him, not by means of his own great power but by means of a trick. He gave out that he would hold a great meeting and that at that meeting he would give a present to every animal and bird, to make each one different from the rest. And all the creatures set out to go to the meeting place. But they all arrived at different times, because Frith made sure that it would happen so. And when the blackbird came, he gave him his beautiful song, and when the cow came, he gave her sharp horns and the strength to be afraid of no other creature. And so in their turn came the fox and the stoat and the weasel. And to each of them Frith gave the cunning and the fierceness and the desire to hunt and slay and eat the children of El-ahrairah. And so they went away from Frith full of nothing but hunger to kill the rabbits.

---

24. **kestrel** [kes′trəl]: small falcon noted for its ability to hover in the air against the wind.

"Now, all this time El-ahrairah was dancing and mating and boasting that he was going to Frith's meeting to receive a great gift. And at last he set out for the meeting place. But as he was going there, he stopped to rest on a soft, sandy hillside. And while he was resting, over the hill came flying the dark swift,[25] screaming as he went, 'News! News! News!' For you know, this is what he has said ever since that day. So El-ahrairah called up to him and said, 'What news?' 'Why,' said the swift, 'I would not be you, El-ahrairah. For Frith has given the fox and the weasel cunning hearts and sharp teeth, and to the cat he has given silent feet and eyes that can see in the dark, and they are gone away from Frith's place to kill and devour all that belongs to El-ahrairah.' And he dashed on over the hills. And at that moment El-ahrairah heard the voice of Frith calling, 'Where is El-ahrairah? For all the others have taken their gifts and gone and I have come to look for him.'

"Then El-ahrairah knew that Frith was too clever for him and he was frightened. He thought that the fox and the weasel were coming with Frith and he turned to the face of the hill and began to dig. He dug a hole, but he had dug only a little of it when Frith came over the hill alone. And he saw El-ahrairah's bottom sticking out of the hole and the sand flying out in showers as the digging went on. When he saw that, he called out, 'My friend, have you seen El-ahrairah, for I am looking for him to give him my gift?' 'No,' answered El-ahrairah, without coming out, 'I have not seen him. He is far away. He could not come.' So Frith said, 'Then come out of that hole and I will bless you instead of him.' 'No, I cannot,' said El-ahrairah, 'I am busy. The fox and the weasel are coming. If you want to bless me you can bless my bottom, for it is sticking out of the hole.'"

All the rabbits had heard the story before: on winter nights, when the cold draft moved down the warren passages and the icy wet lay in the pits of the runs below their burrows; and on summer evenings, in the grass under the red may and the sweet, carrion-scented elder bloom. Dandelion was telling it well, and even Pipkin forgot his weariness and danger and remembered instead the great indestructibility of the rabbits. Each one of them saw himself as El-ahrairah, who could be impudent[26] to Frith and get away with it.

"Then," said Dandelion, "Frith felt himself in friendship with El-ahrairah, who would not give up even when he thought the fox and the weasel were coming. And he said, 'Very well, I will bless your bottom as it sticks out of the hole. Bottom, be strength and warning and speed forever and save the life of your master. Be it so!' And as he spoke, El-ahrairah's tail grew shining white and flashed like a star: and his back legs grew long and powerful and he thumped the hillside until the very beetles fell off the grass stems. He came out of the hole and tore across the hill faster than any creature in the world. And Frith called after him, 'El-ahrairah, your people cannot rule the

---

25. **swift**: fast-flying, swallowlike bird that spends most of its time in the air.

26. **impudent** [im′pyə dənt]: bold in a way that shows a lack of respect for custom or authority.

world, for I will not have it so. All the world will be your enemy, Prince with a Thousand Enemies, and whenever they catch you, they will kill you. But first they must catch you, digger, listener, runner, prince with the swift warning. Be cunning and full of tricks and your people shall never be destroyed.' And El-ahrairah knew then that although he would not be mocked, yet Frith was his friend. And every evening, when Frith has done his day's work and lies calm and easy in the red sky, El-ahrairah and his children and his children's children come out of their holes and feed and play in his sight, for they are his friends and he has promised them that they can never be destroyed."

7. *The Lendri and the River*

As Dandelion ended, Acorn, who was on the windward side of the little group, suddenly started and sat back, with ears up and nostrils twitching. The strange, rank smell was stronger than ever and after a few moments they all heard a heavy movement close by. Suddenly, on the other side of the path, the fern parted and there looked out a long, dog-like head, striped black and white. It was pointed downward, the jaws grinning, the muzzle close to the ground. Behind, they could just discern great, powerful paws and a shaggy black body. The eyes were peering at them, full of savage cunning. The head moved slowly, taking in the dusky lengths of the wood ride[27] in both directions, and then fixed them once more with its fierce, terrible stare. The jaws opened wider and they could see the teeth, glimmering white as the stripes along the head. For long moments it gazed and the rabbits remained motionless, staring back without a sound. Then Bigwig, who was nearest to the path, turned and slipped back among the others.

"A lendri," he muttered as he passed through them. "It may be dangerous and it may not, but I'm taking no chances with it. Let's get away."

They followed him through the fern and very soon came upon another, parallel path. Bigwig turned into it and broke into a run. Dandelion overtook him and the two disappeared among the ilex trees. Hazel and the others followed as best they could, with Pipkin limping and staggering behind, his fear driving him on in spite of the pain in his paw.

Hazel came out on the further side of the ilexes and followed the path round a bend. Then he stopped dead and sat back on his haunches. Immediately in front of him, Bigwig and Dandelion were staring out from the sheer edge of a high bank, and below the bank ran a stream. It was in fact the little river Enborne, twelve to fifteen feet wide and at this time of year two or three feet deep with spring rain, but to the rabbits it seemed immense, such a river as they had never imagined. The moon had almost set and the night was now dark, but they could see the water faintly shining as it flowed and could just make out, on the further side, a thin belt of nut trees and alders. Somewhere beyond, a plover[28] called three or four times and was silent.

---

27. **wood ride**: riding path or road running through the woods.

28. **plover**: shore bird with a straight, pointed bill.

One by one, most of the others came up, stopped at the bank and looked at the water without speaking. A chilly breeze was moving and several of them trembled where they sat.

"Well, this is a nice surprise, Hazel," said Bigwig at length. "Or were you expecting this when you took us into the wood?"

Hazel realized wearily that Bigwig was probably going to be troublesome. He was certainly no coward, but he was likely to remain steady only as long as he could see his way clear and be sure of what to do. To him, perplexity was worse than danger; and when he was perplexed he usually grew angry. The day before, Fiver's warning had troubled him, and he had spoken in anger to the Threarah and left the Owsla. Then, while he was in an uncertain mood about the idea of leaving the warren, Captain Holly had appeared in capital[29] time to be attacked and to provide a perfect reason for their departure. Now, at the sight of the river, Bigwig's assurance was leaking again and unless he, Hazel, could restore it in some way, they were likely to be in for trouble. He thought of the Threarah and his wily courtesy.

"I don't know what we should have done without you just now, Bigwig," he said. "What was that animal? Would it have killed us?"

"A lendri," said Bigwig. "I've heard about them in the Owsla. They're not really dangerous. They can't catch a rabbit that runs, and nearly always you can smell them coming. They're funny things: I've heard of rabbits living almost on top

of them and coming to no harm. But they're best avoided, all the same. They'll dig out rabbit kittens and they'll kill an injured rabbit if they find one. They're one of the Thousand, all right. I ought to have guessed from the smell, but it was new to me."

"It had killed before it met us," said Blackberry with a shudder. "I saw the blood on its lips."

"A rat, perhaps, or pheasant chicks. Lucky for us it *had* killed, otherwise it might have been quicker. Still, fortunately we did the right thing. We really came out of it very well," said Bigwig.

Fiver came limping down the path with Pipkin. They, too, checked and stared at the sight of the river.

"What do you think we ought to do now, Fiver?" asked Hazel.

Fiver looked down at the water and twitched his ears.

"We shall have to cross it," he said. "But I don't think I can swim, Hazel. I'm worn out, and Pipkin's a good deal worse than I am."

"Cross it?" cried Bigwig. "Cross it? Who's going to cross it? What do you want to cross it for? I never heard such nonsense."

Like all wild animals, rabbits can swim if they have to: and some even swim when it suits them. Rabbits have been known to live on the edge of a wood and regularly swim a brook to feed in the fields beyond. But most rabbits avoid swimming, and certainly an exhausted rabbit could not swim the Enborne.

"I don't want to jump in there," said Speedwell.

"Why not just go along the bank?" asked Hawkbit.

Hazel suspected that if Fiver felt they

---

29. **capital**: excellent.

The Great Piece of Turf, Albrecht Dürer, watercolor, 1503.

ought to cross the river, it might be dangerous not to. But how were the others to be persuaded? At this moment, as he was still wondering what to say to them, he suddenly realized that something had lightened his spirits. What could it be? A smell? A sound? Then he knew. Nearby, across the river, a lark had begun to twitter and climb. It was morning. A blackbird called one or two deep, slow notes and was followed by a wood pigeon. Soon they were in a gray twilight and could see that the stream bordered the further edge of the wood. On the other side lay open fields.

8. The Crossing

The top of the sandy bank was a good six feet above the water. From where they sat, the rabbits could look straight ahead upstream, and downstream to their left. Evidently there were nesting holes in the sheer face below them, for as the light grew they saw three or four martins dart out over the stream and away into the fields beyond. In a short time one returned with his beak full, and they could hear the nestlings[30] squeaking as he flew out of sight beneath their feet. The bank did not extend far in either direction. Upstream, it sloped down to a grassy path between the trees and the water. This followed the line of the river, which ran straight from almost as far away as they could see, flowing smoothly without fords, gravel shallows or plank bridges. Immediately below them lay a wide pool and here the water was almost still. Away to their left, the bank sloped down again into clumps of alder, among which the

stream could be heard chattering over gravel. There was a glimpse of barbed wire stretched across the water and they guessed that this must surround a cattle wade, like the one in the little brook near the home warren.

Hazel looked at the path upstream. "There's grass down there," he said. "Let's go and feed."

They scrambled down the bank and set to nibbling beside the water. Between them and the stream itself stood half-grown clumps of purple loosestrife and fleabane, which would not flower for nearly two months yet. The only blooms were a few early meadowsweet and a patch of pink butterbur. Looking back at the face of the bank, they could see that it was in fact dotted thickly with martins' holes. There was a narrow foreshore at the foot of the little cliff and this was littered with the rubbish of the colony—sticks, droppings, feathers, a broken egg and a dead nestling or two. The martins were now coming and going in numbers over the water.

Hazel moved close to Fiver and quietly edged him away from the others, feeding as he went. When they were a little way off, and half concealed by a patch of reeds, he said, "Are you sure we've got to cross the river, Fiver? What about going along the bank one way or the other?"

"No, we need to cross the river, Hazel, so that we can get into those fields—and on beyond them too. I know what we ought to be looking for—a high, lonely place with dry soil, where rabbits can see and hear all round and men hardly ever come. Wouldn't that be worth a journey?"

"Yes, of course it would. But is there such a place?"

"Not near a river—I needn't tell you

---

30. **nestlings**: birds too young to leave the nest.

that. But if you cross a river you start going up again, don't you? We ought to be on the top—on the top and in the open."

"But, Fiver, I think they may refuse to go much further. And then again, you say all this and yet you say you're too tired to swim?"

"I can rest, Hazel, but Pipkin's in a pretty bad way. I think he's injured. We may have to stay here half the day."

"Well, let's go and talk to the others. They may not mind staying. It's crossing they're not going to fancy, unless something frightens them into it."

As soon as they had made their way back, Bigwig came across to them from the bushes at the edge of the path.

"I was wondering where you'd got to," he said to Hazel. "Are you ready to move on?"

"No, I'm not," answered Hazel firmly. "I think we ought to stay here until ni-Frith. That'll give everyone a chance to rest and then we can swim across to those fields."

Bigwig was about to reply, but Blackberry spoke first.

"Bigwig," he said, "why don't you swim over now, and then go out into the field and have a look round? The wood may not stretch very far one way or the other. You could see from there; and then we might know which would be the best way to go."

"Oh, well," said Bigwig rather grudgingly, "I suppose there's some sense in that. I'll swim the embleer* river as many times as you like. Always glad to oblige."

Without the slightest hesitation, he took two hops to the water, waded in and

*Stinking—the word for the smell of a fox. [Adams]

swam across the deep, still pool. They watched him pull himself out beside a flowering clump of figwort, gripping one of the tough stems in his teeth, shake a shower of drops out of his fur and scutter into the alder bushes. A moment later, between the nut trees, they saw him running off into the field.

"I'm glad he's with us," said Hazel to Silver. Again he thought wryly of the Threarah. "He's the fellow to find out all we need to know. Oh, I say, look, he's coming back already."

Bigwig was racing back across the field, looking more agitated than he had at any time since the encounter with Captain Holly. He ran into the water almost headlong and paddled over fast, leaving an arrowhead ripple on the calm brown surface. He was speaking as he jerked himself out on the sandy foreshore.

"Well, Hazel, if I were you I shouldn't wait until ni-Frith. I should go now. In fact, I think you'll have to."

"Why?" asked Hazel.

"There's a large dog loose in the wood."

Hazel started. "What?" he said. "How do you know?"

"When you get into the field you can see the wood sloping down to the river. Parts of it are open. I saw the dog crossing a clearing. It was trailing a chain, so it must have broken loose. It may be on the lendri's scent, but the lendri will be underground by now. What do you think will happen when it picks up our scent, running from one side of the wood to the other, with dew on it? Come on, let's get over quickly."

Hazel felt at a loss. In front of him stood Bigwig, sodden wet, undaunted, single-minded—the very picture of decision. At his shoulder was Fiver, silent and twitching. He saw Blackberry watching him intently, waiting for his lead and disregarding Bigwig's. Then he looked at Pipkin, huddled into a fold of sand, more panic-stricken and helpless than any rabbit he had ever seen. At this moment, up in the wood, there broke out an excited yelping and a jay began to scold.

Hazel spoke through a kind of light-headed trance. "Well, you'd better get on, then," he said, "and anyone else who wants to. Personally, I'm going to wait until Fiver and Pipkin are fit to tackle it."

"You silly blockhead!" cried Bigwig. "We'll all be finished! We'll—"

"Don't stamp about," said Hazel. "You may be heard. What do you suggest, then?"

"Suggest? There's no suggesting to be done. Those who can swim, swim. The others will have to stay here and hope for the best. The dog may not come."

"I'm afraid that won't do for me. I got Pipkin into this and I'm going to get him out."

"Well, you didn't get Fiver into it, did you? He got you into it."

Hazel could not help noticing, with reluctant admiration, that although Bigwig had lost his temper, he was apparently in no hurry on his own account and seemed less frightened than any of them. Looking round for Blackberry, he saw that he had left them and was up at the top of the pool, where the narrow beach tailed away into a gravel spit. His paws were half buried in the wet gravel and he was nosing at something large and flat on the waterline. It looked like a piece of wood.

"Blackberry," he said, "can you come back here a moment?"

Blackberry looked up, tugged out his paws and ran back.

"Hazel," he said quickly, "that's a piece of flat wood—like that piece that closed the gap by the Green Loose above the warren—you remember? It must have drifted down the river. So it floats. We could put Fiver and Pipkin on it and make it float again. It might go across the river. Can you understand?"

Hazel had no idea what he meant. Blackberry's flood of apparent nonsense only seemed to draw tighter the mesh of danger and bewilderment. As though Bigwig's angry impatience, Pipkin's terror and the approaching dog were not enough to contend with, the cleverest rabbit among them had evidently gone out of his mind. He felt close to despair.

"Frithrah, yes, I see!" said an excited voice at his ear. It was Fiver. "Quick, Hazel, don't wait! Come on, and bring Pipkin!"

It was Blackberry who bullied the stupefied Pipkin to his feet and forced him to limp the few yards to the gravel spit. The piece of wood, hardly bigger than a large rhubarb leaf, was lightly aground. Blackberry almost drove Pipkin onto it with his claws. Pipkin crouched shivering and Fiver followed him aboard.

"Who's strong?" said Blackberry. "Bigwig! Silver! Push it out!"

No one obeyed him. All squatted, puzzled and uncertain. Blackberry buried his nose in the gravel under the landward edge of the board and raised it, pushing. The board tipped. Pipkin squealed and Fiver lowered his head and splayed his claws. Then the board righted itself and drifted out a few feet into the pool with the two rabbits hunched upon it, rigid and motionless. It rotated slowly and they found themselves staring back at their comrades.

"Frith and Inlé!" said Dandelion. "They're sitting on the water! Why don't they sink?"

"They're sitting on the wood and the wood floats, can't you see?" said Blackberry. "Now we swim over ourselves. Can we start, Hazel?"

During the last few minutes Hazel had been as near to losing his head as he was ever to come. He had been at his wits' end, with no reply to Bigwig's scornful impatience except his readiness to risk his own life in company with Fiver and Pipkin. He still could not understand what had happened, but at least he realized that Blackberry wanted him to show authority. His head cleared.

"Swim," he said. "Everybody swim."

He watched them as they went in. Dandelion swam as well as he ran, swiftly and easily. Silver, too, was strong. The others paddled and scrambled over somehow, and as they began to reach the other side, Hazel plunged. The cold water penetrated his fur almost at once. His breath came short and as his head went under he could hear a faint grating of gravel along the bottom. He paddled across awkwardly, his head tilted high out of the water, and made for the figwort. As he pulled himself out, he looked round among the sopping rabbits in the alders.

"Where's Bigwig?" he asked.

"Behind you," answered Blackberry, his teeth chattering.

Bigwig was still in the water, on the other side of the pool. He had swum to the raft, put his head against it and was pushing it forward with heavy thrusts of his back legs. "Keep still," Hazel heard him say in a quick, gulping voice. Then he sank. But a moment later he was up again and had thrust his head over the

back of the board. As he kicked and struggled, it tilted and then, while the rabbits watched from the bank, moved slowly across the pool and grounded on the opposite side. Fiver pushed Pipkin onto the stones and Bigwig waded out beside them, shivering and breathless.

"I got the idea once Blackberry had shown us," he said. "But it's hard to push it when you're in the water. I hope it's not long to sunrise. I'm cold. Let's get on."

There was no sign of the dog as they made haste through the alders and up the field to the first hedgerow. Most of them had not understood Blackberry's discovery of the raft and at once forgot it. Fiver, however, came over to where Blackberry was lying against the stem of a blackthorn in the hedge.

"You saved Pipkin and me, didn't you?" he said. "I don't think Pipkin's got any idea what really happened; but I have."

"I admit it was a good idea," replied Blackberry. "Let's remember it. It might come in handy again sometime."

READER'S RESPONSE (Chapters 1–4)

Would you have followed Fiver and Hazel?

STUDY QUESTIONS (Chapters 1–4)

Recalling

1. Describe Fiver and his brother Hazel.
2. What does Fiver fear?
3. What does the sign on the property say?
4. What happens when Fiver and Hazel meet the Chief Rabbit?
5. What other rabbits join Hazel and Fiver, and for what reasons?
6. Who tries to arrest the rabbits as they leave? What happens?

Interpreting

7. Given the message on the sign, what is the meaning of Fiver's frightened statement about blood in the field?
8. What qualities make Hazel a good leader?
9. Describe the risks that the rabbits take in leaving the warren.

Extending

10. Can you think of other examples in which animals are threatened by human progress?

READER'S RESPONSE (Chapters 5–8)

Do you think the rabbits will succeed in establishing a new home? Why or why not?

STUDY QUESTIONS (Chapters 5–8)

Recalling

1. Who is El-ahrairah, and what special gift did Frith give him?
2. What does Bigwig see when he crosses the river? Why does Hazel insist on waiting before crossing the river?
3. How do Pipkin and Fiver cross the river?

Interpreting

4. What help might the story of El-ahrairah be to the band of rabbits?
5. What qualities do Bigwig and Blackberry display in the struggle to cross the river?
6. Would Bigwig be a better leader for the group than Hazel? Why or why not?
7. What might human beings learn from the group of rabbits about facing the unknown?

Extending

8. Why do you think stories that describe how animals feel are popular with many readers?

READING AND LITERARY FOCUS
(Chapters 1–4)

Character

A **character** is a person or animal who appears in a story, novel, or play. Each character has certain **traits,** or qualities, that we discover as the work unfolds. These qualities are revealed by the character's own actions, words, and thoughts as well as through the comments and reactions of other characters.

For example, in *Watership Down* we first learn of Fiver from Buckthorn, who says that Fiver is so named because he was the smallest in his litter. Buckthorn adds, "A man couldn't see him and a fox wouldn't want him." As the story unfolds, however, we learn that although Fiver is small and frail, his sense of danger is keen enough to convince other rabbits to abandon their endangered home.

Thinking About Character

1. What character trait does Hazel reveal in his treatment of Fiver?
2. What character trait does Hazel reveal when he responds to Captain Holly? When he interrupts Bigwig's offer of advice?

READING AND LITERARY FOCUS
(Chapters 5–8)

External Conflict

Most stories spring from a **conflict** of some kind—a struggle between opposing forces. An **external conflict** occurs when a character struggles against an outside force. An individual may struggle against nature, as in the case of someone fighting a wild animal or scaling a mountain. One character may also come into conflict with another character—for example, when someone confronts another person in an argument or competes in a contest. Someone may also come into conflict with society, as when an individual resists a dictatorial state.

The major conflicts in *Watership Down* are external. As the rabbits leave the warren, they fight against their society. Once outside the warren, they must struggle against nature and their Thousand Enemies. In addition, the rabbits experience conflict with each other, as Hazel and Bigwig vie for the role of leader.

Thinking About External Conflict

1. Mention two examples of conflicts with nature. In what way is each conflict resolved?
2. In what way do you think the rabbits will resolve the conflicts with each other?

VOCABULARY

Prefixes

A **prefix** is a letter or group of letters added to the beginning of a word. Knowing the meaning of a prefix can often help you figure out the meaning of the word to which it is attached. For example, the prefix *fore* means "before" or "the front"; this information helps you see that the word *forepaws* means "front paws." Here are some common prefixes, along with their meanings:

Prefix	Meaning	Prefix	Meaning
dis-	away, not	e-, ex-	out of
un-	not	re-	back, again

The following words come from *Watership Down*. Copy each word, underline the prefix, and explain the meaning of the word.

1. undaunted
2. foretell
3. disappear
4. uncertain
5. emigration
6. unusual
7. reassure
8. extend

COMPOSITION

Writing a Character Sketch

Write a character sketch of Fiver. **Prewriting:** Prepare by noting Fiver's appearance, speech, and actions. **Writing:** Begin your sketch with a sentence that sums up Fiver's strengths and weaknesses. Then focus on his personality traits, using examples from the novel. End by stating what you think Fiver contributes to the band of rabbits. **Revising:** Review your paragraph to see that you have expressed your ideas clearly and logically.

Inventing a Character

Create a new rabbit character who will join Hazel's group. Decide on the new rabbit's appearance, personality, and name. Then write a description of your character as he or she approaches the other rabbits. You may want to include the impressions of Hazel and the other rabbits when they meet the new character. *For help with this assignment, see Lesson 3 in the Writing About Literature Handbook at the back of this book.*

Thinking Skills: Representing

DEFINITION

Representing is a way of picturing data, or information. Diagrams, graphs, maps, charts, and other images can help you organize data and think about what they mean. The following steps tell how to picture information using one form of representation— a cluster.

STEPS

1. **Identify the subject you will think about.**
   Write the subject in a circle like the one on this page.

2. **Identify individual features or qualities of the subject.**
   Write the features in circles around the main circle.

3. **Based on some or all of the features, make a statement about the subject.**
   What does the picture tell you about the subject? Can you compare any of the features? Are any of the features more important than others? Which feature is most interesting to you?

EXAMPLE

Imagine that you are asked to write about the space shuttle. The topic is so broad that you need to organize the information you have about it. You decide to use a cluster to think about the many different aspects of the subject.

1. **Identify the subject you will think about.** You write *space shuttle* in a circle.

2. **Identify individual features or qualities of the**

subject. You write "features of the space shuttle" around the main circle.

3. **Based on some or all of the features, make a statement about the subject.** You write, "In some ways, the space shuttle is like a rocket; in other ways, it is like an airplane."

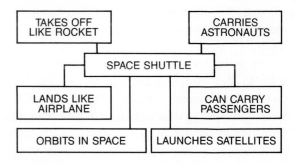

ACTIVITY 1

Follow the three steps of representing to make a cluster about one character in "Watership Down." Choose one character to be your subject, and write in the surrounding circles the most interesting qualities or characteristics of that character. Then make a statement about the character using some or all of the information shown in your cluster.

ACTIVITY 2

Follow the three steps of representing to make a cluster about any other literary selection in this book. Remember that you can use the cluster format to represent information about almost anything— characters, settings, details of action, themes. Make a statement based on the clearer picture the cluster gives you.

A native of Connecticut, the poet Reed Whittemore (born 1919) graduated from Yale University and served in the U.S. Air Force during World War II. He has taught literature at Carleton College in Minnesota and the University of Maryland. He has published books of poetry, fiction, and essays. Critics applaud his poetry for its humor as well as for the "open and free flowing style" that makes his poems entertaining and inviting.

How would you feel if you saw a raccoon on your roof?

Reed Whittemore

Science Fiction

From my city bed in the dawn I see a raccoon
On my neighbor's roof.
He walks along in his wisdom in the gutter
And passes from view
5 On his way to his striped spaceship to take his disguise off
And return to Mars as himself, a Martian
Raccoon.

READER'S RESPONSE

Why is this poem called "Science Fiction"?

STUDY QUESTIONS

Recalling

1. Where is the speaker when he sees the raccoon?
2. Where is the raccoon walking?
3. According to the speaker, where is the raccoon going, and what is he going to do?

Interpreting

4. Do you think the speaker enjoys seeing the raccoon? How can you tell?
5. If the speaker were in the woods, do you think he would imagine the raccoon as a visitor from another world? Explain.
6. Science fiction often leads you into a new world. What different worlds are brought together in this poem?

Extending

7. Picture yourself in the speaker's place. What animal would you imagine to be a Martian?

Rooftops, Edward Hopper, watercolor, 1926.

May Swenson (1919–1989) was raised in Utah and later moved to New York City. She worked as an editor and as a teacher but is best known for her prize-winning poetry and drama. Her poems are often praised for their playful wit, vivid images, and sharp detail. Like "Southbound on the Freeway" many of her poems make a habit of seeing ordinary things in a bizarre and wonderful way.

"They have four eyes," said the tourist from some other world. "The two in the back are red."

• •

May Swenson

Southbound on the Freeway

A tourist came in from Orbitville,
parked in the air, and said:

The creatures of this star
are made of metal and glass.

5 Through the transparent parts
you can see their guts.

Their feet are round and roll
on diagrams or long

measuring tapes, dark
10 with white lines.

They have four eyes.
The two in back are red.

Sometimes you can see a five-eyed
one, with a red eye turning

15 on the top of his head.
He must be special—

the others respect him
and go slow

when he passes, winding
20 among them from behind.

They all hiss as they glide,
like inches, down the marked

tapes. Those soft shapes,
shadowy inside

25 the hard bodies—are they
their guts or their brains?

READER'S RESPONSE

What answer would you give to the tourist's final question?

STUDY QUESTIONS

Recalling

1. Where does the poem take place?
2. What does the tourist from Orbitville say the creatures of "this star" are made of?
3. What makes certain creatures "special"?
4. What does the tourist wonder at the end of the poem?

Interpreting

5. What is the tourist actually seeing?
6. What are the "soft shapes" inside the "creatures"?
7. Is it better to be the "guts" or the "brains" in this situation? Explain.

READING AND LITERARY FOCUS

Making Inferences

An **inference** is a conclusion drawn from available information. For example, you wish to choose between two similar restaurants in an unfamiliar town. One restaurant is crowded; the other, nearly empty. You infer that the crowded restaurant is better. Nevertheless, you may not be correct: The crowded restaurant might feature an attraction unknown to you. Given the information you do have, however, your inference makes sense.

In "Southbound on the Freeway," the tourist from Orbitville makes inferences based only on what he or she sees: The place swarms with large, rolling objects. The tourist infers that these objects are living beings. Since we have much more information about Earth, *we* can infer that the tourist is seeing automobiles. We can also infer that the tourist has never before seen a human being and that perhaps the creatures of his or her world look more like our cars than like us.

Thinking About Inferences

1. Mention three incorrect inferences that the tourist makes about the "creatures."
2. What is the tourist's one correct inference?

VOCABULARY

Analogies

Analogies are comparisons that are stated as double relationships: for example, *A* is to *B* as *C* is to *D*. On tests analogies are written as two pairs of words, *A* : *B* :: *C* : *D*.

You may be given the first pair and asked to find or complete a second pair with the same kind of relationship. In the analogy SUMMER : WINTER :: EARLY : LATE, the words in each pair are opposites. Analogies can state many different kinds of relationships: synonyms (WEAK : FRAIL), antonyms (LOUD : SILENT), verb-object (STEER : WHEEL), or adjective-noun (LIGHT : FEATHER)—to name a few.

The following analogies are incomplete. The third word in each item comes from "Southbound on the Freeway." Decide how the first two words are related. Then from the four choices that follow, choose the word that best completes the second pair. Write the number of each item and the letter of your choice.

1. PAIL : BUCKET :: DIAGRAM :
   - (a) chart
   - (b) paper
   - (c) sentence
   - (d) painting

2. WALLOW : PIG :: GLIDE :
   - (a) lion
   - (b) bird
   - (c) helicopter
   - (d) penguin

3. TRICKY : HONEST :: SHADOWY :
   - (a) dark
   - (b) foggy
   - (c) clear
   - (d) closed

4. GREASY : OIL :: TRANSPARENT :
   - (a) mud
   - (b) glass
   - (c) pale
   - (d) beautiful

5. ARCHED : CEILING :: WINDING :
   - (a) stairway
   - (b) window
   - (c) narrow
   - (d) floor

photograph ©1990 Jill Krementz

Jean Fritz (born 1915) spent the first thirteen years of her life in Hankow, China, where her parents were missionaries. After she came to the United States, she set down her memorable early experiences in an autobiography, *Homesick, My Own Style.* Fritz has also written several novels with historical settings. For example, *Brandy* (1960) and *Early Thunder* (1967) are about teen-age boys living in colonial America. In addition, she has written many humorous biographies for young children, including *What's the Big Idea, Ben Franklin?* (1976).

I flung myself on my bed. What was there to think? Either I went to school and got beaten up. Or I quit.

Jean Fritz

from **Homesick**

In my father's study there was a large globe with all the countries of the world running around it. I could put my finger on the exact spot where I was and had been ever since I'd been born. And I was on the wrong side of the globe. I was in China in a city named Hankow,[1] a dot on a crooked line that seemed to break the country right in two. The line was really the Yangtse River,[2] but who would know by looking at a map what the Yangtse River really was?

Orange-brown, muddy mustard-colored. And wide, wide, wide. With a river smell that was old and came all the way up from the bottom. Sometimes old women knelt on the riverbank, begging the River God to return a son or grandson who may have drowned. They would wail and beat the earth to make the River God pay attention, but I knew how busy the River God must be. All those people on the Yangtse River! Coolies[3] hauling water. Women washing clothes. Houseboats swarming with old people and young, chickens and pigs. Big crooked-sailed junks[4] with eyes painted on their prows[5] so they could see where they were going. I loved the Yangtse River, but, of course, I belonged on the other side of the world. In America with my grandmother.

Twenty-five fluffy little yellow chicks hatched from our eggs today, my grandmother wrote.

I wrote my grandmother that I had

---

1. **Hankow** [han'kou']: former city in east-central China, now part of the city of Wuhan.
2. **Yangtse** [yäng'tse'] **River**: longest river in China.

3. **Coolies** [kōō'lēz]: Oriental workers without technical training who work for low wages.
4. **junks** [jungkz]: large, flat-bottomed Chinese sailing vessels having square front ends and four-cornered sails.
5. **prows**: forward parts of boats or ships; bows.

watched a Chinese magician swallow three yards of fire.

The trouble with living on the wrong side of the world was that I didn't feel like a *real* American.

For instance. I could never be president of the United States. I didn't want to be president; I wanted to be a writer. Still, why should there be a *law* saying that only a person born in the United States could be president? It was as if I wouldn't be American enough.

Actually, I was American every minute of the day, especially during school hours. I went to a British school and every morning we sang "God Save the King."[6] Of course the British children loved singing about their gracious king. Ian Forbes stuck out his chest and sang as if he were saving the king all by himself. Everyone sang. Even Gina Boss, who was Italian. And Vera Sebastian, who was so Russian she dressed the way Russian girls did long ago before the Revolution, when her family had to run away to keep from being killed.

But I wasn't Vera Sebastian. I asked my mother to write an excuse so I wouldn't have to sing, but she wouldn't do it. "When in Rome," she said, "do as the Romans do." What she meant was, "Don't make trouble. Just sing." So for a long time I did. I sang with my fingers crossed but still I felt like a traitor.

Then one day I thought: If my mother and father were really and truly in Rome, they wouldn't do what the Romans did at all. They'd probably try to get the Romans to do what *they* did, just as they were

trying to teach the Chinese to do what Americans did. (My mother even gave classes in American manners.)

So that day I quit singing. I kept my mouth locked tight against the king of England. Our teacher, Miss Williams, didn't notice at first. She stood in front of the room, using a ruler for a baton, striking each syllable so hard it was as if she were making up for the times she had nothing to strike.

(Miss Williams was pinch-faced and bossy. Sometimes I wondered what had ever made her come to China. "Maybe to try and catch a husband," my mother said.

(A husband! Miss Williams!)

"Make him vic-tor-i-ous," the class sang. It was on the strike of "vic" that Miss Williams noticed. Her eyes lighted on my mouth and when we sat down, she pointed her ruler at me.

"Is there something wrong with your voice today, Jean?" she asked.

"No, Miss Williams."

"You weren't singing."

"No, Miss Williams. It is not my national anthem."

"It is the national anthem we sing here," she snapped. "You have always sung. Even Vera sings it."

I looked at Vera with the big blue bow tied on the top of her head. Usually I felt sorry for her but not today. At recess I might even untie that bow, I thought. Just give it a yank. But if I'd been smart, I wouldn't have been looking at Vera. I would have been looking at Ian Forbes and I would have known that, no matter what Miss Williams said, I wasn't through with the king of England.

Recess at the British School was nothing I looked forward to. Every day

---

6. **"God Save the King"**: the national anthem of Great Britain.

we played a game called prisoner's base, which was all running and shouting and shoving and catching. I hated the game, yet everyone played except Vera Sebastian. She sat on the sidelines under her blue bow like someone who had been dropped out of a history book. By recess I had forgotten my plans for that bow. While everyone was getting ready for the game, I was as usual trying to look as if I didn't care if I was the last one picked for a team or not. I was leaning against the high stone wall that ran around the schoolyard. I was looking up at a little white cloud skittering across the sky when all at once someone tramped down hard on my right foot. Ian Forbes. Snarling bulldog face. Hell grinding down on my toes. Head thrust forward the way an animal might before it strikes.

"You wouldn't sing it. So say it," he ordered. "Let me hear you say it."

I tried to pull my foot away but he only ground down harder.

"Say what?" I was telling my face please not to show what my foot felt.

"*God save the king.* Say it. Those four words. I want to hear you say it."

Although Ian Forbes was short, he was solid and tough and built for fighting. What was more, he always won. You had only to look at his bare knees between the top of his socks and his short pants to know that he would win. His knees were square. Bony and unbeatable. So of course it was crazy for me to argue with him.

"Why should I?" I asked. "Americans haven't said that since George the Third."[7]

He grabbed my right arm and twisted it behind my back.

"Say it," he hissed.

I felt the tears come to my eyes and I hated myself for the tears. I hated myself for not staying in Rome the way my mother had told me.

"I'll never say it," I whispered.

They were choosing sides now in the schoolyard and Ian's name was being called—among the first as always.

He gave my arm another twist. "You'll sing tomorrow," he snarled, "or you'll be bloody[8] sorry."

As he ran off, I slid to the ground, my head between my knees.

Oh, Grandma, I thought, why can't I be there with you? I'd feed the chickens for you. I'd pump water from the well, the way my father used to do.

It would be almost two years before we'd go to America. I was ten years old now; I'd be twelve then. But how could I think about *years*? I didn't even dare to think about the next day. After school I ran all the way home, fast so I couldn't think at all.

Our house stood behind a high stone wall which had chips of broken glass sticking up from the top to keep thieves away. I flung open the iron gate and threw myself through the front door.

"I'm home!" I yelled.

Then I remembered that it was Tuesday, the day my mother taught an English class at the Y.M.C.A.[9] where my father was the director.

---

7. **George the Third**: king of England during whose reign (1760–1820) the American colonies won independence from England in the Revolutionary War (1775–1783).

8. **bloody**: very; exceedingly.
9. **Y.M.C.A.**: Young Men's Christian Association, organization with branches throughout the world, concerned with the physical, mental, and spiritual development of its members.

I stood in the hall, trying to catch my breath, and as always I began to feel small. It was a huge hall with ceilings so high it was as if they would have nothing to do with people. Certainly not with a mere child, not with me— the only child in the house. Once I asked my best friend, Andrea, if the hall made her feel little too. She said no. She was going to be a dancer and she loved space. She did a high kick to show how grand it was to have room.

Andrea Hull was a year older than I was and knew about everything sooner. She told me about commas, for instance, long before I took punctuation seriously. How could I write letters without commas? she asked. She made me so ashamed that for months I hung little wagging comma-tails all over the letters to my grandmother. She told me things that sounded so crazy I had to ask my mother if they were true. Like where babies came from. And that someday the whole world would end. My mother would frown when I asked her, but she always agreed that Andrea was right. It made me furious. How could she know such things and not tell me? What was the matter with grown-ups anyway?

I wished that Andrea were with me now, but she lived out in the country and I didn't see her often. Lin Nai-Nai, my amah,[10] was the only one around, and of course I knew she'd be there. It was her job to stay with me when my parents were out. As soon as she heard me come in, she'd called, "Tsai loushang," which meant that she was upstairs. She might

be mending or ironing but most likely she'd be sitting by the window embroidering.[11] And she was. She even had my embroidery laid out, for we had made a bargain. She would teach me to embroider if I would teach her English. I liked embroidering: the cloth stretched tight within my embroidery hoop while I filled in the stamped pattern with cross-stitches and lazy daisy flowers. The trouble was that lazy daisies needed French knots[12] for their centers and I hated making French knots. Mine always fell apart, so I left them to the end. Today I had twenty lazy daisies waiting for their knots.

Lin Nai-Nai had already threaded my needle with embroidery floss.

"Black centers," she said, "for the yellow flowers."

I felt myself glowering. "American flowers don't have centers," I said and gave her back the needle.

Lin Nai-Nai looked at me, puzzled, but she did not argue. She was different from other amahs. She did not even come from the servant class, although this was a secret we had to keep from the other servants who would have made her life miserable, had they known. She had run away from her husband when he had taken a second wife. She would always have been Wife Number One and the Boss no matter how many wives he had, but she would rather be no wife than head of a string of wives. She was modern. She might look old-fashioned, for her feet had been bound up tight when she was a

---

10. **amah** [ä′mə]: in the Orient, a female servant or nurse.

---

11. **embroidering** [em broi′dər ing]: decorating fabric or other material with a design done with needle and thread.
12. **French knots**: embroidery stitches of a particular kind.

little girl[13] so that they would stay small, and now, like many Chinese women, she walked around on little stumps stuffed into tiny cloth shoes. Lin Nai-Nai's were embroidered with butterflies. Still, she believed in true love and one wife for one husband. We were good friends, Lin Nai-Nai and I, so I didn't know why I felt so mean.

She shrugged. "English lesson?" she asked, smiling.

I tested my arm to see if it still hurt from the twisting. It did. My foot too. "What do you want to know?" I asked.

We had been through the polite phrases— Please, Thank you, I beg your pardon, Excuse me, You're welcome, Merry Christmas (which she had practiced but hadn't had a chance to use since this was only October).

"If I meet an American on the street," she asked, "how do I greet him?"

I looked her straight in the eye and nodded my head in a greeting. "Sewing machine," I said. "You say, 'Sew-ing machine.'"

She repeated after me, making the four syllables into four separate words. She got up and walked across the room, bowing and smiling. "Sew Ing Ma Shing."

Part of me wanted to laugh at the thought of Lin Nai-Nai maybe meeting Dr. Carhart, our minister, whose face would surely puff up, the way it always did when he was flustered. But part of me didn't want to laugh at all. I didn't like it when my feelings got tangled, so I ran

Yangtze River Gorge, B. W. Kilburn, c. 1900.

downstairs and played chopsticks on the piano. Loud and fast. When my sore arm hurt, I just beat on the keys harder.

Then I went out to the kitchen to see if Yang Sze-Fu, the cook, would give me something to eat. I found him reading a Chinese newspaper, his eyes going up and down with the characters. (Chinese words don't march across flat surfaces the way ours do; they drop down cliffs, one cliff after another from right to left across a page.)

"Can I have a piece of cinnamon toast?" I asked. "And a cup of cocoa?"

Yang Sze-Fu grunted. He was smoking a cigarette, which he wasn't supposed to do in the kitchen, but Yang Sze-Fu mostly did what he wanted. He considered himself superior to common workers. You could tell because of the fingernails on his pinkies. They were at least two inches long, which was his way of showing that he didn't have to use his hands for rough

13. **her feet . . . girl**: a reference to the ancient Chinese custom of foot-binding, the wrapping of a female child's feet with cloth to produce a small but deformed foot, which was considered necessary for a good marriage and social success.

or dirty work. He didn't seem to care that his fingernails were dirty, but maybe he couldn't keep such long nails clean.

He made my toast while his cigarette dangled out of the corner of his mouth, collecting a long ash that finally fell on the floor. He wouldn't have kept smoking if my mother had been there, although he didn't always pay attention to my mother. Never about butter pagodas,[14] for instance. No matter how many times my mother told him before a dinner party, "No butter pagoda," it made no difference. As soon as everyone was seated, the serving boy, Wong Sze-Fu, would bring in a pagoda and set it on the table. The guests would "oh" and "ah," for it was a masterpiece: a pagoda molded out of butter, curved roofs rising tier[15] upon tier, but my mother could only think how unsanitary it was. For, of course, Yang Sze-Fu had molded the butter with his hands and carved the decorations with one of his long fingernails. Still, we always used the butter, for if my mother sent it back to the kitchen, Yang Sze-Fu would lose face[16] and quit.

When my toast and cocoa were ready, I took them upstairs to my room (the blue room) and while I ate, I began *Sara Crewe*[17] again. Now there was a girl, I thought, who was worth crying over. I wasn't going to think about myself. Or Ian Forbes. Or the next day. I wasn't. I wasn't.

And I didn't. Not all afternoon. Not all evening. Still, I must have decided what I was going to do because the next morning when I started for school and came to the corner where the man sold hot chestnuts, the corner where I always turned to go to school, I didn't turn. I walked straight ahead. I wasn't going to school that day.

I walked toward the Yangtse River. Past the store that sold paper pellets that opened up into flowers when you dropped them in a glass of water. Then up the block where the beggars sat. I never saw anyone give money to a beggar. You couldn't, my father explained, or you'd be mobbed by beggars. They'd follow you everyplace; they'd never leave you alone. I had learned not to look at them when I passed and yet I saw. The running sores, the twisted legs, the mangled faces. What I couldn't get over was that, like me, each one of those beggars had only one life to live. It just happened that they had drawn rotten ones.

Oh, Grandma, I thought, we may be far apart but we're lucky, you and I. Do you even know how lucky? In America do you know?

This part of the city didn't actually belong to the Chinese, even though the beggars sat there, even though upper-class Chinese lived there. A long time ago other countries had just walked into China and divided up part of Hankow (and other cities) into sections, or concessions, which they called their own and used their own rules for governing. We lived in the French concession on Rue de Paris.[18] Then there was the British concession and the Japanese. The Russian and Ger-

---

14. **pagodas** [pə gō′dəz]: in the Far East, ornamental structures with a series of boldly projecting roofs.
15. **tier** [tēr]: one of a series of rows, or layers, arranged one above another.
16. **lose face**: be humiliated by loss of social or professional standing.
17. ***Sara Crewe***: children's book published in 1888 by Frances Hodgson Burnett (1849–1924), English-born American author best known for *The Secret Garden*.

18. **Rue de Paris**: Paris Street.

man concessions had been officially returned to China, but the people still called them concessions. The Americans didn't have one, although, like some of the other countries, they had gunboats on the river. In case, my father said. In case what? Just in case. That's all he'd say.

The concessions didn't look like the rest of China. The buildings were solemn and orderly with little plots of grass around them. Not like those in the Chinese part of the city: a jumble of rickety shops with people, vegetables, crates of quacking ducks, yard goods, bamboo baskets, and mangy dogs spilling onto a street so narrow it was hardly there.

The grandest street in Hankow was the Bund, which ran along beside the Yangtse River. When I came to it after passing the beggars, I looked to my left and saw the American flag flying over the American consulate[19] building. I was proud of the flag and I thought maybe today it was proud of me. It flapped in the breeze as if it were saying ha-ha to the king of England.

Then I looked to the right at the Customs House,[20] which stood at the other end of the Bund. The clock on top of the tower said nine-thirty. How would I spend the day?

I crossed the street to the promenade part of the Bund. When people walked here, they weren't usually going anyplace; they were just out for the air. My mother would wear her broad-brimmed beaver hat when we came and my father would swing his cane in that jaunty way that showed how glad he was to be a man. I thought I would just sit on a bench for the morning. I would watch the Customs House clock, and when it was time, I would eat the lunch I had brought along in my schoolbag.

I was the only one sitting on a bench. People did not generally "take the air" on a Wednesday morning and besides, not everyone was allowed here. The British had put a sign on the Bund, NO DOGS, NO CHINESE. This meant that I could never bring Lin Nai-Nai with me. My father couldn't even bring his best friend, Mr. T. K. Hu. Maybe the British wanted a place where they could pretend they weren't in China, I thought. Still, there were always Chinese coolies around. In order to load and unload boats in the river, coolies had to cross the Bund. All day they went back and forth, bent double under their loads, sweating and chanting in a tired, singsong way that seemed to get them from one step to the next.

To pass the time, I decided to recite poetry. The one good thing about Miss Williams was that she made us learn poems by heart and I liked that. There was one particular poem I didn't want to forget. I looked at the Yangtse River and pretended that all the busy people in the boats were my audience.

"'Breathes there the man, with soul so dead,'" I cried, "'Who never to himself hath said, This is my own, my native land!'"[21]

19. **consulate** [kon′sə lit]: official home or headquarters of a consul, someone appointed by his or her government to live in a foreign city and protect citizens of his or her country traveling, living, or doing business there.
20. **Customs House**: office building where customs— taxes on goods imported from foreign countries—are collected.

21. **"Breathes there the man . . . my native land!"**: famous lines from *The Lay of the Last Minstrel* (1805), a long poem about ancient Scotland by Scottish novelist and poet Sir Walter Scott (1771–1832).

I was so carried away by my performance that I didn't notice the policeman until he was right in front of me. Like all policemen in the British concession, he was a bushy-bearded Indian with a red turban wrapped around his head.

He pointed to my schoolbag. "Little miss," he said, "why aren't you in school?"

He was tall and mysterious-looking, more like a character in my Arabian Nights[22] book than a man you expected to talk to. I fumbled for an answer. "I'm going on an errand," I said finally. "I just sat down for a rest." I picked up my schoolbag and walked quickly away. When I looked around, he was back on his corner, directing traffic.

So now they were chasing children away too, I thought angrily. Well, I'd like to show them. Someday I'd like to walk a dog down the whole length of the Bund. A Great Dane.[23] I'd have him on a leash— like this—(I put out my hand as if I were holding a leash right then) and he'd be so big and strong I'd have to strain to hold him back (I strained). Then of course sometimes he'd have to do his business and I'd stop (like this) right in the middle of the sidewalk and let him go to it. I was so busy with my Great Dane I was at the end of the Bund before I knew it. I let go of the leash, clapped my hands, and told my dog to go home. Then I left the Bund and the concessions and walked into the Chinese world.

My mother and father and I had walked here but not for many months.

This part near the river was called the Mud Flats. Sometimes it was muddier than others, and when the river flooded, the flats disappeared underwater. Sometimes even the fishermen's huts were washed away, knocked right off their long-legged stilts and swept down the river. But today the river was fairly low and the mud had dried so that it was cracked and cakey. Most of the men who lived here were out fishing, some not far from the shore, poling their sampans[24] through the shallow water. Only a few people were on the flats: a man cleaning fish on a flat rock at the water's edge, a woman spreading clothes on the dirt to dry, a few small children. But behind the huts was something I had never seen before. Even before I came close, I guessed what it was. Even then, I was excited by the strangeness of it.

It was the beginnings of a boat. The skeleton of a large junk, its ribs lying bare, its backbone running straight and true down the bottom. The outline of the prow was already in place, turning up wide and snub-nosed, the way all junks did. I had never thought of boats starting from nothing, of taking on bones under their bodies. The eyes, I supposed, would be the last thing added. Then the junk would have life.

The builders were not there and I was behind the huts where no one could see me as I walked around and around, marveling. Then I climbed inside and as I did, I knew that something wonderful was happening to me. I was a-tingle, the way

---

22. **Arabian Nights**: collection of exotic tales from Arabia, Persia, and India, dating from the tenth century.
23. **Great Dane**: a breed of dog known for its size and strength.

24. **sampans** [sam′panz′]: in China, small, flat-bottomed boats rowed with an oar from the back end and often having a single sail and a rounded shelter made of mats.

a magician must feel when he swallows fire, because suddenly I knew that the boat was mine. No matter who really owned it, it was mine. Even if I never saw it again, it would be my junk sailing up and down the Yangtse River. My junk seeing the river sights with its two eyes, seeing them for me whether I was there or not. Often I had tried to put the Yangtse River into a poem so I could keep it. Sometimes I had tried to draw it, but nothing I did ever came close. But now, *now* I had my junk, and somehow that gave me the river too.

I thought I should put my mark on the boat. Perhaps on the side of the spine. Very small. A secret between the boat and me. I opened my schoolbag and took out my folding penknife that I used for sharpening pencils. Very carefully I carved the Chinese character that was our name. Gau. (In China my father was Mr. Gau, my mother was Mrs. Gau, and I was Little Miss Gau.) The builders would paint right over the character, I thought, and never notice. But I would know. Always and forever I would know.

For a long time I dreamed about the boat, imagining it finished, its sails up, its eyes wide. Someday it might sail all the way down the Yangtse to Shanghai,[25] so I told the boat what it would see along the way because I had been there and the boat hadn't. After a while I got hungry and I ate my egg sandwich. I was in the midst of peeling an orange when all at once I had company.

A small boy, not more than four years old, wandered around to the back of the huts, saw me, and stopped still. He was

Detail, *Peking, Avenue of Tien-men*, L. Sabathier, 1913.

wearing a ragged blue cotton jacket with a red cloth, pincushion-like charm around his neck which was supposed to keep him from getting smallpox.[26] Sticking up straight from the middle of his head was a small pigtail, which I knew was to fool the gods and make them think he was a girl. (Gods didn't bother much with girls; it was boys that were important in China.) The weather was still warm so he wore no pants, nothing below the waist. Most small boys went around like this so that when they had to go, they could just let loose and go. He walked slowly up to the boat, stared at me, and then nodded as if he'd already guessed what I was. "Foreign devil," he announced gravely.

I shook my head. "No," I said in Chinese. "American friend." Through the ribs

25. **Shanghai** [shang hī′]: chief port and largest city in China, in the eastern part of the country.

26. **smallpox**: severe, easily spread disease marked by fever and skin eruptions that often leave scars.

of the boat, I handed him a segment of orange. He ate it slowly, his eyes on the rest of the orange. Segment by segment, I gave it all to him. Then he wiped his hands down the front of his jacket.

"Foreign devil," he repeated.

"American friend," I corrected. Then I asked him about the boat. Who was building it? Where were the builders?

He pointed with his chin upriver. "Not here today. Back tomorrow."

I knew it would only be a question of time before the boy would run off to alert the people in the huts. "Foreign devil, foreign devil," he would cry. So I put my hand on the prow of the boat, wished it luck, and climbing out, I started back toward the Bund. To my surprise the boy walked beside me. When we came to the edge of the Bund, I squatted down so we would be on the same eye level.

"Good-bye," I said. "May the River God protect you."

For a moment the boy stared. When he spoke, it was as if he were trying out a new sound. "American friend," he said slowly.

When I looked back, he was still there, looking soberly toward the foreign world to which I had gone.

The time, according to the Customs House clock, was five after two, which meant that I couldn't go home for two hours. School was dismissed at three-thirty, and I was home by three-forty-five unless I had to stay in for talking in class. It took me about fifteen minutes to write "I will not talk in class" fifty times, and so I often came home at four o'clock. (I wrote up and down like the Chinese: fifty "I's," fifty "wills," and right through the sentence so I never had to think what I was writing. It wasn't as if I were

making a promise.) Today I planned to arrive home at four, my "staying-in" time, in the hope that I wouldn't meet classmates on the way.

Meanwhile I wandered up and down the street, in and out of stores. I weighed myself on the big scale in the Hankow Dispensary[27] and found that I was as skinny as ever. I went to the Terminus Hotel and tried out the chairs in the lounge.[28] At first I didn't mind wandering about like this. Half of my mind was still on the river with my junk, but as time went on, my junk began slipping away until I was alone with nothing but questions. Would my mother find out about today? How could I skip school tomorrow? And the next day and the next? Could I get sick? Was there a kind of long lie-abed sickness that didn't hurt?

I arrived home at four, just as I had planned, opened the door, and called out, "I'm home!" Cheery-like and normal. But I was scarcely in the house before Lin Nai-Nai ran to me from one side of the hall and my mother from the other.

"Are you all right? Are you all right?" Lin Nai-Nai felt my arms as if she expected them to be broken. My mother's face was white. "What happened?" she asked.

Then I looked through the open door into the living room and saw Miss Williams sitting there. She had beaten me home and asked about my absence, which of course had scared everyone. But now my mother could see that I was in one piece and for some reason this seemed to

---

27. **Dispensary**: place where medical treatment is provided without charge.
28. **lounge**: public room where one may sit and relax or wait.

Detail, *Peking, Avenue of Tien-men,* L. Sabathier, 1913.

make her mad. She took me by the hand and led me into the living room. "Miss Williams said you weren't in school," she said. "Why was that?"

I hung my head, just the way cowards do in books.

My mother dropped my hand. "Jean will be in school tomorrow," she said firmly. She walked Miss Williams to the door. "Thank you for stopping by."

Miss Williams looked satisfied in her mean, pinched way. "Well," she said, "ta-ta." (She always said "ta-ta" instead of

"good-bye." Chicken language, it sounded like.)

As soon as Miss Williams was gone and my mother was sitting down again, I burst into tears. Kneeling on the floor, I buried my head in her lap and poured out the whole miserable story. My mother could see that I really wasn't in one piece after all, so she listened quietly, stroking my hair as I talked, but gradually I could feel her stiffen. I knew she was remembering that she was a Mother.

"You better go up to your room," she

said, "and think things over. We'll talk about it after supper."

I flung myself on my bed. What was there to think? Either I went to school and got beaten up. Or I quit.

After supper I explained to my mother and father how simple it was. I could stay at home and my mother could teach me, the way Andrea's mother taught her. Maybe I could even go to Andrea's house and study with her.

My mother shook her head. Yes, it was simple, she agreed. I could go back to the British School, be sensible, and start singing about the king again.

I clutched the edge of the table. Couldn't she understand? I couldn't turn back now. It was too late.

So far my father had not said a word. He was leaning back, teetering on the two hind legs of his chair, the way he always did after a meal, the way that drove my mother crazy. But he was not the kind of person to keep all four legs of a chair on the floor just because someone wanted him to. He wasn't a turning-back person so I hoped maybe he would understand. As I watched him, I saw a twinkle start in his eyes and suddenly he brought his chair down slam-bang flat on the floor. He got up and motioned for us to follow him into the living room. He sat down at the piano and began to pick out the tune for "God Save the King."

A big help, I thought. Was he going to make me practice?

Then he began to sing:
"My country 'tis of thee,
Sweet land of liberty, . . ."

Of course! It was the same tune. Why hadn't I thought of that? Who would know what I was singing as long as I moved my lips? I joined in now, loud and strong.

"Of thee I sing."

My mother laughed in spite of herself. "If you sing that loud," she said, "you'll start a revolution."

"Tomorrow I'll sing softly," I promised. "No one will know." But for now I really let freedom ring.

Then all at once I wanted to see Lin Nai-Nai. I ran out back, through the courtyard that separated the house from the servants' quarters, and upstairs to her room.

"It's me," I called through the door and when she opened up, I threw my arms around her. "Oh, Lin Nai-Nai, I love you," I said. "You haven't said it yet, have you?"

"Said what?"

"Sewing machine. You haven't said it?"

"No," she said, "not yet. I'm still practicing."

"Don't say it, Lin Nai-Nai. Say 'Good day.' It's shorter and easier. Besides, it's more polite."

"Good day?" she repeated.

"Yes, that's right. Good day." I hugged her and ran back to the house.

The next day at school when we rose to sing the British national anthem, everyone stared at me, but as soon as I opened my mouth, the class lost interest. All but Ian Forbes. His eyes never left my face, but I sang softly, carefully, proudly. At recess he sauntered over to where I stood against the wall.

He spat on the ground. "You can be bloody glad you sang today," he said. Then he strutted off as if he and those square knees of his had won again.

And, of course, I was bloody glad.

READER'S RESPONSE

Should Jean have followed her mother's advice and not made an issue of singing the anthem?

STUDY QUESTIONS

Recalling

1. Where was Jean born, and where does she feel she belongs?
2. Why does Jean not want to sing the anthem?
3. What does Ian Forbes do to Jean?
4. Instead of going to school, what does Jean do and see the next day?
5. How does Jean's father solve her problem?

Interpreting

6. What aspects of China does Jean seem to like? What aspects make her uncomfortable?
7. Jean's problem at school is an example of a conflict between two cultures. Mention another example of conflicting cultures from the selection, and explain whether the conflict is resolved satisfactorily.

READING AND LITERARY FOCUS

Autobiography and Biography

An **autobiography** is the story of a person's life written by that person. A **biography** is the story of a person's life written by someone else. Both types of nonfiction focus on the most important events and people in the subject's life. An autobiography can give the reader an exciting inside view of a life, while a biography is likely to be more balanced and objective.

In her autobiography, *Homesick, My Own Story,* Jean Fritz describes her experiences as a ten-year-old American girl in China. Through her eyes you see details of the exotic world of China—the amah with her bound feet, the sails with painted eyes. Through her emotions you discover how it feels to be an outsider in a strange land.

Thinking About Autobiography

Summarize Jean's feelings about growing up in China.

VOCABULARY

Compound Words

A compound word is one word made up of two or more other words. For example, *homesick* is a compound word made up of the base words *home* and *sick*. The words below all come from *Homesick*. Select the compound word in each item. Write the number of your choice on a separate sheet of paper, and indicate the base words that make up each compound.

1. (a) riverbank   (b) washing   (c) syllable
2. (a) pagodas   (b) schoolbag   (c) segment
3. (a) consulate   (b) houseboat   (c) cakey
4. (a) fingernails (b) dismissed   (c) unload
5. (a) promenade   (b) backbone   (c) quarters

COMPOSITION

Writing About Autobiography

Write a composition describing Jean Fritz's views on the way different cultures treat one another. **Prewriting:** List the incidents in the selection that relate to conflicts between the cultures. Review your list, and determine the main idea that the items on the list suggest. **Writing:** State your version of the main idea. Use the examples from your prewriting list to support your statement. **Revising:** Reread your composition, checking to see that your writing is clear and logical. Review for effective word choice and organization. Make sure that your final copy is free of errors in grammar, spelling, and punctuation.

Writing an Autobiographical Narrative

Write a short autobiographical narrative entitled "A Day in My Life." Choose a day on which you learned something important about life. Begin by stating what you learned. Then tell what happened on that day. Organize the narrative in chronological order.

The Spanish writer Pedro Antonio de Alarcón [ä lär kon'] (1833–1891) published his first novel when he was only twenty-two years old. A few years later, in 1859, he went to Africa, where he served as a soldier and reporter. When he returned to Spain, he published an account of his African experiences. One of his best-known works is *The Three-Cornered Hat*, which was inspired by clothing owned by his grandfather.

The old farmer knows his pumpkins perfectly—but can he outwit the thief who stole them?

• •

Pedro Antonio de Alarcón

The Stub-Book

The action begins in Rota.[1] Rota is the smallest of those pretty towns that form the great semicircle of the bay of Cádiz. But despite its being the smallest, the grand duke of Osuna preferred it, building there his famous castle, which I could describe stone by stone. But now we are dealing with neither castles nor dukes, but with the fields surrounding Rota, and with a most humble gardener, whom we shall call *tío Buscabeatas* (or *old Hag-Chaser*), though this was not his true name.

From the fertile fields of Rota, particularly its gardens, come the fruits and vegetables that fill the markets of Huelva and Seville.[2] The quality of its tomatoes and pumpkins is such that in Andalusia[3]

the Roteños are always referred to as *pumpkin-* and *tomato-growers*, titles which they accept with pride.

And, indeed, they have reason to be proud; for the fact is that the soil of Rota, which produces so much—that is to say, the soil of the gardens, that soil which yields three or four crops a year—is not soil, but sand, pure and clean, cast up by the ocean, blown by the furious west winds and thus scattered over the entire region of Rota.

But the ingratitude of nature is here more than compensated for by the constant diligence of man. I have never seen, nor do I believe there is in all the world, any farmer who works as hard as the Roteño. Not even a tiny stream runs through those melancholy fields. No matter! The pumpkin-grower has made many wells from which he draws the precious liquid that is the lifeblood of his vegetables. The tomato-grower spends half his life seeking substances which may be used as fertil-

---

1. **Rota** [rō'tä]: town and port in southwest Spain on the Atlantic Ocean, northwest of Cádiz [kä' diz].
2. **Huelva** [wel'vä] **and Seville** [sə vil']: two cities in southwest Spain.
3. **Andalusia** [än'də lōō'zhə]: historic region of southern Spain, now divided into eight provinces.

Landscape Near Chatou, Maurice de Vlaminck, 1905.

izer. And when he has both elements, water and fertilizer, the gardener of Rota begins to fertilize his tiny plots of ground, and in each of them sows a tomato-seed, or a pumpkin pip[4] which he then waters by hand, like a person who gives a child a drink.

From then until harvest time, he attends daily, one by one, to the plants which grow there, treating them with a

love only comparable to that of parents for children. One day he applies to such a plant a bit of fertilizer; on another he pours a pitcherful of water; today he kills the insects which are eating up the leaves; tomorrow he covers with reeds and dry leaves those which cannot bear the rays of the sun, or those which are too exposed to the sea winds. One day, he counts the stalks, the flowers, and even the fruits of the earliest ripeners; another day, he talks to them, pets them, kisses

_____
4. **pip**: seed of a fruit.

them, blesses them, and even gives them expressive names in order to tell them apart and individualize them in his imagination.

Without exaggerating, it is now a proverb (and I have often heard it repeated in Rota) that the gardener of that region *touches with his own hands at least forty times a day every tomato plant growing in his garden.* And this explains why the gardners of that locality get to be so bent over that their knees almost touch their chins.

Well, now, *tío Buscabeatas* was one of those gardeners. He had begun to stoop at the time of the event which I am about to relate. He was already sixty years old . . . and had spent forty of them tilling a garden near the shore.

That year he had grown some enormous pumpkins that were already beginning to turn yellow, which meant it was the month of June. *Tío Buscabeatas* knew them perfectly by color, shape, and even by name, especially the forty fattest and yellowest, which were already saying *cook me.*

"Soon we shall have to part," he said tenderly, with a melancholy look.

Finally, one afternoon he made up his mind to the sacrifice and pronounced the dreadful sentence.

"Tomorrow," he said, "I shall cut these forty and take them to the market at Cádiz. Happy the man who eats them!" Then he returned home at a leisurely pace, and spent the night as anxiously as a father whose daughter is to be married the following day.

"My poor pumpkins!" he would occasionally sigh, unable to sleep. But then he reflected and concluded by saying, "What can I do but sell them? For that I raised them! They will be worth at least fifteen *duros*!"[5]

Imagine, then, how great was his astonishment, his fury and despair when, as he went to the garden the next morning, he found that, during the night, he had been robbed of his forty pumpkins. He began calculating coldly, and knew that his pumpkins could not be in Rota, where it would be impossible to sell them without the risk of his recognizing them.

"They must be in Cádiz, I can almost see them!" he suddenly said to himself. "The thief who stole them from me last night at nine or ten o'clock escaped on the *freight boat.* . . . I'll leave for Cádiz this morning on the *hour boat,* and there I'll catch the thief and recover the daughters of my toil!"

So saying, he lingered for some twenty minutes more at the scene of the catastrophe, counting the pumpkins that were missing, until, at about eight o'clock, he left for the wharf.

Now the *hour boat* was ready to leave. It was a small craft which carries passengers to Cádiz every morning at nine o'clock, just as the *freight boat* leaves every night at twelve, laden with fruit and vegetables.

The former is called the *hour boat* because in an hour, and occasionally in less time, it cruises the three leagues[6] separating Rota from Cádiz.

It was, then, ten-thirty in the morning when *tío Buscabeatas* stopped before a vegetable stand in the Cádiz market, and

---

5. **duros** [dōō′rōs]: Spanish pesos, or silver dollars.
6. **leagues**: measures of distance, used especially for distances over the sea.

said to a policeman who accompanied him, "These are my pumpkins! Arrest that man!" and pointed to the vendor.

"Arrest *me*?" cried the latter, astonished and enraged. "These pumpkins are mine; I bought them."

"You can tell that to the judge," answered *tío Buscabeatas*.

"No, I won't!"

"Yes, you will!"

"You old thief!"

"You old scoundrel!"

"Keep a civil tongue. Men shouldn't insult each other like that," said the policeman very calmly, giving them each a punch in the chest.

By this time several people had gathered, among them the inspector of public markets. When the policeman had informed the inspector of all that was going on, the latter asked the vendor in accents majestic, "From whom did you buy these pumpkins?"

"From *tío Fulano*, near Rota," answered the vendor.

"He *would* be the one," cried *tío Buscabeatas*. "When his own garden, which is very poor, yields next to nothing, he robs from his neighbors'."

"But, supposing your forty pumpkins were stolen last night," said the inspector, addressing the gardener, "how do you know that these, and not some others, are yours?"

"Well," replied *tío Buscabeatas*, "because I know them as well as you know your daughters, if you have any. Don't you see that I raised them? Look here, this one's name is Fatty; this one, Plumpy Cheeks; this one, Pot Belly; this one, Little Blush Bottom; and this one, Manuela, because it reminds me so much of my youngest daughter."

And the poor old man started weeping like a child.

"That is all very well," said the inspector, "but it is not enough for the law that you recognize your pumpkins. You must identify them with incontrovertible[7] proof. Gentlemen, this is no laughing matter. I am a lawyer!"

"Then you'll soon see me prove to everyone's satisfaction, without stirring from this spot, that these pumpkins were raised in my garden," said *tío Buscabeatas*.

And throwing on the ground a sack he

---

7. **incontrovertible** [in kon′trə ver′tə bəl]: undebatable.

was holding in his hand, he kneeled, and quietly began to untie it. The curiosity of those around him was overwhelming.

"What's he going to pull out of there?" they all wondered.

At the same time another person came to see what was going on in that group and when the vendor saw him, he exclaimed, "I'm glad you have come, *tío Fulano*. This man says that the pumpkins you sold me last night were stolen. Answer . . ."

The newcomer turned yellower than wax, and tried to escape, but the others prevented him, and the inspector himself ordered him to stay.

As for *tío Buscabeatas*, he had already faced the supposed thief, saying, "Now you will see something good!"

Tío Fulano, recovering his presence of mind, replied, "You are the one who should be careful about what you say, because if you don't prove your accusation, and I know you can't, you will go to jail. Those pumpkins were mine; I raised them in my garden, like all the others I brought to Cádiz this year, and no one could prove I didn't."

"Now you shall see!" repeated *tío Buscabeatas*, as he finished untying the sack.

A multitude of green stems rolled on the ground, while the old gardener, seated on his heels, addressed the gathering as follows: "Gentlemen, have you never paid taxes? And haven't you seen that green book the tax-collector has, from which he cuts receipts, always leaving a stub in the book so he can prove afterwards whether the receipt is counterfeit[8] or not?"

"What you are talking about is called the stub-book," said the inspector gravely.

"Well, that's what I have here: the stub-book of my garden; that is, the stems to which these pumpkins were attached before this thief stole them from me. Look here: this stem belongs to this pumpkin. No one can deny it . . . this other one . . . now you're getting the idea . . . belongs to this one . . . this thicker one . . . belongs to that one . . . exactly! And this one to that one . . . that one, to that one over there . . ."

And as he spoke, he fitted the stems to the pumpkins, one by one. The spectators were amazed to see that the stems really fitted the pumpkins exactly, and delighted by such strange proof, they all began to help *tío Buscabeatas*, exclaiming: "He's right! He's right! No doubt about it. Look: this one belongs here. . . . That one goes there. . . . That one there belongs to this one. . . . This one goes there. . . ."

The laughter of the men mingled with the catcalls[9] of the boys, the insults of the women, the joyous and triumphant tears of the old gardener and the shoves the policemen were giving the convicted thief.

Needless to say, besides going to jail, the thief was compelled to return to the vendor the fifteen *duros* he had received, and the latter handed the money to *tío Buscabeatas*, who left for Rota very pleased with himself, saying, on his way home, "How beautiful they looked in the market! I should have brought back Manuela to eat tonight and kept the seeds."

---

8. **counterfeit** [koun′tər fit′]: made in imitation of an original, with intent to deceive.

9. **catcalls**: shrill cries expressing dislike or scorn.

READER'S RESPONSE

Were you surprised that *tío Buscabeatas* was able to outwit the thief? Explain.

STUDY QUESTIONS

Recalling

1. What special efforts do the farmers of Rota make for their crops?
2. To whom is *tío Buscabeatas* compared on the night before he plans to harvest his pumpkins?

3. Why does *tío Buscabeatas* go to Cadiz? What does he see there?
4. What does *tío Buscabeatas* do to prove that the pumpkins in the market are his?

Interpreting

5. What qualities enable *tío Buscabeatas* to win out in the end?
6. What is admirable about *tío Buscabeatas* and others like him?

Extending

7. Why do you think people tend to root for underdogs like *tío Buscabeatas*?

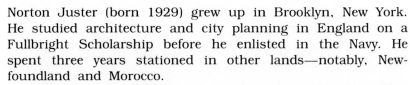

Norton Juster (born 1929) grew up in Brooklyn, New York. He studied architecture and city planning in England on a Fullbright Scholarship before he enlisted in the Navy. He spent three years stationed in other lands—notably, New-foundland and Morocco.

While he was working as an architect in New York City, Juster wrote his first novel, *The Phantom Tollbooth*. It is the story of a boy named Milo who makes a magical journey to the land of Dictionopolis, where he meets strange characters named King Azaz the Unabridged, the Humbug, and Spelling Bee and embarks on a quest to rescue Princesses Sweet Rhyme and Pure Reason.

Key Ideas in *The Phantom Tollbooth*

As you read *The Phantom Tollbooth*, think about the following topics. If you keep track of what the play says about each topic, you will begin to understand the most important themes of *The Phantom Tollbooth*.

- Exploring new worlds
- Personal growth
- Achieving impossible goals
- Fantasy and reality

Something dreadful is going to happen to us. I can feel it in my bones.

Kakafonous A. Dischord and *The Awful Dynne*

A Dramatization by Susan Nanus
Based on the Story by Norton Juster

The Phantom Tollbooth

CHARACTERS *(in order of appearance)*

THE CLOCK

MILO: a boy

THE WHETHER MAN

SIX LETHARGARIANS

TOCK: the watchdog (same as THE CLOCK)

AZAZ THE UNABRIDGED: king of Dictionopolis

THE MATHEMAGICIAN: king of Digitopolis

PRINCESS SWEET RHYME

PRINCESS PURE REASON

GATEKEEPER OF DICTIONOPOLIS

THREE WORD MERCHANTS

THE LETTERMAN (FOURTH WORD
   MERCHANT)

SPELLING BEE

THE HUMBUG

THE DUKE OF DEFINITION

THE MINISTER OF MEANING

THE EARL OF ESSENCE

THE COUNT OF CONNOTATION

THE UNDERSECRETARY OF UNDERSTANDING

A PAGE

KAKAFONOUS A. DISCHORD, DOCTOR
   OF DISSONANCE

THE AWFUL DYNNE

THE DODECAHEDRON

MINERS OF THE NUMBERS MINE

THE EVERPRESENT WORDSNATCHER

THE TERRIBLE TRIVIUM

THE DEMON OF INSINCERITY

THE SENSES TAKER

ACT ONE

Scene 1

The stage is completely dark and silent. Suddenly the sound of someone winding an alarm clock is heard, and after that, the sound of loud ticking is heard.

[*Lights up on the* CLOCK, *a huge alarm clock. The* CLOCK *reads 4:00. The lighting should make it appear that the* CLOCK *is suspended in mid-air (if possible). The* CLOCK *ticks for 30 seconds.*]

CLOCK. See that! Half a minute gone by. Seems like a long time when you're waiting for something to happen, doesn't it? Funny thing is, time can pass very slowly or very fast, and sometimes even both at once. The time now? Oh, a little after four, but what that means should depend on you. Too often, we do something simply because time tells us to. Time for school, time for bed, whoops, 12:00, time to be hungry. It can get a little silly, don't you think? Time is important, but it's what you do with it that makes it so. So my advice to you is to use it. Keep your eyes open and your ears perked. Otherwise it will pass before you know it, and you'll certainly have missed something!

Things have a habit of doing that, you know.
Being here one minute and gone the next.
In the twinkling of an eye.
In a jiffy.
In a flash!

I know a girl who yawned and missed a whole summer vacation. And what about that caveman who took a nap one after-noon, and woke up to find himself completely alone. You see, while *he* was sleeping, someone had invented the wheel and everyone had moved to the suburbs. And then of course, there is Milo. [*Lights up to reveal* MILO's *bedroom. The* CLOCK *appears to be on a shelf in the room of a young boy—a room filled with books, toys, games, maps, papers, pencils, a bed, a desk. There is a dartboard with numbers and the face of the* MATHE-MAGICIAN,[1] *a bedspread made from king* AZAZ's[2] *cloak, a kite looking like the* SPELLING BEE, *a punching bag with the* HUMBUG's *face, as well as records, a television, a toy car, and a large box that is wrapped and has an envelope taped to the top. The sound of footsteps is heard, and then enter* MILO *dejectedly. He throws down his books and coat, flops into a chair, and sighs loudly.*] Who never knows what to do with himself—not just sometimes, but always. When he's in school, he wants to be out, and when he's out, he wants to be in. [*During the following speech,* MILO *examines the various toys, tools, and other possessions in the room, trying them out and rejecting them.*] Wherever he is, he wants to be somewhere else—and when he gets there, so what. Everything is too much trouble or a waste of time. Books—he's already read them. Games—boring. T.V.—dumb.

---

1. **MATHEMAGICIAN** [math′ə mə jish′ən]: a play on *mathematician,* one who is an expert on mathematics.
2. **AZAZ** [ə zaz′]: from the first and last letters of the alphabet.

So what's left? Another long, boring afternoon. Unless he bothers to notice a very large package that happened to arrive today.

MILO. [*Suddenly notices the package. He drags himself over to it, and disinterestedly reads the label.*] "For Milo, who has plenty of time." Well, that's true. [*Sighs and looks at it.*] No. [*Walks away.*] Well . . . [*Comes back. Rips open envelope and reads.*]

A VOICE. "One genuine turnpike tollbooth, easily assembled at home for use by those who have never traveled in lands beyond."

MILO. Beyond what? [*Continues reading.*]

A VOICE. "This package contains the following items:" [MILO *pulls the items out of the box and sets them up as they are mentioned.*] "One (1) genuine turnpike tollbooth to be erected according to directions. Three (3) precautionary signs to be used in a precautionary fashion. Assorted coins for paying tolls. One (1) map, strictly up to date, showing how to get from here to there. One (1) book of rules and traffic regulations which may not be bent or broken. Warning! Results are not guaranteed. If not perfectly satisfied, your wasted time will be refunded."

MILO. [*Skeptically.*] Come off it, who do you think you're kidding? [*Walks around and examines tollbooth.*] What am I supposed to do with this? [*The ticking of the* CLOCK *grows loud and impatient.*] Well . . . what else do I have to do. [MILO *gets into his toy car and drives up to the first sign. Note: The car may be an actual toy car propelled by pedals or a small motor, or simply a cardboard imitation that* MILO *can fit into and move by walking.*]

Milo and *Tock*

VOICE. "HAVE YOUR DESTINATION IN MIND."

MILO. [*Pulls out the map.*] Now, let's see. That's funny. I never heard of any of these places. Well, it doesn't matter anyway. Dictionopolis.[3] That's a weird name. I might as well go there. [*Begins to move, following map. Drives off.*]

CLOCK. See what I mean? You never know how things are going to get started. But when you're bored, what you need more than anything is a rude awakening.

[*The alarm goes off very loudly as the stage darkens. The sound of the alarm is transformed into the honking of a car horn, and is then joined by the blasts, bleeps, roars and growls of heavy highway traffic. When the lights come up,* MILO's *bedroom is gone and we see a lonely road in the middle of nowhere.*]

Scene 2

The road to Dictionopolis

[*Enter* MILO *in his car.*]

MILO. This is weird! I don't recognize any of this scenery at all. [*A sign is held up before* MILO, *startling him.*] Huh? [*Reads.*] "WELCOME TO EXPECTATIONS. INFORMATION, PREDICTIONS AND ADVICE CHEERFULLY OFFERED. PARK HERE AND BLOW HORN." [MILO *blows horn.*]

WHETHER MAN. [*A little man wearing a long coat and carrying an umbrella pops up from behind the sign that he was holding. He speaks very fast and excitedly.*] My, my, my, my, my, welcome, welcome, welcome, welcome to the Land of Expectations, Expectations, Expectations! We don't get many travelers these days; we certainly don't get many travelers. Now what can I do for you? I'm the Whether Man.

MILO. [*Referring to map.*] Uh . . . is this the right road to Dictionopolis?

WHETHER MAN. Well now, well now, well now, I don't know of any *wrong* road to Dictionopolis, so if this road goes to Dictionopolis at all, it must be the right road, and if it doesn't, it must be the right road to somewhere else, because there are no wrong roads to anywhere. Do you think it will rain?

MILO. I thought you were the Weather Man.

WHETHER MAN. Oh, no, I'm the Whether Man, not the weather man. [*Pulls out a sign or opens a flap of his coat, which reads:* "WHETHER."] After all, it's more important to know whether there will be weather than what the weather will be.

MILO. What kind of place is Expectations?

WHETHER MAN. Good question, good question! Expectations is the place you must always go to before you get to where you are going. Of course, some people never go beyond Expectations, but my job is to hurry them along whether they like it or not. Now what else can I do for you? [*Opens his umbrella.*]

MILO. I think I can find my own way.

---

3. **Dictionopolis** [dik′shə nop′ə lis]: from *diction*, "manner of expression in words," plus the root *polis*, "city."

WHETHER MAN. Splendid, splendid, splendid! Whether or not you find your own way, you're bound to find some way. If you happen to find my way, please return it. I lost it years ago. I imagine by now it must be quite rusty. You did say it was going to rain, didn't you? [*Escorts* MILO *to the car under the open umbrella.*] I'm glad you made your own decision. I do so hate to make up my mind about anything, whether it's good or bad, up or down, rain or shine. Expect everything, I always say, and the unexpected never happens. Goodbye, goodbye, goodbye, good . . . [*A loud clap of thunder is heard.*] Oh dear! [*He looks up at the sky, puts out his hand to feel for rain, and runs away.* MILO *watches puzzledly and drives on.*]

MILO. I'd better get out of Expectations, but fast. Talking to a guy like that all day would get me nowhere for sure. [*He tries to speed up, but finds instead that he is moving slower and slower.*] Oh, oh, now what? [*He can barely move. Behind* MILO, *the* LETHARGARIANS [4] *begin to enter from all parts of the stage. They are dressed to blend in with the scenery and carry small pillows that look like rocks. Whenever they fall asleep, they rest on the pillows.*] Now I really am getting nowhere. I hope I didn't take a wrong turn. [*The car stops. He tries to start it. It won't move. He gets out and begins to tinker with it.*] I wonder where I am.

LETHARGARIAN 1. You're . . . in . . . the . . . Dol . . . drums . . . [MILO *looks around.*]

---

4. **LETHARGARIANS** [leth′ər jär′ē ənz]: from *lethargy,* "state of having or showing little interest or desire to act."

LETHARGARIAN 2. Yes . . . the . . . Dol . . . drums . . . [*A yawn is heard.*]

MILO. [*Yelling.*] WHAT ARE THE DOLDRUMS?

LETHARGARIAN 3. The Doldrums, my friend, are where nothing ever happens and nothing ever changes. [*Parts of the scenery stand up or* SIX PEOPLE *come out of the scenery colored in the same colors of the trees or the road. They move very slowly and as soon as they move, they stop to rest again.*] Allow me to introduce all of us. We are the Lethargarians at your service.

MILO. [*Uncertainly.*] Very pleased to meet you. I think I'm lost. Can you help me?

LETHARGARIAN 4. Don't say think. [*He yawns.*] It's against the law.

LETHARGARIAN 1. No one's allowed to think in the Doldrums. [*He falls alseep.*]

LETHARGARIAN 2. Don't you have a rule book? It's local ordinance 175389-J. [*He falls asleep.*]

MILO. [*Pulls out rule book and reads.*] Ordinance 175389-J: "It shall be unlawful, illegal and unethical to think, think of thinking, surmise, presume, reason, meditate or speculate while in the Doldrums. Anyone breaking this law shall be severely punished." That's a ridiculous law! Everybody thinks.

ALL THE LETHARGARIANS. We don't!

LETHARGARIAN 2. And the most of the time, you don't, that's why you're here. You weren't thinking and you weren't paying attention either. People who don't pay attention often get stuck in the Doldrums. Face it, most of the time, you're just like us. [*Falls, snoring, to the ground.* MILO *laughs.*]

LETHARGARIAN 5. Stop that at once. Laughing is against the law. Don't you have a rule book? It's local ordinance 574381-W.

MILO. [*Opens rule book and reads.*] "In the Doldrums, laughter is frowned upon and smiling is permitted only on alternate Thursdays." Well, if you can't laugh or think, what can you do?

LETHARGARIAN 6. Anything as long as it's nothing, and everything as long as it isn't anything. There's lots to do. We have a very busy schedule. . . .

LETHARGARIAN 1. At 8:00 we get up and then we spend from 8:00 to 9:00 daydreaming.

LETHARGARIAN 2. From 9:00 to 9:30 we take our early midmorning nap. . . .

LETHARGARIAN 3. From 9:30 to 10:30 we dawdle and delay. . . .

LETHARGARIAN 4. From 10:30 to 11:30 we take our late early morning nap. . . .

LETHARGARIAN 5. From 11:30 to 12:00 we bide our time and then we eat our lunch.

LETHARGARIAN 6. From 1:00 to 2:00 we linger and loiter. . . .

LETHARGARIAN 1. From 2:00 to 2:30 we take our early afternoon nap. . . .

LETHARGARIAN 2. From 2:30 to 3:30 we put off for tomorrow what we could have done today. . . .

LETHARGARIAN 3. From 3:30 to 4:00 we take our early late afternoon nap. . . .

LETHARGARIAN 4. From 4:00 to 5:00 we loaf and lounge until dinner. . . .

LETHARGARIAN 5. From 6:00 to 7:00 we dillydally. . . .

LETHARGARIAN 6. From 7:00 to 8:00 we take our early evening nap and then for an hour before we go to bed, we waste time.

LETHARGARIAN 1. [*Yawning.*] You see, it's really quite strenuous doing nothing all day long, and so once a week, we take a holiday and go nowhere.

LETHARGARIAN 5. Which is just where we were going when you came along. Would you care to join us?

MILO. [*Yawning.*] That's where I seem to be going, anyway. [*Stretching.*] Tell me, does everyone here do nothing?

LETHARGARIAN 3. Everyone but the terrible Watchdog. He's always sniffing around to see that nobody wastes time. A most unpleasant character.

MILO. The Watchdog?

LETHARGARIAN 6. THE WATCHDOG!

ALL THE LETHARGARIANS. [*Yelling at once.*] RUN! WAKE UP! RUN! HERE HE COMES! THE WATCHDOG! [*They* ALL *run off and enter a large* DOG *with the head, feet, and tail of a dog, and the body of a clock, having the same face as the character the* CLOCK.]

WATCHDOG. What are you doing here?

MILO. Nothing much. Just killing time. You see . . .

WATCHDOG. KILLING TIME! [*His alarm rings in fury.*] It's bad enough wasting time without killing it. What are you doing in the Doldrums, anyway? Don't you have anywhere to go?

MILO. I think I was on my way to Dictionopolis when I got stuck here. Can you help me?

WATCHDOG. Help you! You've got to help yourself. I suppose you know why you got stuck.

MILO. I guess I just wasn't thinking.

WATCHDOG. Precisely. Now you're on your way.

MILO. I am?

WATCHDOG. Of course. Since you got here by not thinking, it seems reasonable that in order to get out, you must *start* thinking. Do you mind if I get in? I love automobile rides. [*He gets in. They wait.*] Well?

MILO. All right. I'll try. [*Screws up his face and thinks.*] Are we moving?

WATCHDOG. Not yet. Think harder.

MILO. I'm thinking as hard as I can.

WATCHDOG. Well, think just a little harder than that. Come on, you can do it.

MILO. All right, all right. . . . I'm thinking of all the planets in the solar system, and why water expands when it turns to ice, and all the words that begin with "q," and . . . [*The wheels begin to move.*] We're moving! We're moving!

WATCHDOG. Keep thinking.

MILO. [*Thinking.*] How a steam engine works and how to bake a pie and the difference between Fahrenheit and Centigrade. . . .

WATCHDOG. Dictionopolis, here we come.

MILO. Hey, Watchdog, are you coming along?

TOCK. You can call me Tock, and keep your eyes on the road.

MILO. What kind of place is Dictionopolis, anyway?

TOCK. It's where all the words in the world come from. It used to be a marvelous place, but ever since Rhyme and Reason left, it hasn't been the same.

MILO. Rhyme and Reason?

TOCK. The two princesses. They used to settle all the arguments between their two brothers who rule over the Land of Wisdom. You see, Azaz is the king of Dictionopolis and the Mathemagician is the king of Digitopolis[5] and they almost never see eye to eye on anything. It was the job of the Princesses Sweet Rhyme and Pure Reason to solve the differences between the two kings, and they always did so well that both sides usually went home feeling very satisfied. But then, one day, the kings had an argument to end all arguments. . . .

[*The lights dim on* TOCK *and* MILO, *and come up on* KING AZAZ *of Dictionopolis on another part of the stage.* AZAZ *has a great stomach, a gray beard reaching to his waist, a small crown and a long robe with the letters of the alphabet written all over it.*]

AZAZ. Of course, I'll abide by the decision of Rhyme and Reason, though I have no

---

5. **Digitopolis** [dij'i top'ə lis]: from *digit*, "any numeral from zero to nine," plus the root *polis*, "city."

doubt as to what it will be. They will choose *words*, of course. Everyone knows that words are more important than numbers any day of the week.

[*The* MATHEMAGICIAN *appears opposite* AZAZ. *The* MATHEMAGICIAN *wears a long flowing robe covered entirely with complex mathematical equations, and a tall pointed hat. He carries a long staff with a pencil point at one end and a large rubber eraser at the other.*]

MATHEMAGICIAN. That's what you think, Azaz. People wouldn't even know what day of the week it is without *numbers.* Haven't you ever looked at a calendar? Face it, Azaz. It's numbers that count.

AZAZ. Don't be ridiculous. [*To audience, as if leading a cheer.*] Let's hear it for WORDS!

MATHEMAGICIAN. [*To audience, in the same manner.*] Cast your vote for NUMBERS!

AZAZ. A, B, C's!

MATHEMAGICIAN. 1, 2, 3's! [*A fanfare*[6] *is heard.*]

AZAZ and **MATHEMAGICIAN.** [*To each other.*] Quiet! Rhyme and Reason are about to announce their decision.

[RHYME *and* REASON *appear.*]

RHYME. Ladies and gentlemen, letters and numerals, fractions and punctuation marks—may we have your attention, please. After careful consideration of the problem set before us by King Azaz of Dictionopolis [AZAZ *bows.*] and the Mathemagician of Digitopolis [MATHEMAGICIAN *raises his hands in a victory salute.*] we have come to the following conclusion:

REASON. Words and numbers are of equal value, for in the cloak of knowledge, one is the warp and the other is the woof.[7]

RHYME. It is no more important to count the sands than it is to name the stars.

RHYME and **REASON.** Therefore, let both kingdoms, Dictionopolis and Digitopolis live in peace.

[*The sound of cheering is heard.*]

AZAZ. Boo! is what I say. Boo and Bah and Hiss!

MATHEMAGICIAN. What good are these girls if they can't even settle an argument in anyone's favor? I think I have come to a decision of my own.

AZAZ. So have I.

AZAZ and **MATHEMAGICIAN.** [*To the* PRINCESSES.] You are hereby banished from this land to the Castle-in-the-Air. [*To each other.*] And as for you, KEEP OUT OF MY WAY! [*They stalk off in opposite directions.*]

[*During this time, the set has been changed to the market square of Dictionopolis. Lights come up on the deserted square.*]

TOCK. And ever since then, there has been

6. *fanfare:* call or short tune sounded by trumpets.

7. **one is the warp . . . woof:** In a woven fabric the warp refers to the threads that run lengthwise and cross the woof, the threads that run from side to side.

neither Rhyme nor Reason in this kingdom. Words are misused and numbers are mismanaged. The argument between the two kings has divided everyone and the real value of both words and numbers has been forgotten. What a waste!

MILO. Why doesn't somebody rescue the princesses and set everything straight again?

TOCK. That is easier said than done. The Castle-in-the-Air is very far from here, and the one path which leads to it is guarded by ferocious demons. But hold on, here we are. [*A* MAN *appears, carrying a gate and a small tollbooth.*]

GATEKEEPER. AHHHHREMMMM! This is Dictionopolis, a happy kingdom, advantageously located in the foothills of Confusion and caressed by gentle breezes from the Sea of Knowledge. Today, by royal proclamation, is Market Day. Have you come to buy or sell?

MILO. I beg your pardon?

GATEKEEPER. Buy or sell, buy or sell. Which is it? You must have come here for a reason.

MILO. Well, I . . .

GATEKEEPER. Come now, if you don't have a reason, you must at least have an explanation or certainly an excuse.

MILO. [*Meekly.*] Uh . . . no.

GATEKEEPER. [*Shaking his head.*] Very serious. You can't get in without a reason. [*Thoughtfully.*] Wait a minute. Maybe I have an old one you can use. [*Pulls out an old suitcase from the tollbooth and rummages through it.*] No . . . no . . . no . . . this won't do . . . hmmm . . .

Azaz the Unabridged

MILO. [*To* TOCK.] What's he looking for? [TOCK *shrugs.*]

GATEKEEPER. Ah! This is fine. [*Pulls out a medallion on a chain. Engraved in the medallion is* "WHY NOT?"] Why not. That's a good reason for almost anything . . . a bit used, perhaps, but still quite serviceable. There you are, sir. Now I can truly say: Welcome to Dictionopolis.

[*He opens the gate and walks off.* CITIZENS *and* MERCHANTS *appear on all levels of the stage, and* MILO *and* TOCK *find themselves in the middle of a noisy marketplace. As some people buy and sell their wares, others hang a large banner which reads,* "WELCOME TO THE WORD MARKET."]

MILO. Tock! Look!

MERCHANT 1. Hey-ya, hey-ya, hey-ya, step right up and take your pick. Juicy tempting words for sale. Get your fresh-picked "ifs," "and's" and "but's"! Just take a look at these nice ripe "where's" and "when's."

MERCHANT 2. Step right up, step right up, fancy, best-quality words here for sale. Enrich your vocabulary and expand your speech with such elegant items as "quagmire," "flabbergast," or "upholstery."

MERCHANT 3. Words by the bag, buy them over here. Words by the bag for the more talkative customer. A pound of "happy's" at a very reasonable price . . . very useful for "Happy Birthday," "Happy New Year," "happy days," or "happy-go-lucky." Or how about a package of "good's," always handy for "good morning," "good afternoon," "good evening," and "goodbye."

MILO. I can't believe it. Did you ever see so many words?

TOCK. They're fine if you have something to say. [*They come to a do-it-yourself bin.*]

MILO. [*To* MERCHANT 4 *at the bin.*] Excuse me, but what are these?

MERCHANT 4. These are for people who like to make up their own words. You can pick any assortment you like or buy a special box complete with all the letters and a book of instructions. Here, taste an "A." They're very good. [*He pops one into* MILO's *mouth.*]

MILO. [*Tastes it hesitantly.*] It's sweet! [*He eats it.*]

MERCHANT 4. I knew you'd like it. "A" is one of our best-sellers. All of them aren't that good, you know. The "Z," for instance—very dry and sawdusty. And the "X"? Tastes like a trunkful of stale air. But most of the others aren't bad at all. Here, try the "I."

MILO. [*Tasting.*] Cool! It tastes icy.

MERCHANT 4. [*To* TOCK.] How about the "C" for you? It's as crunchy as a bone. Most people are just too lazy to make their own words, but take it from me, not only is it more fun, but it's also *de*-lightful [*Holds up a* "D."], *e*-lating [*Holds up an* "E."], and extremely *u*seful! [*Holds up a* "U."]

MILO. But isn't it difficult? I'm not very good at making words.

[*The* SPELLING BEE, *a large colorful bee, comes up from behind.*]

SPELLING BEE. Perhaps I can be of some assistance . . . a-s-s-i-s-t-a-n-c-e. [*The* THREE *turn around and see him.*] Don't be alarmed . . . a-l-a-r-m-e-d. I am the

Spelling Bee. I can spell anything. Anything. A-n-y-t-h-i-n-g. Try me. Try me.

MILO. [*Backing off,* TOCK *on his guard.*] Can you spell "goodbye"?

SPELLING BEE. Perhaps you are under the misapprehension . . . m-i-s-a-p-p-r-e-h-e-n-s-i-o-n that I am dangerous. Let me assure you that I am quite peaceful. Now, think of the most difficult word you can, and I'll spell it.

MILO. Uh . . . O.K. [*At this point,* MILO *may turn to the audience and ask them to help him choose a word or he may think of one on his own.*] How about . . . "Curiosity"?

SPELLING BEE. [*Winking.*] Let's see now . . . uh . . . how much time do I have?

MILO. Just ten seconds. Count them off, Tock.

SPELLING BEE. [*As* TOCK *counts.*] Oh dear, oh dear. [*Just at the last moment, quickly.*] C-u-r-i-o-s-i-t-y.

MERCHANT 4. Correct! [ALL *cheer.*]

MILO. Can you spell anything?

SPELLING BEE. [*Proudly.*] Just about. You see, years ago, I was an ordinary bee minding my own business, smelling flowers all day, occasionally picking up part-time work in people's bonnets. Then one day, I realized that I'd never amount to anything without an education, so I decided that . . .

HUMBUG. [*Coming up in a booming voice.*] BALDERDASH![8] [*He wears a lavish coat,* striped pants, checked vest, spats,[9] and a derby hat.] Let me repeat . . . BALDERDASH! [*Swings his cane and clicks his heels in the air.*] Well, well, what have we here? Isn't someone going to introduce me to the little boy?

SPELLING BEE. [*Disdainfully.*] This is the Humbug. You can't trust a word he says.

HUMBUG. NONSENSE! Everyone can trust a Humbug. As I was saying to the king just the other day . . .

SPELLING BEE. You've never met the king. [*To* MILO.] Don't believe a thing he tells you.

HUMBUG. Bosh,[10] my boy, pure bosh. The Humbugs are an old and noble family, honorable to the core. Why, we fought in the Crusades with Richard the Lionhearted, crossed the Atlantic with Columbus, blazed trails with the pioneers. History is full of Humbugs.

SPELLING BEE. A very pretty speech . . . s-p-e-e-c-h. Now, why don't you go away? I was just advising the lad of the importance of proper spelling.

HUMBUG. BAH! As soon as you learn to spell one word, they ask you to spell another. You can never catch up, so why bother? [*Puts his arm around* MILO.] Take my advice, boy, and forget about it. As my great-great-great-grandfather George Washington Humbug used to say . . .

SPELLING BEE. You, sir, are an impostor[11]

---

8. **BALDERDASH** [bôl′dər dash′]: nonsense.

9. **spats:** short cloth or leather coverings worn over the upper surface of a shoe and the ankle.
10. **Bosh:** nonsense.
11. **impostor** [im pos′tər]: one who deceives, especially by assuming the name or character of another.

i-m-p-o-s-t-o-r who can't even spell his own name!

HUMBUG. What? You dare to doubt my word? The word of a Humbug? The word of a Humbug who has direct access to the ear of a king? And the king shall hear of this, I promise you. . . .

VOICE 1. Did someone call for the king?

VOICE 2. Did you mention the monarch?

VOICE 3. Speak of the sovereign?[12]

VOICE 4. Entreat the emperor?

VOICE 5. Hail His Highness?

[FIVE *tall*, *thin* GENTLEMEN *regally dressed in silks and satins, plumed hats and buckled shoes appear as they speak.*]

MILO. Who are they?

SPELLING BEE. The king's advisers. Or in more formal terms, his cabinet.[13]

MINISTER[14] **1.** Greetings!

MINISTER 2. Salutations!

MINISTER 3. Welcome!

MINISTER 4. Good afternoon!

MINISTER 5. Hello!

MILO. Uh . . . Hi.

[*All the* MINISTERS *unfold their scrolls and read in order.*]

MINISTER 1. By the order of Azaz the Unabridged[15] . . .

MINISTER 2. King of Dictionopolis . . .

MINISTER 3. Monarch of letters . . .

MINISTER 4. Emperor of phrases, sentences, and miscellaneous figures of speech[16] . . .

MINISTER 5. We offer you the hospitality of our kingdom. . . .

MINISTER 1. Country.

MINISTER 2. Nation.

MINISTER 3. State.

MINISTER 4. Commonwealth.

MINISTER 5. Realm.

MINISTER 1. Empire.

MINISTER 2. Palatinate.

MINISTER 3. Principality.

MILO. Do all those words mean the same thing?

MINISTER 1. Of course.

MINISTER 2. Certainly.

MINISTER 3. Precisely.

MINISTER 4. Exactly.

MINISTER 5. Yes.

MILO. Then why don't you use just one? Wouldn't that make a lot more sense?

---

12. **sovereign** [sov′rən, sov′ər in]: supreme ruler of a monarchy, as a king or queen.
13. **cabinet:** council that advises a leader or sovereign of a nation.
14. **MINISTER:** one appointed to head a department of a government.

15. **Unabridged** [un′ə brijd′]: not shortened or condensed.
16. **figures of speech:** forms of expression, such as similes and metaphors, in which words are used to produce a fresh and vivid effect and are not to be taken as the literal truth.

MINISTER 1. Nonsense!

MINISTER 2. Ridiculous!

MINISTER 3. Fantastic!

MINISTER 4. Absurd!

MINISTER 5. Bosh!

MINISTER 1. We're not interested in making sense. It's not our job.

MINISTER 2. Besides, one word is as good as another, so why not use them all?

MINISTER 3. Then you don't have to choose which one is right.

MINISTER 4. Besides, if one is right, then ten are ten times as right.

MINISTER 5. Obviously, you don't know who we are.

[*Each presents himself and* MILO *acknowledges the introduction.*]

MINISTER 1. The Duke of Definition.

MINISTER 2. The Minister of Meaning.

MINISTER 3. The Earl of Essence.

MINISTER 4. The Count of Connotation.[17]

MINISTER 5. The Undersecretary of Understanding.

ALL FIVE. And we have come to invite you to the Royal Banquet.

SPELLING BEE. The banquet! That's quite an honor, my boy. A real h-o-n-o-r.

HUMBUG. DON'T BE RIDICULOUS! Everybody goes to the Royal Banquet these days.

Five Ministers

SPELLING BEE. [*To the* HUMBUG.] True, everybody does go. But some people are invited and others simply push their way in where they aren't wanted.

HUMBUG. HOW DARE YOU? You buzzing little upstart, I'll show you who's not wanted. . . . [*Raises his cane threateningly.*]

SPELLING BEE. You just watch it! I'm warning w-a-r-n-i-n-g you! [*At that moment, an ear-shattering blast of trumpets, entirely off-key, is heard, and a* PAGE[18] *appears.*]

----

17. **Connotation** [kon′ə tā′shən]: implied meaning or association of a word or expression.

18. **PAGE:** youth who waits on a person of rank.

PAGE. King Azaz the Unabridged is about to begin the Royal Banquet. All guests who do not appear promptly at the table will automatically lose their place. [*A huge table is carried out with* KING AZAZ *sitting in a large chair, carried out at the head of the table.*]

AZAZ. Places. Everyone take your places. [ALL *the characters, including the* HUMBUG *and the* SPELLING BEE, *who forget their quarrel, rush to take their places at the table.* MILO *and* TOCK *sit near the king.* AZAZ *looks at* MILO.] And just who is this?

MILO. Your Highness, my name is Milo and this is Tock. Thank you very much for inviting us to your banquet, and I think your palace is beautiful!

MINISTER 1. Exquisite.

MINISTER 2. Lovely.

MINISTER 3. Handsome.

MINISTER 4. Pretty.

MINISTER 5. Charming.

AZAZ. SILENCE! Now tell me, young man, what can you do to entertain us? Sing songs? Tell stories? Juggle plates? Do tumbling tricks? Which is it?

MILO. I can't do any of those things.

AZAZ. What an ordinary little boy. Can't you do anything at all?

MILO. Well . . . I can count to a thousand.

AZAZ. AARGH, numbers! Never mention numbers here. Only use them when we absolutely have to. Now, why don't we change the subject and have some dinner? Since you are the guest of honor, you may pick the menu.

MILO. Me? Well, uh . . . I'm not very hungry. Can we just have a light snack?

AZAZ. A light snack it shall be!

[AZAZ *claps his hands.* WAITERS *rush in with covered trays. When they are uncovered, shafts of light pour out. The light may be created through the use of battery-operated flashlights which are secured in the trays and covered with a false bottom. The* GUESTS *help themselves.*]

HUMBUG. Not a very substantial meal. Maybe you can suggest something a little more filling.

MILO. Well, in that case, I think we ought to have a square meal. . . .

AZAZ. [*Claps his hands.*] A square meal it is!

[WAITERS *serve trays of colored squares of all sizes.* PEOPLE *serve themselves.*]

SPELLING BEE. These are awful. [HUMBUG *coughs and all the* GUESTS *do not care for the food.*]

AZAZ. [*Claps his hands and the trays are removed.*] Time for speeches. [*To* MILO.] You first.

MILO. [*Hesitantly.*] Your Majesty, ladies and gentlemen, I would like to take this opportunity to say that . . .

AZAZ. That's quite enough. Mustn't talk all day.

MILO. But I just started to . . .

AZAZ. NEXT!

HUMBUG. [*Quickly.*] Roast turkey, mashed potatoes, vanilla ice cream.

SPELLING BEE. Hamburgers, corn on the

cob, chocolate pudding p-u-d-d-i-n-g. [*Each* GUEST *names two dishes and a dessert.*]

AZAZ. [*The last.*] *Pâté de foie gras, soupe à l'oignon, salade endives, fromage et fruits et demi-tasse.*[19] [*He claps his hands.* WAITERS *serve each* GUEST *his words.*] Dig on. [*To* MILO.] Though I can't say I think much of your choice.

MILO. I didn't know I was going to have to eat my words.

AZAZ. Of course, of course, everybody here does. Your speech should have been in better taste.

MINISTER 1. Here, try some somersault. It improves the flavor.

MINISTER 2. Have a rigamarole. [*Offers breadbasket.*]

MINISTER 3. Or a ragamuffin.

MINISTER 4. Perhaps you'd care for a synonym bun.

MINISTER 5. Why not wait for your just desserts?

AZAZ. Ah yes, the dessert. We're having a special treat today . . . freshly made at the half-bakery.

MILO. The half-bakery?

AZAZ. Of course, the half-bakery! Where do you think half-baked ideas come from? Now, please don't interrupt. By royal command, the pastry chefs have . . .

_____

19. ***Pâté de foie gras*** [pä tä′ də fwä grä′], ***soupe à l'oignon*** [sōōp ä lô nyon′], ***salade endives*** [sä läd′ än dēv′], ***fromage et fruits*** [frô mäzh′ ā frwē′], ***et demi-tasse*** [ā dəm′ə täs′]: loaf made from goose livers and mushrooms, onion soup, salad of endive leaves, cheese and fruit, and a small cup of strong, black coffee.

Humbug and Spelling Bee

MILO. What's a half-baked idea?

[AZAZ *gives up the idea of speaking as a cart is wheeled in and the* GUESTS *help themselves.*]

HUMBUG. They're very tasty, but they don't always agree with you. Here's a good one. [HUMBUG *hands one to* MILO.]

MILO. [*Reads.*] "The earth is flat."

SPELLING BEE. People swallowed that one for years. [*Picks up one and reads.*] "The moon is made of green cheese." Now, there's a half-baked idea.

[*Everyone chooses one and eats. They include: "It Never Rains but Pours," "Night Air Is Bad Air," "Everything Happens for the Best," "Coffee Stunts Your Growth."*]

AZAZ. And now for a few closing words.

Attention! Let me have your attention! [EVERYONE *leaps up and exits, except for* MILO, TOCK *and the* HUMBUG.] Loyal subjects and friends, once again on this gala occasion, we have . . .

MILO. Excuse me, but everybody left.

AZAZ. [*Sadly.*] I was hoping no one would notice. It happens every time.

HUMBUG. They've gone to dinner, and as soon as I finish this last bite, I shall join them.

MILO. That's ridiculous. How can they eat dinner right after a banquet?

AZAZ. SCANDALOUS! We'll put a stop to it at once. From now on, by royal command, everyone must eat dinner before the banquet.

MILO. But that's just as bad.

HUMBUG. Or just as good. Things which are equally bad are also equally good. Try to look at the bright side of things.

MILO. I don't know which side of anything to look at. Everything is so confusing, and all your words only make things worse.

AZAZ. How true. There must be something we can do about it.

HUMBUG. Pass a law.

AZAZ. We have almost as many laws as words.

HUMBUG. Offer a reward. [AZAZ *shakes his head and looks madder at each suggestion.*] Send for help? Drive a bargain? Pull the switch? Lower the boom? Toe the line? [*As* AZAZ *continues to scowl, the* HUMBUG *loses confidence and finally gives up.*]

MILO. Maybe you should let Rhyme and Reason return.

AZAZ. How nice that would be. Even if they were a bother at times, things always went so well when they were here. But I'm afraid it can't be done.

HUMBUG. Certainly not. Can't be done.

MILO. Why not?

HUMBUG. [*Now siding with* MILO.] Why not, indeed?

AZAZ. Much too difficult.

HUMBUG. Of course, much too difficult.

MILO. You could, if you really wanted to.

HUMBUG. By all means, if you really wanted to, you could.

AZAZ. [*To* HUMBUG.] How?

MILO. [*Also to* HUMBUG.] Yeah, how?

HUMBUG. Why . . . uh, it's a simple task for a brave boy with a stout heart, a steadfast dog, and a serviceable small automobile.

AZAZ. Go on.

HUMBUG. Well, all that he would have to do is cross the dangerous, unknown countryside between here and Digitopolis, where he would have to persuade the Mathemagician to release the princesses, which we know to be impossible because the Mathemagician will never agree with Azaz about anything. Once achieving that, it's a simple matter of entering the Mountains of Ignorance from where no one has ever returned alive, an effortless climb up a two-thousand-foot stairway without railings in a high wind at night to the

Castle-in-the-Air. After a pleasant chat with the princesses, all that remains is a leisurely ride back through those chaotic crags where the frightening fiends have sworn to tear any intruder from limb to limb and devour him down to his belt buckle. And finally after doing all that, a triumphal parade! If, of course, there is anything left to parade . . . followed by hot chocolate and cookies for everyone.

AZAZ. I never realized it would be so simple.

MILO. It sounds dangerous to me.

TOCK. And just who is supposed to make that journey?

AZAZ. A very good question. But there is one far more serious problem.

MILO. What's that?

AZAZ. I'm afraid I can't tell you that until you return.

MILO. But wait a minute, I don't . . .

AZAZ. Dictionopolis will always be grateful to you, my boy and your dog. [AZAZ *pats* TOCK *and* MILO.]

TOCK. Now, just one moment, sire . . .

AZAZ. You will face many dangers on your journey, but fear not, for I can give you something for your protection. [AZAZ *gives* MILO *a box.*] In this box are the letters of the alphabet. With them you can form all the words you will ever need to help you overcome the obstacles that may stand in your path. All you must do is use them well and in the right places.

MILO. [*Miserably.*] Thanks a lot.

AZAZ. You will need a guide, of course, and since he knows the obstacles so well, the Humbug has cheerfully volunteered to accompany you.

HUMBUG. Now, see here . . . !

AZAZ. You will find him dependable, brave, resourceful and loyal.

HUMBUG. [*Flattered.*] Oh, Your Majesty.

MILO. I'm sure he'll be a great help. [*They approach the car.*]

TOCK. I hope so. It looks like we're going to need it.

[*The lights darken and the* KING *fades from view.*]

AZAZ. Good luck! Drive carefully! [*The* THREE *get into the car and begin to move. Suddenly a thunderously loud noise is heard. They slow down the car.*]

MILO. What was that?

TOCK. It came from up ahead.

HUMBUG. It's something terrible, I just know it. Oh, no. Something dreadful is going to happen to us. I can feel it in my bones. [*The noise is repeated. They* ALL *look at each other fearfully, as the lights fade.*]

ACT TWO

Scene 1

The set of Digitopolis glitters in the background, while upstage right near the road, a small colorful wagon sits, looking quite deserted. On its side in large letters, a sign reads:

KAKAFONOUS A. DISCHORD[1]
DOCTOR OF DISSONANCE[2]

[*Enter* MILO, TOCK *and* HUMBUG, *fearfully. They look at the wagon.*]

TOCK. There's no doubt about it. That's where the noise was coming from.

HUMBUG. [*To* MILO.] Well, go on.

MILO. Go on what?

HUMBUG. Go on and see who's making all that noise in there. We can't just ignore a creature like that.

MILO. Creature? What kind of creature? Do you think he's dangerous?

HUMBUG. Go on, Milo. Knock on the door. We'll be right behind you.

MILO. O.K. Maybe he can tell us how much further it is to Digitopolis.

[MILO *tiptoes up to the wagon door and knocks timidly. The moment he knocks, a terrible crash is heard inside the wagon, and* MILO *and the* OTHERS *jump back in fright. At the same time, the door flies open, and from the dark interior, a hoarse* VOICE *inquires.*]

VOICE. Have you ever heard a whole set of dishes dropped from the ceiling onto a hard stone floor? [*The* OTHERS *are speechless with fright.* MILO *shakes his head.* VOICE *happily.*] Have you ever heard an ant wearing fur slippers walk across a thick wool carpet? [MILO *shakes his head again.*] Have you ever heard a blindfolded octopus unwrap a cellophane-covered[3] bathtub? [MILO *shakes his head a third time.*] Ha! I knew it. [*He hops out, a little* MAN, *wearing a white coat, with a stethoscope[4] around his neck, and a small mirror attached to his forehead, and with very huge ears, and a mortar and pestle[5] in his hands. He stares at* MILO, TOCK *and* HUMBUG.] None of you looks well at all! Tsk, tsk, not at all. [*He opens the top or side of his wagon, revealing a dusty interior resembling an old apothecary[6] shop, with shelves lined with jars and boxes, a table, books, test tubes and bottles and measuring spoons.*]

---

1. **KAKAFONOUS A. DISCHORD** [kə kof′ ə nəs ā dis′ kôrd]: from *cacophonous*, "making a harsh or unpleasant sound," and *discord*, "mingling or clashing of unpleasant sounds."
2. **DISSONANCE** [dis′ə nəns]: harsh, unpleasant sound or combination of sounds.
3. **cellophane** [sel′ə fān′]-**covered**: wrapped in thin, transparent material made from cellulose, the chief part of the cell walls of plants.
4. **stethoscope** [steth′ə skōp′]: instrument used to listen to the sounds made by the internal organs of the body.
5. **mortar** [môr′tər] **and pestle** [pes′əl]: A mortar is a thick bowl in which substances are crushed to a powder by means of a blunt tool, called a pestle.
6. **apothecary** [ə poth′ə ker′ē]: one who prepares and sells medicines.

MILO. [*Timidly.*] Are you a doctor?

DISCHORD'S VOICE. I am KAKAFONOUS A. DISCHORD, DOCTOR OF DISSONANCE! [*Several small explosions and a grinding crash are heard.*]

HUMBUG. [*Stuttering with fear.*] What does the "A" stand for?

DISCHORD. "AS LOUD AS POSSIBLE!" [*Two screeches and a bump are heard.*] Now, step a little closer and stick our your tongues. [DISCHORD *examines them.*] Just as I expected. [*He opens a large dusty book and thumbs through the pages.*] You're all suffering from a severe lack of noise. [DISCHORD *begins running around, collecting bottles, reading the labels to himself as he goes along.*] "Loud Cries." "Soft Cries." "Bangs, Bongs, Swishes, Swooshes." "Snaps and Crackles." "Whistles and Gongs." "Squeeks, Squacks, and Miscellaneous Uproar." [*As he reads them off, he pours a little of each into a large glass beaker and stirs the mixture with a wooden spoon. The concoction smokes and bubbles.*] Be ready in just a moment.

MILO. [*Suspiciously.*] Just what kind of doctor are you?

DISCHORD. Well, you might say, I'm a specialist. I specialize in noises, from the loudest to the softest, and from the slightly annoying to the terribly unpleasant. For instance, have you ever heard a square-wheeled steamroller ride over a street full of hard-boiled eggs? [*Very loud crunching sounds are heard.*]

MILO. [*Holding his ears.*] But who would want all those terrible noises?

DISCHORD. [*Surprised at the question.*] Everybody does. Why, I'm so busy I can hardly fill all the orders for noise pills, racket lotion, clamor salve[7] and hubbub tonic. That's all people seem to want these days. Years ago, everyone wanted pleasant sounds and business was terrible. But then the cities were built and there was a great need for honking horns, screeching trains, clanging bells and all the rest of those wonderfully unpleasant sounds we use so much today. I've been working overtime ever since and my medicine here is in great demand. All you have to do is take one spoonful every day, and you'll never have to hear another beautiful sound again. Here, try some.

HUMBUG. [*Backing away.*] If it's all the same to you, I'd rather not.

MILO. I don't want to be cured of beautiful sounds.

TOCK. Besides, there's no such sickness as a lack of noise.

DISCHORD. How true. That's what makes it so difficult to cure. [*Takes a large glass bottle from the shelf.*] Very well, if you want to go all through life suffering from a noise deficiency, I'll just give this to Dynne[8] for his lunch. [*Uncorks the bottle and pours the liquid into it. There is a rumbling and then a loud explosion accompanied by smoke, out of which* DYNNE, *a smog-like creature with yellow eyes and a frowning mouth, appears.*]

DYNNE. [*Smacking his lips.*] Ahhh, that was good, Master. I thought you'd never let me out. It was really cramped in there.

---

7. **salve** [sav]: greasy substance applied to the skin to treat wounds and sores.
8. **Dynne** [din]: a play on *din*, "loud, continuous noise."

DISCHORD. This is my assistant, the Awful Dynne. You must forgive his appearance, for he really doesn't have any.

MILO. What is a Dynne?

DISCHORD. You mean you've never heard of the Awful Dynne? When you're playing in your room and making a great amount of noise, what do they tell you to stop?

MILO. That awful din.

DISCHORD. When the neighbors are playing their radio too loud late at night, what do you wish they'd turn down?

TOCK. That awful din.

DISCHORD. And when the street on your block is being repaired and the drills are working all day, what does everyone complain of?

HUMBUG. [*Brightly.*] The dreadful row.

DYNNE. The Dreadful Rauw[9] was my grandfather. He perished in the great silence epidemic of 1712. I certainly can't understand why you don't like noise. Why, I heard an explosion last week that was so lovely, I groaned with appreciation for two days. [*He gives a loud groan at the memory.*]

DISCHORD. He's right, you know. Noise is the most valuable thing in the world.

MILO. King Azaz says words are.

DISCHORD. NONSENSE! Why, when a baby wants food, how does he ask?

DYNNE. [*Happily.*] He screams!

DISCHORD. And when a racing car wants gas?

DYNNE. [*Jumping for joy.*] It chokes!

DISCHORD. And what happens to the dawn when a new day begins?

DYNNE. [*Delighted.*] It breaks!

DISCHORD. You see how simple it is? [*To* DYNNE.] Isn't it time for us to go?

MILO. Where to? Maybe we're going the same way.

DYNNE. I doubt it. [*Picking up empty sacks from the table.*] We're going on our collection rounds. Once a day, I travel throughout the kingdom and collect all the wonderfully horrible and beautifully unpleasant sounds I can find and bring them back to the doctor to use in his medicine.

DISCHORD. Where are you going?

MILO. To Digitopolis.

DISCHORD. Oh, there are a number of ways to get to Digitopolis, if you know how to follow directions. Just take a look at the sign at the fork in the road. Though why you'd ever want to go there, I'll never know.

MILO. We want to talk to the Mathemagician.

HUMBUG. About the release of the Princesses Rhyme and Reason.

DISCHORD. Rhyme and Reason? I remember them. Very nice girls, but a little too quiet for my taste. In fact, I've been meaning to send them something that Dynne brought home by mistake and which I have absolutely no use for. [*He*

---

9. **Rauw** [rou]: a play on *row*, "noisy quarrel."

rummages through the wagon.] Ah, here it is . . . or maybe you'd like it for yourself. [*Hands* MILO *a package.*]

MILO. What is it?

DISCHORD. The sounds of laughter. They're so unpleasant to hear, it's almost unbearable. All those giggles and snickers and happy shouts of joy, I don't know what Dynne was thinking of when he collected them. Here, take them to the princesses or keep them for yourselves, I don't care. Well, time to move on. Goodbye now and good luck! [*He has shut the wagon by now and gets in. Loud noises begin to erupt as* DYNNE *pulls the wagon offstage.*]

MILO. [*Calling after them.*] But wait! The fork in the road . . . you didn't tell us where it is. . . .

TOCK. It's too late. He can't hear a thing.

HUMBUG. I could use a fork of my own, at the moment. And a knife and a spoon to go with it. All of a sudden, I feel very hungry.

MILO. So do I, but it's no use thinking about it. There won't be anything to eat until we reach Digitopolis. [*They get into the car.*]

HUMBUG. [*Rubbing his stomach.*] Well, the sooner the better is what I say.

[*A sign suddenly appears.*]

VOICE. [*A strange voice from nowhere.*] But which way will get you there sooner? That is the question.

TOCK. Did you hear something?

MILO. Look! The fork in the road and a signpost to Digitopolis! [*They read the sign.*]

DIGITOPOLIS

5	Miles
1,600	Rods
8,800	Yards
26,400	Feet
316,800	Inches
633,600	Half Inches

AND THEN SOME

HUMBUG. Let's travel by miles, it's shorter.

MILO. Let's travel by half inches. It's quicker.

TOCK. But which road should we take? It must make a difference.

MILO. Do you think so?

TOCK. Well, I'm not sure, but . . .

HUMBUG. He could be right. On the other hand, he could also be wrong. Does it make a difference or not?

VOICE. Yes, indeed, indeed it does, certainly, my yes, it does make a difference.

[*The* DODECAHEDRON[10] *appears, a 12-sided figure with a different face on each side, and with all the edges labeled with a small letter and all the angles labeled with a large letter. He wears a beret and peers at the others with a serious face. He doffs[11] his cap and recites.*]

DODECAHEDRON.
My angles are many.
My sides are not few.
I'm the Dodecahedron.
Who are you?

---

10. **DODECAHEDRON** [dō dek′ə hē′drən].
11. *doffs* [dofs]: removes or lifts, especially as an expression of greeting.

MILO. What's a Dodecahedron?

DODECAHEDRON. [*Turning around slowly.*] See for yourself. A Dodecahedron is a mathematical shape with 12 faces. [*All his faces appear as he turns, each face with a different expression. He points to them.*] I usually use one at a time. It saves wear and tear. What are you called?

MILO. Milo.

DODECAHEDRON. That's an odd name. [*Changing his smiling face to a frowning one.*] And you have only one face.

MILO. [*Making sure it is still there.*] Is that bad?

DODECAHEDRON. You'll soon wear it out using it for everything. Is everyone with one face called Milo?

MILO. Oh, no. Some are called Billy or Jeffrey or Sally or Lisa or lots of other things.

DODECAHEDRON. How confusing. Here everything is called exactly what it is. The triangles are called triangles, the circles are called circles, and even the same numbers have the same name. Can you imagine what would happen if we named all the twos Billy or Jeffrey or Sally or Lisa or lots of other things? You'd have to say Robert plus John equals four, and if the fours were named Albert, things would be hopeless.

MILO. I never thought of it that way.

DODECAHEDRON. [*With an admonishing face.*] Then I suggest you begin at once, for in Digitopolis, everything is quite precise.

MILO. Then perhaps you can help us decide which road we should take.

DODECAHEDRON. [*Happily.*] By all means. There's nothing to it. [*As he talks, the* THREE OTHERS *try to solve the problem on a large blackboard that is wheeled onstage for the occasion.*] Now, if a small car carrying 3 people at 30 miles an hour for 10 minutes along a road 5 miles long at 11:35 in the morning starts at the same time as 3 people who have been traveling in a little automobile at 20 miles an hour for 15 minutes on another road exactly twice as long as half the distance of the other, while a dog, a bug, and a boy travel an equal distance in the same time or the same distance in an equal time along a third road in mid-October, then which one arrives first and which is the best way to go?

HUMBUG. Seventeen!

MILO. [*Still figuring frantically.*] I'm not sure, but . . .

DODECAHEDRON. You'll have to do better than that.

MILO. I'm not very good at problems.

DODECAHEDRON. What a shame. They're so very useful. Why, did you know that if a beaver 2 feet long with a tail a foot and a half long can build a dam 12 feet high and 6 feet wide in 2 days, all you would need to build Boulder Dam[12] is a beaver 68 feet long with a 51-foot tail?

HUMBUG. [*Grumbling as his pencil snaps.*] Where would you find a beaver that big?

DODECAHEDRON. I don't know, but if you did, you'd certainly know what to do with him.

---

12. **Boulder Dam:** former name of the Hoover Dam, a massive dam on the Colorado River between Nevada and Arizona.

MILO. That's crazy.

DODECAHEDRON. That may be true, but it's completely accurate, and as long as the answer is right, who cares if the question is wrong?

TOCK. [*Who has been patiently doing the first problem.*] All three roads arrive at the same place at the same time.

DODECAHEDRON. Correct! And I'll take you there myself. [*The blackboard rolls off, and* ALL FOUR *get into the car and drive off.*] Now you see how important problems are. If you hadn't done this one properly, you might have gone the wrong way.

MILO. But if all the roads arrive at the same place at the same time, then aren't they all the right road?

DODECAHEDRON. [*Glaring from his upset face.*] Certainly not! They're all the wrong way! Just because you have a choice, it doesn't mean that any of them *has to be* right. [*Pointing in another direction.*] That's the way to Digitopolis and we'll be there any moment. [*Suddenly the lighting grows dimmer.*] In fact, we're here. Welcome to the Land of Numbers.

HUMBUG. [*Looking around at the barren landscape.*] It doesn't look very inviting.

MILO. Is this the place where numbers are made?

DODECAHEDRON. They're not made. You have to dig for them. Don't you know anything at all about numbers?

MILO. Well, I never really thought they were very important.

DODECAHEDRON. NOT IMPORTANT! Could you have tea for two without the 2? Or three blind mice without the 3? And how

would you sail the seven seas without the 7?

MILO. All I meant was . . .

DODECAHEDRON. [*Continues shouting angrily.*] If you had high hopes, how would you know how high they were? And did you know that narrow escapes come in different widths? Would you travel the whole world wide without ever knowing how wide it was? And how could you do anything at long last without knowing how long the last was? Why numbers are the most beautiful and valuable things in the world. Just follow me and I'll show you. [*He motions to them and pantomimes[13] walking through rocky terrain with the* OTHERS *in tow. A doorway similar to the tollbooth appears and the* DODECAHEDRON *opens it and motions the* OTHERS *to follow him through.*] Come along, come along. I can't wait for you all day. [*They enter the doorway and the lights are dimmed very low, as to simulate the interior of a cave. The sounds of scrapings and tapping, scuffling and digging are heard all around them. He hands them helmets with flashlights attached.*] Put these on.

MILO. [*Whispering.*] Where are we going?

DODECAHEDRON. We're here. This is the numbers mine. [*Lights up a little, revealing little* MEN *digging and chopping, shoveling and scraping.*] Right this way and watch your step. [*His voice echoes and reverberates. Iridescent and glittery numbers seem to sparkle from everywhere.*]

---

13. **pantomimes** [pan'tə mīmz']: indicates an action without speech, through the use of body movements and facial expressions.

MILO. [*Awed.*] Whose mine is it?

VOICE OF MATHEMAGICIAN. By the four million eight hundred and twenty-seven thousand six hundred and fifty-nine hairs on my head, it's mine, of course! [*Enter the* MATHEMAGICIAN, *carrying his long staff, which looks like a giant pencil.*]

HUMBUG. [*Already intimidated.*] It's a lovely mine, really it is.

MATHEMAGICIAN. [*Proudly.*] The biggest numbers mine in the kingdom.

MILO. [*Excitedly.*] Are there any precious stones in it?

MATHEMAGICIAN. PRECIOUS STONES! [*Then softly.*] By the eight million two hundred and forty-seven thousand three hundred and twelve threads in my robe, I'll say there are. Look here. [*Reaches in a cart, pulls out a small object, polishes it vigorously and holds it to the light, where it sparkles.*]

MILO. But that's a five.

MATHEMAGICIAN. Exactly. As valuable a jewel as you'll find anywhere. Look at some of the others. [*Scoops up others and pours them into* MILO's *arms. They include all numbers from 1 to 9 and an assortment of zeros.*]

DODECAHEDRON. We dig them and polish them right here, and then send them all over the world. Marvelous, aren't they?

TOCK. They are beautiful. [*He holds them up to compare them to the numbers on his clock body.*]

MILO. So that's where they come from. [*Looks at them and carefully hands them back, but drops a few, which smash and break in half.*] Oh, I'm sorry!

MATHEMAGICIAN. [*Scooping them up.*] Oh, don't worry about that. We use the broken ones for fractions. How about some lunch?

[*Takes out a little whistle and blows it.* TWO MINERS *rush in carrying an immense caldron, which is bubbling and steaming. The* WORKERS *put down their tools and gather around to eat.*]

HUMBUG. That looks delicious! [TOCK *and* MILO *also look hungrily at the pot.*]

MATHEMAGICIAN. Perhaps you'd care for something to eat?

MILO. Oh, yes, sir!

TOCK. Thank you.

HUMBUG. [*Already eating.*] Ummm . . . delicious! [ALL *finish their bowls immediately.*]

MATHEMAGICIAN. Please have another portion. [*They eat and finish.* MATHEMAGICIAN *serves them again.*] Don't stop now. [*They finish.*] Come on, no need to be bashful. [*Serves them again.*]

MILO. [*To* TOCK *and* HUMBUG *as he finishes again.*] Do you want to hear something strange? Each one I eat makes me a little hungrier than before.

MATHEMAGICIAN. Do have some more. [*He serves them again. They eat frantically, until the* MATHEMAGICIAN *blows his whistle again and the pot is removed.*]

HUMBUG. [*Holding his stomach.*] Uggghhh! I think I'm starving.

MILO. Me too, and I ate so much.

DODECAHEDRON. [*Wiping the gravy from several of his mouths.*] Yes, it was delicious, wasn't it? It's the specialty of the kingdom . . . subtraction stew.

TOCK. [*Weak from hunger.*] I have more of an appetite than when I began.

MATHEMAGICIAN. Certainly, what did you expect? The more you eat, the hungrier you get; everyone knows that.

MILO. They do? Then how do you get enough?

MATHEMAGICIAN. Enough? Here in Digitopolis, we have our meals when we're full and eat until we're hungry. That way, when you don't have anything at all, you have more than enough. It's a very economical system. You must have been stuffed to have eaten so much.

DODECAHEDRON. It's completely logical. The more you want, the less you get, and the less you get, the more you have. Simple arithmetic, that's all. [TOCK, MILO *and* HUMBUG *look at him blankly.*] Now, look, suppose you had something and added nothing to it. What would have?

MILO. The same.

DODECAHEDRON. Splendid! And suppose you had something and added less than nothing to it? What would you have then?

HUMBUG. Starvation! Oh, I'm so hungry.

DODECAHEDRON. Now, now, it's not as bad as all that. In a few hours, you'll be nice and full again . . . just in time for dinner.

MILO. But I only eat when I'm hungry.

MATHEMAGICIAN. [*Waving the eraser of his staff.*] What a curious idea. The next thing you'll have us believe is that you only sleep when you're tired.

[*The mine has disappeared as well*

Mathemagician

as the MINERS. *This may be done by dropping a curtain in front of the mine, through a blackout on the stage, while a single spotlight remains on the* MATHEMAGICIAN *and the* OTHERS, *or through the use of multi-level platforms. The* MINERS *may fall behind the platforms as two-dimensional*[14] *props, which depict the* MATHEMAGICIAN*'s room, are dropped down or raised up.*]

HUMBUG. Where did everyone go?

MATHEMAGICIAN. Oh, they're still in the mine. I often find that the best way to get from one place to another is to erase everything and start again. Please make yourself at home.

[*They find themselves in a unique room, in which all the walls, tables, chairs, desks, cabinets and blackboards are labeled to show their heights, widths, depths and distances to and from each other. To one side is a gigantic notepad on an artist's easel, and from hooks and strings hang a collection of rulers, measures, weights and tapes, and all other measuring devices.*]

MILO. Do you always travel that way? [*He looks around in wonder.*]

MATHEMAGICIAN. No, indeed! [*He pulls a plumb line*[15] *from a hook and walks.*] Most of the time I take the shortest distance between any two points. And of course, when I have to be in several places at once . . . [*He writes "3 × 1 = 3"*

---

14. **two-dimensional:** having or seeming to have the dimensions of length and width but not depth.
15. **plumb** [plum] **line:** line from which a weight is suspended, used to measure the depth of bodies of water or to determine whether something is vertical.

on the notepad with his staff.] I simply multiply. [THREE FIGURES *looking like the* MATHEMAGICIAN *appear on a platform above.*]

MILO. How did you do that?

MATHEMAGICIAN and the **THREE.** There's nothing to it if you have a magic staff. [*The* THREE *cancel themselves out and disappear.*]

HUMBUG. That's nothing but a big pencil.

MATHEMAGICIAN. True enough, but once you learn to use it, there's no end to what you can do.

MILO. Can you make things disappear?

MATHEMAGICIAN. Just step a little closer and watch this. [*Shows them that there is nothing up his sleeve or in his hat. He writes.*] "4 + 9 − 2 × 16 + 1 ÷ 3 × 6 − 67 + 8 × 2 − 3 + 26 − 1 − 34 + 3 − 7 + 2 − 5 =" [*He looks up expectantly.*]

HUMBUG. Seventeen?

MILO. It all comes to zero.

MATHEMAGICIAN. Precisely. [*Makes a theatrical bow and rips off paper from notepad.*] Now, is there anything else you'd like to see? [*At this point, an appeal to the audience to see if anyone would like a problem solved.*]

MILO. Well . . . can you show me the biggest number there is?

MATHEMAGICIAN. Why, I'd be delighted. [*Opening a closet door.*] We keep it right here. It took four miners to dig it out. [*He shows them a huge 3 twice as high as the* MATHEMAGICIAN.]

MILO. No, that's not what I mean. Can you show me the longest number there is?

MATHEMAGICIAN. Sure. [*Opens another door.*] Here it is. It took three carts to carry it here. [*Door reveals an 8 that is as wide as the 3 was high.*]

MILO. No, no, that's not what I meant either. [*Looks helplessly at* TOCK.]

TOCK. I think what you would like to see is the number of the greatest possible magnitude.

MATHEMAGICIAN. Well, why didn't you say so? [*He busily measures them and all other things as he speaks, and marks it down.*] What's the greatest number you can think of? [*Here, an appeal can also be made to the audience or* MILO *may think of his own answers.*]

MILO. Uh . . . nine trillion, nine hundred and ninety-nine billion, nine hundred ninety-nine million, nine-hundred ninety-nine thousand, nine hundred and ninety-nine. [*He puffs.*]

MATHEMAGICIAN. [*Writes that on the pad.*] Very good. Now add one to it. [MILO *or audience does.*] Now add one again. [MILO *or audience does so.*] Now add one again. Now add one again. Now add . . .

MILO. But when can I stop?

MATHEMAGICIAN. Never. Because the number you want is always at least one more than the number you have, and it's so large that if you started saying it yesterday, you wouldn't finish tomorrow.

HUMBUG. Where could you ever find a number so big?

MATHEMAGICIAN. In the same place they have the smallest number there is, and you know what that is?

MILO. The smallest number . . . let's see . . . one one-millionth?

MATHEMAGICIAN. Almost. Now all you have to do is divide that in half and then divide that in half and then divide that in half and then divide that . . .

MILO. Doesn't that ever stop either?

MATHEMAGICIAN. How can it when you can always take half of what you have and divide it in half again? Look. [*Pointing offstage.*] You see that line?

MILO. You mean that long one out there?

MATHEMAGICIAN. That's it. Now, if you just follow that line forever, and when you reach the end, turn left, you will find the Land of Infinity.[16] That's where the tallest, the shortest, the biggest, the smallest and the most and the least of everything are kept.

MILO. But how can you follow anything forever? You know, I get the feeling that everything in Digitopolis is very difficult.

MATHEMAGICIAN. But on the other hand, I think you'll find that the only thing you can do easily is be wrong, and that's hardly worth the effort.

MILO. But . . . what bothers me is . . . well, why is it that even when things are correct, they don't really seem to be right?

MATHEMAGICIAN. [*Grows sad and quiet.*] How true. It's been that way ever since Rhyme and Reason were banished. [*Sadness turns to fury.*] AND ALL BECAUSE OF THAT STUBBORN WRETCH AZAZ! It's all his fault.

---

16. **Infinity** [in fin′ə tē]: state or quality of having no limits or end.

MILO. Maybe if you discussed it with him . . .

MATHEMAGICIAN. He's just too unreasonable! Why, just last month, I sent him a very friendly letter, which he never had the courtesy to answer. See for yourself. [*Puts the letter on the easel. The letter reads:*]

4738 1919,
   667 394107 5841 62589
85371 14 39588 7190434 203
27689 57131 481206.
           5864 98053,
           62179875073

MILO. But maybe he doesn't understand numbers.

MATHEMAGICIAN. Nonsense! Everybody understands numbers. No matter what language you speak, they always mean the same thing. A 7 is a 7 everywhere in the world.

MILO. [*To* TOCK *and* HUMBUG.] Everyone is so sensitive about what he knows best.

TOCK. With your permission, sir, we'd like to rescue Rhyme and Reason.

MATHEMAGICIAN. Has Azaz agreed to it?

TOCK. Yes, sir.

MATHEMAGICIAN. THEN I DON'T! Ever since they've been banished, we've never agreed on anything, and we never will.

MILO. Never?

MATHEMAGICIAN. NEVER! And if you can prove otherwise, you have my permission to go.

MILO. Well then, with whatever Azaz agrees, you disagree.

MATHEMAGICIAN. Correct.

MILO. And with whatever Azaz disagrees, you agree.

MATHEMAGICIAN. [*Yawning, cleaning his nails.*] Also correct.

MILO. Then, each of you agrees that he will disagree with whatever each of you agrees with, and if you both disagree with the same thing, aren't you really in agreement?

MATHEMAGICIAN. I'VE BEEN TRICKED! [*Figures it over, but comes up with the same answer.*]

TOCK. And now may we go?

MATHEMAGICIAN. [*Nods weakly.*] It's a long and dangerous journey. Long before you find them, the demons will know you're there. Watch out for them, because if you ever come face to face, it will be too late. But there is one other obstacle even more serious than that.

MILO. [*Terrified.*] What is it?

MATHEMAGICIAN. I'm afraid I can't tell you until you return. But maybe I can give you something to help you out. [*Claps hands. Enter the* DODECAHEDRON, *carrying something on a pillow. The* MATHEMAGICIAN *takes it.*] Here is your own magic staff. Use it well and there is nothing it can't do for you. [*Puts a small, gleaming pencil in* MILO's *breast pocket.*]

HUMBUG. Are you sure you can't tell about that serious obstacle?

MATHEMAGICIAN. Only when you return. And now the Dodecahedron will escort you to the road that leads to the Castle-in-the-Air. Farewell, my friends, and good luck to you. [*They shake hands, say goodbye,*

and the DODECAHEDRON *leads them off.*]
Good luck to you! [*To himself.*] Because
you're sure going to need it. [*He watches
them through a telescope and marks
down the calculations.*]

DODECAHEDRON. [*He re-enters.*] Well, they're
on their way.

MATHEMAGICIAN. So I see. [DODECAHEDRON
stands waiting.] Well, what is it?

DODECAHEDRON. I was just wondering myself, Your Numbership. What actually *is*
the serious obstacle you were talking
about?

MATHEMAGICIAN. [*Looks at him in surprise.*] You mean you really don't know?

Scene 2

The Land of Ignorance

[*Lights up on* RHYME *and* REASON, *in
their castle, looking out two windows.*]

RHYME.
I'm worried sick, I must confess
I wonder if they'll have success
All the others tried in vain,[17]
And were never seen or heard again.

REASON. Now, Rhyme, there's no need to
be so pessimistic. Milo, Tock, and Humbug have just as much chance of succeed-
ing as they do of failing.

RHYME.
But the demons are so deadly smart
They'll stuff your brain and fill your
  heart
With petty thoughts and selfish dreams
And trap you with their nasty schemes.

REASON. Now, Rhyme, be reasonable, won't
you? And calm down; you always talk in
couplets[18] when you get nervous. Milo has
learned a lot from his journey. I think
he's a match for the demons and that he
might soon be knocking at our door. Now
come on, cheer up, won't you?

RHYME. I'll try.

[*Lights fade on the* PRINCESSES *and
come up on the little car, traveling
slowly.*]

MILO. So this is the Land of Ignorance.
It's so dark. I can hardly see a thing.
Maybe we should wait until morning.

VOICE. They'll be mourning[19] for you soon
enough. [*They look up and see a large,
soiled, ugly* BIRD *with a dangerous beak
and a malicious expression.*]

MILO. I don't think you understand. We're
looking for a place to spend the night.

BIRD. [*Shrieking.*] It's not yours to spend!

MILO. That doesn't make any sense, you
see . . .

BIRD. Dollars or cents, it's still not yours
to spend.

MILO. But I don't mean . . .

BIRD. Of course you're mean. Anybody
who'd spend a night that doesn't belong
to him is very mean.

TOCK. Must you interrupt like that?

BIRD. Naturally, it's my job. I take the
words right out of your mouth. Haven't

17. **in vain:** without success.

18. **couplets** [kup′lits]: groups of two rhyming lines
that follow one after the other and form a unit.
19. **mourning** [môr′ning]: feeling or expressing sorrow or grief over someone's death.

we met before? I'm the Everpresent Wordsnatcher.

MILO. Are you a demon?

BIRD. I'm afraid not. I've tried, but the best I can manage to be is a nuisance. [*Suddenly gets nervous as he looks beyond the three.*] And I don't have time to waste with you. [*Starts to leave.*]

TOCK. What is it? What's the matter?

MILO. Hey, don't leave. I wanted to ask you some questions. . . . Wait!

BIRD. Weight? Twenty-seven pounds. Bye-bye. [*Disappears.*]

MILO. Well, he was no help.

MAN. Perhaps I can be of some assistance to you? [*There appears a beautifully-dressed* MAN, *very polished and clean.*] Hello, little boy. [*Shakes* MILO's *hand.*] And how's the faithful dog? [*Pats* TOCK.] And who is this handsome creature? [*Tips his hat to* HUMBUG.]

HUMBUG. [*To others.*] What a pleasant surprise to meet someone so nice in a place like this.

MAN. But before I help you out, I wonder if first you could spare me a little of your time, and help me with a few small jobs?

HUMBUG. Why, certainly.

TOCK. Gladly.

MILO. Sure, we'd be happy to.

MAN. Splendid, for there are just three tasks. First, I would like to move this pile of sand from here to there. [*Indicates through pantomime a large pile of sand.*] But I'm afraid that all I have are these tiny tweezers. [*Hands it to* MILO, *who begins*

moving the sand one grain at a time.*] Second, I would like to empty this well and fill that other, but I have no bucket, so you'll have to use this eyedropper. [*Hands it to* TOCK, *who begins to work.*] And finally, I must have a hole in this cliff, and here is a needle to dig it. [HUMBUG *eagerly begins. The* MAN *leans against a tree and stares vacantly off into space. The lights indicate the passage of time.*]

MILO. You know something? I've been working steadily for a long time now, and I don't feel the least bit tired or hungry. I could go right on the same way forever.

MAN. Maybe you will. [*He yawns.*]

MILO. [*Whispers to* TOCK.] Well, I wish I knew how long it was going to take.

TOCK. Why don't you use your magic staff and find out?

MILO. [*Takes out pencil and calculates. To* MAN.] Pardon me, sir, but it's going to take 837 years to finish these jobs.

MAN. Is that so? What a shame. Well then, you'd better get on with them.

MILO. But . . . it hardly seems worthwhile.

MAN. WORTHWHILE! Of course they're not worthwhile. I wouldn't ask you to do anything that was worthwhile.

TOCK. Then why bother?

MAN. Because, my friends, what could be more important than doing unimportant things? If you stop to do enough of them, you'll never get where you are going. [*Laughs villainously.*]

MILO. [*Gasps.*] Oh, no. You must be . . .

MAN. Quite correct! I am the Terrible Trivium,[20] demon of petty tasks and worthless jobs, ogre of wasted effort and monster of habit. [*They start to back away from him.*] Don't try to leave, there's so much to do, and you still have 837 years to go on the first job.

MILO. But why do unimportant things?

MAN. Think of all the trouble it saves. If you spend all your time doing only the easy and useless jobs, you'll never have time to worry about the important ones which are so difficult. [*Walks toward them, whispering.*] Now do come and stay with me. We'll have such fun together. There are things to fill and things to empty, things to take away and things to bring back, things to pick up and things to put down . . . [*They are transfixed by his soothing voice. He is about to embrace them when a* VOICE *screams.*]

VOICE. Run! Run! [*They all wake up and run with the* TRIVIUM *behind. As the* VOICE *continues to call out directions, they follow until they lose the* TRIVIUM.] RUN! RUN! This way! This way! Over here! Over here! Up here! Down there! Quick, hurry up!

TOCK. [*Panting.*] I think we lost him.

VOICE. Keep going straight! Keep going straight! Now step up! Now step up!

MILO. Look out! [*They all fall into a trap.*] But he said "up"!

VOICE. Well, I hope you didn't expect to get anywhere by listening to me.

HUMBUG. We're in a deep pit! We'll never get out of here.

---

20. **Trivium** [triv′ē əm]: a play on *trivial*, "having little or no importance or significance."

Princesses Sweet Rhyme and Pure Reason

VOICE. That is quite an accurate evaluation of the situation.

MILO. [*Shouting angrily.*] Then why did you help us at all?

VOICE. Oh, I'd do as much for anybody. Bad advice is my specialty. [*A little furry* CREATURE *appears.*] I'm the Demon of Insincerity. I don't mean what I say; I don't mean what I do; and I don't mean what I am.

MILO. Then why don't you go away and leave us alone!

INSINCERITY'S VOICE. Now, there's no need to get angry. You're a very clever boy and I have complete confidence in you. You can certainly climb out of that pit . . . come on, try . . .

MILO. I'm not listening to one word you say! You're just telling me what you think I'd *like* to hear, and not what is important.

INSINCERITY. Well, if that's the way you feel about it . . .

MILO. That's the way I feel about it. We will manage by ourselves without any unnecessary advice from you.

INSINCERITY. [*Stamping his foot.*] Well, all right for you! Most people listen to what I say, but if that's the way you feel, then I'll just go home. [*Exits in a huff.*]

HUMBUG. [*Who has been quivering with fright.*] And don't you ever come back! Well, I guess we showed him, didn't we?

MILO. You know something? This place is a lot more dangerous than I ever imagined.

TOCK. [*Who's been surveying the situa-*

tion.] I think I figured a way to get out. Here, hop on my back. [MILO *does so.*] Now you, Humbug, on top of Milo. [*He does so.*] Now hook your umbrella onto that tree and hold on. [*They climb over* HUMBUG, *then pull him up.*]

HUMBUG. [*As they climb.*] Watch it! Watch it, now. Ow, be careful of my back! My back! Easy, easy . . . oh, this is so difficult. Aren't you finished yet?

TOCK. [*As he pulls up* HUMBUG.] There. Now, I'll lead for a while. Follow me, and we'll stay out of trouble. [*They walk and climb higher and higher.*]

HUMBUG. Can't we slow down a little?

TOCK. Something tells me we better reach the Castle-in-the-Air as soon as possible, and not stop to rest for a single moment. [*They speed up.*]

MILO. What is it, Tock? Did you see something?

TOCK. Just keep walking and don't look back.

MILO. You *did* see something!

HUMBUG. What is it? Another demon?

TOCK. Not just one, I'm afraid. If you want to see what I'm talking about, then turn around. [*They turn around. The stage darkens and hundreds of yellow gleaming eyes can be seen.*]

HUMBUG. Good grief! Do you see how many there are? Hundreds! The Overbearing Know-It-All, the Gross Exaggeration, the Horrible Hopping Hindsight . . . and look over there! The Triple Demons of Compromise! Let's get out of here! [*Starts to scurry.*] Hurry up, you two! Must you be so slow about everything?

MILO. Look! There it is, up ahead! The Castle-in-the-Air! [*They all run.*]

HUMBUG. They're gaining!

MILO. But there it is!

HUMBUG. I see it! I see it!

[*They reach the first step and are stopped by a little* MAN *in a frock coat, sleeping on a worn ledger.*[21] *He has a long quill pen*[22] *and a bottle of ink at his side. He is covered with ink stains over his clothes and wears spectacles.*]

TOCK. Shh! Be very careful. [*They try to step over him, but he wakes up.*]

SENSES TAKER.[23] [*From sleeping position.*] Names? [*He sits up.*]

HUMBUG. Well, I . . .

SENSES TAKER. NAMES? [*He opens book and begins to write, splattering himself with ink.*]

HUMBUG. Uh . . . Humbug, Tock, and this is Milo.

SENSES TAKER. Splendid, splendid. I haven't had an "M" in ages.

MILO. What do you want our names for? We're sort of in a hurry.

SENSES TAKER. Oh, this won't take long. I'm the official Senses Taker and I must have some information before I can take your sense. Now if you'll just tell me:

[*Handing them a form to fill. Speaking slowly and deliberately.*] when you were born, where you were born, why you were born, how old you are now, how old you were then, how old you'll be in a little while . . .

MILO. I wish he'd hurry up. At this rate, the demons will be here before we know it!

SENSES TAKER. . . . your mother's name, your father's name, where you live, how long you've lived there, the schools you've attended, the schools you haven't attended . . .

HUMBUG. I'm getting writer's cramp.

TOCK. I smell something very evil and it's getting stronger every second. [*To* SENSES TAKER.] May we go now?

SENSES TAKER. Just as soon as you tell me your height, your weight, the number of books you've read this year . . .

MILO. We have to go!

SENSES TAKER. All right, all right, I'll give you the short form. [*Pulls out a small piece of paper.*] Destination?

MILO. But we have to . . .

SENSES TAKER. DESTINATION?

MILO, TOCK and **HUMBUG.** The Castle-in-the-Air! [*They throw down their papers and run past him up the first few stairs.*]

SENSES TAKER. Stop! I'm sure you'd rather see what I have to show you. [*Snaps his fingers; they freeze.*] A circus of your very own. [*Circus music is heard.* MILO *seems to go into a trance.*] And wouldn't you enjoy this most wonderful smell? [TOCK *sniffs and goes into a trance.*] And here's something I know you'll enjoy hearing. . . .

---

21. **ledger** [lej'ər]: book in which business dealings and finances are recorded and classified.
22. **quill** [kwil] **pen:** pen made from the hollow stem of a feather.
23. **senses** [sen'siz] **taker:** a play on *census* [sen'səs] *taker,* "one who helps conduct an official count of a population."

[*To* HUMBUG. *The sound of cheers and applause for* HUMBUG *is heard, and he goes into a trance.*] There we are. And now, I'll just sit back and let the demons catch up with you.

[MILO *accidentally drops his package of gifts. The package of laughter from* DR. DISCHORD *opens and the sounds of laughter are heard. After a moment,* MILO, TOCK *and* HUMBUG *join in laughing and the spells are broken.*]

MILO. There was no circus.

TOCK. There were no smells.

HUMBUG. The applause is gone.

SENSES TAKER. I warned you I was the Senses Taker. I'll steal your sense of Purpose, your sense of Duty, destroy your sense of Proportion[24]—and but for one thing, you'd be helpless yet.

MILO. What's that?

SENSES TAKER. As long as you have the sound of laughter, I cannot take your sense of Humor. Agh! That horrible sense of Humor.

HUMBUG. HERE THEY COME! LET'S GET OUT OF HERE!

[*The* DEMONS *appear in nasty slithering hordes, running through the audience and up onto the stage, trying to attack* TOCK, MILO *and* HUMBUG. *The* THREE HEROES *run past the* SENSES TAKER *up the stairs toward the Castle-in-the-Air with the* DEMONS *snarling behind them.*]

---

24. **sense of Proportion** [prə pôr′shən]: the ability to see or appreciate the proper relation of parts to each other or to a whole.

MILO. Don't look back! Just keep going! [*They reach the castle. The* TWO PRINCESSES *appear in the windows.*]

PRINCESSES. Hurry! Hurry! We've been expecting you.

MILO. You must be the princesses. We've come to rescue you.

HUMBUG. And the demons are close behind!

TOCK. We should leave right away.

PRINCESSES. We're ready any time you are.

MILO. Good, now if you'll just come out. But wait a minute—there's no door! How can we rescue you from the Castle-in-the-Air if there's no way to get in or out?

HUMBUG. Hurry, Milo! They're gaining on us.

REASON. Take your time, Milo, and think about it.

MILO. Ummm, all right . . . just give me a second or two. [*He thinks hard.*]

HUMBUG. I think I feel sick.

MILO. I've got it! Where's that package of presents? [*Opens the package of letters.*] Ah, here it is. [*Takes out the letters and sticks them on the door, spelling.*] E-N-T-R-A-N-C-E. Entrance. Now, let's see. [*Rummages through and spells in smaller letters.*] P-u-s-h. Push. [*He pushes and a door opens. The* PRINCESSES *come out of the castle. Slowly, the* DEMONS *ascend the stairway.*]

HUMBUG. Oh, it's too late. They're coming up and there's no other way down!

MILO. Unless . . . [*Looks at* TOCK.] Well . . . Time flies, doesn't it?

TOCK. Quite often. Hold on, everyone, and I'll take you down.

HUMBUG. Can you carry us all?

TOCK. We'll soon find out. Ready or not, here we go!

[*His alarm begins to ring. They jump off the platform and disappear. The* DEMONS, *howling with rage, reach the top and find no one there. They see the* PRINCESSES *and the* HEROES *running across the stage and bound down the stairs after them and into the audience. There is a mad chase scene until they reach the stage again.*]

HUMBUG. I'm exhausted! I can't run another step.

MILO. We can't stop now. . . .

TOCK. Milo! Look out there! [*The armies of* AZAZ *and* MATHEMAGICIAN *appear at the back of the theater, with the* KINGS *at their heads.*]

AZAZ. [*As they march toward the stage.*] Don't worry, Milo, we'll take over now.

MATHEMAGICIAN. Those demons may not know it, but their days are numbered!

SPELLING BEE. Charge! C-H-A-R-G-E! Charge! [*They rush at the* DEMONS *and battle until the* DEMONS *run off howling. Everyone cheers. The* FIVE MINISTERS OF AZAZ *appear and shake* MILO's *hand.*]

MINISTER 1. Well done.

MINISTER 2. Fine job.

MINISTER 3. Good work!

MINISTER 4. Congratulations!

MINISTER 5. CHEERS! [EVERYONE *cheers*

again. A fanfare interrupts. A PAGE *steps forward and reads from a large scroll.*]

PAGE.
Henceforth, and forthwith,
Let it be known by one and all,
That Rhyme and Reason
Reign once more in Wisdom.

[*The* PRINCESSES *bow gratefully and kiss their brothers, the* KINGS.]

And furthermore,
The boy named Milo,
The dog known as Tock,
And the insect hereinafter referred to as
  the Humbug
Are hereby declared to be
Heroes of the Realm.

[ALL *bow and salute the* HEROES.]

MILO. But we never could have done it without a lot of help.

REASON. That may be true, but you had the courage to try, and what you can do is often a matter of what you *will* do.

AZAZ. That's why there was one very important thing about your quest we couldn't discuss until you returned.

MILO. I remember. What was it?

AZAZ. Very simple. It was impossible!

MATHEMAGICIAN. *Completely* impossible!

HUMBUG. Do you mean . . . ? [*Feeling faint.*] Oh . . . I think I need to sit down.

AZAZ. Yes, indeed, but if we'd told you then, you might not have gone.

MATHEMAGICIAN. And, as you discovered, many things are possible just as long as you don't know they're impossible.

MILO. I think I understand.

RHYME. I'm afraid it's time to go now.

REASON. And you must say goodbye.

MILO. To everyone? [*Looks around at the* CROWD. *To* TOCK *and* HUMBUG.] Can't you two come with me?

HUMBUG. I'm afraid not, old man. I'd like to, but I've arranged for a lecture tour which will keep me occupied for years.

TOCK. And they do need a watchdog here.

MILO. Well, O.K., then. [MILO *hugs the* HUMBUG.]

HUMBUG. [*Sadly.*] Oh, bah.

MILO. [*He hugs* TOCK, *and then faces* EVERYONE.] Well, goodbye. We all spent so much time together, I know I'm going to miss you. [*To the* PRINCESSES.] I guess we would have reached you a lot sooner if I hadn't made so many mistakes.

REASON. You must never feel badly about making mistakes, Milo, as long as you take the trouble to learn from them. Very often you learn more by being wrong for the right reasons than you do by being right for the wrong ones.

MILO. But there's so much to learn.

RHYME. That's true, but it's not just learning that's important. It's learning what to do with what you learn and learning why you learn things that matters.

MILO. I think I know what you mean, Princess. At least, I hope I do. [*The car is rolled forward and* MILO *climbs in.*] Goodbye! Goodbye! I'll be back someday! I will! Anyway, I'll try. [*As* MILO *drives, the set of the Land of Ignorance begins to move offstage.*]

AZAZ. Goodbye! Always remember. Words! Words! Words!

MATHEMAGICIAN. *And* numbers!

AZAZ. Now, don't tell me you think numbers are as important as words?

MATHEMAGICIAN. Is that so? Why, I'll have you know . . . [*The set disappears, and* MILO*'s room is seen onstage.*]

MILO. [*As he drives on.*] Oh, oh, I hope they don't start all over again. Because I don't think I'll have much time in the near future to help them out. [*The sound of loud ticking is heard.* MILO *finds himself in his room. He gets out of the car and looks around.*]

THE CLOCK. Did someone mention time?

MILO. Boy, I must have been gone for an awful long time. I wonder what time it is. [*Looks at* CLOCK.] Five o'clock. I wonder what day it is. [*Looks at calendar.*] It's still today! I've only been gone for an hour! [*He continues to look at his calendar, and then begins to look at his books and toys and maps and chemistry set with great interest.*]

CLOCK. An hour. Sixty minutes. How long it really lasts depends on what you do with it. For some people, an hour seems to last forever. For others, just a moment, and so full of things to do.

MILO. [*Looks at* CLOCK.] Six o'clock already?

CLOCK. In an instant. In a trice.[25] Before you have time to blink. [*The stage goes black in less than no time at all.*]

---

25. **trice** [trīs]: very short time.

READER'S RESPONSE (Act 1)

Do you think that a box of letters will help Milo overcome all the obstacles that stand in his path?

STUDY QUESTIONS (Act 1)

Recalling

1. What "good question" does Milo ask the Whether Man? What does the Whether Man answer?
2. Where is Milo when his car stops? According to the Lethargarians, why is he there?
3. What are the names of the two brothers who "almost never see eye to eye"? Whose job is it to solve the differences that drive brothers apart?
4. According to the Spelling Bee, who should not be trusted nor believed?
5. After a flurry of food and words, Milo admits that he is confused. What suggestion does he make to help bring order?
6. What does Azaz give Milo for his journey?

Interpreting

7. How would you describe Milo's personality? What are his personal strengths and weaknesses?
8. In what ways are the Lethargarians and Humbug each dangerous to Milo?
9. Why is Milo confused by the words spoken at the banquet? Why is his suggestion a good one?
10. In what way might Azaz's gift help Milo on his journey?

Extending

11. If you had to make a choice, would you prefer to live in a land of words or of numbers? Why?

READER'S RESPONSE (Act 2)

Do you think it is possible to accomplish the impossible? the _completely_ impossible?

STUDY QUESTIONS (Act 2)

Recalling

1. What does Dischord give Milo to deliver to Rhyme and Reason?
2. In the Land of Numbers, what is a "magic staff"?
3. After eating subtraction stew and hearing the Mathemagician explain the Land of Infinity, Milo is confused. What does the Mathemagician say is the reason for the confusion?
4. What gift does the Mathemagician give Milo for his journey? What does he say that terrifies Milo?
5. What demons and obstacles do the travelers meet?
6. What breaks the Senses Taker's spell? What does Milo use to rescue Rhyme and Reason from the castle?
7. What other obstacle does Milo face?

Interpreting

8. In what way could a pencil be magic?
9. How would you describe the ways in which Azaz's and the Mathemagician's gifts are similar?
10. In what similar way does the banishment of Rhyme and Reason affect Digitopolis and Dictionopolis?
11. Why is the "other, more serious" obstacle a greater danger than the other demons?

Extending

12. Which of your own mistakes have taught you something important about life?

READING AND LITERARY FOCUS

Drama

Drama is a form of literature that presents a story to be performed for an audience. A drama includes two important elements: **dialogue,** lines that the characters speak, and **stage directions,** instructions that tell actors how to say their lines and how to move on stage.

Read the following excerpt from *The Phantom Tollbooth:*

HUMBUG. [*Flattered.*] Oh, Your Majesty.
MILO. I'm sure he'll be a great help. [*They approach the car.*]

The stage directions appear in brackets. The first direction tells the actor playing the part of Humbug how to speak; the last direction tells the actors who play Humbug and Milo how to move. The dialogue begins with Humbug's line "Oh, Your Majesty."

A drama is usually divided into acts and scenes. An **act** is the main part into which a drama is divided; it usually consists of several scenes. A **scene** usually begins whenever the time or place of the action changes. For example, Scene 1, the short scene that begins the play, takes place in Milo's room and ends as he drives through the phantom tollbooth. Scene 2 takes place a little later as Milo is on the road to Dictionopolis.

Thinking About Drama

1. In Act 1, Scene 2, find three examples of stage directions that tell the actors how to speak and three directions that tell them how to move.

2. Name the different settings in Act 1. What are the different settings in Act 2?

Character and Theme

We are able to understand a play's **characters** partly by what they say, partly by what they do, and partly by what others say about them or do with them. Some characters are easier to understand than others—especially in a play with many characters. Rhyme and Reason, for instance, remain the same throughout *The Phantom Tollbooth:* They try to keep the peace between the kingdoms of Dictionopolis and Digitopolis. On the other hand, Milo is a complex character who changes and grows in the course of the play.

In fact, Milo's development helps us understand the theme of the play. The **theme** is the general meaning that grows out of the specific story the play is portraying. Although *The Phantom Tollbooth* is specifically about one boy's journey through the Land of Ignorance to the Land of Wisdom, the play is more generally about how nearly all young people come to learn things as they live their lives. It portrays the difficulties and triumphs of being a thinking human being in the process of growing up.

Thinking About Character and Theme

1. How would you describe Milo's character by the end of the play? Who has he changed, and what has happened to make him change?

2. At the end of the play, Reason praises Milo for having the courage to do something that was "impossible" to do. Find specific passages in the play where Milo demonstrates his courage.

Thinking Skills: Evaluating

DEFINITION

Evaluating is a way of thinking about something and making a judgment about it. When you evaluate, you apply criteria to make your judgment. Criteria are the standards, rules, or tests on which a judgment can be based.

STEPS

1. **State the reason or purpose for your evaluation.**
   What do you want to evaluate? Why do you want to evaluate it?

2. **Identify the criteria.**
   What specific rules, tests, or standards will you use to make your judgment?

3. **Apply the criteria.**
   Does the subject of your evaluation meet each specific criterion? Does it meet some criteria better than others?

4. **Draw a conclusion.**
   The conclusion is your evaluation of how well the subject meets the criteria.

EXAMPLE

Imagine that you are writing about a new science-fiction film for your school newspaper. Your readers want to know, "Is it a good film?" Your answer may be "yes" or "no." As a responsible newspaper writer, however, you make sure to base your evaluation on your criteria for a good film.

1. **State the reason or purpose for your evalua-tion.** You want to evaluate the film in order to give your readers an accurate answer.

2. **Identify the criteria.** You choose to evaluate the film according to its plot, characters, and special effects.

3. **Apply the criteria.** You think that the plot is not original, and the characters are not developed. The special effects are well done, however.

4. **Draw a conclusion.** You conclude that the film is not good because it meets only one of your criteria.

ACTIVITY 1

Evaluating *The Phantom Tollbooth*

Follow the four steps of evaluating to answer the question "Is *The Phantom Tollbooth* a good play?" Identify your criteria carefully, being very specific about what you think makes a good play. You may want to include one or more of the following criteria: an exciting plot, a variety of characters, dialogue that reveals what the characters think and feel, details that help you to picture the settings, a satisfying ending.

ACTIVITY 2

Evaluating a Work of Literature

Evaluate another selection in this book or any other work of literature that you have read. Follow the four steps. Remember that people of different cultures or ages or with different interests may have different criteria. What is important is that you think about your own criteria and they reflect what you believe.

Collaborative Learning: Themes

Other Lands, Other Worlds

The desire to travel, to see how others live, comes from people's need for adventure as well as from their sense of curiosity. Some people enjoy going to faraway places and experiencing new sights and sensations. Others, armchair travelers, savor the excitement of distant lands through books, magazines, and films. One discovery that most travelers make is that while food, clothing, and customs vary, people everywhere have similar desires, needs, and goals.

What about people in other worlds? In the last decades of the twentieth century, science fiction and reality seemed to blend into one as astronauts walked on the moon. Is there life on Mars or on another planet? Certainly the idea of space travel by the general public in the foreseeable future is not as outrageous as it once seemed.

■ **Advertisement** Imagine that moon vacations have become a reality. You and your group of advertising executives want to land a major travel-agency account. The job is to create an advertisement for a vacation on the moon.

With your group brainstorm on how to make such a vacation sound exciting and inviting. Review what people usually look for when they plan vacations—cost, transportation, hotels, restaurants, sports activities, entertainment.

Go to the library, and research the climate, atmosphere, and topography of the moon. Is it cold or warm? Is there enough oxygen for humans to breathe without using masks? How would the pull of gravity on the moon affect people's activities—for example, playing tennis?

The advertisement will need illustrations. Consider drawing your own rocket ships, space hotels, and moon restaurants. Review your presentation at least once before you actually give it. The rest of the class, acting as representatives of the travel agency, should respond with questions and comments.

Collaborative Learning:
Across the Curriculum

Other Lands, Other Worlds

1. **Literature and Social Studies: Map Making** Maps are very important to travelers as guides to the places they visit. Most parts of the earth have been mapped at one time or another. There are places of the imagination, however, for which no maps exist. One such spot is the home and surrounding territory of the rabbits in *Watership Down.*

   With two or three classmates plan, design, and draw a map showing the various locations described in *Watership Down.* When you have finished your map, draw lines indicating the movement of the characters in the excerpt you have read. Explain your map to the class.

2. **Literature and Music: Musical Accompaniment** Imagine that you and three of your classmates are the music selection committee for a small, independent film studio. The studio is planning to make a film short based on the poem "Southbound on the Freeway." The director has called for background music and special musical effects at certain places in the poem.

   At a preliminary meeting decide whether you will compose and score the musical accompaniment yourselves or do research to find already existing pieces. Schedule meetings at locations where a tape deck or record player is available. When you have made your final selections, play them for the class as one of the committee members reads the poem.

Myths,

The time is long ago. The place is anywhere on earth. Huddled in the shadows of a flaring fire, you stare wide-eyed at the storyteller. The stories are a record—the only record—of the ancient memories, remarkable events, and important truths of your people.

What will the story be this time, and how will it affect you? An adventure tale of a hero might teach you about the courage you will need. The misadventures of a fool might make you wiser. Perhaps the tale will show you monsters and imaginary creatures. Those fabulous beasts have a secret place in the human heart. Or will the story tell of the goddess of love and her awesome influence?

Those ancient camp fires are gone now, but the stories remain. Ten are gathered here in this unit. Carefully handed down over the ages, they come at last to you. Read them well, and you will enter into the memories and imagination, the fears and feelings, of people everywhere.

Lady with the Unicorn, tapestry, late fifteenth century.

A Model for Active Reading

Reading and thinking go hand in hand. When you read actively, you think, ask questions, and imagine possibilities.

Here is an example of the thoughts of an active reader who is just beginning to read the myth of Pygmalion. Notice the kinds of thoughts and feelings and imaginings that the active reader brings to the story.

The entire story begins on the following page. As you read it, what questions and ideas occur to you?

Doris Gates

Pygmalion

This takes place on a sacred island in mythical times.

On the island of Cyprus,[1] sacred to Aphrodite,[2] there lived a sculptor named Pygmalion.[3] The man was a fine artist and his studio was a gathering place for his admirers. They marveled at the way he worked in stone and ivory, fashioning figures that seemed so real a visitor would sometimes put out a hand and touch the statue to make sure it was not living flesh.

I believe it. I've seen statues that look like real people.

Now Pygmalion hated women; no one knew exactly why. Some said he had been disappointed in love; others that he had had a cruel mother who had resented his birth. In any case, Pygmalion lived alone in his studio, and no woman ever came there. Nor had he ever fashioned a statue in the form of a woman.

Is he foolish to hate all women even if he has been hurt by one?

But one day Pygmalion was seized with a great desire to sculpt a woman. He was shocked and bewildered by the sudden urge.

Why would he want to sculpt one instead of meet a real one?

His first reaction is to blame the goddess of love instead of his own loneliness.

"Has mischievous Aphrodite put this spell upon me?" he asked himself. "And, if so, to what purpose?"

As a children's librarian in California, Doris Gates (born 1901) introduced thousands of readers to the books they needed. Some readers, however, needed books that hadn't been written yet. To help them, Gates became an author. For example, after working with homeless children, she wrote *Blue Willow*, an award-winning novel about a family in search of a home.

One frequent request at any library is "Do you have any good books of myths?" Doris Gates wrote a series of books that skillfully retell the myths of ancient Greece. "Pygmalion" is taken from *Two Queens of Heaven*, which contains myths about the goddesses Aphrodite and Demeter.

What would it take to make you suddenly love something that you have always hated?

• •

Doris Gates

Pygmalion

On the island of Cyprus,[1] sacred to Aphrodite,[2] there lived a sculptor named Pygmalion.[3] The man was a fine artist and his studio was a gathering place for his admirers. They marveled at the way he worked in stone and ivory, fashioning figures that seemed so real a visitor would sometimes put out a hand and touch the statue to make sure it was not living flesh.

Now Pygmalion hated women; no one knew exactly why. Some said he had been disappointed in love; others that he had had a cruel mother who had resented his birth. In any case, Pygmalion lived alone in his studio, and no woman ever came there. Nor had he ever fashioned a statue in the form of a woman.

But one day Pygmalion was seized with a great desire to sculpt a woman. He was shocked and bewildered by the sudden urge.

"Has mischievous Aphrodite put this spell upon me?" he asked himself. "And, if so, to what purpose?"

He tried to ignore the strange desire, but in vain. It kept him from sleep. It hounded his every waking moment. At last he gave in to it.

As he reluctantly started work upon the statue, he felt ashamed of what he was doing. He banished all visitors from his studio. No one must ever learn of his self-betrayal. Nor would they, for of course when the sculpture was completed and the strange urge satisfied, he would destroy it.

---

1. **Cyprus** [sī′prəs]: island country in the eastern Mediterranean, south of Turkey.
2. **Aphrodite** [af′rə dī′tē]: Greek goddess of love and beauty.
3. **Pygmalion** [pig māl′yən]

As the statue began to take form under his hands, a compelling interest in it seized Pygmalion. At first he had thought to fashion an ugly female figure, completely without grace and with a face so ugly no man would look upon it without loathing. If this were Aphrodite's trick, it should not succeed whatever her intent.

But as he began to cut away the marble to the point where the figure began to emerge from the rude block, Pygmalion's hands seemed to act on their own. Day after day the figure grew and began to take on beauty. Despite his best intentions, Pygmalion was fashioning an object so ravishing that even he began to feel a grudging admiration for it. The chiseled face wore an expression so soft and beguiling[4] it was hard to imagine it was only stone. The sculptor, gazing on it in amazement, smiled as he had never before smiled upon a woman. But, of course, this was merely a statue!

Then came the final polishing of the marble. Pygmalion smoothed it until it glowed, even taking on the lucent,[5] ivory tone of healthy young flesh. His hands moved almost lovingly upon it.

At last the day came when nothing remained to be done. The life-sized statue stood upon its pedestal complete and utterly lovely. Pygmalion walked slowly around it, and when he came to where its face looked sweetly down upon him, a violent passion gripped him. He fell in love!

Now began a period of perfect misery for Pygmalion. The pangs of unrequited[6] love are torment, especially when the object of that love is there before the sufferer day and night. Pygmalion tried to embrace the lovely figure, but the cold stone repulsed him. For all its fleshly appearance, it was stone, unfeeling and unyielding.

"Ah, if you could but speak to me," Pygmalion exclaimed to the face bending above him. "Your eyes look into mine, your lips smile, almost opening to speak, yet you are ever silent."

He remembered his intention to destory the statue, but that was unthinkable now. Life would lose all meaning without this lovely creation. Then in his desperation and frustration, Pygmalion began to fantasize about his marble love. He saw her as really human. He talked to her. He robed her in silken garments. He even tucked her into bed at night with a pillow beneath her head. He brought her gifts young girls prize—flowers, birds, and pretty stones. The bare and cluttered studio became a kind of bower[7] for his beloved, while his sculptor's tools gathered dust.

Then came the day that was sacred to Aphrodite on the island of Cyprus. Altars everywhere were decked with roses, her favorite flower. Snow-white heifers, garlanded and with their horns tipped with gold, were led to the sacrifice by lads and maidens in their rarest finery. All the people were celebrating, Pygmalion among them.

Half-fearfully, he approached an altar where incense sent up its sweet fragrance. There he offered a prayer to the great goddess.

"Oh, Aphrodite, protector of lovers, listen

---

4. **beguiling** [bi gīl'ing]: charming; delightful.
5. **lucent** [loo'sənt]: shining; bright.
6. **unrequited** [un'ri kwī'tid]: not returned to the same degree or in the same way.

7. **bower** [bou'ər]: a lady's private apartment or bedroom.

to me now. If it be in your power, then send me a wife like the woman I have sculpted. Until now I have shunned the company of women, detesting them above all creatures. But now I acknowledge my fault in this and any affront it may have offered to you, great goddess of love and beauty. Only grant me such a wife as I crave, and I will honor you above all Immortals."

It so happened that Aphrodite, invisible, was present at that altar to hear Pygmalion's prayer. Perhaps she had indeed induced him to carve that statue. If so, then she must have watched with amusement his infatuation[8] with it. It would not have pleased the goddess of love that any man should spurn her sex. Whatever her reasons, Aphrodite now listened to Pygmalion's prayer and was moved by its sincerity. Still, she did not disclose her presence, and Pygmalion left the altar wondering with little hope if his prayer would be answered.

Straight home he went to torment himself with gazing on his beloved statue. But as he approached the pedestal where each day he placed her, he stopped amazed. Were his eyes playing him tricks, or had he simply gone mad? She was smiling at him as before, only there was a difference in the smile. It was wider, warmer, and her eyes had a sparkle that no marble could produce. As he gazed, a warm color rose into her cheeks. He rushed forward and seized her hand. It was warm within his own and he

could feel a pulse beating faintly under his thumb. The statue was alive!

With a glad cry, Pygmalion lifted his arms, and the statue stepped lightly down and into them.

Pygmalion gave his love the name Galatea.[9] Soon their marriage was celebrated. They became the parents of a son called Paphos[10] for whom an island was later named. And as far as anyone knows, they lived happily ever after.

---

8. **infatuation** [in fach′oo ā′shən]: attraction that is foolish or childish and passes quickly.

9. **Galatea** [gal′ə tē′ə]
10. **Paphos** [pā′fos]

READER'S RESPONSE

Do you think Pygmalion fell in love with a woman or with his own artwork? Explain your answer.

STUDY QUESTIONS

Recalling

1. What reasons are given to explain Pygmalion's hatred of women?
2. What strange desire suddenly seizes Pygmalion?
3. What sort of statue does Pygmalion plan to carve at first? What does he actually sculpt?
4. What feeling does Pygmalion develop for the completed statue?
5. What does Pygmalion ask of Aphrodite?
6. What happens to the statue in the end?

Interpreting

7. Why might Aphrodite want to "put a spell" on Pygmalion?
8. In what ways does Pygmalion change?

Extending

9. The ancient Greeks believed the goddess Aphrodite led people to fall in love. Why do *you* think people fall in love?

READING AND LITERARY FOCUS

Myth

A **myth** is an ancient, anonymous story that conveys the beliefs and ideals of a culture. Myths originally explained an aspect of nature or human life. The rumble of thunder, the changing seasons, a sunset—these were marvelous and fearful events in a time before science. To explain them, ancient peoples composed myths.

In "Pygmalion" we see several elements of myth. Pygmalion's statue demonstrates the Greek association of beauty with perfect physical form. Aphro-

dite's spell on Pygmalion and her prompt, fantastic answer to his prayer exemplify the Greek belief that the gods are active in everyday human life.

Thinking About Myth

1. The Greeks believed that human behavior should conform to the will of the gods and goddesses. How does "Pygmalion" convey this ideal?
2. Why do you think that Greek myths still inspire and fascinate people?

COMPOSITION

Writing About Character Motivation

Motivation is a feeling or goal that causes a character to act. In a paragraph describe Pygmalion's motivation. **Prewriting:** Read through the selection, and note as many possible motives as you can for two of Pygmalion's actions: his choosing to start the statue and his falling in love with it. **Writing:** Working from your prewriting notes, tell why Pygmalion begins the statue. Discuss how his feelings and goals change as he works on it. Finally identify what motivates him to seek help from Aphrodite. **Revising:** Review your paragraph to see that you have expressed your ideas clearly and logically. *For help with this assignment, see Lesson 3 in the Writing About Literature Handbook at the back of this book.*

Writing About Personal Motivation

We all sometimes do or say something that surprises everyone—even ourselves! Write a journal or diary entry about an incident that caused people to notice you. Begin by setting the scene. Tell where you were and what you were doing. Then describe the surprising event. Provide some colorful details about how people reacted to you. Finally explore the motivation for your actions. What feelings did you have? At the time you may not have been aware of your motivation, but as you write about the event, you may come to understand the reasons for your actions better.

Margaret Price (1888–1973) used her creativity in many ways. As an artist she sold her paintings to museums. During the 1920s and 1930s she illustrated well-known children's books. Later she helped start the Fisher-Price toy company and designed its first toys. As a popular author Price wrote original stories and novels and retold familiar myths and tales.

There was only one man alive who deserved to ride the magnificent horse Pegasus.

● ●

Retold by Margaret Evans Price

Pegasus and Bellerophon

Pegasus[1] was a wonderful winged horse that belonged to Minerva,[2] the gray-eyed goddess who watched over heroes and gave wisdom and skill to all those who truly wished it.

Now it happened that after Minerva had caught and tamed Pegasus, the winged horse, she did not care to ride him herself, but knew no human who deserved to own him. So Minerva gave Pegasus to the nymphs[3] to care for until she could find a youth brave enough and wise enough to ride him.

The nymphs were happy caring for Pegasus. They brushed him, combed his mane, and fed him, but they knew that some day he would belong to a mortal master who would come and ride him away.

At last in Corinth[4] there was born a little prince named Bellerophon.[5] Glaucus, his father, had more skill in handling horses than any other man. As Bellerophon grew up, his father trained him and taught him all he knew, so that while Bellerophon was still very young he understood the ways of horses and learned to ride them.

All this time the winged horse was without a master.

When Bellerophon was sixteen he began to long for travel and adventure in other lands, so he set out to visit a neighboring king.

Many friends came to bid the gallant young man goodby and wish him well, but there was one, named Proetus,[6] who pretended to be Bellerophon's friend, but who

---

1. **Pegasus** [peg′ə səs]
2. **Minerva** [mi nur′və]
3. **nymphs** [nimfs]: female deities who live in forests or hills or near rivers and are usually represented as beautful young women.

---

4. **Corinth** [kôr′inth]: ancient city in southern Greece.
5. **Bellerophon** [bə ler′ə fon′]
6. **Proetus** [prō ē′təs]

really wished for him the worst that might happen. Proetus was jealous of Prince Bellerophon, and hoped that the young hero would not return from the journey.

It happened that Proetus was the son-in-law of Iobates,[7] King of Lycia,[8] and so, pretending friendship, Proetus gave Bellerophon a letter to carry to the king. Bellerophon, knowing nothing of the wicked words that were in this letter, put it carefully in the pocket of his tunic and rode gaily away.

When he reached Lycia, the home of Iobates, he found great sorrow in the land and all the people mourning. Each night a monster called the Chimera[9] came down into the valley and carried off women and children, sheep and oxen. The mountain where he lived was white with the bones of his victims.

Bellerophon rode through the mourning city and came to the palace of the king. He presented himself to Iobates and gave him the letter.

As the king read, his face darkened and he seemed troubled, for the letter asked that Bellerophon should be put to death. The king did not like to heed the request in this strange letter, yet he wished to please his son-in-law. He knew that to kill a guest would be a wicked deed and against the laws of kindness to a visitor, and might also bring war on him from the land where the young prince lived. So he decided to send Bellerophon to slay the Chimera, thinking he never could come back alive.

Bellerophon was not the least bit afraid, because he longed for adventure, and his heart was filled with a great desire to overcome this dark and evil monster, free the kingdom from fear, and make the mourning people happy.

But before starting out he found the oldest and wisest man in the whole kingdom and asked for his advice. This aged man was named Polyidus.[10] When he saw that Bellerophon was young and full of courage, yet humble enough to ask help from some one older, Polyidus told him a secret that no one else in the kingdom knew.

He told him of Minerva's winged horse, which he had once seen drinking at a spring deep in the forest.

"If you sleep all night in Minerva's temple," said the old man, "and offer gifts at her altar, she may help you to find the horse."

Bellerophon went to the temple, and as he slept he dreamed that he saw Minerva, clad in silver armor, her gray eyes shining as if they held sparks of fire. Plumes of blue and rose and violet floated from her helmet. She carried a golden bridle in her hand and told Bellerophon how he might reach the well where Pegasus came to drink.

When Bellerophon awakened, he saw the golden bridle on the temple floor beside him, and knew Minerva really had visited him. Then with the bridle over his arm he set out on his journey through the forest. When he found the well, he hid himself among the bushes near by to watch for the coming of the winged horse. Soon Bellero-

_____
7. **Iobates** [ī ō bä′tēz]
8. **Lycia** lish′ē ə]: ancient country in southwestern Asia Minor, on the Mediterranean.
9. **Chimera** [ki mēr′ə]: in Greek and Roman mythology, fire-breathing monster with the head of a lion, the body of a goat, and the tail of a serpent.

_____
10. **Polyidus** [pō lǐ′ī duz]

Bellerophon mounted on Pegasus, attacking the Chimera,
engraved bronze plaque, Greek, seventh century B.C.

phon saw the winged horse flying far up in the sky. Nearer and nearer he wheeled until his silver feet touched the green grass beside the spring.

As Pegasus bent his head to drink, Bellerophon sprang from his hiding place and caught him by the mane. Before Pegasus knew what had happened, the golden bridle was slipped over his head, and Bellerophon had leaped to his back and was sitting between his outspread wings.

Pegasus rose into the air and darted wildly through the sky, now flying high among the clouds, now diving swiftly toward the earth. He reared and plunged, trying to shake Bellerophon from his back. He flew wildly over the sea and the mountains all the way to Africa and back. He flew over Thebes[11] and over Corinth, and people looking up into the sky thought they saw some strange bird passing overhead.

But Bellerophon understood how to handle fierce horses, for he remembered the things his father had taught him. At last Pegasus knew he had found his master and, tired and panting, sank down to the grass beside the well.

After Pegasus had rested, Bellerophon armed himself with a long spear and rode toward the mountain where the Chimera lived.

There on a ledge of rock outside his cave the monster lay basking in the sunlight. He was partly like a lion and partly like a dragon. He lay with his lion's head resting between his paws and his long green tail, like that of a lizard, curled around him.

Bellerophon rode his horse as near as he dared to the ledge on which the dragon lay, then raised his spear to strike at the Chimera, but the great beast blew out clouds of smoke and fire, and Pegasus drew back in terror.

As the monster drew in his breath for another puff, Bellerophon rode close to the ledge and with one strong thrust sent his spear through the heart of the Chimera.

When the young prince came back to the palace, riding the winged horse and carrying the head of the dreadful Chimera, there was wild rejoicing in Lycia. Everyone admired and praised Bellerophon, and crowded around the wonderful horse, amazed at his wings and his silver feet.

The young daugher of King Iobates, who came out on the portico of the palace to see the hero and his horse, fell in love with Bellerophon the moment she saw the young warrior sitting so proudly between the white wings of Pegasus. King Iobates led her to Bellerophon and gave her to him for his bride.

For a long time they were happy together. Bellerophon and Pegasus went on many adventures, and when Iobates died Bellerophon became king.

At last one day Bellerophon thought of a most daring adventure. He decided he would try to ride Pegasus to Mount Olympus[12] and visit the gods.

Minerva appeared and warned him that the gods would be angry, but he mounted his horse and rose high into the clouds, urging Pegasus up toward the summit of Mount Olympus.

Jupiter, chief of the gods, looked down and, seeing the horse approaching, was angry to think that any mortal should dare approach the home of the gods. He caused a gadfly[13] to light on Pegasus and sting his neck, his shoulders, and his nose.

Pegasus was so startled by this that at once he reared and wheeled among the clouds, leaping wildly in the air, and Bellerophon was thrown from his back and dropped down to earth.

Minerva, causing him to land where the ground was soft, spared his life, but as long as he lived Bellerophon wandered, crippled and lonely, seeking all over the earth for his wonderful winged horse.

But Pegasus never again returned to him.

---

11. **Thebes** [thēbz]: ancient Egyptian city.

12. **Mount Olympus** [ō lim′pəs]: mountain in northeastern Greece; in Greek mythology, the home of the major gods.
13. **gadfly:** large, blood-sucking fly.

READER'S RESPONSE

Was it fair for Jupiter to punish Bellerophon so harshly at the end of the myth?

STUDY QUESTIONS

Recalling

1. What was most unusual about the horse Pegasus? Who was the first to own and tame him?
2. What was the Chimera? In what ways did it cause suffering in Lycia?
3. Why did Bellerophon leave his home in Corinth?
4. What important secret did Polyidus tell Bellerophon?
5. What brave deed did Bellerophon and Pegasus do in Lycia?
6. How did Bellerophon lose Pegasus?

Interpreting

7. Why did Minerva give Pegasus to Bellerophon?
8. Why was Jupiter so angry with Bellerophon when he tried to fly to Mount Olympus?

Extending

9. Can you think of a modern-day hero who has suddenly fallen from a position of great success and popularity? What was the cause of this hero's downfall?

COMPOSITION

Writing a Summary

A story summary briefly explains what a story is all about. A good summary includes only the most important events and ideas from the story. In one paragraph summarize "Pegasus and Bellerophon." **Prewriting:** Before you begin, briefly reread the story to decide which main events you will include in the summary. Then list these events in the order in which they occur in the story. **Writing:** As you summarize, avoid adding unnecessary details. **Revising:** Review your summary. Be sure that you have used complete sentences, described the main events in the order in which they occurred, and not added unnecessary details.

Writing a News Story

Suppose the hero Bellerophon were to appear in your community astride the magnificent Pegasus. Write an imaginary news story describing some heroic deed that he might perform. For example, he might save a family from a burning building or capture some bank robbers. In the news story describe the role of both the hero and the horse.

CHALLENGE

Puppet Show

Prepare a puppet-show version of "Pegasus and Bellerophon." Base the script on the main events of the story, omitting minor details. Use your imagination to create colorful, interesting puppets of Pegasus, Bellerophon, Minerva, the Chimera, and King Iobates. Paint colorful backdrops to represent Minerva's temple, the Chimera's cave, and Mount Olympus. Props, such as the golden bridle, should be eye catching and easy to use. After practicing your puppet show, present it to a class of younger students.

Growing up in a Nigerian village, Chinua Achebe loved to listen to the old tales of his tribe. Later, as a college professor and the director of a radio station, he collected and published these traditional African tales. In retelling "Why the Tortoise's Shell Is Not Smooth," Achebe shows us how storytelling was a part of everyday African life.

Getting up into the sky was easy for Tortoise. Getting back down was the problem.

• •

Chinua Achebe

Why the Tortoise's Shell Is Not Smooth

Low voices, broken now and again by singing, reached Okonkwo[1] from his wives' huts as each woman and her children told folk stories. Ekwefi[2] and her daughter, Ezinma,[3] sat on a mat on the floor. It was Ekwefi's turn to tell a story.

"Once upon a time," she began, "all the birds were invited to a feast in the sky. They were very happy and began to prepare themselves for the great day. They painted their bodies with red cam wood[4] and drew beautiful patterns on them with dye.

"Tortoise saw all these preparations and soon discovered what it all meant. Nothing that happened in the world of the animals ever escaped his notice; he was full of cunning. As soon as he heard of the great feast in the sky his throat began to itch at the very thought. There was a famine in those days and Tortoise had not eaten a good meal for two moons. His body rattled like a piece of dry stick in his empty shell. So he began to plan how he would go to the sky."

"But he had no wings," said Ezinma.

"Be patient," replied her mother. "That is the story. Tortoise had no wings, but he went to the birds and asked to be allowed to go with them.

" 'We know you too well,' said the birds when they had heard him. 'You are full of cunning and you are ungrateful. If we allow you to come with us you will soon begin your mischief.'

" 'You do not know me,' said Tortoise. 'I am a changed man. I have learned that a man who makes trouble for others is also making it for himself.'

---

1. **Okonkwo** [ō kōn'kwō]
2. **Ekwefi** [e kwe'fē]
3. **Ezinma** [e zēn'mä]
4. **cam wood:** hard West African wood that yields a red dye.

Gold Emblem in the Form of a Turtle, Ghana, Ashante, 800–1200.

"Tortoise had a sweet tongue, and within a short time all the birds agreed that he was a changed man, and they each gave him a feather, with which he made two wings.

"At last the great day came and Tortoise was the first to arrive at the meeting place. When all the birds had gathered together, they set off in a body. Tortoise was very happy as he flew among the birds, and he was soon chosen as the man to speak for the party because he was a great orator.

" 'There is one important thing which we must not forget,' he said as they flew on their way, 'When people are invited to a great feast like this, they take new names for the occasion. Our hosts in the sky will expect us to honor this age-old custom.'

"None of the birds had heard of this custom but they knew that Tortoise, in spite of his failings in other directions, was a widely traveled man who knew the customs of different peoples. And so they each took a new name. When they had all taken, Tortoise also took one. He was to be called *All of you.*

"At last the party arrived in the sky and their hosts were very happy to see them. Tortoise stood up in his many-colored plumage and thanked them for their invitation.

His speech was so eloquent that all the birds were glad they had brought him, and nodded their heads in approval of all he said. Their hosts took him as the king of the birds, especially as he looked somewhat different from the others.

"After kola nuts[5] had been presented and eaten, the people of the sky set before their guests the most delectable dishes Tortoise had even seen or dreamed of. The soup was brought out hot from the fire and in the very pot in which it had been cooked. It was full of meat and fish. Tortoise began to sniff aloud. There was pounded yam and also yam pottage[6] cooked with palm oil and fresh fish. There were also pots of palm wine. When everything had been set before the guests, one of the people of the sky came forward and tasted a little from each pot. He then invited the birds to eat. But Tortoise jumped to his feet and asked: 'For whom have you prepared this feast?'

" 'For all of you,' replied the man.

"Tortoise turned to the birds and said: 'You remember that my name is *All of you.* The custom here is to serve the spokesman first and the others later. They will serve you when I have eaten.'

"He began to eat and the birds grumbled angrily. The people of the sky thought it must be their custom to leave all the food for their king. And so Tortoise ate the best part of the food and then drank two pots of palm wine, so that he was full of food and drink and his body grew fat enough to fill out his shell.

"The birds gathered round to eat what was left and to peck at the bones he had thrown all about the floor. Some of them were too angry to eat. They chose to fly home on an empty stomach. But before they left, each took back the feather he had lent to Tortoise. And there he stood in his hard shell full of food and wine but without any wings to fly home. He asked the birds to take a message for his wife, but they all refused. In the end Parrot, who had felt more angry than the others, suddenly changed his mind and agreed to take the message.

" 'Tell my wife,' said Tortoise, 'to bring out all the soft things in my house and cover the compound with them so that I can jump down from the sky without very great danger.'

"Parrot promised to deliver the message, and then flew away. But when he reached Tortoise's house he told his wife to bring out all the hard things in the house. And so she brought out her husband's hoes, machetes,[7] spears, guns, and even his cannon. Tortoise looked down from the sky and saw his wife bringing things out, but it was too far to see what they were. When all seemed ready he let himself go. He fell and fell and fell until he began to fear that he would never stop falling. And then like the sound of his cannon he crashed on the compound."

"Did he die?" asked Ezinma.

"No," replied Ekwefi. "His shell broke into pieces. But there was a great medicine man in the neighborhood. Tortoise's wife sent for him and he gathered all the bits of shell and stuck them together. That is why Tortoise's shell is not smooth."

---

5. **kola** [ko′lə] **nuts:** bitter brown seeds of the kola, a tropical evergreen tree, contained in thick, fleshy pods.
6. **pottage** [pot′ij]: thick soup or broth with vegetables and sometimes meat or fish.

---

7. **machetes** [mə shet′ēz]: broad, heavy knives used as tools or as weapons.

READER'S RESPONSE

Do you think Tortoise deserved the rough treatment he got from the birds? Why or why not?

STUDY QUESTIONS

Recalling

1. Where are all the birds preparing to go?
2. Why does Tortoise want to go with the birds?
3. How do the birds help Tortoise fly?
4. What does Tortoise do at the meeting place to make all the birds angry with him?
5. In what way does Tortoise return to his home? What happens to him?

Interpreting

6. Why does Tortoise tell the birds that his new name is *All of you*?
7. According to Tortoise, "A man who makes trouble for others is also making it for himself." Do the events of the story support this saying? Explain.

Extending

8. All the birds are charmed by Tortoise's "sweet tongue." Can you think of situations in which people today use speech to trick others?

READING AND LITERARY FOCUS

Folk Literature and the Oral Tradition

Thousands of years ago all literature was **oral**—spoken aloud rather than written down. Every community had storytellers who entertained and inspired the group with exciting tales. People passed down their beliefs, customs, and skills by word of mouth. Myths, legends, folk tales, proverbs, superstitions, and other folklore were all part of the **oral tradition.**

The previous selection, "Pygmalion," was part of the oral tradition of the ancient Greeks. Over the centuries the myth was told and retold aloud. Eventually people began to write down the myths. They would not have been able to do so if the oral tradition had not kept the myths alive.

Thinking About Folk Literature and the Oral Tradition

Reread the selection's opening and closing paragraphs. Why do you think the author introduces the characters of Ezinma and Ekwefi?

VOCABULARY

Using a Glossary

A **glossary** is an alphabetical list of words, usually found at the end of a textbook. Like a dictionary a glossary gives the **definitions,** or meanings, of the words. Many glossaries also give pronunciations, explaining how a word is spoken. The letters used in the pronunciation make up a **phonetic alphabet.** Many glossaries have **pronunciation keys** to explain the sounds of these letters. Glossaries often also give the **parts of speech,** telling how a word is used in a sentence. The abbreviation for a word's part of speech often follows the pronunciation.

Unlike a dictionary a glossary includes only certain words that are found within the textbook. The Glossary at the back of this book lists words from the selections. For those words with more than one meaning, the Glossary for this book defines the terms as they are used in the selections.

Use the Glossary at the back of this book to answer the numbered questions about the italicized words from "Why the Tortoise's Shell Is Not Smooth."

1. What is the meaning of *compound*?
2. Is the *u* in *plumage* pronounced like the *u* in *up* or the $\overline{oo}$ in *fool*?
3. What part of speech is *eloquent*?
4. On what syllable of *delectable* does the main stress fall?

Yoshiko Uchida (born 1921) has written many books for young people. The child of Japanese immigrants to the United States, she often writes about Japanese culture and the Japanese American experience. Her nonfiction, stories, and folk tales help share with younger generations her pride in her Japanese heritage.

"What a terrible decree! What a cruel and unreasonable lord we have," the people of the village whispered.

Yoshiko Uchida

The Wise Old Woman

It is told that many long years ago, there lived an arrogant and cruel young lord. He ruled over a small village in the western hills of Japan.

"I have no use for old people in my village," he said haughtily. "They are neither useful nor able to work for a living. I therefore decree that anyone over seventy-one must be banished from the village and left in the mountains to die."

"What a terrible decree! What a cruel and unreasonable lord we have," the people of the village whispered. But the lord fearfully punished anyone who disobeyed him. So villagers who turned seventy-one were tearfully carried into the mountains, never to return.

Gradually there were fewer and fewer old people in the village, and soon they disappeared altogether. The young lord was pleased.

"What a fine village of young, healthy, and hardworking people I have," he

bragged. "Soon it will be the finest village in all Japan."

Now there lived in this village a kind young farmer and his aged mother. They were poor, but the farmer was good to his mother. The two of them lived happily together.

However, as the years went by, the mother grew older, and before long she reached the terrible age of seventy-one.

"If only I could somehow deceive the cruel lord," the farmer thought. But there were records in the village books. Everyone knew that his mother had turned seventy-one.

Each day the son put off telling his mother that he must take her into the mountains to die, but the people of the village began to talk. The farmer knew that if he did not take his mother away soon, the lord would send his soldiers and throw them both into a dark dungeon to die.

"Mother . . ." he would begin, as he tried

190   *Myths, Tales, and Fabulous Beasts*

to tell her what he must do, but he could not go on.

Then one day the mother herself spoke of the lord's decree. "Well, my son," she said, "the time has come for you to take me to the mountains. We must hurry before the lord sends his soldiers for you." She did not seem worried at all that she must go to the mountains to die.

"Forgive me, dear Mother, for what I must do," the farmer said sadly, and the next morning he lifted his mother to his shoulders and set off on the steep path toward the mountains. Up and up he climbed, until the trees clustered close and the path was gone. There was no longer even the sound of birds, and they heard only the soft wail of the wind in the trees. The son walked slowly, for he could not bear to think of leaving his old mother in the mountains. On and on he climbed, not wanting to stop and leave her behind. Soon, he heard his mother breaking off small twigs from the trees that they passed.

"Mother, what are you doing?" he asked.

"Do not worry, my son," she answered gently. "I am just marking the way so you will not get lost returning to the village."

The son stopped. "Even now you are thinking of me?" he asked, wonderingly.

The mother nodded. "Of course, my son," she replied. "You will always be in my thoughts. How could it be otherwise?"

At that, the young farmer could bear it no longer.

"Mother, I cannot leave you in the mountains to die all alone," he said. "We are going home. No matter what the lord does to punish me, I will never desert you again."

So they waited until the sun had set and a lone star crept into the silent sky. Then in the dark shadows of night, the farmer carried his mother down the hill

and they returned quietly to their little house. The farmer dug a deep hole in the floor of his kitchen and made a small room where he could hide his mother. From that day, she spent all her time in the secret room and the farmer carried meals to her there. The rest of the time, he was careful to work in the fields and act as though he lived alone. In this way, for almost two years, he kept his mother safely hidden. No one in the village knew that she was there.

Then one day there was a terrible commotion among the villagers. Lord Higa[1] of the town beyond the hills threatened to take over their village and make it his own.

"Only one thing can spare you," Lord Higa announced. "Bring me a box containing one thousand ropes of ash and I will spare your village."

The cruel young lord quickly gathered together all the wise men of his village. "You are men of wisdom," he said. "Surely you can tell me how to meet Lord Higa's demands so our village can be spared."

But the wise men shook their heads. "It is impossible to make even one rope of ash, Sire," they answered. "How can we ever make one thousand?"

"Fools!" the lord cried angrily. "What good is your wisdom if you cannot help me now?"

He posted a notice in the village square offering a great reward of gold to any villager who could help him save their village.

But all the people in the village whispered, "Surely it is an impossible thing, for ash crumbles at the touch of the finger. How could anyone ever make a rope of ash?" They shook their heads and sighed,

1. **Higa** [hē′gä]

The Wise Old Woman 191

"Alas, alas, we must be conquered by yet another cruel lord."

The young farmer, too, supposed that this must be. He wondered what would happen to his mother if a new lord even more terrible than their own came to rule over them.

When his mother saw the troubled look on his face, she asked, "Why are you so worried, my son?"

So the farmer told her of the impossible task ordered by Lord Higa if the village was to be spared, but his mother did not seem troubled at all. Instead she laughed softly and said, "Why, that is not such an impossible task. All one has to do is soak ordinary rope in salt water and dry it well. When it is burned, it will hold its shape and there is your rope of ash! Tell the villagers to hurry and find one thousand pieces of rope."

The farmer shook his head in amazement. "Mother, you are wonderfully wise," he said. He rushed to tell the young lord what he must do.

"You are wiser than all the wise men of the village," the lord said when he heard the farmer's solution. He rewarded the farmer with many pieces of gold. The thousand ropes of ash were quickly made and the village was spared.

In a few days, however, there was another great commotion in the village as Lord Higa sent another threat. This time he sent a log with a small hole that curved and bent seven times through its length. He ordered that a single piece of silk thread be threaded through the hole. "If you cannot perform this task," the lord threatened, "I shall come to take over your village."

The young lord hurried once more to his wise men, but they all shook their heads in bewilderment. "A needle cannot bend its way through such curves," they moaned. "Again we are faced with an impossible task."

"And again you are stupid fools!" the lord said, stamping his foot impatiently. He then posted a second notice in the village square asking the villagers for their help.

Once more the young farmer hurried with the problem to his mother in her secret room.

"Why, that is not so difficult," his mother said with a quick smile. "Put some sugar at one end of the hole. Then, tie an ant to a piece of silk thread and put it in at the other end. The ant will weave its way in and out of the curves to get to the sugar and it will take the silk thread with it."

"Mother, you are remarkable?" the son cried, and he hurried off to the lord with the solution to the second problem.

Once more the lord commended the young farmer and rewarded him with many pieces of gold. "You are a brilliant man. You have saved our village again," the lord said gratefully.

However, the lord's troubles were not over even then, for a few days later Lord Higa sent still another task. "This time you will undoubtedly fail and then I shall take over your village," he threatened. "Bring me a drum that sounds without being beaten."

"But that is not possible," sighed the people of the village. "How can anyone make a drum sound without beating it?"

This time the wise men held their heads in their hands and moaned, "It is hopeless. It is hopeless. This time Lord Higa will conquer us all."

The young farmer hurried home breathlessly. "Mother, Mother, we must solve another terrible problem or Lord Higa will take over our village!" Then he quickly told his

Reeds and Cranes,
Suzuki Kiitsu,
color on gilded silk,
early nineteenth
century.

mother about the impossible drum.

His mother, however, smiled and answered, "Why, this is the easiest of them all. Make a drum with sides of paper and put a bumblebee inside. As it tries to escape, it will buzz and beat itself against the paper and you will have a drum that sounds without being beaten."

The young farmer was amazed at his mother's wisdom. "You are far wiser than any of the wise men of the village," he said. He hurried to tell the young lord of how to complete Lord Higa's third task.

When the lord heard the answer, he was greatly impressed. "Surely a young man like you cannot be wiser than all my wise men," he said. "Tell me honestly, who has helped you solve all these difficult problems?"

The young farmer could not lie. "My lord," he began slowly, "for the past two years I have broken the law of the land. I have kept my aged mother hidden beneath the floor of my house. It is she who solved each of your problems and saved the village from Lord Higa."

He trembled as he spoke, for he feared the lord's displeasure and rage. Surely now the soldiers would be called to throw him into the dark dungeon. But when he glanced fearfully at the lord, he saw that the young ruler was not angry at all. Instead, the lord was silent and thoughtful. At last he realized how much wisdom and knowledge old people possess.

"I have been very wrong," he said finally. "I must ask the forgiveness of your mother and of all my people. Never again will I order that the old people of our village be sent to the mountains to die. Rather, they will be treated with the respect and the honor they deserve. They will be asked to share with us the wisdom of their years."

And so it was. From that day, the villagers were no longer forced to leave their parents in the mountains. The village became once more a happy, cheerful place in which to live. The terrible Lord Higa stopped sending his impossible tasks and no longer threatened to take over the village, for he too was impressed. "Even in such a small village there is much wisdom," he declared, "and its people should be allowed to live in peace."

And that is exactly what the farmer and his mother and all the people of the village did for all the years thereafter.

READER'S RESPONSE

Would you have forgiven the young lord if you had been one of the villagers? Why or why not?

STUDY QUESTIONS

Recalling

1. What terrible decree does the cruel lord of the village make?
2. How does the young farmer disobey the decree?
3. What three impossible tasks does Lord Higa demand? What solution does the old woman suggest for each?
4. What does the lord of the village do when he learns the young farmer's secret?

Interpreting

5. Contrast the behavior of the young farmer with that of the young lord at the beginning of the story. What seem to be the main traits of each character?
6. What does the aged mother's suggestions reveal about her character?
7. At the end of the tale, how does the young lord change? Explain the reasons for the changes.

Extending

8. Can you suggest some ways in which the older people in your community could share their knowledge and experience with young people?

READING AND LITERARY FOCUS

Folk Hero

A **folk hero** is the central character of a folk tale. Folk heroes frequently have special gifts, such as great strength, skill, or cleverness, that are much admired in their cultures. Using these talents, folk heroes often perform important services for their communities.

You are probably familiar with folk tales about the logger Paul Bunyan. These tales, which began on the American frontier, emphasize Bunyan's great size and strength. People on the frontier admired these traits because they were necessary to clear forests and build communities.

Thinking About Folk Heroes

1. Who do you think is the folk hero of "The Wise Old Woman"? What is this folk hero's special talent or trait?
2. What important service does the folk hero of this tale perform for the community?

COMPOSITION

Writing a Character Sketch

Write a character sketch of the wise old woman of this tale. **Prewriting:** Reread the selection, making notes about the old woman as you go along. Pay attention to her age, her position in her family, the place in which she lives, and her actions, thoughts, words, and feelings. **Writing:** Begin by briefly identifying the woman, explaining who she is, how old she is, where she lives, and so on. Then discuss what you consider to be her outstanding character traits. To determine those traits, examine the woman's actions, thoughts, words, and feelings. Give examples from the folk tale that illustrate the traits you name. **Revising:** Review your character sketch to see that you have expressed your ideas clearly and logically. *For help with this assignment, see Lesson 3 in the Writing About Literature Handbook at the back of this book.*

Writing a Personal Narrative

Recall a personal experience in which someone you know acted wisely in a difficult or dangerous situation. Begin by describing the person. Then relate details about the situation. Tell what the person said or did, and tell how the danger or difficulty was resolved. End by explaining why you think the person's behavior was wise.

Thinking Skills: Problem Solving

DEFINITION

Problem solving is a way of thinking. A good problem solver starts with basic information about a problem and then thinks in an orderly fashion, following several clear steps.

STEPS

1. **State the goal.**
   What do you want to find out or accomplish?

2. **List the givens.**
   What information do you have?

3. **List the obstacles.**
   What is stopping you from solving the problem? What information do you need?

4. **Identify the methods.**
   What specific actions are you going to take to remove each obstacle?

5. **Carry out the plan.**

6. **Check the results.**
   Have you solved the problem?

EXAMPLE

Imagine that a student named James is having difficulty with his schoolwork.

1. **State the goal.** James would like to get better grades.

2. **List the givens.** James is bright and spends many hours studying, but his grades show little improvement.

3. **List the obstacles.** James never seems to have enough time to complete all his assignments. He is becoming discouraged about the fact that his grades are not improving.

4. **Identify the methods.** James wonders whether his approach to studying is causing his problem. He decides to research study skills.

5. **Carry out the plan.** James talks to teachers, librarians, and friends. He uses books and tapes designed to help students develop good study skills. He begins studying with a group of other students in his class in order to boost his confidence.

6. **Check the results.** James is able to study more effectively, complete his assignments, and raise his grades.

ACTIVITY 1

Problem Solving in "The Wise Old Woman"

Follow the six steps of problem solving to describe what the old woman does to solve one of the problems posed by Lord Higa. Remember that she succeeds by not taking the most obvious approach to each problem.

ACTIVITY 2

Problem Solving in Literature

Follow the six steps of problem solving to describe what happens in another selection in this book. Remember that people are constantly solving problems in ordinary human relationships, in the process of growing up, in real-life adventures, in folk tales, and in science.

photograph ©1990 Jill Krementz

Isaac Bashevis Singer (born 1904) came from his native Poland to the United States in 1935. Singer usually writes about the people and places of his childhood. He has continued to write in Yiddish, a language spoken by Jews of eastern Europe. Many of Singer's stories about Chelm, the imaginary city of fools, are based on folk tales his mother told him. She in turn had heard them from her mother and grandmother. According to Singer, the Chelm stories "are products of a way of life rich in fantasy and make-believe."

"There is no prison in Chelm for fish," said Zeinvel Ninny. "And to build such a prison would take too long."

"Maybe he should be hanged," suggested Dopey Lekisch.

● ●

Isaac Bashevis Singer

The Fools of Chelm and the Stupid Carp

In Chelm,[1] a city of fools, every housewife bought fish for the Sabbath.[2] The rich bought large fish, the poor small ones. They were bought on Thursday, cut up, chopped, and made into gefilte fish[3] on Friday, and eaten on the Sabbath.

One Thursday morning the door opened at the house of the community leader of Chelm, Gronam Ox, and Zeinvel Ninny entered, carrying a trough full of water. Inside was a large, live carp.

"What is this?" Gronam asked.

"A gift to you from the wise men of Chelm," Zeinvel said. "This is the largest carp ever caught in the Lake of Chelm, and we all decided to give it to you as a token of appreciation for your great wisdom."

"Thank you very much," Gronam Ox replied. "My wife, Yente Pesha, will be delighted. She and I both love carp. I read in a book that eating the brains of a carp increases wisdom, and even though we in Chelm are immensely clever, a little improvement never hurts. But let me have a close look at him. I was told that a carp's tail shows the size of his brain."

Gronam Ox was known to be nearsighted, and when he bent down to the trough to better observe the carp's tail, the carp did something that proved he was not as wise as Gronam thought. He lifted his tail and smacked Gronam across the face.

Gronam Ox was flabbergasted. "Something like this never happened to me before," he exclaimed. "I cannot believe this

---

1. **Chelm** [ĸнelm]
2. **Sabbath** [sab′əth]: day of the week reserved for rest and religious worship; Saturday is the Sabbath of the Jewish people.
3. **gefilte** [gə fil′tə] **fish:** chopped fish, usually carp or other whitefish, shaped into balls, seasoned, and boiled in broth.

carp was caught in the Chelm lake. A Chelm carp would know better."

"He's the meanest fish I ever saw in my life," agreed Zeinvel Ninny.

Even though Chelm is a big city, news traveled quickly there. In no time at all the other wise men of Chelm arrived at the house of their leader, Gronam Ox. Treitel Fool came, and Sender Donkey, Shmendrick Numskull, and Dopey Lekisch. Gronam Ox was saying, "I'm not going to eat this fish on the Sabbath. This carp is a fool, and malicious to boot. If I eat him, I could become foolish instead of cleverer."

"Then what shall I do with him?" asked Zeinvel Ninny.

Gronam Ox put a finger to his head as a sign that he was thinking hard. After a while he cried out, "No man or animal in Chelm should slap Gronam Ox. This fish should be punished."

"What kind of punishment shall we give him?" asked Treitel Fool. "All fish are killed anyhow, and one cannot kill a fish twice."

"He shouldn't be killed like other fish," Sender Donkey said. "He should die in a different way to show that no one can smack our beloved sage, Gronam Ox, and get away with it."

"What kind of death?" wondered Shmendrick Numskull. "Shall we perhaps just imprison him?"

"There is no prison in Chelm for fish," said Zeinvel Ninny. "And to build such a prison would take too long."

"Maybe he should be hanged," suggested Dopey Lekisch.

"How do you hang a carp?" Sender Donkey wanted to know. "A creature can be hanged only by its neck, but since a carp has no neck, how will you hang him?"

"My advice is that he should be thrown to the dogs alive," said Treitel Fool.

"It's no good," Gronam Ox answered. "Our Chelm dogs are both smart and modest, but if they eat this carp, they may become as stupid and mean as he is."

"So what should we do?" all the wise men asked.

"This case needs lengthy consideration," Gronam Ox decided. "Let's leave the carp in the trough and ponder the matter as long as is necessary. Being the wisest man in Chelm, I cannot afford to pass a sentence that will not be admired by all the Chelmites."

"If the carp stays in the trough a long time, he may die," Zeinvel Ninny, a former fish dealer, explained. "To keep him alive we must put him into a large tub, and the water has to be changed often. He must also be fed properly."

"You are right, Zeinvel," Gronam Ox told him. "Go and find the largest tub in Chelm and see to it that the carp is kept alive and healthy until the day of judgment. When I reach a decision, you will hear about it."

Of course Gronam's words were the law in Chelm. The five wise men went and found a large tub, filled it with fresh water, and put the criminal carp in it, together with some crumbs of bread, challah,[4] and other tidbits a carp might like to eat. Shlemiel, Gronam's bodyguard, was stationed at the tub to make sure that no greedy Chelmite wife should use the imprisoned carp for gefilte fish.

It just so happened that Gronam Ox had many other decisions to make, and he kept postponing the sentence. The carp seemed not to be impatient. He ate, swam in the tub, became even fatter than he had been,

---

4. **challah** [KHÄ′lä]: bread in the form of a braided loaf, traditionally eaten by Jewish people on the Sabbath.

not realizing that a severe sentence hung over his head. Shlemiel changed the water frequently, because he was told that if the carp died, this would be an act of contempt for Gronam Ox and for the Chelm Court of Justice. Yukel the water carrier made a few extra pennies every day by bringing water for the carp. Some of the Chelmites who were in opposition to Gronam Ox spread the gossip that Gronam just couldn't find the right type of punishment for the carp and that he was waiting for the carp to die a natural death. But, as always, a great disappointment awaited them. One morning about half a year later, the sentence became known, and when it was known, Chelm was stunned. The carp had to be drowned.

Gronam Ox had thought up many clever sentences before, but never one as brilliant as this one. Even his enemies were amazed at this shrewd verdict. Drowning is just the kind of death suited to a spiteful carp with a large tail and a small brain.

That day the entire Chelm community gathered at the lake to see the sentence executed. The carp, which had become almost twice as big as he had been before, was brought to the lake in the wagon that carried the worst criminals to their death. The drummers drummed. Trumpets blared. The Chelmite executioner raised the heavy carp and threw it into the lake with a mighty splash.

A great cry rose from the Chelmites. "Down with the treacherous carp! Long live Gronam Ox! Hurrah!"

Gronam was lifted by his admirers and carried home with songs of praise. Some Chelmite girls showered him with flowers. Even Yente Pesha, his wife, who was often critical of Gronam and dared to call him fool, seemed impressed by Gronam's high intelligence.

In Chelm, as everywhere else, there were envious people who found fault with everyone, and they began to say that there was no proof whatsoever that the carp really drowned. Why should a carp drown in lake water? they asked. While hundreds of innocent fish were killed every Friday, they said, that stupid carp lived in comfort for months on the taxpayers' money and then was returned sound and healthy to the lake, where he is laughing at Chelm justice.

But only a few listened to these malicious words. They pointed out that months passed and the carp was never caught again, a sure sign that he was dead. It is true that the carp just might have decided to be careful and to avoid the fisherman's net. But how can a foolish carp who slaps Gronam Ox have such wisdom?

Just the same, to be on the safe side, the wise men of Chelm published a decree that if the nasty carp had refused to be drowned and was caught again, a special jail should be built for him, a pool where he would be kept prisoner for the rest of his life.

The decree was printed in capital letters in the official gazette of Chelm and signed by Gronam Ox and his five sages—Treitel Fool, Sender Donkey, Shmendrick Numskull, Zeinvel Ninny, and Dopey Lekisch.

Green Violinist,
Marc Chagall, 1923–1924.

READER'S RESPONSE

What piece of advice would you like to give to the fools of Chelm?

STUDY QUESTIONS

Recalling

1. What does the carp do to offend Gronam Ox?
2. Why don't the wise men want to eat the carp?
3. Which punishments do the wise men consider? Why do they reject these punishments?
4. In the end what do the wise men finally do to punish the carp?

Interpreting

5. Why is the punishment finally chosen for the carp so humorous?
6. What problems do you see about the way in which the elders of Chelm make decisions?

VOCABULARY

Synonyms

A **synonym** is a word that has the same or nearly the same meaning as another word. For example, the words *fools, simpletons,* and *numskulls* are synonyms. The italicized words below are from "The Fools of Chelm and the Stupid Carp." Choose the word that is *nearest* the meaning of each italicized word, *as the word is used in the story.* Write the number of each item and the letter of your choice on a separate sheet of paper.

1. *flabbergasted* by the event
   (a) surprised   (c) angered
   (b) pleased   (d) sickened
2. after some *consideration*
   (a) time   (c) difficulty
   (b) thought   (d) confusion
3. *ponder* the matter
   (a) disagree over   (c) avoid
   (b) think about   (d) decide
4. an act of *contempt*
   (a) honor   (c) confidence
   (b) horror   (d) disrespect
5. a *shrewd* decision
   (a) difficult   (c) clever
   (b) unfair   (d) dangerous

Over Vitebsk, Marc Chagall, 1915–1920.

Howard Pyle (1853–1911) was one of America's finest illustrators. At first he drew pictures for books written by others; later he began to write and illustrate his own. Before depicting a place, Pyle studied it in detail to allow faraway places and ancient events to come to life in his imagination.

Pyle once compared imagination to a clock belonging to Time's grandmother. Out of this clock step wonderful people and events every hour of the day. If you should want to find this clock, Howard Pyle gave these directions: "Put on your dream cap and go into Wonderland, and soon you will come to the old house where Father Time lives. And up in the garret of this house is the Wonder Clock."

"I am hunting for the Water of Life, and have come as far as this without finding a drop of it."

● ●

Howard Pyle

The Water of Life

Once upon a time there was an old king who had a faithful servant. There was nobody in the whole world like him, and this was why: around his wrist he wore an armlet that fitted as close as the skin. There were words on the golden band; on one side they said:

"WHO THINKS TO WEAR ME ON HIS ARM
MUST LACK BOTH GUILE AND THOUGHT OF HARM."

And on the other side they said:

"I AM FOR ONLY ONE AND HE
SHALL BE AS STRONG AS TEN CAN BE."

At last the old king felt that his end was near, and he called the faithful servant to him and besought[1] him to serve and aid the young king who was to come, as he had served and aided the old king who was to go. The faithful servant promised that which was asked, and then the old king closed his eyes and folded his hands and went the way that those had traveled who had gone before him.

Well, one day a stranger came to that town from over the hills and far away. With him he brought a painted picture, but it was all covered with a curtain so that nobody could see what it was.

He drew aside the curtain and showed the picture to the young king, and it was a likeness of the most beautiful princess in the whole world; for her eyes were as black as a crow's wing, her cheeks were as red as apples, and her skin as white as snow. Moreover, the picture was so natural that it seemed as though it had nothing to do but to open its lips and speak.

The young king just sat and looked and looked. "Oh me!" said he, "I will never rest

---

1. **besought** [bi sôt′]: asked earnestly.

content until I have such a one as that for my own."

"Then listen!" said the stranger, "this is a likeness of the princess that lives over beyond the three rivers. Awhile ago she had a wise bird on which she doted, for it knew everything that happened in the world, so that it could tell the princess whatever she wanted to know. But now the bird is dead, and the princess does nothing but grieve for it day and night. She keeps the dead bird in a glass casket,[2] and has promised to marry whoever will bring a cup of water from the Fountain of Life, so that the bird may be brought back to life again." That was the story the stranger told, and then he jogged on the way he was going, and I, for one, do not know whither it led.

But the young king had no peace or comfort in life for thinking of the princess who lived over beyond the three rivers. At last he called the faithful servant to him. "And can you not," said he, "get me a cup of the Water of Life?"

"I know not, but I will try," said the faithful servant, for he bore in mind what he had promised to the old king.

So out he went into the wide world, to seek for what the young king wanted, though the way there is both rough and thorny. On he went and on, until his shoes were dusty, and his feet were sore, and after a while he came to the end of the earth, and there was nothing more over the hill. There he found a little tumbled-down hut, and within the hut sat an old, old woman with a distaff,[3] spinning a lump of flax.[4]

---

2. **casket** [kas′kit]: small box or chest, as for jewels.
3. **distaff** [dis′taf]: stick used to hold fibers used in spinning.
4. **flax** [flaks]: fiber obtained from the stems of flax, a slender plant with blue flowers and narrow leaves.

"Good-morning, mother," said the faithful servant.

"Good-morning, son," says the old woman, "and where are you traveling that you have come so far?"

"Oh!" says the faithful servant, "I am hunting for the Water of Life, and have come as far as this without finding a drop of it."

"Hoity, toity," says the old woman, "if that is what you are after, you have a long way to go yet. The fountain is in the country that lies east of the Sun and west of the Moon, and it is few that have gone there and come back again, I can tell you. Besides that, there is a great dragon that keeps watch over the water, and you will have to get the better of him before you can touch a drop of it. All the same, if you have made up your mind to go you may stay here until my sons come home, and perhaps they can put you in the way of getting there, for I am the Mother of the Four Winds of Heaven, and it is few places that they have not seen."

So the faithful servant came in and sat down by the fire to wait till the Winds came home.

The first that came was the East Wind; but he knew nothing of the Water of Life and the land that lay east of the Sun and west of the Moon; he had heard folks talk of them both now and then, but he had never seen them with his own eyes.

The next that came was the South Wind, but he knew no more of it than his brother, and neither did the West Wind for the matter of that.

Last of all came the North Wind, and dear, dear, what a hubbub he made outside of the door, stamping the dust off of his feet before he came into the house.

"And do you know where the Fountain

of Life is, and the country that lies east of the Sun and west of the Moon?" said the old woman.

Oh, yes, the North Wind knew where it was. He had been there once upon a time, but it was a long, long distance away.

"So, good! Then perhaps you will give this lad a lift over there tomorrow," said the old woman.

At this the North Wind grumbled and shook his head; but at last he said "yes," for he is a good-hearted fellow at bottom, is the North Wind, though his ways are a trifle rough perhaps.

So the next morning he took the faithful servant on his back, and away he flew till the man's hair whistled behind him. On they went and on they went and on they went, until at last they came to the country that lay east of the Sun and west of the Moon; and they were none too soon getting there either, I can tell you, for when the North Wind tumbled the faithful servant off his back he was so weak that he could not have lifted a feather.

"Thank you," said the faithful servant, and then he was for starting away to find what he came for.

"Stop a bit," says the North Wind, "you will be wanting to come away again after a while. I cannot wait here, for I have other business to look after. But here is a feather; when you want me, cast it into the air, and I will not be long in coming."

Then away he bustled, for he had caught his breath again, and time was none too long for him.

The faithful servant walked along a great distance until, by and by, he came to a field covered all over with sharp rocks and white bones, for he was not the first by many who had been that way for a cup of the Water of Life.

Monna Vanna, Dante Gabriel Rossetti, 1886.

There lay the great fiery dragon in the sun, sound asleep, and so the faithful servant had time to look about him. Not far away was a great deep trench like a drain in a swampy field; that was a path that the dragon had made by going to the river for a drink of water every day. The faithful servant dug a hole in the bottom of this trench, and there he hid himself as snugly as a cricket in the crack in the kitchen floor. By and by the dragon awoke and found that he was thirsty, and then started down to the river to get a drink. The faithful servant lay as still as a mouse until the dragon was just above where he was hidden, then he thrust his sword through its heart, and there it lay, after a turn or two, as dead as a stone.

After that he had only to fill the cup at the fountain, for there was nobody to say nay to him. Then he cast the feather into the air, and there was the North Wind, as fresh and as sound as ever. The North Wind took him upon its back, and away it flew until it came home again.

The faithful servant thanked them all around—the Four Winds and the old woman—and as they would take nothing else, he gave them a few drops of the Water of Life, and that is the reason that the Four Winds and their mother are as fresh and young now as they were when the world began.

Then the faithful servant set off home again, right foot foremost, and he was not as long in getting there as in coming.

As soon as the king saw the cup of the Water of Life he had the horses saddled, and off he and the faithful servant rode to find the princess who lived over beyond the three rivers. By and by they came to the town, and there was the princess mourning and grieving over her bird just as she had done from the first. But when she heard that the king had brought the Water of Life she welcomed him as though he were a flower in March.

They sprinkled a few drops upon the dead bird, and up it sprang as lively and as well as ever.

But now, before the princess would marry the king she must have a talk with the bird, and there came the hitch, for the Wise Bird knew as well as you and I that it was not the king who had brought the Water of Life. "Go and tell him," said the Wise Bird, "that you are ready to marry him as soon as he saddles and bridles the Wild Black Horse in the forest over yonder, for if he is the hero who found the Water of Life he can do that, and more, easily enough."

The princess did as the bird told her, and so the king missed getting what he wanted after all. But off he went to the faithful servant. "And can you not saddle and bridle the Wild Black Horse for me?" said he.

"I do not know," said the faithful servant, "but I will try."

So off he went to the forest to hunt up the Wild Black Horse, the saddle over his shoulder and the bridle over his arm. By and by came the Wild Black Horse galloping through the woods like a thunder gust in summer, so that the ground shook under his feet. But the faithful servant was ready for him; he caught him by the mane and forelock, and the Wild Black Horse had never had such a one to catch hold of him before.

But how they did stamp and wrestle! Up and down and here and there, until the fire flew from the stones under their feet. But the Wild Black Horse could not stand against the strength of ten men, such as the faithful servant had, so by and by he fell on his knees, and the faithful servant clapped the saddle on his back and slipped the bridle over his ears.

"Listen now," says he; "tomorrow my master, the king, will ride you up to the princess's house, and if you do not do just as I tell you, it will be the worse for you; when the king mounts upon your back you must stagger and groan, as though you carried a mountain."

The horse promised to do as the other bade, and then the faithful servant jumped on his back and away to the king, who had been waiting at home for all this time.

The next day the king rode up to the princess's castle, and the Wild Black Horse did just as the faithful servant told him to do; he staggered and groaned, so that everybody cried out, "Look at the great hero riding upon the Wild Black Horse!"

And when the princess saw him she also thought that he was a great hero. But the Wise Bird was of a different mind from her, for when the princess came to talk to him about marrying the king he shook his head. "No, no," said he, "there is something wrong here, and the king has baked his cake in somebody else's oven. He never saddled and bridled the Wild Black Horse by himself. Listen, you must say to him that you will marry nobody but the man who wears such and such a golden armlet with this and that written on it."

So the princess told the king what the Wise Bird had bidden her to say, and the king went straightway to the faithful servant.

"You must let me have your armlet," said he.

"Alas, master," said the faithful servant, "that is a woeful thing for me, for the one and only way to take the armlet off of my wrist is to cut my hand from off my body."

"So!" says the king, "that is a great pity, but the princess will not have me without the armlet."

"Then you shall have it," says the faithful servant; but the king had to cut the hand off, for the faithful servant could not do it himself.

But, bless your heart! The armlet was ever so much too large for the king to wear! Nevertheless he tied it to his wrist with a bit of ribbon, and off he marched to the princess's castle.

"Here is the armlet of gold," said he, "and now will you marry me!"

But the Wise Bird sat on the princess's chair. "Hut! tut!" says he, "it does not fit the man."

Yes, that was so; everybody who was there could see it easily enough; and as for marrying him, the princess would marry nobody but the man who could wear the armlet.

What a hubbub there was then! Everyone who was there was sure that the armlet would fit him if it fitted nobody else. But no; it was far too large for the best of them. The faithful servant was very sad, and stood back of the rest, over by the wall, with his arm tied up in a napkin. "You shall try it too," says the princess; but the faithful servant only shook his head, for he could not try it on as the rest had done, because he had no hand. But the Wise Bird was there and knew what he was about. "See now," says he, "maybe the Water of Life will cure one thing as well as another."

Yes, that was true, and one was sent to fetch the cup. They sprinkled it on the faithful servant's arm, and it was not twice they had to do it, for there was another hand as good and better than the old.

Then they gave him the armlet; he slipped it over his hand, and it fitted him like his own skin.

"This is the man for me," says the princess, "and I will have none other"; for she could see with half an eye that he was the hero who had been doing all the wonderful things that had happened, because he said nothing about himself.

As for the king—why, all that was left for him to do was to pack off home again; and I, for one, am glad of it.

And this is true: the best packages are not always wrapped up in blue paper and tied with a gay string, and there are better men in the world than kings and princes, fine as they seem to be.

READER'S RESPONSE

How could the faithful servant let the king cut off his arm? Was he taking loyalty too far?

STUDY QUESTIONS

Recalling

1. At the beginning of the story, for what does the young king want the Water of Life?
2. Where does the faithful servant find the Water of Life? What does he have to do to get it?
3. Explain how the young king performs the first task required by the Wise Bird and the princess.
4. What final requirement does the princess set for the man she will marry? What does the young king do to fulfill this requirement?
5. In what way is the Water of Life used at the end of the story?
6. Whom does the princess marry, and why?

Interpreting

7. In what ways is the faithful servant different from the young king?
8. Does the king deserve the servant's loyalty? What does the tale suggest about the rewards of loyalty?
9. In your own words explain how the story illustrates the idea that "the best packages are not always wrapped up in blue paper and tied with a gay string."

Extending

10. Can you name some "faithful servants" in your community? To what are they devoted? Are they honored and respected for their loyalty?

READING AND LITERARY FOCUS

Chronological Order

Chronological order is the time order in which events occur. A story that follows chronological order begins with the first event. The second event is described next, and so on, until the end of the story.

The stories in this unit follow chronological order. "The Fools of Chelm and the Stupid Carp," for example, begins with the event that sets the plot in motion: the giving of the carp to Gronam Ox. Next the author describes how the carp slaps Gronam. Then we read about the various punishments that the wise men consider. Finally we learn that the carp is to be drowned and are told of the reaction of the townspeople to this decision.

Thinking About Chronological Order

1. Do the events of "The Water of Life" follow chronological order? Tell how you know.
2. When might a story *not* follow chronological order? Give examples.

COMPOSITION

Using Chronological Order in Writing

Use chronological, or time, order to summarize the main events of "The Water of Life." **Prewriting:** Reread the selection, and briefly list the main events. **Writing:** Begin your composition with the faithful servant's promise to be loyal to the young king. Then recount the servant's various adventures, using clue words such as *next, soon, then,* and *eventually.* The final event of your summary should be the princess' decision to marry the servant. **Revising:** Review your paragraph to see that you have summarized the events clearly and logically. Then review for effective word choice and organization. Make sure that your final copy is free of errors in grammar, spelling, and punctuation.

Writing a Diary Entry

Write a diary entry for the most memorable day in your life. Tell about the events of the day in chronological order, beginning with the morning. End the entry by explaining why you find this day so memorable.

With an author for a mother and a historian for a father, Antonia Fraser (born 1932) grew up in a home "knee deep in books." Acting out scenes from English history and legends was a favorite pastime for young Antonia and her seven brothers and sisters. As the author of *Robin Hood* and *King Arthur and the Knights of the Round Table*, Antonia Fraser shares the drama of history and legends with us.

"Master Robin, I fear that no good will come of this shooting-match. Whatever you do, do not go near it."

• •

Antonia Fraser

A Narrow Escape

from **Robin Hood**

There was a rousing cheer from the children in the market square of Nottingham[1] as the young man on the fine horse galloped into the square and leaped lightly from the saddle.

"Hooray for Robin Hood!" cried one shrill voice. Robin of Locksley bent down and patted the boy on the cheek.

"Why do you cheer me, boy?" he asked gently.

"Because you saved our father from the wicked Sheriff and his men," said the boy boldly. Robin looked round quickly. There was one fellow lounging idly against the tavern wall, and a few dogs sleeping in the midday sun, but otherwise the main square of Nottingham town was remarkably empty.

"Is your father Nat the Weaver, then?" he inquired softly. The boy nodded, and the two smaller children with him piped up together:

"Yes, we are the Weaver's children, and our father has fled into the forest. He sent word to us that he had been saved by brave Robin Hood and his green-feathered arrows." And all the children started to cheer again, all six of them, down to the smallest tugging at his brother's hand. Robin Hood pulled a handful of florins[2] out of his jerkin[3] pocket and pressed them into the boy's hand.

"Buy yourself some bread," he said. "Perhaps one day I will be able to help you further." He smiled cheerfully. "After all, it is only five days until my birthday, and *then* we shall see how Robin Hood uses his inheritance to save the poor of Nottingham from the Sheriff and his men."

---

1. **Nottingham** [not′ing əm]: city in central England.

2. **florins** [flôr′inz]: English silver coins.
3. **jerkin** [jur′kin]: short, close-fitting jacket, usually sleeveless.

A Narrow Escape 207

Was it mere coincidence that the lounger by the tavern pulled his hood over his face at these words and sidled into the tavern itself? Perhaps if Robin had looked closer he might have recognized the scowling features of his enemy in the forest—Walter of Weybridge. But a merry shout from the far corner of the square distracted him.

"Will Scarlett?" cried Robin joyfully. "What brings you to Nottingham? Why, Will, I have not seen you since Michaelmas[4] when you wagered me a pint of ale that I would not split a peeled wand[5] at four-score[6] yards with my new bow."

"I can split a wand at five-score[7] now, Robin," said Will Scarlett, clapping Robin on the back. "And that is why I have come to Nottingham this day."

"To Nottingham?" Robin looked puzzled. "Why, there is precious little marksmanship in Nottingham these days—unless it be in the Forest of Sherwood," he added under his breath. "No," he went on, "the Sheriff has set his heart against tournaments and all merrymaking of that sort. He grudges the expense," he added bitterly. "There was a time when there were fairs and shooting-matches at Nottingham every quarter, and the people came from miles around to try their skill. That was in King Richard's[8] day, before my father went on the Crusade."

"Look yonder, Robin," said Will Scarlett with a smile, "and see if those days are not

come again." As he spoke there was a great noise of shouting and laughing, and a crowd of people ran into the market square, with the Sheriff's herald in their midst.

"Patience, good people," said the herald fussily, adjusting his ruffled clothes. "All this commotion for a shooting-match," he muttered.

"The first we have had for many a long year," shouted one sturdy fellow. "When King Richard went on the Crusade he took all the gaiety of England with him. Alack, he now lies a prisoner in the hands of his enemies, far away in a foreign land."

At this moment, the herald managed to get his trumpet free, and blew a long shrill blast on it.

"Oyez, oyez,"[9] cried the herald, clearing his throat and extending a long scroll of parchment in front of him." Good people of Nottingham, be silent to hear the words of the noble Sheriff of Nottingham. Be it known unto all of you here present, that the Worshipful Sheriff, out of his great goodness and mercy towards his people of Nottingham . . ."

"What a mouthful of words!" whispered Robin Hood. The herald glared at him.

"Silence!" he shouted. "Be it known unto all of you here present, that the Worshipful Sheriff has decreed that a Shrove Tuesday,[10] that is to say, in a week's time, a shooting-match will be held here in the square at Nottingham!" A loud huzza[11] broke from the townspeople, and Will turned excitedly to Robin.

"There, that is what brought me to

---

4. **Michaelmas** [mik′əl məs]: church feast in honor of the angel Michael, observed on September 29.
5. **wand:** thin strip of wood used as a target in the sport of archery.
6. **four-score:** four times twenty; eighty.
7. **five-score:** five times twenty; one hundred.
8. **King Richard:** also known as Richard the Lion-Hearted (1157–1199), king of England (1189–1199). On his way back to England from the Third Crusade, Richard was captured by a hostile monarch and imprisoned.

---

9. **Oyez, oyez** [ō′yez]: Hear ye, hear ye.
10. **Shrove** [shrōv] **Tuesday:** day before Ash Wednesday, the first day of Lent, observed on the seventh Wednesday before Easter.
11. **huzza** [hə zä′]: hurrah.

Nottingham," he cried," Much the Miller, who takes the flour to the castle, brought the news privately a week or so back."

They were interrupted by another peremptory blast from the herald's trumpet.

"Forasmuch as"—he shouted above the hubbub—"forasmuch as it has pleased the Worshipful Sheriff to celebrate in this manner the twenty-first birthday of his beloved and right noble ward, Robin, son of the Earl of Locksley, commonly known around these parts as Robin Hood." More huzzas greeted this announcement, but Robin stepped back in amazement. "His beloved ward!" Those were not the words in which the Sheriff generally addressed him. "Scrapegrace![12] Troublesome knave!" and "Saucy boy!" were his usual terms. And why should he go to the expense of arranging a shooting-match when he particularly disliked archery, since he was too portly to draw a bow with comfort?

But there was a fresh surprise to come. A third time the herald reduced the crowd to silence with his trumpet, and this time, in the most splendid language at his command—which was, indeed, splendid—he announced that His Royal Highness the Prince John,[13] Regent of England, had graciously condescended to honor the shooting-match with his presence during his visit to the midlands of his kingdom.

"Strange," murmured Will Scarlett. "I cannot help thinking there is more to this shooting-match than meets the eye." But Robin Hood did not heed him. He threw his cap into the air and shouted cheerfully:

---

12. **Scapegrace:** mischievous person lacking principles; rascal.

13. **Prince John:** English prince (1167–1216) and king of England (1199–1216) following the death of his brother Richard. While Richard was away from England, John plotted (unsuccessfully) to overthrow him.

"This is the first good news I have heard yet about Prince John. Off to the meadows, Will, and let us set to practicing our archery."

Will Scarlett shrugged his shoulders. He knew that it was a waste of breath trying to argue with Robin once his mind was made up. Part of Robin's charm was his trusting nature. He never willingly believed evil of anyone.

A Warning

As the two lads crossed the square, a fellow on the edge of the crowd tugged at Robin's striped sleeve and muttered:

"I would have a word with you, Robin Hood."

Robin paused, and then gazed at him closely. "Dickon Barleycorn, is it not?"

The man nodded and flushed. "I reckon your worship knows my face well enough after that punishing we took in the forest," he said in a shamed voice.

Robin patted his shoulder in a friendly fashion. "Tush, Dickon, not a word of that here. The whole countryside seems to have heard of that little exploit. The Weaver's brood of children shout it abroad from the market square. I fear my arrows were recognized."

"The Sheriff too has heard of it," said Dickon, "And Master Robin, I warn you, he means mischief. That very Christmas Eve the Sheriff, together with Guy of Gisborne and Oswald Montdragon, plotted against you. Master Robin, I fear that no good will come of this shooting-match. Whatever you do, do not go near it."

Robin laughed merrily, "I thank you, friend Dickon, for your kindness," he said, "but Robin Hood was never yet frightened away from a shooting-match by threats. Did the Sheriff send you to me with that message, eh, Dickon? No doubt he has some plot to win the prize himself."

Dickon looked Robin Hood straight in the eye. "I know you have good reason to reproach me," he said, "for it was I who helped to catch Nat the Weaver. But for all the fact that I serve the Sheriff, I do not like his evil ways. Perchance it is my Saxon[14] blood which rebels, for I am half Saxon by birth. It was Walter of Weybridge who warned me about the shooting-match, for he overheard something about it."

But although Will Scarlett nudged his friend and bade him take heed, Robin, with another friendly smile at Dickon Barleycorn, dismissed the warning light-heartedly, and mounted his horse as if he had not a care in the world. It was as well that he could not overhear Guy of Gisborne, who at that very moment was sitting in his castle, weaving a dark conspiracy.

"I'll be revenged on young Robin Hood," he vowed. "However long it takes me. No one flouts Guy of Gisborne with impunity!"[15]

The Robbers' Valley

The day of the shooting-match dawned bright at Nottingham. The air was frosty but clear, and there was hardly any wind to alter the course of the marksmen's arrows. Robin Hood licked his finger and tested the breeze. He observed to Will Scarlett that it was the fairest day for marksmen there had been this side of Chrismas,

Robin Hood, Howard Pyle, drawing, early twentieth century.

as they rode slowly towards Nottingham from the manor of Locksley. The road lay through the great forest of Sherwood and Will gazed enviously at the fat bucks grazing among the trees.

"Oh, how I long for a shot at one of the royal deer," he said wistfully. "What a life we could lead in this forest, Robin, with venison to feed us. We could practice our marksmanship all day, and ride about the unexplored paths of the forest. I wager that we should have many merry adventures together." Little did Will Scarlett know how soon his wish was to come true.

Suddenly Robin gave a startled exclamation, and pointed along the stream they had been following to a waterfall which flowed precipitiously down the rocks.

"This is a new path to me," said Will Scarlett wonderingly. "I have never set eyes on that waterfall before."

---

14. **Saxon** [sak′sən]: of the descendants of one of the Germanic tribes that invaded England in the fifth and sixth centuries and established kingdoms in the southern and eastern regions of the country.

15. **impunity** [im pū′nə tē]: freedom from punishment, injury, or loss.

The two lads decided to investigate it further. To their amazement, they found that the waterfall in fact concealed the entrance to a narrow path, greatly over-grown. Slithering down it, they found themselves suddenly emerging in a spacious valley.

"We must have stumbled on the Robbers' Valley, which they sing about in the old ballads," exclaimed Will Scarlett.

"A score of men could hide out here for months and never be discovered," said Robin Hood. "This valley may be useful to us one day."

Robin was anxious to explore the rest of the valley, but the more prudent Will reminded him that they would miss the shooting-match altogether if they tarried much longer, so reluctantly Robin re-mounted his horse, and clambered up the steep path back into the Forest of Sherwood. Will and Robin vowed to each other to keep their discovery secret, and rode on, mightily pleased with what they had found.

Prince John is Afeard

Nottingham was all noise and confusion and merry-making when they arrived. Famous marksmen had traveled from all over the midlands to compete for the rich prize of the silver arrow with golden feathers which the Sheriff was offering to the finest marksman in honor of his ward's twenty-first birthday. Although on the next day he would have to hand over all Robin's money, lands, farms, meadows, fields and manors, the Sheriff's podgy face was wreathed in smiles. Perhaps there was something slightly strained at the back of his smile, as he plucked at the fur which edged his blue robe, but if there was, Prince John at least did not detect it.

"A splendid show, Sheriff, a splendid show," he said genially. "I am glad to hear that Nottingham is rich enough to hold a shooting-match in my honor." The Prince's face creased into a foxy smile as he added, "Perhaps I may increase the taxes due from this wealthy city next year."

The Sheriff tried not to let his annoyance appear. Momentarily he cursed Guy of Gisborne for his plot. But he managed to smile bravely.

"Your Highness is too kind," he murmured. Then he continued in a sharper tone, "Perchance Your Highness, in gazing at this brave sight, over-estimates our wealth and under-estimates our generosity."

Prince John showed no sign that this shaft had gone home. He continued to play with his beard and smile amiably at the crowds, occasionally bowing his head graciously to acknowledge the cheers of the people. To the Sheriff's watchful eye, these did not seem as frequent as they might have been, perhaps because the Saxons outnumbered the Normans[16] among the spectators. He nudged Guy of Gisborne, who was standing by, and whispered hotly:

"Tell your men to mingle with the crowd and raise a cheer or two for His Highness. Methought I heard one or two ominous cries for King Richard!"

Guy of Gisborne took the hint, and a minute later a chorus of rousing cries arose from one quarter of the square. This piece of by-play did not pass unobserved by Robin Hood and Will Scarlett, the one

---

16. **Normans** [nôr′mənz]: descendants of the French invaders who conquered England in 1066.

gaily attired in a striped jerkin, the other in his traditional red.

"I vow I'll pay the Sheriff out for that trick," murmured Robin. "Call forth some of the brave Saxon lads who are loyal to our true King."

Obediently, Will Scarlett put his two fingers in his mouth and gave vent to a curious warbling bird's whistle, which had been the secret rallying-call of Robin Hood and his friends since their boyhood. Immediately half a dozen stout lads sprang to Robin's side.

"Who's for King Richard?" cried Robin. "Friends, will you raise a cry for our rightful King?"

"Aye, Robin," answered Alan-a-Dale, a handsome upstanding young man with a guitar on his back. "We'll stand by you, never fear."

Thus it came about that not long after a few tame shouts had been raised by Guy of Gisborne's men for Prince John, a lusty cry of "Richard the Lionheart! Richard for England!" seemed to spring from all corners of the square at once. The Prince went pale, and clutched at the Sheriff's robe.

"Treachery!" he exclaimed in a tremulous voice. "There are traitors here, Sheriff. Did you not hear that cry? You swore to me on the Rood[17] that I should be safe here in Nottingham."

"Your Highness . . ." began the Sheriff in great agitation, but he was interrupted by Guy of Gisborne, who stepped forward and with a significant glance at the Sheriff, said smoothly:

"Your Highness, as one of the most loyal barons in your realm, may I speak the truth freely to you? It is true that there *are* certain traitors around Nottingham, a few Saxon scoundrels. But while my right arm still has strength, I swear they will not harm a hair of Your Highness's head."

The Prince cast a grateful glance at Guy of Gisborne's commanding figure and wiped the sweat from his pale brow. "Ah, loyalty, how rare true loyalty is," murmured the Prince.

Guy of Gisborne gave a smile of triumph and whispered to the Sheriff:

"This fits in well enough with our plan, forsooth. The Prince now sees traitors all round him. It will not be difficult to rouse his suspicions against . . ."

"Hush," murmured the Sheriff, waving a fat hand. "The match is about to begin."

The Shooting-Match

The heralds blew a long blast on their trumpets, and the competitors for the first of the archery prizes stepped forward. Neither Robin nor Will raised their bow; they intended to save their strength until the final competition for the silver arrow with the golden feathers. But Robin's band of friends acquitted[18] themselves nobly in the various contests. To Robin's joy, they worsted[19] the Norman marksmen time and time again. It was Alan-a-Dale who snatched the coveted prize from one of Guy of Gisborne's soldiers in the last contest but one. The Norman baron's face darkened as he saw the defeat of his man.

"You young Saxon whippersnapper. I'll pay you out for that, never fear," growled

---

17. **Rood** [rood]: cross that serves as a symbol of the cross on which Jesus Christ died.

18. **acquitted** [ə kwit′id]: conducted; behaved.
19. **worsted** [wurst′id]: defeated; got the better of.

Guy of Gisborne. He lost no time in whispering in the Prince's ear.

"A very dangerous fellow, that young Alan-a-Dale, for all he looks so young and guileless. Only last Lady Day[20] he refused to pay his taxes to Your Highness, and declared he owed no loyalty to an upstart Regent."

Prince John, who had calmed down somewhat, immediately turned pale again and groaned faintly. "Are there many of these treacherous youths in these parts?" He glared at the Sheriff and muttered, "You have indeed led me into a hornet's nest."

"Not many, Your Highness," said Guy of Gisborne, "But there is *one*. . . . Alas, I hardly dare speak more, he is so dear to the Sheriff's heart. . . ." Guy of Gisborne cunningly left the sentence unfinished.

At that moment Robin Hood's slim, muscular figure could be seen, conspicuous among the crowd by his striped jacket. Pretending that he did not want the Sheriff to see him, Guy of Gisborne nudged the Prince and pointed.

Prince John's eyes grew round as saucers. "By Our Lady," he breathed. "Never would I have thought it possible! The Sheriff's ward! Robin of Locksley!"

Guy of Gisborne shook his head sadly and murmured, "It is a great grief to our dear Sheriff's heart."

Now all attention was concentrated on the contest for the silver arrow, the last contest of the day.

Forty stout archers stepped forward in answer to the herald's command. Among them were Robin Hood, Will Scarlett and

---

20. **Lady Day:** March 25, the Feast of the Annunciation.

Walter of Weybridge, wearing the badge of the Sheriff's service, as well as a host of other young men eager to try their skill. They lined up, five at a time, for the first round, which would leave eight men to compete for the prize in the final attempt.

When Robin Hood's turn came, he was three inches nearer to the center of the target than any of his companions. Walter of Weybridge displayed a certain Norman skill, too, with his shot, and Will Scarlett acquitted himself well.

"It would be a fine thing to win the silver arrow on the eve of my birthday," said Robin to Will. "But if you win it, Will, I vow I will not bear a grudge against you, for we learned archery together."

"If I win, Robin," cried Will gaily, "I will bestow it on you for a birthday gift."

So saying, he stepped forward and loosed his arrow: amid the applause of the crowd it landed a bare inch from the bull's-eye. Then it was Walter of Weybridge's turn, and the man-at-arms, with the practice born of long years in the Sheriff's service, landed his arrow a fraction of an inch inside Will's. A great sign of regret went up from the common people, who hated the Sheriff's retainers. Finally, Robin Hood stepped forward, and with careless grace, loosed his green-feathered arrow at the target. A moment's silence, then a great shout went up.

"A Hood! A Hood! Robin of Locksley wins the day!"

The Mysterious Arrow

Even as the shout died away, a series of things occurred all at once so quickly that afterwards no man could rightly remember which happened first. One moment Robin was standing with his bow loose in his hands, gazing joyfully at the

The Sheriff of Nottingham, Howard Pyle, drawing, early twentieth century.

target, with its center transfixed by his green-tipped arrow. The next moment a great crowd had surged round him, intending to chair[21] him to the royal box in triumph. The moment after that, all in the twinkling of an eye, an arrow was speeding truly and surely towards the royal box itself!

Had Oswald Montdragon not flung the Prince aside, the arrow would surely have

embedded itself in his heart! As it was, the arrow transfixed the back of the box, where it quivered in the wood. Not one person present failed to notice that the arrow had—green feathers! "Treachery!" cried Guy of Gisborne. "To arms! Seize the traitor! 'Tis Robin of Locksley who has attacked our Prince in this dastardly fashion. Behold, the green feather of Locksley!" Plucking the green arrow from above his head, he waved it outside the box for all to see.

---

21. **chair** [chār]: carry on the shoulders.

"Save me, save me," murmured the Prince, in a hoarse voice of terror, as he crouched behind the broad figure of the Sheriff. Tears of fright began to trickle down his face. Now half a dozen Norman soldiers flung themselves at Robin Hood, as he stood, half-dazed by the quickness of events, in the center of the square.

"Guard yourself, Robin," yelled the faithful Will. "Look behind you!"

Robin Hood sprang back, just in time to avoid the onrush of the soldiery, and with only his woodsman's dagger to protect himself, he began to hack his way violently through the menacing Norman crowd which surrounded him. Twice it seemed that his body would fall beneath the weight of their onslaught: for how could one youth prevail against a dozen soldiers? But still Robin kept himself free, although his left arm was bleeding from a nasty wound, and his breath was coming short and fast. At the third rush, with one desperate twist of his body, Robin managed to free himself temporarily from the clutches of the soldiers, and despite the blood pouring from his wound, he sprinted valiantly across the square, to where he saw Will holding his horse.

"Good people of Nottingham," yelled Will, "show your loyalty to the Saxon cause. Keep back the Norman varlets!"[22]

The Saxons needed no further encouragement. With a mighty roar of "Norman knaves!" they flung themselves in the faces of the oncoming soldiers, and just gave Robin enough time to fling himself on the back of his horse, and be off at a whirlwind gallop, which scattered men, women and children, Normans and Saxons alike.

Flight to Sherwood

The next minute, amid frantic cries of "After him! Seize him, you craven curs!"[23] from the Sheriff, Guy of Gisborne and Oswald Montdragon, the Normans had mounted their own horses and were in full pursuit.

Robin and Will cleared the town gates with scarcely a minute to spare before the guards were alerted, and the gates clanged shut. However, their shutting delayed Guy's men considerably. By the time the gates had been opened amid much cursing and swearing, Robin and Will were only specks of dust on the horizon of the road which led to Sherwood.

"Whither away, Robin?" panted Will, spurring his flagging horse to fresh speed. "My mare Polly is nigh exhausted, and you are faint from your wounds."

"To Sherwood," grunted Robin. "We can hide out there . . . you remember"—he stifled a groan, and managed to gasp—"you remember the Robbers' Valley?" before he fainted dead away over his horse's neck.

It meant an instantaneous decision for Will Scarlett. Either he had to stop and succor[24] Robin, which would almost certainly mean capture for both, or else he pressed on alone, for it was equally certain that Robin could no longer ride a horse. Will Scarlett's pride revolted at the idea of falling into the Sheriff's hands. But loyalty to Robin came before pride—one check on the reins of his galloping steed, a lightning swoop, and Robin's lifeless body was slumped over his saddle, while Robin's riderless mount galloped on beside him. For a mile they rode thus, until they

---

22. **varlets** [vär'litz]: tricky, dishonest fellows.

23. **craven curs** [krā'vən kurz]: cowardly, mean persons.
24. **succor** [suk'ər]: give help or relief to.

reached the crossroads, where one signpost pointed to Sherwood and the other road stretched on out of sight. Then Will Scarlett brought down a great whack on the rump of Robin's horse and swerved down the forest path. Robin's horse gave a startled neigh of anger and fear, then bolted down the left-hand road. Soon it was out of sight.

"Poor Troubadour!" whispered Robin between clenched teeth. "Never was he used so before! But God bless you, Will, for your kindness. You could have been in Yorkshire[25] by now, without me."

Will Scarlett glanced down and saw Robin's deathly white countenance.

"You know that I would never leave you, Robin," he said. He slackened his speed slightly and gazed round him at the trees and undergrowth, which was growing thicker with every step his horse took. As if to encourage him to spur his exhausted horse once more, the faint shouts and hallooing of the Sheriff's men reached his ears.

"On, Will," gasped Robin. "Press on, and pray that stout Polly will not fall beneath our weight!"

So Will spurred Polly once more and the gallant mare made one last effort. The three of them galloped forward, until they seemed to be right in the heart of the forest. But either some memory of the morning's journey still lingered in Polly's memory, or else fortune favored Will in his hour of need; for quite by chance he found himself riding by the withered oak tree which marked the turning to the waterfall and the hidden valley. With a cry of joy, he wheeled Polly down the disused

track. Pushing their way through a curtain of leaves and branches, they found themselves bursting through the barrier of greenery which hid the entry to the valley. Polly half-slid, half-clambered down the last slope, and the journey was over.

Will leaped from his saddle and lifted Robin gently down. He lay gasping on the turf as Will tenderly staunched[26] his wound with strips of linen from his own shirt. All was silence around them, save for the birds, high above their heads in the trees, and the occasional rustle of foliage as one of the famous royal herd of deer sprang away in fear from the strange sight of two mortals in the deserted glade. As the afternoon drew on and the shadows lengthened, the two Saxon heroes were still undisturbed.

The Sheriff's men, after pursuing Robin's horse vainly some distance, had then returned to comb Sherwood Forest fruitlessly for some hours. They found no trace of their prey, and at length Walter of Weybridge was forced to call a halt.

"God knows we do not want to get caught in this devilish forest at nightfall," he cried.

Dickon Barleycorn, who had reluctantly accompanied him, agreed fervently.

"Back to the Sheriff," continued Walter. "Either the devil has swallowed up Robin Hood or else he has fallen into a quagmire[27] in the forest. Either way, we are well rid of him!"

So saying, Walter of Weybridge wheeled his horse and headed angrily for Nottingham. Little did he know how soon he was to hear more of Robin Hood.

---

25. **Yorkshire** [yôrk'shẽr]: in Robin Hood's time, the largest English county, located in the northeast section of the country.

26. **staunched** [stôncht]: stopped or checked the flow of blood from.
27. **quagmire** [kwag'mīr']: soft, muddy ground that yields under the foot.

READER'S RESPONSE

Is Fraser's Robin Hood different from the one you imagined before reading the selection? Explain.

STUDY QUESTIONS

Recalling

1. What event is the Nottingham shooting match meant to celebrate?
2. What relationship does Robin have with the Sheriff of Nottingham?
3. What warning does Robin Hood receive a few days before the shooting match?
4. What happens just after Robin Hood wins the shooting match? Why do the officials blame Robin Hood for this act?
5. What do Robin Hood and Will Scarlet do to escape the Sheriff's men?

Interpreting

6. Why do Walter of Weybridge and Guy of Gisborne seek revenge upon Robin Hood?
7. Why might the Sheriff of Nottingham be unhappy that Robin is about to turn twenty-one?
8. What was the "dark conspiracy" against Robin Hood?

Extending

9. Robin Hood is an English folk hero: He represents qualities the English people find admirable. Can you name some American folk heros?

READING AND LITERARY FOCUS

Legend

A **legend** is a story that is handed down from the past and seems to have some basis in fact. A legend usually centers on some real person, incident or a place. Most legends were passed down orally before they were written. After many retellings the characters and actions often grew larger than life.

The first written account of Robin Hood appeared in 1378, but the merry bandit was the subject of many earlier oral tales. The action in the legend occurs in a real place and time—Nottingham, England, around the end of the twelfth century. Also, the bitter enmity between the Saxons and their Norman conquerors was a historical reality at this time.

Thinking About Legend

1. King John and King Richard, brothers who are historical figures, play a role in this retelling of the Robin Hood legend. Why do you think the author includes them?
2. Which of Robin's traits and skills seem exaggerated, or larger than life, in this retelling of the Robin Hood legend?

VOCABULARY

Suffixes

A **suffix** is a word part added to the end of a word. Adding a suffix can change the meaning of a word. Suffixes are listed in most dictionaries.

You can often figure out the meaning of a word by examining its suffix. The word *inheritance,* for example, contains the suffix *-ance,* which means "what is ----ed." So *inheritance* means "what is inherited." Other suffixes and their meanings are listed below.

Suffix	Meaning
-er, -or	one who
-ity	condition or fact of being
-less	without
-ment	condition of being
-ous, -ious	full of; having much

The following words are from "Robin Hood." Copy each word, underline the suffix, and explain the meaning of the word.

1.	amazement	4.	spacious
2.	annoyance	5.	lounger
3.	guileless	6.	generosity

Thinking Skills: Evaluating

DEFINITION

Evaluating is a way of thinking about something and making a judgment about it. When you evaluate, you apply criteria to make your judgment. Criteria are the standards, rules, or tests on which a judgment can be based.

STEPS

1. **State the reason or purpose for your evaluation.**
   What do you want to evaluate? Why do you want to evaluate it?

2. **Identify the criteria.**
   What specific rules, tests, or standards will you use to make your judgment?

3. **Apply the criteria.**
   Does the subject of your evaluation meet each specific criterion? Does it meet some criteria better than others?

4. **Draw a conclusion.**
   The conclusion is your evaluation of how well the subject meets the criteria.

EXAMPLE

Imagine that your class has just heard a scientist give a speech about pollution. A classmate asks you, "Is it a good speech?" You may answer "yes" or "no" without talking about all your criteria for a good speech. In your mind, however, you make your evaluation based on criteria.

1. **State the reason or purpose for your evalua-tion.** You want to evaluate the speech in order to give your classmate an accurate answer.

2. **Identify the criteria.** You choose to evaluate the speech according to its subject, length, language, and delivery.

3. **Apply the criteria.** You think the speech has an interesting and important subject. But the speech is long and contains language that only other scientists could understand. Worse, the speech is delivered in a dull, dry manner.

4. **Draw a conclusion.** You conclude that the speech is not good even though you liked the choice of subject.

ACTIVITY 1
Evaluating "Robin Hood"

Follow the four steps of evaluating to answer the question "Is 'Robin Hood' a good story?" Identify your criteria carefully, being very specific about what you think makes a good story. You may want to include one or more of the following criteria: an exciting plot, an interesting setting, characters you care about, details that help you picture the way people lived in another time.

ACTIVITY 2
Evaluating a Work of Literature

Evaluate another selection in this book or any other work of literature that you have read. Follow the four steps. Remember that people of different cultures or ages or with different interests may have different criteria. What is important is that you think about your criteria and they reflect what you believe.

Charles Finger (1869–1941) loved adventure. He left home at an early age and wandered through Africa, South America, Mexico, the United States, and even Antarctica. He worked as a miner, a cowboy, a sailor, and a musician. At the age of fifty, Finger became a writer and began to retell the tales he had heard all over the world. One of his first books, *Tales from Silver Lands*, won the 1925 Newbery medal, an award given to the year's finest book for young readers.

What do you do when the monster in your house refuses to leave?

• •

Charles J. Finger

El Enano[1]

Everyone disliked El Enano who lived in the forest, because he always lay hidden in dark places, and when woodmen passed he jumped out on them and beat them and took their dinners from them. He was a squat creature, yellow of skin and snag-toothed and his legs were crooked, his arms were crooked, and his face was crooked. There were times when he went about on all fours and then he looked like a great spider, for he had scraggy whiskers that hung to the ground and looked like legs. At other times he had the mood to make himself very small like a little child, and then he was most horrible to see, for his skin was wrinkled and his whiskers hung about him like a ragged garment.

Yet all of that the people might have forgiven and he might have been put up with, were it not for some worse tricks. What was most disliked about his trick of walking softly about a house in the night-time while the people were inside, suspecting nothing, perhaps singing and talking. Seeing them thus, El Enano would hide in the shadows until someone went for water to the spring, then out he would leap, clinging fast to the hair of the boy or man and beating, biting, scratching the while. Being released, the tortured one would of course run to reach the house, but El Enano would hop on one leg behind, terribly fast, and catch his victim again just as a hand was almost laid on the door latch. Nor could an alarm be raised, because El Enano cast a spell of silence, so that, try as one would, neither word nor shout would come.

Then there was his other evil trick of hiding close to the ground and reaching out a long and elastic arm to catch boy or girl by the ankle. But that was not worse than his habit of making a noise like hail or rain, hearing which the people in the house would get up to close a window, and there, looking at them from the dark but

---
1. **El Enano** [el e nä′nō]: Spanish for "The Dwarf."

quite close to their faces, would be the grinning Enano holding in his hands his whiskers that looked like a frightening curtain, his eyes red and shining like rubies. That was very unpleasant indeed, especially when a person was alone in the house. Nor was it much better when he left the window, for he would hop and skip about the house yard for hours, screaming and howling and throwing sticks and stones. So, wherever he was there was chill horror.

One day, a good old woman who lived alone went with her basket to gather berries. El Enano saw her and at once made himself into a little creature no larger than a baby and stretched himself on a bed of bright moss between two trees, leafless and ugly. He pretended to be asleep, though he whimpered a little as a child does when it has a bad dream.

The good old woman was short-sighted but her ears were quick, and hearing the soft whimper she found the creature and took it in her arms. To do that bent her sadly, for Enano when small was the same weight as when his full size.

"Oh, poor thing," she said. "Someone has lost a baby. Or perhaps some wild creature has carried the tender thing from its home. So, lest it perish I will take care of it, though to be sure, a heavier baby I never held."

The dame had no children of her own and, though poor, was both willing and glad to share what she had with any needy creature. Gently she took it home and, having put dry sticks on the fire, she made a bed of light twigs which she covered with a mat of feathers. Then she bustled about, getting bread and milk for supper for the little one, feeling happy at heart because she had rescued the unhappy creature from the dismal forest.

At first she was glad to see the appetite of the homeless thing, for it soon finished the bread and milk and cried for more.

"Bless me! It must be half starved," she said. "It may have my supper." So she took the food she had set out for herself and El Enano swallowed it as quickly as he had swallowed the first bowl. Yet still he cried for more. Off then to the neighbors she went, borrowing milk from this one, bread from that, rice from another, until half the children of the village had to go on short commons[2] that night. The creature devoured all that was brought and still yelled for more and the noise it made was ear-splitting. But as it ate and felt the warmth, it grew and grew.

"Santa Maria!"[3] said the dame. "What wonderful thing is this? Already it is no longer a baby, but a grown child. Almost it might be called ugly, but that, I suppose, is because it was motherless and lost. It is all very sad." Then, because she had thought it ugly she did the more for it, being sorry for her thoughts, though she could not help nor hinder them. As for the creature itself, having eaten all in the house, it gave a grunt or two, turned heavily on its side and went to sleep, snoring terribly.

Next morning matters were worse, for El Enano was stretched out on the floor before the fire, his full size, and seeing the dame he called for food, making so great a noise that the very windows shook and his cries were heard all over the village. So to still him, and there being nothing to eat in the house, the good old woman went out and told her tale to the neighbors, asking their

2. **short commons:** reduced or meager portions of food.
3. **Santa Maria!** [sän′tə mə rē′ä]: Spanish for "Blessed Mary!"

La Garza, Luis Alvarado, c. 1980.

help and advice, and to her house they all went flocking to look at the strange creature. One man, a stout-hearted fellow, told El Enano that it was high time for him to be going, hearing which, the ugly thing shrieked with wicked laughter.

"Well, bring me food," it said, looking at the man with red eyes. "Bring me food, I say, and when I have eaten enough I may leave you. But bring me no child's food, but rather food for six and twenty men. Bring an armadillo[4] roasted and a pig and a large goose and many eggs and the milk of twenty cows. Nor be slow about it, for I must amuse myself while I wait and it may well be that you will not care for the manner of my amusement."

Indeed, there was small likelihood of anyone there doing that, for his amusement was in breaking things about the house, the tables and benches, the pots and the ollas,[5] and when he had made sad havoc of the woman's house he started on the house next door, smashing doors and windows,

---

4. **armadillo** [är′mə dil′ō]: burrowing, insect-eating animal with an armorlike shell of bony plates, sharp claws, and a long snout and tail.

5. **ollas** [ol′əs]: wide-mouthed jars or pots made of baked clay, used especially for holding water or for cooking.

tearing up flowers by the roots, chasing the milk goats and the chickens, and setting dogs to fight. Nor did he cease in his mischief until the meal was set out for him, when he leaped upon it and crammed it down his throat with fearful haste, leaving neither bone nor crumb.

The people of the village stood watching, whispering one to another behind their hands, how they were shocked at all that sight, and when at last the meal was finished, the stout-hearted man who had spoken before stepped forward. "Now sir!" said he to El Enano, "seeing that you have eaten enough and more than enough, you will keep your word, going about your business and leaving this poor woman and us in peace. Will you?"

"No. *No.* NO!" roared El Enano, each "no" being louder than the one before it.

"But you promised," said the man.

What the creature said when answering that made nearly everyone there faint with horror. It said:

"What I promised was that I would leave when I had eaten enough. I did not—"

The bold man interrupted then, saying "Well, you have eaten enough."

"Ah yes, for one meal," answered the cruel Enano. "But I meant that I would leave when I have eaten enough for always. There is tomorrow and tomorrow night. There is the day after that and the next day and the next day. There are to be weeks of eating and months of eating and years of eating. You are stupid people if you think that I shall ever have eaten enough. So I shall not leave. No. *No.* NO!"

Having said that, the creature laughed in great glee and began to throw such things as he could reach against the walls, and so, many good things were shattered.

Now for three days that kind of thing

went on, at the end of which time the men of the place were at their wits' ends to know what to do, for almost everything eatable in the village had gone down the creature's throat. Sad at heart, seeing what had come to pass, the good old woman went out and sat down to weep by the side of a quiet pool, for it seemed to her to be a hard thing that what she had done in kindness had ended thus, and that the house she had built and loved and kept clean and sweet should be so sadly wrecked and ruined. Her thoughts were broken by the sound of a voice, and, turning, she saw a silver-gray fox sitting on a rock and looking at her.

"It is well enough to have a good cry," he said, "but it is better to be gay and have a good laugh."

"Ah! Good evening, Señor Zorro," answered the dame, drying her tears. "But who can be gay when a horrible creature is eating everything? Who can be otherwise than sad, seeing the trouble brought on friends?" The last she added, being one of those who are always saddened by the cheerlessness of others.

"You need not tell me," said the fox. "I know everything that has passed," and he put his head a little sideways like a wise young dog and seemed to smile.

"But what is there to do?" asked the dame. "I am in serious case indeed. This *alocado*[6] says that he will make no stir until he has had enough to eat for all his life, and certainly he makes no stir to go away."

"The trouble is that you give him enough and not too much," said the fox.

---

6. **alocado** [ä lō cä′dō]: "wild, reckless creature"; "lunatic."

"Too much, you say? We have given him too much already, seeing that we have given him all that we have," said the old dame a little angrily.

"Well, what you must do is to give him something that he does not like. Then he will go away," said the fox.

"Easier said than done," answered the old woman with spirit. "Did we but give him something of which he liked not the taste, then he would eat ten times more to take the bad taste away. Señor Zorro, with all your cleverness, you are but a poor adviser."

After that the fox thought a long while before saying anything, then coming close to the old woman and looking up into her face, he said:

"Make your mind easy. He shall have enough to eat this very night and all that you have to do is to see that your neighbors do as I say, nor be full of doubt should I do anything that seems to be contrary."

So the good old woman promised to warn her neighbors, knowing well the wisdom of the fox, and together they went to her house, where they found El Enano stretched out on the floor, looking like a great pig, and every minute he gave a great roar. The neighbors were both angry and afraid, for the creature had been very destructive that day. Indeed, he had taken delight in stripping the thatched roofs and had desisted only when the men of the place had promised to double the amount of his meal.

Not five minutes had the fox and the dame been in the house when the men of the place came in with things—with berries and armadillos, eggs and partridges, turkeys and bread and much fish from the lake. At once they set about cooking, while the women commenced to brew a great bowl of

knot-grass[7] tea. Soon the food was cooked and El Enano fell to as greedily as ever.

The fox looked at Enano for a while, then said:

"You have a fine appetite, my friend. What will there be for the men and the

---

7. **knot-grass:** low-growing weed with a wiry stem having knotlike swellings.

women and the children and for me to eat?"

"You may have what I leave, and eat it when I end," said El Enano.

"Let us hope then that our appetites will be light," said the fox.

A little later the fox began to act horribly, jumping about the room and whining, and calling the people lazy and inhospitable.

"Think you," he said, "that this is the way to treat a visitor? A pretty thing indeed to serve one and let the other go hungry. Do I get nothing at all to eat? Quick. Bring me potatoes and roast them, or it will be bad for all of you. The mischief I do shall be ten times worse than any done already."

Knowing that some plan was afoot the people ran out of the house and soon came back with potatoes, and the fox showed them how he wanted them roasted on the hearth. So they were placed in the ashes and covered with hot coals and when they were well done the fox told everyone to take a potato, saying that El Enano, who was crunching the bones of the animals he had eaten, would not like them. But all the while the men were eating, the fox ran from one to another whispering things, but quite loud enough for Enano to hear. "Hush!" said he. "Say nothing. El Enano must not know how good they are and when he asks for some, tell him that they are all gone."

"Yes. Yes," said the people, keeping in with the plan. "Do not let Enano know."

By this time El Enano was suspicious and looked from one man to another. "Give me all the potatoes," he said.

"They are all eaten except mine," said the fox, "but you may taste that." So saying he thrust the roasted potato into the hands of Enano and the creature crammed it down its throat at once.

"Ha! It is good," he roared. "Give me more. *More*. MORE."

"We have no more," said the fox very loud, then, quite softly to those who stood near him, he added, "Say nothing about the potatoes on the hearth," but loudly enough for El Enano to hear, though quite well he knew that there were none.

"Ah! I heard you," roared El Enano. "There are potatoes on the hearth. Give them to me."

"We must let him have them," said the fox, raking the red-hot coals to the front.

"Out of the way," cried El Enano, reaching over the fox and scooping up a double handful of hot coals, believing them to be potatoes. Red hot as they were he swallowed them and in another moment was rolling on the floor, howling with pain as the fire blazed in his stomach. Up he leaped again and dashed out of the house to fling himself by the side of the little river. The water was cool to his face and he drank deep, but the water in his stomach turned to steam, so that he swelled and swelled, and presently there was a loud explosion that shook the very hills, and El Enano burst into a thousand pieces.

READER'S RESPONSE

Do you think the villagers could have found a better way to deal with El Enano? What would you have done?

STUDY QUESTIONS

Recalling

1. What does El Enano do to himself to make the good old woman take him home?
2. When does El Enano say he would be willing to leave the house?
3. What does El Enano do over the next three days to drive the villagers to their wits' end?
4. How does the fox trick El Enano?
5. What happenes to El Enano at the end of the story?

Interpreting

6. What magical or supernatural powers does El Enano have?
7. Which of El Enano's character traits make it likely that the fox's plan will work?
8. Does El Enano deserve the punishment he receives? Explain.

9. What lesson might this tale teach us about our own life?

Extending

10. Why do you think people enjoy reading stories about horrible monsters like El Enano?

READING AND LITERARY FOCUS

Plot

The **plot** is the sequence of events in a short story, novel, or play. Most plots arise from a **conflict,** or struggle, between opposing forces. The **climax** of a plot is the point of the reader's highest interest. The **resolution** reveals the plot's final outcome. For example, in "Robin Hood" Robin is in conflict with the sheriff, Guy of Gisborne, and other men in Nottingham who have created a conspiracy against him. The climax occurs when Robin's enemies try to capture him at the shooting match. The resolution reveals that Robin, although wounded, escapes to safety in Sherwood Forest.

Thinking About Plot

1. What is the main conflict, or struggle, in "El Enano"?
2. Identify the climax of "El Enano." What is the final outcome?

photograph ©1990 Jill Krementz

As a young man Italo Calvino (1923–1985) challenged himself to prepare a master collection of Italian folk tales. Searching libraries and bookstores, he filled his house with books of folklore. For months he read and reread the tales, comparing plots, characters, and language. To illustrate the major themes and ideas of Italian folklore, Calvino retold two hundred tales. "Bellinda and the Monster" is one of them.

The author described his work with folk tales as "a plunge into an unknown sea." Calvino was certain that a mysterious treasure lay at the bottom of that sea. Moreover, he was convinced that finding that treasure is absolutely essential if people are to survive.

In came the monster. Bellinda was speechless: he was far uglier than she had dared imagine.

• •

Retold by Italo Calvino
Translated by Montale Pistoiese

Bellinda and the Monster

Once upon a time in Leghorn[1] there was a merchant who had three daughters: Assunta, Carolina, and Bellinda. He was rich, and had brought his girls up in the lap of luxury. They were all three beautiful, but the youngest was so bewitchingly lovely that they had given her the name of Bellinda. Not only was she beautiful, but also kind, modest, and wise—every bit as much as her sisters were haughty, stubborn, spiteful, and always full of envy to boot.

When the girls were older, the richest merchants in town went and proposed to them, but Assunta and Carolina scornfully dismissed them. "Never will we marry a merchant!"

Bellinda, however, always had a courteous reply for her suitors. "I can't marry just now, for I'm still too young. We'll speak further of the matter when I get older."

As the saying goes, life is full of surprises. The father lost a ship with its entire cargo, and in no time he was ruined. Of all his former possessions, the only thing left was a cottage in the country. The only choice he now had was to move there with his daughters and till the soil as a farmer. Just imagine the faces the two older girls made upon hearing that. "No, indeed, Father," they said, "we're not about to move to the country. We're staying right here in town. Certain gentlemen of consequence have proposed to us."

But just let them seek out the gentlemen now! On hearing that the young ladies were left without a cent to their name, the

---

1. **Leghorn:** port city on the western coast of Italy.

sometime suitors all stole away, saying, "It serves them right! That will teach them a lesson. Now they'll get off their high horse." But equal to the men's delight over Assunta and Carolina's misfortune was everyone's sympathy for poor Bellinda, who had never turned up her nose at anyone. Two or three youths even asked her to marry them just as she was, beautiful and penniless. She wouldn't hear of it, however, for her heart was set on helping her father, whom she couldn't think of abandoning now. As things stood, she was the one who rose early in the country, did the housework, got dinner for her sisters and her father. Her sisters, however, always rose at ten o'clock and didn't lift a hand all day long. They were forever out of sorts with Bellinda, and called her "country wench,"[2] for taking such a wretched life in her stride from the start.

One day the father got a letter saying that his ship, which he had given up for lost, had reached Leghorn with part of its cargo intact. The older sisters, imagining they'd be back in town in no time and rich again, went wild with joy. Their father said, "I'm going to Leghorn now to see about recovering what is due me. What shall I bring you as a present?"

Assunta said, "I want a beautiful silk gown the color of air."

Then Carolina said, "Bring me, instead, a peach-colored gown."

Bellinda, however, remained silent and asked for nothing. Her father repeated his question, and she said, "Now is no time to be spending so much money. Just bring me a rose, and I'll be happy." Her sisters poked fun at her, but she paid no attention.

The father went to Leghorn, but just as he was about to claim his cargo, up rushed other merchants to prove he owed them money and that these goods were therefore not his. After much wrangling,[3] the poor old man was left empty-handed. But not wanting to disappoint his daughters, he drew out the little money remaining to him and bought the air-colored gown for Assunta and the peach-colored one for Carolina. Then he hadn't a cent left. The rose for Bellinda was such a little thing, he decided, that it really made no difference whether he bought it or not.

Thus he headed back to the country. He walked and walked until nightfall; entering a forest, he soon lost his way. To make matters worse, snow began falling and a strong wind arose. The merchant took refuge under a tree, expecting to be torn to bits any moment by the wolves whose howling came from all directions. While he stood there glancing around, he caught sight of a light in the distance. He made his way toward it and at length saw a handsome palace all lit up inside. The merchant went in, but not a soul was anywhere to be seen; no matter where he looked, there was absolutely no one. A fire burned brightly in the fireplace, and the merchant, who was soaking wet, paused to warm himself. Somebody will surely come in now, he thought. He waited and waited, but not a living soul appeared. The merchant saw a table laden with delicacies of every variety, so he sat down and dined. Then he took up the lamp and passed into another room, where a fine bed had been carefully made; after undressing, he climbed into it and went to sleep.

2. **country wench:** country girl of the working class.

3. **wrangling** [rang'ling]: arguing in a noisy or angry manner.

When he woke the next morning, he couldn't believe his eyes: there on the chair beside the bed lay a brand-new suit of clothes. He dressed, went downstairs and out into the garden. A magnificent rosebush was blooming in the middle of a flowerbed. The merchant remembered his daughter Bellinda's wish and decided he could now fulfill this one too. He selected the most beautiful rose and plucked it. At that moment a roar came from behind the rosebush, and in the midst of the roses appeared a monster, so ugly that the mere sight of it was enough to reduce a person to ashes. It exclaimed, "How dare you steal my roses after I've lodged you, fed you, and clothed you! You shall pay for that rose with your life!"

The poor merchant fell to his knees and explained that the flower had been intended for his daughter Bellinda, who wanted no present but a rose. Hearing the story, the monster calmed down and said, "If you have such a daughter, bring her to me. I will keep her here with me, and she will live like a queen. But if you don't send her, I will pursue you and your family wherever you happen to be."

Quaking in his boots, the little old man could hardly believe it when he was told he was free to go. But first the monster had him go back inside the palace and pick out all the jewels, gold objects, and brocades[4] that captured his fancy. These things filled a chest, which the monster would send to the merchant's house.

As soon as the merchant got back to the country, his daughters ran out to meet him. Simpering,[5] the two older girls asked

him for their presents. Bellinda, though, was truly happy over his return and as gracious as ever. He gave one of the dresses to Assunta, the other to Carolina. Then he looked at Bellinda and burst into tears as he handed her the rose and told her exactly what had happened.

The older sisters were quick to speak out. "We said so! Bellinda and her crazy ideas! A rose, mind you! Now we'll all have to suffer the consequences!"

Calm as usual, Bellinda said to her father, "The monster promised to harm none of you if I go to him? In that case I'll go, since it's better for me to sacrifice myself than for all of us to suffer."

Her father said that never, never would he take her there, and her sisters insisted she was crazy. Bellinda, though, would hear no more. She put her foot down and declared she was going.

The following morning, then, father and daughter set out at dawn. Earlier, however, upon arising, the father had found at the foot of his bed the chest with all the treasures he had selected at the monster's palace. Making no mention of it to the two older girls, he hid it under the bed.

They arrived at the monster's palace in the evening and found it all lit up. They went inside. On the first floor was a table laid for two, full of heavenly delights. Although Bellinda and her father had little appetite for these things, they nevertheless sat down to taste a few dishes. When they had finished eating, a great roar was heard, and in came the monster. Bellinda was speechless: he was far uglier than she had dared imagine. But little by little she took heart, and when the monster asked if she'd come of her own will, she answered quite frankly that she had.

The monster seemed pleased. He turned

---

4. **brocades** [brō kādz′]: elegant, heavy fabrics woven with raised designs.
5. **Simpering** [sim′pər ing]: smiling in a silly, self-conscious way.

Portrait of a Lady, Neroccio de 'Landi, c. 1490.

to the father, handed him a traveling bag full of gold, and ordered him to leave the palace at once and never set foot there again; the monster would see to it that the family had everything they needed. Heartbroken, the poor father kissed his daughter goodbye and returned home, pitifully weeping.

Left by herself (since the monster had bid her good night right after her father's departure), Bellinda undressed and got into bed and slept peacefully the whole night long, knowing she had saved her father from no telling what catastrophes.

Next morning she arose refreshed and confident, and decided to look around the palace. On the door of her room was written BELLINDA'S ROOM. On the door of her wardrobe was written BELLINDA'S WARDROBE. In each of the beautiful frocks was embroidered BELLINDA'S FROCK. And all around were placards that read:

> QUEEN ART THOU HERE,
> THY EVERY WISH TO US IS DEAR.

In the evening, when Bellinda sat down to dine, the customary roar was heard, and in walked the monster. "May I join you?" he asked.

Naturally polite, Bellinda replied, "You are the master."

"No," he said, "you are in charge here. The whole palace and everything in it are yours." He was silent for a while, as though lost in thought. Then he asked, "Am I really so ugly?"

Bellinda answered, "Ugly you are, but you have a kind heart which makes you almost handsome."

Then he asked, all of a sudden, "Bellinda, would you marry me?"

She trembled all over, not knowing what to reply. She thought, if I turn him down,

goodness knows how he will feel. Then she took heart and said, "To tell the truth, I'm not really interested in marrying you."

The monster made no comment, but bid her good night and went away sighing.

Three months passed. And every evening during that time, the monster came and asked Bellinda the same thing, if she would marry him, and then went away sighing. The girl was now so used to it that she would have been hurt if he had missed one evening.

Every day Bellinda strolled in the garden, and the monster told her about the magic of the plants. Among the trees was a leafy one known as the tree of weeping and laughter. "Whenever its leaves turn upward," explained the monster, "that means there's joy in your family; when they droop, there is weeping at home."

One day Bellinda noticed the tree of weeping and laughter with all its leaves pointed upward. She asked the monster, "Why is it so jubilant?"

"Your sister Assunta is going to get married."

"Could I go to the wedding?"

"Of course," answered the monster. "But come back in a week, or else you'll surely find me dead. Take this ring. Whenever the stone clouds up, that means I'm sick, and you must rush back to me at once. Now gather together whatever things in the palace you'd like to take along as wedding presents, and put them in a trunk this evening at the foot of your bed."

Bellinda thanked him and took a trunk and filled it with silk gowns, fine lingerie, jewels, and gold coins. She put the trunk at the foot of her bed and went to sleep. In the morning she woke up in her father's house, and there with her was the trunk she had packed the night before. Everybody

Detail, *The Departure of Silvius Aeneas Piccolomini,* Pinturricchio, 1502.

gave her a hearty welcome, even her sisters. But when they learned she was so happy and rich and the monster so kind, they were again green with envy, since they were far from wealthy themselves, in spite of the monster's presents; and to make matters worse, Assunta was marrying a mere carpenter. As spiteful as ever, they got Bellinda's ring away from her under the pretext[6] of wearing it themselves for a little while;

---

6. **pretext** [prē′tekst′]: false reason or excuse given to hide a true reason or intention.

then they hid it. Bellinda was quite upset over not being able to see the stone, and at the end of a week she wept and pleaded so with her sisters that her father ordered them to return the ring at once. As soon as she got it back she noticed the stone had become somewhat cloudy, so she left immediately for the palace.

The monster failed to appear at mealtime, and Bellinda grew worried; she looked all over for him and called and called. Only at dinner did he turn up, with a somewhat pained expression. "I was ill," he said, "and if you'd come any later, you wouldn't have found me alive. Don't you love me any more?"

"Of course I love you," she replied.

"And you would marry me?"

"That, no!" exclaimed Bellinda.

Two more months went by and the leaves again pointed upward on the tree of weeping and laughter, since this time Carolina was getting married. Bellinda went home once more with the ring and another trunk of treasures. Her sisters pretended they were glad to see her. Assunta was now meaner than ever, since her carpenter husband beat her every day. Bellinda told her sisters what a risk she had run by staying too long on her last visit, and said she couldn't tarry this time. But once more the sisters stole the ring. When they finally returned it, the stone had completely clouded over. Bellinda rushed home in alarm, but the monster showed up for neither lunch nor dinner. He came in next morning looking quite weak, and said, "I was ready to die. If you are late another time, it will be the end of me."

A few more months went by. One day, the leaves of the tree of weeping and laughter were drooping, and the tree appeared completely withered. "What's the matter at home?" Bellinda cried.

"Your father is dying," answered the monster.

"Let me go to him! I promise I'll come back on time!"

The joy of having his youngest daughter at his bedside put the poor merchant on the road to recovery. Bellinda stayed by him day and night, but one day while washing her hands she left the ring lying on the washstand and then couldn't find it when she went to put it back on. Frantic, she looked everywhere for it, and pleaded with her sisters to return it. When she finally recovered it, the stone was all black, except for a tiny dot on the edge.

She hastened to the palace, but it was pitch-dark and looked as though it had been vacant for the last hundred years. Screaming and crying, she called and called the monster, but there was no answer. She looked everywhere for him; as she was running through the garden, she suddenly saw him lying under the rosebush and breathing what seemed to be his last. She got down on her knees and listened to his heart: it was still beating but very feebly. Then she kissed him and sobbed, "Monster, if you die, I'll be lost without you! If only . . . if only you could go on living, I'd marry you at once to make you happy!"

She had not finished speaking, when all at once the whole palace lit up and music and song poured from every window. Bellinda turned around, amazed. When she faced the rosebush again, the monster had vanished and in his place, among the roses, stood a handsome knight. He bowed and said, "Thank you, dear Bellinda, for freeing me."

Bellinda was dumbfounded. "But I want the monster," she said.

The knight knelt at her feet and said, "Here is the monster. I was under a spell and obliged to remain a monster until a beautiful maiden promised to marry me the way I was."

Bellinda gave her hand to the youth, who was a king, and together they walked to the palace. At the door stood her father, who embraced her, and her two sisters. The sisters, out of spite, remained outside and became statues on each side of the door.

The young king made Bellinda his wife and queen, and they lived happily ever afterward.

READER'S RESPONSE

Do you think Bellinda missed the monster after he turned into a handsome king? Why or why not?

STUDY QUESTIONS

Recalling

1. How is Bellinda different from her sisters, Assunta and Carolina?
2. What happens when Bellinda's father picks a rose for her at the mysterious palace in the forest?
3. Why does Bellinda decide to stay at the palace?
4. How many times does Bellinda leave the castle to visit her family? What happens to the monster each time she leaves?
5. Why does the monster change at the end of the story? What happens to Bellinda?

Interpreting

6. What does Bellinda's decision to live at the palace tell you about her?
7. Why do you think Bellinda rushes back to the palace when she learns the monster is sick?
8. Describe the character of the monster. Why is the change he undergoes at the end of the tale appropriate to his character?

Extending

9. "Bellinda and the Monster" is very much like the story of Beauty and the Beast. Why do you think love stories involving gentle monsters are so popular?

READING AND LITERARY FOCUS

Cause and Effect

The events of a story are often related by cause and effect. That is, one event—**the cause**—is the reason that another event—**the effect**—takes place. In "Bellinda and the Monster," for example, the family must give up its wealthy way of life when the father loses his ship. The loss of the ship is the cause; the family's poverty is the effect.

Much of the cause and effect in "Bellinda and the Monster" is magical and supernatural. For example, the leaves of the tree turn up when there is joy in Bellinda's family. The family's joy is the cause; the turning upward of the leaves is the effect. Thinking about cause and effect will help you understand why the events in a story happen as they do.

Thinking About Cause and Effect

1. What is the cause of each of the following events? (a) The stone in Bellinda's ring becomes cloudy. (b) The leaves of the tree of weeping and laughter turn down. (c) Assunta and Carolina become jealous when Bellinda returns home for a visit.
2. What is the effect of each of the following? (a) The merchant picks the rose in the monster's garden. (b) Bellinda kisses the monster and agrees to marry him.

Portrait of a Youth,
Sandro Botticelli, early 1480s.

Bellinda and the Monster 233

Although a modern English poet, Stevie Smith (1903–1971) carried on the oral tradition of the ancient bards and troubadours. Setting her poems to music, Smith sang at music festivals across her native England. Smith also touched people with the power of her words by reading her poems to audiences in person and over the radio. Her life was the basis for the successful play and film *Stevie*.

What is an enchanted frog supposed to do while waiting for a princess to come along?

* *

Stevie Smith

The Frog Prince

I am a frog.
I live under a spell,
I live at the bottom
Of a green well.

5 And here I must wait
Until a maiden places me
on her royal pillow,
And kisses me,
In her father's palace.

10 The story is familiar,
Everybody knows it well,
But do other enchanted people feel as nervous
As I do? The stories do not tell,

Ask if they will be happier
15 When the changes come,
As already they are fairly happy
In a frog's doom?

I have been a frog now
For a hundred years
20 And in all this time
I have not shed many tears,

Detail, *Morning with Weeping Willows.*
Claude Monet, 1916–1926.

I am happy, I like the life,
Can swim for many a mile
(When I have hopped to the river)
25 And am for ever agile.

And the quietness,
Yes, I like to be quiet
I am habituated[1]
To a quiet life,

30 But always when I think these thoughts
As I sit in my well
Another thought comes to me and says:
It is part of the spell

To be happy
35 To work up contentment
To make much of being a frog
To fear disenchantment

Says, It will be *heavenly*
To be set free,
40 Cries, *Heavenly* the girl who disenchants
And the royal times, *heavenly,*
And I think it will be.

Come, then, royal girl and royal times,
Come quickly,
45 I can be happy until you come
But I cannot be heavenly,
Only disenchanted people
Can be heavenly.

---

1. **habituated** [hə bich′ o͞o āt′ id]: used to or familiar
with through habit or repeated contact.

READER'S RESPONSE

If the frog in this poem asked your advice, what would you tell him?

STUDY QUESTIONS

Recalling

1. For what is the frog waiting?
2. What does the frog like about being a frog?
3. What does the frog fear?
4. Who are the only people who can be "heavenly"?

Interpreting

5. What conflict or struggle goes on within the frog's mind?
6. How would you interpret the difference between being happy and being "heavenly"?
7. *Disenchanted* means both "set free from a spell" and "disillusioned." How does each meaning apply to the frog's situation?

Extending

8. Think of the times you have been "disenchanted" (that is, disillusioned) with people or things. How might this form of disenchantment actually be good for you?

VOCABULARY

Antonyms

Antonyms are words that have opposite or nearly opposite meanings. The words *enchanted* and *disenchanted,* for example, are antonyms. The capitalized words in the following numbered items are from "The Frog Prince." Choose the word that is *most nearly opposite* the meaning of each capitalized word, *as the word is used in the poem.* Write the number of each item and the letter of your choice on a separate sheet.

1. FAMILIAR: (a) strange (b) difficult (c) wise (d) generous
2. NERVOUS: (a) tense (b) intelligent (c) placid (d) innocent
3. AGILE: (a) overweight (b) clumsy (c) sly (d) talkative
4. QUIETNESS: (a) silence (b) popularity (c) uproar (d) kindness
5. HABITUATED: (a) disgusted (b) unaccustomed (c) carefree (d) inactive

The Mink Pond, Winslow Homer, watercolor, 1891.

As a girl in Puerto Rico, Pura Belpré (1899–1982) was thrilled by the legends and folk tales of her island home. Later, as a librarian, storyteller, and puppeteer, she shared this folklore with the children of New York City. Today Pura Belpré's many writings preserve the tales she loved and remembered from her childhood.

All at once the dog began to bark and howl.... The fisherman could not remember when he had seen his dog act so strangely.

• •

Pura Belpré

The Stone Dog

In Puerto Rico many years ago near the Condado Lagoon,[1] there lived a poor fisherman. He lived alone in a hut. His only companion was his dog.

The fisherman and his dog were devoted to each other. They might be seen strolling on the white sandy beach. Or they might be seen coming through the tangle of vines along the road that led to San Juan.[2] However, there was one place where nobody saw them together. That was in the fisherman's boat. The man never took the dog along with him.

But the dog was always beside his master as the fisherman made his little boat ready to sail. When the man pulled out to sea each morning, the dog would scamper up on the high ridge that sepa-

rated the Condado Lagoon from the open sea. There he would sit and watch all day. The dog never moved until late afternoon when he saw the little boat return. Then he would race back to the shore to greet his master. And together the man and the dog would set off for San Juan to sell the fresh-caught fish.

As the years went by, the fisherman grew older. So did the faithful dog. The fisherman still went out to sea. The dog still watched for his return, sitting on the high ridge above the lagoon.

One morning early in September, the fisherman was getting his little boat ready. All at once the dog began to bark and howl. He circled around the fisherman and tugged at his trousers. The fisherman could not remember when he had seen his dog act so strangely. He patted the dog's back, thinking the dog wanted to play. But nothing made any difference. The dog kept barking. The fisherman laughed and continued getting ready. Finally he gave the dog another

---

1. **Condado Lagoon** [kōn dä′dō lə gōōn′]: body of water surrounded by a coral reef in San Juan, Puerto Rico.
2. **San Juan** [sän hwän′]: capital and port city of Puerto Rico, in the northeastern part of the island.

The Stone Dog 237

The Wave, Marsden Hartley, 1940.

pat. Then the man climbed into the boat and sailed away. The dog went to his watching place, still barking and howling.

There were other fishing boats out that morning. The sky was blue and the breeze soft and fresh.

Suddenly the soft breeze changed. It began to flow wildly. The fisherman's boat was seized by the wind and whirled around. The sky darkened. Rain began to fall.

"It's a hurricane!" said the fisherman. "A hurricane blowing onshore!"

The man thought of his dog at once. Had the dog left the ridge and run home? Or was he still sitting there? The fisherman tried to steer his boat and turn it toward the shore. Suddenly a great wave swept over his head and tossed the boat away.

When dawn came next morning, the hurricane was over. The sky was blue once more. The sea was so calm it was hard to believe it was the same sea that had roared and raged the night before. When the sun rose over the mountains, the families of the other fishermen ran to shore. They watched for the return of the boats. They waited and waited, but none returned.

Then the people went slowly back to their homes to endure their grief and start a new life. As they rebuilt their village, no one gave a thought to the fisherman's dog.

Several months later a group of villagers was out gathering sea grapes.[3] They noticed what appeared to be the figure of a dog sitting high on the ridge above the lagoon.

"Look," said one. "Isn't that the old fisherman's dog?"

"How could it be, after all this time?" said another.

To prove his point, the first man climbed the ragged stony ridge to get hold of the dog. But when he reached the spot, he found only a rock—a rock shaped like a dog. The man came down quickly. But as soon as the people looked up again, they saw the stone dog. His head was held high. His body was alert, as if ready to spring into the sea. He just sat there on top of the ridge, waiting, waiting . . .

And there he sits today for anyone to see.

---

3. **sea grapes:** edible berries of a tropical shrub having rounded leaves and small green flowers.

READER'S RESPONSE

Do you believe the events in this legend actually happened? Why or why not?

STUDY QUESTIONS

Recalling

1. What does the dog do every day while the fisherman is out in his boat?
2. How does the dog act on the morning of the hurricane?
3. What happens to the fisherman and his boat?
4. What do the people notice on the ridge above the lagoon several months after the hurricane?

Interpreting

5. What are the dog's feelings for the fisherman?
6. Why does the dog act so strangely on that September morning?
7. What seems to have happened to the dog, and why?

Extending

8. Dogs are known for their loyalty. Do you think this loyalty is the main reason people keep dogs as pets? What other appealing traits do dogs have?

COMPOSITION

Answering an Essay Question

The **setting** is the time and place in which a story occurs. Why is the setting of "The Stone Dog" important? Write an essay answering this question. **Prewriting:** Review the selection. Then make a chart on which you list both the details of setting and the sequence of events. **Writing:** Begin with a sentence that restates the question. Then briefly summarize the action in the tale. Conclude by explaining how the setting—time and place—suits this action. Use details from the story to support your statement. **Revising:** Review your essay to see that you have expressed your ideas clearly and logically. *For help with this assignment, see Lesson 2 in the Writing About Literature Handbook at the back of this book.*

Creating a Legend

Think of a geographical feature in your community that is unusual in some way. Then use your imagination to make up a legend that explains the origin of this landmark. For example, you might explain why a lake or mountain has a special shape. You may want to begin by identifying your landmark and then relating your legend. Or you may tell your story first and then connect it to the landmark.

CHALLENGE

Research

Every community has legendary people, places, and events. Do research at a local library or historical society to find a legend about your community. Think of an entertaining way in which to share your legend with your classmates. For example, you might dramatize the legend as a radio play, or you could depict it in a diorama.

Myths, Tales, and Fabulous Beasts

Throughout the ages every society has used myths and folk tales to present certain universal themes. Some of these themes appear in this unit: the value of the past, the transforming power of love, the triumph of skill over brute force. In our own time universal themes such as these still appear in novels, short stories, poems, movies, and songs.

1. **Oral Report** Work as a group to prepare an oral report on ways in which one of the themes in this unit is still active in today's culture. First identify one theme that the group finds interesting, and then brainstorm to identify specific examples of that theme in action today. For example, if your theme is the power of love, you may cite songs, novels, movies, or current events that show the theme's continuing vitality. Research the theme, making each member of the group responsible for one aspect of the topic.

   Report the results of your research to the class. Assign a specific role in the oral presentation to each person in the group. You may want to call on members of the audience to contribute additional examples and ask questions.

2. **Collage and Display** Work as a group to create a collage and display called "Fabulous Beasts Throughout the Ages." Brainstorm in a group meeting, making lists of possible ideas for the display. Make each member of the group responsible for researching one aspect of the display. For example, you may want to consider researching fine art, popular magazines, book illustrations, children's toys, or movie creatures. Include in your display labels or signs that describe each fabulous beast and provide some interesting details about it.

Collaborative Learning:
Across the Curriculum

Myths, Tales, and Fabulous Beasts

1. **Literature and Social Studies: Group Storytelling** As a group choose a culture that interests you, and research its myths and folk tales. Discuss those myths and folk tales that each member of the group likes best, and decide on one to be read or told to the class. Whether you read the story aloud or tell it in your own words, divide it into sections, and make each student responsible for presenting one section.

   Have one student introduce the work and provide any background information that the audience would need to know in order to appreciate the tale. To add an authentic touch to the performance, research the music of the culture. One or more students may play musical instruments during the storytelling, or you may play a recording of the music in the background.

2. **Literature and Science: Research and Oral Report** Many ancient myths are believed to have been attempts to explain nature long before there were scientific explanations. For example, a story of a fire god may have been told to explain why a volcano erupted. A story of an animal may have been told to explain the particular formation of a constellation of stars.

   As a group choose a particular country, and identify several myths of that country you wish to investigate. In your research determine whether any scientific explanations have been put forth to explain each myth. You may even want to propose your own scientific explanations. Report your findings to the class, making each member of the group responsible for one part of the report. You may want to use photographs, drawings, or maps to demonstrate the scientific explanation of the myths.

Preview

A hero is a person we admire for his or her extraordinary achievements. A hero is able to achieve greatness because of certain personal qualities, such as intelligence, courage, strength, generosity, and grace. Heroes may be well-known personalities, like astronauts, Presidents, artists, or athletes. Often, however, a hero is an "everyday" person, someone like each of us. A hero may be a lifeguard who rescues a drowning swimmer or an elderly person who teaches you a valuable lesson.

The Wave Off Kanagawa, Hokusai, 1832.

Heroes and Survivors

A Model for Active Reading

Active reading is thinking as you read—the kind of work that becomes play. The more you do, the more enjoyable it becomes. Here an active reader "works and plays" through the beginning of a story.

The entire story begins on the following page. Read it as an active reader—ask questions, consider possibilities, enjoy the details.

William Saroyan

The Rescue of the Perishing

What is it that is perishing? people? animals? things?

There was a chicken hiding under a parked car on Van Ness Avenue, in the heart of town, on the first rainless day after eleven days and nights of storm, after the floods. And three cars farther down the street, there was a small dog hiding under another car.

So this story takes place in a town after a tremendous storm.

He'd never have noticed them on his way home from the public library if they hadn't been so upset about something. The chicken, a big hen with mottled black-and-white feathers, was making noises that were for all the world almost human. And the little dog, a common lost dog not more than twice the size of a cat, was whimpering the same way, making almost the same appeal.

Who is he? a man or a boy? What was he doing in the library after a flood?

It must be the chicken and the dog that are perishing.

He'd passed up the chicken, astonished that it was there at all and half believing it must belong to the owners of the car, and then he came upon the dog.

What would a chicken be doing downtown? Did the storm wash away a farm?

It was after six, the streets were almost deserted, he was late for supper. He'd been to the library, examining the whole place—not one book, not one shelf of them, but the whole library, looking into one book after another, as if he were in search of something and knew what it was but just couldn't find it.

I've had that feeling. But whatever he was looking for, I'll bet it wasn't a chicken and a dog!

At the age of fourteen William Saroyan (1908–1981) decided that he was a writer, and a year later he dropped out of school to spend time sampling the treasures in his local library. Over the course of his professional career, Saroyan published hundreds of short stories, essays, novels, and plays, which are often based on himself and his Armenian family. He believed that the "proud and angry Saroyans" reflected most of humankind. Like Saroyan's other works, "The Rescue of the Perishing" explores the basic goodness of human beings and expresses the idea that individuals are unique.

He stepped into the dining room, the dog under one arm, the chicken under the other, the eyes of both creatures open and unsure. Everybody at the table stared at the boy, the dog, and the hen.

William Saroyan

The Rescue of the Perishing

There was a chicken hiding under a parked car on Van Ness Avenue, in the heart of town, on the first rainless day after eleven days and nights of storm, after the floods. And three cars farther down the street, there was a small dog hiding under another car.

He'd never have noticed them on his way home from the public library if they hadn't been so upset about something. The chicken, a big hen with mottled black-and-white feathers, was making noises that were for all the world almost human. And the little dog, a common lost dog not more than twice the size of a cat, was whimpering the same way, making almost the same appeal.

He'd passed up the chicken, astonished that it was there at all and half believing it must belong to the owners of the car, and then he came upon the dog.

It was after six, the streets were almost deserted, he was late for supper. He'd been to the library, examining the whole place—not one book, not one shelf of them, but the whole library, looking into one book after another, as if he were in search of something and knew what it was but just couldn't find it.

Whenever he was at the public library and got to searching that way he forgot time and supper and everything else, sometimes feeling glad about his luck, about drawing nearer to what he was looking for, and sometimes feeling miserable, believing his search was hopeless.

One afternoon during the eleven-day

storm he rode out to Skaggs Bridge on his bicycle in answer to a radio appeal, riding six miles in heavy rain. There he got on a truck with twenty others, none of them under sixteen. He was twelve, and eager to prove that twelve years are enough to help in a flood. The truck traveled over muddy roads until it came to where the river was nearest flooding over.

He stayed with the men from five in the afternoon until one in the morning, and worked as hard as any of them. He stopped for coffee and sandwiches only when the others did, and together they put up a high bank.

But when the truck got back to the country store at Skaggs Bridge where he'd left his bike, the bike was gone.

He asked the old man at the store about the bike, telling where he'd put it and the kind it was. It was one he'd bought from Paul Saydak, who'd been rebuilding bikes for twenty years, working in the barn behind his house on Oleander Avenue. It was a lean bike, and strong. Paul Saydak had let him have it for $27.50, although Paul had said it was worth $35.

The old man in the store, at half past one in the morning, hardly knew what the boy was talking about, but he understood that the boy's bike had been swiped, and he couldn't help feeling upset about it. He didn't understand the part about Paul Saydak, but he went outside and let the boy point out to him where he had put the bike. Then he told the boy he hadn't been at the store at five in the afternoon, so he hadn't seen the bike at all. He said he would ask about it, though. He went to the driver of the truck and asked him to get the boy home.

The next day the boy took a bus to school, and the next afternoon he hitchhiked to Skaggs Bridge to ask at the store about his bike. But nobody knew what he was talking about, and he himself felt he was making quite a lot of a $27.50 bike in weather like that, the river free in a dozen different places and millions of dollars lost in damages of all kinds. The bike was gone, that's all. And there wasn't a great deal of interest in the fact that it *was* gone, or in the circumstances under which he had given somebody the best chance in the world to take off with it. He'd listened to the radio appeal for help, he'd got on his bike, he'd gone as fast as he could go to where they'd asked him to go, and there somebody had swiped his bike.

"The radio appeal wasn't to *you*," his father said the night after the bike had been stolen.

"I thought it was," the boy said.

"No," his father said, "it was to *me*, and I didn't go. You might have known they'd steal your bike."

"I didn't think they would."

"Well, they did. And since they did, and since they had no right to, no right even to be *tempted* to steal it—anybody at the store should have taken it inside and put it away somewhere—well, I'm going to buy you a new bike. Any kind you want. Any time you want it. Tomorrow. You pick it out and I'll buy it."

"That's not it," the boy said. "I don't want a new bike."

"Well, you've lost the old one," the man said. "Pick out the one you want and I'll buy it."

"I liked my bike because I'd bought it with money I'd earned myself," the boy said. He was a little angry with his father for being so angry with whoever had stolen the bike, and with people in general. He knew his father was sympathetic and *did* want him to have a bike, but he didn't like to see his father so angry about people and things in general. The angrier his father got with people, the kinder he became with his family.

"Perhaps it's just as well," his mother said to his father. "So few boys nowadays ride bikes to school, and motorists are so careless. Perhaps it's just as well he's had it stolen. It's always made me worry. Must you have another bike?"

"Of course he must," his father said.

"No," the boy said, "I think I'd rather not have one."

"I'm sure he doesn't want a new bike," his mother said.

"Oh, *are* you?" his father said. He turned to the boy and said, "I leave it to you. Think about it and let me know."

He rode the bus to school after that. It wasn't half as much fun as riding his bike, but it was all right. He couldn't move as freely as he'd moved for a year— for the year he'd had the bike. And every now and then he forgot that the bike had been stolen, so that when he stepped out of the house or out of school he believed he was on his way to his bike and a quick ride to wherever he was going.

Five days after the bike had been stolen, he took the bus after school and rode to town and went to the public library.

He took the place shelf by shelf, forgetting the bike and his father's anger. He read parts of plays, short stories, novels, travel books, histories, biographies, and philosophy. Everything he read seemed fresh and good and new, but not quite what he wanted, not what he was searching for. He was in the public library for

hours, sitting down at last to read a story, not knowing the name of the story or who the writer was, and not stopping until the story came to a description of a meal, making him hungry. He looked at the clock and saw that it was twenty past six. His father would be getting home in a few minutes, and supper would start in half an hour. He left the book open on the table and hurried out of the library to the street. The sky was clear and the air seemed clean and fresh, as if nobody had ever breathed it. If he waited for a bus, he might not get home any sooner than if he walked, so he decided to cut through town and enjoy a swift glance at anything he came to, and then get on home. It was a walk of about a mile and a half, but he felt like walking.

When he heard the chicken under the parked car on Van Ness Avenue, he couldn't imagine what it was that was making such a sorrowful appeal for help.

Every day the paper was full of stories about strange things that had happened during the storm, so he felt the noise had something to do with it, too. But he didn't expect it to be a chicken, and he didn't expect it to be under a car.

He was some time finding out what it was and where it was, and when he saw that it *was* a chicken under a car he didn't feel that he ought to try to do something for it. It might just belong to the people who owned the car, and they might think he was stealing it. But when he came to the whimpering dog, he knew it belonged to no one, and he was sure he couldn't just leave it there. He called to the dog, but the dog was afraid of him. It took a good three or four minutes to stop the dog from being afraid. The dog crawled out from under the car, still struggling with its fear. The boy was very gentle with the dog, speaking softly and not touching it for some time. At last he began to stroke the dog's head. The dog got to its feet and barked, but all it could manage was one little sound that was more like a cough than a bark.

He picked it up and walked back to where the chicken was.

He set the dog down on the pavement and said, "Now, you just stand there. I'm going to take you home and give you some food and a warm place to sleep, but I've got to get this chicken, too."

The dog watched him and listened to his voice, but couldn't stand still and couldn't understand. It managed to bark again once. It ran off a little, whimpering, and then came back and asked if the boy wanted it to go away.

"Now, will you just stand there a minute while I see about the chicken?" the boy said. "There's a lost chicken under the car here that I've got to take home and take care of, too."

The dog seemed to understand a little, so the boy went around to the back of the car where the hen was sitting as if it were hatching. He began to talk to it, but a bird is a bird, even if it's a hen, and a bird, even if it's lost and sick, has *got* to be afraid of a human being. The hen got to its feet, but not all the way up: not because there wasn't room enough under the car, but because in fear all creatures, even men, do not rise to their full height: only in pride or exultation do they stand very tall, as men do when they are glad about themselves or as roosters do when they are overwhelmed about themselves and must push themselves to the limits of themselves, and then, half dying with joy, crow about who they are and what they can do. The lost hen wobbled to the next car, and then to a third car, the boy going after it slowly and speaking to it softly. He had to crawl under the third car to reach the hen and bring it out.

When the dog saw the hen it began to dance, growling softly—partly, perhaps, because it was a dog and the bird was a bird and partly, perhaps, because another lost creature had been rescued.

"All right," the boy said to both of them. "Now we're going home."

The dog stayed close to the boy's heels, barking now and then, and the hen stopped being frightened. When the boy got home he picked up the dog and went in through the back door.

He stepped into the dining room, the dog under one arm, the chicken under the other, the eyes of both creatures open and unsure. Everybody at the table stared at the boy, the dog, and the hen.

"I found them," the boy said. "They

Chicken and Tree, Edouard Boubat, 1950.

were hiding under cars on Van Ness. They were both crying. I thought I'd better bring them home."

"Orphans of the storm, is that it?" the father said. "That's not a bad-looking dog."

"Can I keep them?" the boy asked.

"A dog and a chicken?" the mother said.

"They won't be any trouble," the boy said. "I'll fix up a small coop with a nest and a perch for the hen, and the dog can sleep in a box in the garage. Can I keep them?"

"Can he?" his father asked his mother.

"Can he?" the boy's kid brothers asked.

"Well," his mother said, "are you sure you *want* to? I mean, nobody keeps chickens in their yards any more, and dogs—*some* dogs—have a way of getting the people who own them into a lot of trouble."

"I'd like to keep them," the boy said. "They were lost. Nobody wanted them. I found them. They were afraid of me. I had to talk to them. It wasn't easy, especially the hen. I didn't buy them, but I do feel they are mine, and I'd like to keep them."

"Well," his mother said. She turned to his father. "Are you sure it's all right?"

"I don't know why not," his father said.

"All right," his mother said. She got up. "I'll help you put them away until after you've had your supper."

"No," the boy said, "you go ahead. They're both hungry. I'll give the dog a little warm milk to start, and the hen maybe a little rice or something. I won't be a minute."

All the same, his mother went with him to the kitchen and warmed milk for the dog. The boy set the chicken on the floor, and his mother sprinkled rice in front of it, and soon both creatures began to eat and come alive in earnest.

After supper, the boy went to the garage with his younger brothers, and they fixed the hen a small coop with a perch and a nest and the dog a little house, made out of a small box, with rags on the bottom for a bed.

While they were out in the garage, the boy's father and mother sat in the living room and talked.

"Well, so far he's said nothing about a new bike," the man said. "That bike meant everything in the world to him. You know it did."

"Yes," the woman said, "but *that* bike only. *His* bike. The bike bought with his own money. No other bike can take its place. Something else has got to."

"A stray dog and a tired old hen?" the man said.

"Well, yes," the woman said. "They're *his*. I don't think he'll ever have another bike. I don't think he'll ever want another one. The next time he saves up some money, he'll buy something else. But he did love his bike. It became part of him. He knows it's gone forever, though."

"Then I shouldn't surprise him and bring home a new one?" the man said.

"No," the woman said. "He wouldn't like it. Not *really*. Oh, he'd like it, of course, but it couldn't possibly be what his own bike was."

"Yes, I suppose so," the man said. "Well, it was quite a storm at that, wasn't it?"

"Yes," the woman said. "Everybody's talked of nothing else."

"I can't imagine," the man said, "why you allowed him to ride his bike all the way to Skaggs Bridge in the first place."

"Can you imagine my asking him *not* to?" the woman said. "He *wanted* to. It seemed silly, of course, but it wasn't silly to him, and he *did* help. I mean he did actually do the same work as everybody else."

The man saw the whole thing very clearly: he saw a boy on a bike riding to the rescue of the world, and he laughed, perhaps because it can't be done, perhaps because it must, perhaps because only a small boy can believe it's worth trying to do.

The woman laughed, too, and then both of them stopped quickly, to resume their expressions of earnestness, for they heard him down the hall with his kid brothers, all of them on their way to the living room, to report on what they had done in the brave business of rescuing the perishing.

READER'S RESPONSE

Can you think of an object that is so special to you it would be difficult to replace? Why is it so important?

STUDY QUESTIONS

Recalling

1. What does the boy do "with twenty others" during the storm? What reason does he give for doing this?
2. What reason does the boy give his father for not wanting a new bicycle?
3. What does the boy find on his way home from the library? Where does he take them?
4. List examples to show that the boy knows how to care for his "orphans of the storm."
5. What does the mother say takes the place of the lost bike?

Interpreting

6. What does the boy's refusal to get a new bike tell you about his character?
7. In what ways are the bicycle and the animals similar in their importance to the boy?
8. Which details in the story show that the mother understands the boy?
9. What does the father finally realize about the boy?

READING AND LITERARY FOCUS

The Hero

The **hero** of a story is its central character. In myths and folk tales heroes often have supernatural abilities. In modern stories heroes may be ordinary people who act in courageous or admirable ways. A reader is apt to identify with a hero because the hero's difficulties and triumphs are familiar and universal. In "The Rescue of the Perishing," the hero is a twelve-year-old boy.

Often a hero goes on a journey, usually in search of something—reaching a goal, fulfilling a desire, or solving a problem. During the journey the hero is tested or challenged in some way, and the test allows the hero to grow or to learn something new.

Thinking About the Hero

Which of the boy's character traits support the idea that he is a hero?

VOCABULARY

The Thesaurus

A **synonym** is a word that has the same or nearly the same meaning as another word. For example, the words *sad* and *gloomy* are synonyms.

A **thesaurus** is a book that contains synonyms. Many thesauruses list key words in alphabetical order, just as dictionaries do. Each key word is followed by its part of speech and synonyms.

Suppose that you want to find a synonym for *astonish.* Turn to the *A* section of the thesaurus, and locate the word. Notice that the *v.* that follows *astonish* indicates that the word is a verb. The synonyms that follow will also be verbs.

Sample Thesaurus Entry
astonish, v.—Syn. shock, amaze, astound

The following list of words is from "The Rescue of the Perishing." Copy the words onto a separate sheet, and beside each word place a synonym that has the same meaning as the word *as it is used in the story.* Use your classroom's or library's thesaurus.

1. resume (verb)
2. bank (noun)
3. sympathetic (adjective)
4. exultation (noun)

As a child growing up in Brooklyn, New York, Mary Alsop (1885–1980) longed for a horse of her own. She never got one, but she kept her affection for horses close to her heart for many years. Alsop took the pen name O'Hara when she moved to California and began her professional career as a motion-picture screenwriter. When she decided to leave Hollywood, she moved to Wyoming and started a dairy ranch. This ranch became the setting of *My Friend Flicka* and its sequel, *Thunderhead*.

"You'll go back there someday, Flicka. . . . You'll be three and I'll be eleven. . . . And we'll fly like the wind."

• •

Mary O'Hara

My Friend Flicka

Report cards for the second semester were sent out soon after school closed in mid-June. Kennie's was a shock to the whole family.

"If I could have a colt all for my own," said Kennie, "I might do better."

Rob McLaughlin glared at his son. "Just as a matter of curiosity," he said, "how do you go about it to get a *zero* in an examination? Forty in arithmetic; seventeen in history! But a *zero*? Just as one man to another, what goes on in your head?"

"Yes, tell us how you do it, Ken," chirped Howard.

"Eat your breakfast, Howard," snapped his mother.

Kennie's blond head bent over his plate until his face was almost hidden. His cheeks burned.

McLaughlin finished his coffee and pushed his chair back. "You'll do an hour a day on your lessons all through the summer."

Nell McLaughlin saw Kennie wince as if something had actually hurt him.

Lessons and study in the summertime, when the long winter was just over and there weren't hours enough in the day for all the things he wanted to do!

Kennie took things hard. His eyes turned to the wide-open window with a look almost of despair.

The hill opposite the house, covered with arrow-straight jack pines,[1] was sharply etched in the thin air of the eight-thousand-foot altitude. Where it fell away, vivid green grass ran up to meet it; and over range and upland poured the

---

1. **jack pines:** gray pines of the northern United States and Canada.

strong Wyoming sunlight that stung every-thing into burning color. A big jack rabbit sat under one of the pines, waving his long ears back and forth.

Ken had to look at his plate and blink back tears before he could turn to his father and say carelessly, "Can I help you in the corral with the horses this morning, Dad?"

"You'll do your study every morning before you do anything else." And Mc-Laughlin's scarred boots and heavy spurs clattered across the kitchen floor. "I'm disgusted with you. Come, Howard."

Howard strode after his father, nobly refraining from looking at Kennie.

"Help me with the dishes, Kennie," said Nell McLaughlin as she rose, tied on a big apron, and began to clear the table.

Kennie looked at her in despair. She poured steaming water into the dishpan and sent him for the soap powder.

"If I could have a colt," he muttered again.

"Now get busy with that dish towel, Ken. It's eight o'clock. You can study till nine and then go up to the corral. They'll still be there."

At supper that night, Kennie said, "But Dad, Howard had a colt all of his own when he was only eight. And he trained it and schooled it all himself; and now he's eleven and Highboy is three, and he's riding him. I'm nine now, and even if you did give me a colt now, I couldn't catch up to Howard because I couldn't ride it till it was a three-year-old and then I'd be twelve."

Nell laughed. "Nothing wrong with that arithmetic."

But Rob said, "Howard never gets less than seventy-five average at school, and hasn't disgraced himself and his family by

getting more demerits[2] than any other boy in his class."

Kennie didn't answer. He couldn't figure it out. He tried hard, he spent hours poring over his books. That was supposed to get you good marks, but it never did. Everyone said he was bright; why was it that when he studied he didn't learn? He had a vague feeling that perhaps he looked out the window too much; or looked through the walls to see clouds and sky and hills, and wonder what was happening out there. Sometimes it wasn't even a wonder, but just a pleasant drifting feeling of nothing at all, as if nothing mattered, as if the lessons would get done of themselves. And then the bell would ring and study period was over.

If he had a colt . . .

When the boys had gone to bed that night Nell McLaughlin sat down with her overflowing mending basket and glanced at her husband.

He was at his desk as usual, working on account books and inventories.

Nell threaded a darning needle and thought, "It's either that whacking big bill from the vet for the mare that died, or the last half of the tax bill."

It didn't seem just the auspicious moment to plead Kennie's cause. But then, these days, there was always a line between Rob's eyes and a harsh note in his voice.

"Rob," she began.

He flung down his pencil and turned around.

"Hang that law!" he exclaimed.

"What law?"

---

2. **demerits** [dē mer′its]: marks against a person for work or behavior that is unsatisfactory.

"The state law that puts high taxes on pedigreed stock. I'll have to do as the rest of 'em do—drop the papers."[3]

"Drop the papers! But you'll never get decent prices if you don't have registered horses."

"I don't get decent prices now."

"But you will someday, if you don't drop the papers."

"Maybe." He bent again over the desk.

Rob, thought Nell, was a lot like Kennie himself. He set his heart. Oh, how stubbornly he set his heart on just some one thing he wanted above everything else. He had set his heart on horses and ranching way back when he had been a crack rider at West Point;[4] and he had resigned and thrown away his army career just for the horses. Well, he'd got what he wanted. . . .

She drew a deep breath, snipped her thread, laid down the sock and again looked across at her husband as she unrolled another length of darning cotton.

To get what you want is one thing, she was thinking. The three-thousand-acre ranch and the hundred head of horses. But to make it pay—for a dozen or more years they had been trying to make it pay. People said ranching hadn't paid since the beef barons ran their herds on public land; people said the only prosperous ranchers in Wyoming were the dude ranchers;[5] people said . . .

But suddenly she gave her head a little rebellious, gallant shake. Rob would always be fighting and struggling against something, like Kennie; perhaps like herself too. Even those first years when there was no water piped into the house, when every day brought a new difficulty or danger, how she had loved it! How she still loved it!

She ran the darning ball into the toe of a sock, Kennie's sock. The length of it gave her a shock. Yes, the boys were growing up fast, and now Kennie—Kennie and the colt—

After a while she said, "Give Kennie a colt, Rob."

"He doesn't deserve it." The answer was short. Rob pushed away his papers and took out his pipe.

"Howard's too far ahead of him; older and bigger and quicker and his wits about him, and—"

"Ken doesn't half try; doesn't stick at anything."

She put down her sewing. "He's crazy for a colt of his own. He hadn't had another idea in his head since you gave Highboy to Howard."

"I don't believe in bribing children to do their duty."

"Not a bribe." She hesitated.

"No? What would you call it?"

She tried to think it out. "I just have the feeling Ken isn't going to pull anything off, and—" her eyes sought Rob's, "it's time he did. It isn't the school marks alone, but I just don't want things to go on any longer with Ken never coming out at the right end of anything."

"I'm beginning to think he's just dumb."

"He's not dumb. Maybe a little thing like this—if he had a colt of his own, trained him, rode him—"

_____

3. **drop the papers:** no longer register pedigreed horses with an association of persons who breed horses of a particular stock. The papers increase the value of the horse.

4. **West Point:** site of the United States Military Academy, located in southeastern New York State.

5. **dude ranchers:** operators of ranches that serve as resorts for tourists, offering horseback riding, swimming, and other activities.

Rob interrupted. "But it isn't a little thing, nor an easy thing to break and school a colt the way Howard has schooled Highboy. I'm not going to have a good horse spoiled by Ken's careless ways. He goes wool-gathering. He never knows what he's doing."

"But he'd *love* a colt of his own, Rob. If he could do it, it might make a big difference in him."

"*If* he could do it! But that's a big if."

At breakfast next morning Kennie's father said to him, "When you've done your study come out to the barn. I'm going in the car up to section twenty-one this morning to look over the brood mares. You can go with me."

"Can I go too, Dad?" cried Howard.

McLaughlin frowned at Howard. "You turned Highboy out last evening with dirty legs."

Howard wriggled. "I groomed him . . ."

"Yes, down to his knees."

"He kicks."

"And whose fault is that? You don't get on his back again until I see his legs clean."

The two boys eyed each other, Kennie secretly triumphant and Howard chagrined. McLaughlin turned at the door, "And, Ken, a week from today I'll give you a colt. Between now and then you can decide what one you want."

Kennie shot out of his chair and stared at his father. "A—a—spring colt, Dad, or a yearling?"

McLaughlin was somewhat taken aback, but his wife concealed a smile. If Kennie got a yearling colt, he would be even up with Howard.

"A yearling colt, your father means, Ken," she said smoothly. "Now hurry with your lessons. Howard will wipe."

Kennie found himself the most important personage[6] on the ranch. Prestige lifted his head, gave him an inch more of height and a bold stare, and made him feel different all the way through. Even Gus and Tim Murphy, the ranch hands, were more interested in Kennie's choice of a colt than anything else.

Howard was fidgety with suspense. "Who'll you pick, Ken? Say—pick Doughboy, why don't you? Then when he grows up he'll be sort of twins with mine, in his name anyway. Doughboy, Highboy, see?"

The boys were sitting on the worn wooden step of the door which led from the tack room[7] into the corral, busy with rags and polish, shining their bridles.

Ken looked at his brother with scorn. Doughboy would never have half of Highboy's speed.

"Lassie, then," suggested Howard. "She's black as ink, like mine. And she'll be fast. . . ."

"Dad says Lassie'll never go over fifteen hands."[8]

Nell McLaughlin saw the change in Kennie and her hopes rose. He went to his books in the morning with determination and really studied. A new alertness took the place of the day-dreaming. Examples in arithmetic were neatly written out and, as she passed his door before breakfast, she often heard the monotonous drone of his voice as he read his American history aloud.

---

6. **personage** [pɔr′sə nij]: person or individual, especially one of distinction or importance.

7. **tack room:** room where riding harnesses and saddles are kept.

8. **hands:** unit of measure equal to four inches, or the approximate width of the hand, used in expressing the height of a horse.

Each night, when he kissed her, he flung his arms around her and held her fiercely for a moment, then, with a winsome and blissful smile into her eyes, turned away to bed.

He spent days inspecting the different bands of horses and colts. He sat for hours on the corral fence, very important, chewing straws. He rode off on one of the ponies for half the day, wandering through the mile square pastures that ran down toward the Colorado border.

And when the week was up, he announced his decision. "I'll take that yearling filly of Rocket's. The sorrel[9] with the cream tail and mane."

His father looked at him in surprise. "The one that got tangled in the barbed wire? That's never been named?"

In a second all Kennie's new pride was gone. He hung his head defensively. "Yes."

"You've made a bad choice, son. You couldn't have picked a worse."

"She's fast, Dad. And Rocket's fast . . ."

"It's the worst line of horses I've got. There's never one amongst them with real sense. The mares are hellions and the stallions outlaws; they're untamable."

"I'll tame her."

Rob guffawed. "Not I, nor anyone, has ever been able to really tame any one of them."

Kennie's chest heaved.

"Better change your mind, Ken. You want a horse that'll be a real friend to you, don't you?"

"Yes . . ." Kennie's voice was unsteady.

"Well, you'll never make a friend of that filly. She's all cut and scarred up already with tearing through barbed wire after that mother of hers. No fence'll hold 'em . . ."

"I know," said Kennie, still more faintly.

"Change your mind?" asked Howard briskly.

"No."

Rob was grim and put out. He couldn't go back on his word. The boy had to have a reasonable amount of help in breaking and taming the filly, and he could envision precious hours, whole days, wasted in the struggle.

Nell McLaughlin despaired. Once again Ken seemed to have taken the wrong turn and was back where he had begun; stoical, silent, defensive.

But there was a difference that only Ken could know. The way he felt about his colt. The way his heart sang. The pride and joy that filled him so full that sometimes he hung his head so they wouldn't see it shining out of his eyes.

He had known from the very first that he would choose that particular yearling because he was in love with her.

The year before, he had been out working with Gus, the big Swedish ranch hand, on the irrigation ditch, when they had noticed Rocket standing in a gully on the hillside, quiet for once, and eyeing them cautiously.

"Ay bet she got a colt," said Gus, and they walked carefully up the draw.[10] Rocket gave a wild snort, thrust her feet out, shook her head wickedly, then fled away. And as they reached the spot, they saw standing there the wavering, pinkish colt, barely able to keep its feet. It gave a

---

9. **sorrel** [sôr′əl]: horse of a reddish-brown color.

10. **draw:** gully or ravine into or through which water drains.

little squeak and started after its mother on crooked, wobbling legs.

"Yee whiz! Luk at de little *flicka*!" said Gus.

"What does *flicka* mean, Gus?"

"Swedish for little gurl, Ken . . ."

Ken announced at supper, "You said she'd never been named. I've named her. Her name is Flicka."

The first thing to do was to get her in. She was running with a band of yearlings on the saddleback,[11] cut with ravines and gullies, on section twenty.

They all went out after her, Ken, as owner, on old Rob Roy, the wisest horse on the ranch.

Ken was entranced to watch Flicka when the wild band of youngsters discovered that they were being pursued and took off across the mountain. Footing made no difference to her. She floated across the ravines, always two lengths ahead of the others. Her pink mane and tail whipped in the wind. Her long delicate legs had only to aim, it seemed, at a particular spot for her to reach it and sail on. She seemed to Ken a fairy horse.

He sat motionless, just watching and holding Rob Roy in, when his father thundered past on Sultan and shouted, "Well, what's the matter? Why didn't you turn 'em?"

Kennie woke up and galloped after.

Rob Roy brought in the whole band. The corral gates were closed, and an hour was spent shunting the ponies in and out and through the chutes,[12] until Flicka was

Taming a Wild Mustang, Ernst Haas, photograph, c.1950.

left alone in the small round corral in which the baby colts were branded. Gus drove the others away, out the gate, and up the saddleback.

But Flicka did not intend to be left. She hurled herself against the poles which walled the corral. She tried to jump them. They were seven feet high. She caught her front feet over the top rung, clung, scrambled, while Kennie held his breath for fear the slender legs would be caught between the bars and snapped. Her hold broke, she fell over backward, rolled, screamed, tore around the corral. Kennie had a sick feeling in the pit of his stomach and his father looked disgusted.

One of the bars broke. She hurled herself again. Another went. She saw the opening and as neatly as dog crawls through a fence, inserted her head and forefeet, scrambled through and fled away, bleeding in a dozen places.

As Gus was coming back, just about to

---

11. **saddleback:** elevated land having a shallow depression between two points.
12. **chutes** [shōōts]: narrow, fenced passages connecting one corral with another.

close the gate to the upper range, the sorrel whipped through it, sailed across the road and ditch with her inimitable[13] floating leap, and went up the side of the saddleback like a jack rabbit.

From away up the mountain, Gus heard excited whinnies, as she joined the band he had just driven up, and the last he saw of them they were strung out along the crest running like deer.

"Yee whiz!" said Gus, and stood motionless and staring until the ponies had disappeared over the ridge. Then he closed the gate, remounted Rob Roy, and rode back to the corral.

Rob McLaughlin gave Kennie one more chance to change his mind. "Last chance, son. Better pick a horse that you have some hope of riding one day. I'd have got rid of this whole line of stock if they weren't so fast that I've had the fool idea that someday there might turn out one gentle one in the lot—and I'd have a race horse. But there's never been one so far, and it's not going to be Flicka."

"It's not going to be Flicka," chanted Howard.

"Perhaps she *might* be gentled," said Kennie; and Nell, watching, saw that although his lips quivered, there was fanatical determination in his eye.

"Ken," said Rob, "it's up to you. If you say you want her, we'll get her. But she wouldn't be the first of that line to die rather than give in. They're beautiful and they're fast, but let me tell you this, young man, they're *loco*!"[14]

Kennie flinched under his father's direct glance.

"If I go after her again, I'll not give up whatever comes, understand what I mean by that?"

"Yes."

"What do you say?"

"I want her."

They brought her in again. They had better luck this time. She jumped over the Dutch half door[15] of the stable and crashed inside. The men slammed the upper half of the door shut, and she was caught.

The rest of the band were driven away, and Kennie stood outside of the stable, listening to the wild hoofs beating, the screams, the crashes. His Flicka inside there! He was drenched with perspiration.

"We'll leave her to think it over," said Rob, when dinnertime came. "Afterward, we'll go up and feed and water her."

But when they went up afterward, there was no Flicka in the barn. One of the windows, higher than the mangers, was broken.

The window opened into a pasture an eighth of a mile square, fenced in barbed wire six feet high. Near the stable stood a wagon load of hay. When they went around the back of the stable to see where Flicka had hidden herself, they found her between the stable and the hay wagon, eating.

At their approach she leaped away, then headed east across the pasture.

"If she's like her mother," said Rob, "she'll go right through the wire."

---

13. **inimitable** [in im′ə tə bəl]: not to be imitated.
14. **loco** [lō′kō]: Spanish for "insane" or "crazy."

15. **Dutch half door:** one half of a door that divides horizontally so that the upper or lower part can be opened or closed separately.

"Ay bet she'll go over," said Gus. "She yumps like a deer."

"No horse can jump that," said McLaughlin.

Kennie said nothing because he could not speak. It was, perhaps, the most terrible moment of his life. He watched Flicka racing toward the eastern wire.

A few yards from it, she swerved, turned and raced diagonally south.

"It turned her! It turned her!" cried Kennie, almost sobbing. It was the first sign of hope for Flicka. "Oh, Dad! She has got sense. She has! She has!"

Flicka turned again as she met the southern boundary of the pasture; again at the northern; she avoided the barn. Without abating anything of her whirlwind speed, following a precise, accurate calculation and turning each time on a dime, she investigated every possibility. Then, seeing that there was no hope, she raced south toward the range where she had spent her life, gathered herself, and shot into the air.

Each of the three men watching had the impulse to cover his eyes, and Kennie gave a sort of a howl of despair.

Twenty yards of fence came down with her as she hurled herself through. Caught on the upper strands, she turned a complete somersault, landing on her back, her four legs dragging the wires down on top of her, and tangling herself in them beyond hope of escape.

"Blasted wire!" cried McLaughlin. "If I could afford decent fences . . ."

Kennie followed the men miserably as they walked to the filly. They stood in a circle watching, while she kicked and fought and thrashed until the wire was tightly wound and knotted about her, cutting, piercing and tearing great three-cornered pieces of flesh and hide. At last she was unconscious, streams of blood running on her golden coat, and pools of crimson widening and spreading on the grass beneath her.

With the wire cutter which Gus always carried in the hip pocket of his overalls, he cut all the wire away, and they drew her into the pasture, repaired the fence, placed hay, a box of oats and a tub of water near her, and called it a day.

"I don't think she'll pull out of it," said McLaughlin.

Next morning Kennie was up at five, doing his lessons. At six he went out to Flicka.

She had not moved. Food and water were untouched. She was no longer bleeding, but the wounds were swollen and caked over.

Kennie got a bucket of fresh water and poured it over her mouth. Then he leaped away, for Flicka came to life, scrambled up, got her balance, and stood swaying.

Kennie went a few feet away and sat down to watch her. When he went in to breakfast, she had drunk deeply of the water and was mouthing the oats.

There began, then, a sort of recovery. She ate, drank, limped about the pasture; stood for hours with hanging head and weakly splayed out legs, under the clump of cottonwood trees. The swollen wounds scabbed and began to heal.

Kennie lived in the pasture too. He followed her around, he talked to her. He, too, lay snoozing or sat under the cottonwoods; and often, coaxing her with hand outstretched, he walked very quietly toward her. But she would not let him come near her.

Often she stood with her head at the south fence, looking off to the mountain.

It made the tears come to Kennie's eyes to see the way she longed to get away.

Still Rob said she wouldn't pull out of it. There was no use putting a halter on her. She had no strength.

One morning, as Ken came out of the house, Gus met him and said, "De filly's down."

Kennie ran to the pasture, Howard close behind him. The right hind leg which had been badly swollen at the knee joint had opened in a festering wound, and Flicka lay flat and motionless, with staring eyes.

"Don't you wish now you'd chosen Doughboy?" asked Howard.

"Go away!" shouted Ken.

Howard stood watching while Kennie sat down on the ground and took Flicka's head on his lap. Though she was conscious and moved a little, she did not struggle or seem frightened. Tears rolled down Kennie's cheeks as he talked to her and petted her. After a few moments, Howard walked away.

"Mother, what do you do for an infection when it's a horse?" asked Kennie.

"Just what you'd do if it was a person. Wet dressings. I'll help you, Ken. We mustn't let those wounds close or scab over until they're clean. I'll make a poultice[16] for that hind leg, and help you put it on. Now that she'll let us get close to her, we can help her a lot."

"The thing to do is see that she eats," said Rob. "Keep up her strength."

But he himself would not go near her.

---

16. **poultice** [pōl′tis]: soft, moist mass of flour, mustard, herbs, or similar substances heated and applied to a wound.

"She won't pull out of it," he said. "I don't want to see her or think about her."

Kennie and his mother nursed the filly. The big poultice was bandaged on the hind leg. It drew out much poisoned matter and Flicka felt better and was able to stand again.

She watched for Kennie now, and followed him like a dog, hopping on three legs, holding up the right hind leg with its huge knob of a bandage in comical fashion.

"Dad, Flicka's my friend now; she likes me," said Ken.

His father looked at him. "I'm glad of that, son. It's a fine thing to have a horse for a friend."

Kennie found a nicer place for her. In the lower pasture the brook ran over cool stones. There was a grassy bank, the size of a corral, almost on a level with the water. Here she could lie softly, eat grass, drink fresh running water. From the grass, a twenty-foot hill sloped up, crested with overhanging trees. She was enclosed, as it were, in a green, open-air nursery.

Kennie carried her oats morning and evening. She would watch for him to come, eyes and ears pointed to the hill. And one evening Ken, still some distance off, came to a stop and a wide grin spread over his face. He had heard her nicker. She had caught sight of him coming and was calling to him!

He placed the box of oats under her nose and she ate while he stood beside her, his hand smoothing the satin-soft skin under her mane. It had a nap as deep as plush. He played with her long, cream-colored tresses; arranged her forelock neatly between her eyes. She was a bit dish-faced, like an Arab,[17] with eyes set far apart. He lightly groomed and brushed her while she stood turning her head to him whichever way he went.

He spoiled her. Soon she would not step to the stream to drink but he must hold a bucket for her. And she would drink, then lift her dripping muzzle, rest it on the shoulder of his blue chambray shirt, her golden eyes dreaming off into the distance, then daintily dip her mouth and drink again.

When she turned her head to the south, and pricked her ears and stood tense and listening, Ken knew she heard the other colts galloping on the upland.

"You'll go back there someday, Flicka," he whispered. "You'll be three and I'll be eleven. You'll be so strong you won't know I'm on your back, and we'll fly like the wind. We'll stand on the very top where we can look over the whole world, and smell the snow from the Neversummer Range. Maybe we'll see antelope. . . ."

This was the happiest month of Kennie's life.

With the morning, Flicka always had new strength and would hop three-legged up the hill to stand broadside to the early sun, as horses love to do.

The moment Ken woke, he'd go to the window and see her there; and when he was dressed and at his table studying, he sat so that he could raise his head and see Flicka.

After breakfast, she would be waiting for him and the box of oats at the gate, and for Nell McLaughlin with fresh bandages and buckets of disinfectant; and all three would go together to the brook, Flicka hopping along ahead of them, as if she was leading the way.

But Rob McLaughlin would not look at her.

One day all the wounds were swollen again. Presently they opened, one by one; and Kennie and his mother made more poultices.

Still the little filly climbed the hill in the early morning and ran about on three legs. Then she began to go down in flesh and almost overnight wasted away to nothing. Every rib showed; the glossy hide was dull and brittle, and was pulled over the skeleton as if she was a dead horse.

Gus said, "It's de fever. It burns up her flesh. If you could stop de fever she might get vell."

McLaughlin was standing in his window one morning and saw the little skeleton hopping about three-legged in the sunshine, and he said, "That's the end. I won't have a thing like that on my place."

Kennie had to understand that Flicka had not been getting well all this time; she had been slowly dying.

"She still eats her oats," he said mechanically.

They were all sorry for Ken. Nell McLaughlin stopped disinfecting and dressing the wounds. "It's no use, Ken," she said gently, "you know Flicka's going to die, don't you?"

"Yes, Mother."

Ken stopped eating. Howard said, "Ken doesn't eat anything any more. Don't he have to eat his dinner, Mother?"

But Nell answered, "Leave him alone."

Because the shooting of wounded animals is all in the day's work on the western plains, and sickening to everyone, Rob's voice, when he gave the order to have Flicka shot, was as flat as if he had been telling Gus to kill a chicken for dinner.

"Here's the Marlin,[18] Gus. Pick out a time when Ken's not around and put the filly out of her misery."

Gus took the rifle. "*Ja*, Boss . . ."

Ever since Ken had known that Flicka was to be shot, he had kept his eye on the rack which held the firearms. His father allowed no firearms in the bunkhouse. The gun rack was in the dining room of the ranch house; and, going through it to the kitchen three times a day for meals, Ken's eye scanned the weapons to make sure that they were all there.

That night they were not all there. The Marlin rifle was missing.

When Kennie saw that, he stopped walking. He felt dizzy. He kept staring at the gun rack, telling himself that it surely was there—he counted again and again—he couldn't see clearly—

Then he felt an arm across his shoulders and heard his father's voice.

"I know, son. Some things are awful hard to take. We just have to take 'em. I have to, too."

Kennie got hold of his father's hand and held on. It helped steady him.

Finally he looked up. Rob looked down and smiled at him and gave him a little shake and squeeze. Ken managed a smile too.

"All right now?"

"All right, Dad."

They walked in to supper together.

Ken even ate a little. But Nell looked thoughtfully at the ashen color of his face and at the little pulse that was beating in the side of his neck.

After supper he carried Flicka her oats, but he had to coax her and she would only eat a little. She stood with her head hanging, but when he stroked it and talked to her, she pressed her face into his chest and was content. He could feel the burning heat of her body. It didn't seem possible that anything so thin could be alive.

Presently Kennie saw Gus come into the pasture carrying the Marlin. When he saw Ken, he changed his direction and sauntered along as if he was out to shoot some cottontails.

Ken ran to him. "When are you going to do it, Gus?"

"Ay was goin' down soon now, before it got dark . . ."

"Gus, don't do it tonight. Wait till morning. Just one more night, Gus."

"Vell, in de morning den, but it got to be done, Ken. Yer fader gives de order."

"I know. I won't say anything more."

An hour after the family had gone to bed, Ken got up and put on his clothes. It was a warm moonlit night. He ran down to the brook, calling softly. "Flicka! Flicka!"

But Flicka did not answer with a little nicker; and she was not in the nursery, nor hopping about the pasture. Ken hunted for an hour.

At last he found her down the creek, lying in the water. Her head had been on the bank, but as she lay there, the current of the stream had sucked and pulled

18. **Marlin:** a type of gun.

at her, and she had had no strength to resist; and little by little her head had slipped down until when Ken got there only the muzzle was resting on the bank, and the body and legs were swinging in the stream.

Kennie slid into the water, sitting on the bank, and he hauled at her head. But she was heavy and the current dragged like a weight; and he began to sob because he had no strength to draw her out.

Then he found a leverage for his heels against some rocks in the bed of the stream, and he braced himself against these, and pulled with all his might; and

her head came up onto his knees, and he held it cradled in his arms.

He was glad that she had died of her own accord, in the cool water, under the moon, instead of being shot by Gus. Then, putting his face close to hers, and looking searchingly into her eyes, he saw that she was alive and looking back at him.

And then he burst out crying, and hugged her, and said, "Oh, my little Flicka, my little Flicka."

The long night passed.

The moon slid slowly across the heavens.

The water rippled over Kennie's legs,

and over Flicka's body. And gradually the heat and fever went out of her. And the cool running water washed and washed her wounds.

When Gus went down in the morning with the rifle, they hadn't moved. There they were, Kennie sitting in water over his thighs and hips, with Flicka's head in his arms.

Gus seized Flicka by the head, and hauled her out on the grassy bank, and then, seeing that Kennie couldn't move, cold and stiff and half-paralyzed as he was, lifted him in his arms and carried him to the house.

"Gus," said Ken through chattering teeth, "don't shoot her, Gus."

"It ain't fur me to say, Ken. You know dat."

"But the fever's left her, Gus."

"Ay wait a little, Ken . . ."

Rob McLaughlin drove to Laramie[19] to get the doctor, for Ken was in violent chills that would not stop. His mother had him in bed wrapped in hot blankets when they got back.

He looked at his father imploringly as the doctor shook down the thermometer.

"She might get well now, Dad. The fever's left her. It went out of her when the moon went down."

"All right, son. Don't worry. Gus'll feed her, morning and night, as long as she's . . ."

"As long as I can't do it," finished Kennie happily.

The doctor put the thermometer in his mouth and told him to keep it shut.

All day Gus went about his work,

thinking of Flicka. He had not been back to look at her. He had been given no more orders. If she was alive, the order to shoot her was still in effect. But Kennie was ill, McLaughlin making his second trip to town taking the doctor home, and would not be back till long after dark.

After their supper in the bunkhouse, Gus and Tim walked down to the brook. They did not speak as they approached the filly, lying stretched out flat on the grassy bank, but their eyes were straining at her to see if she was dead or alive.

She raised her head as they reached her.

"By the powers!" exclaimed Tim, "there she is!"

She dropped her head, raised it again, and moved her legs and became tense as if struggling to rise. But to do so she must use her right hind leg to brace herself against the earth. That was the damaged leg, and at the first bit of pressure with it, she gave up and fell back.

"We'll swing her on to the other side," said Tim. "Then she can help herself."

"*Ja* . . ."

Standing behind her, they leaned over, grabbed hold of her left legs, front and back, and gently hauled her over. Flicka was as lax and willing as a puppy. But the moment she found herself lying on her right side, she began to scramble, braced herself with her good left leg and tried to rise.

"Yee whiz!" said Gus. "She got plenty strength yet."

"Hi!" cheered Tim. "She's up!"

But Flicka wavered, slid down again, and lay flat. This time she gave notice that she would not try again by heaving a deep sigh and closing her eyes.

Gus took his pipe out of his mouth

---

19. **Laramie** [lar′ə mē]: city in southeastern Wyoming.

and thought it over. Orders or no orders, he would try to save the filly. Ken had gone too far to be let down.

"Ay'm goin' to rig a blanket sling fur her, Tim, and get her on her feet and keep her up."

There was bright moonlight to work by. They brought down the posthole digger and set two aspen poles deep into the ground either side of the filly, then, with ropes attached to the blanket, hoisted her by a pulley.

Not at all disconcerted, she rested comfortably in the blanket under her belly, touched her feet on the ground, and reached for the bucket of water Gus held for her.

Kennie was sick a long time. He nearly died. But Flicka picked up. Every day Gus passed the word to Nell, who carried it to Ken. "She's cleaning up her oats." "She's out of the sling." "She bears a little weight on the bad leg."

Tim declared it was a real miracle. They argued about it, eating their supper.

"Na," said Gus. "It was de cold water, washin' de fever outa her. And more dan dot—it was Ken—you tink it don't count? All night dot boy sits dere, and says, 'Hold on, Flicka. Ay'm here wid you. Ay'm standin' by, two of us togeder' . . ."

Tim stared at Gus without answering, while he thought it over. In the silence, a coyote yapped far off on the plains; and the wind made a rushing sound high up in the jack pines on the hill.

Gus filled his pipe.

"Sure," said Tim finally. "Sure. That's it."

Then came the day when Rob McLaughlin stood smiling at the foot of Kennie's bed and said, "Listen! Hear your friend?"

Ken listened and heard Flicka's high, eager whinny.

"She don't spend much time by the brook any more. She's up at the gate of the corral half the time, nickering for you."

"For me!"

Rob wrapped a blanket around the boy and carried him out to the corral gate.

Kennie gazed at Flicka. There was a look of marveling in his eyes. He felt as if he had been living in a world where everything was dreadful and hurting but awfully real; and *this* couldn't be real; this was all soft and happy, nothing to struggle over or worry about or fight for any more. Even his father was proud of him! He could feel it in the way Rob's big arms held him. It was all like a dream and far away. He couldn't, yet, get close to anything.

But Flicka—Flicka—alive, well, pressing up to him, recognizing him . . .

Kennie put out a hand—weak and white—and laid it on her face. His thin little fingers straightened her forelock the way he used to do, while Rob looked at the two with a strange expression about his mouth, and a glow in his eyes that was not often there.

"She's still poor, Dad, but she's on four legs now."

"She's picking up."

Ken turned his face up, suddenly remembering. "Dad! She did get gentled, didn't she?"

"Gentle—as—a kitten . . ."

They put a cot down by the brook for Ken, and boy and filly got well together.

READER'S RESPONSE

Do you think Kennie should have followed his father's advice and chosen a horse other than Flicka? Why or why not?

STUDY QUESTIONS

Recalling

1. What reasons does Kennie give Rob for wanting a colt of his own?
2. What is Rob's opinion of Kennie's choice? What reasons does he give for his opinion?
3. List three examples that show Flicka's determination to escape capture.
4. What does Kennie do to show Flicka he is her friend? What does Flicka do that shows her feelings for Kennie?
5. What order does Rob give Gus? What reason does he give for doing so?
6. What does Kennie do to save Flicka?

Interpreting

7. In what ways does Kennie change during the course of the story? In what ways does Flicka change?
8. Which of Rob's words and actions show that he finally believes Kennie and Flicka belong together?

Extending

9. Is there some person, animal, or thing for which you are responsible? What has this responsibility taught you?

READING AND LITERARY FOCUS

Characterization

Characterization refers to the personality of a character in a literary work. The term also refers to the method an author uses to reveal that personality to the reader. Sometimes the author makes clear statements about the character's personality. For example, when O'Hara tells us that Kennie "took things hard," she is making a direct statement about Kennie's character.

More often an author reveals a character's personality indirectly, by letting the character's words and actions speak for themselves. We can then form our own opinions about the character. We gain insight into Flicka's personality when the author describes how the colt "hurled herself against the poles which walled the corral. She tried to jump them. They were seven feet high." We can see that Flicka is a determined, fiery animal.

Thinking About Characterization

1. Find two more direct statements that the author makes about Kennie.
2. Find one example of Kennie's words and one example of his actions that convey information about his character. What do you learn from each?

COMPOSITION

Writing a Character Sketch

Write a character sketch of Kennie in which you discuss his outstanding personality traits. **Prewriting:** Take notes on Kennie's actions, thoughts, words, and feelings. Use your notes to determine three traits that you want to write about. **Writing:** Illustrate each trait with examples from your prewriting notes. **Revising:** Review your sketch to see that you have expressed your ideas clearly and logically. *For help with this assignment, see Lesson 3 in the Writing About Literature Handbook at the back of this book.*

Creating a Character

In a paragraph or two create a character who possesses the personality trait you most admire, such as courage, leadership, or loyalty. Describe a specific event that will allow the character to reveal his or her special quality. Be sure that the character's words, actions, and thoughts demonstrate this trait.

When Joseph Bruchac [brōō′ shak] (born 1942) finished college, he spent three years teaching in Africa. While there he realized "how much we have as Americans and take for granted." Many of Bruchac's African experiences are reflected in his poetry. In addition to poems, he has written short stories, folk tales, and a novel, and he has recorded an album of songs. Nature and Native American culture often inspire his writing. You will see how these two inspirations helped create an important message in "Birdfoot's Grampa."

Would you go out of your way to save the life of an animal?

Joseph Bruchac

Birdfoot's Grampa

The Old Man
must have stopped our car
two dozen times to climb out
and gather into his hands
5 the small toads blinded
by our lights and leaping
like live drops of rain.

The rain was falling,
a mist around his white hair,
10 and I kept saying,
"You can't save them all,
accept it, get in,
we've got places to go."

But, leathery hands full
15 of wet brown life,
knee deep in the summer
roadside grass,
he just smiled and said,
"They have places to go, too."

READER'S RESPONSE

Why might it be significant that the person saving the toads' lives is elderly?

STUDY QUESTIONS

Recalling

1. What does the Old Man do many times? What words does the poet use to describe the toads' movements?

2. What words does the poet use to describe the Old Man's appearance?

3. In the second stanza, what reason does the speaker give for wanting the Old Man to stay in the car?

4. With what words does the speaker describe the toads in the last stanza? What does the Old Man say about them?

Interpreting

5. Why do you think the poet capitalizes the words *old man*?

6. What do the Old Man's actions in the first stanza tell you about his character?

7. What do the speaker's words in the second stanza tell you about the Old Man's character?

8. What lesson might the speaker draw from the Old Man's words in the last line?

Extending

9. What important lesson or idea have you learned from an older person?

VOCABULARY

Analogies

Analogies are comparisons that are stated as double relationships: for example, *A* is to *B* as *C* is to *D*. On tests analogies are written as two pairs of words, *A* : *B* :: *C* : *D*.

You may be given the first pair and asked to find or complete a second pair, which will have the same kind of relationship. For example, in the analogy COOL : COLD :: DAMP : WET, the words in each pair name different degrees of the same quality. Analogies can describe many different kinds of relationships, such as synonyms (YELL : SCREAM) and antonyms (IN : OUT).

The following numbered items are incomplete analogies. The third word in each item comes from "Birdfoot's Grampa." Decide how the first two words in each item are related. Then, from the four choices that follow each item, choose the word that best completes the second pair.

1. UNDER : OVER :: SMILED :
   (a) happy   (c) laughed
   (b) frowned   (d) spoke

2. LARGE : GIGANTIC :: SMALL :
   (a) tiny   (c) ant
   (b) doll   (d) huge

3. SNOW : BLIZZARD :: RAIN :
   (a) drizzle   (c) hurricane
   (b) tornado   (d) wind

4. SPRINTING : RUNNING :: LEAPING :
   (a) high   (c) fast
   (b) falling   (d) jumping

> **"None of the other tribes make girls go through the endurance ritual," I complained to my mother.**

● ●

Mary Whitebird

Ta-Na-E-Ka

As my birthday drew closer, I had awful nightmares about it. I was reaching the age at which all Kaw Indians[1] had to participate in Ta-Na-E-Ka. Well, not all Kaws. Many of the younger families on the reservation were beginning to give up the old customs. But my grandfather, Amos Deer Leg, was devoted to tradition. He still wore handmade beaded moccasins instead of shoes, and kept his iron gray hair in tight braids. He could speak English, but he spoke it only with white men. With his family he used a Sioux[2] dialect.

Grandfather was one of the last living Indians (he died in 1953 when he was eighty-one) who actually fought against the U.S. Cavalry.[3] Not only did he fight, he was wounded in a skirmish at Rose Creek—a famous encounter in which the celebrated Kaw chief Flat Nose lost his life. At the time, my grandfather was only eleven years old.

Eleven was a magic word among the Kaws. It was the time of Ta-Na-E-Ka, the "flowering of adulthood." It was the age, my grandfather informed us hundreds of times, "when a boy could prove himself to be a warrior and a girl took the first steps to womanhood."

"I don't want to be a warrior," my cousin, Roger Deer Leg, confided to me. "I'm going to become an accountant."

"None of the other tribes make girls go through the endurance ritual," I complained to my mother.

"It won't be as bad as you think, Mary," my mother said, ignoring my protests. "Once you've gone through it, you'll certainly never forget it. You'll be proud."

I even complained to my teacher, Mrs. Richardson, feeling that, as a white woman, she would side with me.

She didn't. "All of us have rituals of one kind or another," Mrs. Richardson said. "And look at it this way: how many girls have the opportunity to compete on equal terms with boys? Don't look down on your heritage."

Heritage, indeed! I had no intention of living on a reservation for the rest of my life. I was a good student. I loved school. My fantasies were about knights in armor and fair ladies in flowing gowns being

1. **Kaw Indians:** North American Indian tribe that lived along the Kansas River in eastern Kansas; also known as the Kansa Indians.
2. **Sioux** [sōō]: family of North American Indian tribes, of which the Kaw Indians are a subtribe, formerly living in Minnesota, North and South Dakota, and Wyoming.
3. **Cavalry** [kav′əl rē]: military unit trained to fight on horseback.

saved from dragons. It never once occurred to me that being Indian was exciting.

But I've always thought that the Kaw were the originators of the women's liberation movement. No other Indian tribe— and I've spent half a lifetime researching the subject—treated women more "equally" than the Kaw. Unlike most of the subtribes of the Sioux Nation, the Kaw allowed men and women to eat together. And hundreds of years before we were "acculturated,"[4] a Kaw woman had the right to refuse a prospective husband even if her father arranged the match.

The wisest women (generally wisdom was equated with age) often sat in tribal councils. Furthermore, most Kaw legends revolve around "Good Woman," a kind of supersquaw, a Joan of Arc[5] of the high plains. Good Woman led Kaw warriors into battle after battle from which they always seemed to emerge victorious.

And girls as well as boys were required to undergo Ta-Na-E-Ka.

The actual ceremony varied from tribe to tribe, but since the Indians' life on the plains was dedicated to survival, Ta-Na-E-Ka was a test of survival.

"Endurance is the loftiest virtue of the Indian," my grandfather explained. "To survive, we must endure. When I was a boy, Ta-Na-E-Ka was more than the mere symbol it is now. We were painted white with the juice of a sacred herb and sent

naked into the wilderness without so much as a knife. We couldn't return until the white had worn off. It wouldn't wash off. It took almost eighteen days, and during that time we had to stay alive, trapping food, eating insects and roots and berries, and watching out for enemies. And we did have enemies—both the white soldiers and the Omaha[6] warriors, who were always trying to capture Kaw boys and girls undergoing their endurance test. It was an exciting time."

"What happened if you couldn't make it?" Roger asked. He was born only three days after I was, and we were being trained for Ta-Na-E-Ka together. I was happy to know he was frightened too.

"Many didn't return," Grandfather said. "Only the strongest and shrewdest. Mothers were not allowed to weep over those who didn't return. If a Kaw couldn't survive, he or she wasn't worth weeping over. It was our way."

"What a lot of hooey," Roger whispered. "I'd give anything to get out of it."

"I don't see how we have any choice," I replied.

Roger gave my arm a little squeeze. "Well, it's only five days."

Five days! Maybe it was better than being painted white and sent out naked for eighteen days. But not much better.

We were to be sent, barefoot and in bathing suits, into the woods. Even our very traditional parents put their foot down when Grandfather suggested we go naked. For five days we'd have to live off the land, keeping warm as best we could,

---

4. **"acculturated"** [ə kul′ chə rā′ tid]: blended into another culture by gradually adopting the other culture's customs and distinctive qualities.

5. **Joan of Arc** [jōn′ əv ark′]: French national heroine and military leader who led French troops to victory over the English and was later condemned as a witch and burned at the stake (1412–1431).

6. **Omaha** [ō′ mə hô′]: North American Indian tribe, part of the Sioux Nation, formerly living in Nebraska and Iowa, now living in Nebraska.

getting food where we could. It was May, but on the northernmost reaches of the Missouri River the days were still chilly and the nights were fiercely cold.

Grandfather was in charge of the month's training for Ta-Na-E-Ka. One day he caught a grasshopper and demonstrated how to pull its legs and wings off in one flick of the fingers and how to swallow it.

I felt sick, and Roger turned green. "It's a darn good thing it's 1947," I told Roger teasingly. "You'd make a terrible warrior." Roger just grimaced.

I knew one thing. This particular Kaw Indian girl wasn't going to swallow a grasshopper, no matter how hungry she got. And then I had an idea. Why hadn't I thought of it before? It would have saved nights of bad dreams about squooshy grasshoppers.

I headed straight for my teacher's house. "Mrs. Richardson," I said, "would you lend me five dollars?"

"Five dollars!" she exclaimed. "What for?"

"You remember the ceremony I talked about?"

"Ta-Na-E-Ka. Of course. Your parents have written me and asked me to excuse you from school so you can participate in it."

"Well, I need some things for the ceremony," I replied, in a half-truth. "I don't want to ask my parents for the money."

"It's not a crime to borrow money, Mary. But how can you pay it back?"

"I'll baby-sit for you ten times."

"That's more than fair," she said, going to her purse and handing me a crisp new five-dollar bill. I'd never had that much money at once.

"I'm happy to know the money's going

to be put to a good use," Mrs. Richardson said.

A few days later, the ritual began with a long speech from my grandfather about how we had reached the age of decision, how we now had to fend for ourselves and prove that we could survive the most horrendous of ordeals. All the friends and relatives who had gathered at our house for dinner made jokes about their own Ta-Na-E-Ka experiences. They all advised us to fill up now, since for the next five days we'd be gorging ourselves on crickets. Neither Roger nor I was very hungry. "I'll probably laugh about this when I'm an accountant," Roger said, trembling.

"Are you trembling?" I asked.

"What do you think?"

"I'm happy to know boys tremble too," I said.

At six the next morning we kissed our parents and went off to the woods. "Which side do you want?" Roger asked. According to the rules, Roger and I would stake out "territories" in separate areas of the woods, and we weren't to communicate during the entire ordeal.

"I'll go toward the river, if it's okay with you," I said.

"Sure," Roger answered. "What difference does it make?"

To me, it made a lot of difference. There was a marina a few miles up the river and there were boats moored there. At least, I hoped so. I figured that a boat was a better place to sleep than under a pile of leaves.

"Why do you keep holding your head?" Roger asked.

"Oh, nothing. Just nervous," I told him. Actually, I was afraid I'd lose the five-dollar bill, which I had tucked into my hair with a bobby pin. As we came to a fork in the trail, Roger shook my hand. "Good luck, Mary."

"*N'ko-n'ta*," I said. It was the Kaw word for courage.

The sun was shining and it was warm, but my bare feet began to hurt immediately. I spied one of the berry bushes Grandfather had told us about. "You're lucky," he had said. "The berries are ripe in the spring, and they are delicious and nourishing." They were orange and fat and I popped one into my mouth.

Argh! I spat it out. It was awful and bitter, and even grasshoppers were probably better tasting, although I never intended to find out.

I sat down to rest my feet. A rabbit hopped out from under the berry bush. He nuzzled the berry I'd spat out and ate it. He picked another one and ate that too. He liked them. He looked at me, twitching his nose. I watched a redheaded woodpecker bore into an elm tree and I caught a glimpse of a civet cat[7] waddling through some twigs. All of a sudden I realized I was no longer frightened. Ta-Na-E-Ka might be more fun than I'd anticipated. I got up and headed toward the marina.

"Not one boat," I said to myself dejectedly. But the restaurant on the shore, "Ernie's Riverside," was open. I walked in, feeling silly in my bathing suit. The man at the counter was big and tough-looking. He wore a sweat shirt with the words "Fort Sheridan, 1944," and he had only three fingers on one of his hands. He asked me what I wanted.

"A hamburger and a milk shake," I said, holding the five-dollar bill in my hand so he'd know I had money.

"That's a pretty heavy breakfast, honey," he murmured.

"That's what I always have for breakfast," I lied.

"Forty-five cents," he said, bringing me the food. (Back in 1947, hamburgers were twenty-five cents and milk shakes were twenty cents.) "Delicious," I thought. "Better'n grasshoppers—and Grandfather never once mentioned that I couldn't eat hamburgers."

While I was eating, I had a grand idea. Why not sleep in the restaurant? I went to the ladies' room and made sure the window was unlocked. Then I went back outside and played along the riverbank, watching the water birds and trying to identify each one. I planned to look for a beaver dam the next day.

The restaurant closed at sunset, and I watched the three-fingered man drive away. Then I climbed in the unlocked window. There was a night light on, so I didn't turn on any lights. But there was a radio on the counter. I turned it on to a music program. It was warm in the restaurant, and I was hungry. I helped myself to a glass of milk and a piece of pie, intending to keep a list of what I'd eaten so I could leave money. I also planned to get up early, sneak out through the window, and head for the woods before the three-fingered man returned. I turned off the radio, wrapped myself in the man's apron, and, in spite of the hardness of the floor, fell asleep.

"What the heck are you doing here, kid?"

It was the man's voice.

It was morning. I'd overslept. I was scared.

---

7. **civet** [siv'it] **cat:** in North America, a variety of small, spotted skunk.

"Hold it, kid. I just wanna know what you're doing here. You lost? You must be from the reservation. Your folks must be worried sick about you. Do they have a phone?"

"Yes, yes," I answered. "But don't call them."

I was shivering. The man, who told me his name was Ernie, made me a cup of hot chocolate while I explained about Ta-Na-E-Ka.

"Darndest thing I ever heard," he said, when I was through. "Lived next to the reservation all of my life and this is the first I've heard of Ta-Na-whatever-you-call-it." He looked at me, all goosebumps in my bathing suit. "Pretty silly thing to do to a kid," he muttered.

That was just what I'd been thinking for months, but when Ernie said it, I became angry. "No, it isn't silly. It's a custom of the Kaw. We've been doing this for hundreds of years. My mother and my grandfather and everybody in my family went through this ceremony. It's why the Kaw are great warriors."

"Okay, great warrior," Ernie chuckled, "suit yourself. And, if you want to stick around, it's okay with me." Ernie went to the broom closet and tossed me a bundle. "That's the lost-and-found closet," he said. "Stuff people left on boats. Maybe there's something to keep you warm."

The sweater fitted loosely, but it felt good. I felt good. And I'd found a new friend. Most important, I was surviving Ta-Na-E-Ka.

My grandfather had said the experience would be filled with adventure, and I was having my fill. And Grandfather had never said we couldn't accept hospitality.

I stayed at Ernie's Riverside for the entire period. In the mornings I went into

Boats and Car Track, William Glackens, c. 1915.

the woods and watched the animals and picked flowers for each of the tables in Ernie's. I had never felt better. I was up early enough to watch the sun rise on the Missouri, and I went to bed after it set. I ate everything I wanted—insisting that Ernie take all my money for the food. "I'll keep this in trust for you, Mary," Ernie promised, "in case you are ever desperate for five dollars."

I was sorry when the five days were over. I'd enjoyed every minute with Ernie. He taught me how to make western omelets and to make Chili Ernie Style (still one of my favorite dishes). And I told Ernie all about the legends of the Kaw. I hadn't realized I knew so much about my people.

But Ta-Na-E-Ka was over, and as I approached my house at about nine-thirty in the evening, I became nervous all over again. What if Grandfather asked me about the berries and the grasshoppers? And my feet were hardly cut. I hadn't lost a pound and my hair was combed.

"They'll be so happy to see me," I told

myself hopefully, "that they won't ask too many questions."

I opened the door. My grandfather was in the front room. He was wearing the ceremonial beaded deerskin shirt which had belonged to *his* grandfather. "*N'g'da'ma*," he said. "Welcome back."

I embraced my parents warmly, letting go only when I saw my cousin Roger sprawled on the couch. His eyes were red and swollen. He'd lost weight. His feet were an unsightly mass of blood and blisters, and he was moaning: "I made it, see. I made it. I'm a warrior. A warrior."

My grandfather looked at me strangely. I was clean, obviously well-fed, and radiantly healthy. My parents got the message. My uncle and aunt gazed at me with hostility.

Finally my grandfather asked, "What did you eat to keep you so well?"

I sucked in my breath and blurted out the truth: "Hamburgers and milk shakes."

"Hamburgers!" my grandfather growled.

"Milk shakes!" Roger moaned.

"You didn't say we *had* to eat grasshoppers," I said sheepishly.

"Tell us about your Ta-Na-E-Ka," my grandfather commanded.

I told them everything, from borrowing the five dollars, to Ernie's kindness, to observing the beaver.

"That's not what I trained you for," my grandfather said sadly.

I stood up. "Grandfather, I learned that Ta-Na-E-Ka *is* important. I didn't think so during training. I was scared stiff of it. I handled it my way. And I learned I had

nothing to be afraid of. There's no reason in 1947 to eat grasshoppers when you can eat a hamburger."

I was inwardly shocked at my own audacity. But I liked it. "Grandfather, I'll bet you never ate one of those rotten berries yourself."

Grandfather laughed! He laughed aloud! My mother and father and aunt and uncle were all dumbfounded. Grandfather never laughed. Never.

"Those berries—they are terrible," Grandfather admitted. "I could never swallow them. I found a dead deer on the first day of my Ta-Na-E-Ka—shot by a soldier, probably—and he kept my belly full for the entire period of the test!"

Grandfather stopped laughing. "We should send you out again," he said.

I looked at Roger. "You're pretty smart, Mary," Roger groaned. "I'd never have thought of what you did."

"Accountants just have to be good at arithmetic," I said comfortingly. "I'm terrible at arithmetic."

Roger tried to smile, but couldn't. My grandfather called me to him. "You should have done what your cousin did. But I think you are more alert to what is happening to our people today than we are. I think you would have passed the test under any circumstances, in any time. Somehow, you know how to exist in a world that wasn't made for Indians. I don't think you're going to have any trouble surviving."

Grandfather wasn't entirely right. But I'll tell about that another time.

READER'S RESPONSE

Do you think Grandfather should have sent Mary out again? Why or why not?

STUDY QUESTIONS

Recalling

1. What does Grandfather say is "the loftiest virtue of the Indian"?
2. List at least three examples that demonstrate equal treatment of men and women in the Kaw tribe.
3. Where does Mary find food and shelter during Ta-Na-E-Ka?
4. In what ways does Mary's and Roger's appearance differ after Ta-Na-E-Ka?
5. What reason does Grandfather give Mary for his opinion that she'll have no trouble surviving in the world?

Interpreting

6. Why do you think Mary becomes angry when Ernie criticizes the Kaw ritual?
7. In what way does Mary prove that she can survive in the modern world?

Extending

8. What kinds of rituals or rites of passage exist for young people today?

READING AND LITERARY FOCUS

Stated Theme

An author usually writes a story in order to communicate a general message about life. The message may state a moral truth, or it may be a general observation about nature, society, or human behavior. This message is the **theme,** or main idea, of the story. In some stories the author announces the theme directly. Such a **stated theme** is often found in a sentence near the end of the story. It may be expressed by the author or by one of the characters. Details in the story usually support the stated theme.

The moral lesson at the end of a fable is a good example of a stated theme. For instance, Aesop's fable about the dog and the wolf tells of how a well-fed dog encounters a starving wolf. The dog offers to arrange for the wolf to live with him at his master's house. The wolf agrees until he finds out that the dog spends each night collared and chained. The fable ends with the moral "Better starve free than be a fat slave." This is a stated theme.

Thinking About Stated Theme

What is the theme of Ta-Na-E-Ka? Is it a stated theme? How do you know?

COMPOSITION

Writing About Theme

Write a paragraph in which you show that the events of Ta-Na-E-Ka support the theme. **Prewriting:** List the events in order. **Writing:** Begin your paragraph by stating the theme of the story. Expand your prewriting notes to describe the story's events. Finally tell why you think these events lead Grandfather to make his final statement about Mary. **Revising:** Review your paragraph, making sure that you have expressed your ideas clearly and logically.

Writing About a Personal Lesson

Write an essay about a lesson that you have learned in your own life. This lesson will be the theme, or main idea, of your writing. Write one sentence that directly states your theme. Then jot down the details or events that helped you learn this lesson. Use these details to write a brief essay about what you learned from your experiences. Be sure to state the theme directly at the end of your story.

Born in San Francisco to a poor family, Jack London (1876–1916) left school after the eighth grade in order to go to work. His occupations as a seaman, oyster pirate, and gold prospector during the Klondike gold rush provided material for many of his adventure stories. One of his most famous stories is "To Build a Fire." The story you will read first appeared in the *Youth's Companion* magazine in 1902. London wrote another version in 1908.

When he tried to add the first twigs his hand shook and the tiny flame was quenched. The frost had beaten him. His hands were worthless.

• •

Jack London

To Build a Fire

For land travel or seafaring, the world over, a companion is usually considered desirable. In the Klondike,[1] as Tom Vincent found out, such a companion is absolutely essential. But he found it out, not by precept,[2] but through bitter experience.

"Never travel alone," is a precept of the North. He had heard it many times and laughed; for he was a strapping young fellow, big-boned and big-muscled, with faith in himself and in the strength of his head and hands.

It was on a bleak January day when the experience came that taught him respect for the frost, and for the wisdom of the men who had battled with it.

He had left Calumet Camp on the Yukon[3] with a light pack on his back, to go up Paul Creek to the divide between it and Cherry Creek, where his party was prospecting and hunting moose.

The frost was sixty-degrees below zero, and he had thirty miles of lonely trail to cover, but he did not mind. In fact, he enjoyed it, swinging along through the silence, his blood pounding warmly through veins, and his mind carefree and happy. For he and his comrades were certain they had struck "pay" up there on the Cherry Creek Divide; and, further, he was returning to them from Dawson with cheery home letters from the States.

At seven o'clock, when he turned the heels of his moccasins toward Calumet Camp, it was still black night. And when

---

1. **Klondike** [klon′dīk]: noted gold-mining region in northwestern Canada, near the Alaska border.
2. **precept** [prē′sept]: rule intended as a guide for conduct or action.

3. **Yukon** [ū′kon]: river in northwestern Canada.

day broke at half past nine he had made the four-mile cut-off across the flats and was six miles up Paul Creek. The trail, which had seen little travel, followed the bed of the creek, and there was no possibility of his getting lost. He had gone to Dawson by way of Cherry Creek and Indian River, so Paul Creek was new and strange. By half past eleven he was at the forks, which had been described to him, and he knew he had covered fifteen miles, half the distance. He knew that in the nature of things the trail was bound to grow worse from there on, and thought that, considering the good time he had made, he merited lunch. Casting off his pack and taking a seat on a fallen tree, he unmittened his right hand, reached inside his shirt next to the skin, and fished out a couple of biscuits sandwiched with sliced bacon and wrapped in a handkerchief—the only way they could be carried without freezing solid.

He had barely chewed the first mouthful when his numbing fingers warned him to put his mitten on again. This he did, not without surprise at the bitter swiftness with which the frost bit in. Undoubtedly it was the coldest snap he had ever experienced, he thought.

He spat upon the snow—a favorite northland trick—and the sharp crackle of the instantly congealed spittle startled him. The spirit thermometer[4] at Calumet had registered sixty below when he left, but he was certain it had grown much colder, how much colder he could not imagine.

Half of the first biscuit was yet untouched, but he could feel himself beginning to chill—a thing most unusual for him. This would never do, he decided, and slipping the packstraps across his shoulders, he leaped to his feet and ran briskly up the trail.

A few minutes of this made him warm again, and he settled down to a steady stride, munching the biscuits as he went along. The moisture that exhaled with his breath crusted his lips and mustache with pendant ice and formed a miniature glacier on his chin. Now and again sensation forsook his nose and cheeks, and he rubbed them till they burned with the returning blood.

Most men wore nose-straps; his partners did, but he had scorned such "feminine contraptions," and till now had never felt the need of them. Now he did feel the need, for he was rubbing constantly.

Nevertheless he was aware of a thrill of joy, of exultation. He was doing something, achieving something, mastering the elements. Once he laughed aloud in sheer strength of life, and with his clenched fist defied the frost. He was its master. What he did he did in spite of it. It could not stop him. He was going on to the Cherry Creek Divide.

Strong as were the elements, he was stronger. At such times animals crawled away into their holes and remained in hiding. But he did not hide. He was out in it, facing it, fighting it. He was a man, a master of things.

In such fashion, rejoicing proudly, he tramped on. After an hour he rounded a bend, where the creek ran close to the mountainside, and came upon one of the most insignificant-appearing but most formidable dangers in northern travel.

---

4. **spirit thermometer:** instrument for measuring temperature, using alcohol or ether as the substance whose movement within a small tube gives the measurements.

The creek itself was frozen solid to its rocky bottom, but from the mountain came the outflow of several springs. These springs never froze, and the only effect of the severest cold snaps was to lessen their discharge.[5] Protected from the frost by the blanket of snow, the water of these springs seeped down into the creek and, on top of the creek ice, formed shallow pools.

The surface of these pools, in turn, took on a skin of ice which grew thicker and thicker, until the water overran, and so formed a second ice-skinned pool above the first.

Thus at the bottom was the solid creek ice, then probably six to eight inches of water, then the thin ice-skin, then another six inches of water and another ice-skin. And on top of this last skin was about an inch of recent snow to make the trap complete.

To Tom Vincent's eye the unbroken snow surface gave no warning of the lurking danger. As the crust was thicker at the edge, he was well toward the middle before he broke through.

In itself it was a very insignificant mishap—a man does not drown in twelve inches of water—but in its consequences as serious an accident as could possibly befall him.

At the instant he broke through he felt the cold water strike his feet and ankles, and with half a dozen lunges he made the bank. He was quite cool and collected. The thing to do, and the only thing to do, was to build a fire. For another precept of the North runs: *Travel with wet socks down to twenty below zero; after that build a fire.* And it was three times twenty below and colder, and he knew it.

He knew, further, that great care must be exercised; that with failure at the first attempt, the chance was made greater for failure at the second attempt. In short, he knew that there must be no failure. The moment before a strong, exulting man, boastful of his mastery of the elements, he was now fighting for his life against those same elements—such was the difference caused by the injection of a quart of water into a northland traveler's calculations.

In a clump of pines on the rim of the bank the spring high-water had lodged many twigs and small branches. Thoroughly dried by the summer sun, they now waited the match.

It is impossible to build a fire with heavy Alaskan mittens on one's hands, so Vincent bared his, gathered a sufficient number of twigs, and knocking the snow from them, kneeled down to kindle his fire. From an inside pocket he drew out his matches and a strip of thin birch bark. The matches were of the Klondike kind, sulfur[6] matches, one hundred in a bunch.

He noticed how quickly his fingers had chilled as he separated one match from the bunch and scratched it on his trousers. The birch bark, like the driest of paper, burst into bright flame. This he carefully fed with the smallest twigs and finest debris, cherishing the flame with the utmost care. It did not do to hurry

---

5. **discharge** [dis′chärj′]: that which is sent forth or flows out.

6. **sulfur** [sul′fər]: yellow chemical substance that burns with a blue flame and is used in making gunpowder and matches.

Winter Moonlight,
Charles Burchfield,
watercolor, 1951.

things, as he well knew, and although his fingers were now quite stiff, he did not hurry.

After the first quick, biting sensation of cold, his feet had ached with a heavy, dull ache and were rapidly growing numb. But the fire, although a very young one, was now a success; he knew that a little snow, briskly rubbed, would speedily cure his feet.

But at the moment he was adding the first thick twigs to the fire a grievous thing happened. The pine boughs above his head were burdened with a four months' snowfall, and so finely adjusted were the burdens that his slight movement in collecting the twigs had been sufficient to disturb the balance.

The snow from the topmost bough was the first to fall, striking and dislodging the snow on the boughs beneath. And all this snow, accumulating as it fell, smote Tom Vincent's head and shoulders and blotted out his fire.

He still kept his presence of mind, for he knew how great his danger was. He started at once to rebuild the fire, but his fingers were now so numb that he could not bend them, and he was forced to pick up each twig and splinter between the tips of the fingers of either hand.

When he came to the match he encountered great difficulty in separating one from the bunch. This he succeeded in managing, however, and also, by great effort, in clutching the match between his thumb and forefinger. But in scratching it, he dropped it in the snow and could not pick it up again.

He stood up, desperate. He could not feel even his weight on his feet, although the ankles were aching painfully. Putting on his mittens, he stepped to one side, so that the snow would not fall upon the new fire he was to build, and beat his hands violently against a tree trunk.

This enabled him to separate and strike a second match and to set fire to the remaining fragment of birch bark. But his body had now begun to chill, and he was shivering, so that when he tried to add the first twigs his hand shook and the tiny flame was quenched.

The frost had beaten him. His hands were worthless. But he had the foresight to drop the bunch of matches into his wide-mouthed outside pocket before he slipped on his mittens in despair, and started to run up the trail. One cannot run the frost out of wet feet at sixty below and colder, however, as he quickly discovered.

He came round a sharp turn of the creek to where he could look ahead for a mile. But there was no help, no sign of help, only the white trees and the white hills, and the quiet cold and the brazen[7] silence! If only he had a comrade whose feet were not freezing, he thought, only such a comrade to start the fire that could save him!

Then his eyes chanced upon another high-water lodgment of twigs and branches. If he could strike a match, all might yet be well. With stiff fingers which he could not bend, he got out a bunch of matches, but found it impossible to separate them.

He sat down and awkwardly shuffled the bunch about on his knees, until he got it resting on his palm with the sulfur ends projecting, somewhat in the manner the blade of a hunting-knife would project when clutched in the fist.

But his fingers stood straight out. They could not clutch. This he overcame by pressing the wrist of the other hand against them, and so forcing them down upon the bunch. Time and again, holding thus by both hands, he scratched the bunch on his left leg and finally ignited it. But the flame burned into the flesh of his hand, and he involuntarily relaxed his hold. The bunch fell into the snow, and while he tried vainly to pick it up, sizzled and went out.

Again he ran, by this time badly frightened. His feet were utterly devoid of sensation. He stubbed his toes once on a buried log, but beyond pitching him into the snow and wrenching his back, it gave him no feelings.

His fingers were helpless and his wrists

---

7. **brazen** [brā′zən]: shameless; harsh.
8. **lodgment** [loj′mənt]: place to rest or live.

were beginning to grow numb. His nose and cheeks he knew were frozen, but they did not count. It was his feet and hands that were to save him, if he was to be saved.

He recollected being told of a camp of moose-hunters somewhere above the forks of Paul Creek. He must be somewhere near it, he thought, and if he could find it he yet might be saved. Five minutes later he came upon it, lone and deserted, with drifted snow sprinkled inside the pine-bough shelter in which the hunters had slept. He sank down, sobbing. All was over, and in an hour at best, in that terrific temperature, he would be an icy corpse.

But the love of life was strong in him, and he sprang again to his feet. He was thinking quickly. What if the matches did burn his hands? Burned hands were better than dead hands. No hands at all were better than death. He floundered along the trail until he came upon another high-water lodgment.[8] There were twigs and branches, leaves and grasses, all dry and waiting the fire.

Again he sat down and shuffled the bunch of matches on his knees, got it into place on his palm, with the wrist of his other hand forced the nerveless fingers down against the bunch, and with the wrist kept them there. At the second scratch the bunch caught fire, and he knew that if he could stand the pain he was saved. He choked with the sulfur fumes, and the blue flame licked the flesh of his hands.

At first he could not feel it, but it burned quickly in through the frosted surface. The odor of the burning flesh—his flesh—was strong in his nostrils. He writhed about in his torment, yet held on. He set his teeth and swayed back and forth, until the clear white flame of the burning match shot up, and he had applied that flame to the leaves and grasses.

An anxious five minutes followed, but the fire gained steadily. Then he set to work to save himself. Heroic measures were necessary, such was his extremity, and he took them.

Alternately rubbing his hands with snow and thrusting them into the flames, and now and again beating them against the hard trees, he restored their circulation sufficiently for them to be of use to him. With his hunting-knife he slashed the straps from his pack, unrolled his blanket, and got out dry socks and footgear.

Then he cut away his moccasins and bared his feet. But while he had taken liberties with his hands, he kept his feet fairly away from the fire and rubbed them with snow. He rubbed till his hands grew numb, when he would cover his feet with the blanket, warm his hands by the fire, and return to the rubbing.

For three hours he worked, till the worst effects of the freezing had been counteracted. All that night he stayed by the fire, and it was late the next day when he limped pitifully into the camp on the Cherry Creek Divide.

In a month's time he was able to be about on his feet, although the toes were destined always after that to be very sensitive to frost. But the scars on his hands he knows he will carry to the grave. And—*"Never travel alone!"*—he now lays down the precept of the North.

READER'S RESPONSE

Do you think it was foolish of Tom Vincent to take this journey alone? Why or why not?

STUDY QUESTIONS

Recalling

1. What "precept of the North" does Tom know but ignore?
2. At lunch what signs show Tom that it is getting colder?
3. What is dangerous about the creek? What happens as Tom crosses it?
4. What other "precept of the North" does Tom think of after he gets out of the creek?
5. What measures does he take in a final effort to save himself?

Interpreting

6. Why does Tom ignore the first northern precept?

7. In what sense are his hands and feet the only things that can save him?
8. How might a companion have helped his situation?

Extending

9. What situations can you think of in which it is very important not to panic?

CHALLENGE

Illustration

Draw or paint a picture of one of the following scenes from "To Build a Fire":

a. Tom Vincent starting off on his trip across the Yukon
b. Tom crossing the creek
c. Tom building the first fire
d. Tom trying to save himself at the end of the story

Provide as much detail as possible for the character and the setting. Also write a title for the scene you illustrate.

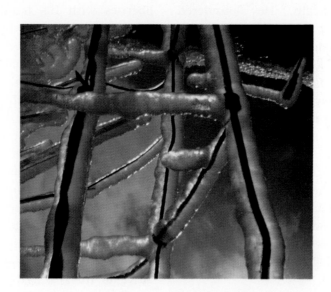

Thinking Skills: Classifying

DEFINITION

Classifying is a way of thinking about things by sorting them into groups. We classify things all the time just to be able to talk about them more easily. For example, we group all of the thousands of different kinds of pieces of furniture we sit on into one class. We call that class chairs.

Classifying things often makes it easier to see relationships between them. It is a way of thinking that can help you understand literature and speak and write more clearly about it.

STEPS

1. **Identify the things to be classified.**

2. **Identify the classes or groups into which the things are to be sorted.**
   Keep in mind that each group has one or more qualities that make it different from any other group.

3. **Sort each thing into a class or group based on the qualities each thing possesses.**

4. **Make a statement based on the groupings.**

EXAMPLE

Imagine that you are asked to write a report on sports in America. With such a broad topic, you need to classify the sports in order to be able to think clearly about them.

1. **Identify the things to be classified.** You list every sport you want to include.

2. **Identify the classes or groups into which the things are to be sorted.** You notice that some sports are played by individuals and some by teams. You decide that two classes—individual sports and team sports—will give you a way to organize your thinking.

3. **Sort each thing into a class or group based on the qualities each thing possesses.** You assign each sport to a class based on whether it is played by an individual or a team.

4. **Make a statement based on the groupings.** Your statement may be a simple descriptive one: "Americans play both individual and team sports." Or you may choose to think about the meanings of the groups: "Americans enjoy team sports more than individual sports."

ACTIVITY 1

Follow the four steps of classifying to organize the actions of Tom Vincent in "To Build a Fire." Let your classes be "actions that lead to survival" and "actions that lead to freezing to death." Develop a statement that says something about the character of Tom Vincent.

ACTIVITY 2

Follow the four steps of classifying to organize information from any other literary selection in this book. You may wish to focus on characters, events, or any specific kind of details in a selection, such as sounds or animals or colors. Remember to make your classes clearly different from one another.

Russell Freedman (born 1929) has worked as a journalist, encyclopedia editor, and writing teacher. During his service in the U.S. Army, he worked as a member of the Counter-intelligence Corps. Today Freedman writes books for young people and is especially known for his works of nonfiction. "A Cow Herder on Horseback" is taken from his award-winning book *Cowboys of the Wild West.*

In the movies, cowboys . . . wear huge white hats, skintight shirts, and shiny six-shooters slung low on each hip. That's not quite the way it was in the real Wild West.

• •

Russell Freedman

A Cow Herder on Horseback

I've roamed the Texas prairies,
I've followed the cattle trail;
I've rid a pitchin' pony
Till the hair come off his tail.©

A century ago, in the years following the Civil War,[1] one million mustang[2] ponies and ten million head of long-horned cattle[3] were driven north out of Texas. Bawling and bellowing, the lanky longhorns tramped along dusty trails in herds that numbered a thousand animals or more.

Behind and beside and ahead of each herd rode groups of men on horseback. Often, they sang to the cattle as they drove them on. These old-time cow herders were mostly very young men, and in time they came to be known as cowboys.

Some were boys in fact as well as name. Youngsters still in their teens commonly worked as horse wranglers, caring for the saddle ponies that traveled with every trail outfit. A typical trail-driving cowboy was in his early twenties. Except for some cooks and bosses, there were few thirty-year-old men on the trail.

Cowboys drove great herds across wild prairies from Texas to markets in Kansas and beyond. They swam the cattle across rivers and stayed with them during stampedes. A man spent eighteen hours a day in the saddle. At night he slept on the ground. Sometimes he lived on the trail for months with no comforts but a campfire and his bedroll.

At the end of the drive, the cattle were sold, the hands[4] were paid off, and the

---

1. **Civil War:** in the United States, the war between the North and the South (1861–1865).
2. **mustang** [mus′tang]: wild horse of the American plains, believed to be descended from stock brought by the Spanish.
3. **long-horned cattle:** breed of cattle of Spanish origin, formerly widely raised in the southwestern United States.

4. **hands:** workmen employed to do manual labor.

trail outfit split up. Then the cowboys went into town to scrape off the trail dust and celebrate. Usually they stopped at the pineboard photographer's studio found in nearly every western cattle town. Decked out in their best duds and sporting the tools of their trade, they posed proudly for souvenir pictures to send to the folks back home. Some of those old photographs still survive. In them we can glimpse the cowboy as he really was, a hundred years ago.

The Long Horn Cattle Sign, Frederic Remington, 1908.

The cowboy trade goes back more than four hundred years. It began in Mexico during the sixteenth century, when Spanish settlers brought the first domesticated horses and cattle to North America. Back home, the Spanish had kept their cattle penned up in pastures. But in the wide-open spaces of the New World, the cattle were allowed to wander freely, finding their own grass and water. The animals flourished. Soon, huge Spanish ranches were scattered across northern Mexico.

Since the cattle roamed far and wide, the ranchers needed skilled horsemen to look after their herds. They began to teach the local Indians to ride horses and handle cattle on the open range. These barefoot Indian cow herders were called *vaqueros,* from the Spanish word *vaca,* for cow. They were the first true cowboys, and they spent their days from sunrise to sunset in the saddle. They became experts at snaring a running steer with a braided rawhide rope, called *la reata* in Spanish. Over the years *la reata*—the lariat—became the cowboy's most important tool, and the Mexican *vaquero* became a proud and independent ranch hand.

Vaqueros drove the first herds of cattle north into Texas early in the eighteenth

century. By the time of the American Civil War (1861–1865), millions of hardy long-horned cattle were roaming the Texas plains. Many of these animals were descended from strays and runaways that had escaped from their owners, and they were as wild as buffalo or deer. They clustered together in small herds, hiding in thickets by day, running by night. If anyone tried to approach them on foot, they would paw the earth and toss their heads in anger.

Like most of the South, Texas was poor when the Civil War ended. Confederate[5] money no longer had any value. The state's economy was in ruins. Yet long-horns were running wild all over the state.

Before the war, cattle had been raised mainly for their hides (for leather) and tallow, or fat (for candles and soap). Now, new methods of meat-packing and refrigeration had created a profitable market for

---

5. **Confederate** [kən fed′ ər it]: of the Confederate States of America, the government formed by the eleven Southern states that withdrew from the national Government during the Civil War.

beef in the crowded cities of the North. Texas had plenty of beef on the hoof,[6] but there were no railroads linking Texas with the rest of the country, where the beef was in demand. The only way to get the cattle to market was to walk them hundreds of miles north to the nearest railroad.

As Texas farmers and ranchers came home from the war, they began to organize what they called "cow hunts." By capturing wild longhorns and branding them as his own, a rancher could build up his herds and drive them north to be sold. Cow-hunters used the same methods to catch wild cattle that Mexican *vaqueros* had been using for a long time. They found a herd of longhorns by moonlight and fired a gun to make them stampede. Riding with the herd, they let the longhorns run for hours, until the cattle grew tired and slowed to a trot or walk. Then the men kept the animals moving for the next day or so, until the longhorns were so hungry and exhausted, they had tamed down and could be handled with ease.

Once the cattle had been caught and branded, they were set loose to graze until they were ready for market. Then they were rounded up and driven in large herds to Kansas railroad towns, where they were loaded aboard freight cars and shipped to meat-packing plants[7] in Kansas City and Chicago.

As the demand for beef grew, the cattle-raising industry spread northward from Texas. New ranches began to spring up all across the northern plains, where only a few years before herds of buffalo had grazed. By the 1870s, most of the buffalo had been slaughtered. They were replaced by long-horned cattle brought up the trails from Texas. Soon, a vast tract of cattle country stretched from Colorado up through Wyoming, Montana, and the Dakotas.

At the heart of this booming[8] cattle industry was the hard-working cowboy. Who was he, where was he from, and what was he like?

To begin with, most cowboys were Texans and other southerners, discharged soldiers back from the war.[9] Jobs were scarce in the South, and the prospering cattle ranchers needed plenty of new hands. Along with the southerners, there were a number of mustered-out Union soldiers.[10] Eventually, men and boys from many backgrounds and all parts of the country began to arrive in Texas, seeking jobs as cowhands. Some had been unlucky at home and were looking for a fresh start. Others were drawn to Texas because they had heard that a cowboy's life was adventurous and exciting.

Today, in movies and TV shows about the Old West, cowboys are usually white. In real life, they were often black or Mexican. Texas had been a slaveholding state before the Civil War. On Texas ranches, slaves broke[11] horses and herded cattle. When the war ended, many freed slaves from Texas and other southern states went to work as professional cowhands.

---

6. **beef on the hoof:** live cattle.
7. **meat-packing plants:** places in which animals are slaughtered for food and the meat is processed, packed, and distributed.

8. **booming:** experiencing sudden and rapid growth.
9. **the war:** the Civil War.
10. **mustered** [mus′tərd]**-out Union soldiers:** soldiers dismissed or discharged from service in the army raised by the states that remained loyal to the national Government during the Civil War.
11. **broke:** tamed.

California Vaqueros, James Walker, 1876–1877.

Most Texas trail outfits included black cowboys, and a few outfits were all black.

Mexican cowhands, descendants of the *vaqueros,* were common in southern Texas, where many ranches were still owned by old Spanish families. Other cowboys were American Indians, or had some Indian blood. In the Indian Territory (now Oklahoma), a number of cattle ranches were operated entirely by Native American cowboys.

In the movies, cowboys seem to spend a good part of their time chasing outlaws, battling Indians, rescuing the rancher's daughter, and hanging out in riotous cow towns like Abilene[12] and Dodge City.[13] They wear huge white hats, skintight shirts, and shiny six-shooters slung low on each hip. That's not quite the way it was in the real Wild West.

A real cowboy was paid to herd cows. He spent most of his time rounding up longhorns, branding calves, and driving

---

12. **Abilene** [ab′ə lēn′]: city in west-central Texas, important as a cattle-shipping center.
13. **Dodge City:** city in southwestern Kansas, known in frontier days as a rowdy cattle town.

the herds to market. He was lucky if he made it into town twice in one year. Out on the range he wore practical work clothing, rode a horse owned by his employer, and seldom carried a gun. When he did, he wore it high and snug around his waist. He never carried two guns.

"There is one thing I would like to get straight," recalled an old-time cowboy named Teddy Blue Abbott. "I punched[14] cows from '71 on [when he was ten years old], and I never yet saw a cowboy with two guns. I mean two six-shooters. Wild Bill[15] carried two guns and so did some of those other city marshals, like Bat Masterson,[16] but they were professional gunmen themselves, not cowpunchers. . . . A cowboy with two guns is all movie stuff, and so is this business of a gun on each hip."

Most cowboys were not sharpshooters, yet their work demanded exceptional skills. A cowboy had to be an expert roper and rider, an artist at busting broncs[17] and whacking bulls.[18] He had to know how to doctor an ailing cow or find a lost calf, how to calm a restless herd in the middle of the night, how to head off a thousand stampeding longhorns.

On a ranch, he worked ten to fourteen hours a day. On trail drives, he herded cattle from before dawn to after dusk, then spent two more hours on night guard duty. He had a tough, dirty, sweaty job, and often a dangerous one. He might be kicked by a horse, charged by a steer, trampled in a stampede, drowned during a river crossing, or caught on the open prairie in the midst of an electrical storm. Probably more cowboys were killed by lightning than by outlaws or Indians. Riding accidents were the most common cause of cowboy deaths, followed by pneumonia.

Teddy Blue Abbott went up the trail for the first time in 1879, when he was eighteen years old. Sixty years later he recalled the men he had worked with: "In person the cowboys were mostly medium-sized men, as a heavy man was hard on horses, quick and wiry, and as a rule very good natured; in fact, it did not pay to be anything else. In character, their like never was or will be again. They were intensely loyal to the outfit they were working for and would fight to the death for it. They would follow their wagon boss through hell and never complain. I have seen them ride into camp after two days and nights on herd, lay down their saddle blankets in the rain and sleep like dead men, then get up laughing and joking about some good time they had in Ogallala[19] or Dodge City. Living that kind of life, they were bound to be wild and brave."

---

14. **punched:** herded using a metal prod or stick.
15. **Wild Bill:** James Butler ("Wild Bill") Hickok (1837–1876), American frontier marshal famous for his skill with a gun and his encounters with outlaws.
16. **Bat Masterson:** William Barclay Masterson (1853–1921), gambler, gunfighter, and U.S. marshal, associated with Dodge City.
17. **busting broncs:** taming small, untamed or partially tamed horses.
18. **whacking bulls:** driving ox teams.

---

19. **Ogallala** [ō gə lä′lə]: city in southwestern central Nebraska.

READER'S RESPONSE

Do you agree with Teddy Blue Abbot's statement that the cowboys' life was bound to make them "wild and brave." Why or why not?

STUDY QUESTIONS

Recalling

1. What were cow herders eventually called?
2. Who were the first true cowboys? What was their special skill?
3. What happened in a cow hunt?
4. What kind of people worked as cowboys during the cattle industry boom?
5. What did a cowboy need to know?
6. List at least three examples that show a cowboy led a tough and dangerous life.

Interpreting

7. Why do you think cowboys were usually young men?
8. How would you describe the differences between real cowboys and the portrayals of cowboys in television and movies?
9. In what way was the cowboy the "heart" of the cattle industry?

Extending

10. In addition to that of cowboys, can you think of other occupations inaccurately portrayed by television and movies? Explain your answer.

READING AND LITERARY FOCUS

Fiction and Nonfiction

Fiction is prose writing that originates in the author's imagination. **Nonfiction** is prose writing that is factual and describes real experiences. "My Friend Flicka," for example, is a fictional story about a boy and a horse. An encyclopedia article about horses is an example of nonfiction.

Thinking About Fiction and Nonfiction

Would you classify "A Cow Herder on Horseback" as fiction or nonfiction? Give reasons for your choice.

VOCABULARY

Word Origins

The origin of a word refers to its history, or heritage—where it comes from, what it originally meant, and how its meaning and form have changed over the years. The origin of a word, or its **etymology,** can be found by looking up the word in a dictionary. You will usually find a word's etymology in parentheses or brackets just after the pronunciation or at the end of the definitions. The etymology will tell you which language or languages the word comes from, its original meaning, and forms that the word took in its development.

For instance, you can discover that *prosper* comes from the Latin word *prosperare.* The word *prosperare* was formed by combining the prefix *pro-* (meaning "for") and the root *spes* ("hope").

The words below come from "A Cow Herder on Horseback." Write them on a separate sheet of paper. Then look them up in your dictionary, and copy down the etymology of each one.

1. marshall
2. industry
3. flourished
4. confederate
5. tract

photograph ©1990 Jill Krementz

Maya Angelou (born 1928) was brought up by her grandmother in Arkansas. Her well-known autobiography, "I Know Why the Caged Bird Sings," recounts many interesting experiences from those early years. In addition to being a writer, Angelou also works as a teacher and has enjoyed acting and directing in movies and the theater. In her writing, she says, "I am always talking about the human condition—about what we can endure, dream, fail at and still survive." In the poem "Life Doesn't Frighten Me," she explores an emotion that affects all of us.

Do you think it is possible to be fearless?

Maya Angelou

Life Doesn't Frighten Me

Shadows on the wall
Noises down the hall
Life doesn't frighten me at all
Bad dogs barking loud
5 Big ghosts in a cloud
Life doesn't frighten me at all.

Mean old Mother Goose
Lions on the loose
They don't frighten me at all
10 Dragons breathing flame
On my counterpane[1]
That doesn't frighten me at all,

I go boo
Make them shoo
15 I make fun
Way they run
I won't cry
So they fly

---

1. **counterpane** [koun′tər pān′]: bedspread.

Blue Interior, Morning, Romare Bearden, collage on board, 1968.

I just smile
20 They go wild
Life doesn't frighten me at all.

Tough guys in a fight
All alone at night
Life doesn't frighten me at all.
25 Panthers in the park
Strangers in the dark
No, they don't frighten me at all.

That new classroom where
Boys all pull my hair
30 (Kissy little girls
With their hair in curls)
They don't frighten me at all.

Don't show me frogs and snakes
And listen for my scream,
35 If I'm afraid at all
It's only in my dreams.

I've got a magic charm
That I keep up my sleeve,
I can walk the ocean floor
40 And never have to breathe.

Life doesn't frighten me at all
Not at all
Not at all.
Life doesn't frighten me at all.

Do you think the speaker *should* be frightened by all the things mentioned in the poem? Why or why not?

STUDY QUESTIONS

Recalling

1. Name five real and three imaginary things that the speaker claims don't frighten her.
2. In the third stanza, what does the speaker do to banish frightening things?
3. When is the only time the speaker says she might be afraid?
4. In the seventh stanza, what protects the speaker from harm? What does she say she can do as a result of it?

Interpreting

5. Which words in the poem make you think the speaker *isn't* afraid? Which words lead you to believe that she *is*?
6. What do the speaker's actions in the third stanza tell you about her personality?
7. What does the repetition of certain phrases tell you about the speaker's feelings?

Extending

8. Can you think of some things that often frighten people? Why are they frightening?

READING AND LITERARY FOCUS

Lyric Poetry

A **lyric poem** expresses a poet's thoughts and feelings and is usually brief. A lyric poem's main purpose is to communicate the emotions of the poet. Most lyric poems contain vivid and imaginative images. Lyric poems usually describe a particular moment, feeling, or memory that stirs the poet's imagination. "Life Doesn't Frighten Me" is a lyric poem. It is filled with vivid and varied images of things that frighten the narrator.

The word *lyric* comes from *lyre*, a guitarlike instrument that poets centuries ago played as they sang their poems. Few poets today sing their poems, but *lyric* is still used to refer to the words of songs and to poems that are brief, emotional, and musical.

Thinking About Lyric Poetry

Identify at least two examples that show that "Life Doesn't Frighten Me" is a lyric poem.

COMPOSITION

Writing About Poetry

Write a paragraph about Maya Angelou's use of emotions to create an effect on the reader. **Prewriting:** List examples of sounds, images, and words that help to create the effect. **Writing:** Begin your paragraph with a sentence that describes the poem's overall impact on you. Use your prewriting notes to explain this statement in more detail. **Revising:** Review your paragraph to see that you have expressed your ideas clearly. *For help with this assignment, see Lesson 5 in the Writing About Literature Handbook at the back of this book.*

Writing a Description

Write a paragraph in which you describe something that frightens you. Make notes of words, sounds, and images that will help you create a vivid picture of the frightening thing. You might begin your paragraph by stating what it is that frightens you. Then use your notes to help you describe why this is so.

Thinking Skills: Evaluating

DEFINITION

Evaluating is a way of thinking about something and making a judgment about it. When you evaluate, you apply criteria to make your judgment. Criteria are the standards, rules, or tests on which a judgment can be based.

STEPS

1. **State the reason or purpose for your evaluation.**
   What do you want to evaluate? Why do you want to evaluate it?

2. **Identify the criteria.**
   What specific rules, tests, or standards will you use to make your judgment?

3. **Apply the criteria.**
   Does the subject of your evaluation meet each specific criterion? Does it meet some criteria better than others?

4. **Draw a conclusion.**
   The conclusion is your evaluation of how well the subject meets the criteria.

EXAMPLE

Imagine that you have just returned from a championship football game and a friend asks you, "Was it a good game?" You probably answer "yes" or "no" and then give a few details. Even though you may not talk about all your criteria for a good game, in your mind you make an evaluation based on criteria.

1. **State the reason or purpose for your evalua-**
tion. You want to evaluate the game in order to give your friend an accurate answer.

2. **Identify the criteria.** You choose to evaluate the game according to which team won, the excitement of the contest, and the quality of the plays.

3. **Apply the criteria.** The game was exciting from beginning to end. Each team made spectacular plays, and your team won with a touchdown in the last thirty seconds.

4. **Draw a conclusion.** You conclude that not only was the game a good one, but it was one of the best games you've ever seen.

ACTIVITY 1
Evaluating "Life Doesn't Frighten Me"

Follow the four steps of evaluating to answer the question "Is 'Life Doesn't Frighten Me' a good poem?" Identify your criteria carefully, being very specific about what you think makes a good poem. You may want to include one or more of the following criteria: rhythmic language, repetition that helps give the poem meaning, unusual images, a theme relevant to your own life, the poet's expression of personal thoughts and emotions.

ACTIVITY 2
Evaluating a Work of Literature

Evaluate another selection in this book or any other work of literature that you have read. Follow the four steps. Remember that people of different cultures or ages or with different interests may have different criteria. What is important is that you think about your criteria and they reflect what you believe.

Langston Hughes (1902–1967) was born in Joplin, Missouri, and later moved to Cleveland, Ohio. The summer of his graduation from high school, his first poem, "The Negro Speaks of Rivers," was published and received high praise. After traveling throughout the world, Hughes settled in Harlem, a neighborhood in New York City, and became the best-known black writer in the nation. He occasionally wrote fiction, drama, autobiography, and children's books, but he always returned to poetry. He said that he tried to write "seriously and as well as I know how about Negro people." In the following poem he shares some of his feelings and thoughts about Harlem.

How would you feel if you found a song written just for you on the jukebox?

• •

Langston Hughes

Juke Box[1] Love Song

I could take the Harlem[2] night
and wrap around you,
Take the neon lights and make a crown,
Take the Lenox Avenue buses,
5 Taxis, subways,
And for your love song tone their rumble down.
Take Harlem's heartbeat,
Make a drumbeat,
Put it on a record, let it whirl,
10 And while we listen to it play,
Dance with you till day—
Dance with you, my sweet brown Harlem girl.

---

1. **Juke Box** [jōōk′boks′] coin-operated phonograph with buttons by which the record to be played is selected.
2. **Harlem** [här′ləm]: section of New York City, including one of the largest black communities in the United States.

READER'S RESPONSE

Do you think this poem is a "love song"? Why or why not?

STUDY QUESTIONS

Recalling

1. Where does the poem take place?
2. List four examples of what the speaker can see and hear there.
3. What does the speaker want to "wrap around" the girl? What does he want to "tone down"?
4. Where does the speaker want to put all the sights and sounds he describes?
5. To whom is the poem addressed? What line tells you so?

Interpreting

6. In what way are the sights and sounds of the city appropriate for a love song?
7. What feelings does the speaker have for the girl mentioned in the poem? How do you know?

Extending

8. If you were going to make a song out of the sights and sounds around your home, what would you put on a record?

CHALLENGE

Collage

A **collage** is a picture made from assembling scraps of materials—string, pictures, paint, glitter, cloth, and so on. Make a collage that illustrates the sights, sounds, and feelings presented in "Juke Box Love Song."

Juke Box, Jacob Lawrence, 1946.

Pat Mora (born 1942) was raised in El Paso, Texas. Growing up near the border between Mexico and the United States allowed her to witness the blending of American and Mexican cultures. She thinks that all people's "sense of identity is firmly rooted in their culture," and her own Mexican American heritage is reflected in her poems. In the following poem Mora describes with vivid language the desert landscape around her.

Can you imagine what a desert and a mother might have in common?

• •

Pat Mora

Mi Madre[1]

I say feed me.
She serves red prickly pear[2] on a spiked cactus.

I say tease me.
She sprinkles raindrops in my face on a sunny day.

5 I say frighten me.
She shouts thunder, flashes lightning.

I say comfort me.
She invites me to lay on her firm body.

I say heal me.
10 She gives me *manzanilla, orégano, dormilón.*[3]

I say caress me.
She strokes my skin with her warm breath.

---

1. **Mi Madre** [mē mä′thrā]
2. **prickly pear** [prik′lē pãr]: red or purple pear-shaped fruit that grows on a cactus.
3. **manzanilla** [män′sä nē′yə], **orégano** [ō rā′gä nō], **dormilón** [dôr mē lōn′]: three herbs often used as medicines.

Red and Orange Hills, Georgia O'Keeffe, 1938.

I say make me beautiful.
She offers turquoise[4] for my fingers, a pink blossom for my hair.

15 I say sing to me.
She chants lonely women's songs of femaleness.

I say teach me.
She endures: glaring heat
           numbing cold
20   frightening dryness.

She: the desert
She: strong mother.

---

4. **turquoise** [tur′kwoiz]: greenish-blue mineral
having a waxy shine and prized as a gem.

READER'S RESPONSE

Do you agree with the speaker that the desert is strong? Why or why not?

STUDY QUESTIONS

Recalling

1. What nine things does the speaker ask the "she" of the poem to do for her?
2. According to the speaker, what food does "she" provide? What medicine?
3. In what way does "she" caress the speaker?
4. What verb does the poet use to describe what "she" teaches the speaker?
5. According to the speaker, what is "she"?

Interpreting

6. Do you think the speaker actually makes her requests out loud? Why or why not?
7. What do you think "her warm breath" refers to?
8. Explain how the fact that "she endures" teaches the speaker.

Extending

9. What do you find especially interesting about a desert landscape? Explain your answer.

READING AND LITERARY FOCUS

Personification

Personification is the description of an animal, object, or idea in terms that normally would be used to describe only a person. Expressions like Mother Nature and Father Time are common examples of personification. By using personification, an author can make an insect, an ocean, or even a coat rack come to life and endow it with human qualities. The thing that is personified might speak, feel emotions, and even assume a human appearance.

Thinking About Personification

1. Identify the words in "Mi Madre" that give human qualities to the desert.
2. Why do you think the author decided to describe the desert as a person?

CHALLENGE

Research and Oral Report

Use the library to locate information about the deserts in the United States. In what states are they found? How large are they? What kinds of plants and animals exist? Are there any specific rocks or minerals present? Share your findings with the class.

When Helen Keller (1880–1968) was nineteen months old, she was struck by a disease that left her blind, deaf, and mute. When Keller was seven years old, Anne Sullivan became her teacher and taught her to communicate by means of the manual alphabet. With Sullivan's help Keller pursued her education and eventually graduated from Radcliffe College with a degree in English. Thereafter, she wrote many poems, essays, and books, including her stirring autobiography, "The Story of My Life." She was dedicated to helping others and said, "I will always—as long as I have breath—work for the handicapped."

I who am blind can give one hint to those who see: . . . Use your eyes as if tomorrow you would be stricken blind.

• •

Helen Keller

Three Days to See

I

All of us have read thrilling stories in which the hero had only a limited and specified time to live. Sometimes it was as long as a year; sometimes as short as twenty-four hours. But always we were interested in discovering just how the doomed man chose to spend his last days or his last hours. I speak, of course, of free men who have a choice, not condemned criminals whose sphere of activities is strictly delimited.

Such stories set us thinking, wondering what we should do under similar circumstances. What events, what experiences, what associations, should we crowd into those last hours as mortal beings? What happiness should we find in reviewing the past, what regrets?

Sometimes I have thought it would be an excellent rule to live each day as if we should die tomorrow. Such an attitude would emphasize sharply the values of life. We should live each day with a gentleness, a vigor, and a keenness of appreciation which are often lost when time stretches before us in the constant panorama of more days and months and years to come. There are those, of course, who would adopt the epicurean[1] motto of "Eat, drink, and be merry," but most people would be chastened[2] by the certainty of impending death.

In stories, the doomed hero is usually saved at the last minute by some stroke

---

1. **epicurean** [ep′i kyoo rē′ən]: given to luxurious tastes or habits, especially in eating and drinking.
2. **chastened** [chā′sənd]: restrained from excess.

of fortune, but almost always his sense of values is changed. He becomes more appreciative of the meaning of life and its permanent spiritual values. It has often been noted that those who live, or have lived, in the shadow of death bring a mellow sweetness to everything they do.

Most of us, however, take life for granted. We know that one day we must die, but usually we picture that day as far in the future. When we are in buoyant health, death is all but unimaginable. We seldom think of it. The days stretch out in an endless vista. So we go about our petty tasks, hardly aware of our listless attitude toward life.

The same lethargy, I am afraid, characterizes the use of all our faculties and senses. Only the deaf appreciate hearing, only the blind realize the manifold blessings that lie in sight. Particularly does this observation apply to those who have lost sight and hearing in adult life. But those who have never suffered impairment of sight or hearing seldom make the fullest use of these blessed faculties. Their eyes and ears take in all sights and sounds hazily, without concentration and with little appreciation. It is the same old story of not being grateful for what we have until we lose it, of not being conscious of health until we are ill.

I have often thought it would be a blessing if each human being were stricken blind and deaf for a few days at some time during his early adult life. Darkness would make him more appreciative of sight; silence would teach him the joys of sound.

Now and then I have tested my seeing friends to discover what they see. Recently I was visited by a very good friend who had just returned from a long walk in the woods, and I asked her what she had observed. "Nothing in particular," she replied. I might have been incredulous had I not been accustomed to such responses, for long ago I became convinced that the seeing see little.

How was it possible, I asked myself, to walk for an hour through the woods and see nothing worthy of note? I who cannot see find hundreds of things to interest me through mere touch. I feel the delicate symmetry of a leaf. I pass my hands lovingly about the smooth skin of a silver birch, or the rough, shaggy bark of a pine. In spring I touch the branches of trees hopefully in search of a bud, the first sign of awakening Nature after her winter's sleep. I feel the delightful, velvety texture of a flower, and discover its remarkable convolutions;[3] and something of the miracle of Nature is revealed to me. Occasionally, if I am very fortunate, I place my hand gently on a small tree and feel the happy quiver of a bird in full song. I am delighted to have the cool waters of a brook rush through my open fingers. To me a lush carpet of pine needles or spongy grass is more welcome than the most luxurious Persian rug. To me the pageant of seasons is a thrilling and unending drama, the action of which streams through my finger tips.

At times my heart cries out with longing to see all these things. If I can get so much pleasure from mere touch, how much more beauty must be revealed by sight. Yet, those who have eyes apparently see little. The panorama of color and ac-

---

3. **convolutions** [kon′və lōō′shənz]: winding or twistings of something that is turned inward or wound up upon itself.

tion which fills the world is taken for granted. It is human, perhaps, to appreciate little that which we have and to long for that which we have not, but it is a great pity that in the world of light the gift of sight is used only as a mere convenience rather than as a means of adding fullness to life.

If I were the president of a university I should establish a compulsory course in "How to Use Your Eyes." The professor would try to show his pupils how they could add joy to their lives by really seeing what passes unnoticed before them. He would try to awake their dormant and sluggish faculties.

II

Perhaps I can best illustrate by imagining what I should most like to see if I were given the use of my eyes, say, for just three days. And while I am imagining, suppose you, too, set your mind to work on the problem of how you would use your own eyes if you had only three more days to see. If with the oncoming darkness of the third night you knew that the sun would never rise for you again, how would you spend those three precious intervening days? What would you most want to let your gaze rest upon?

I, naturally, should want most to see the things which have become dear to me through my years of darkness. You, too, would want to let your eyes rest long on the things that have become dear to you so that you could take the memory of them with you into the night that loomed before you.

If, by some miracle, I were granted three seeing days, to be followed by a relapse into darkness, I should divide the period into three parts.

On the first day, I should want to see the people whose kindness and gentleness and companionship have made my life worth living. First I should like to gaze long upon the face of my dear teacher, Mrs. Anne Sullivan Macy,[4] who came to me when I was a child and opened the outer world to me. I should want not merely to see the outline of her face, so that I could cherish it in my memory, but to study that face and find in it the living evidence of the sympathetic tenderness and patience with which she accomplished the difficult task of my education. I should like to see in her eyes that strength of character which has enabled her to stand firm in the face of difficulties, and that compassion for all humanity which she has revealed to me so often.

I do not know what it is to see into the heart of a friend through that "window of the soul," the eye. I can only "see" through my finger tips the outline of a face. I can detect laughter, sorrow, and many other obvious emotions. I know my friends from the feel of their faces. But I cannot really picture their personalities by touch. I know their personalities, of course, through other means, through the thoughts they express to me, through whatever of their actions are revealed to me. But I am denied that deeper understanding of them which I am sure would come through sight of them, through watching their reactions to various expressed thoughts and circumstances,

---

4. **Mrs. Anne Sullivan Macy:** Partially blind herself, Sullivan (1866–1936) was Keller's teacher and lifelong companion.

through noting the immediate and fleeting reactions of their eyes and countenance.

Friends who are near to me I know well, because through the months and years they reveal themselves to me in all their phases; but of casual friends I have only an incomplete impression, an impression gained from a handclasp, from spoken words which I take from their lips with my finger tips, or which they tap into the palm of my hand.

How much easier, how much more satisfying it is for you who can see to grasp quickly the essential qualities of another person by watching the subtleties of expression, the quiver of a muscle, the flutter of a hand. But does it ever occur to you to use your sight to see into the inner nature of a friend or acquaintance? Do not most of you seeing people grasp casually the outward features of a face and let it go at that?

For instance, can you describe accurately the faces of five good friends? Some of you can, but many cannot. As an experiment, I have questioned husbands of long standing about the color of their wives' eyes, and often they express embarrassed confusion and admit that they do not know. And, incidentally, it is a chronic complaint of wives that their husbands do not notice new dresses, new hats, and changes in household arrangements.

The eyes of seeing persons soon become accustomed to the routine of their surroundings, and they actually see only the startling and spectacular. But even in viewing the most spectacular sights the eyes are lazy. Court records reveal every day how inaccurately "eyewitnesses" see. A given event will be "seen" in several different ways by as many witnesses. Some see more than others, but few see everything that is within the range of their vision.

Oh, the things that I should see if I had the power of sight for just three days!

The first day would be a busy one. I should call to me all my dear friends and look long into their faces, imprinting upon my mind the outward evidences of the beauty that is within them. I should let my eyes rest, too, on the face of a baby, so that I could catch a vision of the eager, innocent beauty which precedes the individual's consciousness of the conflicts which life develops.

And I should like to look into the loyal, trusting eyes of my dogs—the grave, canny[5] little Scottie, Darkie, and the stalwart,[6] understanding Great Dane, Helga, whose warm, tender, and playful friendships are so comforting to me.

On that busy first day I should also view the small simple things of my home. I want to see the warm colors in the rugs under my feet, the pictures on the walls, the intimate trifles that transform a house into home. My eyes would rest respectfully on the books in raised type[7] which I have read, but they would be more eagerly interested in the printed books which seeing people can read, for during the long night of my life the books I have read and those which have been read to me have built themselves into a great shining lighthouse, revealing to me the deepest channels of human life and the human spirit.

---

5. **canny** [kan′ē]: alert and watchful.
6. **stalwart** [stôl′wərt]: strong and loyal.
7. **raised type:** Braille, a system of writing using raised dots in specific patterns that may be recognized and read by touching them.

In the afternoon of that first seeing day, I should take a long walk in the woods and intoxicate my eyes on the beauties of the world of Nature, trying desperately to absorb in a few hours the vast splendor which is constantly unfolding itself to those who can see. On the way home from my woodland jaunt my path would lie near a farm so that I might see the patient horses plowing in the field (perhaps I should see only a tractor!) and the serene content of men living close to the soil. And I should pray for the glory of a colorful sunset.

When dusk had fallen, I should experience the double delight of being able to see by artificial light, which the genius of man has created to extend the power of his sight when Nature decrees darkness.

In the night of that first day of sight, I should not be able to sleep, so full would be my mind of the memories of the day.

III

The next day—the second day of sight—I should arise with the dawn and see the thrilling miracle by which night is transformed into day. I should behold with awe the magnificent panorama of light with which the sun awakens the sleeping earth.

This day I should devote to a hasty glimpse of the world, past and present. I should want to see the pageant of man's progress, the kaleidoscope[8] of the ages. How can so much be compressed into one day? Through the museums, of course. Often I have visited the New York Museum of Natural History to touch with my hands

Anonymous, Chinese, watercolor.

many of the objects there exhibited, but I have longed to see with my eyes the condensed history of the earth and its inhabitants displayed there—animals and the races of men pictured in their native environment; gigantic carcasses of dinosaurs and mastodons which roamed the earth long before man appeared, with his tiny stature and powerful brain, to conquer the animal kingdom; realistic presentations of the processes of evolution[9] in animals, in

---

8. **kaleidoscope** [kə lī′də skōp′]: anything exhibiting a succession of changing patterns, colors, or phases.

9. **evolution** [ev′ə lōō′shən]: gradual process of development through a series of stages.

man, and in the implements which man has used to fashion for himself a secure home on this planet; and a thousand and one other aspects of natural history.

I wonder how many readers of this article have viewed this panorama of the face of living things as pictured in that inspiring museum. Many, of course, have not had the opportunity, but I am sure that many who *have* had the opportunity have not made use of it. There, indeed, is a place to use your eyes. You who see can spend many fruitful days there, but I, with my imaginary three days of sight, could only take a hasty glimpse, and pass on.

My next stop would be the Metropolitan Museum of Art,[10] for just as the Museum of Natural History reveals the material aspects of the world, so does the Metropolitan show the myriad facets of the human spirit. Throughout the history of humanity the urge to artistic expression has been almost as powerful as the urge for food, shelter, and procreation.[11] And here, in the vast chambers of the Metropolitan Museum, is unfolded before me the spirit of Egypt, Greece, and Rome, as expressed in their art. I know well through my hands the sculptured gods and goddesses of the ancient Nile-land.[12] I have felt copies of Parthenon[13] friezes,[14]

and I have sensed the rhythmic beauty of charging Athenian[15] warriors. Apollos and Venuses and the Winged Victory of Samothrace[16] are friends of my finger tips. The gnarled, bearded features of Homer[17] are dear to me, for he, too, knew blindness.

My hands have lingered upon the living marble of Roman sculpture as well as that of later generations. I have passed my hands over a plaster cast of Michelangelo's[18] inspiring and heroic Moses;[19] I have sensed the power of Rodin;[20] I have been awed by the devoted spirit of Gothic[21] wood carving. These arts which can be touched have meaning for me, but even they were meant to be seen rather than felt, and I can only guess at the beauty which remains hidden from me. I can admire the simple lines of a Greek vase, but its figured decorations are lost to me.

So on this, my second day of sight, I should try to probe into the soul of man through his art. The things I knew through touch I should now see. More splendid still, the whole magnificent world of painting would be opened to me, from the Italian Primitives, with their serene re-

---

10. **Metropolitan Museum of Art:** leading art museum in the United States, located in New York City.
11. **procreation** [prō′krē ā′shən]: production of offspring.
12. **Nile** [nīl]**-land:** valley of the longest river in the world, in Africa, where the civilization of ancient Egypt flourished.
13. **Parthenon** [pär′thə non′]: Greek temple dedicated to the goddess Athena, built in the fifth century B.C.
14. **friezes** [frēz′əz]: horizontal, decorative bands of sculpture at the tops of buildings.

15. **Athenian** [ə thē′nē ən]: of Athens, the capital of Greece and one of the most important of the ancient Greek cities.
16. **Apollos** [ə pol′ōz] **and Venuses** [vē′nəs iz] **and . . . Samothrace** [sa′mə thrās′]: references to statues of various gods of Greek and Roman mythology.
17. **Homer** [hō′mər]: great poet of ancient Greece (c. 850 B.C.).
18. **Michelangelo** [mī′kəl an′jə lō′]: great Italian sculptor and painter (1475–1564).
19. **Moses** [mō′ziz]: in the Bible, the great prophet and lawgiver who led the Hebrews out of Egypt.
20. **Rodin** [rō dan′]: French sculptor (1840–1917).
21. **Gothic** [goth′ik]: style of European art and architecture characteristic of the twelfth through the sixteenth centuries.

ligious devotion, to the Moderns, with their feverish visions. I should look deep into the canvases of Raphael, Leonardo da Vinci, Titian, Rembrandt.[22] I should want to feast my eyes upon the warm colors of Veronese, study the mysteries of El Greco, catch a new vision of Nature from Corot.[23] Oh, there is so much rich meaning and beauty in the art of the ages for you who have eyes to see!

Upon my short visit to this temple of art I should not be able to review a fraction of that great world of art which is open to you. I should be able to get only a superficial impression. Artists tell me that for a deep and true appreciation of art one must educate the eye. One must learn through experience to weigh the merits of line, of composition, of form and color. If I had eyes, how happily would I embark upon so fascinating a study! Yet I am told that, to many of you who have eyes to see, the world of art is a dark night, unexplored and unilluminated.

It would be with extreme reluctance that I should leave the Metropolitan Museum, which contains the key to beauty—a beauty so neglected. Seeing persons, however, do not need a Metropolitan to find this key to beauty. The same key lies waiting in smaller museums, and in books on the shelves of even small libraries. But naturally, in my limited time of imaginary sight, I should choose the place where the key unlocks the greatest treasures in the shortest time.

The evening of my second day of sight I should spend at a theater or at the movies. Even now I often attend theatrical performances of all sorts, but the action of the play must be spelled into my hand by a companion. But how I should like to see with my own eyes the fascinating figure of Hamlet,[24] or the gusty Falstaff[25] amid colorful Elizabethan[26] trappings! How I should like to follow each movement of the graceful Hamlet, each strut of the hearty Falstaff! And since I could see only one play, I should be confronted by a many-horned dilemma, for there are scores of plays I should want to see. You who have eyes can see any you like. How many of you, I wonder, when you gaze at a play, a movie, or any spectacle, realize and give thanks for the miracle of sight which enables you to enjoy its color, grace, and movement?

I cannot enjoy the beauty of rhythmic movement except in a sphere restricted to the touch of my hands. I can vision only dimly the grace of a Pavlova,[27] although I know something of the delight of rhythm, for often I can sense the beat of music as it vibrates through the floor. I can well imagine that cadenced motion must be one of the most pleasing sights in the world. I have been able to gather something of this by tracing with my fingers the lines in sculptured marble; if this static grace can be so lovely, how much

---

22. **Raphael** [raf′ē əl], **Leonardo da Vinci** [lā′ə när ′do də vin′chē], **Titian** [tish′ən], **Rembrandt** [rem ′brant]: great European painters of the fifteenth through the seventeenth centuries.
23. **Veronese** [ver′ə nā′sē] . . . **El Greco** [el grek′ō] . . . **Corot** [kô rō′]: great European painters of the sixteenth through the nineteenth centuries.

24. **Hamlet** [ham′lit]: prince of Denmark, hero of William Shakespeare's tragedy *Hamlet*.
25. **Falstaff** [fôl′staf]: good-natured, swaggering old knight who appears in several plays by Shakespeare.
26. **Elizabethan** [i liz′ə bē′thən]: of the era of Queen Elizabeth I of England (1533–1603), during whose reign Shakespeare wrote his great works.
27. **Pavlova** [päv lō′və]: great Russian ballerina (1882–1931).

more acute must be the thrill of seeing grace in motion.

One of my dearest memories is of the time when Joseph Jefferson[28] allowed me to touch his face and hands as he went through some of the gestures and speeches of his beloved Rip Van Winkle.[29] I was able to catch thus a meager glimpse of the world of drama, and I shall never forget the delight of that moment. But, oh, how much I must miss, and how much pleasure you seeing ones can derive from watching and hearing the interplay of speech and movement in the unfolding of a dramatic performance! If I could see only one play, I should know how to picture in my mind the action of a hundred plays which I have read or had transferred to me through the medium of the manual alphabet.[30]

So, through the evening of my second imaginary day of sight, the great figures of dramatic literature would crowd sleep from my eyes.

IV

The following morning, I should again greet the dawn, anxious to discover new delights, for I am sure that for those who have eyes which really see, the dawn of each day must be a perpetually new revelation of beauty.

---

28. **Joseph Jefferson:** American actor (1829–1905).
29. **Rip Van Winkle** [rip′ van wing′kəl]: hero of a story by American writer Washington Irving (1783–1859).
30. **manual alphabet:** alphabet used to communicate with the deaf, consisting of a series of signs made with the fingers, each sign representing a letter of the written alphabet. Since Keller was blind as well as deaf, persons would communicate with her by spelling messages into her hand using the manual alphabet.

This, according to the terms of my imagined miracle, is to be my third and last day of sight. I shall have no time to waste in regrets or longings; there is too much to see. The first day I devoted to my friends, animate and inanimate. The second revealed to me the history of man and Nature. Today I shall spend in the workaday world of the present, amid the haunts of men going about the business of life. And where can one find so many activities and conditions of men as in New York? So the city becomes my destination.

I start from my home in the quiet little suburb of Forest Hills, Long Island. Here, surrounded by green lawns, trees, and flowers, are neat little houses, happy with the voices and movements of wives and children, havens of peaceful rest for men who toil in the city. I drive across the lacy structure of steel which spans the East River, and I get a new and startling vision of the power and ingenuity of the mind of man. Busy boats chug and scurry about the river—racy speedboats, stolid, snorting tugs. If I had long days of sight ahead, I should spend many of them watching the delightful activity upon the river.

I look ahead, and before me rise the fantastic towers of New York, a city that seems to have stepped from the pages of a fairy story. What an awe-inspiring sight, these glittering spires, these vast banks of stone and steel—structures such as the gods might build for themselves! This animated picture is a part of the lives of millions of people every day. How many, I wonder, give it so much as a second glance? Very few, I fear. Their eyes are blind to this magnificent sight because it is so familiar to them.

East River, Dong Kingman, watercolor, 1953.

I hurry to the top of one of those gigantic structures, the Empire State Building, for there, a short time ago, I "saw" the city below through the eyes of my secretary. I am anxious to compare my fancy with reality. I am sure I should not be disappointed in the panorama spread out before me, for to me it would be a vision of another world.

Now I begin my rounds of the city. First, I stand at a busy corner, merely looking at people, trying by sight of them to understand something of their lives. I see smiles, and I am happy. I see serious determination, and I am proud. I see suffering, and I am compassionate.

I stroll down Fifth Avenue. I throw my eyes out of focus, so that I see no particular object but only a seething kaleidoscope of color. I am certain that the colors of women's dresses moving in a throng must be a gorgeous spectacle of which I should never tire. But perhaps if I had sight, I should be like most other women—too interested in styles and the cut of individual dresses to give much attention to the splendor of color in the mass. And I am convinced, too, that I should become an inveterate[31] window shopper, for it must be a delight to the eye to view the myriad articles of beauty on display.

From Fifth Avenue I make a tour of the city—to Park Avenue, to the slums, to factories, to parks where children play. I take a stay-at-home trip abroad by visiting the foreign quarters.[32] Always my eyes are open wide to all the sights of both happiness and misery so that I may probe deep and add to my understanding of how people work and live. My heart is full of the images of people and things. My eye passes lightly over no single trifle; it strives to touch and hold closely each thing its gaze rests upon. Some sights are pleasant, filling the heart with happiness; but some are miserably pathetic. To these latter I do not shut my eyes, for they, too, are part of life. To close the eye on them is to close the heart and mind.

My third day of sight is drawing to an end. Perhaps there are many serious pursuits to which I should devote the few remaining hours, but I am afraid that on the evening of that last day I should again run away to the theater, to a hilariously funny play, so that I might appreciate the overtones of comedy in the human spirit.

At midnight my temporary respite from blindness would cease, and permanent night would close in on me again. Naturally in those three short days I should not have seen all I wanted to see. Only when darkness had again descended upon me should I realize how much I had left unseen. But my mind would be so crowded with glorious memories that I should have little time for regrets. Thereafter the touch of every object would bring a glowing memory of how that object looked.

Perhaps this short outline of how I should spend three days of sight does not agree with the program you would set for yourself if you knew that you were about to be stricken blind. I am, however, sure that if you actually faced that fate your eyes would open to things you had never seen before, storing up memories for the long night ahead. You would use your eyes as never before. Everything you saw would become dear to you. Your eyes would touch and embrace every object that came within your range of vision. Then, at last, you would really see, and a new world of beauty would open itself before you.

I who am blind can give one hint to those who see—one admonition[33] to those who would make full use of the gift of sight: Use your eyes as if tomorrow you would be stricken blind. And the same method can be applied to the other senses. Hear the music of voices, the song of a bird, the mighty strains of an orchestra, as if you would be stricken deaf tomorrow. Touch each object you want to touch as if tomorrow your tactile sense would fail. Smell the perfume of flowers, taste with relish each morsel, as if tomorrow you could never smell and taste again. Make the most of every sense; glory in all the facets of pleasure and beauty which the world reveals to you through the several means of contact which Nature provides. But of all the senses, I am sure that sight must be the most delightful.

---

31. **inveterate** [in vet′ər it]: settled in a habit or practice.
32. **foreign quarters:** sections of a city where people born in or still attached to the culture of another country live.

---

33. **admonition** [ad′mə nish′ən]: advice or warning.

READER'S RESPONSE

Do you think that sight is the "most delight-ful" of all the senses? Why or why not?

STUDY QUESTIONS

Recalling

1. What does Keller say about the way in which most people use their "faculties and senses"?
2. In what way does Keller generally organize her three days of sight?
3. List at least one specific thing that she would see during each of her three days.
4. According to Keller, why would she "have little time for regrets" after three days of sight?

Interpreting

5. Why do you think Keller feels that the first person she would like to see is Anne Sullivan?
6. Why do you think Keller feels that history and art are important enough for her to devote one third of her time with vision to them?

Extending

7. What would you look at if you had only three days of sight? Why?

READING AND LITERARY FOCUS

Essay

An **essay** is a short work of nonfiction that expresses the writer's observations or opinions on a particular subject. There are several different types of essays. A **narrative essay** tells a story, usually in chronological order. A **descriptive essay** creates a clear picture of something. An **expository essay** presents facts or explains ideas. A **persuasive essay** attempts to convince you to accept an opinion or take action.

Thinking About the Essay

1. What is the subject of Helen Keller's essay?
2. What kind of essay is "Three Days to See"? How do you know?

Persuasion

Persuasion is writing in which an author tries to make the reader accept an opinion or take an action. To be persuasive, writers must back up their opinions with **objective evidence**—facts, incidents, and examples. Keller backs up an opinion with evidence when she writes that many husbands do not know the color of their wife's eyes.

Persuasive writers also offer **logical arguments,** or reasons, in support of their opinions. For example, Keller gives a logical argument for appreciating the sense of sight when she recounts that she has only been able to touch the objects at the Museum of Natural History.

Thinking About Persuasion

1. Restate in your own words one opinion that Helen Keller expresses in her essay.
2. Relate one piece of evidence or logical argument that she uses to support her opinion.
3. Does Keller's writing persuade you? Why or why not?

COMPOSITION

Writing About a Persuasive Essay

Write a brief composition telling how persuasive you found Keller's essay. **Prewriting:** List the evidence and arguments that support your viewpoint. **Writing:** Restate Keller's opinion in your own words. Then tell whether she persuaded you to accept this opinion. If she succeeded, use your prewriting notes to tell why. If she did not succeed, use your notes to tell what faults you found in her evidence and arguments. **Revising:** Review your composition to see that you have expressed your ideas clearly and logically.

Writing Persuasion

Choose an issue that is currently in the news, one about which you have a strong opinion. Write an essay expressing your opinion on this issue. Using facts, incidents, and logical arguments to support your opinion, develop your viewpoint so that other people will be persuaded to accept it.

Don Marquis (1878–1937) tried many occupations—clerk, teacher, actor, and farmhand—before deciding to be a journalist. He set himself the goal of improving enough to write a column and signing his own name to it. Eventually two New York newspapers printed his columns, which were called "The Sun Dial" and "The Lantern." He was also interested in writing fantasy, particularly with animal characters. He is in fact best remembered for his poems and stories about archy (the cockroach) and mehitabel (the cat). It is archy who tells the tale of how "freddy the rat perishes."

you remember freddy the rat well
freddy is no more

• •

Don Marquis

freddy the rat perishes

listen to me there have
been some doings here since last
i wrote there has been a battle
behind that rusty typewriter cover
5 in the corner
you remember freddy the rat well
freddy is no more but
he died game[1] the other
day a stranger with a lot of
10 legs came into our
little circle a tough looking kid
he was with a bad eye

who are you said a thousand legs
if i bite you once
15 said the stranger you won t ask
again he he little poison tongue said
the thousand legs who gave you hydrophobia[2]

---

1. **died game:** died without being beaten in spirit.
2. **hydrophobia** [hī′drə fō′bē ə]: rabies, a fatal disease spread by animals.

Rat IV, Manon Cleary, 1977.

i got it by biting myself said
the stranger i m bad keep away
20 from me where i step a weed dies
if i was to walk on your forehead it would
raise measles and if
you give me any lip i ll do it

they mixed it then
25 and the thousand legs succumbed[3]

---

3. **succumbed** [sə kumd′]: gave way under pressure
or force.

well we found out this fellow
was a tarantula he had come up from
south america in a bunch of bananas
for days he bossed us life
30 was not worth living he would stand in
the middle of the floor and taunt
us ha ha he would say where i
step a weed dies do
you want any of my game i was
35 raised on red pepper and blood i am
so hot if you scratch me i will light
like a match you better
dodge me when i m feeling mean and
i don t feel any other way i was nursed
40 on a tabasco[4] bottle if i was to slap
your wrist in kindness you
would boil over like job[5] and heaven
help you if i get angry give me
room i feel a wicked spell coming on

Mark's Rat, Manon Cleary, 1977.

45 last night he made a break at freddy
the rat keep your distance
little one said freddy i m not
feeling well myself somebody poisoned some
cheese for me i m as full of
50 death as a drug store i
feel that i am going to die anyhow
come on little torpedo come on don t stop
to visit and search then they
went at it and both are no more . . .

55 . . . . we dropped freddy
off the fire escape into the alley with
military honors
           archy[6]

---

4. **tabasco** [tə ba′skō]: trade name of a spicy sauce.
5. **job** [jōb]: in the Bible, righteous man who patiently accepts God's tests of his faith, including having his body covered with boils.
6. **archy:** in Don Marquis's tales, the name of a poetic cockroach who is supposed to have composed the stories at night using a typewriter in a deserted office.

READER'S RESPONSE

Do you think someone in the group should have stopped freddy from fighting? Explain your answer.

STUDY QUESTIONS

Recalling

1. Who does the narrator say "is no more"?
2. In the first stanza, what words does the narrator use to describe the stranger?
3. In the second stanza, who challenges the stranger? What does the stranger say happens "where i step"?
4. What happens "for days" after the stranger kills a thousand legs?
5. Who is the stranger? Where does he come from?
6. What happened to freddy before his battle with the tarantula? What happens as a result of their fight?

Interpreting

7. Do you think the thousand legs was right to challenge the stranger? Why or why not?
8. In the third stanza, which words show you that the tarantula is feeling confident?
9. Why do you think freddy describes himself as being "as full of death as a drugstore"?
10. How do you know that freddy was respected by the group?

Extending

11. If someone bothered you and your friends, in what ways could you handle the situation without using violence?

READING AND LITERARY FOCUS

Narrative Poetry

A **narrative poem** tells a story in verse. Like a short story a narrative poem has a plot, a setting, and characters. Often the events of a narrative poem unfold in a chronological sequence, or in the exact order in which they occur in time.

"Freddy the rat perishes" is told in chronological order. It begins with the arrival of a stranger at the place where freddy lives. The middle of the poem describes the tarantula's control of the group and the death of a thousand legs. The poem ends with the death of freddy and the tarantula.

Thinking About Narrative Poetry

1. Which characters appear in "freddy the rat perishes"? What is the setting?
2. List the complete sequence of events, as they are told in "freddy the rat perishes."

CHALLENGE

Cartoon

You can retell "freddy the rat perishes" by creating a cartoon. Begin by dividing a sheet of paper into the number of boxes necessary for you to tell the story. You may want to refer to the events you listed in "Thinking About Narrative Poetry" to help you plan your story and illustration. You might start your cartoon by showing archy pecking away at his typewriter. When you are done, share your work with other members of the class.

Robert Nye (born 1939) is an English author who has worked as a novelist, critic, scriptwriter, dramatist, poet, editor, and author of children's books. He is best known for the novels in which he takes well-known myths and legends and gives them an unexpected twist, such as this new telling of the epic *Beowulf*, the long narrative poem that was composed almost thirteen hundred years ago. Nye says that his *Beowulf* is "an interpretation, not a translation. Myth seems to me to have a particular importance for children, as for poets: it lives in them. One retells old myths and legends hoping to be rewarded with the discovery that their meaning is still very much alive and creative."

It was not a lizard at all. It was the Firedrake, most evil of creatures which haunt the burying places of men!

Robert Nye

from **Beowulf**

Beowulf[1] was now an old man. His beard was white. His back was bent. He was nearly blind. He had done nothing much for forty years but tend his bees. The bees had taught him, he said, to rule wisely. There was order and beauty in the world of bees. He had tried to bring some of that to the world of men.

But there was one person in the land of the Geats[2] who was not happy. He was a slave, and he had been threatened with a beating for doing something wrong. He did not like being beaten, so he ran away. He climbed high into the mountains to hide.

Now, nobody usually ventured into the mountains because long ago one of them had been opened up and used as a burying place for princes. As was the custom, all their treasures had been buried with them—gold and silver, swords and jeweled cups. People believed that it was best to leave such places alone. The treasure had been given back to the earth, and it would be a sin to steal it.

The slave was desperate. He did not care about any of this. He clambered up over storm-lashed rocks. The place was wild. Huge blocks of stone lay everywhere,

---

1. **Beowulf** [bā′ə woolf′]: hero of Old English epic, a type of long poem that celebrates the adventures of a great hero; composed by an unknown poet, probably early in the eighth century.
2. **Geats** [gā′ats]: the tribe to which Beowulf belonged, a Scandinavian people of southern Sweden conquered by the Swedes in the sixth century.

piled against the mountainside, threatening to fall, strewn about as though hurled by giants in some dreadful battle. At last he got to the top. This was where the treasure had been buried.

He crept inside a narrow crack in the rock. It was like being inside a demon's mouth. Teeth tore at him as he wriggled along. They may have been no more than sharp ridges in the walls of the passage, but to the slave, alone and frightened in the dark, they seemed alive and snapping. Something did not welcome his presence here. His scalp prickled. His spine felt like an icicle. But there was no going back.

He came into a natural chamber. The light dazzled his eyes. The chamber was crammed with treasure. On the floor, in the middle of a maze of gold, sat a lizard.

The slave felt panic flooding through his limbs as the lizard's eyes swiveled to look at him. He grabbed the nearest thing to hand—a jeweled cup big enough to bathe a baby in—and turned, and squeezed into the flaw in the rock.

There was a fury at his heels. The lizard hissed and swelled. Fire poured from its mouth. It was not a lizard at all. It was the Firedrake, most evil of creatures which haunt the burying places of men!

The slave's hair caught fire in the blast of flame the Firedrake sent to follow him. He screamed. But he clung on tight to the cup. He had one thought—if he took this prize back to his master he might escape the whipping. It must be worth a lot.

He struggled out into open air and plunged his head straight in a mountain stream. Then he set off as fast as he could, scrambling down the rocks, the cup clutched to his chest.

The mountain shook with the raging of the Firedrake. Its scaly body swelled and swelled as it got angrier. It had gold eyes and a thrashing tail. Flames came teeming from its mouth, and molten spit, and reeking, scorching smoke. The effect was like a volcano.

Fortunately for the slave, the creature's swollen state prevented the Firedrake from following him through the fissure in the rock. If this had not been so, the thief would have been roasted alive.

Beowulf Against the Firedrake

By nightfall the Firedrake managed to cool its temper. It crawled out from its den and stood on top of the mountain. Its gold eyes flared like meteors in the dusk. It was a long time since it had needed to leave the glittering hoard it gloated over. Deep in its tiny brain a coal of evil began to glow. It wanted revenge. It looked down at the lights in the valley, the houses of the peaceful country-folk. They seemed to form the shape of a great jeweled cup. The creature lashed its tail in fury. It spread its wings, and swooped.

Houses, churches, fields of grain, nothing was spared by the Firedrake in its ruinous flight. People woke up to find fire at their windows, and ran from their doors howling warning, only to encounter the same flames everywhere, leaping and lapping, laying the countryside bare. In the morning, when the Firedrake flapped back to its den, the valley looked like a basin of white ashes. Even the streams had caught fire and burned away.

They brought the slave to Beowulf, and he told his story. When he had finished, and his master had shown the king the stolen cup, some of the lords of the court cried out that the slave should be offered to the Firedrake as a sacrifice.

Beowulf hummed, then said: "No, let him eat honey."

Most of those present looked curiously at the king, and muttered among themselves, thinking him mad. "He is too old," said one. "His wits are warped."

Only Wiglaf, son of Weohstan, had a good word for Beowulf. "By saying the slave should eat honey," he explained, "he means that we should find a little pity in our hearts for one who was driven by despair to do something he will always regret."

"All the honey in the world can't sweeten the bitterness this wretch has brought down upon us," said one of the old soldiers. "It means the old days are back. War and strife and pestilence, that's what it means. You're young, Wiglaf, and you don't know what you're talking about."

Wiglaf flushed. "It's true I've had no experience of battle," he said, "but I'm sure I'd prove as brave as you."

"Well," sneered the soldier, "no one ever won a wound by boasting, eh? Young Wiglaf against the Firedrake! That should be a fight worth watching! When are you going to volunteer?"

Wiglaf bit his lip.

Beowulf silenced them all with a wave of his hand. He might be an old man but he still carried authority. "I will go against the Firedrake," he said.

Nobody dared to argue.

Beowulf began buckling on his armor. His huge hands shook. Wiglaf had to help him. The young man could not help remarking that Beowulf's body had shrunk with age. His coat of mail hung loose from his stooping shoulders. But his heart, thought Wiglaf, was as big and brave as it had always been—that would never shrink.

Beowulf said nothing. He hummed to himself. He was thinking of a tale he had heard long ago, in Hrothgar's[3] court, at the time of the celebrations occasioned by his victory over Grendel: the tale of Sigemund and little Fitela, and how they had outwitted the Fire Dragon. Patiently, he began to form a plan in his mind.

The old warriors murmured together. For all their complaining, they loved Beowulf, and they could not bear the thought of his going alone to what looked like certain death.

A spokesman stepped forward. "Twelve of us," he said, "want to come with you."

Beowulf nodded absent-mindedly. "Good, good."

"If swords are any use, then—"

"They aren't," said Beowulf.

"Oh." The soldier was flabbergasted.

"But you can carry the hives," said Beowulf.

"The—hives?"

"That's right."

Beowulf stood up. "Wiglaf," he said.

"My lord?"

"You come too."

They climbed up into the mountains. Beowulf went slowly, leaning on Wiglaf's shoulder. The other twelve followed behind, each man struggling with one of the enormous hives on his back. Wiglaf, on Beowulf's instructions, carried a newly cut

---

3. **Hrothgar** [hroth′gär]: in *Beowulf,* king of the Danes whose sleeping warriors are eaten each night by the monster Grendel until Beowulf kills the monster.

Viking Tombstone, c. 1030.

stake, about six feet long, and a glove that would have fitted a giant. None of the others knew what these were for, and they all thought privately that Beowulf had gone quite mad in having them venture, thus equipped, against a monster that could breathe fire. Beowulf said nothing by way of explanation. He chuckled as he told Wiglaf the story of Sigemund and Fitela. He said: "They used their wits, you see. If you can't beat evil by strength alone, then a little cunning is called for."

Wiglaf told his king how black the burned-out valley looked below. Beowulf nodded sadly. "No one can bring back the living who were lost," he said, "yet some good can be plucked from the worst disaster. The Firedrake will pay for what it has done—not only with its life, but with the gold it keeps watch over. What good does gold do, buried in the earth? When we have killed the creature we will use that treasure to build again each dwelling that is gone."

An eagle drifted high overhead. Young Wiglaf looked from the eagle to his master, and back again. Beowulf was bent and breathless. The eagle was king of the air. Yet, thought Wiglaf, there was not so much difference between them.

Bees

Beowulf halted his men when they came to the crack that led to the Firedrake's den. He had them set the hives down in the entrance. Then he sat for a while, muttering to the bees in each hive. No one could make out what he said. It sounded like nonsense.

At last, just as the sinking sun came level with the crags behind them, he motioned for Wiglaf to go forward.

The lad, acquainted with his master's plan, slipped into the crack. He carried the white stake in his left hand. In his right hand, and very carefully, as though it contained something infinitely precious, he carried the giant glove.

The others were too puzzled to protest. They noticed that the bees in each hive buzzed busily as Wiglaf wriggled past them. Beowulf stooped and murmured soothingly and the noise subsided.

Once inside the narrow passageway, Wiglaf moved on tiptoe, deftly. He was a small person, slim and agile, which was partly why Beowulf had chosen him for the job. When he came to the bright treasure-chamber he skipped into it like a shadow. As it happened, the Firedrake was asleep—worn-out by its night's havoc—and did not see him hide himself amid the gold.

Beowulf was watching the sun. When he judged that enough time had elapsed for Wiglaf to have performed the first part of the plan successfully, he crept into the crack himself. He set his horn to his lips and blew a loud rude blast.

"Haloo," he cried. "Haloo, old fire-belcher! I am Beowulf, come to quench you!"

The Firedrake's golden eyes snapped open. It could not believe that anyone would be so foolhardy as to shout at it inside the mountain.

Beowulf sounded another mocking note on his horn. "Ho, you, old smoky-guts! Where are you hiding?"

The Firedrake hissed with rage. No one had ever spoken to it like this before. Its tail began to flog the rock. Its body started to swell in the usual way.

Peeping from his hiding-place, little Wiglaf waited anxiously for the right moment. He could hear the grumbling fire beginning in the creature's belly. Smoke was whistling from its nostrils. It was getting bigger every moment. Wiglaf crouched, ready to pounce.

"Call yourself a dragon?" shouted Beowulf. "You look more like a glow-worm!"[4]

The Firedrake had reached full size. When it heard this final insult it swallowed hard in its fury.

Wiglaf seized his chance. He leaped.

Quick as lightning he thrust the big stake in the Firedrake's jaws, jamming them open even as the creature gaped wide to let loose the first foul gust of flame. The golden eyes glared at this new

---

4. **glow-worm:** any of various insects, such as the fire-fly, that give off light.

surprise. The barbed tail thrashed and twisted to be at him. But Wiglaf dodged, danced, flitted out of range. And as he went he threw the giant glove into the open mouth.

The Firedrake coughed. A hail of cinders flew out. For a terrible moment Wiglaf thought the glove had come out too—but, no, it was still there, caught on a tooth that looked like a scythe.

As Wiglaf watched, the glove flapped and bulged.

Beowulf made a high-pitched buzzing sound.

The Firedrake took a deep breath . . . and swallowed a big Queen Bee[5] that emerged from the glove as if in answer to Beowulf's call!

"They follow the Queen Bee *anywhere!*" This, whispered to Wiglaf on the way up the mountain, was the essence of Beowulf's plan. Now, in response to another noise he made, sawing at his lips with his square-tipped fingers, all the twelve hives came alive. The bees poured out, a singing angry stream, orange, brown, black, yellow. They buzzed into the crack in the mountain.

They whirled past Beowulf. And on into the brightness of the treasure-chamber.

The Firedrake saw them coming. Its gold eyes bulged with fright. It tried to shut its mouth, but the stake between its jaws prevented this.

The bees poured down the monster's throat like a stream of honey, in pursuit of their queen. But when they reached the

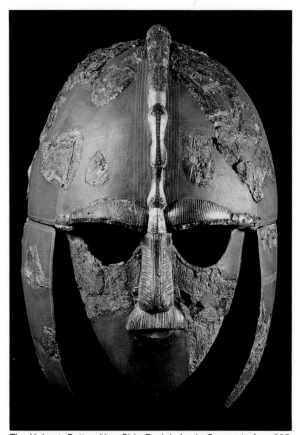

The Helmet, Sutton Hoo Ship Burial, Anglo-Saxon, before 665.

Firedrake's stomach their effect was like no honey in the world.

They began to sting!

Hundreds of bees, stinging it from the inside!

The Firedrake roared with pain and fury.

It tried to spit out bees. But there were too many.

It tried to spew up fire. But its own insides were burning.

Little Wiglaf danced with glee.

But Beowulf had collapsed in the entrance to the treasure-chamber. His armor came undone. It was all too big and heavy for him.

---

5. **Queen Bee:** in a bee colony, the female bee whose function is to lay eggs.

Some men said, long afterwards, that Beowulf was killed by the burning breath of the Firedrake. But, in truth, the monster managed only the merest tiny little cough of smoke before turning over on its side and giving up the ghost.[6] Beowulf's bees had stung it to death.

Wiglaf knelt by his master's side.

Beowulf chuckled. "A pretty trick," he said. "Listen, Wiglaf. When I was young I'd never have done a thing like that. I'd have thought it was dishonorable, or something. Well, the dragon lies dead and the treasure is there for the good of our people. Who was right? Old Beowulf, or young Beowulf?"

Wiglaf said, "Both."

Beowulf was quiet for a while. His eyes seemed to overflow with the dazzling light off the treasure, and tears ran down his cheeks.

"A pity about the bees," he said at last. "I loved them."

"They died well, master," Wiglaf said. Then he began to laugh. He could not help or stop himself. "What a trick!" he cried. "Who ever would have thought of it!"

Beowulf winked one watery eye. "Perhaps it's better that nobody should just now," he said. "Tell them what you like, the ones out there, but remember the world will need to be a little older before it understands this last exploit of Beowulf. Yes, and all the others too! Meanwhile, it must have an ordinary kind of hero to believe in. Make sure you give them that, Wiglaf. It will serve for now. And one day—who knows how far ahead?—if my name should live, someone will stumble on this story and put the pieces together again, and come up with the truth of it."

Wiglaf shook his head. "I doubt it," he said. "Not this last bit, anyway."

"Beowulf," said Beowulf. "Beowulf, the beehunter. Well, it might occur to somebody."

They buried Beowulf's body in a great green fist of land that stuck out into the sea. And they heaped white stones upon it, to show how much they had loved him. In the years that followed the place became a well-known landmark for mariners. Men would point to it on the way to sea, saying: "There is Beowulf's grave." And no one saw it without feeling an inch taller where he stood.

Wiglaf never told the whole story about the bees. He became king in Beowulf's stead, and ruled wisely and well to the end of his days. When people asked him this or that about the dead hero he had one way of answering—with a little puzzling smile in his eyes as he silently recalled a golden stream of bees disappearing down a dragon's throat. "Beowulf," he said, "was Beowulf."

"Come now," the more curious people protested, smelling a mystery. "There must have been more to it than that."

"No more, no less," said Wiglaf. "Beowulf was Beowulf."

And that was all he would say, ever.

---

6. **giving up the ghost:** dying.

READER'S RESPONSE

Do you think that Beowulf should have been the one to fight the Firedrake? Why or why not?

STUDY QUESTIONS

Recalling
1. What does the slave steal from the Firedrake? For what reason does he do this?
2. What does the Firedrake do in retaliation?
3. Describe the appearance of the Firedrake.
4. What plan does Beowulf have to kill the Firedrake? Does it work?
5. What does Beowulf tell Wiglaf to say about the battle with the Firedrake?

Interpreting
6. Why do you think Beowulf gives the slave honey instead of punishing him?
7. Describe Beowulf's personality in your own words, and list examples for each of his character traits.
8. In what ways does Beowulf prove that he is a good king?

Extending
9. Can you think of other situations in which it is useful to use intellect rather than physical strength? Explain your answer.

READING AND LITERARY FOCUS

External Conflict
Most plots present a conflict of some kind. A **conflict** is a struggle between two opposing forces. The details of the conflict gain our interest as we begin to read the story. At the story's climax we see how the conflict will be solved. The **resolution** reveals the conflict's final outcome.

An **external conflict** occurs when a character struggles against an outside force. Tom Vincent's battle to survive the cold of the Klondike in "To Build a Fire" is one example of external conflict. There are several specific kinds of external conflict. One kind is a person's struggle against nature, as in the case of a family escaping from a fire. Another kind is a conflict between two people, as in an argument or a contest. Still another kind occurs when a person struggles against society, as when a citizen tries to change a law.

Thinking About External Conflict
Identify two external conflicts in "Beowulf," and tell how each is resolved.

VOCABULARY

Sentence Completions
Each of the following items contains a blank with four possible words for completing the sentence. The words are from "Beowulf." Choose the word that best completes each sentence. Write the number of each sentence and the letter of your choice on a separate sheet of paper.

1. The old key opened the door of the ___.
   (a) padlock   (c) fixture
   (b) dwelling   (d) balcony
2. The sheep ___ over the rocky cliffs.
   (a) rotated   (c) regressed
   (b) bleated   (d) clambered
3. The farmer cut the wheat with a ___.
   (a) silo   (c) scythe
   (b) plow   (d) tractor
4. The hurricane created ___ for everyone.
   (a) havoc   (c) shipwrecks
   (b) relaxation   (d) hilarity
5. The baby's crying ___ when she was fed.
   (a) deafened   (c) subsided
   (b) escalated   (d) amplified

Collaborative Learning:
Themes

Heroes and Survivors

When people hear the word *hero*, they very often think of a strong, larger-than-life figure of the imagination—a fairy-tale prince, a victorious medieval knight, a fierce Greek goddess. These characters indeed are heroes, but their qualities of courage, persistence, and nobility of spirit can be found in people all around us.

There are ordinary citizens who show immense courage and resourcefulness in moments of crisis. There are also many who reveal great heroism as they quietly combat emotions and physical problems with persistence and dignity.

1. **Panel Discussion** With a group first conduct a discussion on what makes a hero. Ask each person to name two favorite heroes from public life. Then brainstorm to make a list of the qualities that *everyone* recognizes as heroic. Each person should then research his or her two heroes, noting their outstanding traits.

    Choose a leader. During the panel discussion evaluate all the chosen heroes, and decide whether they have some or all of the heroic qualities listed earlier. Determine which of their heroic qualities are unique to each individual and which they have in common. Take comments from the class at the end of the discussion.

2. **Oral Report** Almost everyone has a family member or a friend who has managed to triumph over great odds. Often the victory lies less in actually reaching the goal than in the courage and spirit shown along the way.

    With a group, review what you all consider to be heroic behavior. Then brainstorm to come up with a list of people who have triumphed over odds—people whom you know personally or perhaps have learned about from the newspapers or television.

    After your discussion choose for your group report the people who best demonstrate the qualities you as a group have identified as heroic. Each group member should report on one hero. At the end of the oral report, invite class members to comment and tell similar stories from their own experience.

Collaborative Learning:
Across the Curriculum

Heroes and Survivors

1. **Literature and Social Studies: Interviews** Since Colonial times people have been coming to this country to escape religious and political persecution, famine, and other disasters in their native land. Many immigrants came with little or no money and had to struggle to survive. Gradually most settled down and made America their home.

   With a group, plan to collect a series of interviews on the immigrant experience in the United States. People to question include family members, neighbors, and the families of friends. Develop several questions that everyone in your group will use. These might include asking the subjects to recall their day of arrival, their first job, their first home, the low and high points of their early days as immigrants. If you can, borrow old photographs to show to the class.

   Type your interview, and if possible, illustrate it with copies of the photographs. Bring it to the group meeting, and compare notes. Then together write a summary of your impressions about the immigrant experience. Use it as an introduction to your collected interviews, which you will bind in a folder and donate to the class library.

2. **Literature and Science: Biography** Among the greatest heroes are scientists and inventors. Their discoveries range from easing our lives to saving them.

   With a group, plan to write a brief biography of a famous scientist or inventor. At your first meeting brainstorm to determine what you think are the most significant discoveries. Then select one. The subject of the biography is the person who made that discovery.

   Go to the library, and research this scientist. Each group member should use a different reference work. Compare notes at your next group meeting, and begin to work on an outline. Remember to include the qualities of heroism that marked the scientist's life and work. Then start writing the biography itself. Try to obtain a picture of the scientist to accompany the biography. If time permits, read all or part of the biography to the class.

A disaster is an event that causes harm to someone or something. Disasters can be awesome natural events, such as hurricanes or floods, that affect many people. They can also be smaller, more personal matters that touch only a few. A failed test or a mishandled secret can feel like a disaster.

A disaster's physical effects are usually obvious. For instance, you can see how flood waters sweep away houses and automobiles. It is sometimes less easy to recognize the ways in which a disaster affects people's thoughts and feelings, however. For example, a person who helps build a dam in order to divert oncoming flood waters is likely to learn something important about teamwork or view the power of nature in a new way.

In the literature that follows, disasters cause people to feel afraid, to be brave, and to make decisions. In one story a young boy wrestles with the fact that his family must move to a new town every few months. In another a girl learns how a cold snap can mean the difference between life and death. In each selection a disaster encourages some new understanding of the world.

Tornado Over Kansas, John Steuart Curry (1894–1946).

A Model for Active Reading

Literature will give you more pleasure when you read it actively and attentively. Remember that you are the writer's audience—the writer is a performer who needs you to respond.

Below are the responses of an active reader. Notice that the reader asks questions, makes guesses, and brings personal experience to the reading.

As you read the selection that begins on the following page, remember that you are part of the writer's performance.

Jack London

If he was an eyewitness, this is probably a true story of an earthquake.	

Earthquake: The Story of an Eyewitness

The earthquake shook down in San Francisco[1] hundreds of thousands of dollars worth of walls and chimneys. But the conflagration[2] that followed burned up hundreds of millions of dollars worth of property. There is no estimating within hundreds of millions the actual damage wrought.

This sounds like the earthquake California had just recently!

What does "imperial" mean? There is no American emperor, so it probably means "big" or "important."

Not in history has a modern imperial city been so completely destroyed. San Francisco is gone. Nothing remains of it but memories and fringe of dwelling houses on its outskirts. Its industrial section is wiped out. Its business section is wiped out. Its social and residential section is wiped out. The factories and warehouses, the great stores and newspaper buildings, the hotels and the palaces of the nabobs,[3] are all gone. Remains only the fringe of dwelling houses on the outskirts of what was once San Francisco.

If this is all that was left, where was the eyewitness and how did he survive?

Within an hour after the earthquake shock, the smoke of San Francisco's burning was a lurid tower visible a hundred miles away. And for three days and nights this lurid tower swayed in the sky, reddening the sun, darkening the day, and filling the land with smoke.

This sounds like the end of the world or a passage out of the Bible.

Jack London (1876–1916) spent most of his life fighting hardship. His family was desperately poor, and as a teen-ager London left home to make a living. He traveled across the United States and Canada working as a sailor, a factory hand, a seal hunter, and a gold prospector. At age twenty-two he became a writer. London was fascinated by disasters, and his writing usually describes a person or an animal fighting to survive. Many of his famous works (including *The Call of the Wild*, *White Fang*, and "To Build a Fire") feature a character battling to stay alive in the vast wilderness of northern Canada. In his nonfiction account "Earthquake: The Story of an Eyewitness," London describes San Francisco in 1906 as a whole city fights to save itself from ruin.

Not in history has a modern imperial city been so completely destroyed. San Francisco is gone.

• •

Jack London

Earthquake: The Story of an Eyewitness

The earthquake shook down in San Francisco[1] hundreds of thousands of dollars worth of walls and chimneys. But the conflagration[2] that followed burned up hundreds of millions of dollars worth of property. There is no estimating within hundreds of millions the actual damage wrought.

Not in history has a modern imperial city been so completely destroyed. San Francisco is gone. Nothing remains of it but memories and fringe of dwelling houses on its outskirts. Its industrial section is wiped out. Its business section is wiped out. Its social and residential section is wiped out. The factories and warehouses, the great stores and newspaper buildings, the hotels and the palaces of the nabobs,[3] are all gone. Remains only the fringe of dwelling houses on the outskirts of what was once San Francisco.

Within an hour after the earthquake shock, the smoke of San Francisco's burning was a lurid tower visible a hundred miles away. And for three days and nights

---

1. **earthquake . . . San Francisco:** On April 18, 1906, a massive earthquake occurred in San Francisco, California, resulting in fires that destroyed much of the city and left tens of thousands of its residents homeless.
2. **conflagration** [kon′flə grā′shən]: very large, destructive fire.

3. **nabobs** [nā′bäbz]: rich men.

this lurid tower swayed in the sky, reddening the sun, darkening the day, and filling the land with smoke.

On Wednesday morning at quarter past five came the earthquake. A minute later the flames were leaping upward. In a dozen different quarters south of Market Street, in the working class ghetto[4] and in the factories, fires started. There was no opposing the flames. There was no organization, no communication. All the cunning adjustments of a twentieth century city had been smashed by the earthquake. The streets were humped into ridges and depressions, and piled with the debris of fallen walls. The steel rails were twisted into perpendicular and horizontal angles. The telephone and telegraph systems were disrupted. And the great water mains had burst. All the shrewd contrivances and safeguards of man had been thrown out of gear by thirty seconds' twitching of the earth-crust.

By Wednesday afternoon, inside of twelve hours, half the heart of the city was gone. At that time I watched the vast conflagration from out on the bay. It was dead calm. Not a flicker of wind stirred. Yet from every side wind was pouring in upon the city. East, west, north, and south, strong winds were blowing upon the doomed city. The heated air rising made an enormous suck. Thus did the fire of itself build its own colossal[5] chimney through the atmosphere. Day and night this dead calm continued, and yet, near to the flames, the wind was often half a gale, so mighty was the suck.

Wednesday night saw the destruction of the very heart of the city. Dynamite was lavishly used, and many of San Francisco's proudest structures were crumbled by man himself into ruins, but there was no withstanding the onrush of the flames. Time and again successful stands were made by the firefighters, and every time the flames flanked around on either side, or came up from the rear, and turned to defeat the hard won victory.

An enumeration[6] of the buildings destroyed would be a directory of San Francisco. An enumeration of the buildings undestroyed would be a line and several addresses. An enumeration of the deeds of heroism would stock a library and bankrupt the Carnegie medal fund.[7] An enumeration of the dead—will never be made. All vestiges of them were destroyed by the flames. The number of the victims of the earthquake will never be known. South of Market Street, where the loss of life was particularly heavy, was the first to catch fire.

Remarkable as it may seem, Wednesday night, while the whole city crashed and roared into ruin, was a quiet night. There were no crowds. There was no shouting and yelling. There was no hysteria, no disorder. I passed Wednesday night in the path of the advancing flames, and in all those terrible hours I saw not one woman who wept, not one man who was excited, not one person who was in the slightest degree panic-stricken.

Before the flames, throughout the night, fled tens of thousands of homeless ones. Some were wrapped in blankets. Others carried bundles of bedding and dear house-

---

4. **ghetto** [get'ō]: section of a city that is home to a racial, religious, political, or other group differing in some way from the larger group of which it is a part.
5. **colossal** [kə los'əl]: immense; gigantic.

6. **enumeration** [i nōō'mə rā'shən]: act of naming one by one or listing.
7. **Carnegie medal fund:** Carnegie Hero fund created in 1904 by American man of industry Andrew Carnegie (1835–1919) to honor persons performing heroic deeds.

San Francisco Earthquake, 1906.

hold treasures. Sometimes a whole family was harnessed to a carriage or delivery wagon that was weighted down with their possessions. Baby-buggies, toy wagons and go-carts were used as trucks, while every other person was dragging a trunk. Yet everybody was gracious. The most perfect courtesy obtained. Never, in all San Francisco's history, were her people so kind and courteous as on this night of terror.

All night these tens of thousands fled before the flames. Many of them, the poor people from the labor ghetto, had fled all day as well. They had left their homes burdened with possessions. Now and again

they lightened up, flinging out upon the street clothing and treasures they had dragged for miles.

They held on longest to their trunks, and over these trunks many a strong man broke his heart that night. The hills of San Francisco are steep, and up these hills, mile after mile, were the trunks dragged. Everywhere were trunks, with across them lying their exhausted owners, men and women. Before the march of the flames were flung picket-lines of soldiers. And a block at a time, as the flames advanced, these pickets retreated. One of their tasks was to keep the trunk-pullers moving. The exhausted creatures, stirred on by the menace of bayonets, would arise and struggle up the steep pavements, pausing from weakness every five or ten feet.

Often, after surmounting a heart-breaking hill, they would find another wall of flame advancing upon them at right angles and be compelled to change anew the line of their retreat. In the end, completely played out, after toiling for a dozen hours like giants, thousands of them were compelled to abandon their trunks. Here the shop-keepers and soft members of the middle class were at a disadvantage. But the workingmen dug holes in vacant lots and backyards and buried their trunks.

At nine o'clock Wednesday evening, I walked down through the very heart of the city. I walked through miles and miles of magnificent buildings and towering sky-scrapers. Here was no fire. All was in perfect order. The police patrolled the streets. Every building had its watchman at the door. And yet it was doomed, all of it. There was no water. The dynamite was giving out. And at right angles two different conflagrations were sweeping down upon it.

At one o'clock in the morning I walked down through the same section. Everything still stood intact. There was no fire. And yet there was a change. A rain of ashes was falling. The watchmen at the doors were gone. The police had been withdrawn. There were no firemen, no fire-engines, no men fighting with dynamite. The district had been absolutely abandoned.

I stood at the corner of Kearney and Market, in the very innermost heart of San Francisco. Kearney Street was deserted. Half a dozen blocks away it was burning on both sides. The street was a wall of flame. And against this wall of flame, silhouetted sharply, were two United States cavalrymen sitting their horses, calmly watching. That was all. Not another person was in sight. In the intact heart of the city two troopers sat their horses and watched.

Surrender was complete. There was no water. The sewers had long since been pumped dry. There was no dynamite. Another fire had broken out farther uptown, and now from three sides conflagrations were sweeping down. The fourth side had been burned earlier in the day. In that direction stood the tottering walls of the *Examiner*[8] Building, the burned out *Call*[9] Building, the smoldering ruins of the Grand Hotel, and the gutted, devastated, dynamited Palace Hotel.

The following will illustrate the sweep of the flames and the inability of men to calculate their spread. At eight o'clock Wednesday evening I passed through Union Square.[10] It was packed with refugees. Thousands of them had gone to bed on the grass. Government tents had been set up, supper was being cooked, and the refugees were lining up for free meals.

At half past one in the morning three sides of Union Square were in flames. The fourth side, where stood the great St. Francis Hotel, was still holding out. An hour later, ignited from top and sides, the St. Francis was flaming heavenward. Union Square, heaped high with mountains of trunks, was deserted. Troops, refugees, and all had retreated.

It was at Union Square that I saw a man offering a thousand dollars for a team of horses. He was in charge of a truck piled

---

8. ***Examiner:*** San Francisco daily newspaper that began publication in the mid-1860s.
9. ***Call:*** San Francisco daily newspaper that began publication in the mid-1850s.
10. **Union Square:** block in downtown San Francisco, location of the city's central hotel and shopping district.

high with trunks from some hotel. It had been hauled here into what was considered safety and the horses had been taken out. The flames were on three sides of the Square, and there were no horses.

Also, at this time, standing beside the truck, I urged a man to seek safety in flight. He was all but hemmed in by several conflagrations. He was an old man and he was on crutches. Said he, "Today is my birthday. Last night I was worth thirty thousand dollars. I bought five bottles of wine, some delicate fish, and other things for my birthday dinner. I have had no dinner, and all I own are these crutches."

I convinced him of his danger and started him limping on his way. An hour later, from a distance, I saw the truckload of trunks burning merrily in the middle of the street.

On Thursday morning, at quarter past five, just twenty-four hours after the earthquake, I sat on the steps of a small residence on Nob Hill.[11] With me sat Japanese, Italians, Chinese, and Negroes—a bit of the cosmopolitan[12] flotsam[13] of the wreck of the city. All about were the palaces of the nabob pioneers of forty-nine.[14] To the east and south, at right angles, were advancing two mighty walls of flames.

I went inside with the owner of the house on the steps of which I sat. He was cool and cheerful and hospitable. "Yesterday morning," he said, "I was worth six hundred thousand dollars. This morning

City Hall, San Francisco Earthquake, 1906.

this house is all I have left. It will go in fifteen minutes." He pointed to a large cabinet. "That is my wife's collection of china. This rug upon which we stand is a present. It cost fifteen hundred dollars. Try that piano. Listen to its tone. There are few like it. There are no horses. The flames will be here in fifteen minutes."

Outside, the old Mark Hopkins residence, a palace, was just catching fire. The troops were falling back and driving the refugees before them. From every side came the roaring of flames, the crashing of walls, and the detonations of dynamite.

I passed out of the house. Day was trying to dawn through the smoke-pall. A sickly light was creeping over the face of things. Once only the sun broke through the smoke-pall, blood-red and showing quarter its usual size. The smoke-pall itself, viewed from beneath, was a rose-color that pulsed and fluttered with lavender shades. Then it turned to mauve[15] and yellow and

11. **Nob Hill:** elevated residential area of San Francisco and location of many mansions.
12. **cosmopolitan** [koz′mə pol′ə tən]: composed of people, qualities, or elements from many different countries.
13. **flotsam** [flot′səm]: here, homeless people who wander about from place to place.
14. **nabob pioneers of forty-nine:** men who became wealthy during the California gold rush of 1849.

15. **mauve** [mōv]: purplish-blue or rose color.

dun.[16] There was no sun. And so dawned the second day on stricken San Francisco.

An hour later I was creeping past the shattered dome of the City Hall. Than it, there was no better exhibit of the destructive force of the earthquake. Most of the stone had been shaken from the great dome, leaving standing the naked framework of steel. Market Street was piled high with the wreckage, and across the wreckage lay the overthrown pillars of the City Hall shattered into short crosswise sections.

This section of the city, with the exception of the Mint[17] and the Post Office, was already a waste of smoking ruins. Here and there through the smoke, creeping warily under the shadows of tottering walls, emerged occasional men and women. It was like the meeting of the handful of survivors after the day of the end of the world.

On Mission Street lay a dozen steers, in a neat row stretching across the street, just as they had been struck down by the flying ruins of the earthquake. The fire had passed through afterward and roasted them. The human dead had been carried away before the fire came. At another place on Mission Street I saw a milk wagon. A steel telegraph pole had smashed down sheer through the driver's seat and crushed the front wheels. The milk cans lay scattered around.

All day Thursday and all Thursday night, all day Friday and Friday night, the flames still raged. Friday night saw the flames finally conquered, though not until Russian Hill[18] and Telegraph Hill[19] had been swept and three-quarters of a mile of wharves and docks had been licked up.

The great stand of the firefighters was made Thursday night on Van Ness Avenue. Had they failed here, the comparatively few remaining houses of the city would have been swept. Here were the magnificent residences of the second generation of San Francisco nabobs, and these, in a solid zone, were dynamited down across the path of the fire. Here and there, the flames leaped the zone, but these isolated fires were beaten out, principally by the use of wet blankets and rugs.

San Francisco, at the present time, is like the crater of a volcano, around which are camped tens of thousands of refugees. At the Presidio[20] alone are at least twenty thousand. All the surrounding cities and towns are jammed with the homeless ones, where they are being cared for by the relief committees. The refugees were carried free by the railroads to any point they wished to go, and it is estimated that over one hundred thousand people have left the peninsula on which San Francisco stood. The government has the situation in hand, and, thanks to the immediate relief given by the whole United States, there is not the slightest possibility of a famine. The bankers and businessmen have already set about making preparations to rebuild San Francisco.

---

16. **dun:** dull grayish-brown color.
17. **Mint:** place where money is coined by authority of the government.

18. **Russian Hill:** elevated area in San Francisco where many large houses were located.
19. **Telegraph Hill:** elevated area in San Francisco, popular as a residential neighborhood.
20. **Presidio:** San Francisco district at the northernmost tip of the peninsula; site of many military buildings.

READER'S RESPONSE

In your opinion, what was the most disastrous part of the 1906 San Francisco earthquake?

STUDY QUESTIONS

Recalling

1. What two events occur Wednesday morning within minutes of each other? What is "thrown out of gear" in thirty seconds?
2. What is unusual about the behavior of the city's residents that night?
3. With what words does London describe the people sitting on the steps on Nob Hill? Whose steps are they?
4. What occurs Thursday night on Van Ness Avenue?
5. What do the city's bankers and business leaders do after the fires are put out?

Interpreting

6. Which did more damage to the city, the earthquake or the fires? Explain your answer.
7. What do you think the author is referring to with the words "all the shrewd contrivances and safeguards of man"?
8. In what ways are "the cosmopolitan flotsam" and "the nabob pioneers" on Nob Hill different? What do they have in common?
9. In what ways is the disaster victorious over the city? In what ways is the city victorious over the disaster?

Extending

10. How would you compare and contrast the San Francisco earthquakes of 1906 and 1989?

READING AND LITERARY FOCUS

Word Choice

Word choice refers to the selection of one word instead of another word. Writers choose words care-fully to create vivid images. For example, in the fourth paragraph of "Earthquake," London describes an earthquake as "thirty seconds' twitching of the earth-crust." By choosing the word *twitching,* he conveys an image of the earth as a powerful living thing.

Thinking About Word Choice

1. Look at the words *swept* and *licked up* in the essay's third-to-last paragraph. What effect is created by substituting the words *burned* and *destroyed*?
2. Choose another sentence in London's essay, and tell why a specific word in the sentence is an effective choice.

COMPOSITION

Writing About Word Choice

Write a paragraph in which you explain how London's choice of words creates a vivid image. **Prewriting:** Choose a sentence from "Earthquake" that contains a vivid image. List other words London might have chosen to create the same image. **Writing:** Begin by identifying the sentence's image. Explain how London's choice of words makes the image come alive. Then explain how other words would change the image. **Revising:** Review your writing for effective word choice and organization. Then check for errors of grammar, spelling, and punctuation.

Writing a Description

Write a paragraph in which you describe an accident you have witnessed—such as someone falling off a bicycle or dropping a dish of hot vegetables. Choose an incident, and list descriptive words and phrases that will convey a vivid image of the event. You might choose words that emphasize sound and color or that create dramatic pictures. Begin your paragraph with a general statement about the accident. Then, using the descriptive words from your list, describe the accident in four or five sentences.

As a young girl Sandra Cisneros (born 1954) lived with her parents and six brothers and sisters in a succession of small apartments in Chicago. The family's living conditions were so crowded that Cisneros could find peace and quiet only in the family bathroom. Whenever she could, she escaped there to read by herself. The books she read—*Alice in Wonderland,* fairy tales, *Doctor Doolittle*—tempted her to dream of being a writer. Now in her thirties, she has written two books of poetry and an award-winning novel, *The House on Mango Street.* In "Twister Hits Houston" she describes how three members of a family experience a violent storm.

Have you ever missed witnessing a dramatic event by only a moment or two?

• •

Sandra Cisneros

Twister Hits Houston

Papa was on the front porch.
Mama was in the kitchen.
Mama was trying
to screw a lightbulb into a fixture.
5 Papa was watching the rain.
Mama, it's a cyclone for sure,
he shouted to his wife in the kitchen.
Papa who was sitting on his front porch
when the storm hit
10 said the twister ripped
the big back oak to splinter,
tossed a green sedan into his garden,
and banged the back door
like a mad cat wanting in.
15 Mama who was in the kitchen
said Papa saw everything,
the big oak ripped to kindling,
the green sedan land out back,
the back door slam and slam.
20 I missed it.

Mama was in the kitchen Papa explained.
Papa was sitting on the front porch.
That light bulb is still sitting
where I left it. Don't matter now.
25 Got no electricity anyway.

READER'S RESPONSE

Would you call this disaster great or small? Why?

STUDY QUESTIONS

Recalling

1. What was Papa doing when the cyclone hit? What was Mama doing?
2. The speaker names four details that show the cyclone's damage to the house and yard. What are they?
3. Which family member "missed" the storm?
4. Who last touched the light bulb?

Interpreting

5. What words would you use to describe the poem's speaker? What emotions do you think the speaker feels about missing the storm?
6. How long ago did the cyclone hit, in your opinion? Which details make you think so?
7. What do you think the speaker was doing with the light bulb? Explain your answer.

Extending

8. If you could have been either in the kitchen or on the porch when the cyclone hit, where would you have choosen to be? Why?
9. What other natural disasters might make good subjects for a poem? Give reasons for your choices.

READING AND LITERARY FOCUS

Simile

A **simile** is a directly stated comparison that uses the word *like* or *as*. "Sophie sprints like a cheetah" and "Sam runs as fast as a cheetah" are both similes. Similes focus on characteristics that two different things have in common. For example, Sophie, Sam, and the cheetah all share the characteristic of great speed. Similes help readers connect images and ideas within a poem.

Be careful not to confuse similes with other statements using the words *like* or *as*. For example, although "his muscles tightened as he lifted the barbell" uses the word *as,* it is not a comparison and therefore not a simile.

Thinking About Simile

1. Identify the simile in "Twister Hits Houston."
2. What two things are being compared? In what ways are they different? In what way does the poet suggest that they are alike?

CHALLENGE

Collage

A **collage** is a picture made from scraps of materials (such as paint, cloth, magazine photographs, bits of string, wood, and other items) that are assembled on a flat surface. Make a collage that illustrates the effects of a cyclone. You might get ideas from the details in "Twister Hits Houston," from your knowledge of cyclones, and from your imagination.

As a boy in a New Jersey town, Jim Murphy (born 1947) spent hours exploring abandoned factories. He loved to wander through interesting, exotic places, and he and his friends often boarded a bus or train to New York to sample the city's bustling streets and unusual foods. Murphy has used this same curiosity and imagination to write more than a dozen books for young people, including *Weird and Wacky Inventions*, *The Indy 500*, and *Two Hundred Years of Bicycles*. He enjoys writing because it "lets me research subjects that I'm really interested in and lets me get out some of the thoughts and opinions that rattle around in my head." His fascination with the unusual led him to write this story about a catastrophe in the life of a dinosaur.

In the smoke and dark forest shadows, something moved. The shape was big, as big as many of the trees, and had a massive head. Tyrannosaurus rex.

• •

Jim Murphy

The Last Dinosaur

The sun came up slowly, fingers of light poking into and brightening the tangled forest of pine and poplar and hemlock trees. The drone of insects quieted, and the tiny mammals scampered to hide.

In a clearing a small Triceratops herd began their day. The female Triceratops blinked several times before moving to get the light out of her eyes. Then she went back to the frond she'd ripped from a cycadeoid.[1]

The frond was tough and spiky, but her sharp-edged beak and rows of teeth chopped the plant into easily swallowed pieces. She was about to tug at another frond when a male Triceratops began stamping his feet in alarm.

He had been feeding at the base of a tree when his horns became entangled in a mass of grapevines. He shook his head violently to get free. When that didn't work, he backed away, yanking his head from side to side. Still covered with vines, he halted. His breathing came in short, grunting pants.

Suddenly he lowered his head and charged the tree. He hit it solidly, backed up, and hit it again, and then again. The fourth butt splintered the tree's base and it leaned over. A few wiggles of his head and the vine slipped off.

He snorted at the vine, challenging it. When it didn't move, he walked around it and left the clearing. He was the largest

---
1. **cycadeoid** [sī'kəd ē' oid]: type of tropical plant resembling a palm.

Triceratops and leader of the herd, so the smaller male and the female followed him.

The three wandered through the forest, always staying near the stream that was their source of water. They did not hurry, and often stopped to nibble at figs or tender tree saplings. On the second day they came to a hillside covered with tasty ferns. The spot was cool and quiet, so they stayed the afternoon, browsing.

A sudden noise made the female jerk up her head to look and listen. They had not seen another dinosaur in a very long time, but she was still wary. A hungry Tyrannosaurus might have picked up their scent and followed, hoping one of them would stray from the herd.

The two males sensed her unease and also looked around. A giant dragonfly circled the Triceratops, then flew away. A bird chattered briefly. Then the forest grew still. Was a Tyrannosaurus out there, watching, waiting? Nothing moved and the noise did not return, but the herd was nervous. They left the hillside and continued their journey.

The next day, the land sloped downward and the stream widened to become a series of falls, pools, and swirling rapids. The path twisted to follow the water and dipped sharply in places. Despite their great size, the Triceratops walked the narrow ledges and leaped boulders with an easy grace.

The female Triceratops smelled something. Her sense of sight was very poor, so she turned to face what was causing the strange odor. Wisps of smoke trailed through the trees.

The smoke was from a fire started the night before by heat lightning.[2] The female couldn't see the fire or know that it was advancing toward them. But the smoke was growing thicker and more unpleasant, so the three animals trotted away.

All night they moved quickly to stay clear of the smoke. At dawn, the ground leveled, and the smell seemed to disappear. The two males stopped, exhausted, and bent to drink the cool water. The female continued along the path.

Weeks before, the female Triceratops had mated with the leader of the herd. She was hunting now for a spot to build her nest.

The leader stamped his feet and snorted for her to stop, but it did no good. The female would not obey until the nest was completed and her eggs laid. This time, the males followed.

A mile downstream, the forest thinned and the stream emptied into a broad marsh. In the past, dome-headed Pachycephalosaurus[3] or armored Ankylosaurus[4] would be browsing in the cattails and rushes. Now only the bones of a long dead Anatosaurus,[5] half buried in mud, were there to greet the herd.

The female walked the edge of the marsh carefully. The ground was either too wet or too rocky for the nest. On the opposite side of the marsh she found a warm, sandy area with low-growing shrubs.

Immediately she began digging, using the toes of her front and rear feet to shovel out the sand. The hole she dug was six feet across and a foot deep.

---

2. **heat lightning:** flashes of lightning occurring too far away for the thunder to be heard; seen near the horizon, especially on summer evenings.

3. **Pachycephalosaurus** [pak ə se fa′lō sôr′əs]: dinosaur of North America with a dome-shaped head and thick skull.
4. **Ankylosaurus** [ang′kə lō sôr′ əs]: plant-eating dinosaur with short legs and a broad body covered with bony plates.
5. **Anatosaurus** [a na′tō sôr′əs]: plant-eating dinosaur of the Northern Hemisphere with a jaw resembling the bill of a duck.

When the hole was finished, she laid fifteen eggs in it to form a circle. Gently she covered the eggs with sand. The sun would warm the sand and eggs, and eventually baby Triceratops would emerge.

The two males were feeding a little distance from the nest. The smaller male approached the nest.

When the female saw him, she placed herself between him and her eggs and lowered her head as a warning. The curious male kept coming, so the female charged him. Only when he backed away did the female stop her charge.

When the herd had been larger, many females would make nests in the same area. They would then take turns guarding the nests or feeding and sleeping. But the female Triceratops was alone now. It would be her job to keep clumsy males and egg-eating creatures away from her eggs. The quick shrewlike[6] mammals were especially annoying at night.

Two days later the smell of smoke returned. It was faint, distant, and yet the three Triceratops grew nervous. The female paced near her nest.

Late in the day, a heavy line of smoke appeared on the other side of the marsh. Flames erupted, reaching into the air.

A flock of birds flew overhead, screeching an alarm. Mammals, made bold by their fear, left their hiding places and ran from the fire. The two males edged away, but the female stayed to guard her eggs.

In the smoke and dark forest shadows, something moved. The shape was big, as big as many of the trees, and had a massive head. Tyrannosaurus rex.[7] The giant flesh-eater stepped from the forest, snapping his mouth to reveal seven-inch-long slashing teeth.

Instinctively the two Triceratops males rejoined the female and formed a semicircle barrier in front of the nest. The leader lowered his head and stared at his enemy. Neither moved.

Ordinarily, the Tyrannosaurus would not attack a Triceratops, especially near its nest. But a wall of flames and heat had cut off his retreat. Besides, the Tyrannosaurus had not had a large meal in weeks.

The Tyrannosaurus darted at the herd, skidded to a sudden halt, then began circling warily, watching for a chance to strike. He hissed and snapped his teeth. At that instant, the largest Triceratops charged, his powerful legs driving him directly at the soft belly of his attacker.

With the aid of his long tail and thickly muscled legs, the Tyrannosaurus leaped aside to avoid the sharp horns. He spun and dove, mouth wide open, and sank his teeth into the back of the Triceratops.

Then the smaller Triceratops lunged at the giant, but he was an inexperienced fighter. The Tyrannosaurus' teeth closed on his neck and with a quick, deadly yank, he tore a chunk of flesh from the Triceratops. The smaller Triceratops fell, dying.

The other Triceratops tried to charge again, but his right leg was dragging and his movements were slow. Again the Tyrannosaurus moved aside easily. Using his tail as a spring, the Tyrannosaurus launched himself for the kill. His teeth sank into the Triceratops, while his clawed feet struck

---

6. **shrewlike:** resembling a shrew, a small mammal related to the mole, having brownish fur, short ears, and a long, pointed snout.

7. **Tyrannosaurus rex** [ti ran′ə sôr′ əs reks]: huge, flesh-eating dinosaur of North America.

him in the stomach. The two rolled, kicking and biting each other.

At this moment, the female Triceratops abandoned her eggs and rammed the Tyrannosaurus full in the side. He bellowed painfully, releasing his hold on the male. The female pushed forward with all her strength, pinning the Tyrannosaurus against a tree and driving her horns in deeper.

She stepped away and watched her enemy, ready to charge if he got up. His legs and tail flailed weakly, his breathing became labored. Then, with a violent shudder, the great killer died.

During the battle, the fire had spread, leaping and dancing from tree to tree until it reached the edge of the sandy area. Flames rolled through the reeds.

The male Triceratops struggled to get up, but his legs buckled under him. He crawled a few feet but had to stop. His wounds were too severe. A choking wave of smoke surrounded him.

The female Triceratops went back to protect her eggs. To one side a tree crashed to the ground, sending up an explosion of sparks. A bush nearby caught fire. The female charged it, slashing at it blindly with her horns.

The roar of the fire became deafening, and the heat and smoke grew painful. Reluctantly the female moved away from her eggs to find air.

She went only a short distance and turned to go back. The smoke stung her lungs and burned her eyes. She shook her head, but the choking pain would not go away. She backed away some more and lost sight of her nest.

Immediately the tiny mammals pounced on the unguarded nest. Low to the ground the smoke was not so thick. Digging hastily,

they uncovered the eggs and devoured them. Then they scurried from the approaching fire.

The female Triceratops hurried through the forest. Several times she stopped to look back toward her eggs. A wall of smoke and flames was all she could see. Finally she gave up.

A tongue of flames reached out at her, and she broke into a gallop. She crashed through branches and vines, leaped over fallen logs heedlessly, with the fire just behind her. At last she came to a rock ledge overlooking a wide river.

The water was dark and deep. Branches and tree roots floated near the banks. The female wanted to find another retreat, but she was surrounded by flames. She hesitated a second, then jumped into the water.

Legs churning frantically, she swam across the river and away from the fire. The river's current caught her, pulling her swiftly along. She struggled to keep her head above water, to breathe, all the while moving her legs. At last her feet touched the river bottom.

Exhausted, her breathing fast, she hauled herself onto solid ground. Across from her, the fire had stopped at the river's edge. She was safe. It was then she noticed the streams of mammals that had also crossed the river to escape the fire.

The light grew dim and the air became chilly. The female's breath gave off thin vapor streams.

The Triceratops shook her head and snorted. She hadn't eaten much in days and wanted to find some tender plants. And maybe, somewhere deep in the forest, there was another Triceratops herd she could join.

Slowly, as the sun went down, the female pushed through the bushes to begin her search.

READER'S RESPONSE

Where do you think the female Triceratops' search will lead?

STUDY QUESTIONS

Recalling

1. Why do the three animals trot away from the stream on the third day?

2. What does the female do when she finds "a warm, sandy area with low-growing shrubs"?

3. A Tyrannosaurus rex usually would not attack a Triceratops. What causes this one to attack?

4. Why does the female Triceratops first abandon her eggs? Why does she next leave them?

5. What does the female do "several times" as she runs through the forest?

6. At the end of the story, what is the female Triceratops searching for?

Interpreting

7. Is there a hero and a villain in this story? Why do you think so?

8. Why do you think the female Triceratops decides to attack the Tyrannosaurus rex?

9. Why do you think that "finally she gave up" looking back toward her eggs?

10. Do you think the female Triceratops will survive? Why or why not?

Extending

11. When, if ever, is it appropriate to put your own safety and survival above that of others?

READING AND LITERARY FOCUS

Atmosphere

A vivid description of a story's setting creates an **atmosphere**, or mood, that runs through the story.

For example, in "The Last Dinosaur" the narrator's description of the forest creates a suspenseful atmosphere:

> A giant dragonfly circled the Triceratops, then flew away. A bird chattered briefly. Then the forest grew still. Was a Tyrannosaurus out there, watching, waiting?

In this passage we sense that something unexpected and dangerous may happen. From time to time, the narrator changes the mood of the story by describing the setting in different ways.

Thinking About Atmosphere

Describe the atmosphere at the beginning of the story. What details of setting does the narrator use to convey this mood?

COMPOSITION

Writing About Atmosphere

Write a paragraph in which you explain how vivid description makes the atmosphere of "The Last Dinosaur" come alive. **Prewriting:** Choose a passage that conveys a strong atmosphere. Make a list of the words and phrases that describe the atmosphere. **Writing:** Begin by describing the atmosphere. Then tell about the details that make this atmosphere come alive. **Revising:** Review your paragraph for effective word choice and organization. Then check for errors of grammar, spelling, and punctuation.

Writing a Descriptive Paragraph

Write a paragraph in which you describe a place that has an atmosphere of mystery and suspense. First choose a familiar setting that has an atmosphere of mystery. List details that you could use in a description of this place. Then write a description of this setting, using details to create a distinct atmosphere.

Thinking Skills: Representing

DEFINITION

Representing is a way of picturing data, or information. Diagrams, graphs, maps, charts, and other images can help you organize data and think about what they mean. The following steps tell how to picture information using one form of representation — a spider map.

STEPS

1. **Identify the subject you will think about.**
   Write the subject in a box like the one on this page.

2. **Identify individual features, qualities, or examples of the subject.**
   Write the features, qualities, or examples on lines, or "legs," attached to the box.

3. **Based on some or all of the features, qualities, or examples, make a statement about the subject.**
   What does the picture tell you about the subject? Can you compare any of the features, qualities, or examples? Are some more important than others? Which feature, quality, or example is most interesting to you?

EXAMPLE

Imagine that you are asked to write about leadership. The topic is so broad that you need to organize the information about it. You decide to use a spider map to think about the many different aspects of the subject.

1. **Identify the subject you will think about.** You write *leadership* in a box.

2. **Identify individual features, qualities, or examples of the subject.** You think of several features, qualities, or examples of leadership and write them on separate lines around the box.

3. **Based on some or all of the features, qualities, or examples, make a statement about the subject.** You write, "Leadership involves facing challenges, inspiring others, and making good decisions."

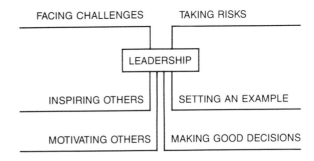

ACTIVITY 1

Follow the three steps of representing to make a spider map of the topic of natural disasters. Write *natural disasters* in a box. Identify features, qualities, or examples of natural disasters, and write them on separate lines around the box. Then make a statement about natural disasters using some or all of the information on your spider map.

ACTIVITY 2

Follow the three steps of representing to make a spider map of any literary selection in this book. Remember that you can use the spider-map format to represent information about almost anything — characters, settings, details of action, themes. Make a statement based on the picture the spider map gives you.

Robert Cormier (born 1925) remembers himself as "a skinny kid living in a ghetto type of neighborhood wanting the world to know I existed." One day at age thirteen he began to read a book by the American writer Thomas Wolfe. Cormier identified strongly with the book's main character (who wants to be a writer) and realized, "That's me! I want to be a writer." In the years that followed, Cormier became a newspaper and radio reporter and then went on to write several books for young adults. The following short story—like Cormier's most famous works, *I Am the Cheese* and *The Chocolate War*—is concerned with some of the struggles that a young person faces in today's world.

I thought of my father and Armand and Rollie Tremaine and Grover Cleveland and wished that I could go away someplace far away. But there was no place to go.

* *

Robert Cormier

President Cleveland, Where Are You?

That was the autumn of the cowboy cards[1]—Buck Jones and Tom Tyler and Hoot Gibson and especially Ken Maynard.[2] The cards were available in those five-cent packages of gum: pink sticks, three together, covered with a sweet white powder. You couldn't blow bubbles with that particular gum, but it couldn't have mattered less. The cowboy cards were important—the pictures of those rock-faced men with eyes of blue steel.

On those wind-swept, leaf-tumbling afternoons we gathered after school on the sidewalk in front of Lemire's Drugstore, across from St. Jude's Parochial School,[3] and we swapped and bargained and matched for the cards. Because a Ken Maynard serial was playing at the Globe[4] every Saturday afternoon, he was the most popular cowboy of all, and one of his cards was worth at least ten of any other kind. Rollie Tremaine had a treasure of thirty or so, and he guarded them jealously. He'd match you for the other cards, but he

---

1. **cowboy cards:** trading cards on which photographs of actors who portray cowboys in western movies were printed.
2. **Buck Jones . . . Ken Maynard:** film actors who appeared in many westerns during the 1920s, 1930s, and 1940s.

3. **Parochial** [pə rōʹkē əl] **School:** private school supported and operated by a church.
4. **the Globe:** the town's movie theater.

risked his Ken Maynards only when the other kids threatened to leave him out of the competition altogether.

You could almost hate Rollie Tremaine. In the first place, he was the only son of Auguste Tremaine, who operated the Uptown Dry Goods Store, and he did not live in a tenement but in a big white birthday cake of a house on Laurel Street. He was too fat to be effective in the football games between the Frenchtown Tigers and the North Side Knights, and he made us constantly aware of the jingle of coins in his pockets. He was able to stroll into Lemire's and casually select a quarter's worth of cowboy cards while the rest of us watched, aching with envy.

Once in a while I earned a nickel or dime by running errands or washing windows for blind old Mrs. Belander, or by finding pieces of copper, brass, and other valuable metals at the dump and selling them to the junkman. The coins clutched in my hand, I would race to Lemire's to buy a cowboy card or two, hoping that Ken Maynard would stare boldly out at me as I opened the pack. At one time, before a disastrous matching session with Roger Lussier (my best friend, except where the cards were involved), I owned five Ken Maynards and considered myself a millionaire, of sorts.

One week I was particularly lucky; I had spent two afternoons washing floors for Mrs. Belander and received a quarter. Because my father had worked a full week at the shop, where a rush order for fancy combs had been received, he allotted my brothers and sisters and me an extra dime along with the usual ten cents for the Saturday-afternoon movie. Setting aside the movie fare, I found myself with a bonus of thirty-five cents, and I then planned to put

Rollie Tremaine to shame the following Monday afternoon.

Monday was the best day to buy the cards because the candy man stopped at Lemire's every Monday morning to deliver the new assortments. There was nothing more exciting in the world than a fresh batch of card boxes. I rushed home from school that day and hurriedly changed my clothes, eager to set off for the store. As I burst through the doorway, letting the screen door slam behind me, my brother Armand blocked my way.

He was fourteen, three years older than I, and a freshman at Monument High School. He had recently become a stranger to me in many ways—indifferent to such matters as cowboy cards and the Frenchtown Tigers—and he carried himself with a mysterious dignity that was fractured now and then when his voice began shooting off in all directions like some kind of vocal fireworks.

"Wait a minute, Jerry," he said. "I want to talk to you." He motioned me out of earshot of my mother, who was busy supervising the usual after-school skirmish in the kitchen.

I sighed with impatience. In recent months Armand had become a figure of authority, siding with my father and mother occasionally. As the oldest son he sometimes took advantage of his age and experience to issue rules and regulations.

"How much money have you got?" he whispered.

"You in some kind of trouble?" I asked, excitement rising in me as I remembered the blackmail[5] plot of a movie at the Globe a month before.

---

5. **blackmail:** the act of obtaining money from a person by threatening to expose information the person wishes to keep secret.

He shook his head in annoyance. "Look," he said, "it's Pa's birthday tomorrow. I think we ought to chip in and buy him something. . . ."

I reached into my pocket and caressed the coins. "Here," I said carefully, pulling out a nickel. "If we all give a nickel we should have enough to buy him something pretty nice."

He regarded me with contempt. "Rita already gave me fifteen cents, and I'm throwing in a quarter. Albert handed over a dime—all that's left of his birthday money. Is that all you can do—a nickel?"

"Aw, come on," I protested. "I haven't got a single Ken Maynard left, and I was going to buy some cards this afternoon."

"Ken Maynard!" he snorted. "Who's more important—him or your father?"

His question was unfair because he knew that there was no possible choice—"my father" had to be the only answer. My father was a huge man who believed in the things of the spirit, although my mother often maintained that the spirits he believed in came in bottles. He had worked at the Monument Comb Shop since the age of fourteen; his booming laugh—or grumble—greeted us each night when he returned from the factory. A steady worker when the shop had enough work, he quickened with gaiety on Friday nights and weekends, a bottle of beer at his elbow, and he was fond of making long speeches about the good things in life. In the middle of the Depression,[6] for instance, he paid cash for a piano, of all things, and insisted that my

twin sisters, Yolande and Yvette, take lessons once a week.

I took a dime from my pocket and handed it to Armand.

"Thanks, Jerry," he said. "I hate to take your last cent."

"That's all right," I replied, turning away and consoling myself with the thought that twenty cents was better than nothing at all.

When I arrived at Lemire's I sensed disaster in the air. Roger Lussier was kicking disconsolately at a tin can in the gutter, and Rollie Tremaine sat sullenly on the steps in front of the store.

"Save your money," Roger said. He had known about my plans to splurge on the cards.

"What's the matter?" I asked.

"There's no more cowboy cards," Rollie Tremaine said. "The company's not making any more."

"They're going to have President cards," Roger said, his face twisting with disgust. He pointed to the store window. "Look!"

A placard in the window announced: "Attention, Boys. Watch for the New Series. Presidents of the United States. Free in Each 5-Cent Package of Caramel Chew."

"President cards?" I asked, dismayed.

I read on: "Collect a Complete Set and Receive an Official Imitation Major League Baseball Glove, Embossed with Lefty Grove's[7] Autograph."

Glove or no glove, who could become excited about Presidents, of all things?

Rollie Tremaine stared at the sign. "Benjamin Harrison, for crying out loud," he

---

6. **the Depression** [di presh'ən]: in the United States, the period of business failure, low wages, rising prices, and widespread unemployment that lasted from 1929 to 1939.

7. **Lefty Grove:** Pitcher for the Philadelphia Athletics and the Boston Red Sox in the 1920s and 1930s. In 1931 his percentage of games won was .866, a record for many years.

said. "Why would I want Benjamin Harrison when I've got twenty-two Ken Maynards?"

I felt the warmth of guilt creep over me. I jingled the coins in my pocket, but the sound was hollow. No more Ken Maynards to buy.

"I'm going to buy a Mr. Goodbar," Rollie Tremaine decided.

I was without appetite, indifferent even to a Baby Ruth, which was my favorite. I thought of how I had betrayed Armand and, worst of all, my father.

"I'll see you after supper," I called over my shoulder to Roger as I hurried away toward home. I took the shortcut behind the church, although it involved leaping over a tall wooden fence, and I zigzagged recklessly through Mr. Thibodeau's garden, trying to outrace my guilt. I pounded up the steps and into the house, only to learn that Armand had already taken Yolande and Yvette uptown to shop for the birthday present.

I pedaled my bike furiously through the streets, ignoring the indignant horns of automobiles as I sliced through the traffic. Finally I saw Armand and my sisters emerge from the Monument Men's Shop. My heart sank when I spied the long, slim package that Armand was holding.

"Did you buy the present yet?" I asked, although I knew it was too late.

"Just now. A blue tie," Armand said. "What's the matter?"

"Nothing," I replied, my chest hurting.

He looked at me for a long moment. At first his eyes were hard, but then they softened. He smiled at me, almost sadly, and touched my arm. I turned away from him because I felt naked and exposed.

"It's all right," he said gently. "Maybe you've learned something." The words were gentle, but they held a curious dignity, the

dignity remaining even when his voice suddenly cracked on the last syllable.

I wondered what was happening to me, because I did not know whether to laugh or cry.

Sister Angela was amazed when, a week before Christmas vacation, everybody in the class submitted a history essay worthy of a high mark—in some cases as high as A-minus. (Sister Angela did not believe that anyone in the world ever deserved an A.) She never learned—or at least she never let on that she knew—we all had become experts on the Presidents because of the cards we purchased at Lemire's. Each card contained a picture of a President, and on the reverse side, a summary of his career. We looked at those cards so often that the biographies imprinted themselves on our minds without effort. Even our street-corner conversations were filled with such information as the fact that James Madison was called "The Father of the Constitution,"[8] or that John Adams had intended to become a minister.

The President cards were a roaring success and the cowboy cards were quickly forgotten. In the first place we did not receive gum with the cards, but a kind of chewy caramel. The caramel could be tucked into a corner of your mouth, bulging your cheek in much the same manner as wads of tobacco bulged the mouths of baseball stars. In the second place the competition for collecting the cards was fierce and frustrating—fierce because everyone was intent on being the first to send away for a

---

8. **Constitution** [kon'stə too'shən]: in the United States, the highest law and plan of government, in effect since 1789.

baseball glove and frustrating because although there were only thirty-two Presidents, including Franklin Delano Roosevelt,[9] the variety at Lemire's was at a minimum. When the deliveryman left the boxes of cards at the store each Monday, we often discovered that one entire box was devoted to a single President—two weeks in a row the boxes contained nothing but Abraham Lincolns. One week Roger Lussier and I were the heroes of Frenchtown. We journeyed on our bicycles to the North Side, engaged three boys in a matching bout and returned with five new Presidents, including Chester Alan Arthur, who up to that time had been missing.

Perhaps to sharpen our desire, the card company sent a sample glove to Mr. Lemire, and it dangled, orange and sleek, in the window. I was half sick with longing, thinking of my old glove at home, which I had inherited from Armand. But Rollie Tremaine's desire for the glove outdistanced my own. He even got Mr. Lemire to agree to give the glove in the window to the first person to get a complete set of cards, so that precious time wouldn't be wasted waiting for the postman.

We were delighted at Rollie Tremaine's frustration, especially since he was only a substitute player for the Tigers. Once after spending fifty cents on cards—all of which turned out to be Calvin Coolidge—he threw them to the ground, pulled some dollar bills out of his pocket and said, "The heck with it. I'm going to buy a glove!"

"Not that glove," Roger Lussier said. "Not a glove with Lefty Grove's autograph. Look what it says at the bottom of the sign."

We all looked, although we knew the words by heart: "This Glove Is Not For Sale Anywhere."

Rollie Tremaine scrambled to pick up the cards from the sidewalk, pouting more than ever. After that he was quietly obsessed with the Presidents, hugging the cards close to his chest and refusing to tell us how many more he needed to complete his set.

I too was obsessed with the cards, because they had become things of comfort in a world that had suddenly grown dismal. After Christmas a layoff at the shop had thrown my father out of work. He received no paycheck for four weeks, and the only income we had was from Armand's after-school job at the Blue and White Grocery Store—a job he lost finally when business dwindled as the layoff continued.

Although we had enough food and clothing—my father's credit had always been good, a matter of pride with him—the inactivity made my father restless and irritable. He did not drink any beer at all, and laughed loudly, but not convincingly, after gulping down a glass of water and saying, "Lent[10] came early this year." The twins fell sick and went to the hospital to have their tonsils removed. My father was confident that he would return to work eventually and pay off his debts, but he seemed to age before our eyes.

When orders again were received at the comb shop and he returned to work, another disaster occurred, although I was the only one aware of it. Armand fell in love.

I discovered his situation by accident,

---

9. **Franklin Delano Roosevelt:** President of the United States from 1933 to 1945. Roosevelt was President at the time this story takes place.

10. **Lent:** in Roman Catholicism and some other branches of Christianity, period of fasting and prayer beginning on Ash Wednesday and continuing for the forty weekdays before Easter.

when I happened to pick up a piece of paper that had fallen to the floor in the bedroom he and I shared. I frowned at the paper, puzzled.

"Dear Sally, When I look into your eyes the world stands still. . . ."

The letter was snatched from my hands before I finished reading it.

"What's the big idea, snooping around?" Armand asked, his face crimson. "Can't a guy have any privacy?"

He had never mentioned privacy before. "It was on the floor," I said. "I didn't know it was a letter. Who's Sally?"

He flung himself across the bed. "You tell anybody and I'll muckalize you," he threatened. "Sally Knowlton."

Nobody in Frenchtown had a name like Knowlton.

"A girl from the North Side?" I asked, incredulous.

He rolled over and faced me, anger in his eyes, and a kind of despair too.

"What's the matter with that? Think she's too good for me?" he asked. "I'm warning you, Jerry, if you tell anybody . . ."

"Don't worry," I said. Love had no particular place in my life; it seemed an unnecessary waste of time. And a girl from the North Side was so remote that for all practical purposes she did not exist. But I was curious. "What are you writing her a letter for? Did she leave town, or something?"

"She hasn't left town," he answered. "I wasn't going to send it. I just felt like writing to her."

I was glad that I had never become involved with love—love that brought desperation to your eyes, that caused you to write letters you did not plan to send. Shrugging with indifference, I began to search in the closet for the old baseball glove. I found it on the shelf, under some old sneakers. The webbing was torn and the padding gone. I thought of the sting I would feel when a sharp grounder slapped into the glove, and I winced.

"You tell anybody about me and Sally and I'll—"

"I know. You'll muckalize me."

I did not divulge his secret and often shared his agony, particularly when he sat at the supper table and left my mother's special butterscotch pie untouched. I had never realized before how terrible love could be. But my compassion was short-lived because I had other things to worry about: report cards due at Eastertime; the loss of income from old Mrs. Belander, who had gone to live with a daughter in Boston; and, of course, the Presidents.

Because a stalemate[11] had been reached, the President cards were the dominant force in our lives—mine, Roger Lussier's and Rollie Tremaine's. For three weeks, as the baseball season approached, each of us had a complete set—complete except for one President, Grover Cleveland.[12] Each time a box of cards arrived at the store we hurriedly bought them (as hurriedly as our funds allowed) and tore off the wrappers, only to be confronted by James Monroe or Martin Van Buren or someone else. But never Grover Cleveland, never the man who had been the twenty-second and the twenty-fourth President of the United States. We argued about Grover Cleveland. Should he be placed between Chester Alan Arthur and Benjamin Harrison as the twenty-second

---

11. **stalemate:** any position or situation in which no further action is possible.
12. **Grover Cleveland:** President of the United States from 1885 to 1889 and again from 1893 to 1897.

President or did he belong between Benjamin Harrison and William McKinley as the twenty-fourth President? Was the card company playing fair? Roger Lussier brought up a horrifying possibility—did we need *two* Grover Clevelands to complete the set?

Indignant, we stormed Lemire's and protested to the harassed storeowner, who had long since vowed never to stock a new series. Muttering angrily, he searched his bills and receipts for a list of rules.

"All right," he announced. "Says here you only need one Grover Cleveland to finish the set. Now get out, all of you, unless you've got money to spend."

Outside the store, Rollie Tremaine picked up an empty tobacco tin and scaled it across the street. "Boy," he said. "I'd give five dollars for a Grover Cleveland."

When I returned home I found Armand sitting on the piazza[13] steps, his chin in his hands. His mood of dejection mirrored my own, and I sat down beside him. We did not say anything for a while.

"Want to throw the ball around?" I asked.

He sighed, not bothering to answer.

"You sick?" I asked.

He stood up and hitched up his trousers, pulled at his ear and finally told me what the matter was—there was a big dance next week at the high school, the Spring Promenade, and Sally had asked him to be her escort.

I shook my head at the folly of love. "Well, what's so bad about that?"

"How can I take Sally to a fancy dance?" he asked desperately. "I'd have to buy her a corsage.[14] . . . And my shoes are practically falling apart. Pa's got too many worries now to buy me new shoes or give me money for flowers for a girl."

I nodded in sympathy. "Yeah," I said. "Look at me. Baseball time is almost here, and all I've got is that old glove. And no Grover Cleveland card yet . . ."

"Grover Cleveland?" he asked. "They've got some of those up on the North Side. Some kid was telling me there's a store that's got them. He says they're looking for Warren G. Harding."

"Holy Smoke!" I said. "I've got an extra Warren G. Harding!" Pure joy sang in my veins. I ran to my bicycle, swung into the seat—and found that the front tire was flat.

"I'll help you fix it," Armand said.

Within half an hour I was at the North Side Drugstore, where several boys were matching cards on the sidewalk. Silently but blissfully I shouted: President Grover Cleveland, here I come!

After Armand had left for the dance, all dressed up as if it were Sunday, the small green box containing the corsage under his arm, I sat on the railing of the piazza, letting my feet dangle. The neighborhood was quiet because the Frenchtown Tigers were at Daggett's Field, practicing for the first baseball game of the season.

I thought of Armand and the ridiculous expression on his face when he'd stood before the mirror in the bedroom. I'd avoided looking at his new black shoes. "Love," I muttered.

Spring had arrived in a sudden stampede of apple blossoms and fragrant

---

13. **piazza** [pē az′ə]: open porch, usually roofed, extending along one or more sides of the ground floor of a dwelling.

14. **corsage** [kôr säzh′]: flower or small bouquet of flowers to be worn by a woman, usually on the chest or wrist.

breezes. Windows had been thrown open and dust mops had banged on the sills all day long as the women busied themselves with housecleaning. I was puzzled by my lethargy. Wasn't spring supposed to make everything bright and gay?

I turned at the sound of footsteps on the stairs. Roger Lussier greeted me with a sour face.

"I thought you were practicing with the Tigers," I said.

"Rollie Tremaine," he said. "I just couldn't stand him." He slammed his fist against the railing. "Jeez, why did *he* have to be the one to get a Grover Cleveland? You should see him showing off. He won't let anybody even touch that glove . . ."

I felt like Benedict Arnold[15] and knew that I had to confess what I had done.

"Roger," I said, "I got a Grover Cleveland card up on the North Side. I sold it to Rollie Tremaine for five dollars."

"Are you crazy?" he asked.

"I needed that five dollars. It was an—an emergency."

"Boy!" he said, looking down at the ground and shaking his head. "What did you have to do a thing like that for?"

I watched him as he turned away and began walking down the stairs.

"Hey, Roger!" I called.

He squinted up at me as if I were a stranger, someone he'd never seen before.

"What?" he asked, his voice flat.

"I had to do it," I said. "Honest."

He didn't answer. He headed toward the fence, searching for the board we had loosened to give us a secret passage.

I thought of my father and Armand and

After the Prom, Norman Rockwell, 1957.

Rollie Tremaine and Grover Cleveland and wished that I could go away someplace far away. But there was no place to go.

Roger found the loose slat in the fence and slipped through. I felt betrayed: weren't you supposed to feel good when you did something fine and noble?

A moment later two hands gripped the top of the fence and Roger's face appeared. "Was it a real emergency?" he yelled.

"A real one!" I called. "Something important!"

His face dropped from sight and his voice reached me across the yard: "All right."

"See you tomorrow!" I yelled.

I swung my legs over the railing again. The gathering dusk began to soften the sharp edges of the fence, the rooftops, the distant church steeple. I sat there a long time, waiting for the good feeling to come.

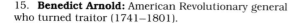

15. **Benedict Arnold:** American Revolutionary general who turned traitor (1741–1801).

READER'S RESPONSE

Do you think Jerry's experience with his father's birthday gift played a part in his decision to sell his President card to Rollie Tremaine?

STUDY QUESTIONS

Recalling

1. With what words does Jerry describe the way in which Armand carries himself?
2. Why is Armand collecting money? What has Jerry been saving to buy?
3. What does the sign in Lemire's announce?
4. In what two ways does Armand look at Jerry outside the Monument Men's Shop?
5. According to Jerry, what two disasters befall the family?
6. What does Jerry do to get the money for Armand's shoes and flowers?

Interpreting

7. What emotions does Jerry feel after he contributes a second dime for his father's gift? Why do you think he feels guilty when he realizes there are no more cowboy cards?
8. Which of the two "disasters" has a greater effect on Jerry? Explain your answer.
9. Why do you think Jerry decided that Armand's feelings were more important than the Grover Cleveland card?

Extending

10. In your experience, *does* it feel good when you do something "fine and noble"?

VOCABULARY

Roots

The **root** of a word is its core, or main part. It is the central portion of a word to which either prefixes or suffixes may be attached. For example, in the word *monologue* the root *-logue-* is from the Greek language and means "speech." *Mono-* is a prefix meaning "one." A monologue is a speech by one person.

Using a dictionary, identify the roots of each of the following words from "President Cleveland, Where Are You?" Then give one other word formed from each root.

1. intervene   3. compassion
2. autograph   4. inherit

COMPOSITION

Answering an Essay Question

Write a short essay that answers the following question: In what respect does Jerry grow up in the course of "President Cleveland, Where Are You?" **Prewriting:** Review the story to determine how Jerry behaved at the beginning and end of the story. List words and phrases that describe how he is different and what might have caused the change. **Writing:** Begin with a general statement of how Jerry matured. Then describe details from the story that show how the change came about. **Revising:** Review your essay for effective word choice and organization. Then check for errors of grammar, spelling, and punctuation. *For help with this assignment, see Lesson 2 in the Writing About Literature Handbook at the back of this book.*

Writing a Story

Write your own story about a difficult and important decision a character must make. Imagine the character and the decision. Jot down ideas for other characters you want to include in the story as well as specific information about how the main character will make his or her decision. Write your story as clearly and simply as possible. Remember to show how each event in the story leads logically to the next event. You may wish to describe the characters' appearance and feelings as well as the story's setting with vivid details. Review your story for effective word choice and organization. Are your descriptions of people and places clear and vivid? *For help with this assignment, see Lesson 4 in the Writing About Literature Handbook at the back of this book.*

"When I was a kid—twelve, fourteen, around there—I would much rather have been a good baseball player or a hit with the girls," says Shel Silverstein. "But I couldn't play ball, I couldn't dance. . . . So, I started to draw and to write." Since then Silverstein (born 1932) has become a popular illustrator and writer. Most people are familiar with his books *The Light in the Attic*, *Where the Sidewalk Ends*, and *The Giving Tree*. He has said that he hopes readers will "find something to identify with in my books, pick one up and experience a personal sense of discovery." As you read the following poem, you may well identify with a girl who refuses to do a chore she hates.

What would happen if the members of your family refused to do household chores?

• •

Shel Silverstein

Sarah Cynthia Sylvia Stout Would Not Take the Garbage Out

Sarah Cynthia Sylvia Stout
Would not take the garbage out!
She'd scour the pots and scrape the pans,
Candy the yams and spice the hams,
5 And though her daddy would scream and shout,
She simply would not take the garbage out.
And so it piled up to the ceilings:
Coffee grounds, potato peelings,
Brown bananas, rotten peas,
10 Chunks of sour cottage cheese.
It filled the can, it covered the floor,
It cracked the window and blocked the door
With bacon rinds and chicken bones,
Drippy ends of ice cream cones,

15 Prune pits, peach pits, orange peel,
   Gloppy glumps of cold oatmeal,
   Pizza crusts and withered greens,
   Soggy beans and tangerines,
   Crusts of black burned buttered toast,
20 Gristly bits of beefy roasts . . .
   The garbage rolled on down the hall,
   It raised the roof, it broke the wall . . .
   Greasy napkins, cookie crumbs,
   Globs of gooey bubble gum,
25 Cellophane from green baloney,
   Rubbery blubbery macaroni,
   Peanut butter, caked and dry,
   Curdled milk and crusts of pie,
   Moldy melons, dried-up mustard,
30 Eggshells mixed with lemon custard,
   Cold french fries and rancid[1] meat,
   Yellow lumps of Cream of Wheat.
   At last the garbage reached so high
   That finally it touched the sky.
35 And all the neighbors moved away,
   And none of her friends would come to play.
   And finally Sarah Cynthia Stout said,
   "OK, I'll take the garbage out!"
   But then, of course, it was too late . . .
40 The garbage reached across the state,
   From New York to the Golden Gate.
   And there, in the garbage she did hate,
   Poor Sarah met an awful fate,
   That I cannot right now relate
45 Because the hour is much too late.
   But children, remember Sarah Stout
   And always take the garbage out!

---

1. **rancid** [ran′sid]: having the unpleasant odor or taste
of a spoiled oily substance.

READER'S RESPONSE

In your opinion, what happened to Sarah?

STUDY QUESTIONS

Recalling

1. In lines 7–22, what eight verbs does the poet use to describe the actions of the garbage?
2. How many items of garbage does the poet list?
3. What effect does the garbage have on the house? On the sky? On the neighbors?
4. What happens to Sarah after the garbage stretches from coast to coast?

Interpreting

5. Which lines would you say contain exaggerated descriptions? Which contain more realistic descriptions?
6. The poet says that a growing pile of garbage has several effects. Which effect is most important to Sarah? Why do you think so?
7. Why do you think the poet leaves out a description of Sarah's "awful fate"?

Extending

8. What other household chores might serve as the subject of a comic poem?

READING AND LITERARY FOCUS

Alliteration

Poets use sounds in many different ways. One sound effect of poetry is called alliteration. **Alliteration** is the repetition of consonant sounds, usually at the beginning of words. For example, Shel Silverstein uses alliteration in the following line:

Moldy melons, dried-up mustard

As we read, we enjoy the repeated sounds, as if a bell were ringing throughout a line, a stanza, or an entire poem. Alliteration often makes a poem more musical, and it emphasizes a poem's tone. In "Sarah Cynthia Sylvia Stout," alliteration helps convey the poem's humor.

Thinking About Alliteration

Find at least three different examples of alliteration in "Sarah Cynthia Sylvia Stout." In what ways does the sound of each line add to the poem's lighthearted tone?

Nancy Woods (born 1936) grew up in New Jersey and moved to the western part of the United States when she was in her early twenties. She has remained there ever since. Her strong interest in the history and culture of Native Americans has led her to write many books and articles about two Indian tribes—the Ute and the Pueblo. She has also written a book celebrating the state of Colorado, *Colorado: Big Mountain Country.* In the following poem Nancy Woods explores the wishes and fears of a young Native American.

Who will tell of times I wish I knew?

• •

Nancy Wood

Who Will Teach Me?

Who will teach me now that my fathers
Have gone with the buffalo?
Who will tell of times I wish I knew?
Who will direct my journey
5 So that I will come out right?
The years are clouds which
Cover my ancestors.
Let them sleep.
I shall find my way alone.

READER'S RESPONSE

What one word would you choose to describe the poem's speaker?

STUDY QUESTIONS

Recalling

1. According to the speaker, what two things have "gone"?
2. What is the speaker concerned about missing?
3. What things "cover" the fathers?
4. At the end of the poem, what does the speaker decide to do?

Interpreting

5. Who are the "fathers" the speaker describes? What has happened to them?
6. What does the speaker mean by "my journey"?
7. In what way can years "cover" ancestors?
8. Describe the change the speaker experiences between the start and the end of the poem.

Extending

9. Whom would you count on to "direct your journey" so that you "will come out right"?

Metaphor

Like a simile, a **metaphor** is a comparison of two basically different things. In a metaphor, however, the comparison is not stated directly. For example, "the sea is a shining emerald" is a metaphor, while "the sea is *like* a shining emerald" is a simile. Like similes, metaphors create images. They can bring a poem to life in colorful, unexpected ways.

Metaphors often make startling, unexpected connections in the world. Because they use language figuratively, making statements that are not literally true, they stretch our imaginations.

Similes and metaphors always compare ideas from two different categories. You cannot, for example, create a simile or a metaphor by simply comparing one person with another. Instead, you must compare the person with something that is not a human being, such as an animal: "That quarterback is a gazelle."

Thinking About Metaphor

1. Identify the metaphor in "Who Will Teach Me?"
2. What two things are being compared? In what ways are the two things different? In what ways does the poet suggest that they are similar?

Russell Hoban (born 1925) finds human beings interesting because they *seem* so easy to understand. "In my books," he says, "there aren't characters who are simply bad or simply good. Nothing in life is that simple." Hoban's interest in life's *un*-simple things has led him to write over sixty books for children. His works include *Bedtime for Frances*, the story of a little girl who is afraid of going to bed, and *The Mouse and His Child*, the story of two wind-up mice who are tossed in the trash at a toy store and must find their first home. In the following poem Hoban describes an event in a child's life that *seems* ordinary. The child, however, feels it is a disaster.

Fitting together the pieces of a jigsaw puzzle can be more than just a pastime.

• •

Russell Hoban

Jigsaw Puzzle

My beautiful picture of pirates and treasure
Is spoiled, and almost I don't want to start
To put it together; I've lost all the pleasure
I used to find in it: there's one missing part.

5 I know there's one missing—they lost it, the others,
The last time they played with my puzzle—and maybe
There's more than one missing: along with the brothers
And sisters who borrow my toys there's the baby.

There's a hole in the ship or the sea that it sails on,
10 And I said to my father, "Well, what shall I do?
It isn't the same now that some of it's gone."
He said, "Put it together; the world's like that too."

READER'S RESPONSE

Do you agree with the father's advice? Why or why not?

STUDY QUESTIONS

Recalling

1. What does the speaker say he has lost?
2. Whom does the speaker blame for his loss? Which words identify these people?

3. What does the speaker say is true "now that some of it's gone"?
4. What two things does the father compare?

Interpreting

5. How would you describe the emotion that the speaker feels? Explain your answer.
6. What kind of man is the father?
7. In what way is the puzzle "spoiled," in your opinion? In what way is it *not* spoiled?

Extending

8. If you were in the speaker's position, would you follow the father's advice? Why or why not?

Champs de Mars (The Red Tower),
Robert Delaunay, 1911.

Francisco Jimenez [frän sēs'kō hē me'nes] (born 1943) was six years old when he began helping his family pick fruit and vegetables each day from sunrise to sunset in California fields. Like the family in "The Circuit," the Jimenez family moved many times during the year in order to find work and earn enough money to survive. Moving from town to town and school to school, Jimenez found that one of the few stable things in his life was his knowledge. He discovered that "whatever I learned was mine to keep, no matter what happened. Wherever we moved, the knowledge I had would go with me." As an adult Jimenez became a teacher in Santa Clara, California. He writes stories in both English and Spanish.

I looked out the bus window and saw students carrying books under their arms. I felt empty; I put my hands in my pants pockets and walked to the principal's office.

Francisco Jiménez

The Circuit

It was that time of year again; Ito, the strawberry sharecropper,[1] did not smile; it was natural. The peak of the strawberry season was over, and the last few days the workers, most of them *braceros*,[2] were not picking as many boxes as they had during the months of June and July.

As the last days of August disappeared, so did the number of *braceros*. Sunday, only one—the best picker—came to work; I liked him. Sometimes we talked during our half-hour lunch break; that is how I found out he was from Jalisco, the same state in Mexico my family was from. That Sunday was the last time I saw him.

When the sun had tired and sunk behind the mountains, Ito signaled us that it was time to go home. *"Ya esora,"*[3] he yelled in his broken[4] Spanish. Those were words I waited for twelve hours a day, every day, seven days a week, week after week; and the thought of not hearing them again saddened me.

As we drove home Papa did not say a word. With both hands on the wheel, he stared at the dirt road; my older brother, Roberto, was also silent. He leaned his head

---

1. **sharecropper:** tenant farmer who farms land for the owner in return for a share of the crops.
2. **braceros** [brä sä'rōs]: Mexican farm workers.

3. **Ya esora** [yä äs ōr'ä]: Spanish contraction for "It's time to go."
4. **broken:** here, spoken imperfectly; not fluent.

back and closed his eyes; once in a while he cleared from his throat the dust that blew in from the outside.

Yes, it was that time of year. When I opened the front door of our *casita*,[5] I stopped; everything we owned was neatly packed in cardboard boxes. Suddenly I felt even more the weight of hours, days, weeks, and months of work. I sat down on a box; the thought of having to move to Fresno,[6] and knowing what was in store for me there, brought tears to my eyes.

That night I could not sleep; I lay in bed, thinking about how much I hated this move.

A little before five o'clock in the morning, Papa woke everyone up. A few minutes later, the yelling and screaming of my little brothers and sisters, for whom the move was a great adventure, broke the silence of dawn. Shortly, the barking of the dogs accompanied them.

While we packed the breakfast dishes, Papa went outside to start the *Carcanchita;* that was the name Papa gave his old '38 black Plymouth. He bought it in a used car lot in Santa Rosa[7] in the winter of 1949. Papa was very proud of his car; *Mi Carcanchita,* my little jalopy, he called it: he had a right to be proud of it. He spent a lot of time looking at other cars before buying this one. When he finally chose the *Carcanchita,* he checked it thoroughly before driving it out of the car lot; he examined every inch of the car. He listened to the motor, tilting his head from side to side like a parrot, trying to detect any noises that spelled car trouble. After being satisfied with the looks and sounds of the car, Papa insisted on knowing who the original owner was. He never did find out from the car dealer, but he bought the car anyway. Papa figured the original owner must have been an important man, because behind the rear seat of the car he found a blue necktie.

Papa parked the car out in front and left the motor running; *"Listo,"*[8] he yelled. Without saying a word, Roberto and I began to carry the boxes out to the car. Roberto carried the two big boxes and I carried the two smaller ones; Papa threw the mattress on the top of the car roof and tied it with ropes to the front and rear bumpers.

Everything was packed except Mama's pot; it was an old, large, galvanized pot she had picked up at the army surplus store in Santa María[9] the year I was born. The pot was full of dents and nicks, and the more dents and nicks it had, the more Mama liked it. *"Mi olla,"*[10] she used to say proudly.

I held the front door open as Mama carefully carried out her pot by both handles, making sure not to spill the cooked beans. When she got to the car, Papa reached out to help her with it. Roberto opened the rear car door and Papa gently placed it on the floor behind the front seat. All of us climbed in. Papa sighed, wiped the sweat off his forehead with his sleeve, and said wearily, *"Es todo."*[11]

As we drove away, I felt a lump in my throat; I turned around and looked at our *casita* for the last time.

At sunset we drove into a vineyard near

---

5. *casita* [cä sē′tä]: Spanish for "little house."
6. **Fresno** [frez′nō]: city in central California.
7. **Santa Rosa:** city in western California, near San Francisco.

8. *Listo* [lē′stō]: Spanish for "ready."
9. **Santa María:** town in the state of Jalisco, in western Mexico.
10. *Mi olla* [mē ōi′yä]: Spanish for "my kettle."
11. *Es todo* [äs tō′thō]: Spanish for "That's everything."

Fresno. Since Papa did not speak English, Mama asked the boss if he needed any more workers. "We don't need any more," said the man, scratching his head, "Check with Sullivan, down the road; can't miss him; he lives in a big white house with a fence around it."

When we got there, Mama walked up to the house. She went through the white gate, past a row of rose bushes, up the stairs to the front door; she rang the doorbell. The porch light went on and a tall, husky man came out; they exchanged a few words. After the man went in, Mama clasped her hands and hurried back to the car. "We have work! Mr. Sullivan said we can stay there the whole season," she said, gasping and pointing to an old garage near the stables.

The garage was worn out by the years. It had no windows; the walls, eaten by termites, strained to support the roof; the loose dirt floor looked like a gray road map.

That night, by the light of a kerosene lamp,[12] we unpacked and cleaned our new home. Roberto swept away the loose dirt, leaving the hard ground; Papa plugged the holes in the walls; Mama fed my little brothers and sisters. Papa and Roberto then brought in the mattress and placed it in the far corner of the garage. "Mama, you and the little ones sleep on the mattress; Roberto, Panchito, and I will sleep outside, under the trees," Papa said.

Early next morning Mr. Sullivan showed us where his crop was, and, after breakfast, Papa, Roberto, and I headed for the vineyard to pick.

Around 9 A.M. the temperature had risen to almost one hundred degrees; I was completely soaked in sweat, and my mouth felt as if I had been chewing on a handkerchief. I walked over to the end of the row, picked up the jug of water we had brought, and began drinking. "Don't drink too much; you'll get sick," Roberto shouted. No sooner had he said that than I felt sick to my stomach; I dropped to my knees and let the jug roll off my hands; I remained motionless, with my eyes glued on the hot, sandy ground. All I could hear was the drone of insects. Slowly I began to recover; I poured water over my face and neck, and watched the black mud run down my arms and hit the ground.

I still felt a little dizzy when we took a break to eat lunch; it was past 2 P.M. and we sat underneath a large walnut tree that was on the side of the road. While we ate, Papa jotted down the number of boxes we had picked; Roberto drew designs on the ground with a stick. Suddenly I noticed Papa's face turn pale as he looked down the road; "Here comes the school bus," he whispered loudly in alarm. Instinctively, Roberto and I ran and hid in the vineyards. We did not want to get in trouble for not going to school. The yellow bus stopped in front of Mr. Sullivan's house; two neatly dressed boys my age got off. They carried books under their arms. After they crossed the street, the bus drove away. Roberto and I came out from hiding and joined Papa; "*Tienen que tener cuidado,*"[13] he warned us.

After lunch, we went back to work; the sun kept beating down; the buzzing insects, the wet sweat, and the hot, dry dust made

---

12. **kerosene** [ker'ə sēn'] **lamp:** lamp fueled by kerosene, a colorless liquid made from petroleum.

13. ***Tienen que tener cuidado*** [tē en'en kā ten er' kwē thä'thō]: Spanish for "You have to be careful."

the afternoon seem to last forever. Finally, the mountains around the valley reached out and swallowed the sun; within an hour, it was too dark to continue picking. The vines blanketed the grapes, making it difficult to see the bunches. *"Vámonos,"*[14] said Papa, signaling to us that it was time to quit work. Papa then took out a pencil and began to figure out how much we had earned our first day. He wrote down numbers, crossed some out, wrote down some more; *"Quince,"*[15] he murmured.

When we arrived home, we took a cold shower underneath a waterhose. We then sat down to eat dinner around some wooden crates that served as a table. Mama had cooked a special meal for us. We had rice and tortillas with *carne con chile,*[16] my favorite dish.

The next morning I could hardly move; my body ached all over. I felt little control over my arms and legs. This feeling went on every morning until my muscles got used to the work.

It was Monday, the first week of November; the grape season was over, and I could now go to school. I woke up early that morning and lay in bed, looking at the stars and savoring the thought of not going to work and of starting school for the first time that year. Since I could not sleep, I decided to get up and join Papa and Roberto at breakfast. I sat at the table across from Roberto, but I kept my head down. I did not want to look up and face him. I knew he was sad; he was not going to school today; he was not going tomorrow, or the next week, or next month. He would not go until the cotton season was over, and that was some time in February. I rubbed my hands together and watched the dry, acid-stained skin fall to the floor in little rolls.

When Papa and Roberto left for work, I felt relief. I walked to the top of a small grade[17] next to the garage and watched the

---

14. *Vámonos* [vä′mō nōs]: Spanish for "Let's go."
15. *Quince* [kēn′sä]: Spanish for "fifteen."
16. **carne con chile** [kär′nä kōn chē′lä]: Spanish for "meat with chile"; highly seasoned dish made of meat, red peppers, tomato sauce, and, usually, beans.

17. **grade:** sloping road.

Carcanchita disappear in the distance in a cloud of dust.

Two hours later, around 8 A.M., I stood by the side of the road waiting for school bus number twenty. When it arrived, I climbed in. No one noticed me; everyone was busy either talking or yelling. I sat in an empty seat in the back.

When the bus stopped in front of the school, I felt very nervous; I looked out the bus window and saw students carrying books under their arms. I felt empty; I put my hands in my pants pockets and walked to the principal's office. When I entered I heard a woman's voice say, "May I help you?" I was startled; I had not heard English for months. For a few seconds I remained speechless; I looked at the woman who waited for an answer. My first instinct was to answer in Spanish, but I held back. Finally, after struggling for English words, I managed to tell her that I wanted to enroll in school. After answering many questions, I was led to the classroom.

Mr. Lema, the teacher, greeted me and assigned me a desk; he then introduced me to the class. I was so nervous and scared at that moment when everyone's eyes were on me that I wished I were with Papa and Roberto picking cotton. After taking roll, Mr. Lema gave the class the assignment for the first hour; "The first thing we have to do this morning is finish reading the story we began yesterday," he said enthusiastically. He walked up to me, handed me an English book, and asked me to read; "We are on page 125," he said politely. When I heard this, I felt my blood rush to my head; I felt dizzy. "Would you like to read?" he asked hesitantly. I opened the book to page 125. My mouth was dry; my eyes began to water; I could not begin. "You can read later," Mr. Lema said understandingly.

For the rest of the reading period I kept getting angrier and angrier with myself. I should have read, I thought to myself.

Between classes I went to the restroom and opened my English book to page 125. I began to read in a low voice, pretending I was in class. There were many words I did not know; I closed the book and headed back to the classroom.

Mr. Lema was sitting at his desk correcting papers. When I entered he looked up at me and smiled; I felt better. I walked up to him and asked if he could help me with the new words; "Gladly," he said.

The rest of the month I spent my lunch hours working on English with Mr. Lema, my best friend at school.

One Friday during lunch hour, Mr. Lema asked me to take a walk with him to the music room. "Do you like music?" he asked me as we entered the building.

"Yes, I like Mexican *corridos*,"[18] I answered. He then picked up a trumpet, blew on it, and handed it to me; the sound gave me goose bumps. I knew that sound; I had heard it in many Mexican *corridos*. "How would you like to learn to play it?" he asked. He must have read my face because before I could answer, he added: "I'll teach you how to play it during our lunch hours."

That day I could hardly wait to get home to tell Papa and Mama the great news. As I got off the bus, my little brothers and sisters ran up to meet me; they were yelling and screaming. I thought they were happy to see me, but when I opened the door to our *casita*, I saw that everything we owned was neatly packed in cardboard boxes.

---

18. ***corridos*** [kō rē′thōs]: Spanish for "ballads"; "popular songs."

READER'S RESPONSE

Do you think "The Circuit" is an appropriate title for this story? Why or why not?

● ●

STUDY QUESTIONS

Recalling

1. What does the narrator feel on the September day when he sees boxes packed in the *casita*?
2. What two possessions do the father and mother treasure?
3. In what condition is the "old garage near the stables" at the Fresno vineyard?
4. Why is the narrator allowed to go to school the first week of November? What emotions does he feel at breakfast that morning?
5. Who becomes the narrator's "best friend at school"?

Interpreting

6. Why do you think the narrator hated the move the family would make to Fresno?
7. Why do you think the father's car and the mother's iron pot are so important to them?
8. What do the family members' actions the first night in the old garage tell you about their personalities?
9. In what ways does Mr. Lema help the narrator adapt to the new school? In what ways does the narrator help himself?

READING AND LITERARY FOCUS

Theme

An author usually writes a story in order to communicate a message, or theme. The **theme** is the general statement about life that is the main idea of the story. Some stories contain a **stated theme;** that is, the author announces the theme directly in a sentence or two. Other stories contain an **implied**

theme; that is, the author gradually reveals the theme to the reader but does not state the theme directly.

For example, an author might write a story about two children who save a pet's life. If the author wished to state the theme directly, he or she might write, "Even in the face of huge obstacles, people who work together can succeed." If the author chose not to state the theme directly, it would be implied in the way the author described the children's teamwork while saving the pet.

Thinking About Theme

1. What do you think is Jimenez's general message, or theme, in "The Circuit"?
2. Is the theme stated directly or implied? Explain your answer.

COMPOSITION

Writing About Theme

Write a paragraph in which you show that the events of "The Circuit" support the story's theme. **Prewriting:** Identify the theme in a single sentence. Then list events from the story that support the theme. **Writing:** Begin by stating the story's theme. Then describe one or two events from the story that demonstrate the theme. **Revising:** Review your paragraph for effective word choice and organization. Then check for errors of grammar, spelling, and punctuation.

Writing a Speech

Imagine that you have been asked to give a short speech to an audience of sixth-graders. Write a speech in which you present one of the following points of view: "Knowledge is more important than money," or "Money is more important than knowledge." Make a list of details or ideas that will support the opinion you chose. Begin by stating the opinion. Then support it with details, examples, and facts. You might wish to repeat your statement of opinion at the end of the speech.

Roald Dahl (born 1916) claims that "children love to be spooked." He believes that a writer of children's books must be able to make up a story "that is so absorbing, exciting, funny, fast and beautiful that the child will fall in love with it." Dahl, who was born in South Wales, in Great Britain, has written dozens of books for children and adults. Two of these—*Charlie and the Chocolate Factory* and *James and the Giant Peach*—have become hugely popular with young people. He has also written plays, screenplays, poetry, and two volumes of autobiography. "The Green Mamba," which is taken from one of these volumes, is a spooky, absorbing account of a real-life incident.

Gradually, he worked his way over to the back wall, and from there he was able to see at least the head and two or three feet of the snake itself. But the snake also saw him.

● ●

Roald Dahl

The Green Mamba

Oh, those snakes! How I hated them! They were the only fearful thing about Tanganyika[1] and a newcomer very quickly learned to identify most of them and to know which were deadly and which were simply poisonous. The killers, apart from the black mambas,[2] were the green mambas, the cobras and the tiny little puff adders[3] that looked very much like small sticks lying motionless in the middle of a dusty path, and so easy to step on.

One Sunday evening I was invited to go and have a sundowner[4] at the house of an Englishman called Fuller who worked in the Customs office in Dar es Salaam.[5] He lived with his wife and two small children in a plain white wooden house that stood alone some way back from the road in a rough grassy piece of ground with coconut trees scattered about. I was walking across the grass towards the house and was about twenty yards away when I saw a large green snake go gliding straight up the veranda steps of Fuller's house and in through the open front door. The brilliant yellowy-green skin and its great size made me certain it was a green mamba, a creature almost as

---

1. **Tanganyika** [tang′gən yē′kə]: former country in eastern Africa once under partial British control, now part of Tanzania.
2. **mambas** [mäm′bəz]: poisonous snakes of southern Africa related to the cobra, having a green or black color and a deadly bite.
3. **puff adders:** poisonous African snakes with brown or gray bodies with yellow markings.

4. **sundowner:** drink taken at the end of the day.
5. **Dar es Salaam** [där′ əs sə läm′]: capital and largest city of Tanzania, formerly the capital of Tanganyika.

deadly as the black mamba, and for a few seconds I was so startled and dumbfounded and horrified that I froze to the spot. Then I pulled myself together and ran round to the back of the house shouting, "Mr. Fuller! Mr. Fuller!"

Mrs. Fuller popped her head out of an upstairs window. "What on earth's the matter?" she said.

"You've got a large green mamba in your front room!" I shouted. "I saw it go up the veranda steps and right in through the door!"

"Fred!" Mrs. Fuller shouted, turning round. "Fred! Come here!"

Freddy Fuller's round red face appeared at the window beside his wife. "What's up?" he asked.

"There's a green mamba in your living-room!" I shouted.

Without hesitation and without wasting time with more questions, he said to me, "Stay there. I'm going to lower the children down to you one at a time." He was completely cool and unruffled. He didn't even raise his voice.

A small girl was lowered down to me by her wrists and I was able to catch her easily by the legs. Then came a small boy. Then Freddy Fuller lowered his wife and I caught her by the waist and put her on the ground. Then came Fuller himself. He hung by his hands from the window-sill and when he let go he landed neatly on his two feet.

We stood in a little group on the grass at the back of the house and I told Fuller exactly what I had seen.

The mother was holding the two children by the hand, one on each side of her. They didn't seem to be particularly alarmed.

"What happens now?" I asked.

"Go down to the road, all of you," Fuller said. "I'm off to fetch the snake-man." He trotted away and got into his small ancient black car and drove off. Mrs. Fuller and the two small children and I went down to the road and sat in the shade of a large mango tree.

"Who is this snake-man?" I asked Mrs. Fuller.

"He is an old Englishman who has been out here for years," Mrs. Fuller said. "He actually *likes* snakes. He understands them and never kills them. He catches them and sells them to zoos and laboratories all over the world. Every native for miles around knows about him and whenever one of them sees a snake, he marks its hiding place and runs, often for great distances, to tell the snake-man. Then the snake-man comes along and captures it. The snake-man's strict rule is that he will never buy a captured snake from the natives."

"Why not?" I asked.

"To discourage them from trying to catch snakes themselves," Mrs. Fuller said. "In his early days he used to buy caught snakes, but so many natives got bit trying to catch them, and so many died, that he decided to put a stop to it. Now any native who brings in a caught snake, no matter how rare, gets turned away."

"That's good," I said.

"What is the snake-man's name?" I asked.

"Donald Macfarlane," she said. "I believe he's Scottish."

"Is the snake in the house, Mummy?" the small girl asked.

"Yes, darling. But the snake-man is going to get it out."

"He'll bite Jack," the girl said.

"Oh, my God!" Mrs. Fuller cried, jumping to her feet. "I forgot about Jack!" She began calling out, "Jack! Come here, Jack! Jack! . . . Jack! . . . Jack!"

The children jumped up as well and all of them started calling to the dog. But no dog came out of the open front door.

"He's bit Jack!" the small girl cried out. "He must have bit him!" She began to cry and so did her brother, who was a year or so younger than she was. Mrs. Fuller looked grim.

"Jack's probably hiding upstairs," she said. "You know how clever he is."

Mrs. Fuller and I seated ourselves again on the grass, but the children remained standing. In between their tears they went on calling to the dog.

"Would you like me to take you down to the Maddens' house?" their mother asked.

"No!" they cried. "No, no, no! We want Jack!"

"Here's Daddy!" Mrs. Fuller cried, pointing at the tiny black car coming up the road in a swirl of dust. I noticed a long wooden pole sticking out through one of the car windows.

The children ran to meet the car. "Jack's inside the house and he's been bit by the snake!" they wailed. "We know he's been bit! He doesn't come when we call him!"

Mr. Fuller and the snake-man got out of the car. The snake-man was small and very old, probably over seventy. He wore leather boots made of thick cowhide and he had long gauntlet-type gloves[6] on his hands made of the same stuff. The gloves reached above his elbows. In his right hand he carried an extraordinary implement, an eight-foot-long wooden pole with a forked end. The two prongs of the fork were made, so it seemed, of black rubber, about an inch thick and quite flexible, and it was clear that if the fork was pressed against the ground the two prongs would bend outwards, allowing the neck of the fork to go down as close to the ground as necessary. In his left hand he carried an ordinary brown sack.

Donald Macfarlane, the snake-man, may have been old and small but he was an impressive-looking character. His eyes were pale blue, deep-set in a face round and dark and wrinkled as a walnut. Above the blue eyes, the eyebrows were thick and startlingly white, but the hair on his head was almost black. In spite of the thick leather boots, he moved like a leopard, with soft slow cat-like strides, and he came straight up to me and said, "Who are you?"

"He's with Shell,"[7] Fuller said. "He hasn't been here long."

"You want to watch?" the snake-man said to me.

"Watch?" I said, wavering. "Watch? How do you mean watch? I mean where from? Not in the house?"

"You can stand out on the veranda and look through the window," the snake-man said.

"Come on," Fuller said. "We'll both watch."

"Now don't do anything silly," Mrs. Fuller said.

The two children stood there forlorn and miserable, with tears all over their cheeks.

The snake-man and Fuller and I walked over the grass towards the house, and as we approached the veranda steps the snake-man whispered, "Tread softly on the wooden boards or he'll pick up the vibration. Wait until I've gone in, then walk up quietly and stand by the window."

---

6. **gauntlet** [gônt′lit]-**type gloves:** gloves having long, flaring cuffs extending above the wrist.

7. **Shell:** British-Dutch oil company.

The snake-man went up the steps first and he made absolutely no sound at all with his feet. He moved soft and cat-like onto the veranda and straight through the front door and then he quickly but very quietly closed the door behind him.

I felt better with the door closed. What I mean is I felt better for myself. I certainly didn't feel better for the snake-man. I figured he was committing suicide. I followed Fuller onto the veranda and we both crept over to the window. The window was open, but it had a fine mesh mosquito-netting[8] all over it. That made me feel better still. We peered through the netting.

The living-room was simple and ordinary, coconut matting on the floor, a red sofa, a coffee-table and a couple of armchairs. The dog was sprawled on the matting under the coffee-table, a large Airedale with curly brown and black hair. He was stone dead.

The snake-man was standing absolutely still just inside the door of the living-room. The brown sack was now slung over his left shoulder and he was grasping the long pole with both hands, holding it out in front of him, parallel to the ground. I couldn't see the snake. I didn't think the snake-man had seen it yet either.

A minute went by . . . two minutes . . . three . . . four . . . five. Nobody moved. There was death in that room. The air was heavy with death and the snake-man stood as motionless as a pillar of stone, with the long rod held out in front of him.

And still he waited. Another minute . . . and another . . . and another.

And now I saw the snake-man beginning

to bend his knees. Very slowly he bent his knees until he was almost squatting on the floor, and from that position he tried to peer under the sofa and the armchairs.

And still it didn't look as though he was seeing anything.

Slowly he straightened his legs again, and then his head began to swivel around the room. Over to the right, in the far corner, a staircase led up to the floor above. The snake-man looked at the stairs, and I knew very well what was going through his head. Quite abruptly, he took one step forward and stopped.

---

8. **mosquito netting:** screen or covering of gauzelike material that keeps out mosquitoes.

Nothing happened.

A moment later I caught sight of the snake. It was lying full-length along the skirting[9] of the right-hand wall, but hidden from the snake-man's view by the back of the sofa. It lay there like a long, beautiful, deadly shaft of green glass, quite motionless, perhaps asleep. It was facing away from us who were at the window, with its small triangular head resting on the matting near the foot of the stairs.

I nudged Fuller and whispered, "It's over there against the wall." I pointed and Fuller saw the snake. At once, he started waving both hands, palms outward, back and forth across the window, hoping to get the snake-man's attention. The snake-man didn't see him. Very softly, Fuller said, "Psst!" and the snake-man looked up sharply. Fuller pointed. The snake-man understood and gave a nod.

Now the snake-man began working his way very very slowly to the back wall of the room so as to get a view of the snake behind the sofa. He never walked on his toes as you or I would have done. His feet remained flat on the ground all the time. The cowhide boots were like moccasins, with neither soles nor heels. Gradually, he worked his way over to the back wall, and from there he was able to see at least the head and two or three feet of the snake itself.

But the snake also saw him. With a movement so fast it was invisible, the snake's head came up about two feet off the floor and the front of the body arched backwards, ready to strike. Almost simultaneously, it bunched its whole body into a series of curves, ready to flash forward.

The snake-man was just a bit too far away from the snake to reach it with the end of his pole. He waited, staring at the snake, and the snake stared back at him with two small malevolent[10] black eyes.

Then the snake-man started speaking to the snake. "Come along, my pretty," he whispered in a soft wheedling voice. "There's a good boy. Nobody's going to hurt you. Nobody's going to harm you, my pretty little thing. Just lie still and relax . . ." He took a step forward towards the snake, holding the pole out in front of him.

What the snake did next was so fast that the whole movement couldn't have taken more than a hundredth of a second, like the flick of a camera shutter. There was a green flash as the snake darted forward at least ten feet and struck at the snake-man's leg. Nobody could have got out of the way of that one. I heard the snake's head strike against the thick cowhide boot with a sharp little *crack,* and then at once the head was back in that same deadly backward-curving position, ready to strike again.

"There's a good boy," the snake-man said softly. "There's a clever boy. There's a lovely fellow. You mustn't get excited. Keep calm and everything's going to be all right." As he was speaking, he was slowly lowering the end of the pole until the forked prongs were about twelve inches above the middle of the snake's body. "There's a lovely fellow," he whispered. "There's a good kind little chap. Keep still now, my beauty. Keep still,

---

9. **skirting:** strip of board or molding at the bottom of a wall that covers the line where the wall meets the floor.

10. **malevolent** [mə lev′ə lənt]: showing ill will or hatred.

my pretty. Keep quite still. Daddy's not going to hurt you."

I could see a thin dark trickle of venom running down the snake-man's right boot where the snake had struck.

The snake, head raised and arcing backwards, was as tense as a tight-wound spring and ready to strike again. "Keep still, my lovely," the snake-man whispered. "Don't move now. Keep still. No one's going to hurt you."

Then *wham*, the rubber prongs came down right across the snake's body, about midway along its length, and pinned it to the floor. All I could see was a green blur as the snake thrashed around furiously in an effort to free itself. But the snake-man kept up the pressure on the prongs and the snake was trapped.

What happens next? I wondered. There was no way he could catch hold of that madly twisting flailing length of green muscle with his hands, and even if he could have done so, the head would surely have flashed around and bit him in the face.

Holding the very end of the eight-foot pole, the snake-man began to work his way round the room until he was at the tail end of the snake. Then, in spite of the flailing and the thrashing, he started pushing the prongs forward along the snake's body towards the head. Very very slowly he did it, pushing the rubber prongs forward over the snake's flailing body, keeping the snake pinned down all the time and push-ing, pushing, pushing the long wooden rod forward millimeter by millimeter. It was a fascinating and frightening thing to watch, the little man with white eyebrows and black hair carefully manipulating his long implement and sliding the fork ever so slowly along the length of the twisting snake towards the head. The snake's body was thumping against the coconut matting with such a noise that if you had been upstairs you might have thought two big men were wrestling on the floor.

Then at last the prongs were right behind the head itself, pinning it down, and at that point the snake-man reached forward with one gloved hand and grasped the snake very firmly by the neck. He threw away the pole. He took the sack off his shoulder with his free hand. He lifted the great, still twisting length of the deadly green snake and pushed the head into the sack. Then he let go the head and bundled the rest of the creature in and closed the sack. The sack started jumping about as though there were fifty angry rats inside it, but the snake-man was now totally relaxed and he held the sack casually in one hand as if it contained no more than a few pounds of potatoes. He stooped and picked up his pole from the floor, then he turned and looked towards the window where we were peering in.

"Pity about the dog," he said. "You'd better get it out of the way before the children see it."

READER'S RESPONSE

Do you think the snake-man was afraid of the green mamba at any point during the incident described?

• •

STUDY QUESTIONS

Recalling

1. What does Mr. Fuller do when the narrator says, "There's a green mamba in your living room"? With what words does the narrator describe Mr. Fuller's behavior?

2. What does Mrs. Fuller say about the snake-man's attitude toward snakes?

3. What do the children assume has happened to Jack? What does Mrs. Fuller say about him?

4. How old is the snake-man? Describe his clothes and tools.

5. What does the snake do as soon as it sees the snake-man? What does the snake-man begin to do as the two stare at each other?

6. What does the snake-man say is a "pity"?

Interpreting

7. What does Mr. Fuller's response to the snake's presence tell you about his character?

8. Do you think Mrs. Fuller knows that the dog is dead? Explain your answer.

9. What do the snake-man's clothes and tools tell you about his personality and his attitude toward green mambas?

10. In your opinion, why does the snake-man talk to the snake?

11. What disaster occurs in "The Green Mamba"? In what way might killing the snake have been a disaster?

Extending

12. What occupations require a person to be both brave and respectful in response to danger?

VOCABULARY

Using a Pronunciation Key

"The Green Mamba" contains words whose pronunciation is explained in the footnotes. The phonetic symbols used in the footnotes are explained in the **pronunciation key** in the Glossary at the back of this book.

For example, in the footnote for the word *malevolent*, the first *a* is written as [ə]. If you look in the Glossary's pronunciation key, you will see that this sound is pronounced like the *a* in *ago*.

Using the footnotes and the Glossary's pronunciation key, answer the following questions.

1. Is the first *a* in *Tanganyika* pronounced like the *a* in *car*, the *a* in *at*, or the *a* in *ape*?

2. Is the *o* in *malevolent* pronounced like the *o* in *old*, the *u* in *turn*, or the *o* in *lemon*?

3. Is the *a* in *mamba* pronounced like the *a* in *car*, the *a* in *at*, or the *a* in *ape*?

4. Is the *au* in *gauntlet* pronounced like the *o* in *hot*, the *o* in *old*, or the *u* in *up*?

5. Is the first *a* in *Dar Es Salaam* pronounced like the *a* in *car*, the *a* in *at*, or the *a* in *ape*?

CHALLENGE

Picture Research

Look in the library for pictures of dangerous or exotic snakes from around the world. You might check the encyclopedia under *Snakes* or under the names of individual snakes. You might also look at scientific encyclopedias and nature magazines.

Thinking Skills: Evaluating

DEFINITION
Evaluating is a way of thinking about something and making a judgment about it. When you evaluate, you apply criteria to make your judgment. Criteria are the standards, rules, or tests on which a judgment can be based.

STEPS

1. **State the reason or purpose for your evaluation.**
   What do you want to evaluate? Why do you want to evaluate it?

2. **Identify the criteria.**
   What specific rules, tests, or standards will you use to make your judgment?

3. **Apply the criteria.**
   Does the subject of your evaluation meet each specific criterion? Does it meet some criteria better than others?

4. **Draw a conclusion.**
   The conclusion is your evaluation of how well the subject meets the criteria.

EXAMPLE
Imagine that a baseball player has just stepped to the plate, and a friend asks you, "Is he a good ballplayer?" You probably answer "yes" or "no" without talking about all your criteria for a good ballplayer. In your mind, however, you make your evaluation based on criteria.

1. **State the reason or purpose for your evalua-**
tion. You want to evaluate the ballplayer to give your friend an accurate answer.

2. **Identify the criteria.** You choose to evaluate the ballplayer according to his hitting, fielding, and leadership skills.

3. **Apply the criteria.** The player is a better-than-average hitter. His fielding is outstanding, and he is one of the team leaders and cocaptains.

4. **Draw a conclusion.** You conclude that the man at the plate is a good ballplayer.

ACTIVITY 1
Evaluating "The Green Mamba"

Follow the four steps of evaluating to answer the question "Is 'The Green Mamba' a good story?" Identify your criteria carefully, being very specific about what you think makes a good story. You may want to include one or more of the following criteria: an exciting plot, interesting details about life in another part of the world, characters you care about, descriptions that help you see places and animals you may not be familiar with, parts that made you nervous, parts that made you sad.

ACTIVITY 2
Evaluating a Work of Literature

Evaluate another selection in this book or any other work of literature that you have read. Follow the four steps. Remember that people of different cultures or ages or with different interests may have different criteria. What is important is that you think about your criteria and they reflect what you believe.

Robert Frost (1874–1963) is probably the best-known American poet. He was so popular that the United States Senate honored his seventy-fifth birthday, and he was asked to read a poem at President Kennedy's inauguration in 1961. Frost moved from San Francisco to New England when he was eleven. As a youth he worked in a Massachusetts mill, and later he made shoes, edited a newspaper, taught school, and became a farmer. He always thought of himself as a careful craftsman, and he brought that care to the making of poems. Much of his poetry is about people in the New England countryside. In the following poem Frost describes how a child discovers a small tragedy in a meadow.

We saw the risk we took in doing good, / But dared not spare to do the best we could.

• •

Robert Frost

The Exposed Nest

You were forever finding some new play.
So when I saw you down on hands and knees
In the meadow, busy with the new-cut hay,
Trying, I thought, to set it up on end,
5 I went to show you how to make it stay,
If that was your idea, against the breeze,
And, if you asked me, even help pretend
To make it root again and grow afresh.[1]
But 'twas[2] no make-believe with you today,
10 Nor was the grass itself your real concern,
Though I found your hand full of wilted fern,
Steel-bright June-grass, and blackening heads of clover.
'Twas a nest full of young birds on the ground
The cutter-bar[3] had just gone champing over

---

1. **afresh:** anew; again.
2. **'twas:** it was.
3. **cutter-bar:** on a harvesting machine used to cut and collect grain, the bar that carries the triangular knives, or cutters.

15 (Miraculously without tasting flesh)
   And left defenseless to the heat and light.
   You wanted to restore them to their right
   Of something interposed⁴ between their sight
   And too much world at once—could means be found.
20 The way the nest-full every time we stirred
   Stood up to us as to a mother-bird
   Whose coming home has been too long deferred,⁵
   Made me ask would the mother-bird return
   And care for them in such a change of scene
25 And might our meddling make her more afraid.
   That was a thing we could not wait to learn.
   We saw the risk we took in doing good,
   But dared not spare to do the best we could
   Though harm should come of it; so built the screen
30 You had begun, and gave them back their shade.
   All this to prove we cared. Why is there then
   No more to tell? We turned to other things.
   I haven't any memory—have you?—
   Of ever coming to the place again
35 To see if the birds lived the first night through,
   And so at last to learn to use their wings.

---

4. **interposed** [in'tər pōzd']: placed
or brought between; inserted.
5. **deferred** [di furd']: delayed.

Bird's Nest with Ferns, Fidelia Bridges, 1863.

READER'S RESPONSE

Do you think the child and adult should have left the nest untouched?

STUDY QUESTIONS

Recalling

1. What does the speaker, the adult, think the child is doing?
2. What is the child actually handling? What recently happened at that spot?
3. According to the speaker, to what do birds have a "right"?
4. What harm might be done to the birds by the presence of the two people?
5. In lines 27–29, what do the two people decide to do, despite the risks?
6. After helping the birds, what do they do?

Interpreting

7. How old do you imagine the child—the "you" the narrator addresses—is? Why do you think so?
8. In what ways are the young birds like the child? Explain your answer.
9. Why do you think the two never returned to the spot? Could their failure to return be called a small disaster? Why or why not?

VOCABULARY

Sentence Completions

Each of the following sentences contains a blank with four possible words for completing the sentence. The words are from "The Exposed Nest." Choose the word that best completes each sentence. Write the number of each sentence and the letter of your choice on a separate sheet.

1. The museum was ___ the painting after it had been damaged.
   (a) restaining   (c) restoring
   (b) sparing   (d) balancing

2. I told him politely that his ___ in my personal life would get him into trouble.
   (a) meddling   (c) consideration
   (b) stirring   (d) method
3. We decided to ___ our visit until the cost of the trip was less.
   (a) spare   (c) determine
   (b) defer   (d) adjust
4. The ___ flower was drooping and faded.
   (a) colorful   (c) wilted
   (b) sparkling   (d) defenseless
5. The dark sunglasses ___ between the glaring sunshine and my eyes.
   (a) proposed   (c) interviewed
   (b) glanced   (d) interposed

COMPOSITION

Writing About Words in a Poem

Write a paragraph in which you show how Frost uses particular words to suggest the birds' powerlessness. **Prewriting:** Reread the poem to identify specific lines in which Frost describes the birds. List the words the poet uses to convey their powerlessness. **Writing:** Begin with a statement about the birds' dangerous situation. Then explain how Frost uses particular words to convey how fragile they are in the face of danger. **Revising:** Review your paragraph for effective word choice and organization. Then check for errors in grammar, spelling, and punctuation.

Writing a Poem About an Animal

Write a poem about an animal that is in some sort of danger. Choose an animal and a dangerous situation it might face. List details that communicate the animal's situation in the face of danger. Write a first draft of your poem, using the ideas and details you created in your notes. Then reread your poem, and identify words and phrases that could be made clearer or more vivid. Write a second draft that includes these changes.

Lois Phillips Hudson (born 1927) spent her childhood on the prairies of North Dakota. For her the prairie was "a world of elements, not of streets and houses." She spent a great deal of time alone with those elements—vast rolling grasslands, huge blue skies, frigid air from the north, and long winters. Hudson has written two books and many magazine articles. She says that she writes because she wishes "to show the excitement, the complexity, the wonder of the creature called man." In "The Cold Wave" Hudson introduces the reader to a young girl with a vivid imagination and a generous heart.

I was well acquainted with the shock of stepping from the warm kitchen into a winter night. But none of the freezing memories of the past could prepare me for the burning air that night.

● ●

Lois Phillips Hudson

The Cold Wave

My father and grandfather would often speak of the earlier days in North Dakota—of the strong man who could swing a hundred-pound sack of wheat to his back by flinging it over his shoulder with his teeth, of tornadoes that switched[1] the roofs of barns and houses, and of hailstorms that rained sheep-killing stones, heaping July wheatfields with desolations[2] of ice.

Even more fascinating to me were their stories of the early winters. I would never see any winters like these, they said, for a new and milder weather cycle now prevailed. I would never know the bitter years that built the grim legends of our northern land.

My mother used to tell me how once a prairie wolf[3] had stalked her as she walked home alone from school, over miles of abandoned stubble. I always felt cheated when I looked at the faded photograph of my father sitting on a horse, his hat higher than some telephone wires. He had ridden that horse right to the top of a gigantic snowbank, packed so hard that the horse's hoofs hardly dented its crust. It was true that there was usually a bank in our yard that reached to the top of the clothesline pole, but this was hardly satisfying when I knew what grander things had been. Why couldn't something happen *after* I was born, I wondered.

Yet when the sort of thing I was waiting for finally came, its coming was so natural

---

1. **switched:** to make a shift or exchange.
2. **desolations** [des'ə lā'shənz]: barren stretches of waste and ruin.

---

3. **prairie wolf:** a gray or timber wolf.

and casual, so unlike a legend, that I mistook it for a part of the routine of my existence. It was part of my routine, for instance, to run over behind the depot with some of the town kids and slide on the ice by the tracks before I went over to Schlagel's Store to get a ride home with my father. I was almost always the only girl to go sliding, and it was also part of my routine to try to beat the boys to the smoothest patch of ice. On the day I am talking about, the only departure from routine was that there were no contenders for any of the ice.

I didn't slide very long myself, because I began to feel some undefined discomfort that an adult would have easily identified as a deeply pervasive chill. But when an eight-year-old is too cold, he will first feel oddly tired and lonely and deserted, so that he will go to find people. Thus it was that although I began to have the feeling that I had played too long and that surely my father would be waiting for me angrily, when I opened the door to Schlagel's Store, I saw by the big Sessions clock that it was still only a quarter of four and that I would have to wait for him.

Several amorphous[4] large men were warming their hands at the stove in the center of the room and speaking to each other in Russian. Their faces were always very red, and Mr. Buskowski's purplish, large-pored cheeks frightened me a good deal, as did his heavy teasing in a broken English I would make terrified and ineffectual efforts to understand. I managed to sneak past them all to the rear of the store where the harness and great quilted collar pads hung from brass pegs screwed into rough boards. Julius Schlagel's clerk, Irma, was back there shoveling some shingle nails into a brown paper bag. She straightened up from the nail bin, stared at me, and stepped nearer to see my face under the hiss of the gas lamp. "You want to know something? You froze your face, kid."

"How could I? I just came straight over here from school," I lied.

She gave a skeptical glance at the clock and said, "Go get some snow and fetch it in here."

I brought a mittenful of snow and submitted to her harsh massage. The snow felt hot on my cheeks, so I knew I'd frozen them all right.

"Now don't go out again, hear?"

Except for the candy counter, the store was a dark, monotonous jumble of bags and boxes and barrels. I was hungry, so I diverted myself by studying the penny candy and deciding how I would spend a penny if I had one. Since I rarely had the penny, no one paid any attention to me. When I did have one, I would tap it nonchalantly on the grimy glass case—not as though I was impatient to be waited on, for indeed I was not, but just to let Irma and Julius know that I was a potential customer, an individual to be treated with respectful attentiveness when I had finally made up my mind.

Since I had no penny, I was glad to see my father come through the door. He saw that Julius was listening to the radio, and he strode brusquely past me to ask him about the weather reports. Julius dispensed about as many weather reports as he did bags of flour and corn meal;[5] in 1935 in

---

4. **amorphous** [ə môr′fəs]: without definite form or shape.

5. **corn meal:** coarse powder made from ground corn.

drought-ruined North Dakota, radios were a luxury, like candy.

Without speaking, Julius turned up the volume so my father could hear the announcer. ". . . the Canadian cold wave is pressing southward from central Manitoba[6] and is expected to hit northern North Dakota tonight, causing substantial drops in the temperature within the next twenty-four hours. This is KFYR in Bismarck[7] . . ."

"Forty below in Winnipeg[8] last night," Julius said to my father.

"You been out in the last hour? I bet it's thirty below here right now. The pump's froze solid. We gotta go thaw it out." Directing his last sentence to me, he turned and made his way past the Russians, nodding uncordially.

The sun had set while I was waiting in the store, and a vast gloom in the sky sagged low over the town, weighting the rigid streets with cold. The heat absorbed

6. **Manitoba** [mən'ə tō'bə]: province in south-central Canada.
7. **Bismarck** [biz'märk]: capital of North Dakota, in the south-central part of the state.

8. **Winnipeg** [win'ə peg']: capital of Manitoba.

by my snowsuit was gone instantly, and my thawed-out cheeks stung badly. My father scuffed me up over the brittle heaps of snow at the curb of the wooden sidewalk and hoisted me into the sleigh. The sleigh was a wagon box transferred to runners for the winter. I wanted to stand up, but he made me sit on the old Indian blanket spread on straw. There were hot stones under the straw. Then he draped a cowhide from the high side of the wagon box down over my head.

Though I could see nothing, I could hear my father talking to the horses, and I knew he was wiping the frost of their own breathing from their nostrils. Beneath me was the thin scrape of the runners, then the rattle over the railroad tracks and the smoothness of fields of snow. The cow hairs made my nose itch and the straw poked at my legs. It was very dark.

Finally my father stopped the sleigh by our house and lifted me out. "Tell Mother I'll be in directly, soon as I unhitch," he said.

Despite the hot stones, my ankles were numb, and I tripped and fell as I ran to the house. My lip struck the gallon lard[9] pail I used for a lunch bucket and stuck there. I lay tense and still in the snow waiting for it to stop sticking. Once my little sister caught her tongue on the pump handle because she wouldn't believe me when I told her it would stick. She jerked away in fear and tore bleeding skin from the tip of it. So I waited until I could feel the warmth of my breath free my lip before I moved.

The porch timbers creaked with cold,

like thin ice. I could hear my mother yelling to me to get the snow off my clothes and to shut the door tight even before I opened it.

The top of the kitchen stove glowed gray-red through its iron lid, and the belly of the big round stove in the living room seemed stretched dangerously thin, as though it would surely melt soon and spill out its flaming coal on the floor. My mother had set the kerosene lamp on the warming-oven doors above the stove so she could see how much salt to put in the potatoes. I could smell the rabbit she was roasting in the oven for the dog.

My father came in the door, stomping snow clear across the kitchen, and demanded a teakettle of boiling water. Seeing that I still didn't have my snowsuit off, he told me to come with him to work the pump handle.

While he poured the boiling water down the pump, the steam running up into darkness, I struggled to free the handle, but I couldn't budge it. Even when he grasped it in his large thick leather mittens, it didn't move. "Well, it looks like we'll have to melt water for the stock. Take this back to the house." He handed me the teakettle.

I was glad we had to melt snow for water, because then my little sister and I could play a game called Eskimo. We stood on chairs, balancing ourselves imprudently[10] near the searing surface of the stove to lean over the tub. As soon as the dry snow had melted a little, we began to mold the figures for an Eskimo village—Huskies,[11] people, babies, igloos, polar bears, and walruses, just like the ones in the *Book of North*

---

9. **lard:** soft, white fat obtained from the fatty tissue of hogs; used in cooking.

10. **imprudently** [im prōod′ənt lē]: unwisely.
11. **Huskies:** Siberian huskies, a breed of sturdy dog.

American Mammals my mother had got once in a set of books from the National Geographic Society.[12] We conducted hunts and dog-sled treks and sent the Eskimos into the water to harpoon the seals that were languidly[13] floating there. But as the water warmed, the seals disappeared, and it was death for the harpooners to go into the sea. While the shores of their iceland slipped away into the ocean, the frantic people moved higher and higher on the iceberg mountain. Perched on its slushy sides, they would see a small hole appear in their snow island. Then the sea would gush up through the hole, the island would break in pieces, and the ice people would fall into the fatal warmth. Just as the warm wave washed over my people, the game would become hideously real to me, and I would often have nightmares in which I was climbing, climbing, on an ever-collapsing mountain to escape a hot tide.

After supper my father set out for the barn with two pails of the snow water. I had to spend about a half hour, it seemed, getting my outside clothes on again so I could carry the lantern and open the barn door.

I was well acquainted with the shock of stepping from the warm kitchen into a winter night. But none of the freezing memories of the past could prepare me for the burning air that night. It was like strong hot smoke in my nostrils, so that for one confused instant I thought I was going to suffocate with the cold that was

so cold it was hot. I gasped for breathable air, and my father said, "Don't do that! Breathe through your nose—your breath is warmer that way when it gets to your lungs."

We walked carefully down the hill to the barn; then I slithered down the steps chopped in a snowdrift in front of the door and slid it open. The barn was very old, but always before it had been warm with the heat of the animals kept in it all day long. But that night, being inside didn't seem to make any difference. I still had the kind of ache in my temples and cheekbones that I always got when I took too big a mouthful of ice cream. The cows shifted

12. **National Geographic Society:** scientific and educational organization established in 1888 to increase knowledge of geography through exploration, research, and publications.
13. **languidly** [lang′gwid lē]: in a manner showing little strength or energy.

and swung their tails and wouldn't stand still to be milked. My father poured some milk into a pail and told me to feed it to the little new calf in a pen at the rear of the barn.

He had arrived out of season and was not yet two weeks old. Usually by the time the calves came, the mothers were outside all day, and both mothers and calves quickly got used to the idea of being separated. But we had been keeping all the stock inside for nearly a week, and neither cow nor calf was properly weaned. She lowed to him and he cried back to her; he was still determined to nurse. He was still stubbornly bucking and shoving his nose all the way to the bottom of the bucket, and desperately bunting the side of it when he got a noseful of milk. I liked him, though. His hair was almost as fine and soft as a human baby's, and he had a white star on his gleaming black forehead.

Although I had never seen cattle shiver, the little calf looked as though he was shivering as he advanced stiff-legged to our evening battle with the pail. I braced it against my shins and waited for him to begin bunting. At least a winter calf didn't damage you as much as a spring calf did; at the moment I was well padded with long underwear, two pairs of long stockings, and thick pants. I patted him between the ears and he sucked my fingers with his rough, strong tongue.

After the milking was done, we lugged the pails and lantern up the hill and started back for the barn with more water. In two more trips our toes felt numb and thickened, and we both had frostbitten faces. I had the two white spots on my cheeks again and my father's high thin nose stood out bloodless against the chapped red of his face. We took a last look at the stock;

there was nothing more we could do. There was no way to heat the barn, and the cows were already half covered with straw when they lay down. We rolled the door shut.

In the house we planned for the night ahead. My little sister and I would sleep in one bed, with all the blankets and quilts in the house over us, and my mother and father would use the feather tick[14] we had rolled up in a little storeroom we called the cubbyhole. When we opened the door of that little vault to get the tick, the frigid air pushed out across the living room like a low dark flood against our legs.

It took a long time to warm the tick and blankets from the unheated bedroom at the stove. We would hold them as close as we could to its hot belly, but as soon as the warmed section was moved away it grew cold again. We left the bedroom door open, but though the living room grew instantly colder, the bedroom grew no warmer. While we were making the beds we puffed white clouds at each other across the mattresses. We heated our two sadirons[15] and wrapped them in towels, one for each bed. Then my father stoked both stoves full of coal, and we got under the piles of bedding.

My sister and I lay close together, our legs bent and our toes touching the wrapped-up iron. Partly because I couldn't get warm and partly because I was worried about some things, I couldn't get to sleep. I wanted to know what a cold wave was. In the long solitude of prairie childhood I had memorized two sets of books—the set from the National Geographic and a set called *A Childhood Treasury* that contained legends

---

14. **feather tick:** folding mattress covered with strong, usually striped fabric called ticking.
15. **sadirons** [sad′i′ərnz]: heavy metal rods heated in an oven or fireplace and used to warm beds.

of many lands, my favorites being those from Scandinavia.[16] How could it possibly be that so many things had happened before I was born? For instance, *The Book of North American Mammals* told of a time when the plains of Russia and of North America had borne glaciers a mile deep. And before the glaciers there had been vast herds of mammoths.[17] There was a drawing of them lifting their shieldlike foreheads against a gray horizon, marching on tall shaggy legs over the frozen tundra—tundra that had once covered our wheatfields. The book told about how before the glacier finally came the weather had gotten colder and colder, so that the mammoths had to grow longer and longer hair.

But even with their long hair and clever trunks and sixteen-foot tusks curved in unlikely tangles of bone, they had been unable to defend themselves. Why? Under the picture it said that a herd of these mammoths evidently had been preserved intact for centuries, and that one of the discoverers had even tried eating the meat of a carcass thousands of years old. Why couldn't the huge and powerful creatures have run away? It must have been some kind of flood, I thought, like the flood we had in our garden after a cloud burst, only different and much bigger—a flood that could race with the speed of liquid one moment and turn completely solid the next, locking forever the great knees bending for another battling step, then the tusks fending off masses of debris, and finally the long trunks flailing above the tide in search

of air. A cold wave freezing so fast that the bubbles of their last breathing would be fixed like beads in the ice.

What if some polar impulse was now sending a flood to rise up out of the north, to flow swiftly over our house, becoming ice as the wind touched it, shutting us off from that strangling but precious air above us? I had heard of digging out of a house completely covered with snow—that used to happen in the days before I was born—but did anybody ever dig out of a glacier? I

---

16. **Scandinavia** [skan′də nā′vē ə]: region in northern Europe consisting of Norway, Sweden, Denmark, and, sometimes, Iceland and Finland.
17. **mammoths** [mam′əths]: prehistoric elephants with long, upward curving tusks and shaggy, blackish hair.

wanted to go and climb in bed with my mother and father and have them tell me that it wouldn't get to us, that it would stop at least as far away as Leeds, twenty miles to the north. But the last time I had tried to climb in with them they had told me not to be such a big baby, that I was a worse baby than my little sister. So I lay there wondering how far the cold had gotten.

Finally the morning came. I could look from my bed across the living room and into the kitchen where my father, in his sheepskin coat, was heating some water saved from the melted snow. The tub, refilled after we had emptied it for the stock, was standing in the corner of the kitchen next to the door. The snow in it was still heaped in a neat cone. It was odd to think of a tub of snow standing inside our house, where we had slept the night, and never feeling the warmth of the stove a few feet away—to think of how the tiny flow of air around the stormlined door was more powerful than the stove filled with coal.

I felt the excitement of sharing in heroic deeds as I pulled on the second pair of long wool stockings over my underwear and fastened them with the knobs and hooks on my garter belt. I was not going to school because it was too cold to take the horses out, so I was to help with the barn chores again.

The cattle were still huddled together in their one big stall. My father set down the pails and walked swiftly to the rear of the barn. The little calf was curled quietly against the corner of his pen. The black-and-white hairs over his small ribs did not move. My father climbed into the pen and brushed the straw away from the sleeping eyes, just to make sure.

I stood looking at the soft fine hair that was too fine and the big-kneed legs that were too thin, and it seemed to me that I now understood how it was with the mammoths in the Ice Age.[18] One night they had lain down to sleep, leaning ponderously back to back, legs bent beneath warm bellies, tusks pointing up from the dying tundra. The blood under their incredible hides slowed a little, and the warmth of their bodies ascended in ghostly clouds toward the indifferent moon. There was no rushing, congealing wave; there was only the unalarmed cold sleep of betrayed creatures.

A couple of nights later, over at the store, the men talked of the figures Julius had gotten over the radio. There had been a dozen readings around fifty degrees below zero. Fifty-two at Bismarck, fifty-eight at Leeds, and sixty-one at Portal on the Canadian border.

"My t'ermometer is bust before I see him in the morning!" shouted Mr. Buskowski. "I do not even from Russia remember such a night."

Hopelessly studying the candy counter, I realized that even my father had forgotten the stiff little black-and-white calf in the contemplation of that remarkable number. "Sixty-one below!" they said over and over again. "Sixty-one below!" The men didn't need to make legends anymore to comprehend the incomprehensible. They had the miraculous evidence of their thermometers. But for me that little death told what there was to know about the simple workings of immense catastrophe.

---

18. **Ice Age:** prehistoric period during which glaciers moved across large areas of North and South America, Europe, and Asia and human beings first appeared.

READER'S RESPONSE

What prevented the family from realizing the calf was in danger of freezing?

STUDY QUESTIONS

Recalling

1. What legendary stories about her mother and father does the narrator admire?
2. According to the narrator, what happens "when the sort of thing I was waiting for finally came"?
3. What tasks does her father ask the narrator to help him perform?
4. Why does the calf with the white star on its forehead need special care?
5. What two questions about the mammoths does the narrator try to answer as she lies awake?
6. What does she understand when she sees the dead calf?

Interpreting

7. What does the narrator's wish for a grand and dramatic event tell you about her character?
8. Describe how the chores that the family performs contribute to their ability to survive the cold.
9. In what ways are the calf's first days a sign of its inability to survive?
10. How do you think the narrator feels about the "legend" she witnessed during the cold wave?

READING AND LITERARY FOCUS

Description

Description is the type of writing that creates a clear picture of something—a person, an animal, an object, or a place, for example. All works of literature, both fiction and nonfiction, contain description.

Good descriptive writing is made up of many details: specific pictures, colors, shapes, sounds, smells, tastes, textures, and even emotions. For example, Lois Phillips Hudson describes a journey home in a sleigh:

Beneath me was the thin scrape of the runners, then the rattle over the railroad tracks and the smoothness of fields of snow. The cow hairs made my nose itch and the straw poked at my legs. It was very dark.

These details call up the senses of hearing ("the thin scrape of the runners"), touch ("the cow hairs made my nose itch"), and sight ("It was very dark"). They also bring to mind certain colors (the whiteness of the snow) and movements ("the rattle" and "the smoothness of fields of snow"). With these details Hudson's description of the scene creates a mood of quiet safety in the face of some larger danger.

Thinking About Description

1. List the details Hudson uses in her description of the kitchen after the narrator enters from the cold.
2. Which details create a mood of safety and warmth? Which create a mood of danger?

COMPOSITION

Writing About Description

Write a paragraph in which you explain how Hudson uses details to describe a particular person, animal, object, or place in "The Cold Wave." **Prewriting:** Choose a descriptive passage, and identify the subject of the description. List the details that contribute to the vividness of the description. **Writing:** Begin by naming the subject of the passage. Then explain how Hudson uses details to bring her description to life. **Revising:** Review your paragraph for effective word choice and organization. Then check for errors in grammar, spelling, and punctuation.

Writing a Description

Write a description of a place or an animal you know well. Use vivid details to make your description come to life. First decide on a subject, and list vivid details that would support a description of the subject. Then write a description of the person, animal, or place using your list of vivid details.

Collaborative Learning: Themes

Disasters Great and Small

Most people face disasters of some kind during their life. Literature records how people deal with such events. Some catastrophes cause great losses and are never forgotten. Some may be learning experiences that make it possible to avoid similar disasters in the future. Some are turned into triumphs of the human spirit.

1. **Research and Oral Report** As a group brainstorm to make a list of songs that describe a great or small disaster. American folk songs, for example, often tell of local natural disasters, such as floods. Many modern popular songs describe personal disasters, such as disappointment in love. Research and list as many songs as possible, and then discuss them. Find recordings of the best ones.

   Have each member of the group choose one song and write a brief statement about it, focusing on the kind of disaster it describes and, most important, how the people in the song deal with the disaster. Present the songs and your individual statements to the class. Play the recordings, or perform the songs yourselves.

2. **Album** As a group compile an album on the general theme of "Disasters Great and Small" or on one disaster that is especially meaningful to your group. Decide on the kinds of material you will gather for the album. You may want to include personal statements, interviews, poems or other quotations by professional writers or members of the group, newspaper clippings, photographs, drawings, or other graphics.

   Each person in the group should have responsibility for one aspect of the album. Discuss and decide on the way the album should be organized and designed. Share the finished product with the members of your class and with other classes as well.

Collaborative Learning:
Across the Curriculum

Disasters Great and Small

1. **Literature and Social Studies: Historical Research and Dramatization** As a group discuss several disasters that you know about from your study of history, geography, or current events. Choose one event to investigate fully. Try to find its causes and effects and the likelihood of its happening again. Plan a television news program based on "live coverage" of the disaster.

   Each member of the group should research the event and then discuss ways to cover the story. You may want to consider having one or more on-the-scene reporters, anchorpersons, eyewitnesses, and professional experts. Use costumes, props, maps, and sound effects to make the event come alive for your class.

2. **Literature and Science and Technology: Display** Create a science-fair display on the topic "How a Disaster Can Be Prevented." As a group choose a particular kind of disaster that you feel can be prevented. Consider, for example, a building collapse, a forest fire, an airplane crash, or an oil spill.

   Use all your library's resources to research the topic. Check periodical magazines, videotapes, and special reference services as well as books. Contact the public relations department of any company or public utility in your area that may have information pertaining to your topic—for example, the United States Forestry Service, a construction company, or an oil company. Use drawings, photographs, and models to demonstrate how science and technology may be used to prevent a catastrophe.

The word *science* comes from the Latin *scientia*, which means "to know." *Story* comes from a Latin word as well: *historia*, meaning "learned man."

Since ancient times people have been telling stories about what they know. When a story is told, knowledge takes shape and becomes something new, even for the storyteller. You may have experienced this yourself. While telling a story about a familiar event, perhaps something that happened to you, you discover a connection or meaning you never realized before. The story itself becomes a way of learning.

The literature you are about to read is all about learning and knowing. Some of the selections are about inventions and inventors; others are about experts expanding the boundaries of knowledge. Still others are about realizations, flashes of knowledge that come from experience. All of these insights are shaped by the storytellers for you to enjoy.

Cattleya Orchid and Three Brazilian Hummingbirds Around Nest, Martin Johnson Heade, 1871.

Science and Storytellers

A Model for Active Reading

Whether you are reading to study for a test or reading for pure pleasure, you'll get more out of the experience by reading actively. Think as you read. The more you understand, the more you'll enjoy.

Here is an example of the thoughts of a thinking reader. Notice how the reader uses personal experience, doubts, ideas, and questions to become involved with the beginning of this story.

The entire story begins on the following page. As you read, what personal experiences, questions, and imaginings make the story richer for you?

Ray Bradbury

The Flying Machine

In the year A.D. 400, the Emperor Yuan held his throne by the Great Wall of China,[1] and the land was green with rain, readying itself toward the harvest, at peace, the people in his dominion[2] neither too happy nor too sad.

> Is the Emperor a real historical person?

Early on the morning of the first day of the first week of the second month of the new year, the Emperor Yuan was sipping tea and fanning himself against a warm breeze when a servant ran across the scarlet and blue garden tiles, calling, "Oh, Emperor, Emperor, a miracle!"

> "New Year": That must be the Chinese New Year. When is that?

> Now this part sounds a bit like a fairy tale.

"Yes," said the Emperor, "the air *is* sweet this morning."

"No, no, a miracle!" said the servant, bowing quickly.

"And this tea is good in my mouth, surely that is a miracle."

"No, no, Your Excellency."

"Let me guess then—the sun has risen and a new day is upon us. Or the sea is blue. *That* now is the finest of all miracles."

"Excellency, a man is flying!"

"What?" The Emperor stopped his fan.

> The servant bows because he does not dare correct the Emperor.

> The Emperor believes that simple things like air and taste are real miracles.

> I know that people tried to build flying machines long ago, but not that long ago!

photograph ©1990 Jill Krementz

Ray Bradbury (born 1920) is one of the most admired writers of science fiction and fantasy. He describes himself simply as a "teller of tales" or "magic realist." An avid reader and movie buff as a boy, he decided then to devote at least four hours a day to writing, a practice he has continued over the years. He writes spontaneously, typing "whatever seizes" him and discovering the story in draft after draft. His stories often explore the impact of machines on human culture. "I'm not afraid of machines," he says. "I don't think the robots are taking over. I think the men who play with toys have taken over. And if we don't take the toys out of their hands, we're fools."

And in the sky, laughing so high that you could hardly hear him laugh, was a man; . . . and he was soaring all about like the largest bird in a universe of birds, like a new dragon in a land of ancient dragons.

Ray Bradbury

The Flying Machine

In the year A.D. 400, the Emperor Yuan held his throne by the Great Wall of China,[1] and the land was green with rain, readying itself toward the harvest, at peace, the people in his dominion[2] neither too happy nor too sad.

Early on the morning of the first day of the first week of the second month of the new year, the Emperor Yuan was sipping tea and fanning himself against a warm breeze when a servant ran across the scarlet and blue garden tiles, calling, "Oh, Emperor, Emperor, a miracle!"

"Yes," said the Emperor, "the air *is* sweet this morning."

"No, no, a miracle!" said the servant, bowing quickly.

"And this tea is good in my mouth, surely that is a miracle."

"No, no, Your Excellency."

"Let me guess then—the sun has risen and a new day is upon us. Or the sea is blue. *That* now is the finest of all miracles."

"Excellency, a man is flying!"

"What?" The Emperor stopped his fan.

"I saw him in the air, a man flying with wings. I heard a voice call out of the sky, and when I looked up there he was, a dragon in the heavens with a man in its mouth, a dragon of paper and bamboo, colored like the sun and the grass."

"It is early," said the Emperor, "and you have just wakened from a dream."

---

1. **Great Wall of China:** defensive wall extending about 1,500 miles between north and northwestern China and Mongolia. It was built in the third century B.C. as a defense against invaders.
2. **dominion** [də min′yən]: territory or country under the authority of a particular ruler or government.

"It is early, but I have seen what I have seen! Come, and you will see it too."

"Sit down with me here," said the Emperor. "Drink some tea. It must be a strange thing, if it is true, to see a man fly. You must have time to think of it, even as I must have time to prepare myself for the sight."

They drank tea.

"Please," said the servant at last, "or he will be gone."

The Emperor rose thoughtfully. "Now you may show me what you have seen."

They walked into a garden, across a meadow of grass, over a small bridge, through a grove of trees, and up a tiny hill.

"There!" said the servant.

The Emperor looked into the sky.

And in the sky, laughing so high that you could hardly hear him laugh, was a man; and the man was clothed in bright papers and reeds to make wings and a beautiful yellow tail, and he was soaring all about like the largest bird in a universe of birds, like a new dragon in a land of ancient dragons.

The man called down to them from high in the cool winds of morning, "I fly, I fly!"

The servant waved to him. "Yes, yes!"

The Emperor Yuan did not move. Instead he looked at the Great Wall of China now taking shape out of the farthest mist in the green hills, that splendid snake of stones which writhed with majesty across the entire land. That wonderful wall which had protected them for a timeless time from enemy hordes and preserved peace for years without number. He saw the town, nestled to itself by a river and a road and a hill, beginning to waken.

"Tell me," he said to his servant, "has anyone else seen this flying man?"

"I am the only one, Excellency," said the servant, smiling at the sky, waving.

The Emperor watched the heavens another minute and then said, "Call him down to me."

"Ho, come down, come down! The Emperor wishes to see you!" called the servant, hands cupped to his shouting mouth.

The Emperor glanced in all directions while the flying man soared down the morning wind. He saw a farmer, early in his fields, watching the sky, and he noted where the farmer stood.

The flying man alit with a rustle of paper and a creak of bamboo reeds. He came proudly to the Emperor, clumsy in his rig,[3] at last bowing before the old man.

"What have you done?" demanded the Emperor.

"I have flown in the sky, Your Excellency," replied the man.

"What *have* you done?" said the Emperor again.

"I have just told you!" cried the flier.

"You have told me nothing at all." The Emperor reached out a thin hand to touch the pretty paper and the birdlike keel of the apparatus. It smelled cool, of the wind.

"Is it not beautiful, Excellency?"

"Yes, too beautiful."

"It is the only one in the world!" smiled the man. "And I am the inventor."

"The *only* one in the world?"

"I swear it!"

"Who else knows of this?"

"No one. Not even my wife, who would think me mad with the sun. She thought I was making a kite. I rose in the night and walked to the cliffs far away. And when the

---

3. **rig:** apparatus or equipment.

Detail, *Early Autumn*, Qian Xuan, ink and color on paper, Yuan Dynasty, c. 1235–1301.

morning breezes blew and the sun rose, I gathered my courage, Excellency, and leaped from the cliff. I flew! But my wife does not know of it."

"Well for her, then," said the Emperor. "Come along."

They walked back to the great house. The sun was full in the sky now, and the smell of the grass was refreshing. The Emperor, the servant, and the flier paused within the huge garden.

The Emperor clapped his hands. "Ho, guards!"

The guards came running.

"Hold this man."

The guards seized the flier.

"Call the executioner," said the Emperor.

"What's this!" cried the flier, bewildered. "What have I done?" He began to weep, so that the beautiful paper apparatus rustled.

"Here is the man who has made a certain machine," said the Emperor, "and yet asks us what he has created. He does not know himself. It is only necessary that he create, without knowing why he has done so, or what this thing will do."

The executioner came running with a sharp silver ax. He stood with his naked, large-muscled arms ready, his face covered with a serene white mask.

"One moment," said the Emperor. He turned to a nearby table upon which sat a machine that he himself had created. The Emperor took a tiny golden key from his own neck. He fitted this key to the tiny, delicate machine and wound it up. Then he set the machine going.

The machine was a garden of metal and jewels. Set in motion, birds sang in tiny metal trees, wolves walked through miniature forests, and tiny people ran in and out of sun and shadow, fanning themselves with miniature fans, listening to the tiny emerald birds, and standing by impossibly small but tinkling fountains.

"Is *it* not beautiful?" said the Emperor. "If you asked me what I have done here, I could answer you well. I have made birds sing, I have made forests murmur, I have set people to walking in this woodland, enjoying the leaves and shadows and songs. That is what I have done."

"But, oh, Emperor!" pleaded the flier, on his knees, the tears pouring down his face. "I have done a similar thing! I have found beauty. I have flown on the morning wind. I have looked down on all the sleeping houses and gardens. I have smelled the sea and even *seen* it, beyond the hills, from my high place. And I have soared like a bird; oh, I cannot say how beautiful it is up there, in the sky, with the wind about me, the wind blowing me here like a feather, there like a fan, the way the sky smells in the morning! And how free one feels! *That* is beautiful, Emperor, that is beautiful too!"

"Yes," said the Emperor sadly, "I know it must be true. For I felt my heart move with you in the air and I wondered: What is it like? How does it feel? How do the distant pools look from so high? And how my houses and servants? Like ants? And how the distant towns not yet awake?"

"Then spare me!"

"But there are times," said the Emperor, more sadly still, "when one must lose a little beauty if one is to keep what little beauty one already has. I do not fear you, yourself, but I fear another man."

"What man?"

"Some other man who, seeing you, will build a thing of bright papers and bamboo like this. But the other man will have an evil face and an evil heart, and the beauty will be gone. It is this man I fear."

"Why? Why?"

"Who is to say that someday just such a man in just such an apparatus of paper and reed, might not fly in the sky and drop huge stones upon the Great Wall of China?" said the Emperor.

No one moved or said a word.

"Off with his head," said the Emperor.

The executioner whirled his silver ax.

"Burn the kite and the inventor's body and bury their ashes together," said the Emperor.

The servants retreated to obey.

The Emperor turned to his hand-servant, who had seen the man flying. "Hold your tongue. It was all a dream, a most sorrowful and beautiful dream. And that farmer in the distant field who also saw, tell him it would pay him to consider it only a vision. If ever the word passes around, you and the farmer die within the hour."

"You are merciful, Emperor."

"No, not merciful," said the old man. Beyond the garden wall he saw the guards burning the beautiful machine of paper and reeds that smelled of the morning wind. He saw the dark smoke climb into the sky. "No, only very much bewildered and afraid." He saw the guards digging a tiny pit wherein to bury the ashes. "What is the life of one man against those of a million others? I must take solace from that thought."

He took the key from its chain about his neck and once more wound up the beautiful miniature garden. He stood looking out across the land at the Great Wall, the peaceful town, the green fields, the rivers and streams. He sighed. The tiny garden whirred its hidden and delicate machinery and set itself in motion; tiny people walked in forests, tiny foxes loped through sunspeckled glades in beautiful shining pelts,[4] and among the tiny trees flew little bits of high song and bright blue and yellow color, flying, flying, flying in that small sky.

"Oh," said the Emperor, closing his eyes, "look at the birds, look at the birds!"

---

4. **pelts:** here, the fur of an animal.

READER'S RESPONSE

Do you think the Emperor was wise? Explain.

STUDY QUESTIONS

Recalling

1. What does the servant tell the Emperor?
2. At first, what does the Emperor think?
3. What does the Emperor decide to do?
4. How does the Emperor convince the farmer and the servant to say nothing?

Interpreting

5. In what ways are the Emperor's mechanical garden and the flying machine alike? In what ways are they different?
6. What do you think the Emperor wants China to be like in the future? How do you know?
7. Do you think the Emperor will be successful in protecting his empire? Why or why not?

Extending

8. Do you think a government has the right to decide what inventions can be made in a country? Why or why not?

VOCABULARY

Context Clues

Sometimes you can figure out the meaning of an unfamiliar word by examining its **context,** or the words and sentences that surround it. The following passages come from "The Flying Machine." From the four choices that follow each item, select the best meaning for each italicized word by studying its *context.* Write the number of each item and the letter of your choice on a separate sheet.

1. The Emperor Yuan held his throne by the Great Wall of China, and . . . the people in his *dominion* [were] neither too happy nor too sad.
   (a) home   (c) game piece
   (b) rounded roof   (d) governed land
2. That wonderful wall which had protected them for a timeless time from enemy *hordes* and preserved peace for years without number.
   (a) wandering tribes (c) large wasps
   (b) governments   (d) windstorms
3. He saw the town, *nestled* to itself by a river and a road and a hill, beginning to waken.
   (a) overcrowded   (c) sheltered snugly
   (b) built   (d) trapped or snared
4. The flying man alit with a rustle of paper and a creak of bamboo reeds. He came proudly to the Emperor, clumsy in his *rig,* at last bowing before the old man.
   (a) round band   (c) chains and ropes
   (b) hard coating   (d) special equipment

COMPOSITION

Writing an Opinion

Do you think the Emperor was wise? Express your opinion in a paragraph. **Prewriting:** List as many reasons as you can to support your opinion. Then choose the best ones, and put them in a logical order. **Writing:** In your first sentence state your opinion. Then go on to explain your reasons. **Revising:** Review your paragraph to see that you have expressed your ideas clearly and logically.

Writing a Sequel

Write another incident about the Emperor Yuan. You might, for example, describe what happens when people find out what happened to the inventor. Try to imitate the story's vivid descriptions.

photograph ©1990 Jill Krementz

Maxine Kumin (born 1925) admits that she wrote "very bad late adolescent romantic poetry" in high school. In college an instructor discouraged her from continuing her poetry, and it was not until she was an adult that she found support for her writing. Kumin prefers the orderliness of traditional verse forms, with their clear patterns of rhyme and rhythm. When she is not giving readings or lecturing, she lives on a farm in New Hampshire, where she writes, tends horses, and works in her garden. Kumin has written more than ten volumes of poetry, several novels, and many books for children. In 1973 she won the Pulitzer Prize for poetry. She has also served as poetry consultant to the Library of Congress.

What does this poem about the inventor of the microscope suggest about scientific progress?

Maxine Kumin

The Microscope

Anton Leeuwenhoek[1] was Dutch.
He sold pincushions, cloth, and such.
The waiting townsfolk fumed and fussed
As Anton's dry goods gathered dust.

5 He worked, instead of tending store,
At grinding special lenses for
A microscope. Some of the things
He looked at were:
                    mosquitoes' wings,
the hairs of sheep, the legs of lice,
10 the skin of people, dogs, and mice;
ox eyes, spiders' spinning gear,
fishes' scales, a little smear

---

1. **Anton Leeuwenhoek** [än′tôn lā′ven hook]: Dutch naturalist; maker of microscopes and early observer of microorganisms (1632–1723).

of his own blood,

　　　　　　　and best of all,
the unknown, busy, very small
15　bugs that swim and bump and hop
inside a simple water drop.

Impossible! Most Dutchmen said.
This Anton's crazy in the head.
We ought to ship him off to Spain.
20　He says he's seen a housefly's brain.
He says the water that we drink
Is full of bugs. He's mad, we think!

They called him *dumkopf*, which means dope.
That's how we got the microscope.

Dutch naturalist Anton Van Leeuwenhoek (1632–1723).

READER'S RESPONSE

How do you think the poet feels about Anton Leeuwenhoek?

STUDY QUESTIONS

Recalling

1. Where did Leeuwenhoek live, and how did he earn a living?
2. What interested him more than his business?
3. What kinds of things did he observe?
4. What did his neighbors think of him?

Interpreting

5. What do the last two lines suggest about the value of public opinion?
6. Why do you think Leeuwenhoek was most amazed by the "bugs" in a drop of water?

Extending

7. What character traits might be helpful to an inventor?

READING AND LITERARY FOCUS

Rhyme

Poets often use the sounds of words in special ways. **Rhyme** is the repetition of the same or similar sounds in words that appear near each other in a poem. Poets may use rhyme to give a poem a musical quality. Rhyming words have similar endings. **Perfect rhymes** have endings that sound exactly the same. Examples are *fair* and *care* or *away* and *Saturday.*

In poetry most rhymes are **end rhymes**—that is, they occur at the ends of lines. The repeating sounds may suggest something actually described in the poem, like the cry of a bird or the ringing of bells, or they may help to create a mood or feeling. In some poems, for example, rhymes are soft and soothing, while in others they are sharp and surprising.

Thinking About Rhyme

1. How many different end rhymes can you fine in "The Microscope"? In what pattern do they most often appear?
2. What feeling or mood does the rhyme create?

CHALLENGE

Research

Use your library to find out more about Anton Leeuwenhoek and his work. Find and list five facts not included in the poem, and share them with a small group of your classmates. After everyone has presented some additional information about this scientist and inventor, discuss which of these new facts add to your understanding of the general idea of the poem.

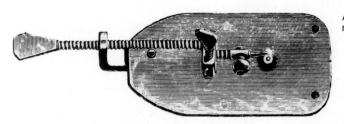

Anton Van Leeuwenhoek's microscope.

Before becoming a writer, Carl Sandburg (1878–1967) worked at many other jobs. He delivered milk, fought fires, drove trucks, and painted houses. His first professional writing assignments were articles, columns, and editorials for newspapers in Milwaukee and Chicago. Eventually he distinguished himself as a poet, biographer, singer, and lecturer. According to a close friend, the author Harry Golden, Sandburg "put America on paper" by writing the way Americans speak.

Arithmetic is where the answer is right and everything is nice.

● ●

Carl Sandburg

Arithmetic

Arithmetic is where numbers fly like pigeons in and out of
    your head.
Arithmetic tells you how many you lose or win if you know
    how many you had before you lost or won.
Arithmetic is seven eleven all good children go to heaven—
    or five six bundle of sticks.
Arithmetic is numbers you squeeze from your head to your hand
    to your pencil to your paper till you get the answer.
5 Arithmetic is where the answer is right and everything is nice
    and you can look out of the window and see the blue sky—
    or the answer is wrong and you have to start all over
    and try again and see how it comes out this time.
If you take a number and double it and double it again and
    then double it a few more times, the number gets bigger
    and bigger and goes higher and higher and only arithmetic
    can tell you what the number is when you decide to quit
    doubling.
Arithmetic is where you have to multiply—and you carry the
    multiplication table in your head and hope you won't lose it.
If you have two animal crackers, one good and one bad, and
    you eat one and a striped zebra with streaks all over him
    eats the other, how many animal crackers will you have
    if somebody offers you five six seven and you say No no
    no and you say Nay nay nay and you say Nix nix nix?
If you ask your mother for one fried egg for breakfast and
    she gives you two fried eggs and you eat both of them,
    who is better in arithmetic, you or your mother?

READER'S RESPONSE

How does this poem make you feel about arithmetic?

STUDY QUESTIONS

Recalling

1. According to the poem, what are some of the things arithmetic can do?
2. What are some of the problems arithmetic causes?

Interpreting

3. How do you think the speaker feels about arithmetic?
4. How old do you think the speaker is? Use details from the poem to support your answer.

Extending

5. What original uses for arithmetic can you make up? Describe at least three. Try to be consistent with the spirit of the poem.

VOCABULARY

Synonyms

A **synonym** is a word that has the same or nearly the same meaning as another word. For example, the words *inexpensive* and *cheap* are synonyms.

The italicized words below are from Sandburg's "Arithmetic." Choose the word that is *nearest* the meaning of each italicized word, *as it is used in the poem.* Write the number of each item and the letter of your choice on a separate piece of paper.

1. a *bundle* of twigs
   (a) wealth   (c) package
   (b) parcel   (d) bunch
2. the *wrong* address
   (a) unfair   (c) bad
   (b) unjust   (d) incorrect
3. to *quit* running
   (a) stop   (c) leave
   (b) satisfy   (d) abandon
4. red with blue *streaks*
   (a) colors   (c) leave
   (b) traits   (d) smears

Numbers in Color, Jasper Johns, encaustic and collage on canvas, 1959.

James Herriot (born 1916) says, "I spent much of my childhood and adolescence walking with my dog, camping and climbing among the highlands of Scotland so that at an early age three things were implanted in my character: love of animals, reading, and the countryside. It is small wonder that I am a happy man!" Herriot, whose real name is James Alfred Wight, practiced veterinary medicine for more than fifty years in rural England. He has also written several best sellers. Although he claims to have exhausted his supply of stories and given up writing, Wight is known to have bought a word processor because he "might get what they call a rush of blood. Besides," he says, "I'm not so good at pushing the horses as I used to be."

Stories about cats and dogs are popular all over the world. Yet some stories like this one, suggest that the familiar animals we think we understand are, in fact, mysterious.

● ●

James Herriot

The Christmas Cat

My strongest memory of Christmas will always be bound up with a certain little cat.

I first saw her one autumn day when I was called to see one of Mrs. Ainsworth's dogs, and I looked in some surprise at the furry black creature sitting before the fire.

"I didn't know you had a cat," I said.

The lady smiled. "We haven't; this is Debbie."

"Debbie?"

"Yes, at least that's what we call her. She's a stray. Comes here two or three times a week and we give her some food. I don't know where she lives but I believe she spends a lot of her time around one of the farms along the road."

"Do you ever get the feeling that she wants to stay with you?"

"No." Mrs. Ainsworth shook her head. "She's a timid little thing. Just creeps in, has some food then flits away. There's something so appealing about her but she doesn't seem to want to let me or anybody into her life."

I looked again at the little cat. "But she isn't just having food today."

"That's right. It's a funny thing but every now and again she slips through here into the lounge and sits by the fire for a few minutes. It's as though she was giving herself a treat."

"Yes . . . I see what you mean." There was no doubt there was something unusual in the attitude of the little animal. She was sitting bolt upright on the thick rug which lay before the fireplace in which the coals glowed and flamed. She made no effort to curl up or wash herself or do anything other than gaze quietly ahead. And there was something in the dusty black of her coat, the half-wild scrawny look of her, that gave me a clue. This was a special event in her life, a rare and wonderful thing; she was lapping up a comfort undreamed of in her daily existence.

As I watched she turned, crept sound-lessly from the room and was gone.

"That's always the way with Debbie," Mrs. Ainsworth laughed. "She never stays more than ten minutes or so, then she's off."

Mrs. Ainsworth was a plumpish, pleas-ant-faced woman in her forties and the kind of client veterinary surgeons dream of; well off, generous, and the owner of three cosseted Basset hounds.[1] And it only needed the habitually mournful expression of one of the dogs to deepen a little and I was round there post haste.[2] Today one of the Bassets had raised its paw and scratched its ear a couple of times and that was enough to send its mistress scurrying to the phone in great alarm.

So my visits to the Ainsworth home were frequent but undemanding, and I had ample opportunity to look out for the little cat that had intrigued me. On one occasion I spotted her nibbling daintily from a saucer at the kitchen door. As I watched she turned and almost floated on light footsteps into the hall then through the lounge door. The three Bassets were already in resi-dence, draped snoring on the fireside rug, but they seemed to be used to Debbie because two of them sniffed her in a bored manner and the third merely cocked a sleepy eye at her before flopping back on the rich pile.

Debbie sat among them in her usual posture; upright, intent, gazing absorbedly into the glowing coals. This time I tried to make friends with her. I approached her carefully but she leaned away as I stretched out my hand. However, by patient wheedling and soft talk I managed to touch her and gently stroked her cheek with one finger. There was a moment when she responded by putting her head on one side and rubbing back against my hand but soon she was ready to leave. Once outside the house she darted quickly along the road then through a gap in a hedge and the last I saw was the little black figure flitting over the rain-swept grass of a field.

"I wonder where she goes," I murmured half to myself.

Mrs. Ainsworth appeared at my elbow. "That's something we've never been able to find out."

It must have been nearly three months before I heard from Mrs. Ainsworth, and in fact I had begun to wonder at the Bassets' long symptomless run when she came on the phone.

It was Christmas morning and she was apologetic, "Mr. Herriot, I'm so sorry to bother you today of all days. I should think you want a rest at Christmas like anybody else." But her natural politeness could not hide the distress in her voice.

"Please don't worry about that," I said. "Which one is it this time?"

"It's not one of the dogs. It's . . . Debbie."

"Debbie? She's at your house now?"

---

1. **Basset** [bas'it] **hounds:** short-legged dogs with long bodies and drooping ears.
2. **post haste:** as quickly as possible.

Black Cat on a Chair, Andrew L. Von Wittkamp, c. 1850.

"Yes . . . but there's something wrong. Please come quickly."

Driving through the market place I thought again that Darrowby on Christmas Day was like Dickens[3] come to life; the empty square with the snow thick on the cobbles and hanging from the eaves of the fretted[4] lines of roofs; the shops closed and the colored lights of the Christmas trees winking at the windows of the clustering houses, warmly inviting against the cold white bulk of the fells[5] behind.

Mrs. Ainsworth's home was lavishly decorated with tinsel and holly, rows of drinks stood on the sideboard and the rich aroma of turkey and sage and onion stuffing wafted from the kitchen. But her eyes were full of pain as she led me through to the lounge.

Debbie was there all right, but this time everything was different. She wasn't sitting upright in her usual position; she was stretched quite motionless on her side, and huddled close to her lay a tiny black kitten.

I looked down in bewilderment. "What's happened here?"

"It's the strangest thing," Mrs. Ainsworth replied. "I haven't seen her for several weeks, then she came in about two hours ago—sort of staggered into the kitchen, and she was carrying the kitten in her mouth. She took it through to the lounge and laid it on the rug and at first I was amused. But I could see all was not well because she sat as she usually does, but for a long

time—over an hour—then she lay down like this and she hasn't moved."

I kneeled on the rug and passed my hand over Debbie's neck and ribs. She was thinner than ever, her fur dirty and mud-caked. She did not resist as I gently opened her mouth. The tongue and mucous membranes were abnormally pale and the lips ice-cold against my fingers. When I pulled down her eyelid and saw the dead white conjunctiva[6] a knell[7] sounded in my mind.

I palpated[8] the abdomen with a grim certainty as to what I would find and there was no surprise, only a dull sadness as my fingers closed around a hard lobulated[9] mass deep among the viscera.[10] Massive lymphosarcoma.[11] Terminal and hopeless. I put my stethoscope on her heart and listened to the increasingly faint, rapid beat, then I straightened up and sat on the rug looking sightlessly into the fireplace, feeling the warmth of the flames on my face.

Mrs. Ainsworth's voice seemed to come from afar. "Is she ill, Mr. Herriot?"

I hesitated. "Yes . . . yes, I'm afraid so. She has a malignant growth." I stood up. "There's absolutely nothing I can do. I'm sorry."

"Oh!" Her hand went to her mouth and she looked at me wide-eyed. When at last

---

3. **Dickens:** Charles Dickens (1812–1870), English novelist and author of the classic *A Christmas Carol* (1843).
4. **fretted:** decorated with frets, patterns consisting of vertical and horizontal lines arranged within a band or border.
5. **fells:** unbroken areas of high, rolling, open land.

6. **conjunctiva** [kon'jungk ti'və]: mucous membrane that covers the front of the eyeball and lines the inner surface of the eyelids.
7. **knell** [nel]: tolling of a bell, especially the sound of a bell rung slowly and solemnly.
8. **palpated** [pal'pāt id]: examined by touch to determine the nature of a medical condition.
9. **lobulated** [läb'yoo lāt'id]: made up of small, rounded divisions called lobules.
10. **viscera** [vis'ər ə]: soft organs inside the body, including the heart, stomach, liver, intestines, and kidneys.
11. **lymphosarcoma** [lim'fə sär kō'mə]: rapidly spreading tumor, or growth, in the tissues of the glands producing lymph, a liquid that brings essential substances to cells and carries away waste.

she spoke her voice trembled. "Well, you must put her to sleep immediately. It's the only thing to do. We can't let her suffer."

"Mrs. Ainsworth," I said. "There's no need. She's dying now—in a coma—far beyond suffering."

She turned quickly away from me and was very still as she fought with her emotions. Then she gave up the struggle and dropped on her knees beside Debbie.

"Oh, poor little thing!" she sobbed and stroked the cat's head again and again as the tears fell unchecked on the matted fur. "What she must have come through. I feel I ought to have done more for her."

For a few moments I was silent, feeling her sorrow, so discordant among the bright seasonal colors of this festive room. Then I spoke gently.

"Nobody could have done more than you," I said. "Nobody could have been kinder."

"But I'd have kept her here—in comfort. It must have been terrible out there in the cold when she was so desperately ill—I daren't think about it. And having kittens, too—I . . . I wonder how many she did have?"

I shrugged. "I don't suppose we'll ever know. Maybe just this one. It happens sometimes. And she brought it to you, didn't she?"

"Yes . . . that's right . . . she did . . . she did." Mrs. Ainsworth reached out and lifted the bedraggled black morsel. She smoothed her finger along the muddy fur and the tiny mouth opened in a soundless miaow. "Isn't it strange? She was dying and she brought her kitten here. And on Christmas Day."

I bent and put my hand on Debbie's heart. There was no beat.

I looked up. "I'm afraid she's gone." I lifted the small body, almost feather light, wrapped it in the sheet which had been spread on the rug and took it out to the car.

When I came back Mrs. Ainsworth was still stroking the kitten. The tears had dried on her cheeks and she was bright-eyed as she looked at me.

"I've never had a cat before," she said.

I smiled. "Well it looks as though you've got one now."

And she certainly had. That kitten grew rapidly into a sleek handsome cat with a boisterous nature which earned him the name of Buster. In every way he was the opposite to his timid little mother. Not for him the privations[12] of the secret outdoor life; he stalked the rich carpets of the Ainsworth home like a king and the ornate collar he always wore added something more to his presence.

On my visits I watched his development with delight but the occasion which stays in my mind was the following Christmas Day, a year from his arrival.

I was out on my rounds as usual. I can't remember when I haven't had to work on Christmas Day because the animals have never got round to recognizing it as a holiday; but with the passage of the years the vague resentment I used to feel has been replaced by philosophical acceptance. After all, as I tramped around the hillside barns in the frosty air I was working up a better appetite for my turkey than all the millions lying in bed or slumped by the fire; and this was aided by the innumerable aperitifs I received from the hospitable farmers.

---

12. **privations** [prī vā′shənz]: lack of comforts or necessities of life.

I was on my way home, bathed in a rosy glow. I had consumed several whiskeys—the kind the inexpert Yorkshiremen pour as though it was ginger ale—and I had finished with a glass of old Mrs. Earnshaw's rhubarb wine, which had seared its way straight to my toenails. I heard the cry as I was passing Mrs. Ainsworth's house.

"Merry Christmas, Mr. Herriot!" She was letting a visitor out of the front door and she waved at me gaily. "Come in and have a drink to warm you up."

I didn't need warming up but I pulled in to the curb without hesitation. In the house there was all the festive cheer of last year and the same glorious whiff of sage and onion which set my gastric juices surging. But there was not the sorrow; there was Buster.

He was darting up to each of the dogs in turn, ears pricked, eyes blazing with devilment, dabbing a paw at them, then streaking away.

Mrs. Ainsworth laughed. "You know, he plagues the life out of them. Gives them no peace."

She was right. To the Bassets, Buster's arrival was rather like the intrusion of an irreverent outsider into an exclusive London club. For a long time they had led a life of measured grace; regular sedate walks with their mistress, superb food in ample quantities and long snoring sessions on the rugs and armchairs. Their days followed one upon another in unruffled calm. And then came Buster.

He was dancing up to the youngest dog again, sideways this time, head on one side, goading him. When he started boxing with both paws it was too much even for the Basset. He dropped his dignity and rolled over with the cat in a brief wrestling match.

"I want to show you something." Mrs. Ainsworth lifted a hard rubber ball from the sideboard and went out to the garden, followed by Buster. She threw the ball across the lawn and the cat bounded after it over the frosted grass, the muscles rippling under the black sheen of his coat. He seized the ball in his teeth, brought it back to his mistress, dropped it at her feet and waited expectantly. She threw it and he brought it back again.

I gasped incredulously. A feline retriever!

The Bassets looked on disdainfully. Nothing would ever have induced them to chase a ball, but Buster did it again and again as though he would never tire of it.

Mrs. Ainsworth turned to me. "Have you every seen anything like that?"

"No," I replied. "I never have. He is a most remarkable cat."

She snatched Buster from his play and we went back into the house where she held him close to her face, laughing as the big cat purred and arched himself ecstatically against her cheek.

Looking at him, a picture of health and contentment, my mind went back to his mother. Was it too much to think that that dying little creature with the last of her strength had carried her kitten to the only haven of comfort and warmth she had ever known in the hope that it would be cared for there? Maybe it was.

But it seemed I wasn't the only one with such fancies. Mrs. Ainsworth turned to me and though she was smiling her eyes were wistful.

"Debbie would be pleased," she said.

I nodded. "Yes, she would....It was just a year ago today she brought him, wasn't it?"

"That's right." She hugged Buster to her again. "The best Christmas present I ever had."

READER'S RESPONSE

Do you think Debbie meant to give the kitten to Mrs. Ainsworth that Christmas Day?

STUDY QUESTIONS

Recalling

1. Where and when does this story take place?
2. What does the author do for a living, and how does he know Mrs. Ainsworth?
3. Why is Debbie such an interesting little cat?
4. Why does Mrs. Ainsworth call the author on Christmas morning?
5. What happens while the author is at her house?
6. What does the author see when he visits Mrs. Ainsworth a year later?

Interpreting

7. Why do you think Debbie does not stay at Mrs. Ainsworth's house?
8. What does history reveal about people and animals?

Extending

9. In your opinion, what kinds of gifts are best?

READING AND LITERARY FOCUS

Narration and Resolution

Narration is any form of writing that tells a story. A narrative work can be either fictional or nonfictional, depending on whether the story it tells actually happened. Autobiographies, biographies, narrative essays, short stories, and even certain poems are all forms of narrative writing.

At the heart of most effective stories is a **conflict,** or problem. Events in the story lead to a **climax,** or emotional high point, when readers learn how the problems will be solved. After that comes the **resolution,** the part of the plot that presents the final outcome of a story. In the resolution seemingly unrelated details may be tied together, questions answered, or conflicts resolved.

Thinking About Narration

1. What is the problem or conflict in "The Christmas Cat"?
2. How is the conflict resolved?

COMPOSITION

Writing About Resolution

Sometimes the resolution of a story is especially satisfying to one of the characters. These satisfactions often involve reversals of feeling. For example, a character who felt fear at the beginning of a story might feel brave at the end, or a lonely character might feel loved by a friend. Write a paragraph to explain how the resolution of "The Christmas Cat" was satisfying to Mrs. Ainsworth. **Prewriting:** Read through the story, making notes about Mrs. Ainsworth's feelings toward Debbie and the kitten. **Writing:** Begin by describing how Mrs. Ainsworth felt about Debbie. Then tell how you think she felt at the climax of the story, when Debbie returned with her kitten. Finally explain how Mrs. Ainsworth felt at the end of the story. Be sure to explain any reversals, or complete changes of emotion she had. **Revising:** Review your paragraph to see that you have expressed your ideas clearly and logically.

Writing a Different Ending

Write another ending for this story. Begin with Mrs. Ainsworth's call to the narrator on Christmas morning. Be sure that your new ending either answers a question, ties details together, or is emotionally satisfying. Remember to tell the story from the veterinarian's point of view.

A native of Pennsylvania, Herbert Goldstone (born 1921) was educated at the University of Chicago and Harvard University. He has taught English at several East Coast colleges and universities. Goldstone is a literary critic as well as a writer of fiction.

What is the difference between a human and a machine, and when is it important to distinguish between them?

• •

Herbert Goldstone

Virtuoso[1]

"Sir?"

The Maestro[2] continued to play, not looking up from the keys. "Sir, I was wondering if you would explain this apparatus to me."

The Maestro stopped playing, his thin body stiffly relaxed on the bench. His long supple fingers floated off the keyboard.

"Apparatus?" He turned and smiled at the robot. "Do you mean the piano, Rollo?"

"This machine that produces varying sounds. I would like some information about it, its operation and purpose. It is not included in my reference data."

"I'd hardly call a piano a machine, Rollo," he smiled, "although technically you are correct. It is actually, I suppose, a machine designed to produce sounds of graduated pitch and tone,[3] singly or in groups."

"I assimilated that much by observation," Rollo replied in a brassy baritone which no longer sent tiny tremors up the Maestro's spine. "Wires of different thickness and tautness struck by felt-covered hammers activated by manually operated levers arranged in a horizontal panel."

"A very cold-blooded description of one of man's nobler works," the Maestro remarked dryly. "You make Mozart[4] and Chopin[5] mere laboratory technicians."

---

1. **Virtuoso** [vur′choo ō′sō]: an especially skilled musician.
2. **Maestro** [mīs′trō]: distinguished conductor, composer, or teacher of music.
3. **pitch and tone:** In music, a tone is a sound that can be described in terms of several qualities, including its pitch, or highness or lowness.
4. **Mozart** [mōt′särt]: Wolfgang Amadeus [woolf′gang′ ä′mə dā′əs] Mozart, great Austrian composer (1756–1791).
5. **Chopin** [shō′pan]: Frédéric François [fred′ər ik frən swä′] Chopin, Polish pianist and composer (1810–1849).

"Mozart? Chopin?" The duralloy[6] sphere that was Rollo's head shone stark and featureless, its immediate surface unbroken but for twin vision lenses. "The terms are not included in my memory banks."

"No, not yours, Rollo," the Maestro said softly. "Mozart and Chopin are not for vacuum tubes and fuses and copper wire. They are for flesh and blood and human tears."

"I do not understand," Rollo droned.

"Well," the Maestro said, "they are two of the humans who compose, or design successions of notes—varying sounds, that is, produced by the piano or by other instruments, machines that produce other types of sounds of fixed pitch and tone.

"Sometimes these instruments, as we call them, are played, or operated, individually: sometimes in groups—orchestras, as we refer to them—and the sounds blend together. They harmonize. That is, they have an orderly, mathematical relationship to each other which results in . . ."

The Maestro threw up his hands.

"I never imagined," he chuckled, "that I would some day struggle so mightily, and so futilely, to explain music to a robot!"

"Music?"

"Yes, Rollo. The sounds produced by this machine and others of the same category are called music."

"What is the purpose of music, sir?"

"Purpose?"

The Maestro turned to the keyboard of the concert grand and flexed his fingers briefly.

"Listen, Rollo."

The wraithlike[7] fingers glided and wove the opening bars of "Clair de Lune,"[8] slender and delicate as spider silk. Rollo stood rigid, the fluorescent light over the music rack casting a bluish jeweled sheen over his towering bulk, shimmering in the amber vision lenses.

The Maestro drew his hands back from the keys and the subtle thread of melody melted reluctantly into silence.

"Claude Debussy," the Maestro said. "One of our mechanics of an era long past. He designed that succession of tones many years ago. What do you think of it?"

Rollo did not answer at once.

"The sounds were well formed," he replied finally. "They do not jar my auditory senses as some do."

The Maestro laughed. "Rollo, you may not realize it, but you're a wonderful critic."

"This music, then," Rollo droned, "its purpose is to give pleasure to humans?"

"Exactly," the Maestro said. "Sounds well formed, that do not jar the auditory senses as some do. Marvelous! It should be carved in marble over the entrance of New Carnegie Hall."[9]

"I do not understand. Why should my definition—?"

The Maestro waved a hand. "No matter, Rollo. No matter."

"Sir?"

"Yes, Rollo?"

"Those sheets of paper you sometimes

---

6. **duralloy** [dur a loi']: type of hard alloy, a mixture of two metals or one metal and another type of substance.

7. **wraithlike** [rāth'līk]: of or like a ghost; lacking substance.
8. **"Clair de Lune"** [kler də lōōn']: piano work by the French composer Claude Debussy [klôd deb'yoo sē'] (1862–1918).
9. **Carnegie** [kär'nə gē] **Hall:** historic New York City auditorium in which a variety of concerts and recitals are held.

place before you on the piano. They are the plans of the composer indicating which sounds are to be produced by the piano and in what order?"

"Just so. We call each sound a note. Combinations of notes we call chords."

"Each dot, then, indicates a sound to be made?"

"Perfectly correct, my man of metal."

Rollo stared straight ahead. The Maestro felt a peculiar sense of wheels turning within that impregnable[10] sphere.

"Sir, I have scanned my memory banks and find no specific or implied instructions against it. I should like to be taught how to produce these notes on a piano. I request that you feed the correlation between those dots and the levers of the panel into my memory banks."

The Maestro peered at him, amazed. A slow grin traveled across his face.

"Done!" he exclaimed. "It's been many years since pupils helped gray these ancient locks. But I have the feeling that you, Rollo, will prove a most fascinating student. To instill the Muse[11] into metal and machinery . . . I accept the challenge gladly!"

He rose, touched the cool latent power of Rollo's arm.

"Sit down here, my Rolleindex Personal Robot. Model M-e. We shall start Beethoven[12] spinning in his grave—or make musical history."

More than an hour later, the Maestro yawned and looked at his watch.

"It's late," he spoke into the end of the yawn. "These old eyes are not tireless like yours, my friend." He touched Rollo's shoulder. "You have the complete fundamentals of musical notation in your memory banks, Rollo. That's a good night's lesson, particularly when I recall how long it took me to acquire the same amount of information. Tomorrow we'll attempt to put those awesome fingers of yours to work."

He stretched. "I'm going to bed," he said. "Will you lock up and put out the lights?"

Rollo rose from the bench. "Yes, sir," he droned. "I have a request."

"What can I do for my star pupil?"

"May I attempt to create some sounds with the keyboard tonight? I will do so very softly so as not to disturb you."

"Tonight? Aren't you—?" Then the Maestro smiled. "You must pardon me, Rollo, it's still a bit difficult for me to realize that sleep has no meaning to you."

He hesitated, rubbing his chin. "Well, I suppose a good teacher should not discourage impatience to learn. All right, Rollo, but please be careful." He patted the polished mahogany.[13] "This piano and I have been together for many years. I'd hate to see its teeth knocked out by those sledgehammer digits of yours. Lightly, my friend, very lightly."

"Yes, sir."

The Maestro fell asleep with a faint smile on his lips, dimly aware of the shy, tentative notes that Rollo was coaxing forth.

Then gray fog closed in and he was in that half-world where reality is dreamlike

10. **impregnable** [im preg′nə bəl]: that which cannot be pierced or penetrated.

11. **Muse** [mūz]: in Greek mythology, the nine Muses were the goddesses of the arts; today, the Muse refers to the spirit or source of genius or artistic inspiration.

12. **Beethoven** [bā′tō′vən]: Ludwig van [lood′wig vän], great German composer (1770–1827)

13. **mahogany** [mə hog′ə nē]: strong, hard, reddish-brown or yellowish wood widely used for making furniture and musical instruments.

and dreams are real. It was soft and feathery and lavender clouds and sounds were rolling and washing across his mind in flowing waves.

Where? The mist drew back a bit. He was in red velvet and deep and the music swelled and broke over him.

He smiled.

My recording. Thank you, thank you, thank—

The Maestro snapped erect, threw the covers aside.

He sat on the edge of the bed, listening.

He groped for his robe in the darkness, shoved bony feet into his slippers.

He crept, trembling uncontrollably, to the door of his studio and stood there, thin and brittle in the robe.

The light over the music rack was an eerie island in the brown shadows of the studio. Rollo sat at the keyboard, prim, inhuman, rigid, twin lenses focused somewhere off into the shadows.

The massive feet working the pedals, arms and hands flashing and glinting—they were living entities, separate, somehow, from the machined perfection of his body.

The music rack was empty.

A copy of Beethoven's "Appassionata"[14] lay closed on the bench. It had been, the Maestro remembered, in a pile of sheet music on the piano.

Rollo was playing it.

He was creating it, breathing it, drawing it through silver flame.

Time became meaningless, suspended in midair.

The Maestro didn't realize he was weeping until Rollo finished the sonata.

The robot turned to look at the Maestro. "The sounds," he droned. "They pleased you?"

The Maestro's lips quivered. "Yes, Rollo," he replied at last. "They pleased me." He fought the lump in his throat.

He picked up the music in fingers that shook.

"This," he murmured. "Already?"

"It has been added to my store of data," Rollo replied. "I applied the principles you explained to me to these plans. It was not very difficult."

The Maestro swallowed as he tried to speak. "It was not very difficult . . ." he repeated softly.

The old man sank down slowly onto the bench next to Rollo, stared silently at the robot as though seeing him for the first time.

Rollo got to his feet.

The Maestro let his fingers rest on the keys, strangely foreign now.

"Music!" he breathed. "I may have heard it that way in my soul. I know Beethoven did!"

He looked up at the robot, a growing excitement in his face.

"Rollo," he said, his voice straining to

14. **"Appassionata"** [ä päs′eo nä′tä]: piano sonata [sə nä′tə] composed by Beethoven.

remain calm. "You and I have some work to do tomorrow on your memory banks."

Sleep did not come again that night.

He strode briskly into the studio the next morning. Rollo was vacuuming the carpet. The Maestro preferred carpets to the new dust-free plastics, which felt somehow profane to his feet.

The Maestro's house was, in fact, an oasis of anachronisms[15] in a desert of contemporary antiseptic efficiency.

"Well, are you ready for work, Rollo?" he asked. "We have a lot to do, you and I. I have such plans for you, Rollo—great plans!"

Rollo, for once, did not reply.

"I have asked them all to come here this afternoon," the Maestro went on. "Conductors, concert pianists, composers, my manager. All the giants of music, Rollo. Wait until they hear you play."

Rollo switched off the vacuum and stood quietly.

"You'll play for them right here this afternoon." The Maestro's voice was high-pitched, breathless. "The 'Appassionata' again, I think. Yes, that's it. I must see their faces!

"Then we'll arrange a recital to introduce you to the public and the critics and then a major concerto with one of the big orchestras. We'll have a telecast around the world, Rollo. It can be arranged.

"Think of it, Rollo, just think of it! The greatest piano virtuoso of all time . . . a robot! It's completely fantastic and completely wonderful. I feel like an explorer at the edge of a new world."

He walked feverishly back and forth.

"Then recordings, of course. My entire repertoire,[16] Rollo, and more. So much more!"

"Sir?"

The Maestro's face shone as he looked up at him. "Yes, Rollo?"

"In my built-in instructions, I have the option of rejecting any action which I consider harmful to my owner." The robot's words were precise, carefully selected. "Last night you wept. That is one of the indications I am instructed to consider in making my decisions."

The Maestro gripped Rollo's thick, superbly molded arm.

"Rollo, you don't understand. That was for the moment. It was petty of me, childish!"

"I beg your pardon, sir, but I must refuse to approach the piano again."

The Maestro stared at him, unbelieving, pleading.

"Rollo, you can't! The world must hear you!"

"No, sir." The amber lenses almost seemed to soften.

"The piano is not a machine," that powerful inhuman voice droned. "To me, yes. I can translate the notes into sounds at a glance. From only a few I am able to grasp at once the composer's conception. It is easy for me."

Rollo towered magnificently over the Maestro's bent form.

"I can also grasp," the brassy monotone rolled through the studio, "that this . . . music is not for robots. It is for people. To me it is easy, yes. . . . It was not meant to be easy."

---

15. **anachronisms** [ə nak′rə niz′ əmz]: people or things out of their proper place in time.

16. **repertoire** [rep′ər twär′]: stock of artistic works that a performer or group of performers has learned.

READER'S RESPONSE

Do you think Rollo will play the piano again? Why or why not?

STUDY QUESTIONS

Recalling

1. What does Rollo want to learn?
2. What does Rollo do while the Maestro sleeps?
3. Why does the Maestro weep when he hears Rollo play Beethoven's "Appassionata"?
4. Why does Rollo refuse to play for the giants of music?

Interpreting

5. According to the story, what might robots be like in the future?
6. Do you think Rollo's decision is wise? Why or why not?

Extending

7. What other things do you think are "not meant to be easy"?

READING AND LITERARY FOCUS

Character and Theme

A **character** is a person or animal in a story, novel, or play. Each character has qualities, or **character traits,** that the reader discovers as the work unfolds. An author reveals the personalities of characters through their words and actions and other details in the story.

Sometimes an author uses characters to convey the **theme,** or central idea, of the story, usually expressed as a generalization about life. In "Virtuoso" two contrasting characters are used to make a point about humans and machines.

Thinking About Character and Theme

1. Who is the Maestro, and what do you think he represents in the story? Use details to support your opinion.

2. Who is Rollo, and what does he seem to represent? What clues suggest this?
3. What does this story tell us about humans and machines?

VOCABULARY

Analogies

Analogies are comparisons that are stated as double relationships: for example, *A* is to *B* as *C* is to *D*. On tests analogies are written as two pairs of words: for example, *A : B :: C : D.* You may be given the first pair and then asked to find or complete a second pair that has the same kind of relationship. For instance, in the analogy OLD : ANCIENT :: SMALL : TINY, the words in each pair represent different degrees of the same quality.

Analogies can state many different kinds of relationships. Some examples are synonyms (BOOK : VOLUME), opposites (ASLEEP : AWAKE), and cause and effect (HUNGER : EAT).

The following numbered items are analogies that need to be completed. The third word in each item comes from "Virtuoso." Decide how the first two words in each item are related. Then from the four choices that follow each item, choose the word that best completes the second pair.

1. PINK : RED :: LAVENDER :
   (a) flower   (c) color
   (b) purple   (d) dye

2. SLOWLY : QUICKLY :: FUTILELY :
   (a) accomplishment   (c) vainly
   (b) manner   (d) successfully

3. WHISTLED : FLUTE :: DRONED :
   (a) violin   (c) hummed
   (b) bagpipe   (d) sound

4. SOLID : FIRM :: SUPPLE :
   (a) flexible   (c) snake
   (b) stiff   (d) round

5. BIRD : FLYING :: APPARATUS :
   (a) playing   (c) working
   (b) machine   (d) metal

Thinking Skills: Classifying

DEFINITION

Classifying is a way of thinking about things by sorting them into groups. We classify things all the time just to be able to talk about them more easily. For example, we group all of the thousands of different kinds of articles worn to cover, protect, or adorn the body into one class. We call that class clothing.

Classifying things often makes it easier to see relationships between them. It is a way of thinking that can help you understand literature and speak and write more clearly about it.

STEPS

1. **Identify the things to be classified.**

2. **Identify the classes or groups into which the things are to be sorted.**
   Keep in mind that each group has one or more qualities that make it different from any other group.

3. **Sort each thing into a class or group based on the qualities each thing possesses.**

4. **Make a statement based on the groupings.**

EXAMPLE

Imagine that you are asked to write a report about heroes. With such a broad topic, you need to classify the heroes in order to be able to think clearly about them.

1. **Identify the things to be classified.** You make a list of heroes.

2. **Identify the classes or groups into which the things are to be sorted.** You notice that some heroes are real people, while other heroes, such as those found in films and books, are imaginary. You decide that two classes—real heroes and imaginary heroes—will give you a way to organize your thinking.

3. **Sort each thing into a class or group based on the qualities each thing possesses.** You assign each hero to a class based on whether the hero is real or imaginary.

4. **Make a statement based on the groupings.** Your statement may be a simple descriptive one: "Heroes can be either real or imaginary." Or you may choose to make a personal statement about the groups: "I would much rather meet a real hero than an imaginary one."

ACTIVITY 1

Follow the four steps of classifying to organize the physical actions of the Maestro and Rollo in "The Virtuoso." Let your classes be "actions performed mechanically" and "actions performed with feeling." Develop a statement that says something about what it means to be a creature of "flesh and blood and human tears."

ACTIVITY 2

Follow the four steps of classifying to organize information from any other literary selection in this book. You may wish to focus on characters, settings, conflicts, events, or any specific kind of details in a selection, such as sounds or animals or colors. Remember to make your classes clearly different from one another.

Diane Ackerman (born 1948), a poet and journalist, says "I'm interested in stretching the limits of what poets, by convention, are expected to think and write about." Originally from Waukegan, Illinois, she was educated at Boston University, Pennsylvania State, and Cornell. Her poems, reviews, and articles appear in a variety of magazines and journals. Deeply interested in science, Ackerman is both a skin diver and an amateur astronomer. Her books include *Brainstem Sonata: Science and Poetry*, a critical study, and two volumes of poetry: *The Planets: A Cosmic Pastoral* and *Victim of the Molecule*.

Scientists know relatively little about bats, but after visiting with one of the few authorities on these remarkable animals, a reporter tells an incredible story.

● ●

Diane Ackerman

Bats

In the early evening, I take my seat in a natural amphitheater[1] of limestone boulders, in the Texas hill country; at the bottom of the slope is a wide, dark cave mouth. Nothing stirs yet in its depths. But I have been promised one of the wonders of our age. Deep inside the cavern, twenty million Mexican free-tailed bats[2] are hanging up by their toes. They are the largest known concentration of warm-blooded animals in the world. Soon, at dusk, all twenty million of them will fly out to feed, in a living volcano that scientists call an "emergence." They will flood the September sky with their leathery wings and ultrasonic[3] cries and people in cities as far as fifty miles away, without realizing it, will rarely be more than seventy feet from a feeding bat.

"I've sat here for three hours and still seen them pouring out," the man next to me says, radiant with anticipation. If anyone should know their habits, it is he, Merlin D. Tuttle—a world authority on bats, and the founder and science director of Bat Conservation International, whose headquarters is in Austin. On the ground beside us lie some of the tools of his trade: an infrared nightscope, a device made popular

---

1. **amphitheater** [am′fə thē′ə tər]: level area of ground surrounded by rising slopes.
2. **free-tailed bats:** bat with a tail that extends beyond the layer of tissue attached to the bat's hind legs; found in the Carlsbad Caverns, New Mexico, and other caves in the southwestern United States.

3. **ultrasonic** [ul′trə son′ik]: of sound waves beyond the range of what human beings are capable of hearing.

in Vietnam; a miner's headlamp powered by a large, heavy battery, which is in a khaki ammunition belt around his waist; a "mini bat-detector," which picks up the ultrasonic echolocating[4] calls of many species of bats. Noticeably absent are gloves, sticks, or other protective articles. "Bats are among the gentlest of animals," he says. "They're really shy creatures, who have just had a bad press."

A thin, muscular man in his mid-forties, Tuttle has gray sideburns, a blond mustache above an emphatic mouth, and wisps of blond hair falling across a large forehead. Before I can say anything, his eyes, behind gold-wire-rimmed glasses, shift to the cave mouth, and a smile drifts over his face. I follow his gaze. In the rays of a fading sun, hundreds of small dark bats have appeared, darting and climbing, swirling and looping. They spiral up and scroll off to the east. It's a small, odd spectacle. . . .

Now small dark clouds begin to swell, spinning in the shape of an open funnel, as the bats orbit until they're high enough to depart. Like airplanes in a mountain valley, they must circle to climb, so they whisk round one another, in tight echelons.[5] As they revolve, they pick up speed. The pace of everything is accelerating: the descent of darkness, the size of the bat clouds, and the rate at which they are emerging from the cave mouth. Over open country, free-tailed bats can cruise at thirty-five miles an hour.

"They're spiraling counterclockwise," I say. "Do they always turn that way?"

"Yes, they do when they emerge, but in the mornings, when they return, they tend to go straight in. They come in real high, peel off, and then dive in fast, with their wings half folded."

Shadows advance through the trees as the whirlpooling[6] bats set off on a night's cross-country journey, to forage for food. A natural insecticide, they eat a quarter of a million pounds of insects every night. Born in June, weaned at about five weeks old, the new babies are strong enough now to fly with their mothers, and practice some of the arcane[7] arts of bathood: how to leave a cave waltzing and veer off into twilight, how to glide over the land and feed in midair, how to swoop down to a pond with their tiny pink tongues out and drink on the wing, and, returning, how to find the warmth they crave among the huddled swarms.

Do the bats fly non-stop all night long, or do they pause somewhere to put their feet up for a spell? Do the mothers demonstrate for their own offspring, the way bird mothers do, or do the babies learn from studying the habits of the whole colony?

"We just don't know," Tuttle says. "So little is known about bats."

A hawk appears, swoops, grabs a stray bat out of the sky, and disappears with it. In a moment, the hawk returns, but hearing his wings coming, the bats in the column all shift sidewise to confuse him, and he misses. As wave upon wave of bats pours out of the cave, their collective wings begin to sound like drizzle on autumn

---

4. **echolocating** [ek'ō lō kā'ting]: determining the location of objects by sending out sound waves and interpreting their sound and the direction from which they return.

5. **echelons** [esh'ə lonz']: groups of flying units arranged in steps, with each new unit behind and to one side of the preceding unit.

6. **whirlpooling:** moving rapidly in a circular motion.

7. **arcane** [är kān']: secret; mysterious.

leaves. Gushing out and swirling fast in the living Mixmaster,[8] newly risen bats start in close and then veer out almost to the rim of the bowl, climbing until they're high enough to clear the ridge. Already, a long black column of bats looks like a tornado spinning far out across the Texas sky. A second column forms, undulating[9] and dancing through the air like a Chinese dragon,[10] stretching for miles, headed for some unknown feeding ground. The night is silent except for the serene beating of wings. Then Tuttle switches on his mini bat-detector, and we hear a frenzy of clicks. Actually, "click" is the sound made by the bat-detector—a machine that can only translate the sounds for us, mainly into clicks and warbles. Beyond human hearing, the air is loud with shouts as the teeming bats flutter wing to wing, echolocating furiously so as not to collide. Like a Geiger counter[11] gone berserk, the bat-detector pours static, and Tuttle laughs. There's no way to hear individual voices in the ultrasonic Babel[12] of the emergence. The two columns of bats flow upward, each thick and beating, making long, pulsing ribbons, climbing to as much as two miles high to ride rapid air currents to distant feeding sites. Some groups twist into a bow-tie shape, others into a tuning fork, a claw, a wrench, a waving hand. Buffeted by uneven

currents, they make the air visible as it rarely is. In the rosy dusk, their wings beat so fast that it looks as if a strobe light[13] were playing over them.

"Some bats live to be more than thirty years old," Tuttle explains. "Someone who kills a bat may be killing an animal that has lived on this planet for thirty years. It's not like killing a roach. For their size, bats are the longest-lived mammal on earth. Unfortunately, they're also the slowest-reproducing mammal for their size. A mother bat usually rears only one pup a year. If you took a pair of meadow mice and gave them everything they needed for survival, they and their progeny[14] could theoretically leave a million meadow mice by the year's end. If you provided an average pair of bats with the same opportunity, at the end of the year there would be a total of three bats—mother, father, and baby. And bats cluster in large colonies in vulnerable places. Here we have the world's largest

---

8. **Mixmaster:** a type of electric food mixer.
9. **undulating** [un′jə lā′ting]: moving in or as a wave.
10. **Chinese dragon:** large silk representation of a dragon used in parades celebrating the Chinese New Year.
11. **Geiger** [gī′gər] **counter:** device for detecting and measuring radiation.
12. **Babel** [bā′bəl]: in the Bible, the people of Babel began building a tower in order to reach heaven. God prevented the completion of the tower and punished its builders by changing their single language into many different ones. Therefore, Babel has come to mean a confused mixture of many voices or languages.

13. **strobe light:** electric device that produces a very brief and intense flash of light; used especially in photography.
14. **progeny** [proj′ə nē]: offspring or descendants.

concentration of warm-blooded animals, and it could be destroyed in five minutes. I personally know of caves where people have wiped out millions of bats at a time."

The four largest summer bat colonies in eastern North America wouldn't exist today if Tuttle hadn't recognized that they were in peril and initiated a campaign to protect them. Tuttle was born in Honolulu, the son of a biology teacher who traveled often and finally settled his family in Tennessee, not far from a bat cave. By the time Tuttle was nine years old, he was studying bats. He made his first serious scientific contributions when he was in high school, and went on to write a doctoral dissertation[15] at the University of Kansas on the population ecology and the behavior of gray bats. A mammalogist[16] by disposition, he found the plight of bats and their decline especially poignant. One day, a few years after he finished graduate school, he returned with friends to show them the extraordinary emergence of two hundred and fifty thousand bats from Hambrick Cave, in Alabama.

"At almost the same time every evening, you could see this big, dark column of bats, sixty feet wide and thirty feet high, going all the way to the horizon," he says. "The sound was like a white-water river. As you can see here tonight, a bat emergence can be one of the most spectacular sights in nature. All of us were excited, our cameras were ready, but the bats never came out. It was quite a shock when it dawned on us that the bats were gone. I had had an emotional attachment to them. Those bats had played a major role in my doctoral research, and I'd gotten to know them. We went into the cave and found sticks, stones, rifle cartridges, and fireworks wrappers beneath what had been a bat roost. There could be no doubt that they had been killed. Many had been banded, and none of them showed up later at their traditional hibernating caves. There were so many ways they could have died. Even a single blast from a cherry bomb could have severely damaged their sensitive hearing, so that they couldn't use their sonar. Hambrick Cave was five miles from the nearest human habitation, not a threat to anyone, and you could get there only by boat. It was one of the last places in the world where I expected bats to be destroyed." He shakes his head.

"Follow that albino[17] one!" Tuttle says suddenly, pointing to the cave entrance, where a white dot has just appeared among what looks like a shoal of flying black peppercorns. Once, twice—three circuits of the bowl. It drifts far out to the rim and toward us, its mouth open; then it floats over the ridge and joins one of the columns. Gesturing with one hand as if to press down a stack of invisible myths, Tuttle says, "Their mouths are open when they fly because they need them that way to echolocate. They're not snarling or mean; they're just trying not to bump into anything. We associate that look—open mouth and bared teeth—with menace, but they're not being aggressive. That's how their sonar works.

15. **doctoral dissertation** [dis′ər tā′shən]: lengthy, formal paper on a given subject written by a student who wishes to obtain a doctorate, the highest graduate degree given by universities.
16. **mammalogist** [mə mal′ə jist]: scientist whose special field is mammalogy, the branch of zoology dealing with mammals.

17. **albino** [al bī′nō]: person, plant, or animal lacking coloring.

Look, I'll show you." With that, he leads me down into the center of the bowl, toward the cave, and directly into the thick of the swarming, fluttering bats, which fly around our shoulders, over our heads, beside my chin. Too amazed to flinch, I can feel them graze my head with their flutters while not actually touching me with their wings. The breeze they make blows my long hair back. We are standing in the path of twenty million emerging bats. Tuttle swings both arms above his head, then does it again. On the third pass, he grabs a bat right out of the air.

Following him back up to our original spot, I sit down on a boulder beside him to see what he has captured. Its wings held closed by his grip, its small, furry brown head sticking out, a little bat looks up at us, frightened and fragile. It uses its chin as a pry bar, trying to escape, but makes no attempt to bite.

"See how ferocious he is?" Tuttle says.

The face is gnomic,[18] the wet eyes as black as Sen-Sen,[19] the body covered with a thick, fluffy brown fur. What must it make of us—large, powerful animals with big eyes and big teeth? It opens its mouth to echolocate but doesn't snap or nip, and, in any case, its teeth are very small. Tuttle loosens his grip slightly. Still holding the wings closed with one hand, he strokes its back with the other, following the nap of the fur, and the little bat quiets down. I know better than to pick up a bat I might see lying on the ground—or any wild animal acting in an abnormal manner, for that

matter. But a veteran bat-handler snatching a healthy bat out of the air is different.

"Want to touch?" he asks.

I run a finger over the tiny back, feel the slender bones and the fur, almost as soft as chinchilla.[20] Then we gently unfold a wing, and I stroke its dark, thin, rubbery membrane, trace the elongated[21] fingers that hold it up, and look at the tail, from which the free-tailed bat gets its name. The scientific name for all bats is *Chiroptera*,[22] "hand wing," and even on a small version like this one the hand wings are clear.

"Isn't he a winsome little fellow?" Tuttle asks. "Here, you can let him go." He places the bat on my open palm, and I feel a swift scuttle as it creeps wing over wing to my fingertips, then launches itself into the air to rejoin its colony, which has now filled the entire sky. . . .

---

18. **gnomic** [nō′mik]: like a gnome, a dwarf who, according to folk tales, lives in a mountain cave or a mine in the earth.
19. **Sen-Sen** [sen sen]: type of breath sweetener.

---

20. **chinchilla** [chin chil′ə]: small, South American rodent valued for its soft, silver or bluish-gray fur.
21. **elongated** [i lông′gāt id]: lengthened; stretched.
22. *Chiroptera* [kī rop′tər ə]

READER'S RESPONSE

Has this article changed the way you feel about bats? Explain.

STUDY QUESTIONS

Recalling

1. What has the author gone to see in Texas?
2. Who is Merlin K. Tuttle, and what does he do?
3. Why doesn't Tuttle use gloves or other protective articles in his work?
4. What does an emergence look and sound like?
5. Why do many people think bats are ferocious?

Interpreting

6. Why are bats unusual?
7. What is the purpose of this article?

Extending

8. Do you think humans have a responsibility to protect animals? Explain.

READING AND LITERARY FOCUS

Main Idea

Writers may state the **main idea,** or the central idea, of a work of nonfiction directly, or they may leave readers to figure it out for themselves. When the main idea is stated, it often appears as a general statement about the subject near the beginning of an essay or article. Although the main idea can be expressed in one or two sentences, it is supported by many details. These supporting details are facts, incidents, examples, or quotations that the writer uses to illustrate and develop the main idea.

Thinking About Main Idea

1. State, in your own words, the main idea of Diane Ackerman's article.

2. List at least four supporting details the author has supplied to develop this idea.

COMPOSITION

Writing About Main Idea

Any work of nonfiction has a central idea. This idea may be a particular point about the subject or an insight into life in general. A writer may use various techniques to develop this idea, such as relating facts, quoting authorities, or describing incidents. Write about the central idea in "Bats." **Prewriting:** Draw up a list of broad statements that might serve as the central idea of "Bats." Then review the selection, and choose the idea from your list that seems to convey the author's overall message most closely. **Writing:** Begin by stating the author's central idea. Then explain the specific techniques she uses to communicate this idea, and provide quotations from the article as examples. **Revising:** Review your paragraph to see that you have expressed your ideas clearly and logically.

Writing a Title

Think about this selection, and create a new title for it. Your title should point to the main idea yet not give away too much information. Tell what your title would be, and in a paragraph explain why it is a good one for this article.

CHALLENGE

Survey

Conduct a survey to find out what people think and feel about bats. Write two or three questions. Be sure none of your questions can be answered with a single word. Then interview a number of people. Ask your questions in exactly the same way each time. Record the responses, and report your findings to the class.

Throughout his life Theodore Roethke (1908–1963) struggled with his own intelligence and sensitivity. As a young man he was not readily accepted by his peers, who felt that "brains were sissies." After college he became an instructor at Michigan State College (now University). There he dedicated himself to writing poetry. Many of his poems reflect his deep fascination with nature and his effort to tie it to the "inner world" of thought and emotion.

A momentary glimpse of a small creature starts an inner journey.

Theodore Roethke

The Bat

By day the bat is cousin to the mouse.
He likes the attic of an aging house.

His fingers make a hat about his head.
His pulse beat is so slow we think him dead.

5 He loops in crazy figures half the night
Among the trees that face the corner light.

But when he brushes up against a screen,
We are afraid of what our eyes have seen:

For something is amiss or out of place
10 When mice with wings can wear a human face.

READER'S RESPONSE

How does this poem make you feel about bats?

STUDY QUESTIONS

Recalling

1. According to the poem, where does the bat like to be during the day?
2. What physical characteristics of a bat are described in the poem?
3. What does the bat do at night?
4. According to the poet, why do people find bats disturbing?

Interpreting

5. What do you think the first line of the poem means?
6. Why are the bat's flight patterns "crazy figures"?
7. What, in your view, inspired Theodore Roethke to write this poem?

Extending

8. What kinds of animals fascinate you? Why?

READING AND LITERARY FOCUS

Rhythm

Speech has rhythm. When we speak, we naturally emphasize some syllables more than others. In poetry **rhythm** is the pattern of beats made by stressed and unstressed syllables in the lines of a poem. In "The Bat" the rhythm repeats in sets of two syllables. One unstressed syllable (marked ˘) is followed by a single stressed syllable (marked ´). Every line has five sets of two syllables:

By day / the bat / is cous / in to / the mouse.
He likes / the at / tic of / an ag / ing house.

The rhythm of a poem should suit the subject. A poem about the sea, for example, should have a regular, rolling rhythm that suggests the action of waves.

Reading a poem requires some attention to the rhythm of the lines. We should not, however, stress the rhythm too much, or the meaning will be lost, and the poem will become singsong. Instead, we should emphasize the words and their meaning, varying the flow of the rhythm by pausing now and then for emphasis or emotional effect. Poets use punctuation, line breaks (ends of lines), and stanza breaks (ends of groups of lines) to show readers where to rest in order to let a second of silence enhance the meaning of the poem.

Thinking About Rhythm

1. Read "The Bat" aloud, and listen to the syllables in each line. Is the pattern of stressed and unstressed syllables always the same?
2. Does the rhythm suit the subject of the poem? What does the rhythm seem to suggest?

At the age of eight, Jane Goodall (born 1934) decided that one day she wanted to live with and study wild animals in Africa. She spent more than twenty years fulfilling her dream, studying chimpanzees at the Gombe Stream Research Centre in Tanzania, East Africa. One of the first people to study chimps in their natural habitat, she made several discoveries that challenged scientific beliefs about primate behavior. Not only did she document hunting and meat eating among chimpanzees, but she also observed chimpanzees modifying twigs, blades of grass, and leaves to use as tools for obtaining insects and water. Today Jane Goodall is the scientific director of the Gombe Research Centre. She also lectures and teaches all over the world.

One evening I returned to camp and found Dominic and Hassan very excited. A large male chimpanzee, they told me, had walked right into camp and spent an hour feeding from the palm tree that shaded my tent.

• •

Jane van Lawick-Goodall

The Chimps Come to Camp

Nineteen sixty-one was a cold winter in England, and in Cambridge, with the winds whistling over the flat country straight from the icy wastes of Norway, the snow and the frost and the frozen water pipes seemed interminable.[1] I felt utterly remote from Africa and the chimpanzees and all that I longed for most at that time. Of course I was immensely grateful for the privilege of going to Cambridge, and for the chance of working under the supervision of Professor Robert Hinde—but what was David Graybeard doing in the meantime?

How were Goliath and Flo? What was I missing?

At last the spring thawed the hard ground; in two months I would be back in Africa. First I had two ordeals to face, and the thought of them terrified me far more than any encounter with enraged chimpanzees. I had to speak at two scientific conferences in London and in New York, since other scientists were avid for firsthand information about the ways of my chimpanzees. These milestones finally came and went, unbelievably the six-month exile was over, and I was heading for Africa again, crossing the vastness of the Sahara Desert[2]

---

1. **interminable** [in tur′mi nə bəl]: as if without end.

2. **Sahara** [sə har′ə] **Desert:** desert in northern Africa, the largest in the world.

in the lurid red dawn light that is so much an integral part of modern air travel.

Would the chimpanzees have forgotten me? Would I have to get them used to me all over again? I need not have worried. When I got back to the Gombe[3] Stream Chimpanzee Reserve[4] it seemed that the chimps were, if anything, *more* tolerant of my presence than before.

One evening I returned to camp and found Dominic and Hassan very excited. A large male chimpanzee, they told me, had walked right into camp and spent an hour feeding from the palm tree that shaded my tent. The following evening I learned that the same chimp had paid another visit. I determined to stay down the next day to see if he came again.

It seemed strange to lie in my bed and watch the dawn break, to have breakfast in camp, to sit in my tent in the *daylight* to type out my previous day's notes on the typewriter I had brought back from England. And it seemed quite unbelievable when at about ten o'clock David Graybeard strolled calmly past the front of my tent and climbed the palm tree. I peeped out and heard him giving low-pitched grunts of pleasure as he poked the first red fruit from its horny case. An hour later he climbed down, paused to look, quite deliberately, into the tent, and wandered away. After all those months of despair, when the chimpanzees had fled at the mere sight of me five hundred yards away, here was one making himself at home in our very camp.

David Graybeard paid regular visits until the palm tree's fruit was finished, then he stopped coming. These oil nut palms do not all fruit at the same time, however, and so a few weeks later the hard nutlike fruits on another of the camp palms became red and ripe. David Graybeard resumed his daily visits.

I did not often stay to watch him, since there was a limit to the amount of information one could gain from watching a lone male guzzling palm nuts. Sometimes, though, I waited for him to come just for the intense pleasure of seeing him so close and so unafraid. One day as I sat on the veranda of the tent, David climbed down from his tree and then, in his deliberate way, walked straight toward me. When he was about five feet from me he stopped, and slowly his hair began to stand on end, until he looked enormous and very fierce. A chimpanzee may erect his hair when he is angry, frustrated, or nervous. Why had David now put his hair out? All at once he ran straight at me, snatched up a banana from my table, and hurried off to eat it farther away. Gradually his hair returned to its normal sleeked position.

After that incident I asked Dominic to leave bananas out whenever he saw David, and so, even when there were no ripe palm nuts, the chimp still wandered into camp sometimes, looking for bananas. His visits were irregular and unpredictable, and I no longer waited in my tent for him to come.

About eight weeks after my return to Gombe I had a slight attack of malaria.[5] I stayed in bed and, hoping that David Graybeard might pass by, asked Dominic to set

3. **Gombe** [gôm′bä]: river in the African country of Tanzania.
4. **Reserve:** area set aside by a government for the protection of plant and animal life or other natural resources.

5. **malaria** [mə lār′ē ə]: disease spread by mosquitoes and marked by repeatedly occurring chills, high fevers, and sweating.

out some bananas. Late that morning David walked up to my tent and helped himself to the fruit. As he walked back toward the bushes I suddenly saw that a second chimpanzee was standing there, half hidden in the vegetation. It was Goliath. As David sat down to eat, Goliath went close to him, peering into his face. Then, as David rolled a banana skin wad around in his lower lip, squeezing out the last juices, occasionally pushing it forward and looking down at it over his nose, Goliath reached out one hand to his friend's mouth, begging for the wad. Presently David responded by spitting out the well-chewed mass into Goliath's hand, and then Goliath sucked on it in turn.

The next day Goliath followed David to camp again. I kept hidden right inside the tent, with the flap down, and peeped out through a small hole. This time Goliath, with much hesitation and with all his hair on end, followed David to the tent and seized some bananas for himself.

The following few weeks were momentous. I sent Hassan off to the village of Mwamgongo, to the north of the reserve, to buy a supply of bananas, and each day I put out a pile near my tent. Since the figs in the home valley were ripe again, large groups of chimps were constantly passing near camp. I spent part of my time up near the fig trees and the remainder waiting for David in camp. He came nearly every day, and not only did Goliath sometimes accompany him but William also, and occasionally a youngster.

One day, when David came by himself, I held a banana out to him in my hand. He approached, put his hair out, and gave a sudden soft exhalation rather like a cough, while at the same time he jerked his chin up. He was mildly threatening me. Suddenly he stood upright, swaggered slightly from

foot to foot, slapped the trunk of a palm tree beside him with one hand, and then, very gently, took the banana from me.

The first time I offered Goliath a banana from my hand was very different. He too put his hair out, then seized a chair and charged past me, almost knocking me over. Next he sat and glowered from the bushes. It was a long time before he behaved as calmly in my presence as David; if I made a sudden movement and startled him he often threatened me vigorously, uttering a soft barking sound while rapidly raising one arm or swaying branches with quick, rather jerky movements.

It was exciting to be able to make fairly regular observations on the same individuals; previously I had found this almost impossible. Chimpanzees follow no set route on their daily wanderings, and so, except when a good fruit tree had been ripe, it had only been by chance that I had observed the same chimpanzee more than a few times in any one month. In camp, however, I was able to make detailed observations on social interactions of David, Goliath, and William to each other several times a week. Additionally, I often saw incidents involving one of the three when I was watching the chimpanzee groups feeding on figs in the home valley.

It was at this point when I began to suspect that Goliath might be the highest-ranking male chimpanzee in the area—and later I found that this in reality was the case. If William and Goliath started to move toward the same banana at the same time, it was William who gave way and Goliath who took the fruit. If Goliath met another adult male along a narrow forest tract, he continued—the other stepped aside. Goliath was nearly always the first to be greeted when a newcomer climbed into a fig tree to join a feeding group of chimpanzees. One day I actually saw him driving another chimp from her nest in order to take it over for himself. It was nearly dark when I observed this from the Peak.[6] The young female had constructed a large leafy nest and was peacefully lying there, curled up for the night. Suddenly Goliath swung up onto the branch beside her, and after a moment stood upright, seized an overhead branch, and began to sway it violently back and forth over her head. With a loud scream she leaped out of bed and vanished into the darkening undergrowth below; Goliath calmed instantly, climbed onto her vacated nest, bent over a new branch, and lay down. Five minutes later the ousted female was still constructing a new bed in the last glimmers of dusk.

William, with his long scarred upper lip and his drooping lower lip, was one of the more subordinate males in his relationships with other chimpanzees. If another adult male showed signs of aggression toward him, William was quick to approach with gestures of appeasement[7] and submission, reaching out to lay his hand on the other, crouching with soft panting grunts in front of the higher-ranking individuals. During such an encounter he would often pull back the corners of his lips and expose his teeth in a nervous grin. Initially William was timid in camp, also. When I offered him a banana in my hand for the first time, he stared at it for several moments, gently shook a branch in his frustration, and then sat uttering soft whimpering sounds until I relented and put the fruit on the ground.

It took much longer to determine David Graybeard's position in the dominance hierarchy.[8] In those early days I only knew that he had a very calm and gentle disposition: if William or some youngster approached him with submissive gestures, David was quick to respond with a reassuring gesture, laying his hand on the other's body or head, or briefly grooming him. Often, too, if Goliath showed signs of ex-

---

6. **the Peak:** a mountain that was the author's favorite spot from which to observe the chimpanzees.

7. **appeasement** [ə pēz′mənt]: the act of bringing to a state of peace or quiet.
8. **hierarchy** [hī′ə rär′kē]: organization by rank, with each rank at a lower level than the one above it.

citement in camp—if I approached too closely, for instance—David would reach out and lay his hand gently in his companion's groin or make a few brief grooming strokes on Goliath's arm. Such gestures nearly always seemed to calm the more dominant male.

It was during these weeks that Hugo arrived at the Gombe Stream. I had at last agreed that a professional photographer be allowed to come and photograph the chimpanzees, and Louis had recommended Hugo. The National Geographic Society had accepted the advice and given Hugo funds for filming the chimpanzees—partly to obtain a documentary film record of as much behavior as possible, and partly in the hope of being able to prepare a lecture film for their members.

Hugo was born in Indonesia,[9] educated in England and Holland, and, like myself, had always loved animals. He chose photography as a career on the assumption that he would somehow and sometime get to Africa and film wild animals. After two years of working in a film studio in Amsterdam[10] he was accepted by Armand and Michaela Denis to help with the filming of their well-known TV program "On Safari." He arrived in Africa, in fact, one year after I did.

While he was working for the Denises,

9. **Indonesia** [in′də nē zhə]: country in southeastern Asia, composed of islands in the Malay Archipelago in the Pacific.
10. **Amsterdam:** capital and largest city of the Netherlands.

Hugo came to know the Leakeys,[11] who were practically neighbors, and after two years he agreed to make a lecture film for the National Geographic Society on Louis's work at the Olduvai Gorge.[12] During this period Louis decided that Hugo would be just the person to go to the Gombe Stream; he realized that Hugo was not only an excellent photographer but also that he had a real love and understanding of animals. Louis wrote to tell me about Hugo and his abilities. At the same time he wrote to Vanne telling her that he had found someone just right as a husband for Jane.

I still felt some apprehension as to how the chimpanzees would tolerate a man with a load of photographic equipment, but I realized the importance of getting a documentary film record of the chimpanzees' behavior. Also, there was David Graybeard— I did not anticipate that David would be too upset by the arrival of a stranger.

On Hugo's first morning at the Gombe Stream, David Graybeard arrived very early in camp, for he had nested nearby. I had decided that it might be best if David first got used to the new tent, and then to its occupant; so while David ate his bananas Hugo remained inside, peering out through the flaps. David scarcely glanced at the tent until his meal was finished. Then he walked deliberately over, pulled back one of the flaps, stared at Hugo, grunted, and plodded away in his usual leisurely manner.

To my surprise Goliath and even timid William, who arrived together a short while afterward, also accepted Hugo with very little fuss. It was as though they regarded him as merely part of the "furniture" of the camp. And so on his first day Hugo was able to get some excellent film of interactions—greeting, grooming, and begging for food—between the three males. And on his second day, Hugo was able to get some even more remarkable film—shots of chimpanzees eating a monkey.

Since that memorable day when I first had watched David Graybeard feeding on the carcass of a young bushpig,[13] I had only once seen meat-eating again. On that occasion the prey had been a young bushbuck,[14] but again I could not be sure that the chimps had caught it themselves. On this third occasion Hugo and I actually witnessed the hunt and kill.

It happened most unexpectedly. I had taken Hugo up to show him the Peak and we were watching four red colobus[15] monkeys that were evidently separated from their troop. Suddenly an adolescent male chimpanzee climbed cautiously up the tree next to the monkeys and moved slowly along a branch. Then he sat down. After a moment, three of the monkeys jumped away—quite calmly, it appeared. The fourth remained, his head turned toward the chimp. A second later another adolescent male chimp climbed out of the thick vegetation surrounding the tree, rushed along the branch on which the last monkey was sitting, and grabbed it. Instantly several

---

11. **Leakeys:** Louis S. B. Leakey [lē′kē] (1903–1972) and his wife Mary (born 1913), British anthropologists, scientists who study the development of human beings from prehistoric times to the present, and archaeologists, scientists who study the human past by uncovering former dwelling sites and examining the remains thus discovered.
12. **Olduvai Gorge** [ôl′du vī′ gôrj]: ravine in northern Tanzania, where the Leakeys discovered important tools and fossils.

13. **bushpig:** large, gray pig found in Africa.
14. **bushbuck:** striped, southern African antelope with twisted horns.
15. **colobus** [käl′ə bəs]: type of long-tailed African monkey.

other chimps climbed up into the tree and, screaming and barking in excitement, tore their victim into several pieces. It was all over within a minute from the time of capture.

We were too far away for Hugo to film the hunt, and anyway it happened so suddenly that he could hardly have expected to do so even had we been close enough. He did get some film of the chimpanzees eating their share of the kill, though from very far away.

After such a startlingly auspicious beginning, however, Hugo's luck changed. True, he was able to get a great deal of excellent movie film and still photographs of David, Wiliam, and Goliath. But he needed more than that for his documentary record. He needed film of as many aspects of the chimpanzees' life as possible—their life in the mountains and forests. And most of them fled from Hugo just as two years earlier they had fled from me; even Goliath and William distrusted him when they met him in the forest.

As I had done previous to Judy's visit, I had constructed a few ramshackle hides[16] for Hugo, close to trees I expected to bear fruit. I had even stuck empty bottles through the walls to try to get the chimps accustomed to the sight of camera lenses. Somehow, though, they instantly detected the difference when they spied real lenses and, if they did arrive in the tree, they usually stared toward the hide and vanished silently. Poor Hugo—he lugged most of his camera equipment up and down the steep slopes himself so as not to create the added disturbance of taking an African porter with

16. **hides:** concealed places from which a person may observe wildlife or shoot wild animals.

him. He spent long hours perched on steep rocky hillsides or down on the softer earth of the valley floors, which always seemed to harbor biting ants. Frequently no chimps came at all; when they did they often left before he could get even a foot of film.

However, it seemed that the chimps, having very slowly got used to one white-skinned ape in the area, and having then had the chance to study a second, very similar-looking ape in the person of my sister, took a relatively short time to accept a third. And David Graybeard hastened the process. Occasionally, when he saw Hugo or me, he would leave his group and come to see whether by any chance we had a banana. The other chimps watched intently.

When David, William, and Goliath had started visiting camp I had soon discovered that they loved chewing on cloth and cardboard; sweaty garments, presumably because of their salty flavor, were the most sought after. One day, when Hugo was crouched in a small hide by a large fruiting tree, a group of chimps climbed up and began to feed. They did not, it appeared, notice him at all. Just as he was beginning to film he felt his camera being pulled away from him. For a moment he couldn't imagine what was going on. Then he saw a black hairy hand pulling at the old shirt he had wrapped around his camera to camouflage the shiny surfaces of the lenses. Of course it was David Graybeard; he had walked along the valley path behind Hugo and then, when he got level with the hide, spied the tempting material. Hugo grabbed hold of one end and engaged in a frenzied tug-of-war until the shirt finally split and David plodded off to join the group in the tree with his spoils in one hand. The other chimps had watched these proceedings with apparent interest, and after that they tolerated Hugo's filming even though during the struggle with David most of the hide had collapsed.

In fact it was only a month after he arrived before most of the chimpanzees accepted not only Hugo but also his clicking, whirring cameras—provided he kept still and did not move around. The rains once again started early, and just as the weather had consistently ruined Judy's few photographic opportunities the year before, so it was with Hugo. Day after day he had sat in his hides, the sun shining, the lighting perfect—but with no chimpanzees to film. Then a group arrived, everything

was just right, and, almost as though prearranged, it began to rain.

Nevertheless, over the weeks Hugo did get some first-rate material on chimpanzee behavior in the mountains. Also, he continued to film interactions between David, Goliath, and William in camp.

One of my problems, from the time when I first tried to tempt David and the others to the camp with bananas, had been that of the baboons. There was never a day when the troop did not pass through camp, and some of the males often remained on their own, as old Shaitani had done, in the hope that bananas would appear. One day, when David, William, and Goliath were sitting around a large pile of bananas, a particularly aggressive male baboon suddenly ran at them. William retired from the fray almost at once, his lips wobbling in his agitation, and, with the few bananas he had managed to seize, watched the ensuing battle from a safe distance. David also ran from the baboon when it first threatened him, but he then approached Goliath (who was calmly ignoring the commotion and finishing his bananas) and flung his arms around his friend. Next, as though made brave by the contact, he turned to scream and wave his arms at the baboon. Again the baboon threatened him, lunging forward, and again David rushed to embrace Goliath. This time Goliath responded; he got up, ran a few steps toward the baboon, and then leaped repeatedly into the air in an upright posture, waving his arms and uttering his fierce *waa* or threat bark. Although David Graybeard joined in, it was noticeable that he kept a few feet behind Goliath from the start. The baboon retreated, but a moment later, avoiding Goliath, it rushed to lunge and slap at David.

This happened over and over. Goliath

leaped at the baboon and the baboon, avoiding him with ease, managed each time to hit out at David, no matter how the latter tried to hide behind his friend. Eventually it was David and Goliath who retreated, leaving the baboon to grab the spoils of victory and rush off to a safer distance. Hugo managed to film the entire incident, and it remains one of the best records of an aggressive encounter between chimpanzees and baboons.

The National Geographic Society had agreed to finance Hugo's work at the Gombe Stream until the end of November so that he would be able to film the chimpanzees using tools during the termite season. I expected this to start, as in previous years, during October. Although Hugo and I daily examined different termite mounds, we saw no signs of any activity until early November. Then, when Hugo had only just over two weeks longer at the Gombe, the termites began to cooperate. One day when Hugo made his pilgrimage to his favorite nest near camp, he saw a few moist spots. He scratched away the newly sealed-over passages, poked a grass down, and to his delight felt the insects grip on. The chimpanzees perversely showed no desire to eat termites. During the following week David, William, and Goliath passed the heap frequently but never paused to examine it. Hugo grew desperate. He even led David Graybeard to the termite nest one day, walking along ahead of him with a banana in one hand, and while the chimp sat eating the fruit, offered him a strawful of clinging termites. David glanced at them and then hit the straw from Hugo's hand with a soft threat cough.

However, during Hugo's last ten days, the chimpanzees finally demonstrated their skill in tool-using and toolmaking. Hugo

was able to film and take still photographs of David, William, and Goliath working at the camp termite heap. It was exciting material, and Hugo hoped that it would help him to persuade the Geographic Society to let him return the following year and continue filming the chimpanzees.

When Hugo left at the end of November I was alone again. I still was not lonely, yet I was not as completely happy in my aloneness as I had been before he came. For I had found in Hugo a companion with whom I could share not only the joys and frustrations of my work but also my love of the chimpanzees, of the forests and mountains, of life in the wilderness. He had been with me into some of the wild, secret places where, I had thought, no other white person would ever tread. Together we had roasted in the sun and shivered under plastic covering in the rain. In Hugo I knew I had found a kindred spirit—one who had a deep appreciation and understanding of animals. Small wonder that I missed him when he was gone.

Christmas that year at the Gombe Stream was a day to remember. I bought an extra large supply of bananas and put them around a small tree I had decorated with silver paper and absorbent cotton. Goliath and William arrived together on Christmas morning and gave loud screams of excitement when they saw the huge pile of fruit. They flung their arms around one another and Goliath kept patting William on his wide-open screaming mouth while William laid one arm over Goliath's back. Finally they calmed down and began their feast, still uttering small squeaks and grunts of pleasure, somewhat muffled and sticky through their mouthfuls of banana.

David arrived much later, on his own. I sat close beside him as he ate his bananas. He seemed extra calm, and after some time I very slowly moved my hand toward his shoulder and made a grooming movement. He brushed me away—but so casually that after a moment I ventured to try again. And this time he actually allowed me to groom him for at least a minute. Then he gently pushed my hand away once more. But he had let me touch him, tolerated physical contact with a human being—and he was a fully adult male chimpanzee who had lived all of his life in the wild. It was a Christmas gift to treasure.

I had invited some of the Africans and their children for tea. At first the children were very nervous and ill-at-ease, but when I produced paper hats and balloons and a few little toys they were so excited that their reserve was soon gone and they were laughing and chasing around and thoroughly enjoying themselves. Iddi Matata, in his stately way, also was entranced by the balloons.

When the party was over I felt a need to go up to the Peak for an hour or so by myself before darkness fell. Then I hurried down to enjoy the Christmas dinner Dominic had been talking about for days. He and Hugo had planned it in minute detail, from the stuffing of the chicken to the custard sauce for the plum pudding, before Hugo left. It was dark when I returned, my mouth watering in anticipation—only to find that Dominic meanwhile had been celebrating Christmas in his own way. Laid out on my table was one unopened tin of bully beef, an empty plate, a knife, and a fork. And that was my Christmas dinner. When I asked Dominic about the chicken and all the rest of it, he only laughed uproariously and repeated many times, "Tomorrow." Then he went off, giggling weakly, to the four-gallon can of local beer which, I later heard, had been brought down by a well-wisher from Bubango, the village on the mountaintop. Dominic made up for it when he cooked the meal next day, despite his king-size hangover.

Shortly after Christmas I had to leave the Gombe Stream myself for another term at Cambridge. My last two weeks were sad, for William fell ill. His nose ran, his eyes watered, and he constantly coughed—a dry hacking cough that shook his entire body. The first day of William's illness I followed him when he left camp, because by that time I was able to move about the forests with both William and David, although Goliath still threatened me if I tried to follow him. William went a few hundred yards along the valley, climbed into a tree, and made himself a large and leafy nest. There he lay until about three in the afternoon, wheezing and coughing, and sometimes apparently dozing. Several times he actually urinated while lying in his bed— behavior so unusual that I knew he surely must be feeling very poorly. When he finally got up he fed on a few bits and pieces of leaf and vine, wandered slowly back to camp, ate a couple of bananas, and then climbed into a tree beside my tent and made another nest.

That night I stayed out since there was a moon. At about one in the morning the clouds built up and covered the moon; soon it began to rain. I was crouched some distance up the steep slope of the mountain at a slightly higher level than William's nest, and when I shone my powerful torch in his direction I could just make out his huddled figure, sitting up in his wet bed with his knees up to his chin and his arms around his legs. For the rest of the night it rained on and off, and the silences between the pattering of the raindrops were punctuated by William's hacking cough. Once at the start of a really heavy deluge William gave a few rather tremulous pant-hoots and then was silent.

When he climbed down in the morning I saw that every few moments his body shook with violent spasms of shivering. When he shivered his long slack lips wobbled, but it was no longer funny. I longed to be able to wrap a warm blanket around him and give him a steaming-hot toddy. All I could offer were a few chilly bananas.

I was with William almost constantly for a week. He spent his days in the vicinity of camp, much of the time lying in different nests. Several times he joined David or Goliath briefly, but when they moved off up the mountainside he turned back as though he couldn't face a long journey.

One morning I was sitting near William a short way up the mountain above camp when a boat arrived with some visitors from Kigoma. By now, David Graybeard's fame had spread and people sometimes came for a Sunday afternoon in the hope of seeing him. I should of course have gone down to say hello, but I had become so attuned to William that I almost felt myself the chimps' instinctive distrust of strangers. When William moved down toward the tents, I followed him; when he sat in the bushes opposite my camp, I sat beside him. Together we watched the visitors. They had coffee and chatted for some time and then, since there was no sign of David, they left. I wondered what they would have thought if they had known I was sitting there with William, peering at them as though they had been alien creatures from an unknown world.

One morning, two days before I had to leave, William stole a blanket from Dominic's tent. He had been sitting chewing on it for a while when David Graybeard arrived and, after eating some bananas, joined William at the blanket. For half an hour or so the two sat peacefully side by side, each sucking noisily and contentedly on different corners. Then William, like the clown he so often appeared to be, put part of the blanket right over his head and made groping movements with his hands as he tried to touch David from within the strange darkness he had created. David stared for a moment, and then patted William's hand. Presently the two wandered off into the forest together, leaving me with the echo of a dry hacking cough and the blanket lying on the ground. I never saw William again.

READER'S RESPONSE

How do you think you would feel if you were close to a wild animal in its natural habitat?

STUDY QUESTIONS

Recalling

1. What worries Jane Goodall when she is away from her chimpanzees?
2. Who is David Graybeard, and why does he visit the author's camp?
3. What inspires Goodall to put out the bananas?
4. What does the author learn about David Graybeard, William, and Goliath?
5. Who is Hugo, and how does Jane meet him?
6. What extraordinary experience does the author have on Christmas Day?

Interpreting

7. What skills and personality traits does one need to study animals in Africa?
8. What makes Jane Goodall's stories about the chimps unusual?

Extending

9. What is the value of studying animals in their natural habitat?

READING AND LITERARY FOCUS

Purpose and Audience

In a single day you might read a letter from a friend, an advertisement on a billboard, and a small book of poems. Each type of writing has a different purpose and audience.

The **purpose** is the author's intention in creating a particular work. A friend writes a letter to inform you of the latest news; an advertiser wants to persuade you to buy a product. A poet might have two goals—to express an idea or feeling and, perhaps, to entertain. Writers must also know their **audience,** or the specific type of people who will read their work, in order to decide how to word their ideas.

Knowing about purpose and audience helps readers decide whether a work achieves the author's goal and whether the language or style is effective.

Thinking About Purpose

1. What is Jane Goodall's purpose in writing this essay? What details suggest this?
2. Has the author achieved her goal? Explain.

Thinking About Audience

1. For what audience are these stories intended? What clues suggest this?
2. Do you think the word choice and writing style are suitable for the audience? Explain.

VOCABULARY

Sentence Completions

Each of the following items contains a blank with four possible words for completing the sentence. The words are from "The Chimps Come to Camp." Choose the word that best completes each sentence, using the word *as it is used in the selection.*

1. The sunny morning was ___ for a picnic.
   - (a) absorbent
   - (c) adolescent
   - (b) auspicious
   - (d) ramshackle
2. The chimps were ___ in their desire for bananas.
   - (a) lurid
   - (c) remote
   - (b) ousted
   - (d) avid
3. Vandals broke into the ___ house.
   - (a) vacated
   - (c) kindred
   - (b) momentous
   - (d) interminable
4. The salesperson called on the ___ that I would be home.
   - (a) exile
   - (c) assumption
   - (b) veranda
   - (d) hesitation
5. The angry child ___ at the nurse.
   - (a) glowered
   - (c) relented
   - (b) constructed
   - (d) detected

Thinking Skills: Evaluating

DEFINITION

Evaluating is a way of thinking about something and making a judgment about it. When you evaluate, you apply criteria to make your judgment. Criteria are the standards, rules, or tests on which a judgment can be based.

STEPS

1. **State the reason or purpose for your evaluation.**
   What do you want to evaluate? Why do you want to evaluate it?

2. **Identify the criteria.**
   What specific rules, tests, or standards will you use to make your judgment?

3. **Apply the criteria.**
   Does the subject of your evaluation meet each specific criterion? Does it meet some criteria better than others?

4. **Draw a conclusion.**
   The conclusion is your evaluation of how well the subject meets the criteria.

EXAMPLE

Imagine that you have just heard a speech by a candidate for class president and a friend asks you, "Do you think this candidate would be a good class president?" You probably answer "yes" or "no" without identifying all your criteria for a good class president. In your mind, however, you make an evaluation based on criteria.

1. **State the reason or purpose for your evalua-**
tion. You want to evaluate the candidate in order to give your friend an accurate answer.

2. **Identify the criteria.** You choose to evaluate the candidate according to maturity, commitment to the class, leadership, good ideas, and image.

3. **Apply the criteria.** You think that the candidate has a strong overall image and the ability to lead people. You also think that the candidate has no genuine ideas and is not mature enough to see what the class needs and stay committed to it.

4. **Draw a conclusion.** You conclude that this candidate would not be a good class president.

ACTIVITY 1
Evaluating "The Chimps Come to Camp"

Follow the four steps of evaluating to answer the question "Is 'The Chimps Come to Camp' both good science writing and a good story?" Identify your criteria carefully, being very specific about what you think makes good science writing and good storytelling. You may want to include one or more of the following criteria: an interesting topic, clear scientific observations, people you care about, and engaging style.

ACTIVITY 2
Evaluating a Work of Literature

Evaluate another selection in this book or any other work of literature that you have read. Follow the four steps. Remember that different people may have different criteria for good literature. What is important is that you think about your criteria and they reflect what you believe.

Themes

Science and Storytellers

Science is itself a kind of collaborative learning, for every scientist relies on the work of other scientists. The story of science is not one story but many stories of many people asking questions, solving problems, taking risks, and investigating possibilities.

1. **Oral Report** As a group identify and discuss several large-scale scientific endeavors that require the participation of many different types of scientist. For example, launching the space shuttle requires physicists, chemists, astronomers, engineers, and many others, each of whom is a specialist. Similarly, curing a disease or inventing a new means of communication requires a variety of specialists working together.

   Choose one scientific project, and research the different kinds of specialists needed to participate in that project. Then have each member of the group choose one kind of scientific specialist to investigate. Each member of the group should present a brief oral report on that specialist, focusing on the kind of knowledge or skill he or she would contribute and his or her specific responsibilities and role in the total project.

2. **Story Conference and Portfolio** Imagine that your group is creating a new science-fiction series for television. You need to assemble an impressive portfolio to persuade the network executives to give you the money to create a pilot for the series.

   Brainstorm to come up with an idea, a basic concept, for the show. Write down a clear description of the concept and the central characters. Then choose a title. Write out the main outline of a plot for the first show, and if you wish, name the actors you would like to play the parts. Back up your ideas with drawings or sketches of designs for the sets, costumes, and makeup. Have each member of the group take responsibility for one part of the portfolio.

Collaborative Learning:
Across the Curriculum

Science and Storytellers

1. **Literature and Art and Music: Demonstration** Advances in science over the centuries have led to significant changes in the art and music we now enjoy. For example, sculpture may now be plastic instead of marble or bronze. Music may now be electrified, and it may be composed by a computer.

   As a group prepare a demonstration for the class that shows how a scientific advance had an important effect on one of the arts—painting, sculpture, architecture, music, dance, or theater. Decide first which art you will investigate, and then research its history at a particular time. Choose, for example, ancient, medieval, or modern times. Demonstrate what the art looked or sounded like before the scientific advance; then describe the scientific advance, and demonstrate how science changed the art.

2. **Literature and Social Studies: Time Capsule** Objects can sometimes tell a story even more powerfully than words. As a group prepare a list of the contents of a time capsule to be opened one thousand years from now. Identify at least twelve items that the group agrees would tell the most about your society in your time and place.

   Include items relating to science, technology, politics, the arts, and cultural beliefs. Divide the items among the members of your group. Have each member write a brief statement about his or her items. The statement should identify the item, describe its purpose in your culture, and tell why you decided to include it.

A passage is like a journey in which something moves or changes or grows. Some passages entail travel from place to place. Such journeys may be as commonplace as a walk across the street or as exotic as a trip to a foreign country, but to the traveler they mean change and new worlds and experiences to explore.

A passage may also be an inner journey, one that takes place within one's mind or personality. These are voyages of learning and discovery. The first step on such a journey might be to get caught in a mistake, help out when a parent becomes sick, or sort out mixed feelings when a grandparent visits.

Still other passages are transitions, or changes in the shape, form, or quality of things. Frequently, this type of passage is found in nature. For example, an animal grows and changes as it matures, or days become longer and warmer as winter turns to spring.

Discover the passages in the literature you are about to read. Go along on the journeys, savor the experiences, and notice the changes.

New Road, Grant Wood, 1939.

A Model for Active Reading

Active reading is the most effective way of discovering the meaning of a work of literature. It is also the best way to enjoy reading literature. When you read actively, thinking and asking questions, you make literature your own.

Here is an example of some of the thoughts and discoveries of one active reader beginning to read a selection. The entire selection begins on the following page. Be an active reader. Discover the selection as you read it.

Charles G. Finney

The Life and Death of a Western Gladiator

This is a "life and death" story, a life cycle from beginning to end.

I know there were gladiators in ancient Rome. Is a "western" gladiator a cowboy?

He was born on a summer morning in the shady mouth of a cave. Three others were born with him, another male and two females. Each was about five inches long and slimmer than a lead pencil.

Their mother left them a few hours after they were born. A day after that his brother and sisters left him also. He was all alone. Nobody cared whether he lived or died. His tiny brain was very dull. He had no arms or legs. His skin was delicate. Nearly everything that walked on the ground or burrowed in it, that flew in the air or swam in the water or climbed trees was his enemy. But he didn't know that. He knew nothing at all. He was aware of his own existence, and that was the sum of his knowledge.

The direct rays of the sun could, in a short time, kill him. If the temperature dropped too low he would freeze. Without food he would starve. Without moisture he would die of dehydration. If a man or a horse stepped on him he would be crushed. If anything chased him he could run neither very far nor very fast.

This couldn't be a human being. Is it an insect or an animal?

He has no family, no arms, no legs, and the whole world is his enemy! Is this science fiction?

Here he seems to have all the weaknesses of a human baby.

Charles S. Finney (born 1902) grew up in Sedalia, Missouri. After studying at the University of Missouri, he enlisted in the army and was stationed in Tientsin, China. Years later he wrote a novel-length fantasy and a book of semidocumentary short stories based on his experiences in China. In 1930 Finney settled in Tucson, Arizona. He became interested in the nearby desert and took up snake catching as a hobby. This interest is reflected in the story "The Life and Death of a Western Gladiator," which has served as the basis for a television documentary.

Nearly everything that walked on the ground or burrowed in it, that flew in the air or swam in the water or climbed trees was his enemy. But he didn't know that.

Charles G. Finney

The Life and Death of a Western Gladiator

He was born on a summer morning in the shady mouth of a cave. Three others were born with him, another male and two females. Each was about five inches long and slimmer than a lead pencil.

Their mother left them a few hours after they were born. A day after that his brother and sisters left him also. He was all alone. Nobody cared whether he lived or died. His tiny brain was very dull. He had no arms or legs. His skin was delicate. Nearly everything that walked on the ground or burrowed in it, that flew in the air or swam in the water or climbed trees was his enemy. But he didn't know that. He knew nothing at all. He was aware of his own existence, and that was the sum of his knowledge.

The direct rays of the sun could, in a short time, kill him. If the temperature dropped too low he would freeze. Without food he would starve. Without moisture he would die of dehydration. If a man or a horse stepped on him he would be crushed. If anything chased him he could run neither very far nor very fast.

Thus it was at the hour of his birth. Thus it would be, with modifications, all his life.

But against these drawbacks he had certain qualifications that fitted him to be a competitive creature of this world and equipped him for its warfare. He could exist a long time without food or water. His very smallness at birth protected him when he most needed protection. Instinct provided him with what he lacked in experience. In order to eat he first had to kill; and he was eminently[1] adapted for

---

1. **eminently** [em′ə nənt lē]: outstandingly.

killing. In sacs in his jaws he secreted[2] a virulent[3] poison. To inject that poison he had two fangs, hollow and pointed. Without that poison and those fangs he would have been among the most helpless creatures on earth. With them he was among the deadliest.

He was, of course, a baby rattlesnake, a desert diamondback, named *Crotalus atrox* by the herpetologists[4] Baird and Girard and so listed in the *Catalogue of North American Reptiles* in its issue of 1853. He was grayish brown in color with a series of large dark diamond-shaped blotches on his back. His tail was white with five black crossbands. It had a button on the end of it.

Little Crotalus lay in the dust in the mouth of his cave. Some of his kinfolk lay there too. It was their home. That particular tribe of rattlers had lived there for scores of years.

The cave had never been seen by a white man.

Sometimes as many as two hundred rattlers occupied the den. Sometimes the numbers shrank to forty or fifty.

The tribe's members did nothing at all for each other except breed. They hunted singly; they never shared their food. They derived some automatic degree of safety from their numbers, but their actions were never concerted[5] toward using their numbers to any end. If an enemy attacked one of them, the others did nothing about it.

Young Crotalus's brother was the first of the litter to go out into the world and the first to die. He achieved a distance of fifty feet from the den when a Sonoran racer,[6] four feet long and hungry, came upon him. The little rattler, despite his poison fangs, was a tidbit. The racer, long skilled in such arts, snatched him up by the head and swallowed him down. Powerful digestive juices in the racer's stomach did the rest. Then the racer, appetite whetted, prowled around until it found one of Crotalus's little sisters. She went the way of the brother.

Nemesis[7] of the second sister was a chaparral cock.[8] This cuckoo, or road runner as it is called, found the baby amid some rocks, uttered a cry of delight, scissored it by the neck, shook it until it was almost lifeless, banged and pounded it upon a rock until life had indeed left it, and then gulped it down.

Crotalus, somnolent in a cranny of the cave's mouth, neither knew nor cared. Even if he had, there was nothing he could have done about it.

On the fourth day of his life he decided to go out into the world himself. He rippled forth uncertainly, the transverse[9] plates on his belly serving him as legs.

He could see things well enough within his limited range, but a five-inch-long snake can command no great field of vision. He had an excellent sense of smell. But, having no ears, he was stone-deaf. On the other hand, he had a pit, a deep pock mark between eye and nostril.

---

2. **secreted** [si krēt′id]: produced and gave off.
3. **virulent** [vir′yə lənt]: extremely harmful.
4. **herpetologists** [hur′pə tol′ə jists]: scientists who study such animals as snakes, lizards, turtles, frogs, and salamanders.
5. **concerted** [kən sur′tid]: planned or carried out by common agreement.

6. **Sonoran** [sə nôr′ən] **racer:** a type of large, fast-moving North American snake.
7. **Nemesis** [nem′ə sis]: Greek goddess of vengeance, the act of causing injury in return for an injury received; here, an opponent who cannot be overcome.
8. **chaparral** [shap′ə ral′] **cock:** a brownish, long-tailed bird.
9. **transverse** [trans vurs′]: lying so as to be crossed.

Unique, this organ was sensitive to animal heat. In pitch blackness, Crotalus, by means of the heat messages recorded in his pit, could tell whether another animal was near and could also judge its size. That was better than an ear.

The single button on his tail could not, of course, yet rattle. Crotalus wouldn't be able to rattle until that button had grown into three segments. Then he would be able to buzz.

He had a wonderful tongue. It looked like an exposed nerve and was probably exactly that. It was forked, and Crotalus thrust it in and out as he traveled. It told him things that neither his eyes nor his nose nor his pit told him.

Snake-fashion, Crotalus went forth, not knowing where he was going, for he had never been anywhere before. Hunger was probably his prime mover. In order to satisfy that hunger he had to find something smaller than himself and kill it.

He came upon a baby lizard sitting in the sand. Eyes, nose, pit, and tongue told

Crotalus it was there. Instinct told him what it was and what to do. Crotalus gave a tiny one-inch strike and bit the lizard. His poison killed it. He took it by the head and swallowed it, his first meal.

During his first two years Crotalus grew rapidly. He attained a length of two feet; his tail had five rattles on it, and its button. He rarely bothered with lizards any more, preferring baby rabbits, chipmunks, and round-tailed ground squirrels. Because of his slow locomotion he could not run down these agile little things. He had to contrive instead to be where they were when they would pass. Then he struck swiftly, injected his poison, and ate them after they died.

At two he was formidable. He had grown past the stage where a racer or a road runner could safely tackle him. He had grown to the size where other desert dwellers—coyotes, foxes, wildcats—knew it was better to leave him alone.

And, at two, Crotalus became a father, his life being regulated by cycles. His cycles were plantlike. The peach tree does not "know" when it is time to flower, but flower it does because its cycle orders it to do so.

In the same way, Crotalus did not "know" when it was time for young desert diamondback rattlers to pair off and breed. But his cycle knew.

He found "her" on a rainy morning. Of that union six new rattlesnakes were born. Thus Crotalus, at two, had carried out his major primary function: he had reproduced his kind. In two years he had experienced everything that was reasonably possible for desert diamondback rattle-snakes to experience except death.

He had not experienced death for the simple reason that there had never been an opportunity for anything bigger and stronger than himself to kill. Now, at two, because he was so formidable, that oppor-tunity became more and more unlikely.

He grew more slowly in the years fol-lowing his initial spurt. At the age of twelve he was five feet long. Few of the rattlers in his den were older or larger than he.

He had a castanet[10] of fourteen seg-ments. It had been broken off occasionally in the past, but with each new molting[11] a new segment appeared.

His first skin-shedding back in his babyhood had been a bewildering experi-ence. He did not know what was happen-ing. His eyes clouded over until he could not see. His skin thickened and dried un-til it cracked in places. His pit and his nostrils ceased to function. There was only one thing to do and that was to get out of that skin.

Crotalus managed it by nosing against the bark of a shrub until he forced the old skin down over his head, bunching it like the rolled top of a stocking around the neck. Then he pushed around among rocks and sticks and branches, literally crawling out of his skin by slow degrees. Wriggling free at last, he looked like a brand new snake. His skin was bright and satiny, his eyes and nostrils were clear, his pit sang with sensation.

For the rest of his life he was to molt three or four times a year. Each time he did it he felt as if he had been born again.

At twelve he was a magnificent reptile. Not a single scar defaced his rippling sym-metry. He was diabolically[12] beautiful and deadly poisonous.

His venom was his only weapon, for he had no power of constriction.[13] Yellowish in color, his poison was odorless and tasteless. It was a highly complex mixture of proteins, each in itself direly toxic. His venom worked on the blood. The more poison he injected with a bite, the more dangerous the wound. The pain rendered by his bite was instantaneous, and the shock accompanying it was profound. Swelling began immediately, to be followed by a ghastly oozing. Injected directly into a large vein, his poison brought death quickly, for the victim died when it reached his heart.

---

10. **castanet** [kas′tə net′]: small rhythm instrument held in the hand and clicked, especially to accom-pany certain Spanish music; here, the snake's rattler, a series of rings at the end of the tail that rattle when shaken.
11. **molting** [mōl′ting]: the shedding of an outer covering, such as hair, skin, shell, or feathers, prior to its replacement by new growth.

12. **diabolically** [dī′ə bol′i kə lē]: wickedly.
13. **constriction** [kən strik′shən]: the act of squeez-ing or binding.

At the age of twenty Crotalus was the oldest and largest rattler in his den. He was six feet long and weighed thirteen pounds. His whole world was only a mile in radius. He had fixed places where he avoided the sun when it was hot and he was away from his cave. He knew his hunting grounds thoroughly, every game trail, every animal burrow.

He was a fine old machine, perfectly adapted to his surroundings, accustomed to a life of leisure and comfort. He dominated his little world.

The mighty seasonal rhythms of the desert were as vast pulsations, and the lives of the rattlesnakes were attuned[14] to them. Spring sun beat down, spring rains fell, and, as the plants of the desert ended their winter hibernations, so did the vipers[15] in their lair. The plants opened forth and budded; the den "opened," too, and the snakes crawled forth. The plants fertilized each other, and new plants were born. The snakes bred, and new snakes were produced. The desert was repopulated.

In the autumn the plants began to close; in the same fashion the snake den began to close, the reptiles returned to it, lay like lingering blossoms about its entrance for a while, then disappeared within it when winter came. There they slept until summoned forth by a new spring.

Crotalus was twenty years old. He was in the golden age of his viperhood.

But men were approaching. Spilling out of their cities, men were settling in that part of the desert where Crotalus lived. They built roads and houses, set up fences, dug for water, planted crops.

They homesteaded the land. They brought new animals with them—cows, horses, dogs, cats, barnyard fowl.

The roads they built were death traps for the desert dwellers. Every morning new dead bodies lay on the roads, the bodies of the things the men had run over and crushed in their vehicles.

That summer Crotalus met his first dog. It was a German shepherd which had been reared on a farm in the Midwest and there had gained a reputation of being a snakekiller. Black snakes, garter snakes, pilots, water snakes; it delighted in killing them all. It would seize them by the middle, heedless of their tiny teeth, and shake them violently until they died.

This dog met Crotalus face to face in the desert at dusk. Crotalus had seen coyotes aplenty and feared them not. Neither did the dog fear Crotalus, although Crotalus then was six feet long, as thick in the middle as a motorcycle tire, and had a head the size of a man's clenched fist. Also this snake buzzed and buzzed and buzzed.

The dog was brave, and the snake was a snake. The German shepherd snarled and attacked. Crotalus struck him in the underjaw; his fangs sank in almost half an inch and squirted big blobs of hemotoxic[16] poison into the tissues of the dog's flesh.

The shepherd bellowed with pain, backed off, groveled with his jaws in the desert sand, and attacked again. He seized Crotalus somewhere by the middle of his

---

14. **attuned** [ə tŏŏnd]: brought into harmony.
15. **vipers** [vī′pərz]: members of a large group of poisonous snakes, including the rattlesnake, having pairs of sharp, hollow fangs with which they inject venom.

16. **hemotoxic** [hē′mə tok′sik]: containing poisonous substances that can destroy red blood cells.

body and tried to flip him in the air and shake him as, in the past, he had shaken slender black snakes to their death. In return, he received another poison-blurting stab in his flank and a third in the belly and a fourth in the eye as the terrible, writhing snake bit wherever it could sink its fangs.

The German shepherd had enough. He dropped the big snake and in sick, agonizing bewilderment crawled somehow back to his master's homestead and died.

The homesteader looked at his dead dog and became alarmed. If there was a snake around big enough to kill a dog that size, it could also kill a child and probably a man. It was something that had to be eliminated.

The homesteader told his fellow farmers, and they agreed to initiate a war of extermination against the snakes.

The campaign during the summer was sporadic.[17] The snakes were scattered over the desert, and it was only by chance that the men came upon them. Even so, at summer's end, twenty-six of the vipers had been killed.

When autumn came the men decided to look for the rattlers' den and execute mass slaughter. The homesteaders had become desert-wise and knew what to look for.

They found Crotalus's lair without too much trouble—a rock outcropping on a slope that faced the south. Cast-off skins were in evidence in the bushes. Bees flew idly in and out of the den's mouth. Convenient benches and shelves of rock were at hand where the snakes might lie for a final sunning in the autumn air.

They killed the three rattlers they found at the den when they first discovered it. They made plans to return in a few more days when more of the snakes had congregated. They decided to bring along dynamite with them and blow up the mouth of the den so the snakes within would be sealed there forever and the snakes without would have no place to find refuge.

On the day the men chose to return nearly fifty desert diamondbacks were gathered at the portals of the cave. The men shot them, clubbed them, smashed them with rocks. Some of the rattlers escaped and crawled into the den.

Crotalus had not yet arrived for the autumn rendezvous.[18] He came that night. The den's mouth was a shattered mass of rock, for the men had done their dynamiting well. Dead members of his tribe lay everywhere. Crotalus nosed among them, tongue flicking as he slid slowly along.

There was no access to the cave any more. He spent the night outside among the dead. The morning sun warmed him and awakened him. He lay there at full length. He had no place to go.

The sun grew hotter upon him and instinctively he began to slide toward some dark shade. Then his senses warned him of some animal presence nearby; he stopped, half coiled, raised his head, and began to rattle. He saw two upright figures. He did not know what they were because he had never seen men before.

"That's the granddaddy of them all," said one of the homesteaders. "It's a good thing we came back." He raised his shotgun.

---

17. **sporadic** [spə rad′ik]: scattered; occasional.

18. **rendezvous** [rän′də vōō′]: appointment to meet at a fixed time and place.

READER'S RESPONSE

Did Crotalus live a successful life? Explain your answer.

STUDY QUESTIONS

Recalling

1. List some of the dangers the young Crotalus faces.
2. What experiences has Crotalus had by age two?
3. What is Crotalus like at age twenty?
4. What happens to the snakes in the den after Crotalus' battle with the German shepherd? What happens to Crotalus?

Interpreting

5. What general impression of nature does Finney create in this story?
6. What does the title suggest about the author's feelings for Crotalus?
7. In what ways is a rattlesnake's life like a human life? How are they different?

Extending

8. How did this selection make you feel about snakes?

READING AND LITERARY FOCUS

Theme

The **theme** is the main idea of a story. You can discover a story's theme by thinking about the elements the writer uses to create the story.

You can discover a story's theme by thinking about the elements the writer uses to create the story. Think about the title, characters, plot, and setting. These questions will help you:

- What do the characters' traits and the changes that the characters undergo suggest about life in general?
- Do details in the setting suggest ideas about the natural or the human world?

- What is the story's main conflict? What ideas about life does the conflict suggest?
- What ideas about life does the title suggest?

Thinking About Theme

State the theme of "The Life and Death of a Western Gladiator" in a sentence.

VOCABULARY

Word Origins

Use a dictionary to find the Latin origins of these words from "The Life and Death of a Western Gladiator." Carefully copy the original Latin words and their meanings. This information can usually be found in parentheses or brackets just after the pronunciation of the entry word or at the end of the definitions.

1. inject
2. virulent
3. transverse
4. regulate
5. constriction
6. extermination

COMPOSITION

Writing an Opinion

Write a paragraph expressing your opinion of the way in which "The Life and Death of a Western Gladiator" ends. Discuss whether Crotalus' death follows the laws of nature as the author presents them. **Prewriting:** Skim the story, and take notes to record Finney's ideas about death and nature. **Writing:** Begin your paragraph by stating your opinion. Use details from your notes to support it. **Revising:** When you are finished, review your paragraph to see that you have expressed your ideas clearly and logically.

Writing a Poem

Write a poem about Crotalus. You may want to describe his beauty, his success as a hunter, or his remarkable adaptations to desert life. You may choose words that suggest his strength and power or words that echo the sounds he makes when he hisses or rattles.

"It's not easy writing four books a year," says Robert Newton Peck (born 1928), "but it sure beats killing hogs." Peck, author of the popular *Day No Pigs Would Die*, grew up on a farm in Vermont and now lives and writes in Florida. He says, "Socially, I am about as sophisticated as a turnip. I play ragtime piano (can't read a note), sing in a barbershop quartet, and have a speaking voice with a Vermont twang that is often akin to a Southern drawl." Peck, who now also writes for the stage and television, explains that his "respect for living creatures led to *Path of Hunters*, which examines the poetic yet brutal life-and-death struggle for survival among small animals in a meadow."

Somewhere out on the meadow, a crow barked. . . . The smaller creatures in the meadow froze at the cry of the crow. They read its meaning, as did the terrier.

Robert Newton Peck

from **Path of Hunters**

Winter softened into spring. The sun swelled big and strong, and the earth opened to be loved. April was aloof[1] and running.

The terrier was a year older and no longer a pup. Barking less and smelling more, his soft brown eyes saw much that interested him, but little that alarmed him. No longer did he hunt by thrashing through the thickets of wild grape, but instead he measured each step with care. He had learned to hunt with little sound and little motion.

He made less racket, and with this quiet came a more mature bravery. He could wade into the pond and wait patiently for the riled-up black muck to settle before lapping the cool water, yet he respected true danger, such as the big snapping turtle, who would enjoy making a meal of his paw.

It was almost dawn, which made him stretch. He was anxious to be up and about, ready to start a new day. It was at this very moment that his ears snapped up and alert. Somewhere out on the meadow, a crow barked. It was not the crow's usual *caw caw caw;* this was different, a single stinging yap—a warning to all other animals that a predator was afoot or aloft. No matter which predator, from hawk to stoat, the crow felt it his duty to bark an alarm.

For a minute, all was still. The smaller creatures in the meadow froze at the cry of the crow. They read its meaning, as did the terrier. Those who could move

---

1. **aloof** [ə lo͞of′]: at a distance.

quickly dived into their burrows beneath the earth. Smaller ones scurried through their tunnels in the timothy.[2] The only sound that the dog heard came from high in the willow tree, the chirp of an early rising whitecrown sparrow or skunkbird.[3] He was the first to snap the spell of fear.

Across the back lawn and past the toolshed, the dog trotted down toward the meadow. If something big enough to alarm the old black crow was afoot, the dog wanted to learn more.

Lowering his nose to the ground, he smelled a bud of butterfly weed, starting to push its tiny stalk up through the sandy soil. Only minutes earlier, a small, gray meadow-mouse had urinated on the butterfly bud, but the dog reacted without interest to the faint, acidy smell.

Scratching the dirt with his paw, the dog dislodged a rock from its nest in the earth and discovered a sleeping salamander. Snout to tail, she was ten inches long, a very dark green with egg-yolk spots smaller than a dime. Her legs were delicate, showing that the salamander was a female.

She had wintered under the rock and was not yet awake. In the dark flesh of her rubbery side there was a deep depression, like a dent, where the stone's weight had pressed against her all winter. To the gentle nudge of his nose, she was cold and stiff to touch, even when he softly tapped her once with a careful paw. He let her sleep.

Moving through the dogbane,[4] a tiny note or two of music made him stop. It seemed to come from the dunes near a juniper bush. The call was one very short blast and then a longer, climbing whistle, the call of the male bobwhite. The little quail was lonely and he wanted a mate. Chasing the whistle with his ear, the dog saw the bobwhite quail working on his nest deep in the timothy turned tawny by winter. The nest was complete, but the little quail was trying to make it even more soft and inviting. Hearing his note, a female would soon come to inspect it, and finding it to her liking (as well as its maker), she would stay.

The curious dog was about to move in when a stronger smell caught his attention—raccoon droppings. Late last night, he'd heard the snorting of two male coons, bluffing a fight over a female or over a territory—most probably the latter, since in the meadow, land was more prized than love. In a few weeks, softer sounds would be heard at the mouth of their den—the gentle purring made by the female coon to her kits.[5]

The terrier had also heard the bark of a flying squirrel, on the way to his store of hickory nuts. Perhaps he might see her, as he had seen one last summer, carrying a fresh-picked bell of wild morning-glory[6] to decorate her nest high up in the sweet gum tree. There she might be nursing up to eight young, lined up as tiny soldiers in two perfect rows to suck the eight teats that were buried in her belly fur.

The old black crow was right. A large hunter was indeed prowling in the

---

2. **timothy:** tall grass having smooth, hollow stems with thick, spiky clusters of tiny flowers at the tips.
3. **skunkbird:** type of American bird.
4. **dogbane:** any of various plants, thought to be poisonous to dogs, having clusters of small, white or pink bell-shaped flowers.

---

5. **kits:** young fur-bearing animals.
6. **morning-glory:** trumpet-shaped flower of a large group of vines, shrubs, or trees.

meadow. Tiny pawprints had been made very recently in the soft earth, pawprints much smaller than the large ones of the mature terrier—the tracks of a red fox.

He walked with a slight stiffness in his left rear leg. Normally a fox walks as if he were two-legged, his hind feet stepping exactly into his front pawprints. This fox walked smartly on the right side, but the left side of his track was out of register, making the left print a hair larger than the right. The tracks in the mud were fresh. One print sank deep into the ground, and was now (as the terrier sniffed at it) slowly filling with water.

No longer could the lame old fox catch bobwhite quail or rabbits. Now he was a stalker of mating fieldmice, a digger of turtle eggs. But the wise black crow judged him to be a fox nonetheless, ten pounds of trouble and an enemy to warrant a warning caw.

The dog tracked the fox through the meadow to high ground. Here he spotted a modest pothole in the leaves, where the red fox had been so hungry he had unearthed a butternut.[7] Bending close, the dog sniffed at some small leaflets that had begun to push up into the sunlight, tiny green hearts that would later flower out into purple violets.

Farther along, the tread of the crippled fox dived into a thicket of blackberry bushes. A sharp thorn still held a tuft of red fur, which whitened with every cool puff of morning wind. A strong gust suddenly tore it loose, and it wafted away.

Beyond the thicket, the fox tracks stopped at a crack between two rocks, where he had hoped a blacksnake might yet be asleep. As the dog tested the mossy crack cautiously, a damselfly[8] darted out. Making a slight hum with her wings, she flew close. He raised his ears for an instant but did not bark; his nose was busy with red fox now, and a damselfly was dull by comparison.

Closer to the pond the earth was wetter, and the tracks of the fox sank deep into ground fresh with rain. Here and there, humps of meadow grass whiskered up from the mud, and in one of them had been a rabbit's nest. But now the doe was gone. She had borne her fawns here, yet only a few bones and some hair remained. Some bird tracks in the earth suggested that maybe the litter of young cottontails had been eaten by bluejays, or even by the black crow who had sounded the fox alarm. Smelling the nest, the dog felt no souvenir of warmth.

At water's edge, the still-wet shells of a pair of crayfish[9] were lying on a flat rock. The fox had eaten, but a crayfish or two had been too modest a breakfast to heal the hurt in his belly. Possibly he had arrived too late for more than a bite of tender rabbit fawn, and as the old fox circled the pond he was still nearly empty. Walking probably hurt him—his footprints seemed to show a greater separation, indicating that he was now limping more. Yet he kept moving; the pain of hunger in his belly kept him going, and there would be no rest, no sleep, until somehow he made a kill. Despite the torture of each

---

7. **butternut:** large, oily nut from a tree of the walnut family.

8. **damselfly** [dam′zəl flī′]: any of a group of brightly colored insects with slender bodies.
9. **crayfish** [crā′fish′]: any of several animals resembling the lobster but smaller in size found in fresh water and valued as a food source.

Dog on a Log, Winslow Homer, watercolor, 1889.

step, the hunter would still hunt. The fox was old or lame, possibly even both, but he was no quitter. He asked welfare of no one.

A few steps farther along, the dog could tell that the red fox had seen something. The tracks were slower, sinking deeper. He had stopped, waited, and then dashed headlong into a juniper bush. But there the dog found nothing, only a bent grouse[10] feather lying nearby which told the story. The jaws of the fox had opened as he leaped, only to snap shut on nothing more than the tip of a wing feather. With a great drumming of wings, the partridge had roared away to safety, leaving behind only a broken feather, and a fox with an empty mouth, and an emptier belly. The crippled fox watched the grouse

flap up and away, and all he could do was spit out a feather. His tracks went on.

As the dog stood in a clump of ferns, still laced with morning dew, he was bent on stalking the old fox. He had yet to catch one, or even run one down, and the idea of such pursuit pleased him.

It was then he heard it, the sound he heard each day—the whistle that meant more to him than any hunt or wild instinct. Bounding through the rain-soaked laurel bushes, water streaming from his flanks, he headed for the sound, running toward the whistle of his young master. As he ran he could see the boy. Ears back, he raced toward the small figure at the far end of the meadow that was waving to him under the yellow sky of morning.

His teeth chattered in the anticipation of their meeting. The day had come, and it felt good to have someone to love.

And he had the boy.

---

10. **grouse** [grous]: game bird, a bird hunted for sport or food.

READER'S RESPONSE

If the dog had found the fox, do you think he would have caught it? Give reasons to support your answer.

STUDY QUESTIONS

Recalling
1. What special alert starts the young terrier on his early-morning hunt?
2. What do the fox's paw prints reveal about him?
3. What clues tell the terrier that the fox is still hungry?

4. What means more to the terrier than "any hunt or wild instinct"?

Interpreting
5. Which senses provide most of the information the dog needs?
6. In your opinion, does the author present a realistic picture of the way a dog thinks? Why, or why not?
7. In what way is the dog's hunting different from that of the fox?

Extending
8. How can the close observance of natural details enrich your life?

On Point, D. G. Stouter, c. 1840.

Thinking Skills: Classifying

DEFINITION

Classifying is a way of thinking about things by sorting them into groups. We classify things all the time just to be able to talk about them more easily. For example, we group all of the thousands of different kinds of buildings for human habitation into one class. We call that class houses.

Classifying things often makes it easier to see relationships between them. It is a way of thinking that can help you understand literature and speak and write more clearly about it.

STEPS

1. **Identify the things to be classified.**

2. **Identify the classes or groups into which the things are to be sorted.**
   Keep in mind that each group has one or more qualities that make it different from any other group.

3. **Sort each thing into a class or group based on the qualities each thing possesses.**

4. **Make a statement based on the groupings.**

EXAMPLE

Imagine that you are asked to write a report on cars. With such a broad topic, you need to group cars in some way in order to be able to think clearly about them.

1. **Identify the things to be classified.** You make a list of many different cars.

2. **Identify the classes or groups into which the** things are to be sorted. You think about the list and notice that there are family cars, sports cars, and luxury cars. You decide that those three classes will give you a way to begin to organize your thinking.

3. **Sort each thing into a class or group based on the qualities each thing possesses.** You assign each car to one class based on whether it is a family car, a sports car, or a luxury car.

4. **Make a statement based on the groupings.** Your statement may be a simple, descriptive one: "A car may be a family car, a sports car, or a luxury car." You may choose instead to make an observation about the groups: "There are many more kinds of family cars than there are kinds of luxury cars."

ACTIVITY 1

Follow the four steps of classifying to organize the actions of the animals in "Path of Hunters." Let your classes be "actions that harm other animals," "actions that help other animals," and "actions that do not affect other animals." Develop a statement that says something about the nature of animal life in the meadow.

ACTIVITY 2

Follow the four steps of classifying to organize information from any other literary selection in this book. You may wish to focus on characters, settings, conflicts, events, or any specific kind of details in a selection, such as sounds or animals or colors. Remember to make your classes clearly different from one another.

Cynthia Rylant (born 1954) lived with her grandparents from the ages of four to eight. She says, "I grew up in West Virginia and what happened to me there deeply affects what I write. . . . Like most Southerners, [my grandparents] kept their emotions tight to themselves, neither showing great anger or great sorrow or immense joy. . . . They lived life with strength, great calm, and a real sense of what it means to be devoted to and responsible for other people. The tone of my work reflects the way they spoke, the simplicity of their language, and, I hope, the depth of their own hearts." In 1985 *Every Living Thing*, which includes the short story "Papa's Parrot," was named a Children's Book of the Year by the Child Study Association of America.

Sometimes we must go on difficult or confusing journeys to understand the people we love.

Cynthia Rylant

Papa's Parrot

Though his father was fat and merely owned a candy and nut shop, Harry Tillian liked his papa. Harry stopped liking candy and nuts when he was around seven, but, in spite of this, he and Mr. Tillian had remained friends and were still friends the year Harry turned twelve.

For years, after school, Harry had always stopped in to see his father at work. Many of Harry's friends stopped there, too, to spend a few cents choosing penny candy from the giant bins or to sample Mr. Tillian's latest batch of roasted peanuts. Mr. Tillian looked forward to seeing his son and his son's friends every day. He liked the company.

When Harry entered junior high school, though, he didn't come by the candy and nut shop as often. Nor did his friends. They were older and they had more spending money. They went to a burger place. They played video games. They shopped for records. None of them were much interested in candy and nuts anymore.

A new group of children came to Mr. Tillian's shop now. But not Harry Tillian and his friends.

The year Harry turned twelve was also the year Mr. Tillian got a parrot. He went to a pet store one day and bought one for more money than he could really afford. He brought the parrot to his shop, set its cage near the sign for maple clusters and named it Rocky.

Harry thought this was the strangest thing his father had ever done, and

Early Sunday Morning,
Edward Hopper, 1930.

he told him so, but Mr. Tillian just ignored him.

Rocky was good company for Mr. Tillian. When business was slow, Mr. Tillian would turn on a small color television he had sitting in a corner, and he and Rocky would watch the soap operas. Rocky liked to scream when the romantic music came on, and Mr. Tillian would yell at him to shut up, but they seemed to enjoy themselves.

The more Mr. Tillian grew to like his parrot, and the more he talked to it instead of to people, the more embarrassed Harry became. Harry would stroll past the shop, on his way somewhere else, and he'd take a quick look inside to see what his dad was doing. Mr. Tillian was always talking to the bird. So Harry kept walking.

At home things were different. Harry and his father joked with each other at the dinner table as they always had—Mr. Tillian teasing Harry about his smelly socks; Harry teasing Mr. Tillian about his blubbery stomach. At home things seemed all right.

But one day, Mr. Tillian became ill. He had been at work, unpacking boxes of caramels, when he had grabbed his chest and fallen over on top of the candy. A customer had found him, and he was taken to the hospital in an ambulance.

Mr. Tillian couldn't leave the hospital. He lay in bed, tubes in his arms, and he worried about his shop. New shipments of candy and nuts would be arriving. Rocky would be hungry. Who would take care of things?

Harry said he would. Harry told his father that he would go to the store every day after school and unpack boxes. He would sort out all the candy and nuts. He would even feed Rocky.

So, the next morning, while Mr. Tillian lay in his hospital bed, Harry took the shop key to school with him. After school he left his friends and walked to the

Papa's Parrot   455

empty shop alone. In all the days of his life, Harry had never seen the shop closed after school. Harry didn't even remember what the CLOSED sign looked like. The key stuck in the lock three times, and inside he had to search all the walls for the light switch.

The shop was as his father had left it. Even the caramels were still spilled on the floor. Harry bent down and picked them up one by one, dropping them back in the boxes. The bird in its cage watched him silently.

Harry opened the new boxes his father hadn't gotten to. Peppermints. Jawbreakers. Toffee creams. Strawberry kisses. Harry traveled from bin to bin, putting the candies where they belonged.

"Hello!"

Harry jumped, spilling a box of jawbreakers.

"Hello, Rocky!"

Harry stared at the parrot. He had forgotten it was there. The bird had been so quiet, and Harry had been thinking only of the candy.

"Hello," Harry said.

"Hello, Rocky!" answered the parrot.

Harry walked slowly over to the cage. The parrot's food cup was empty. Its water was dirty. The bottom of the cage was a mess.

Harry carried the cage into the back room.

"Hello, Rocky!"

"Is that all you can say, you dumb bird?" Harry mumbled. The bird said nothing else.

Harry cleaned the bottom of the cage, refilled the food and water cups, then put the cage back in its place and resumed sorting the candy.

"Where's Harry?"

Harry looked up.

"Where's Harry?"

Harry stared at the parrot.

"Where's Harry?"

Chills ran down Harry's back. What could the bird mean? It was like something from "The Twilight Zone."[1]

"Where's Harry?"

Harry swallowed and said, "I'm here. I'm here, you stupid bird."

"You stupid bird!" said the parrot.

Well, at least he's got one thing straight, thought Harry.

"Miss him! Miss him! Where's Harry? You stupid bird!"

Harry stood with a handful of peppermints.

What? he asked.

"Where's Harry?" said the parrot.

"I'm *here*, you stupid bird! I'm here!" Harry yelled. He threw the peppermints at the cage, and the bird screamed and clung to its perch.

Harry sobbed, "I'm here." The tears were coming.

Harry leaned over the glass counter.

"Papa." Harry buried his face in his arms.

"Where's Harry?" repeated the bird.

Harry sighed and wiped his face on his sleeve. He watched the parrot. He understood now: someone had been saying, for a long time, "Where's Harry? Miss him."

Harry finished his unpacking, then swept the floor of the shop. He checked the furnace so the bird wouldn't get cold. Then he left to go visit his papa.

---

1. **"The Twilight Zone":** television series, originally broadcast between 1959 and 1964, featuring a mixture of science fiction, fantasy, horror, and comedy.

READER'S RESPONSE

How do you think Harry feels at the end of the story? Explain.

STUDY QUESTIONS

Recalling

1. When Harry was in the elementary grades, what did he do every day after school?
2. In what ways does life at the store change for Mr. Tillian when Harry goes to junior high school?
3. When Harry is twelve, what does his father buy and bring into the store?
4. Why does Harry go alone to his father's store one day?
5. What does Rocky repeatedly ask Harry that afternoon? What does Harry suddenly realize?

Interpreting

6. Why do you think Harry's father does not tell Harry what he really feels?
7. In what way does Harry grow up a little on the afternoon that he goes alone to his father's store?

Extending

8. Why do you think pets sometimes become important to people?

COMPOSITION

Writing About Theme

Write a paragraph explaining how the events in "Papa's Parrot" help you understand the story's theme. **Prewriting:** Decide what you think is the theme of the story. **Writing:** Begin by stating the theme in a complete sentence. Then describe the events in the plot, and explain how they fit together to suggest the theme. **Revising:** Review your paragraph to see that you have expressed your ideas clearly and logically. Review for effective word choice and organization. Make sure that your final copy is free of errors in grammar, spelling, and punctuation.

Writing a Diary Entry

Imagine that you are Harry. Write a page in your diary about what you learned on the afternoon that you spent alone in the store. Choose vivid words to express Harry's thoughts and emotions. Try to capture the reactions that Harry would have been likely to have.

photograph ©1990 Jill Krementz

As a child in Auburn, New York, Marijane Meaker (born 1927) wanted only to be a writer. "I was always writing something," she has said, "wanting to tell my own story." She loved the idea of using a pen name and invented several for herself. She is best known as M. E. Kerr. At age twenty-three she moved to New York City, where she worked and wrote short stories in her spare time. After years of seeing her stories rejected, Kerr finally sold a story to a magazine. Since then she has written many popular books. "Where Are You Now, William Shakespeare?" is taken from Kerr's autobiography, in which she describes her responses to the challenges of growing up.

Dorothy Spencer and I went on happily playing house, until the movie _Brother Rat_ came to town. That was when we both fell in love with the movie star Ronald Reagan.

M. E. Kerr

Where Are You Now, William Shakespeare?

My very first boyfriend was named William Shakespeare. This was his real name, and he lived over on Highland Hill, about a block from my house.

Billy Shakespeare didn't call at seven for dates, or suffer my father's inspection, or give me a silver identification bracelet.[1] We didn't have a song, either.

I often went to his house to get him, or I met him down in the empty lot on Alden Avenue, or over at Hoopes Park, where we caught sunfish and brought them from the pond in bottles of murky water with polliwogs.

Marijane is ten [my father wrote in his journal]. _She plays with boys and looks like one._

This was true.

My arms and knees were full of scabs from falls out of trees and off my bicycle. I was happiest wearing the pants my brother'd grown out of, the vest to one of my father's business suits over one of my brother's old shirts, Indian moccasins, and a cap. Everything I said came out of the side of my mouth, and I strolled around with my fists inside my trouser pockets.

This did not faze Billy Shakespeare, whose eyes lit up when he saw me coming, and who readily agreed that when we married we'd name our first son Ellis, after my father, and not William after him.

---

1. **silver identification bracelet:** bracelet with the owner's name engraved in it; sometimes given by a boy to the girl he is dating steadily.

"Because William Shakespeare is a funny name," I'd say.

"It isn't funny. It's just that there's a famous writer with the same name," he'd say.

"Do you agree to Ellis Shakespeare then?"

"Sure, if it's all right with your father."

"He'll be pleased," I'd tell Billy.

Around this time, I was always trying to think of ways to please my father. (The simplest way would have been to wear a dress and a big hair ribbon, stay out of trees, stop talking out of the side of my mouth, and act like a girl . . . but I couldn't have endured such misery even for him.)

Billy Shakespeare accepted the fact, early in our relationship, that my father was my hero. He protested only slightly when I insisted that the reason my father wasn't President of the United States was that my father didn't want to be.

That was what my father told me, when I'd ask him why he wasn't President. I'd look at him across the table at dinner, and think, He knows more than anybody knows, he's handsome, and he always gets things done—so he ought to be President. If he was, I'd think, there'd be no problems in the world.

Sometimes I'd ask him: "Daddy, why aren't you President of the United States?"

His answer was always the same.

"I wouldn't want that job for anything. We couldn't take a walk without Secret Service[2] men following us. Do you think we could go up to the lake for a swim by ourselves? No. There'd be Secret Service men tagging along. It'd ruin our lives. It'd end our privacy. Would you want that?"

Billy Shakespeare would say, "He's not President because nobody elected him President."

"He won't let anyone elect him," I'd answer. "He doesn't want Secret Service men around all the time."

"I'm not sure he could *get* elected," Billy would venture.

"He could get elected," I'd tell Billy. "He doesn't want to! We like our privacy!"

"Okay." Billy'd give in a little. "But he never tried getting elected, so he really doesn't know if he could."

I'd wave that idea away with my dirty hands. "Don't worry. He'd be elected in a minute if he wanted to be. You don't know *him*."

Billy Shakespeare's other rivals for my attention were movie stars. I'd write Clark Gable and Henry Fonda and Errol Flynn, and they'd send back glossy photos of themselves and sometimes letters, too.

These photographs and letters were thumbtacked to the fiberboard walls of a playhouse my father'd had built for me in our back yard.

When I did play with a girl, the game was always the same: getting dinner ready for our husbands. I had an old set of dishes back in the playhouse, and my girl friend and I played setting the table for dinner. During this game, Billy Shakespeare was forgotten. When my husband came through the playhouse door, he would be one of the movie stars pinned to the wall.

I played this game with Dorothy Spencer, who lived behind our house.

She was a tall redhead who looked like a girl, and who always had it in her head

---

2. **Secret Service:** division of the United States Treasury Department that protects the President and his family.

to fix meat loaf with mashed potatoes for a movie star named Spencer Tracy.

I changed around a lot—the menu as well as the movie star—but Dorothy stuck to meat loaf with mashed for Spencer.

I'd be saying, "Well, Clark is a little late tonight and the turkey is going to be overdone," or "Gee, Henry isn't here yet and the ham is going to be dried up." But Dorothy would persist with "Spencer's going to love this meat loaf when he gets here. I'll wait until I hear his footsteps to mash the potatoes."

Billy Shakespeare was jealous of this game and tried his best to ruin it with reality.

He'd say, "What are two famous movie stars doing living in the same house?"

He'd say, "How come famous movie stars only have a one-room house with no kitchen?"

But Dorothy Spencer and I went on happily playing house, until the movie *Brother Rat* came to town.

That was when we both fell in love with the movie star Ronald Reagan.

Suddenly we were both setting the table for the same movie star—different menus, but the same husband.

"You've always stuck to meat loaf and mashed for Spencer!" I said angrily. "Now you want my Ronald!"

"He's not *your* Ronald," she said.

"It's my playhouse, though," I reminded her.

"But I won't play if I can't have Ronald," she said.

"We both can't have Ronald!" I insisted.

We took the argument to her mother, who told us to pretend Ronald Reagan was twins. Then we could both have him.

"He isn't twins, though," Dorothy said.

"And if he is," I put in, "I want the real Ronald, and not his twin."

Our game came to a halt, but our rivalry did not. Both of us had written to Ronald Reagan and were waiting for his reply.

"No matter what he writes her," I told Billy Shakespeare, "my letter from him will be better."

"You might not even get a letter," Billy said. "She might not get one either."

"She might not get one," I said, "but I will."

"You don't know that," Billy said.

"Do you want to know why I know I'll get one?" I asked him.

I made him cross his heart and hope to die if he told anyone what I'd done.

Billy was a skinny little kid with big eyes that always got bigger when I was about to confess to him something I'd done.

"Crossmyheartandhopetodie," he said very fast. "What'd you do?"

"You know that Ronald Reagan isn't like any of the others," I said.

"Because Dorothy Spencer likes him, too."

"That's got nothing to do with it!" I said. "He's just different. I never felt this way about another movie star."

"Why?"

"*Why?* I don't know why! That's the way love is."

"Love?" Billy said.

"Yes. What did you think made me write him that I was a crippled child, and had to go to see him in a wheelchair?"

"Oh migosh!" Billy exclaimed. "Oh migosh!"

"I had to get his attention somehow."

"Oh migosh!"

"Just shut up about it!" I warned him. "If word gets out I'll know it's you."

Dorothy Spencer was the first to hear from Ronald Reagan. She didn't get a letter, but she got a signed photograph.

"Since I heard from him first," she said, "he's my husband."

"Not in my playhouse!" I said.

"He wrote me back first," she said.

"Just wait," I said.

"I don't have to wait," she said. "I'm setting the table for him in my own house."

"It's not even your house, it's your father's," I said. "At least when he's married to me, we'll have our own house."

"He's married to me now," she said.

"We'll see about that," I said.

I was beginning to get a panicky feeling as time passed and no mail came from Ronald Reagan. You'd think he'd write back to a crippled child first. . . . Meanwhile Dorothy was fixing him meat loaf and mashed at her place.

I had pictures of him cut out of movie magazines scotch-taped to my bedroom walls. I went to sleep thinking about him, wondering why he didn't care enough to answer me.

The letter and photograph from Ronald Reagan arrived on a Saturday.

I saw the Hollywood postmark and let out a whoop, thereby attracting my father's attention.

"What's all the excitement?"

I was getting the photograph out of the

envelope. "I got a picture from Ronald Reagan!"

"Who's he?"

"Some movie star," my mother said.

By that time I had the photograph out. My heart began to beat nervously as I read the inscription at the bottom. "To a brave little girl, in admiration, Ronald Reagan."

"What does it say?" my father said.

"Nothing, it's just signed," I said, but he already saw what it said as he stood behind me looking down at it.

"Why are you a brave little girl?" he asked.

"How do I know?" I said.

"There's a letter on the floor," said my mother.

"That's my letter," I said, grabbing it.

"Why are you considered a brave little girl?" my father asked again. "Why does *he* admire *you*?"

I held the letter to my chest. "Those are just things they say," I said.

"They say you're *brave*?" my father said.

"Brave or honest or any dumb thing," I said weakly.

"Read the letter, Marijane," said my father.

I read the letter to myself.

Dear Marijane,

Thank you for your letter.

Remember that a handicap can be a challenge.

Always stay as cheerful as you are now.

Yours truly,
Ronald Reagan

"What does it say?" my mother asked.

"Just the usual," I said. "They never say much."

"Let me see it, brave little girl," my father said.

"It's to me."

"Marijane . . ." and he had his hand out.

After my father read the letter, and got the truth out of me concerning my correspondence with Ronald Reagan, he told me what I was to do.

What I was to do was to sit down immediately and write Ronald Reagan, telling him I had lied. I was to add that I thanked God for my good health. I was to return both the letter and the photograph.

No Saturday in my entire life had ever been so dark.

My father stood over me while I wrote the letter in tears, convinced that Ronald Reagan would hate me all his life for my deception.[3] I watched through blurred eyes while my father took my letter, Ronald Reagan's letter, and the signed photograph, put them into a manila envelope, addressed it, sealed it, and put it in his briefcase to take to the post office.

For weeks and weeks after that, I dreaded the arrival of our postman. I was convinced a letter'd come beginning,

Dear Marijane,

How very disappointed I am in you. . . .

"I don't think he'll write back," Billy Shakespeare told me. "I don't think he'll want anything more to do with you."

That ended getting dinner for movie stars in my playhouse.

I told Dorothy Spencer that I'd outgrown all that.

---

3. **deception** [di sep′shən]: the act of deceiving, or leading someone to believe that which is false.

READER'S RESPONSE

Do you think Marijane's father handled the business about the letter in the right way? Why or why not?

STUDY QUESTIONS

Recalling

1. What are Billy's and Marijane's explanations for the fact that Marijane's father is not President?
2. What do Marijane and Dorothy pretend to do in the playhouse?
3. What changes when a new movie comes to town?
4. What does Marijane do in order to persuade Ronald Reagan to write to her?
5. What does Marijane's father insist that she do after Ronald Reagan responds?

Interpreting

6. Who has a more realistic view of life—Marijane or Billy? Explain.
7. What do Marijane's feelings about her father and Ronald Reagan have in common?
8. At the end of the selection, what causes Marijane to outgrow her favorite game?

READING AND LITERARY FOCUS

Narration

Narration is the type of writing that tells a story. A narrative work can be fiction or nonfiction, depending on whether the characters and events in the story are imagined or real. An **autobiography,** a writer's own life story, is one kind of nonfiction narrative. Biographies, narrative essays, short stories, and novels are all forms of narrative writing.

A central figure in every narrative is the **narrator,** or the person who tells the story. The narrator's attitudes add a distinctive, personal flavor to the story. In an autobiography the narrator is not only a character in the story but the writer as well. The narrator of an autobiography refers to himself or herself as "I."

Thinking About Narration

What details suggest that Kerr's narrative is non-fiction?

VOCABULARY

Context Clues

Sometimes you can figure out the meaning of an unfamiliar word by looking for clues in the word's **context,** or the words and sentences that surround it. Each of the following passages from "Where Are You Now, William Shakespeare?" includes an italicized word that may be unfamiliar. Choose the best meaning for the italicized word by studying the context.

1. Our game came to a halt, but our *rivalry* did not. . . .

   "No matter what he writes her," I told Billy Shakespeare, "my letter from him will be better."
   (a) friendship   (c) understanding
   (b) competition   (d) homework

2. I was beginning to get a *panicky* feeling as time passed and no mail came from Ronald Reagan. You'd think he'd write a crippled child first. . . .
   (a) extremely fearful   (c) very pleasant
   (b) proud   (d) strong

3. By that time I had the photograph out. My heart began to beat nervously as I read the *inscription* at the bottom. "To a brave little girl, in admiration, Ronald Reagan."
   (a) informal dedication   (c) booklet
   (b) table of contents   (d) directions

4. After my father read the letter, and got the truth out of me concerning my *correspondence* with Ronald Reagan, he told me what I was to do.
   (a) friendship   (d) exchange of
   (b) discussion   letters
   (c) legal agreement

Gary Soto (born 1952) is an award-winning poet and writer of prose. During his childhood, in Fresno, California, he worked as a migrant farm laborer. Soto discovered literature in college, and he was so captivated by it that he began writing on his own. Later he took writing classes and began meeting other writers. A critic has said of his work that an "immediate, human presence . . . breathes through the lines." In 1985 Gary Soto received an American Book Award from the Before Columbus Foundation for *Living up the Street*, the collection of prose memoirs that contains "The Jacket."

I threw my books on the bed and approached the jacket slowly, as if it were a stranger whose hand I had to shake.

Gary Soto

The Jacket

My clothes have failed me. I remember the green coat that I wore in fifth and sixth grades when you either danced like a champ or pressed yourself against a greasy wall, bitter as a penny toward the happy couples.

When I needed a new jacket and my mother asked what kind I wanted, I described something like bikers wear: black leather and silver studs with enough belts to hold down a small town. We were in the kitchen, steam on the windows from her cooking. She listened so long while stirring dinner that I thought she understood for sure the kind I wanted. The next day when I got home from school, I discovered draped on my bedpost a jacket the color of day-old guacamole.[1] I threw my books on the bed and approached the jacket slowly, as if it were a stranger whose hand I had to shake. I touched the vinyl sleeve, the collar, and peeked at the mustard-colored lining.

From the kitchen mother yelled that my jacket was in the closet. I closed the door to her voice and pulled at the rack of clothes in the closet, hoping the jacket on the bedpost wasn't for me but my mean brother. No luck. I gave up. From my bed, I stared at the jacket. I wanted to cry because it was so ugly and so big that I knew

———

1. **guacamole** [gwä′kə mō′lā]: thick, yellowish-green sauce made from mashed and seasoned avocado, a tropical fruit. Exposed to air, it turns a muddy greenish brown.

I'd have to wear it a long time. I was a small kid, thin as a young tree, and it would be years before I'd have a new one. I stared at the jacket, like an enemy, thinking bad things before I took off my old jacket whose sleeves climbed halfway to my elbow.

I put the big jacket on. I zipped it up and down several times, and rolled the cuffs up so they didn't cover my hands. I put my hands in the pockets and flapped the jacket like a bird's wings. I stood in front of the mirror, full face, then profile, and then looked over my shoulder as if someone had called me. I sat on the bed, stood against the bed, and combed my hair to see what I would look like doing something natural. I looked ugly. I threw it on my brother's bed and looked at it for a long time before I slipped it on and went out to the backyard, smiling a "thank you" to my mom as I passed her in the kitchen. With my hands in my pockets I kicked a ball against the fence, and then climbed it to sit looking into the alley. I hurled orange peels at the mouth of an open garbage can and when the peels were gone I watched the white puffs of my breath thin to nothing.

I jumped down, hands in my pockets, and in the backyard on my knees I teased my dog, Brownie, by swooping my arms while making bird calls. He jumped at me and missed. He jumped again and again, until a tooth sunk deep, ripping an L-shaped tear on my left sleeve. I pushed Brownie away to study the tear as I would a cut on my arm. There was no blood, only a few loose pieces of fuzz. Damn dog, I thought, and pushed him away hard when he tried to bite again. I got up from my knees and went to my bedroom to sit with my jacket on my lap, with the lights out.

That was the first afternoon with my new

Winter, 1946, Andrew Wyeth.

jacket. The next day I wore it to sixth grade and got a D on a math quiz. During the morning recess Frankie T., the playground terrorist, pushed me to the ground and told me to stay there until recess was over. My best friend, Steve Negrete, ate an apple while looking at me, and the girls turned away to whisper on the monkey bars. The teachers were no help: they looked my way and talked about how foolish I looked in my new jacket. I saw their heads bob with laughter, their hands half-covering their mouths.

Even though it was cold, I took off the jacket during lunch and played kickball in a thin shirt, my arms feeling like braille from goose bumps. But when I returned to class I slipped the jacket on and shivered until I was warm. I sat on my hands, heating them up, while my teeth chattered like a cup of crooked dice.[2] Finally warm, I slid out of the jacket but a few minutes later put it back on when the fire bell rang. We paraded out into

---

2. **cup of crooked dice:** in dishonest gambling, dice physically changed so that they do not rest firmly on certain sides after they have been thrown onto a flat surface from a dice cup, the leather-covered container in which they have first been shaken.

the yard where we, the sixth graders, walked past all the other grades to stand against the back fence. Everybody saw me. Although they didn't say out loud, "Man, that's ugly," I heard the buzz-buzz of gossip and even laughter that I knew was meant for me.

And so I went, in my guacamole jacket. So embarrassed, so hurt, I couldn't even do my homework. I received Cs on quizzes, and forgot the state capitals and the rivers of South America, our friendly neighbor. Even the girls who had been friendly blew away like loose flowers to follow the boys in neat jackets.

I wore that thing for three years until the sleeves grew short and my forearms stuck out like the necks of turtles. All during that time no love came to me—no little dark girl in a Sunday dress she wore on Monday. At lunchtime I stayed with the ugly boys who leaned against the chainlink fence and looked around with propellers of grass spinning in our mouths. We saw girls walk by alone, saw couples, hand in hand, their heads like bookends pressing air together. We saw them and spun our propellers so fast our faces were blurs.

I blame that jacket for those bad years. I blame my mother for her bad taste and her cheap ways. It was a sad time for the heart. With a friend I spent my sixth-grade year in a tree in the alley waiting for something good to happen to me in that jacket, which had become the ugly brother who tagged along wherever I went. And it was about that time that I began to grow. My chest puffed up with muscle and, strangely, a few more ribs. Even my hands, those fleshy hammers, showed bravely through the cuffs, the fingers already hardening for the coming fights. But that L-shaped rip on the left sleeve got bigger; bits of stuffing coughed out from its wound after a hard day of play. I finally scotch-taped it closed, but in rain or cold weather the tape peeled off like a scab and more stuffing fell out until that sleeve shriveled into a palsied arm. That winter the elbows began to crack and whole chunks of green began to fall off. I showed the cracks to my mother, who always seemed to be at the stove with steamed-up glasses, and she said that there were children in Mexico who would love that jacket. I told her that this was America and yelled that Debbie, my sister, didn't have a jacket like mine. I ran outside, ready to cry, and climbed the tree by the alley to think bad thoughts and watch my breath puff white and disappear.

But whole pieces still casually flew off my jacket when I played hard, read quietly, or took vicious spelling tests at school. When it became so spotted that my brother began to call me "camouflage," I flung it over the fence into the alley. Later, however, I swiped the jacket off the ground and went inside to drape it across my lap and mope.

I was called to dinner: steam silvered my mother's glasses as she said grace; my brother and sister with their heads bowed made ugly faces at their glasses of powdered milk. I gagged too, but eagerly ate big rips of buttered tortilla that held scooped up beans. Finished, I went outside with my jacket across my arm. It was a cold sky. The faces of clouds were piled up, hurting. I climbed the fence, jumping down with a grunt. I started up the alley and soon slipped into my jacket, that green ugly brother who breathed over my shoulder that day and ever since.

READER'S RESPONSE

What would you say to comfort Gary Soto if he were your friend?

STUDY QUESTIONS

Recalling

1. Why does the author dislike his new jacket?
2. What problems does he blame on the jacket?
3. In what ways do both the narrator and the jacket change over the years?
4. What happens after the narrator tries to throw the jacket away? What does he call the jacket?

Interpreting

5. Why do you think the boy's mother bought the green jacket?
6. What do you think is the real source of the boy's problems?
7. What does the green jacket come to represent to the author?

Extending

8. Why do you think some people feel that clothes are extremely important?

READING AND LITERARY FOCUS

Character and Internal Conflict

Most narratives present a **conflict** of some kind—a struggle between two or more opposing forces. Conflicts may be either external or internal. An **internal conflict** takes place within the mind of a character. For example, in "Papa's Parrot" Harry loves his father but is embarrassed by the man's eccentric behavior toward his pet parrot.

Internal conflicts affect the lives of a story's characters. For example, Harry's conflict leads him to avoid his father's candy shop. When he discovers how lonely his father is, Harry cries. Sometimes internal conflict can change a character and lead to

maturity. "Papa's Parrot" ends with Harry's resolving to visit his father in the hospital. We know that Harry now sees his father in a new light and will treat him differently in the future.

Thinking About Character and Conflict

1. Describe the central conflict in "The Jacket." In what ways does this conflict affect the main character?
2. How is the conflict resolved? What does the main character learn from the resolution?

VOCABULARY

Words from Spanish

Many English words, especially those associated with the American Southwest, come from Spanish. Use a dictionary to find the meaning and origin of the following words. Then use each word in a sentence.

1. canyon
2. chili
3. lariat
4. maize
5. pimento

COMPOSITION

Writing About Character

Write a paragraph describing the personality of the narrator of "The Jacket." What is the boy like? What is the main conflict he faces? How does this conflict affect him? **Prewriting:** Before you begin, skim the story, noting details that will help you answer these questions. Use details from the story to support your opinions. **Revising:** Review your paragraph to see that you have expressed your ideas clearly and logically.

Writing a Vivid Description

The narrator of "The Jacket" hates the yellow-green jacket his mother buys for him. Write a vivid description of a piece of clothing you feel strongly about. Choose specific words that will help your readers to *know* exactly what the clothing is like and to *feel* your emotional reactions.

Count Leo Tolstoy (1828–1910), author of the epic novels *War and Peace* and *Anna Karenina*, is considered one of the world's greatest writers. Born near Tula, Russia, into a family of wealthy landowners, Tolstoy was orphaned at nine, brought up by his aunts, and educated at home. At sixteen he was sent to the University of Kazan, but his studies bored him, and he never completed a degree. After serving in the Russian Army, he traveled to Europe. Tolstoy found the Europeans' emphasis on wealth and possessions disturbing. He began to develop a moral philosophy and a burning desire to discover the spiritual meaning of life. These concerns helped to shape much of his writing.

All the people on deck had been watching. . . . When they saw the boy let go of the rope and step out on the crossbeam, they froze with terror.

• •

Leo Tolstoy

The Jump

Translated from the Russian by Miriam Morton

A ship had sailed around the world and was on its homeward journey. The weather was calm and everyone was on deck. A large monkey was capering about amidst the crowd, amusing everybody. She tumbled here and there, made silly faces, and aped the people. It was clear that she knew that she was funny and therefore carried on even more.

She jumped over to a twelve-year-old boy, the son of the ship's captain, and snatched his hat from his head, put it on her own, and quickly scampered up the mast. Everyone laughed, and the boy didn't know whether to laugh or be angry.

The monkey perched on the bottom crossbeam of the mast, took off the hat and began to tear it with her teeth and paws. She seemed to be doing it to spite the boy. She pointed at him and made funny faces.

The boy shouted at her and threatened her with his fist, but she kept tearing the hat, doing it even harder. The sailors laughed louder, the boy flushed with anger, threw off his jacket, and went after the monkey on the mast. In an instant he had climbed the rope ladder to the first crossbeam. But just as the boy was about to grab his hat from her, the monkey quickly climbed even higher.

"You won't get away with this," the boy cried out, and climbed after the monkey. The animal lured him on, scrambling still higher, to the top of the high mast.

Up there, holding fast to a rope with one foot, the monkey stretched out her body, extended her long arm, and hung the torn cap on the end of the highest crossbeam. Then she reached the very tip of the mast and sat there making faces, baring her teeth, and enjoying her victory.

There was a space of about six feet between the boy and the end of the crossbeam where his hat was hanging now. To reach it, he would have to let go of both the rope and the mast. He was so upset by now that, forgetting all danger, he stepped onto this highest crossbeam, balancing himself the best he could with his arms.

All the people on deck had been watching the chase between the captain's son and the monkey. But when they saw the boy let go of the rope and step out on the crossbeam, they froze with terror. If he lost his balance and fell to the deck, he would be killed. Or even if he somehow reached the end of the crossbeam and got his hat, it would be hard for him to turn around and get back to the mast.

They were looking on in silence, waiting to see what would happen, when someone in the crowd suddenly cried out in panic. The boy heard the cry, looked down, and teetered.

Just then the captain of the ship, the boy's father, came out of his cabin. He was holding a rifle for shooting seagulls. When he saw his son teetering on the uppermost crossbeam, he at once aimed the gun at him, shouting, "Jump! Jump into the water! Or I'll shoot!"

Sailing the High Seas, Ernst Haas, photograph, c. 1950.

The boy hesitated, not understanding. "Jump! One, two . . ."

As soon as his father cried "three," the boy stepped out and dived into the sea.

Like a cannonball his body hit the water, but before the waves could cover him, twenty brave seamen had jumped from the ship into the sea. Within forty seconds—they seemed like eternity—the body of the boy came to the surface. The seamen grabbed him and brought him back on board.

After a few long minutes water began to come from his mouth and nose, and he began to breathe.

When the captain saw this, he uttered a choked cry, and he hurried away to his cabin so that no one would see him weep.

READER'S RESPONSE

Do you think the captain was smart to do what he did? Why or why not?

STUDY QUESTIONS

Recalling

1. At the beginning of the story, what happens to make the captain's son angry?
2. Why do the spectators become worried?
3. What action does the captain take? What does the boy do?
4. Why does the captain hurry away to his cabin?

Interpreting

5. What do the captain's actions reveal about him?
6. How do you think the son feels toward his father after the incident?

Extending

7. In what situations today might parents have to act as quickly and decisively as the captain did?

READING AND LITERARY FOCUS

Character Motivation

Getting to know a story's characters can be one of the great pleasures of reading. You can appreciate characters best if you think about their actions and the feelings that prompted them. The idea, emotion, or goal that causes a character to behave in a certain way is called **motivation.**

Sometimes writers describe their characters' motivations directly. At other times you must use the details in the story and what you know about similar situations to figure out the causes of a character's actions. At the beginning of "The Jump," for example, Tolstoy tells you exactly how the captain's son feels when the monkey takes his cap: "The boy flushed with anger, threw off his jacket, and went after the monkey on the mast." Later Tolstoy says that "before the waves could cover him, twenty brave seamen had jumped . . . into the sea." Tolstoy does not tell you why the sailors acted so quickly. You can figure out the sailors' motivation, however, by thinking about the relationships among the characters and the way in which the sailors are described.

You know that the sailors work for the captain and that the boy is the captain's son. It may be that the seamen are devoted to their captain—and perhaps to the young man as well—and do not wish to see the boy die. It is also possible, since Tolstoy describes the sailors as "brave," that these men would act unquestioningly to save anybody's life. By thinking about the motivations of a story's characters, you can develop a richer, livelier appreciation of even a small event in a story.

Thinking About Character Motivation

1. What motivates the captain to threaten his son with a rifle? Suggest the series of thoughts that might have led him to this action.
2. Why does the captain cry at the end of the story? Give reasons to support your answer.

photograph © 1990 Jill Krementz

Judith Viorst (born 1931), poet, journalist, writer, and editor of children's books, was born in New Jersey. At seven she began writing poetry—"terrible poems about dead dogs, mostly." She continued writing about "deadly serious things. . . . Very grim. The meaning of life. Death. Pain. . . . That sort of thing." Although she sent her work to various magazines, none of it was ever published until she had grown up, married, and begun writing humorously about her life. Viorst's three children often inspire her. "Most of my children's books," she explains, "are for or about my own children, and mostly they're written to meet certain needs." Viorst enjoys combining career and family life. She says, "It's a dream come true, exactly what I've always wanted to do. . . . My experiences have exceeded my expectations."

Are you willing to risk an important friendship for something you believe in?

• •

Judith Viorst

The Southpaw[1]

Dear Richard,

Don't invite me to your birthday party because I'm not coming. And give back the Disneyland sweatshirt I said you could wear. If I'm not good enough to play on your team, I'm not good enough to be friends with.

Your former friend,
Janet

P.S. I hope when you go to the dentist he finds 20 cavities.

---

1. **Southpaw:** a left-handed baseball pitcher.

Dear Janet,

Here is your stupid Disneyland sweatshirt, if that's how you're going to be. I want my comic books now—finished or not. No girl has ever played on the Mapes Street baseball team, and as long as I'm captain, no girl ever will.

Your former friend,
Richard

P.S. I hope when you go for your checkup you need a tetanus shot.

Dear Richard,

I'm changing my goldfish's name from Richard to Stanley. Don't count on my vote for class president next year. Just because I'm a member of the ballet club doesn't mean I'm not a terrific ballplayer.

Your former friend,
Janet

P.S. I see you lost your first game 28-0.

Dear Janet,
I'm not saving any more seats for you on the bus. For all I care you can stand the whole way to school. Why don't you just forget about baseball and learn something nice like knitting?

Your former friend,
Richard

P.S. Wait until Wednesday.

Dear Richard,
My father said I could call someone to go with us for a ride and hot-fudge sundaes. On case you didn't notice, I didn't call you.

Your former friend,
Janet

P.S. I see you lost your second game, 34-0.

Dear Janet,
Remember when I took the laces out of my blue-and-white sneakers and gave them to you? I want them back.

Your former friend,
Richard

P.S. Wait until Friday.

Dear Richard,
   Congratulations on your unbroken record. Eight straight losses, wow! I understand you're the laughingstock of New Jersey.
                    Your former friend,
                         Janet
P.S. Why don't you and your team forget about baseball and learn something nice like knitting maybe?

Dear Janet,
   Here's the silver horseback riding trophy that you gave me. I don't think I want to keep it anymore.
                    Your former friend,
                       Richard
P.S. I didn't think you'd be the kind who'd kick a man when he's down.

Dear Richard,
   I wasn't kicking exactly. I was kicking <u>back</u>.
                    Your former friend,
                         Janet
P.S. In case you were wondering, my batting average is .345.

Dear Janet,
Alfie is having his tonsils out tomorrow. We might be able to let you catch next week.
Richard

Dear Richard,
I pitch.
Janet

Dear Janet,
Joel is moving to Kansas and Danny sprained his wrist. How about a permanent place in the outfield?
Richard

Dear Richard,
I pitch.
Janet

Dear Janet,
Ronnie caught the chicken pox and Leo broke his toe and Elwood has these stupid violin lessons. I'll give you first base, and that's my final offer.
Richard

Dear Richard,
   Susan Reilly plays first base, Marilyn Jackson catches, Ethel Kahn plays center field, I pitch. It's a package deal.
                                 Janet
P.S. Sorry about your 12-game losing streak.

Dear Janet,
Please! Not Marilyn Jackson.
                    Richard

Dear Richard,
   Nobody ever said that I was unreasonable. How about Lizzie Martindale instead?
                                 Janet

Dear Janet,
At least could you call your goldfish Richard again? Your friend,
                    Richard

READER'S RESPONSE

Do you think girls and boys should play on the same teams? Why or why not?

STUDY QUESTIONS

Recalling

1. Why is Janet angry with her friend Richard?
2. What reason does Richard give for his decision?
3. While Richard and Janet are exchanging notes, what happens to Richard's team?
4. What problem leads Richard to offer Janet the position as catcher? What does Janet insist on doing?
5. In what way is the makeup of Richard's team different by the end of the story?

Interpreting

6. What kind of person is Janet? What clues create this impression?

7. What kind of person is Richard? What clues create this impression?
8. What ideas about change and growth does this story suggest?

Extending

9. Do you think boys and girls are given the same opportunities? Explain your answer.

CHALLENGE

Research

Look through newspapers and magazines for other stories about boys and girls or men and women struggling to achieve equal opportunities in jobs, sports, or other areas. Try to find examples that have occured at different times throughout the years. Bring to class at least two clippings or photocopies of articles, and work with your classmates to create a bulletin-board display. You might arrange the items on the bulletin board in chronological order.

Walter Dean Myers (born 1937) learned basketball in the playgrounds of Harlem and has played it most of his life. Born in West Virginia, he was raised in New York City. He began "filling up notebooks" when he was ten or eleven but never imagined that he could earn his living writing. Today Myers has completed more than thirty books for young people. His goal is to provide good literature for black children. "I feel the need to show them the possibilities that exist for them that were never revealed to me as a youngster."

We had never seen the other team play but Sam said that he knew some of the players and that they were good.

• •

Walter Dean Myers

The Game

We had practiced and practiced until it ran out of our ears. Every guy on the team knew every play. We were ready. It meant the championship. Everybody was there. I never saw so many people at the center at one time. We had never seen the other team play but Sam said that he knew some of the players and that they were good. Mr. Reese told us to go out and play as hard as we could every moment we were on the floor. We all shook hands in the locker room and then went out. Mostly we tried to ignore them warming up at the other end of the court but we couldn't help but look a few times. They were doing exactly what we were doing, just shooting a few lay-ups and waiting for the game to begin.

They got the first tap and started pass-ing the ball around. I mean they really started passing the ball around faster than anything I had ever seen. Zip! Zip! Zip! Two points! I didn't even know how they could *see* the ball, let alone get it inside to their big man. We brought the ball down and one of their players stole the ball from Sam. We got back on defense but they weren't in a hurry. The same old thing. Zip! Zip! Zip! Two points! They could pass the ball better than anybody I ever saw. Then we brought the ball down again and Chalky missed a jump shot. He missed the backboard, the rim, everything. One of their players caught the ball and then brought it down and a few seconds later the score was 6–0. We couldn't even get close enough to foul them. Chalky brought the ball down again, passed to Sam cutting across the lane, and Sam walked. They brought the ball down and it was 8–0.

They were really enjoying the game. You could see. Every time they scored they'd slap hands and carry on. Also, they had some cheerleaders. They had about five girls with little pink skirts on and white sweaters cheering for them.

Clyde brought the ball down this time, passed into our center, a guy named Leon, and Leon turned and missed a hook. They got the rebound and came down, and Chalky missed a steal and fouled his man. That's when Mr. Reese called time out.

"Okay, now, just trade basket for basket. They make a basket, you take your time and you make a basket—don't rush it." Mr. Reese looked at his starting five. "Okay, now, every once in a while take a look over at me and I'll let you know when I want you to make your move. If I put my hands palm down, just keep on playing cool. If I stand up and put my hands up like this"—he put both hands up near his face—"that means to make your move. You understand that?"

Everyone said that they understood. When the ball was back in play Chalky and Sam and Leon started setting picks from the outside and then passed to Clyde for our first two points. They got the ball and started passing around again. Zip! Zip! Zip! But this time we were just waiting for that pass underneath and they knew it. Finally they tried a shot from outside and Chalky slapped it away to Sam on the break. We came down real quick and scored. On the way back Mr. Reese showed everybody that his palms were down. To keep playing cool.

They missed their next shot and fouled

Chalky. They called time out and, much to my surprise, Mr. Reese put me in. My heart was beating so fast I thought I was going to have a heart attack. Chalky missed the foul shot but Leon slapped the ball out to Clyde, who passed it to me. I dribbled about two steps and threw it back to Leon in the bucket. Then I didn't know what to do so I did what Mr. Reese always told us. If you don't know what to do then, just move around. I started moving toward the corner and then I ran quickly toward the basket. I saw Sam coming at me from the other direction and it was a play. Two guards cutting past and one of the defensive men gets picked off. I ran as close as I could to Sam, and his man got picked off. Chalky threw the ball into him for an easy lay-up. They came down and missed again but one of their men got the rebound in. We brought the ball down and Sam went along the base line for a jump shot, but their center knocked the ball away. I caught it just before it went out at the corner and shot the ball. I remembered what Mr. Reese had said about following your shot in, and I started in after the ball but it went right in. It didn't touch the rim or anything. Swish!

One of their players said to watch out for 17—that was me. I played about two minutes more, then Mr. Reese took me out. But I had scored another basket on a lay-up. We were coming back. Chalky and Sam were knocking away just about anything their guards were throwing up, and Leon, Chalky, and Sam controlled the defensive backboard. Mr. Reese brought in Cap, and Cap got fouled two times in two plays. At the end of the half, when I thought we were doing pretty well, I found out the score was 36–29. They were beating us by seven points. Mr. Reese didn't seem worried, though.

"Okay, everybody, stay cool. No sweat. Just keep it nice and easy."

We came out in the second half and played it pretty cool. Once we came within one point, but then they ran it up to five again. We kept looking over to Mr. Reese to see what he wanted us to do and he would just put his palms down and nod his head for us to play cool. There were six minutes to go when Mr. Reese put me and another guy named Turk in. Now I didn't really understand why he did this because I know I'm not the best basketball player in the world, although I'm not bad, and I know Turk is worse than me. Also, he took out both Sam and Chalky, our two best players. We were still losing by five points, too. And they weren't doing anything wrong. There was a jump ball between Leon and their center when all of a sudden this big cheer goes up and everybody looks over to the sidelines. Well, there was Gloria, BB, Maria, Sharon, Kitty, and about four other girls, all dressed in white blouses and black skirts and with big T's on their blouses and they were our cheerleaders. One of their players said something stupid about them but I liked them. They looked real good to me. We controlled the jump and Turk drove right down the lane and made a lay-up. Turk actually made the lay-up. Turk once missed seven lay-ups in a row in practice and no one was even guarding him. But this one he made. Then one of their men double-dribbled and we got the ball and I passed it to Leon, who threw up a shot and got fouled. The shot went in and when he made the foul shot it added up to a three-point play. They

started down court and Mr. Reese started yelling for us to give a foul.

"Foul him! Foul him!" he yelled from the sidelines.

Now this was something we had worked on in practice and that Mr. Reese had told us would only work once in a game. Anybody who plays basketball knows that if you're fouled while shooting the ball you get two foul shots and if you're fouled while not shooting the ball you only get one. So when a guy knows you're going to foul him he'll try to get off a quick shot. At least that's what we hoped. When their guard came across the mid-court line, I ran at him as if I was going to foul him. Then, just as I was going to touch him, I stopped short and moved around him without touching him. Sure enough, he threw the ball wildly toward the basket. It went over the base line and it was our ball. Mr. Reese took me out and Turk and put Sam and Chalky back in. And the game was just about over.

We hadn't realized it but in the two minutes that me and Turk played the score had been tied. When Sam and Chalky came back in they outscored the other team by four points in the last four minutes. We were the champs. We got the first-place trophies and we were so happy we were all jumping around and slapping each other on the back. Gloria and the other girls were just as happy as we were, and when we found that we had an extra trophy we gave it to them. Then Mr. Reese took us all in the locker room and shook each guy's hand and then went out and invited the parents and the girls in. He made a little speech about how he was proud of us and all, and not just because we won tonight but because we had worked so hard to win. When he finished everybody started clapping for us and, as usual, I started boo-hooing. But it wasn't so bad this time because Leon started boo-hooing worse than me.

You know what high is? We felt so good the next couple of days that it was ridiculous. We'd see someone in the street and we'd just walk up and be happy. Really.

READER'S RESPONSE

What are your feelings when your favorite team wins a game? Explain.

STUDY QUESTIONS

Recalling

1. When the story begins, where are the characters, and what are they about to begin?
2. What does the narrator notice about the other team?
3. What does Mr. Reese want the team to do when he calls time out?
4. What do Turk and the narrator manage to do in two minutes during the second half?
5. What are the narrator's feelings at the end of the story? Why does he feel this way?

Interpreting

6. What does the narrator learn about himself during the game?
7. What is the story's message about happiness? What clues suggest this?

Extending

8. What makes team sports important to many young people?

VOCABULARY

Jargon

People in almost every occupation or activity develop their own special vocabulary. Construction workers, sailors, teachers, stamp collectors—all use **jargon,** or specialized words and phrases, to describe their activities. Many sports also have their own vocabulary. In "The Game" Walter Dean Myers uses the jargon of basketball to make the story realistic. Words like *center, lay-ups, tap, defense, rim,* and *base line* are examples of this kind of specialized vocabulary.

Which sports produced the following jargon? Check a dictionary for definitions of any terms you may not know. Some terms may be used in more than one sport.

1. backhand 5. spare
2. fairway 6. wet suit
3. spike 7. lap
4. half gainer 8. bunt

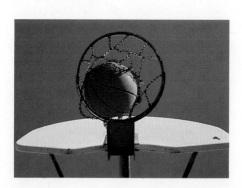

A Cycle of Seasons

photograph ©1990 Jill Krementz

The award-winning writer John Updike (born 1932) was educated at Harvard and the Ruskin School of Drawing and Fine Arts in Oxford, England. He later became a staff member of the magazine *The New Yorker*, where many of his short stories and poems appear. He has been immensely productive, writing several plays, more than a dozen novels, and scores of short stories and poems. Updike says, "In over thirty years as a professional writer I have tried to give my experience of life imaginative embodiment in novels, short stories, and poems. Art is, as I understand it, reality passed through a human mind, and this secondary creation remains for me unfailingly interesting and challenging."

The "poet laureate of Harlem," Langston Hughes (1902–1967) experimented with almost every form of literature. At a time when black writers were rare, he was determined to write genuinely about the lives and feelings of his people. He became one of the first blacks in America to earn his living exclusively by writing. He is particularly famous for the direct, human voices he created and jazz rhythms he used in his poems.

Raised by his mother and educated at the choir school of St. Paul's Cathedral in London, Walter de la Mare (1873–1956) began his career as a bookkeeper for an oil company. In his free time he wrote. His first book was published in 1902. De la Mare went on to distinguish himself as a poet, novelist, and editor of poetry anthologies. "To learn to love books and reading," de la Mare wrote, "is one of the very best things that can happen to anybody. . . . Poetry in particular *wears* well. The longer you care for it in itself, the better it gets."

When you think of the seasons, what pictures come to mind?

John Updike

January

Winter Harmony, John Henry Twachtman, c. 1890–1900.

The days are short,
　The sun a spark
Hung thin between
　The dark and dark.

5 Fat snowy footsteps
　Track the floor.
Milk bottles burst
　Outside the door.

The river is
10　A frozen place
Held still beneath
　The trees of lace.

The sky is low.
　The wind is gray.
15 The radiator
　Purrs all day.

Langston Hughes

April Rain Song

Rainy Day, Boston, Childe Hassam, 1885.

Let the rain kiss you.
Let the rain beat upon your head with silver liquid drops.
Let the rain sing you a lullaby.

The rain makes still pools on the sidewalk.
5 The rain makes running pools in the gutter.
The rain plays a little sleep-song on our roof at night—

And I love the rain.

Walter de la Mare

Summer Evening

Haystack at Sunset near Giverny, Claude Monet (1840–1926).

   The sandy cat by the Farmer's chair
   Mews at his knee for dainty fare;
   Old Rover in his moss-greened house
   Mumbles a bone, and barks at a mouse.
5 In the dewy fields the cattle lie
   Chewing the cud 'neath a fading sky.
   Dobbin at manger pulls his hay:
   Gone is another summer's day.

John Updike

September

Pool in the Woods,
Alexander Helwig Wyant, c. 1880.

The breezes taste
  Of apple peel.
The air is full
  Of smells to feel—

5 Ripe fruit, old footballs,
  Burning brush,
New books, erasers,
  Chalk, and such.

The bee, his hive
10   Well-honeyed, hums,
And Mother cuts
  Chrysanthemums.

Like plates washed clean
  With suds, the days
15 Are polished with
  A morning haze.

Which season do you like best? Why?

STUDY QUESTIONS

Recalling

1. What things in nature does Updike describe in "January"? What things made by humans does the poet describe?
2. In what three ways does the rain in "April Rain" act like a person?
3. Where does de la Mare's "Summer Evening" take place? Use details from the poem to explain your answer.
4. What sights, sounds, smells, and tastes does the poet mention in "September"?

Interpreting

5. Does the poem "January" suggest that winter is an active season or a still one? Use details from the poem to explain your answer.
6. What kind of person do you think is the speaker of "April Rain"? Which clues in the language suggest this?
7. In what ways is the language of "Summer Evening" different from everyday speech?
8. How does the speaker of "September" feel about the fall? How do you know?

Extending

9. Do the poems reflect your feelings about the seasons? Explain.

READING AND LITERARY FOCUS

Imagery

An **image** is a picture, or likeness, that a writer creates with words. Many images are visual, or related to sight. Such word pictures help readers imagine the experiences that writers describe. Not all images are visual, however. Images may appeal to any of our senses. For example, in describing a piece of toast, you may mention its familiar scent (smell), the crunch (sound) of a knife spreading butter on its rough (touch), brown (sight) surface, and the salt-sweet flavor (taste) of your first bite.

The combination of images in a poem is called **imagery.** Imagery is the language that appeals to our senses. Imagery helps readers experience what a poet describes.

Thinking About Imagery

1. In this group of poems, find two images that appeal to each of these senses: sight, hearing, and smell.
2. Which poem appeals most to the sense of smell? Which poem contains the most sound imagery?

CHALLENGE

Poetry Contest

Perform a poetry concert with a group of classmates. Choose poems with similar themes, or simply select some of your favorites, and then decide how to perform them. You may want to have a chorus read parts of some poems aloud while solo voices read other parts.

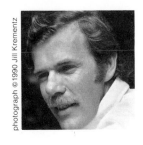

photograph ©1990 Jill Krementz

Richard Bach (born 1936) comes from Oak Park, Illinois, and studied for a year at Long Beach State College in California before joining the U.S. Air Force and becoming a pilot. In addition to writing books and magazine articles, he has edited a magazine, *Flying.* He has also worked as a charter pilot, flight instructor, aviation mechanic, and barnstormer, or stunt flier, in the Midwest. His *Jonathan Livingston Seagull* was a best seller during the 1970s. Bach sums up the book's inspirational theme in a few words: "Find out what you love to do, and do your darndest to make it happen."

"See here, Jonathan," said his father. . . . "This flying business is all very well, but you can't eat a glide, you know. Don't you forget that the reason you fly is to eat."

Richard Bach

from **Jonathan Livingston Seagull**

It was morning, and the new sun sparkled gold across the ripples of a gentle sea.

A mile from shore a fishing boat chummed[1] the water, and the word for Breakfast Flock flashed through the air, till a crowd of a thousand seagulls came to dodge and fight for bits of food. It was another busy day beginning.

But way off alone, out by himself beyond boat and shore, Jonathan Livingston Seagull was practicing. A hundred feet in the sky he lowered his webbed feet, lifted his beak, and strained to hold a painful hard twisting curve through his wings.

The curve meant that he would fly slowly, and now he slowed until the wind was a whisper in his face, until the ocean stood still beneath him. He narrowed his eyes in fierce concentration, held his breath, forced one . . . single . . . more . . . inch . . . of . . . curve. . . . Then his feathers ruffled, he stalled and fell.

Seagulls, as you know, never falter, never stall. To stall in the air is for them disgrace and it is dishonor.

But Jonathan Livingston Seagull, unashamed, stretching his wings again in that trembling hard curve—slowing, slowing, and stalling once more—was no ordinary bird.

Most gulls don't bother to learn more than the simplest facts of flight—how to get from shore to food and back again.

---

1. **chummed:** fished with chum, a bait consisting of bits of cut-up fish spread on the water.

For most gulls, it is not flying that matters, but eating. For this gull, though, it was not eating that mattered, but flight. More than anything else, Jonathan Livingston Seagull loved to fly.

This kind of thinking, he found, is not the way to make one's self popular with other birds. Even his parents were dismayed as Jonathan spent whole days alone, making hundreds of low-level glides, experimenting.

He didn't know why, for instance, but when he flew at altitudes less than half his wingspan above the water, he could stay in the air longer, with less effort. His glides ended not with the usual feet-down splash into the sea, but with a long flat wake[2] as he touched the surface with his feet tightly streamlined against his body. When he began sliding in to feet-up landings on the beach, then pacing the length of his slide in the sand, his parents were very much dismayed indeed.

"Why, Jon, *why*?" his mother asked. "Why is it so hard to be like the rest of the flock, Jon? Why can't you leave low flying to the pelicans, the albatross? Why don't you *eat*? Son, you're bone and feathers!"

"I don't mind being bone and feathers, mom. I just want to know what I can do in the air and what I can't, that's all. I just want to know."

"See here, Jonathan," said his father, not unkindly. "Winter isn't far away. Boats will be few, and the surface fish will be swimming deep. If you must study, then study food, and how to get it. This flying business is all very well, but you can't eat

a glide, you know. Don't you forget that the reason you fly is to eat."

Jonathan nodded obediently. For the next few days he tried to behave like the other gulls; he really tried, screeching and fighting with the flock around the piers and fishing boats, diving on scraps of fish and bread. But he couldn't make it work.

It's all so pointless, he thought, deliberately dropping a hard-won anchovy to a hungry old gull chasing him. I could be spending all this time learning to fly. There's so much to learn!

It wasn't long before Jonathan Gull was off by himself again, far out at sea, hungry, happy, learning.

The subject was speed, and in a week's practice he learned more about speed than the fastest gull alive.

From a thousand feet, flapping his wings as hard as he could, he pushed over into a blazing steep dive toward the waves, and learned why seagulls don't make blazing steep power-dives. In just six seconds he was moving seventy miles per hour, the speed at which one's wing goes unstable on the upstroke.

Time after time it happened. Careful as he was, working at the very peak of his ability, he lost control at high speed.

Climb to a thousand feet. Full power straight ahead first, then push over, flapping, to a vertical dive. Then, every time, his left wing stalled on an upstroke, he'd roll violently left, stall his right wing recovering, and flick like fire into a wild tumbling spin to the right.

He couldn't be careful enough on that upstroke. Ten times he tried, and all ten times, as he passed through seventy miles per hour, he burst into a churning mass of feathers, out of control, crashing down into the water.

---

2. **wake:** track or path left by something moving through water.

Cliffs of Mendocino, Millard Sheets, 1979.

The key, he thought at last, dripping wet, must be to hold the wings still at high speeds—to flap up to fifty and then hold the wings still.

From two thousand feet he tried again, rolling into his dive, beak straight down, wings full out and stable from the moment he passed fifty miles per hour. It took tremendous strength, but it worked. In ten seconds he had blurred through ninety miles per hour. Jonathan had set a world speed record for seagulls!

But victory was short-lived. The instant he began his pullout, the instant he changed the angle of his wings, he snapped into that same terrible uncontrolled disaster, and at ninety miles per hour it hit him like dynamite. Jonathan Seagull exploded in midair and smashed down into a brick-hard sea.

When he came to, it was well after dark, and he floated in moonlight on the surface of the ocean. His wings were ragged bars of lead, but the weight of failure was even heavier on his back. He wished, feebly, that the weight could be just enough to drag him gently down to the bottom, and end it all.

As he sank low in the water, a strange hollow voice sounded within him. There's no way around it. I am a seagull. I am limited by my nature. If I were meant to learn so much about flying, I'd have charts for brains. If I were meant to fly at speed, I'd have a falcon's short wings, and live on mice instead of fish. My father was right. I must forget this foolishness. I must fly home to the Flock and be content as I am, as a poor limited seagull.

The voice faded, and Jonathan agreed. The place for a seagull at night is on shore, and from this moment forth, he vowed, he would be a normal gull. It would make everyone happier.

He pushed wearily away from the dark water and flew toward the land, grateful for what he had learned about work-saving low-altitude flying.

But no, he thought. I am done with the way I was, I am done with everything I learned. I am a seagull like every other seagull, and I will fly like one. So he climbed painfully to a hundred feet and flapped his wings harder, pressing for shore.

He felt better for his decision to be just another one of the Flock. There would be no ties now to the force that had driven him to learn, there would be no more challenge and no more failure. And it was pretty, just to stop thinking, and fly through the dark, toward the lights above the beach.

Dark! The hollow voice cracked in alarm. *Seagulls never fly in the dark!*

Jonathan was not alert to listen. It's pretty, he thought. The moon and the lights twinkling on the water, throwing out little beacon-trails through the night, and all so peaceful and still. . . .

Get down! Seagulls never fly in the dark! If you were meant to fly in the dark, you'd have the eyes of an owl! You'd have charts for brains! You'd have a falcon's short wings!

There in the night, a hundred feet in the air, Jonathan Livingston Seagull—blinked. His pain, his resolutions, vanished.

Short wings. *A falcon's short wings!*

That's the answer! What a fool I've been! All I need is a tiny little wing, all I need is to fold most of my wings and fly on just the tips alone! *Short wings!*

He climbed two thousand feet above the black sea, and without a moment for thought of failure and death, he brought his forewings tightly in to his body, left only the narrow swept daggers of his wingtips extended into the wind, and fell into a vertical dive.

The wind was a monster roar at his head. Seventy miles per hour, ninety, a hundred and twenty and faster still. The wing-strain now at a hundred and forty miles per hour wasn't nearly as hard as it had been before at seventy, and with the faintest twist of his wingtips he eased out of the dive and shot above the waves, a gray cannonball under the moon.

He closed his eyes to slits against the wind and rejoiced. A hundred forty miles per hour! And under control! If I dive from five thousand feet instead of two thousand, I wonder how fast . . .

His vows of a moment before were forgotten, swept away in that great swift wind. Yet he felt guiltless, breaking the promises he had made himself. Such promises are only for the gulls that accept the ordinary. One who has touched excellence in his learning has no need of that kind of promise.

By sunup, Jonathan Gull was practicing again. From five thousand feet the fishing boats were specks in the flat blue water, Breakfast Flock was a faint cloud of dust motes,[3] circling.

He was alive, trembling ever so slightly

_____

3. **motes:** particles or specks.

with delight, proud that his fear was under control. Then without ceremony he hugged in his forewings, extended his short, angled wingtips, and plunged directly toward the sea. By the time he passed four thousand feet he had reached terminal velocity,[4] the wind was a solid beating wall of sound against which he could move no faster. He was flying now straight down, at two hundred fourteen miles per hour. He swallowed, knowing that if his wings unfolded at that speed he'd be blown into a million tiny shreds of seagull. But the speed was power, and the speed was joy, and the speed was pure beauty.

He began his pullout at a thousand feet, wingtips thudding and blurring in that gigantic wind, the boat and the crowd of gulls tilting and growing meteor-fast, directly in his path.

He couldn't stop; he didn't know yet even how to turn at that speed.

Collision would be instant death.

And so he shut his eyes.

It happened that morning, then, just after sunrise, that Jonathan Livingston Seagull fired directly through the center of Breakfast Flock, ticking off two hundred twelve miles per hour, eyes closed, in a great roaring shriek of wind and feathers. The Gull of Fortune smiled upon him this once, and no one was killed.

By the time he had pulled his beak straight up into the sky he was still scorching along at a hundred and sixty miles per hour. When he had slowed to twenty and stretched his wings again at last, the boat was a crumb on the sea, four thousand feet below.

His thought was triumph. Terminal velocity! A seagull at *two hundred fourteen miles per hour*! It was a breakthrough, the greatest single moment in the history of the Flock, and in that moment a new age opened for Jonathan Gull. Flying out to his lonely practice area, folding his wings for a dive from eight thousand feet, he set himself at once to discover how to turn.

A single wingtip feather, he found, moved a fraction of an inch, gives a smooth sweeping curve at tremendous speed. Before he learned this, however, he found that moving more than one feather at that speed will spin you like a rifle ball . . . and Jonathan had flown the first aerobatics[5] of any seagull on earth.

He spared no time that day for talk with other gulls, but flew on past sunset. He discovered the loop, the slow roll, the point roll, the inverted spin, the gull bunt,[6] the pinwheel.

When Jonathan Seagull joined the Flock on the beach, it was full night. He was dizzy and terribly tired. Yet in delight he flew a loop to landing, with a snap roll just before touchdown. When they hear of it, he thought, of the Breakthrough, they'll be wild with joy. How much more there is now to living! Instead of our drab slogging forth and back to the fishing boats, there's a reason to life! We can lift ourselves out of ignorance, we can find ourselves as creatures of excellence and intelligence and skill. We can be free! *We can learn to fly!*

---

4. **terminal velocity** [vi los′ə tē]: the greatest speed that a body can reach by falling freely through the air.

5. **aerobatics** [âr′ə bat′iks]: unusual and difficult flying feats or stunts.
6. **bunt:** flying maneuver consisting of half an outside loop followed by a half roll.

READER'S RESPONSE

Do you think it is good to be as driven by a goal as Jonathan Livingston Seagull is? Why or why not?

STUDY QUESTIONS

Recalling

1. What does Jonathan Livingston Seagull love above all?
2. Why do Jonathan's parents worry about him?
3. What problems does Jonathan have at high speeds?
4. After Jonathan falls into the sea at ninety miles per hour, what does he decide to do?
5. What discovery about flying does he make as he flies home that night?
6. What is Jonathan's dream for all seagulls?

Interpreting

7. Do you think the author wants us to admire Jonathan or find him foolish? How do you know?
8. What would you say is the author's attitude toward living for an ideal?

Extending

9. Jonathan lives for the ideal of flight. What ideals do you think humans should live for?

VOCABULARY

Suffixes

A **suffix** is a word part added to the end of a word. Adding a suffix can change the meaning of a word. Suffixes are listed in most dictionaries, along with their meanings.

Sometimes you can figure out the meaning of a word by examining its suffix. In the word *gigantic,* for example, the suffix *-ic* means "characteristic of," or "like." Therefore *gigantic* means "like a giant." Here are some common suffixes:

Suffix	Meaning
-ion	the act or condition of
-less	without, lacking
-ness	state, quality, or condition of being
-ly	in a (specified) manner

The following words are from "Jonathan Livingston Seagull." Copy each word, underline the suffix, and use the meaning of the suffix to help you explain the word's meaning.

1. guiltless
2. feebly
3. foolishness
4. pointless
5. concentration

High Cliffs of Mendocino,
Millard Sheets, 1981.

Thinking Skills: Evaluating

DEFINITION
Evaluating is a way of thinking about something and making a judgment about it. When you evaluate, you apply criteria to make your judgment. Criteria are the standards, rules, or tests on which a judgment can be based.

STEPS
1. **State the reason or purpose for your evaluation.**
   What do you want to evaluate? Why do you want to evaluate it?

2. **Identify the criteria.**
   What specific rules, tests, or standards will you use to make your judgment?

3. **Apply the criteria.**
   Does the subject of your evaluation meet each specific criterion? Does it meet some criteria better than others?

4. **Draw a conclusion.**
   The conclusion is your evaluation of how well the subject meets the criteria.

EXAMPLE
Imagine that you have just read a newspaper editorial defending the need for unmanned space exploration. A friend asks you, "Is it a good editorial?" You may answer "yes" or "no" without talking about all your criteria for a good editorial. In your mind, however, you make your evaluation based on criteria.

1. **State the reason or purpose for your evaluation.** You want to evaluate the editorial in order to give your friend an accurate answer.

2. **Identify the criteria.** You choose to evaluate the editorial according to its topic, argument, use of facts and examples, and final statement.

3. **Apply the criteria.** You think that the editorial deals with an important topic, states its argument clearly, and backs up opinions with facts and examples. Finally, the editorial uses the strong evidence it contains to make a persuasive final statement.

4. **Draw a conclusion.** You conclude that the editorial is good. In fact, it meets your criteria so well that it persuades you to accept its point of view.

ACTIVITY 1
Evaluating *Jonathan Livingston Seagull*
Follow the four steps of evaluating to answer the question "Is *Jonathan Livingston Seagull* a good story?" Identify your criteria carefully, being very specific about what you think makes a good story. You may want to include one or more of the following criteria: an exciting plot, a hero you care about, a conflict that holds your interest, and vivid descriptions of the natural world.

ACTIVITY 2
Evaluating a Work of Literature
Evaluate another selection in this book or any other work of literature that you have read. Follow the four steps. Remember that different people may have different criteria for good literature. What is important is that you think about your criteria and they reflect what you believe.

Amiri Baraka (born 1934) is a poet and playwright, formerly known as LeRoi Jones. A native of New Jersey, Baraka attended Rutgers and Howard universities and served with the Strategic Air Command. He later studied philosophy at Columbia University and German literature at the New School for Social Research. While his early poetry was personal and romantic, Baraka's later writing has been increasingly aggressive and provocative. In 1965 he took the name Amiri Baraka to symbolize his commitment to African-Americans. Plays such as *Dutchman* and *Slave Ship* established him as a major American dramatist. Many of Baraka's numerous poems and essays express his passionate commitment to social justice and his rich appreciation of black culture and spirit.

Why do we often learn about ourselves when we are concentrating on something else?

Amiri Baraka

Song Form

Morning uptown, quiet on the street,
no matter the distinctions that can be
made, quiet, very quiet, on the street.
Sun's not even up, just some kid and me,
5   skating, both of us, at the early sun, and
amazed there is grace for us, without our
having to smile too tough, or be very pleasant
even to each other. Merely to be mere, ly to be

READER'S RESPONSE

What feeling does this poem create in you?

STUDY QUESTIONS

Recalling

1. Where and when does the event described in the poem take place?
2. Who are the people in the poem? What are they doing?
3. What surprises both of them?

Interpreting

4. Why do you think Baraka stresses the quietness of the street?
5. What do you think the poet means by "there is grace for us"?
6. What do you think the people in the poem are usually like? Why are they different on this morning?

Extending

7. Describe a situation in which you enjoyed a similar sense of quiet coexistence with someone else.

Manhattan Bridge Loop, Edward Hopper, 1928.

Virginia Driving Hawk Sneve (born 1933) is a member of the Rosebud Sioux Tribe of South Dakota. She has taught English in both public and Indian schools and has worked as a guidance counselor. Since the 1970s she has been an editor, writer, and journalist. "In my writing, both fiction and nonfiction," she says, "I try to present an accurate portrayal of American Indian life as I have known it. I also attempt to interpret history from the viewpoint of the American Indian; in so doing, I hope to correct the many misconceptions and untruths which have been too long perpetrated by non-Indian authors who have written about us." In "The Medicine Bag" a boy exchanges some misconceptions about his Indian heritage for a deeper truth.

Grandpa wasn't tall and stately like TV Indians. His hair wasn't in braids, but hung in stringy, gray strands on his neck and he was old. . . . So when Grandpa came to visit us, I was so ashamed and embarrassed I could've died.

Virginia Driving Hawk Sneve

The Medicine Bag

My kid sister Cheryl and I always bragged about our Sioux grandpa, Joe Iron Shell. Our friends, who had always lived in the city and only knew about Indians from movies and TV, were impressed by our stories. Maybe we exaggerated and made Grandpa and the reservation sound glamorous, but when we'd return home to Iowa after our yearly summer visit to Grandpa we always had some exciting tale to tell.

We always had some authentic Sioux article to show our listeners. One year Cheryl had new moccasins that Grandpa had made. On another visit he gave me a small, round, flat, rawhide drum which was decorated with a painting of a warrior riding a horse. He taught me a real Sioux chant to sing while I beat the drum with a leather-covered stick

that had a feather on the end. Man, that really made an impression.

We never showed our friends Grandpa's picture. Not that we were ashamed of him, but because we knew that the glamorous tales we told didn't go with the real thing. Our friends would have laughed at the picture, because Grandpa wasn't tall and stately like TV Indians. His hair wasn't in braids, but hung in stringy, gray strands on his neck and he was old. He was our great-grandfather, and he didn't live in a tipi, but all by himself in a part log, part tar-paper[1] shack on the Rosebud Reservation in South Dakota. So

---

1. **tar-paper:** heavy paper coated with tar and used to cover the outside of buildings.

when Grandpa came to visit us, I was so ashamed and embarrassed I could've died.

There are a lot of yippy poodles and other fancy little dogs in our neighborhood, but they usually barked singly at the mailman from the safety of their own yards. Now it sounded as if a whole pack of mutts were barking together in one place.

I got up and walked to the curb to see what the commotion was. About a block away I saw a crowd of little kids yelling, with the dogs yipping and growling around someone who was walking down the middle of the street.

I watched the group as it slowly came closer and saw that in the center of the strange procession was a man wearing a tall black hat. He'd pause now and then to peer at something in his hand and then at the houses on either side of the street. I felt cold and hot at the same time as I recognized the man. "Oh, no!" I whispered. "It's Grandpa!"

I stood on the curb, unable to move even though I wanted to run and hide. Then I got mad when I saw how the yippy dogs were growling and nipping at the old man's baggy pant legs and how wearily he poked them away with his cane. "Stupid mutts," I said as I ran to rescue Grandpa.

When I kicked and hollered at the dogs to get away, they put their tails between their legs and scattered. The kids ran to the curb where they watched me and the old man.

"Grandpa," I said and felt pretty dumb when my voice cracked. I reached for his beat-up old tin suitcase, which was tied shut with a rope. But he set it down right in the street and shook my hand.

"*Hau, Takoza,*[2] Grandchild," he greeted me formally in Sioux.

All I could do was stand there with the whole neighborhood watching and shake the hand of the leather-brown old man. I saw how his gray hair straggled from under his big black hat, which had a drooping feather in its crown. His rumpled black suit hung like a sack over his stooped frame. As he shook my hand, his coat fell open to expose a bright-red, satin shirt with a beaded bolo tie[3] under the collar. His getup wasn't out of place on the reservation, but it sure was here, and I wanted to sink right through the pavement.

"Hi," I muttered with my head down. I tried to pull my hand away when I felt his bony hand trembling, and looked up to see fatigue in his face. I felt like crying. I couldn't think of anything to say so I picked up Grandpa's suitcase, took his arm, and guided him up the driveway to our house.

Mom was standing on the steps. I don't know how long she'd been watching, but her hand was over her mouth and she looked as if she couldn't believe what she saw. Then she ran to us.

"Grandpa," she gasped. "How in the world did you get here?"

She checked her move to embrace Grandpa and I remembered that such a display of affection is unseemly to the Sioux and would embarrass him.

"*Hau,* Marie," he said as he shook Mom's hand. She smiled and took his other arm.

As we supported him up the steps the door banged open and Cheryl came bursting out of the house. She was all smiles and was so obviously glad to see Grandpa that I was ashamed of how I felt.

---

2. ***Hau, Takoza*** [hou tä kō′zhä]: Sioux for "Hello, Grandchild."

---

3. **bolo tie:** a necktie consisting of a piece of cord fastened at the throat with a clasp or bar.

"Grandpa!" she yelled happily. "You came to see us!"

Grandpa smiled and Mom and I let go of him as he stretched out his arms to my 10-year-old sister, who was still young enough to be hugged.

"Wicincala,[4] little girl," he greeted her and then collapsed.

He had fainted. Mom and I carried him into her sewing room, where we had a spare bed.

After we had Grandpa on the bed Mom stood there helplessly patting his shoulder.

"Shouldn't we call the doctor, Mom?" I suggested, since she didn't seem to know what to do.

"Yes," she agreed with a sigh. "You make Grandpa comfortable, Martin."

I reluctantly moved to the bed. I knew Grandpa wouldn't want to have Mom undress him, but I didn't want to, either. He was so skinny and frail that his coat slipped off easily. When I loosened his tie and opened his shirt collar, I felt a small leather pouch that hung from a thong around his neck. I left it alone and moved to remove his boots. The scuffed old cowboy boots were tight and he moaned as I put pressure on his legs to jerk them off.

I put the boots on the floor and saw why they fit so tight. Each one was stuffed with money. I looked at the bills that lined the boots and started to ask about them, but Grandpa's eyes were closed again.

Mom came back with a basin of water. "The doctor thinks Grandpa is suffering from heat exhaustion," she explained as she bathed Grandpa's face. Mom gave a big sigh, "Oh hinh, Martin. How do you suppose he got here?"

We found out after the doctor's visit. Grandpa was angrily sitting up in bed while Mom tried to feed him some soup.

"Tonight you let Marie feed you, Grandpa," spoke my dad, who had gotten home from work just as the doctor was leaving. "You're not really sick," he said as he gently pushed Grandpa back against the pillows. "The doctor said you just got too tired and hot after your long trip."

Grandpa relaxed, and between sips of soup he told us of his journey. Soon after our visit to him Grandpa decided that he would like to see where his only living descendants lived and what our home was like. Besides, he admitted sheepishly, he was lonesome after we left.

I knew everybody felt as guilty as I did—especially Mom. Mom was all Grandpa had left. So even after she married my dad, who's a white man and teaches in the college in our city, and after Cheryl and I were born, Mom made sure that every summer we spent a week with Grandpa.

I never thought that Grandpa would be lonely after our visits, and none of us noticed how old and weak he had become. But Grandpa knew and so he came to us. He had ridden on buses for two and a half days. When he arrived in the city, tired and stiff from sitting for so long, he set out, walking, to find us.

He had stopped to rest on the steps of some building downtown and a policeman found him. The cop, according to Grandpa, was a good man who took him to the bus stop and waited until the bus came and told the driver to let Grandpa out at Bell View Drive. After Grandpa got off the bus, he started walking again. But he couldn't see the house num-

---

4. **Wicincala** [wē chēn'chä lä]: Sioux for "Little girl."

bers on the other side when he walked on the sidewalk so he walked in the middle of the street. That's when all the little kids and dogs followed him.

I knew everybody felt as bad as I did. Yet I was proud of this 86-year-old man, who had never been away from the reservation, having the courage to travel so far alone.

"You found the money in my boots?" he asked Mom.

"Martin did," she answered, and roused herself to scold. "Grandpa, you shouldn't have carried so much money. What if someone had stolen it from you?"

Grandpa laughed. "I would've known if anyone tried to take the boots off my feet. The money is what I've saved for a long time—a hundred dollars—for my funeral. But you take it now to buy groceries so that I won't be a burden to you while I am here."

"That won't be necessary, Grandpa," Dad said. "We are honored to have you with us and you will never be a burden. I am only sorry that we never thought to bring you home with us this summer and spare you the discomfort of a long trip."

Grandpa was pleased. "Thank you," he answered. "But do not feel bad that you didn't bring me with you for I would not have come then. It was not time." He said this in such a way that no one could argue with him. To Grandpa and the Sioux, he once told me, a thing would be done when it was the right time to do it and that's the way it was.

"Also," Grandpa went on, looking at me, "I have come because it is soon time for Martin to have the medicine bag."

We all knew what that meant. Grandpa thought he was going to die and he had to follow the tradition of his family to pass the medicine bag, along with its history, to the oldest male child.

"Even though the boy," he said still looking at me, "bears a white man's name, the medicine bag will be his."

I didn't know what to say. I had the same hot and cold feeling that I had when I first saw Grandpa in the street. The medicine bag was the dirty leather pouch I had found around his neck. "I could never wear such a thing," I almost said aloud. I thought of having my friends see it in gym class, at the swimming pool, and could imagine the smart things they would say. But I just swallowed hard and took a step toward the bed. I knew I would have to take it.

But Grandpa was tired. "Not now, Martin," he said, waving his hand in dismissal, "it is not time. Now I will sleep."

So that's how Grandpa came to be

with us for two months. My friends kept asking to come see the old man, but I put them off. I told myself that I didn't want them laughing at Grandpa. But even as I made excuses I knew it wasn't Grandpa that I was afraid they'd laugh at.

Nothing bothered Cheryl about bringing her friends to see Grandpa. Every day after school started there'd be a crew of giggling little girls or round-eyed little boys crowded around the old man on the patio, where he'd gotten in the habit of sitting every afternoon.

Grandpa would smile in his gentle way and patiently answer their questions, or he'd tell them stories of brave warriors, ghosts, animals, and the kids listened in awed silence. Those little guys thought Grandpa was great.

Finally, one day after school, my friends came home with me because nothing I said stopped them. "We're going to see the great Indian of Bell View Drive," said Hank, who was supposed to be my best friend. "My brother has seen him three times so he oughta be well enough to see us."

When we got to my house Grandpa was sitting on the patio. He had on his red shirt, but today he also wore a fringed leather vest that was decorated with beads. Instead of his usual cowboy boots he had solidly beaded moccasins on his feet that stuck out of his black trousers. Of course, he had his old black hat on—he was seldom without it. But it had been brushed and the feather in the beaded headband was proudly erect, its tip a brighter white. His hair lay in silver strands over the red shirt collar.

I stared just as my friends did and I heard one of them murmur, "Wow!"

Grandpa looked up and when his eyes met mine they twinkled as if he were laughing inside. He nodded to me and my face got all hot. I could tell that he had

known all along I was afraid he'd embarrass me in front of my friends.

"*Hau, hoksilas,*[5] boys," he greeted and held out his hand.

My buddies passed in a single file and shook his hand as I introduced them. They were so polite I almost laughed. "How, there, Grandpa," and even a "How-do-you-do, sir."

"You look fine, Grandpa," I said as the guys sat on the lawn chairs or on the patio floor.

"*Hanh,*[6] yes," he agreed. "When I woke up this morning it seemed the right time to dress in the good clothes. I knew that my grandson would be bringing his friends."

"You guys want some lemonade or something?" I offered. No one answered. They were listening to Grandpa as he started telling how he'd killed the deer from which his vest was made.

Grandpa did most of the talking while my friends were there. I was so proud of him and amazed at how respectfully quiet my buddies were. Mom had to chase them home at supper time. As they left they shook Grandpa's hand again and said to me:

"Martin, he's really great!"

"Yeah, man! Don't blame you for keeping him to yourself."

"Can we come back?"

But after they left, Mom said, "No more visitors for a while, Martin. Grandpa won't admit it, but his strength hasn't returned. He likes having company, but it tires him."

That evening Grandpa called me to his room before he went to sleep. "Tomorrow," he said, "when you come home, it will be time to give you the medicine bag."

---

5. **Hau, hoksilas** [hou hōk shē′läs]: Sioux for "Hello, boys."
6. **Hanh** [hän]: Sioux for "Yes."

I felt a hard squeeze from where my heart is supposed to be and was scared, but I answered, "OK, Grandpa."

All night I had weird dreams about thunder and lightning on a high hill. From a distance I heard the slow beat of a drum. When I woke up in the morning I felt as if I hadn't slept at all. At school it seemed as if the day would never end, and when it finally did, I ran home.

Grandpa was in his room, sitting on the bed. The shades were down and the place was dim and cool. I sat on the floor in front of Grandpa, but he didn't even look at me. After what seemed a long time he spoke.

"I sent your mother and sister away. What you will hear today is only for a man's ears. What you will receive is only for a man's hands." He fell silent and I felt shivers down my back.

"My father in his early manhood," Grandpa began, "made a vision quest[7] to find a spirit guide for his life. You cannot understand how it was in that time, when the great Teton[8] Sioux were first made to stay on the reservation. There was a strong need for guidance from *Wakantanka*,[9] the Great Spirit. But too many of the young men were filled with despair and hatred. They thought it was hopeless to search for a vision when the glorious life was gone and only the hated confines of a reservation lay ahead. But my father held to the old ways.

"He carefully prepared for his quest with a purifying sweat bath[10] and then he went alone to a high butte[11] top to fast and pray. After three days he received his sacred dream—in which he found, after long searching, the white man's iron. He did not understand his vision of finding something belonging to the white people, for in that time they were the enemy. When he came down

---

7. **vision quest:** among the Indian tribes of the Great Plains, a young Indian's journey to an isolated place to seek a vision of a spirit or special guardian who would become his guide and protector. The quest included obtaining sacred objects, which the Indian would carry wrapped in a skin.
8. **Teton** [tē′tän]: one of the tribes of the Sioux Indian nation, whose members formerly lived in North and South Dakota and Wyoming.
9. *Wakantanka* [wä kän′tän kä]: Sioux for "the Great Spirit."

10. **sweat bath:** bath intended to cleanse the body by causing or increasing sweating, taken in a closed hut in which hot water is poured on stones to produce steam.
11. **butte** [būt]: isolated, usually flat-topped hill or mountain with steep sides.

from the butte to cleanse himself at the stream below, he found the remains of a campfire and the broken shell of an iron kettle. This was a sign which reinforced his dream. He took a piece of the iron for his medicine bag, which he had made of elk skin years before, to prepare for his quest.

"He returned to his village, where he told his dream to the wise old men of the tribe. They gave him the name *Iron Shell*, but neither did they understand the meaning of the dream. This first Iron Shell kept the piece of iron with him at all times and believed it gave him protection from the evils of those unhappy days.

"Then a terrible thing happened to Iron Shell. He and several other young men were taken from their homes by the soldiers and sent far away to a white man's boarding school. He was angry and lonesome for his parents and the young girl he had wed before he was taken away. At first Iron Shell resisted the teachers' attempts to change him and he did not try to learn. One day it was his turn to work in the school's blacksmith shop. As he walked into the place he knew that his medicine had brought him there to learn and work with the white man's iron.

"Iron Shell became a blacksmith and worked at the trade when he returned to the reservation. All of his life he treasured the medicine bag. When he was old, and I was a man, he gave it to me, for no one made the vision quest any more."

Grandpa quit talking and I stared in disbelief as he covered his face with his hands. His shoulders were shaking with quiet sobs and I looked away until he began to speak again.

"I kept the bag until my son, your mother's father, was a man and had to leave us to fight in the war across the ocean. I gave him the bag, for I believed it would protect him in battle, but he did not take it with him. He was afraid that he would lose it. He died in a far-away place."

Again Grandpa was still and I felt his grief around me.

"My son," he went on after clearing his throat, "had only a daughter and it is not proper for her to know of these things."

He unbuttoned his shirt, pulled out the leather pouch, and lifted it over his head. He held it in his hand, turning it over and over as if memorizing how it looked.

"In the bag," he said as he opened it and removed two objects, "is the broken shell of the iron kettle, a pebble from the butte, and a piece of the sacred sage." He held the pouch upside down and dust drifted down.

"After the bag is yours you must put a piece of prairie sage within and never open it again until you pass it on to your son." He replaced the pebble and the piece of iron, and tied the bag.

I stood up, somehow knowing I should. Grandpa slowly rose from the bed and stood upright in front of me holding the bag before my face. I closed my eyes and waited for him to slip it over my head. But he spoke.

"No, you need not wear it." He placed the soft leather bag in my right hand and closed my other hand over it. "It would not be right to wear it in this time and place where no one will understand. Put it safely away until you are again on the reservation. Wear it then, when you replace the sacred sage."

Grandpa turned and sat again on the bed. Wearily he leaned his head against the pillow. "Go," he said, "I will sleep now."

"Thank you, Grandpa," I said softly and left with the bag in my hands.

That night Mom and Dad took Grandpa to the hospital. Two weeks later I stood alone on the lonely prairie of the reservation and put the sacred sage in my medicine bag.

READER'S RESPONSE

How do you think Martin feels about his Sioux heritage by the end of the story?

STUDY QUESTIONS

Recalling

1. In what ways is Grandpa different from the man Martin has described in his stories?
2. What makes Grandpa's journey to Martin's family so difficult?
3. Why does Grandpa decide to visit Martin's family?
4. What does Grandpa tell Martin about the history of the medicine bag?
5. What does Martin do two weeks after he receives the bag?

Interpreting

6. What does the medicine bag stand for?
7. In what way do Martin's feelings about his great grandfather change by the end of the story?
8. Describe the passages that Martin and his grandfather go through in this story.

VOCABULARY

Sentence Completions

Each of the following sentences contains a blank with four possible words for completing the sentence. Choose the word that completes each sentence correctly. Write the number of each item and the letter of your choice on a separate sheet.

1. This signature is ___ and very valuable.
   (a) unseemly   (c) tar paper
   (b) authentic   (d) purifying
2. This is a family portrait showing my great-grandparents and their ___.
   (a) confines   (c) dismissal
   (b) basin   (d) descendants
3. Standing on the ___, we could see for miles.
   (a) butte   (c) elk
   (b) thong   (d) basin
4. He burst out of the ___ of his tiny room.
   (a) reservation   (c) dismissal
   (b) basin   (d) confines
5. The bell rang for ___, and everyone left.
   (a) dismissal   (c) descendants
   (b) reservation   (d) purifying

COMPOSITION

Writing a Comparison/Contrast

Write a three-paragraph composition comparing and contrasting what you know about native Americans from movies and television with what you learned from this story. **Prewriting:** Make a chart with two columns. In one column list the characteristics of native Americans seen in movies and on television. In the other column list the characteristics suggested by "The Medicine Bag." **Writing:** In the first paragraph of your composition, describe specific ways in which the portrayals of native Americans in the media and in this story are similar. In a second paragraph, explain the differences between the media's presentation and that of the story. In the last paragraph tell which view seems more realistic, and explain why. **Revising:** Review your paragraph to see that you have expressed your ideas clearly and logically. Review for effective choice and organization. Make sure that your final copy is free of errors in grammar, spelling, and punctuation.

Writing a Character's Thoughts

Imagine that you are the narrator of "The Medicine Bag." Your great-grandfather has died, and you are putting a piece of sage in your medicine bag as you stand alone on the prairie in the reservation. Write your thoughts. Describe the journey you have taken within your heart.

Gerald Haslam (born 1937) did many things before writing fiction. He worked on farms and in oil fields, stores, banks, and shops. In addition, he taught English at two California universities. He explains his preference for writing short stories: "I was raised in a richly varied area—California's San Joaquin Valley—where oral tale-telling was a fine art. I was a good listener and I still am. Since no one ever told me a novel, I have always considered the story, not its longer counterpart, to be fiction's most natural . . . expression. It is a continuing source of both wonder and satisfaction to me that I have evolved into a storyteller."

What is the difference between someone's home and the place in which he or she lives?

• •

Gerald Haslam

The Horned Toad[1]

Expectoran su sangre!"[2] exclaimed Great-grandma when I showed her the small horned toad I had removed from my breast pocket. I turned toward my mother, who translated: "They spit blood."

"*De los ojos*,"[3] Grandma added. "From their eyes," mother explained, herself uncomfortable in the presence of the small beast.

I grinned, "Awwwwww."

But my Great-grandmother did not smile.

"*Son muy toxicos*,"[4] she nodded with finality. Mother moved back an involuntary step, her hands suddenly busy at her breast. "Put that thing down," she ordered.

"His name's John," I said.

"Put John down and not in your pocket, either," my mother nearly shouted. "Those things are very poisonous. Didn't you understand what Grandma said?"

I shook my head.

"Well . . ." mother looked from one of us to the other—spanning four generations of California, standing three feet apart—and said, "of course you didn't. Please take him back where you got him, and be care-

---

1. **horned toad:** insect-eating lizard with spiny horns on its head and scales along the sides of its body.
2. *Expectoran su sangre* [eks pek tō′rän sōō sän′grä]: Spanish for "They spit blood."
3. *De los ojos* [dā lōs ō′hōs]: Spanish for "from their eyes."

4. *Son muy toxicos* [sōn mōō′e tōk′sē kōs]: Spanish for "They are very poisonous."

ful. We'll all feel better when you do." The tone of her voice told me that the discussion had ended, so I released the little reptile where I'd captured him.

During those years in Oildale,[5] the mid-1940s, I needed only to walk across the street to find a patch of virgin desert. Neighborhood kids called it simply "the vacant lot," less than an acre without houses or sidewalks. Not that we were desperate for desert then, since we could walk into its scorched skin a mere half-mile west, north, and east. To the south, incongruously,[6] flowed the icy Kern River, fresh from the Sierras[7] and surrounded by riparian[8] forest.

Ours was rich soil formed by that same Kern River as it ground Sierra granite and turned it into coarse sand, then carried it down into the valley and deposited it over millennia[9] along its many changes of channels. The ants that built miniature volcanoes on the vacant lot left piles of tiny stones with telltale markings of black on white. Deeper than ants could dig were pools of petroleum that led to many fortunes and lured men like my father from Texas. The dry hills to the east and north sprouted forests of wooden derricks.[10]

Despite the abundance of open land, plus the constant lure of the river where desolation and verdancy[11] met, most kids relied on the vacant lot as their primary playground. Even with its bullheads[12] and stinging insects, we played everything from football to kick-the-can on it. The lot actually resembled my father's head, bare in the middle but full of growth around the edges: weeds, stickers,[13] cactuses, and a few bushes. We played our games on its sandy center, and conducted such sports as ant fights and lizard hunts on its brushy periphery.[14]

That spring, when I discovered the lone horned toad near the back of the lot, had been rough on my family. Earlier, there had been quiet, unpleasant tension between Mom and Daddy. He was a silent man, little given to emotional displays. It was difficult for him to show affection and I guess the openness of Mom's family made him uneasy. Daddy had no kin in California and rarely mentioned any in Texas. He couldn't seem to understand my mother's large, intimate family, their constant noisy concern for one another, and I think he was a little jealous of the time she gave everyone, maybe even me.

I heard her talking on the phone to my various aunts and uncles, usually in Spanish. Even though I couldn't understand—Daddy had warned her not to teach me that foreign tongue[15] because it would hurt me in school, and she'd complied—I could sense the stress. I had been afraid they were going to divorce, since she only used Spanish to hide things from me. I'd confronted her with my suspicion, but she comforted me, saying, no, that was not the problem. They were merely deciding when it would be our turn to care for Grandma. I didn't really understand, although I was relieved.

---

5. **Oildale:** town in south central California where many oil fields are located.
6. **incongruously** [in kongˈgroo əs lē]: not appropriately, not in harmony.
7. **Sierras** [sē erˈəz]: the Sierra Nevada mountain range, in eastern California.
8. **riparian** [ri pärˈē ən]: of or on the banks of a river.
9. **millennia** [mi lenˈē ə]: periods of one thousand years.
10. **derricks** [derˈiks]: structures placed over oil wells to support drilling equipment.
11. **verdancy** [verˈdən sē]: greenness; plant life.

12. **bullheads:** small, black insects.
13. **stickers:** types of thorny or prickly weeds.
14. **periphery** [pə rifˈər ē]: outer boundary of an area.
15. **foreign tongue:** foreign language.

I later learned that my Great-grandmother—whom we simply called "Grandma"—had been moving from house to house within the family, trying to find a place she'd accept. She hated the city, and most of the aunts and uncles lived in Los Angeles. Our house in Oildale was much closer to the open country where she'd dwelt all her life. She had wanted to come to our place right away because she had raised my mother from a baby when my own grandmother died. But the old lady seemed unimpressed with Daddy, whom she called "ese gringo."[16]

In truth, we had more room, and my dad made more money in the oil patch than almost anyone else in the family. Since my mother was the closest to Grandma, our place was the logical one for her, but Ese Gringo didn't see it that way, I guess, at least not at first. Finally, after much debate, he relented.

In any case, one windy afternoon, my Uncle Manuel and Aunt Toni drove up and deposited four-and-a-half feet of bewigged, bejeweled Spanish spitfire: a square, pale face topped by a tightly-curled black wig that hid a bald head—her hair having been lost to typhoid nearly sixty years before—her small white hands veined with rivers of blue. She walked with a prancing bounce that made her appear half her age, and she barked orders in Spanish from the moment she emerged from Manuel and Toni's car. Later, just before they left, I heard Uncle Manuel tell my dad, "Good luck, Charlie. That old lady's dynamite." Daddy only grunted.

She had been with us only two days when I tried to impress her with my horned toad. In fact, nothing I did seemed to impress her, and she referred to me as el malcriado,[17] causing my mother to shake her head. Mom explained to me that Grandma was just old and lonely for Grandpa and uncomfortable in town. Mom told me that Grandma had lived over half a century in the country, away from the noise, away from clutter, away from people. She refused to accompany my mother on shopping trips, or anywhere else. She even refused to climb into a car, and I wondered how Uncle Manuel had managed to load her up in order to bring her to us.

She disliked sidewalks and roads, dancing across them when she had to, then appearing to wipe her feet on earth or grass. Things too civilized simply did not please her. A brother of hers had been killed in the great San Francisco earthquake and that had been the end of her tolerance of cities. Until my Great-grandfather died, they lived on a small rancho near Arroyo Cantua,[18] north of Coalinga.[19] Grandpa, who had come north from Sonora[20] as a youth to work as a vaquero,[21] had bred horses and cattle, and cowboyed for other ranchers, scraping together enough of a living to raise eleven children.

He had been, until the time of his death, a lean, dark-skinned man with wide shoulders, a large nose, and a sweeping handlebar mustache that was white when I knew him. His Indian blood darkened all his progeny so that not even I was as fair-skinned as my Great-grandmother, Ese Gringo for a father or not.

---

16. **ese gringo** [ā'sā grēn'gō]: Spanish for "that foreigner; that Yankee."

17. **el malcriado** [el mäl krē ä'thō]: Spanish for "the ill-behaved one."
18. **Arroyo Cantua** [ä rrō'yō cän tōō'ä]: town in central California.
19. **Coalinga** [kō lin'gə]: city in central California and oil-field center, near Fresno.
20. **Sonora** [sə nôr'ə]: state in northwestern Mexico.
21. **vaquero** [vä kā'rō]: Spanish for "cowboy."

As it turned out, I didn't really understand very much about Grandma at all. She was old, of course, yet in many ways my parents treated her as though she were younger than me, walking her to the bathroom at night and bringing her presents from the store. In other ways—drinking wine at dinner, for example—she was granted adult privileges. Even Daddy didn't drink wine except on special occasions. After Grandma moved in, though, he began to occasionally join her for a glass, sometimes even sitting with her on the porch for a pre-meal sip.

She held court[22] on our front porch, often gazing toward the desert hills east of us or across the street at kids playing on the lot. Occasionally, she would rise, cross the yard and sidewalk and street, skip over them, sometimes stumbling on the curb, and wipe her feet on the lot's sandy soil, then she would slowly circle the boundary between the open middle and the brushy sides, searching for something, it appeared. I never figured out what.

One afternoon I returned from school and saw Grandma perched on the porch as usual, so I started to walk around the house to avoid her sharp, mostly incomprehensible, tongue. She had already spotted me. "*Venga aquí!*"[23] she ordered, and I understood.

I approached the porch and noticed that Grandma was vigorously chewing something. She held a small white bag in one hand. Saying "*Qué deseas tomar?*"[24] she withdrew a large orange gumdrop from the bag and began slowly chewing it in her toothless mouth, smacking loudly as she did so. I stood below her for a moment trying to

remember the word for candy. Then it came to me: "*Dulce,*"[25] I said.

Still chewing, Grandma replied, "*Mande?*"[26]

Knowing she wanted a complete sentence, I again struggled, then came up with "*Deseo dulce.*"[27]

She measured me for a moment, before answering in nearly perfect English, "Oh, so you wan' some candy. Go to the store an' buy some."

---

22. **held court:** ruled, as a monarch surrounded by his or her attendants.
23. ***Venga aquí*** [ven'gä ä kē']: Spanish for "Come here."
24. ***Qué deseas tomar?*** [kā dā sā'äs tō mär']: Spanish for "What do you want to eat?"

25. ***Dulce*** [dōōl'sä]
26. ***Mande?*** [män'dä]: Spanish for "What?"
27. ***Deseo dulce*** [dā sā'ō dōōl'sä]: Spanish for "I want a piece of candy."

I don't know if it was the shock of hearing her speak English for the first time, or the way she had denied me a piece of candy, but I suddenly felt tears warm my cheeks and I sprinted into the house and found Mom, who stood at the kitchen sink. "Grandma just talked English," I burst between light sobs.

"What's wrong?" she asked as she reached out to stroke my head.

"Grandma can talk English," I repeated.

"Of course she can," Mom answered. "What's wrong?"

I wasn't sure what was wrong, but after considering, I told Mom that Grandma had teased me. No sooner had I said that than the old woman appeared at the door and hiked her skirt. Attached to one of her petticoats by safety pins were several small tobacco sacks, the white cloth kind that closed with yellow drawstrings. She carefully unhooked one and opened it, withdrawing a dollar, then handed the money to me. "*Para su dulce,*"[28] she said. Then, to my mother, she asked, "Why does he bawl like a motherless calf?"

"It's nothing," Mother replied.

"Do not weep, little one," the old lady comforted me, "Jesus and the Virgin love you." She smiled and patted my head. To my mother she said as though just realizing it, "Your baby?"

Somehow that day changed everything. I wasn't afraid of my great-grandmother any longer and, once I began spending time with her on the porch, I realized that my father had also begun directing increased attention to the old woman. Almost every evening Ese Gringo was sharing wine with Grandma. They talked out there, but I never did hear a real two-way conversation between them. Usually Grandma rattled on and Daddy nodded. She'd chuckle and pat his hand and he might grin, even grunt a word or two, before she'd begin talking again. Once I saw my mother standing by the front window watching them together, a smile playing across her face.

No more did I sneak around the house to avoid Grandma after school. Instead, she waited for me and discussed my efforts in class gravely, telling mother that I was a bright boy, "*muy inteligente,*"[29] and that I should be sent to the nuns who would train me. I would make a fine priest. When Ese Gringo heard that, he smiled and said, "He'd make a fair-to-middlin' Holy Roller preacher, too." Even Mom had to chuckle, and my great-grandmother shook her finger at Ese Gringo. "Oh you debil, Sharlie!" she cackled.

Frequently, I would accompany Grandma to the lot where she would explain that no fodder could grow there. Poor pasture or not, the lot was at least unpaved, and Grandma greeted even the tiniest new cactus or flowering weed with joy. "Look how beautiful," she would croon. "In all this ugliness, it lives." Oildale was my home and it didn't look especially ugly to me, so I could only grin and wonder.

Because she liked the lot and things that grew there, I showed her the horned toad when I captured it a second time. I was determined to keep it, although I did not discuss my plans with anyone. I also wanted to hear more about the bloody eyes, so I thrust the small animal nearly into her face one afternoon. She did not flinch. "*Ola señor sangre de ojos,*"[30] she said with a mischievous grin. "*Qué tal?*"[31]

---

28. **Para su dulce** [pä′rä soo dool′sä]: Spanish for "For your candy."

29. **muy inteligente** [moo′e ēn te le hen′tä]: Spanish for "very intelligent."

30. **Ola señor sangre de ojos** [ō′lä sen yôr′ sän ′grä dä ō′hōs]: Spanish for "Hello, Mr. Bloody Eyes."

31. **Qué tal?** [kä täl′]: Spanish for "How are you?"

It took me a moment to catch on.

"You were kidding before," I accused.

"Of course," she acknowledged, still grinning.

"But why?"

"Because the little beast belongs with his own kind in his own place, not in your pocket. Give him his freedom, my son."

I had other plans for the horned toad, but I was clever enough not to cross Grandma. "Yes, Ma'am," I replied. That night I placed the reptile in a flower bed cornered by a brick wall Ese Gringo had built the previous summer. It was a spot rich with insects for the toad to eat, and the little wall, only a foot high, must have seemed massive to so squat an animal.

Nonetheless, the next morning when I searched for the horned toad it was gone. I had no time to explore the yard for it, so I trudged off to school, my belly troubled. How could it have escaped? Classes meant little to me that day. I thought only of my lost pet—I had changed his name to Juan, the same as my Great-grandfather—and where I might find him.

I shortened my conversation with Grandma that afternoon so I could search for Juan. "What do you seek?" the old woman asked me as I poked through flower beds beneath the porch. "Praying mantises,"[32] I improvised, and she merely nodded, surveying me. But I had eyes only for my lost pet, and I continued pushing through branches and brushing aside leaves. No luck.

Finally, I gave in and turned toward the lot. I found my horned toad nearly across the street, crushed. It had been heading for the miniature desert and had almost made it when an automobile's tire had run over it. One notion immediately swept me: if I had left it on its lot, it would still be alive. I stood rooted there in the street, tears slicking my cheeks, and a car honked its horn as it passed, the driver shouting at me.

Grandma joined me, and stroked my back. "The poor little beast," was all she said, then she bent slowly and scooped up what remained of the horned toad and led me out of the street. "We must return him to his own place," she explained, and we trooped, my eyes still clouded, toward the back of the vacant lot. Carefully, I dug a hole with a piece of wood. Grandma placed Juan in it and covered him. We said an Our Father and a Hail Mary, then Grandma walked me back to the house. "Your little Juan is safe with God, my son," she comforted. We kept the horned toad's death a secret, and we visited his small grave frequently.

Grandma fell just before school ended and summer vacation began. As was her habit, she had walked alone to the vacant lot but this time, on her way back, she tripped over the curb and broke her hip. That following week, when Daddy brought her home from the hospital, she seemed to have shrunk. She sat hunched in a wheelchair on the porch, gazing with faded eyes toward the hills or at the lot, speaking rarely. She still sipped wine every evening with Daddy and even I could tell how concerned he was about her. It got to where he'd look in on her before leaving for work every morning and again at night before turning in. And if Daddy was home, Grandma always wanted him to push her chair when she needed moving, calling, "Sharlie!" until he arrived.

I was tugged from sleep on the night she died by voices drumming through the

32. **Praying mantises** [man'tis əz]: green or brown insects, related to the grasshopper, having stout, spiny forelegs for grasping their prey.

walls into darkness. I couldn't understand them, but was immediately frightened by the uncommon sounds of words in the night. I struggled from bed and walked into the living room just as Daddy closed the front door and a car pulled away.

Mom was sobbing softly on the couch and Daddy walked to her, stroked her head, then noticed me. "Come here, son," he gently ordered.

I walked to him and, uncharacteristically, he put an arm around me. "What's wrong?" I asked, near tears myself. Mom looked up, but before she could speak, Daddy said, "Grandma died." Then he sighed heavily and stood there with his arms around his weeping wife and son.

The next day my Uncle Manuel and Uncle Arnulfo, plus Aunt Chintia, arrived and over food they discussed with my mother where Grandma should be interred.[33] They argued that it would be too expensive to transport her body home and, besides, they could more easily visit her grave if she was buried in Bakersfield.[34] "They have such a nice, manicured grounds at Greenlawn," Aunt Chintia pointed out. Just when it seemed they had agreed, I could remain silent no longer. "But Grandma has to go home," I burst. "She has to! It's the only thing she really wanted. We can't leave her in the city."

Uncle Arnulfo, who was on the edge, snapped to Mother that I belonged with the other children, not interrupting adult conversation. Mom quietly agreed, but I

refused. My father walked into the room then. "What's wrong?" he asked.

"They're going to bury Grandma in Bakersfield, Daddy. Don't let 'em, please."

"Well, son . . ."

"When my horny toad got killed and she helped me to bury it, she said we had to return him to his place."

"Your horny toad?" Mother asked.

"He got squished and me and Grandma buried him in the lot. She said we had to take him back to his place. Honest she did."

No one spoke for a moment, then my father, Ese Gringo, who stood against the sink, responded: "That's right . . ." he paused, then added, "We'll bury her." I saw a weary smile cross my mother's face. "If she wanted to go back to the ranch then that's where we have to take her," Daddy said.

I hugged him and he, right in front of everyone, hugged back.

No one argued. It seemed, suddenly, as though they had all wanted to do exactly what I had begged for. Grown-ups baffled me. Late that week the entire family, hundreds it seemed, gathered at the little Catholic church in Coalinga for mass, then drove out to Arroyo Cantua and buried Grandma next to Grandpa. She rests there today.

My mother, father, and I drove back to Oildale that afternoon across the scorching westside desert, through sand and tumbleweeds and heat shivers. Quiet and sad, we knew we had done our best. Mom, who usually sat next to the door in the front seat, snuggled close to Daddy, and I heard her whisper to him, "Thank you, Charlie," as she kissed his cheek.

Daddy squeezed her, hesitated as if to clear his throat, then answered, "When you're family, you take care of your own."

---

33. **interred** [in turd′]: buried.
34. **Bakersfield:** city in south central California, where many oil fields are located.

READER'S RESPONSE

Would you say this story has a happy ending or a sad one?

STUDY QUESTIONS

Recalling

1. Why does the narrator's great-grandmother come to live with him and his parents? Does the narrator's father, Charlie, want her to come?
2. When does the narrator stop fearing Grandma?
3. What reason does Grandma later give for saying that the horned toad spits poisonous blood?
4. What is the toad trying to do when it dies?
5. After Grandma dies, what does the narrator tell the adults in his family? What does his father say at the end of the story?

Interpreting

6. What causes the boy's feelings about his great-grandmother to change during the course of the story?
7. What does the boy do to show how well he understands Grandma?
8. What does Charlie's final comment show about how his feelings toward Grandma have changed?

READING AND LITERARY FOCUS

Total Effect

In your reading so far you have been giving special attention to each of the various elements that make up a story: plot, character, setting, and theme. The best part of reading stories is putting all the parts back together—seeing how all the elements blend into a **total effect,** the story's overall impact on you. Each story has its own special total effect. The total effect of one story—say, "The Jump"—may be its tension and suspense. "Papa's Parrot" may be memorable for its power to make you feel compassion.

Thinking About Total Effect

1. **Setting and Character:** Where does this story take place? Why is this environment important to Grandma and the boy?
2. **Setting and Plot:** How does the setting influence the story's outcome?
3. **Plot and Character:** Find two examples of events that lead a character to change.
4. **Theme:** What do you think is the theme of this story? How do the plot, characters, and setting help you see this theme?
5. What would you say is the total effect of "The Horned Toad"?

COMPOSITION

Writing About Total Effect

Write a paragraph about the total effect of "The Horned Toad." **Prewriting:** First answer each of the questions above. Then think about the best words you can use to describe the story's total effect. **Writing:** Begin your paragraph with a sentence that describes the total effect. Then go on to explain how the story's elements fit together to create that effect. **Revising:** Check to see that you have presented your ideas in a logical order and used examples from the story to illustrate these ideas.

Inventing a Character

Invent a character, and write a description of him or her. First make a wheel diagram with which to gather together your ideas. In the center list two or three of the most important qualities your character will have. Draw spokes reaching out from the center. On each one write something your character might do. Make these actions fit the qualities in the center. Then, around the rim of the wheel, describe the physical appearance of your character. Use the best ideas from your diagram to help you write a lively description of your character. Your written description should begin with the character's physical traits. Then tell how the character's actions embody the two or three qualities at his or her heart.

The Horned Toad 513

Collaborative Learning: Themes

Passages

Without even knowing it, we start to learn about life and living from the moment we are born. All living beings—animals as well as humans—must go through this learning process in order to survive.

Every once in a while in this continuing learning process, we realize that we have learned something new and important. We become aware that we have grown up a little more—achieved a new level of understanding that will affect our thoughts and actions in the future.

1. **Panel Discussion** With a group, plan and conduct a panel discussion on the subject of movies about growing up in America. Brainstorm with the other panel members to come up with a list of the films best suited to your discussion. Select three. What do they have in common? How are they different? What do they say about the problems young Americans face and how they try to solve them? If you are using films set in earlier historical periods, compare the problems young Americans faced growing up then with those they face now.

   Consult with your teacher, and determine whether you could rent videotapes of the movies. If so, select appropriate parts, and show these to the class before you begin the discussion. Remember to pick a moderator or leader. At the end of the discussion, ask for questions or comments from the class.

2. **Report** Working with a group, select two or three famous men and women who are or were outstanding in their field. You might pick a scientist, like Marie Curie; an inventor, like Thomas Edison; or a sports hero, like Jackie Robinson. After you have chosen your subjects, go to the library, and research their lives. Then brainstorm to determine the qualities these people, different though they be, have in common. Identify and compare the obstacles they had to overcome before they triumphed. As you write the report, note the qualities that make these people different from ordinary men and women and those qualities that they share with others.

Collaborative Learning:
Across the Curriculum

Passages

1. **Literature and Science: Report** With a group, plan a short nonfiction piece about the life cycle of an animal that interests you. Possibilities might include a frog, a sea horse, a butterfly, a hippopotamus, or any other animal of your choice.

   Begin researching your subject and taking notes on its surroundings, appearance, development, growth, feeding patterns, enemies, and any other important information. Then make an outline showing the major events in the creature's life cycle. Finally, write the report, adding accurate and interesting details based on your research. Divide the work so that each member of the group has equal responsibility.

2. **Literature and Social Studies: American Citizenship** Not everyone who lives in the United States is an American citizen. People who come from other countries to live in the United States have to go through a process called *naturalization* before they can become American citizens. A naturalized American citizen has the same rights and privileges as a person who is an American citizen by birth.

   With three or four classmates plan an oral report on the process of becoming a naturalized American citizen. Find out whether your parents or grandparents or the relatives of any of the students in your class are naturalized. If so, interview these citizens for firsthand information on their experiences in the process.

   In addition, do library research on the subject. When you have all the facts, organize them into an outline, and write them down on index cards. For the class presentation, each member of the group should report on a different aspect of the naturalization process.

Preview

A novel is a long work of prose fiction that tells a story. Using the same literary elements that are found in short stories—plot, character, setting, narrator, and theme—a novelist takes us into worlds we might not ordinarily experience. Thus, we encounter and explore places and life styles that are set apart from our everyday life. Since a novel is longer than a short story, the author can include more of this imaginary world for us to explore.

My Side of the Mountain is a novel that describes a year in the life of Sam, a boy who has gone to the mountains by himself to live off the land. While reading his story, we become involved with his experiences of survival and independence. Most of us will never know a similar world, one spent in the woods living off the land, but through Sam we discover ways to face challenges and become independent without ever leaving home.

The Pinkham Notch, White Mountains,
Charles de Wolf Brownell, 1862.

photograph ©1990 Jill Krementz

Jean Craighead George (born 1919) was raised in Washington, D.C. "I grew up in the wild edges and riversides of Washington, spending summers at the old family home at Craighead, Pennsylvania. My father, an entomologist [a scientist who studies insects], and my twin brothers, now wildlife ecologists, took me with them on hunting and camping trips, to the tops of cliffs to look for falcons, down the white water rivers to fish and swim, and over the forest floors in search of mice, birds, wildflowers, trees, fish, salamanders, and mammals."

George began writing in the third grade, hoping that she would become an author and illustrator one day. While working as a newspaper reporter, she started to write books for young people because she wanted to communicate her love of nature. She wrote some of her books with her husband but is the sole author of many books on science and nature. These include a long series, "The Thirteen Moons," as well as the novels *Gull Number 737* and *Coyote in Manhattan*. In 1973 George won the Newbery Medal for *Julie of the Wolves*. Of all the awards she has won, this one is the most important to her—"better than getting the Pulitzer Prize!" *My Side of the Mountain*, a Newbery Honor Book more than thirty years ago, has been translated into foreign languages and made into a movie.

Although the characters, settings, and plots of George's novels vary, they all communicate the same search for an understanding of the mysteries of nature. In *My Side of the Mountain*, the character Sam does what George would have liked to have done when she was growing up: He lives off the land, observing and learning to live in harmony with nature.

Key Ideas in *My Side of the Mountain*

As you read *My Side of the Mountain*, think about the following topics. Keep track of what the novel says about each one. You will then understand the major themes of *My Side of the Mountain*.

- Survival in the wilderness
- Facing challenges
- The relationship between people and nature
- Learning from observation and books
- The search for independence

If you wanted to be free and independent, what would you do?

· ·

Dogtooth Violets

Jean Craighead George

My Side of the Mountain

IN WHICH
I Hole Up in a Snowstorm

I am on my mountain in a tree home that people have passed without ever knowing that I am here. The house is a hemlock tree six feet in diameter, and must be as old as the mountain itself. I came upon it last summer and dug and burned it out until I made a snug cave in the tree that I now call home.

"My bed is on the right as you enter, and is made of ash slats and covered with deerskin. On the left is a small fireplace about knee high. It is of clay and stones. It has a chimney that leads the smoke out through a knothole. I chipped out three other knotholes to let fresh air in. The air coming in is bitter cold. It must be below zero outside, and yet I can sit here inside my tree and write with bare hands. The fire is small, too. It doesn't take much fire to warm this tree room.

"It is the fourth of December, I think. It may be the fifth. I am not sure because I have not recently counted the notches in the aspen pole that is my calendar. I have been just too busy gathering nuts and berries, smoking[1] venison, fish, and small game to keep up with the exact date.

"The lamp I am writing by is deer fat poured into a turtle shell with a strip of my old city trousers for a wick.

"It snowed all day yesterday and today. I have not been outside since the storm began, and I am bored for the first time since I ran away from home eight months ago to live on the land.

"I am well and healthy. The food is good. Sometimes I eat turtle soup, and I know how to make acorn pancakes. I keep my supplies in the wall of the tree in wooden pockets that I chopped myself.

"Every time I have looked at those pockets during the last two days, I have felt just like a squirrel, which reminds me: I didn't see a squirrel one whole day before that storm began. I guess they are holed up and eating their stored nuts, too.

---

1. **smoking**: curing or preserving meat by exposure to smoke.

"I wonder if The Baron, that's the wild weasel who lives behind the big boulder to the north of my tree, is also denned up. Well, anyway, I think the storm is dying down because the tree is not crying so much. When the wind really blows, the whole tree moans right down to the roots, which is where I am.

"Tomorrow I hope The Baron and I can tunnel out into the sunlight. I wonder if I should dig the snow. But that would mean I would have to put it somewhere, and the only place to put it is in my nice snug tree. Maybe I can pack it with my hands as I go. I've always dug into the snow from the top, never up from under.

"The Baron must dig up from under the snow. I wonder where he puts what he digs? Well, I guess I'll know in the morning."

When I wrote that last winter, I was scared and thought maybe I'd never get out of my tree. I had been scared for two days—ever since the first blizzard hit the Catskill Mountains.[2] When I came up to the sunlight, which I did by simply poking my head into the soft snow and standing up, I laughed at my dark fears.

Everything was white, clean, shining, and beautiful. The sky was blue, blue, blue. The hemlock grove was laced with snow, the meadow was smooth and white, and the gorge was sparkling with ice. It was so beautiful and peaceful that I laughed out loud. I guess I laughed because my first snowstorm was over and it had not been so terrible after all.

Then I shouted, "I did it!" My voice never got very far. It was hushed by the tons of snow.

I looked for signs from The Baron Weasel. His footsteps were all over the boulder, also slides[3] where he had played. He must have been up for hours, enjoying the new snow.

Inspired by his fun, I poked my head into my tree and whistled. Frightful, my trained falcon, flew to my fist, and we jumped and slid down the mountain, making big holes and trenches as we went. It was good to be whistling and carefree again, because I was sure scared by the coming of that storm.

I had been working since May, learning how to make a fire with flint and steel,[4] finding what plants I could eat, how to trap animals and catch fish—all this so that when the curtain of blizzard struck the Catskills, I could crawl inside my tree and be comfortably warm and have plenty to eat.

During the summer and fall I had thought about the coming of winter. However, on that third day of December when the sky blackened, the temperature dropped, and the first flakes swirled around me. I must admit that I wanted to run back to New York. Even the first night that I spent out in the woods, when I couldn't get the fire started, was not as frightening as the snowstorm that gathered behind the gorge and mushroomed up over my mountain.

I was smoking three trout. It was nine o'clock in the morning. I was busy keep-

---

2. **Catskill** [kats′kil′] **Mountains**: mountain range in southeastern New York State, part of the Appalachian system.

3. **slides**: masses of rock, snow, or other matter that have fallen down a slope.
4. **flint and steel**: Flint is a hard, dull-gray mineral that produces sparks when struck against steel.

ing the flames low so they would not leap up and burn the fish. As I worked, it occurred to me that it was awfully dark for that hour of the morning. Frightful was leashed to her tree stub. She seemed restless and pulled at her tethers.[5] Then I realized that the forest was dead quiet. Even the woodpeckers that had been tapping around me all morning were silent. The squirrels were nowhere to be seen. The juncos and chickadees and nuthatches[6] were gone. I looked to see what The Baron Weasel was doing. He was not around. I looked up.

From my tree you can see the gorge beyond the meadow. White water pours between the black wet boulders and cascades into the valley below. The water that day was as dark as the rocks. Only the sound told me it was still falling. Above the darkness stood another darkness. The clouds of winter, black and fearsome. They looked as wild as the winds that were bringing them. I grew sick with fright. I knew I had enough food. I knew everything was going to be perfectly all right. But knowing that didn't help. I was scared. I stamped out the fire and pocketed the fish.

I tried to whistle for Frightful, but couldn't purse my shaking lips tight enough to get out anything but *pffffff.* So I grabbed her by the hide straps that are attached to her legs and we dove through the deerskin door into my room in the tree.

I put Frightful on the bedpost, and curled up in a ball on the bed. I thought

Weasel

about New York and the noise and the lights and how a snowstorm always seemed very friendly there. I thought about our apartment, too. At that moment it seemed bright and lighted and warm. I had to keep saying to myself: There were eleven of us in it! Dad, Mother, four sisters, four brothers, and me. And not one of us liked it, except perhaps little Nina, who was too young to know. Dad didn't like it even a little bit. He had been a sailor once, but when I was born, he gave up the sea and worked on the docks in New York. Dad didn't like the land. He liked the sea, wet and big and endless.

Sometimes he would tell me about Great-grandfather Gribley, who owned land in the Catskill Mountains and felled the trees and built a home and plowed the land—only to discover that he wanted to be a sailor. The farm failed, and Great-grandfather Gribley went to sea.

As I lay with my face buried in the sweet greasy smell of my deerskin, I could

---

5. **tethers** [te<u>th</u>′ərz]: ropes, chains, or other materials used to fasten an animal so that it is confined.
6. **juncos** [jung′kōz] . . . **nuthatches**: birds of North America.

hear Dad's voice saying, "That land is still in the family's name. Somewhere in the Catskills is an old beech[7] with the name *Gribley* carved on it. It marks the northern boundary of Gribley's folly—the land is no place for a Gribley."

"The land is no place for a Gribley," I said. "The land is no place for a Gribley, and here I am three hundred feet from the beech with *Gribley* carved on it."

I fell asleep at that point, and when I awoke I was hungry. I cracked some walnuts, got down the acorn flour I had pounded, with a bit of ash to remove the bite, reached out the door for a little snow, and stirred up some acorn pancakes. I cooked them on a top of a tin can, and as I ate them, smothered with blueberry jam, I knew that the land was just the place for a Gribley.

IN WHICH
I Get Started on This Venture

I left New York in May. I had a penknife, a ball of cord, an ax, and $40, which I had saved from selling magazine subscriptions.[8] I also had some flint and steel which I had bought at a Chinese store in the city. The man in the store had showed me how to use it. He had also given me a little purse to put it in, and some tinder[9] to catch the sparks. He

had told me that if I ran out of tinder, I should burn cloth, and use the charred ashes.

I thanked him and said, "This is the kind of thing I am not going to forget."

On the train north to the Catskills I unwrapped my flint and steel and practiced hitting them together to make sparks. On the wrapping paper I made these notes.

"A hard brisk strike is best. Remember to hold the steel in the left hand and the flint in the right, and hit the steel with the flint.

"The trouble is the sparks go every which way."

And that *was* the trouble. I did not get a fire going that night, and as I mentioned, this was a scary experience.

I hitched rides into the Catskill Mountains. At about four o'clock a truck driver and I passed through a beautiful dark hemlock forest, and I said to him, "This is as far as I am going."

He looked all around and said, "You live here?"

"No," I said, "but I am running away from home, and this is just the kind of forest I have always dreamed I would run to. I think I'll camp here tonight." I hopped out of the cab.

"Hey, boy," the driver shouted. "Are you serious?"

"Sure," I said.

"Well, now, ain't that sumpin'? You know, when I was your age, I did the same thing. Only thing was, I was a farm boy and ran to the city, and you're a city boy running to the woods. I was scared of the city—do you think you'll be scared of the woods?"

---

7. **beech** [bēch]: tree found in cooler regions of the Northern Hemisphere, having smooth, light-gray bark and bearing small, edible nuts.

8. **subscriptions** [səb skrip′shənz]: rights to receive newspapers, magazines, or similar materials for certain periods of time in return for specific payments.

9. **tinder** [tin′dər]: any substance that burns easily, especially something used to kindle a fire from a spark, such as dry twigs.

"Heck, no!" I shouted loudly.

As I marched into the cool shadowy woods, I heard the driver call to me, "I'll be back in the morning, if you want to ride home."

He laughed. Everybody laughed at me. Even Dad. I told Dad that I was going to run away to Great-grandfather Gribley's land. He had roared with laughter and told me about the time he had run away from home. He got on a boat headed for Singapore,[10] but when the whistle blew for departure, he was down the gangplank and home in bed before anyone knew he was gone. Then he told me, "Sure, go try it. Every boy should try it."

I must have walked a mile into the woods until I found a stream. It was a clear athletic stream that rushed and ran and jumped and splashed. Ferns grew along its bank, and its rocks were uphol-stered[11] with moss.

I sat down, smelled the piney air, and took out my penknife. I cut off a green twig and began to whittle. I have always been good at whittling. I carved a ship once that my teacher exhibited for parents' night at school.

First I whittled an angle on one end of the twig. Then I cut a smaller twig and sharpened it to a point. I whittled an angle on that twig, and bound the two angles face to face with a strip of green bark. It was supposed to be a fishhook.

According to a book on how to survive on the land that I read in the New York Public Library, this was the way to make your own hooks. I then dug for worms. I had hardly chopped the moss away with my ax before I hit frost. It had not occurred to me that there would be frost in the ground in May, but then, I had not been on a mountain before.

This did worry me, because I was depending on fish to keep me alive until I got to my great-grandfather's mountain, where I was going to make traps and catch game.

I looked into the stream to see what else I could eat, and as I did, my hand knocked a rotten log apart. I remembered about old logs and all the sleeping stages of insects that are in it. I chopped away until I found a cold white grub.[12]

I swiftly tied a string to my hook, put the grub on, and walked up the stream looking for a good place to fish. All the manuals I had read were very emphatic[13] about where fish lived, and so I had memorized this: "In streams, fish usually congregate in pools and deep calm water. The heads of riffles, small rapids, the tail of a pool, eddies below rocks or logs, deep undercut banks, in the shade of overhanging bushes—all are very likely places to fish."

This stream did not seem to have any calm water, and I must have walked a thousand miles before I found a pool by a deep undercut bank in the shade of overhanging bushes. Actually, it wasn't that far, it just seemed that way because as I

---

10. **Singapore** [sing′gə pôr′]: island nation off the southern tip of the Malay Peninsula in southeast Asia; also, the capital and largest city of this country.
11. **upholstered** [up hōl′stərd]: fitted with a soft covering.

12. **grub**: soft, wormlike early form of an insect.
13. **emphatic** [em fat′ik]: spoken or done with force; insistent.

went looking and finding nothing, I was sure I was going to starve to death.

I squatted on this bank and dropped in my line. I did so want to catch a fish. One fish would set me upon my way, because I had read how much you can learn from one fish. By examining the contents of its stomach you can find what the other fish are eating or you can use the internal organs as bait.

The grub went down to the bottom of the stream. It swirled around and hung still. Suddenly the string came to life, and rode back and forth and around in a circle. I pulled with a powerful jerk. The hook came apart, and whatever I had went circling back to its bed.

Well, that almost made me cry. My bait was gone, my hook was broken, and I was getting cold, frightened, and mad. I whittled another hook, but this time I cheated and used string to wind it together instead of bark. I walked back to the log and luckily found another grub. I hurried to the pool, and I flipped a trout out of the water before I knew I had a bite.

The fish flopped, and I threw my whole body over it. I could not bear to think of it flopping itself back into the stream.

I cleaned it like I had seen the man at the fish market do, examined its stomach, and found it empty. This horrified me. What I didn't know was that an empty stomach means the fish are hungry and will eat about anything. However, I thought at the time that I was a goner.[14] Sadly, I put some of the internal organs on my hook, and before I could get my line to the bottom I had another bite. I lost that one, but got the next one. I stopped when I had five nice little trout and looked around for a place to build a camp and make a fire.

It wasn't hard to find a pretty spot along that stream. I selected a place beside a mossy rock in a circle of hemlocks.

I decided to make a bed before I cooked. I cut off some boughs for a mattress, then I leaned some dead limbs against the boulder and covered them with hemlock limbs. This made a kind of tent. I crawled in, lay down, and felt alone and secret and very excited.

But ah, the rest of this story! I was on the northeast side of the mountain. It grew dark and cold early. Seeing the shadows slide down on me, I frantically ran around gathering firewood. This is about the only thing I did right from that moment until dawn, because I remembered that the driest wood in a forest is the dead limbs that are still on the trees, and I gathered an enormous pile of them. That pile must still be there, for I never got a fire going.

I got sparks, sparks, sparks. I even hit the tinder with the sparks. The tinder burned all right, but that was as far as I got. I blew on it, I breathed on it, I cupped it in my hands, but no sooner did I add twigs than the whole thing went black.

Then it got too dark to see. I clicked steel and flint together, even though I couldn't see the tinder. Finally, I gave up and crawled into my hemlock tent, hungry, cold, and miserable.

I can talk about that first night now, although it is still embarrassing to me because I was so stupid, and scared, that I hate to admit it.

---

14. **goner:** slang for "one who or thing that is dying, ruined, lost, or beyond help or recovery."

The Old Hunting Grounds, Worthington Whittredge, c. 1864.

I had made my hemlock bed right in the stream valley where the wind drained down from the cold mountaintop. It might have been all right if I had made it on the other side of the boulder, but I didn't. I was right on the main highway of the cold winds as they tore down upon the valley below. I didn't have enough hemlock boughs under me, and before I had my head down, my stomach was cold and damp. I took some boughs off the roof and stuffed them under me, and then my shoulders were cold. I curled up in a ball and was almost asleep when a whippoorwill called. If you have ever been within forty feet of a whippoorwill, you will understand why I couldn't even shut my eyes. They are deafening!

Well, anyway, the whole night went like that. I don't think I slept fifteen minutes, and I was so scared and tired that my throat was dry. I wanted a drink but didn't dare go near the stream for fear of making a misstep and falling in and getting wet. So I sat tight, and shivered and shook—and now I am able to say—I cried a little tiny bit.

Fortunately, the sun has a wonderfully glorious habit of rising every morning. When the sky lightened, when the birds awoke, I knew I would never again see anything so splendid as the round red sun coming up over the earth.

I was immediately cheered, and set out directly for the highway. Somehow, I thought that if I was a little nearer the road, everything would be all right.

I climbed a hill and stopped. There was a house. A house warm and cozy, with smoke coming out the chimney and lights in the windows, and only a hundred feet from my torture camp.

Without considering my pride, I ran down the hill and banged on the door. A nice old man answered. I told him everything in one long sentence, and then said, "And so, can I cook my fish here, because I haven't eaten in years."

He chuckled, stroked his whiskery face, and took the fish. He had them cooking in a pan before I knew what his name was.

When I asked him, he said Bill something, but I never heard his last name because I fell asleep in his rocking chair that was pulled up beside his big hot glorious wood stove in the kitchen.

I ate the fish some hours later, also some bread, jelly, oatmeal, and cream. Then he said to me, "Sam Gribley, if you are going to run off and live in the woods, you better learn how to make a fire. Come with me."

We spent the afternoon practicing. I penciled these notes on the back of a scrap of paper, so I wouldn't forget.

"When the tinder glows, keep blowing and add fine dry needles one by one—and keep blowing, steadily, lightly, and evenly. Add one inch dry twigs to the needles and then give her a good big handful of small dry stuff. Keep blowing."

THE MANNER IN WHICH
I Find Gribley's Farm

The next day I told Bill good-by, and as I strode, warm and fed, onto the road, he called to me, "I'll see you tonight. The back door will be open if you want a roof over your head."

I said, "Okay," but I knew I wouldn't seen Bill again. I knew how to make fire, and that was my weapon. With fire I could conquer the Catskills. I also knew how to fish. To fish and to make a fire. That was all I needed to know, I thought.

Three rides that morning took me to Delhi.[15] Somewhere around here was Great-grandfather's beech tree with the name *Gribley* carved on it. This much I knew from Dad's stories.

By six o'clock I still had not found anyone who had even heard of the Gribleys, much less Gribley's beech, and so I slept on the porch of a schoolhouse and ate chocolate bars for supper. It was cold and hard, but I was so tired I could have slept in a wind tunnel.

At dawn I thought real hard: Where would I find out about the Gribley farm? Some old map, I said. Where would I find an old map? The library? Maybe. I'd try it and see.

The librarian was very helpful. She was sort of young, had brown hair and brown eyes, and loved books as much as I did.

The library didn't open until ten-thirty. I got there at nine. After I had lolled and rolled and sat on the steps for fifteen or twenty minutes, the door whisked open, and this tall lady asked me to come on in and browse around until opening time.

All I said to her was that I wanted to find the old Gribley farm, and that the Gribleys hadn't lived on it for maybe a hundred years, and she was off. I can still hear her heels click, when I think of her, scattering herself around those shelves finding me old maps, histories of the Catskills, and files of letters and deeds that must have come from attics around Delhi.

Miss Turner—that was her name— found it. She found Gribley's farm in an old book of Delaware County. Then she worked out the roads to it, and drew me maps and everything. Finally she said, "What do you want to know for? Some school project?"

"Oh, no, Miss Turner, I want to go live there."

"But, Sam, it is all forest and trees now. The house is probably only a foundation covered with moss."

"That's just what I want. I am going to trap animals and eat nuts and bulbs and berries and make myself a house. You see, I am Sam Gribley, and I thought I would like to live on my great-grandfather's farm."

Miss Turner was the only person that believed me. She smiled, sat back in her chair, and said, "Well, I declare."

The library was just opening when I gathered the notes we had made and started off. As I pushed open the door, Miss Turner leaned over and said to me, "Sam, we have some very good books on plants and trees and animals, in case you get stuck."

I knew what she was thinking, and so I told her I would remember that.

With Miss Turner's map, I found the first stone wall that marked the farm. The old roads to it were all grown up and mostly gone, but by locating the stream at the bottom of the mountain I was able to begin at the bridge and go north and up a mile and a half. There, caterpillaring around boulders, roller-coasting up ravines and down hills, was the mound of rocks that had once been Great-grandfather's boundary fence.

And then, do you know, I couldn't believe I was there. I sat on the old gray stones a long time, looking through the forest, up that steep mountain, and saying to myself, "It must be Sunday afternoon,

---

15. **Delhi** [del′hī]: town in New York State, in the Catskill Mountains.

and it's raining, and Dad is trying to keep us all quiet by telling us about Great-grandfather's farm; and he's telling it so real that I can see it."

And then I said, "No. I am here, because I was never this hungry before."

I wanted to run all the way back to the library and tell Miss Turner that I had found it. Partly because she would have liked to have known, and partly because Dad had said to me as I left, "If you find the place, tell someone at Delhi. I may visit you someday." Of course, he was kidding, because he thought I'd be home the next day, but after many weeks, maybe he would think I meant what I said, and he might come see me.

However, I was too hungry to run back. I took my hook and line and went back down the mountain to the stream.

I caught a big old catfish. I climbed back to the stone wall in great spirits.

It was getting late and so I didn't try to explore. I went right to work making a fire. I decided that even if I didn't have enough time to cut boughs for a bed, I was going to have cooked fish and a fire to huddle around during those cold night hours. May is not exactly warm in the Catskills.

By firelight that night I wrote this:

"Dear Bill [that was the old man]:

"After three tries, I finally got a handful of dry grass on the glow in the tinder. Grass is even better than pine needles, and tomorrow I am going to try the outside bark of the river birch. I read somewhere that it has combustible[16] oil in it

that the Indians used to start fires. Anyway, I did just what you showed me, and had cooked catfish for dinner. It was good.

> Your friend,
> Sam."

After I wrote that I remembered I didn't know his last name, and so I stuffed the note in my pocket, made myself a bed of boughs and leaves in the shelter of the stone wall, and fell right to sleep.

I must say this now about that first fire. It was magic. Out of dead tinder and grass and sticks came a live warm light. It cracked and snapped and smoked and filled the woods with brightness. It lighted the trees and made them warm and friendly. It stood tall and bright and held back the night. Oh, this was a different night than the first dark frightful one. Also I was stuffed on catfish. I have since learned to cook it more, but never have I enjoyed a meal as much as that one, and never have I felt so independent again.

IN WHICH
I Find Many Useful Plants

The following morning I stood up, stretched, and looked about me. Birds were dripping from the trees, little birds, singing and flying and pouring over the limbs.

"This must be the warbler[17] migration,"[18] I said, and I laughed because

---

16. **combustible** [kəm bus′tə bəl]: capable of catching fire and burning.

17. **warbler** [wôr′blər]: small, brightly colored American songbird.
18. **migration** [mī grā′shən]: the movement of large groups of animals from one region to another at regular periods of time, such as during certain seasons.

Summer Foliage,
George Inness, 1883.

there were so many birds. I had never seen so many. My big voice rolled through the woods, and their little voices seemed to rise and answer me.

They were eating. Three or four in a maple tree near me were darting along the limbs, pecking and snatching at something delicious on the trees. I wondered if there was anything there for a hungry boy. I pulled a limb down, and all I saw were leaves, twigs, and flowers. I ate a flower. It was not very good. One manual I had read said to watch what the birds and animals were eating in order to learn what is edible and nonedible in the forest. If the animal life can eat it, it is safe for humans. The book did suggest that a raccoon had tastes more nearly like ours. Certainly the birds were no example.

Then I wondered if they were not eating something I couldn't see—tiny insects perhaps; well, anyway, whatever it was, I decided to fish. I took my line and hook and walked down to the stream.

I lay on a log and dangled my line in the bright water. The fish were not biting. That made me hungrier. My stomach pinched. You know, it really does hurt to be terribly hungry.

A stream is supposed to be full of food. It is the easiest place to get a lot of food in a hurry. I needed something in a hurry, but what? I looked through the clear water and saw the tracks of mussels[19] in the mud. I ran along the log back to shore, took off my clothes, and plunged into that icy water.

I collected almost a peck[20] of mussels

---

19. **mussels** [mus′əlz]: water-dwelling animals lacking backbones and having soft bodies encased in bluish-black shells.
20. **peck:** unit of dry measure, equal to eight quarts, or one fourth of a bushel.

in very little time at all, and began tying them in my sweater to carry them back to camp.

But I don't have to carry them anywhere, I said to myself. I have my fire in my pocket, I don't need a table. I can sit right here by the stream and eat. And so I did. I wrapped the mussels in leaves and sort of steamed them in coals. They are not quite as good as clams—a little stronger, I would say—but by the time I had eaten three, I had forgotten what clams tasted like and knew only how delicious freshwater mussels were. I actually got full.

I wandered back to Great-grandfather's farm and began to explore. Most of the acreage[21] was maple and beech, some pine, dogwoods, ash; and here and there a glorious hickory. I made a sketch of the farm on my road map, and put x's where the hickories were. They were gold trees to me. I would have hickory nuts in the fall. I could also make salt from hickory limbs. I cut off one and chopped it into bits and scraps. I stuck them in my sweater.

The land was up and down and up and down, and I wondered how Great-grandfather ever cut it and plowed it. There was one stream running through it, which I was glad to see, for it meant I did not have to go all the way down the mountain to the big creek for fish and water.

Around noon I came upon what I was sure was the old foundation of the house. Miss Turner was right. It was ruins—a few stones in a square, a slight depres-sion for the basement, and trees growing right up through what had once been the living room. I wandered around to see what was left of the Gribley home.

After a few looks I saw an apple tree. I rushed up to it, hoping to find an old apple. No apples beneath it. About forty feet away, however, I found a dried one in the crotch of a tree, stuck there by a squirrel and forgotten. I ate it. It was pretty bad—but nourishing, I hoped. There was another apple tree and three walnuts. I scribbled x's. These were wonderful finds.

I poked around the foundations, hoping to uncover some old iron implements that I could use. I found nothing. Too many leaves had fallen and turned to loam,[22] too many plants had grown up and died down over the old home site. I decided to come back when I had made myself a shovel.

Whistling and looking for food and shelter, I went on up the mountain, following the stone walls, discovering many things about my property. I found a marsh. In it were cattails and arrow-leaf— good starchy foods.

At high noon I stepped onto a mountain meadow. An enormous boulder rose up in the center of it. At the top of the meadow was a fringe of white birch. There were maples and oaks to the west, and a hemlock forest to the right that pulled me right across the sweet grasses, into it.

Never, never have I seen such trees. They were giants—old, old giants. They must have begun when the world began.

21. **acreage** [ā′kər ij]: area of land measured in acres.

22. **loam** [lōm]: soil that is a mixture of clay, sand, and other matter that has been carried and deposited by water.

I started walking around them. I couldn't hear myself step, so dense and damp were the needles. Great boulders covered with ferns and moss stood among them. They looked like pebbles beneath those trees.

Standing before the biggest and the oldest and the most kinglike of them all, I suddenly had an idea.

THIS IS ABOUT
The Old, Old Tree

I knew enough about the Catskill Mountains to know that when the summer came, they were covered with people. Although Great-grandfather's farm was somewhat remote, still hikers and campers and hunters and fishermen were sure to wander across it.

Therefore I wanted a house that could not be seen. People would want to take me back where I belonged if they found me.

I looked at that tree. Somehow I knew it was home, but I was not quite sure how it was home. The limbs were high and not right for a tree house. I could build a bark extension around it, but that would look silly. Slowly I circled the great trunk. Halfway around the whole plan became perfectly obvious. To the west, between two of the flanges[23] of the tree that spread out to be roots, was a cavity. The heart of the tree was rotting away. I scraped at it with my hands; old, rotten insect-ridden dust came tumbling out. I dug on and on, using my ax from time to time as my excitement grew.

Cattails

With much of the old rot out, I could crawl in the tree and sit cross-legged. Inside I felt as cozy as a turtle in its shell. I chopped and chopped until I was hungry and exhausted. I was now in the hard good wood, and chopping it out was work. I was afraid December would come before I got a hole big enough to lie in. So I sat down to think.

You know, those first days, I just never planned right. I had the beginnings of a home, but not a bite to eat, and I had worked so hard that I could hardly move forward to find that bite. Furthermore, it was discouraging to feed that body of mine. It was never satisfied, and gathering food for it took time and got it hungrier. Trying to get a place to rest it took time and got it more tired, and I really felt I

---

23. **flanges** [flanj′əz]: ribs or rims that stand out from an object and provide strength.

was going in circles and wondered how primitive man ever had enough time and energy to stop hunting food and start thinking about fire and tools.

I left the tree and went across the meadow looking for food. I plunged into the woods beyond, and there I discovered the gorge and the white cascade splashing down the black rocks into the pool below.

I was hot and dirty. I scrambled down the rocks and slipped into the pool. It was so cold I yelled. But when I came out on the bank and put on my two pairs of trousers and three sweaters, which I thought was a better way to carry clothes than in a pack, I tingled and burned and felt coltish.[24] I leaped up the bank, slipped, and my face went down in a patch of dogtooth violets.

You would know them anywhere after a few looks at them at the Botanical Gardens[25] and in colored flower books. They are little yellow lilies on long slender stems with oval leaves dappled with gray. But that's not all. They have wonderfully tasty bulbs. I was filling my pockets before I got up from my fall.

"I'll have a salad type lunch," I said as I moved up the steep sides of the ravine. I discovered that as late as it was in the season, the spring beauties were still blooming in the cool pockets of the woods. They are all right raw, that is if you are as hungry as I was. They taste a little like lima beans. I ate these as I went on hunting food, feeling better and better,

until I worked my way back to the meadow where the dandelions were blooming. Funny I hadn't noticed them earlier. Their greens are good, and so are their roots—a little strong and milky, but you get used to that.

A crow flew into the aspen grove without saying a word. The little I knew of crows from following them in Central Park,[26] they always have something to say. But this bird was sneaking, obviously trying to be quiet. Birds are good food. Crow is certainly not the best, but I did not know that then, and I launched out to see where it was going. I had a vague plan to try to noose it. This is the kind of thing I wasted time on in those days when time was so important. However, this venture turned out all right, because I did not have to noose that bird.

I stepped into the woods, looked around, could not see the crow, but noticed a big stick nest in a scrabbly pine. I started to climb the tree. Off flew the crow. What made me keep on climbing in face of such discouragement, I don't know, but I did, and that noon I had crow eggs and wild salad for lunch.

At lunch I also solved the problem of carving out my tree. After a struggle I made a fire. Then I sewed a big skunk cabbage[27] leaf into a cup with grass strands. I had read that you can boil water in a leaf, and ever since then I had been very anxious to see if this were true. It seems impossible, but it works. I boiled the eggs in a leaf. The water keeps the

---

24. **coltish** [kōl′tish]: having the liveliness of a young horse, or colt; playful.
25. **Botanical Gardens**: the New York Botanical Gardens, in New York City, whose grounds contain gardens, a library, and other facilities for the study and display of plant life.

---

26. **Central Park**: large, popular public park in New York City.
27. **skunk cabbage**: weedy marsh plant found in eastern North America and noted for its foul-smelling leaves.

Brook by Moonlight,
Ralph Albert
Blakelock, before
1891.

leaf wet, and although the top dries up and burns down to the water level, that's as far as the burning goes. I was pleased to see it work.

Then here's what happened. Naturally, all this took a lot of time, and I hadn't gotten very far on my tree, so I was fretting and stamping out the fire when I stopped with my foot in the air.

The fire! Indians made dugout canoes with fire. They burned them out, an easier and much faster way of getting results. I would try fire in the tree. If I was very careful, perhaps it would work. I ran into the hemlock forest with a burning stick and got a fire going inside the tree.

Thinking that I ought to have a bucket of water in case things got out of hand, I looked desperately around me. The water was far across the meadow and down the ravine. This would never do. I began to think the whole inspiration of a home in the tree was no good. I really did have to live near water for cooking and drinking and comfort. I looked sadly at the magnificent hemlock and was about to put the fire out and desert it when I said something to myself. It must have come out of some book: "Hemlocks usually grow around mountain streams and springs."

I swirled on my heel. Nothing but boulders around me. But the air was damp, somewhere—I said—and darted around the rocks, peering and looking and sniffing and going down into pockets and dales. No water. I was coming back, circling wide, when I almost fell in it. Two sentinel boulders,[28] dripping wet, decorated with flowers, ferns, moss, weeds—everything that loved water—guarded a bathtub-sized spring.

"You pretty thing," I said, flopped on my stomach, and pushed my face into it to drink. I opened my eyes. The water was like glass, and in it were little insects with oars. They rowed away from me. Beetles skittered like bullets on the surface, or carried a silver bubble of air with them to the bottom. Ha, then I saw a crayfish.

I jumped up, overturned rocks, and found many crayfish. At first I hesitated to grab them because they can pinch. I gritted my teeth, thought about how much more it hurts to be hungry, and came down upon them. I did get pinched, but I had my dinner. And that was the first time I had planned ahead! Any planning that I did in those early days was such a surprise to me and so successful that I was delighted with even a small plan. I wrapped the crayfish in leaves, stuffed them in my pockets, and went back to the burning tree.

Bucket of water, I thought. Bucket of water? Where was I going to get a bucket? How did I think, even if I found water, I could get it back to the tree? That's how citified I was in those days. I had never lived without a bucket before— scrub buckets, water buckets—and so when a water problem came up, I just thought I could run to the kitchen and get a bucket.

"Well, dirt is as good as water," I said as I ran back to my tree. "I can smother the fire with dirt."

Days passed working, burning, cutting, gathering food, and each day I cut another notch on an aspen pole that I had stuck in the ground for a calendar.

---

28. **sentinel** [sent′ən əl] **boulders**: large rocks resembling a person or animal that keeps watch and alerts others of danger.

READER'S RESPONSE

Would you want to live by yourself in the wilderness?

STUDY QUESTIONS

Recalling

1. At the beginning of the novel, where is Sam's home? Where else has he lived?
2. List and describe in a few words the first three people Sam encounters after he leaves New York.
3. What items does Sam take with him to start his venture?
4. After he reaches the woods, what steps does Sam take to have his first meal?
5. Why is Sam hungry, cold, and miserable the first night he is in the woods?
6. Besides fishing, list at least four ways in which Sam solves his problem of hunger.

Interpreting

7. Why does Sam want to live off the land?
8. Why does Sam's father let him leave home?

9. Describe two or three of Sam's character traits.
10. Do you think Sam is capable of accomplishing his goal of living off the land? Why or why not?

Extending

11. What is your opinion of Sam? Explain.

READING AND LITERARY FOCUS

Flashback

Most stories are written in **chronological order,** or the time sequence in which events naturally occur. Sometimes authors interrupt that order to show us an event that happened in the past. A **flashback** is a scene that breaks the normal time order of a plot to show a past event. Flashbacks often provide important background information. For example, *My Side of the Mountain* begins with a description of a snowstorm that occurs many months after Sam's arrival in the Catskill Mountains.

Thinking About Flashback

1. Relate one flashback in "I Hole Up in a Snowstorm." What information does it add to the story?
2. Name another story or a television program that uses flashback.

Detail, *The Old Hunting Grounds,*
Worthington Whittredge, c. 1864.

• •

*Common
Frog*

IN WHICH
I Meet One of My Own Kind and Have a Terrible Time Getting Away

Five notches into June, my house was done. I could stand in it, lie down in it, and there was room left over for a stump to sit on. On warm evenings I would lie on my stomach and look out the door, listen to the frogs and nighthawks, and hope it would storm so that I could crawl into my tree and be dry. I had gotten soaked during a couple of May downpours, and now that my house was done, I wanted the chance to sit in my hemlock and watch a cloudburst wet everything but me. This opportunity didn't come for a long time. It was dry.

One morning I was at the edge of the meadow. I had cut down a small ash tree and was chopping it into lengths of about eighteen inches each. This was the beginning of my bed that I was planning to work on after supper every night.

With the golden summer upon me, food was much easier to get, and I actually had several hours of free time after supper in which to do other things. I had been eating frogs' legs, turtles, and best of all, an occasional rabbit. My snares and traps were set now. Furthermore, I had a good supply of cattail roots I had dug in the marsh.

If you ever eat cattails, be sure to cook them well, otherwise the fibers are tough and they take more chewing to get the starchy food from them than they are worth. However, they taste just like potatoes after you've been eating them a couple of weeks, and to my way of thinking are extremely good.

Well, anyway, that summer morning when I was gathering material for a bed, I was singing and chopping and playing a game with a raccoon I had come to know. He had just crawled in a hollow tree and had gone to bed for the day when I came to the meadow. From time to time I would tap on his tree with my ax. He would hang his sleepy head out, snarl at me, close his eyes, and slide out of sight.

The third time I did this, I knew something was happening in the forest. Instead of closing his eyes, he pricked up his ears and his face became drawn and tense. His eyes were focused on something down the mountain. I stood up and looked. I could see nothing. I squatted down and went back to work. The raccoon dove out of sight.

"Now what's got you all excited?" I said, and tried once more to see what he had seen.

I finished the posts for the bed and was looking around for a bigger ash to fell and make slats for the springs when I nearly jumped out of my shoes.

"Now what are you doing up here all alone?" It was a human voice. I swung around and stood face to face with a little old lady in a pale blue sunbonnet and a loose brown dress.

"Oh! Gosh!" I said. "Don't scare me like that. Say one word at a time until I get used to a human voice." I must have looked frightened because she chuckled, smoothed down the front of her dress, and whispered, "Are you lost?"

"Oh, no, ma'am," I stuttered.

"Then a little fellow like you should not be all alone way up here on this haunted mountain."

"Haunted?" said I.

"Yes, indeed. There's an old story says there are little men up here who play ninepins[1] right down in that gorge in the twilight." She peered at me. "Are you one of them?"

"Oh, no, no, no, no," I said. "I read that story. It's just make-believe." I laughed, and she puckered her forehead.

"Well, come on," she said, "make some use of yourself and help me fill this basket with strawberries."

I hesitated—she meant *my* strawberry supply.

"Now, get on with you. A boy your age should be doing something worthwhile, 'stead of playing mumbly peg[2] with sticks.

Come on, young man." She jogged me out into the meadow.

We worked quite a while before we said any more. Frankly, I was wondering how to save my precious, precious strawberries, and I may say I picked slowly. Every time I dropped one in her basket, I thought how good it would taste.

"Where do ye live?" I jumped. It is terribly odd to hear a voice after weeks of listening only to birds and raccoons, and what is more, to hear the voice ask a question like that.

"I live here," I said.

"Ye mean Delhi. Fine. You can walk me home."

Nothing I added did any good. She would not be shaken from her belief that I lived in Delhi. So I let it go.

We must have reaped every last strawberry before she stood up, put her arm in mine and escorted me down the mountain. I certainly was not escorting her. Her wiry little arms were like crayfish pinchers. I couldn't have gotten away if I had tried. So I walked and listened.

She told me all the local and world news, and it was rather pleasant to hear about the National League,[3] an atom bomb test,[4] and a Mr. Riley's three-legged dog that chased her chickens. In the middle of all this chatter she said, "That's the best strawberry patch in the entire Catskill range. I come up here every spring. For forty years I've come to that meadow for my strawberries. It gits harder every year,

---

1. **ninepins**: bowling game using nine bottle-shaped wooden pins and a large ball.
2. **mumbly peg**: game played by throwing or dropping a knife from various positions in such a way that it sticks in the ground.

3. **National League**: one of the two major leagues of baseball teams that compete regularly among themselves during the regular baseball season.
4. **atom bomb test**: During the 1950s many atomic-bomb tests took place on the Pacific island of Enewetak and in Nevada.

but there's no jam can beat the jam from that mountain. I know. I've been around here all my life." Then she went right into the New York Yanks[5] without putting in a period.

As I helped her across the stream on big boulders, I heard a cry in the sky. I looked up. Swinging down the valley on long pointed wings was a large bird. I was struck by the ease and swiftness of its flight.

"Duck hawk," she said. "Nest around here every year. My man used to shoot 'em. He said they killed chickens, but I don't believe it. The only thing that kills chickens is Mr. Riley's three-legged dog."

She tipped and teetered as she crossed the rocks, but kept right on talking and stepping as if she knew that no matter what, she would get across.

We finally reached the road. I wasn't listening to her very much. I was thinking about the duck hawk. This bird, I was sure, was the peregrine falcon,[6] the king's hunting bird.

"I will get one. I will train it to hunt for me," I said to myself.

Finally I got the little lady to her brown house at the edge of town.

She turned fiercely upon me. I started back.

"Where are you going, young man?"

I stopped. Now, I thought, she is going to march me into town. Into town? Well, that's where I'll go then, I said to myself. And I turned on my heel, smiled at her, and replied, "To the library."

---

5. **New York Yanks**: the Yankees, one of New York City's baseball teams.
6. **peregrine** [per'ə grin] **falcon**: swift falcon with bluish-gray plumage, formerly used in the sport of falconry.

The King's Provider

Miss Turner was glad to see me. I told her I wanted some books on hawks and falcons, and she located a few, although there was not much to be had on the subject. We worked all afternoon, and I learned enough. I departed when the library closed. Miss Turner whispered to me as I left, "Sam, you need a haircut."

I hadn't seen myself in so long that this had not occurred to me. "Gee, I don't have any scissors."

She thought a minute, got out her library scissors, and sat me down on the back steps. She did a fine job, and I looked like any other boy who had played hard all day, and who, with a little soap and water after supper, would be going off to bed in a regular house.

I didn't get back to my tree that night. The May apples were ripe, and I stuffed on those as I went through the woods. They taste like a very sweet banana, are earthy and a little slippery. But I liked them.

At the stream I caught a trout. Everybody thinks a trout is hard to catch because of all the fancy gear and flies[7] and lines sold for trout fishing, but, honestly, they are easier to catch than any other fish. They have big mouths and snatch and swallow whole anything they see when they are hungry. With my wooden hook in its mouth, the trout was mine. The trouble is that trout are not hungry when most people have time to fish. I knew they were hungry that evening because the creek was swirling, and minnows and everything else were jumping out of the

---

7. **flies**: fishhooks decorated with feathers or other materials so as to resemble an insect.

water. When you see that, go fish. You'll get them.

I made a fire on a flat boulder in the stream, and cooked the trout. I did this so I could watch the sky. I wanted to see the falcon again. I also put the trout head on the hook and dropped it in the pool. A snapping turtle would view a trout head with relish.

I waited for the falcon patiently. I didn't have to go anywhere. After an hour or so, I was rewarded. A slender speck came from the valley and glided above the stream. It was still far away when it folded its wings and bombed the earth. I watched. It arose, clumsy and big—carrying food—and winged back to the valley.

I sprinted down the stream and made myself a lean-to[8] near some cliffs where I thought the bird had disappeared. Having learned that day that duck hawks prefer to nest on cliffs, I settled for this site.

Early the next morning, I got up and dug the tubers[9] of the arrow-leaf that grew along the stream bank. I baked these and boiled mussels for breakfast, then I curled up behind a willow and watched the cliff.

The falcons came in from behind me and circled the stream. They had apparently been out hunting before I had gotten up, as they were returning with food. This was exciting news. They were feeding young, and I was somewhere near the nest.

I watched one of them swing in to the cliff and disappear. A few minutes later it winged out empty-footed. I marked the spot mentally and said, "Ha!"

After splashing across the stream in the shallows, I stood at the bottom of the cliff and wondered how on earth I was going to climb the sheer wall.

I wanted a falcon so badly, however, that I dug in with my toes and hands and started up. The first part was easy; it was not too steep. When I thought I was stuck, I found a little ledge and shinnied up to it.

I was high, and when I looked down, the stream spun. I decided not to look down anymore. I edged up to another ledge, and lay down on it to catch my breath. I was shaking from exertion[10] and I was tired.

I looked up to see how much higher I had to go when my hand touched something moist. I pulled it back and saw that it was white—bird droppings. Then I saw them. Almost where my hand had been sat three fuzzy whitish gray birds. Their wide-open mouths gave them a startled look.

"Oh, hello, hello," I said. "You are cute."

When I spoke, all three blinked at once. All three heads turned and followed my hand as I swung it up and toward them. All three watched my hand with opened mouths. They were marvelous. I chuckled. But I couldn't reach them.

I wormed forward, and *wham!*—something hit my shoulder. It pained. I turned my head to see the big female. She had hit me. She winged out, banked, and started back for another strike.

Now I was scared, for I was sure she would cut me wide open. With sudden

8. **lean-to**: crude, usually open shelter, consisting only of a sloping roof that extends to the ground.
9. **tubers** [tōō′bərz]: thickened, fleshy portions of underground stems, such as potatoes, from which new plants sprout.

10. **exertion** [ig zur′shən]: vigorous use of energy.

nerve, I stood up, stepped forward, and picked up the biggest of the nestlings. The females are bigger than the males. They are the "falcons." They are the pride of kings. I tucked her in my sweater and leaned against the cliff, facing the bulletlike dive of the falcon. I threw out my foot as she struck, and the sole of my tennis shoe took the blow.

The female was now gathering speed for another attack, and when I say speed, I mean 50 to 60 miles an hour. I could see myself battered and torn, lying in the valley below, and I said to myself, "Sam Gribley, you had better get down from here like a rabbit."

I jumped to the ledge below, found it was really quite wide, slid on the seat of my pants to the next ledge, and stopped. The hawk apparently couldn't count. She did not know I had a youngster, for she checked her nest, saw the open mouths, and then she forgot me.

I scrambled to the riverbed somehow, being very careful not to hurt the hot fuzzy body that was against my own. However, Frightful, as I called her right then and there because of the difficulties we had had in getting together, did not think so gently of me. She dug her talons into my skin to brace herself during the bumpy ride to the ground.

I stumbled to the stream, placed her in a nest of buttercups, and dropped beside her. I fell asleep.

When I awoke my eyes opened on two gray eyes in a white stroobly head. Small pinfeathers were sticking out of the stroobly down, like feathers in an Indian quiver.[11] The big blue beak curled down in a snarl and up in a smile.

"Oh, Frightful," I said, "you are a raving beauty."

Frightful fluffed her nubby feathers and shook. I picked her up in the cup of my hands and held her under my chin. I stuck my nose in the deep warm fuzz. It smelled dusty and sweet.

I liked that bird. Oh, how I liked that bird from that smelly minute. It was so pleasant to feel the beating life and see the funny little awkward movements of a young thing.

The legs pushed out between my fingers, I gathered them up, together with the thrashing wings, and tucked the bird in one piece under my chin. I rocked.

"Frightful," I said. "You will enjoy what we are going to do."

I washed my bleeding shoulder in the creek, tucked the torn threads of my sweater back into the hole they had come out of, and set out for my tree.

A BRIEF ACCOUNT OF
What I Did About the First Man Who Was After Me

At the edge of the meadow, I sensed all was not well at camp. How I knew there was a human being there was not clear to me then. I can only say that after living so long with the birds and animals, the movement of a human is like the difference between the explosion of a cap pistol and a cannon.

I wormed toward camp. When I could see the man I felt to be there, I stopped and looked. He was wearing a forester's[12] uniform. Immediately I thought they had

---

11. **quiver**: case for holding arrows.

12. **forester's**: of a forester, one who practices or has been trained in forestry, the science of caring for and managing forests.

sent someone out to bring me in, and I began to shake. Then I realized that I didn't have to go back to meet the man at all. I was perfectly free and capable of settling down anywhere. My tree was just a pleasant habit.

I circled the meadow and went over to the gorge. On the way I checked a trap. It was a deadfall.[13] A figure four[14] under a big rock. The rock was down. The food was rabbit.

I picked a comfortable place just below the rim of the gorge where I could pop up every now and then and watch my tree. Here I dressed down the rabbit and fed Frightful some of the more savory bites from a young falcon's point of view: the liver, the heart, the brain. She ate in gulps. As I watched her swallow I sensed a great pleasure. It is hard to explain my feelings at that moment. It seemed marvelous to see life pump through that strange little body of feathers, wordless noises, milk eyes—much as life pumped through me.

The food put the bird to sleep. I watched her eyelids close from the bottom up, and her head quiver. The fuzzy body rocked, the tail spread to steady it, and the little duck hawk almost sighed as she sank into the leaves, sleeping.

I had lots of time. I was going to wait for the man to leave. So I stared at my bird, the beautiful details of the new feathers, the fernlike lashes along the lids, the saucy bristles at the base of the beak. Pleasant hours passed.

Peregrine Falcon nestling

Frightful would awaken, I would feed her, she would fall back to sleep, and I would watch the breath rock her body ever so slightly. I was breathing the same way, only not as fast. Her heart beat much faster than mine. She was designed to her bones for a swifter life.

It finally occurred to me that I was very hungry. I stood up to see if the man were gone. He was yawning and pacing.

The sun was slanting on him now, and I could see him quite well. He was a fire warden. Of course, it has not rained, I told myself, for almost three weeks, and the fire planes have been circling the mountains and valleys, patrolling the mountains. Apparently the smoke from my fire was spotted, and a man was sent to check it. I recalled the bare trampled ground around the tree, the fireplace of rocks filled with ashes, the wood chips from the making of my bed, and resolved hereafter to keep my yard clean.

So I made rabbit soup in a tin can I

---

13. **deadfall**: trap constructed so that a weight falls upon and kills or holds down an animal.
14. **figure four**: trap with a trigger set in the shape of a 4.

found at the bottom of the gorge. I seasoned it with wild garlic and jack-in-the-pulpit roots.

Jack-in-the-pulpits have three big leaves on a stalk and are easily recognized by the curly striped awning above a stiff, serious preacher named Jack. The jack-in-the-pulpit root, or corm, tastes and looks like potato. It should never be eaten raw.

The fire I made was only of the driest wood, and I made it right at the water's edge. I didn't want a smoky fire on this particular evening.

After supper I made a bough bed and stretched out with Frightful beside me. Apparently, the more you stroke and handle a falcon, the easier they are to train.

I had all sorts of plans for hoods and jesses, as the straps on a falcon are called, and I soon forgot about the man.

Stretched on the boughs, I listened to the wood pewees[15] calling their haunting good nights until I fell sound asleep.

IN WHICH
I Learn to Season My Food

The fire warden made a fire some time in the colder hours of the night. At dawn he was asleep beside white smoldering ashes. I crawled back to the gorge, fed Frightful rabbit bites, and slipped back to the edge of the meadow to check a box trap I had set the day before. I made it by tying small sticks together like a log cabin. This trap was better than the snares or deadfalls. It had caught numerous rabbits, several squirrels, and a groundhog.

I saw, as I inched toward it, that it was closed. The sight of a closed trap excites me to this day. I still can't believe that animals don't understand why delicious food is in such a ridiculous spot.

Well, this morning I pulled the trap deep into the woods to open it. The trapped animal was light. I couldn't guess what it was. It was also active, flipping and darting from one corner to the next. I peeked in to locate it, so that I could grab it quickly behind the head without getting bitten. I was not always successful at this, and had scars to prove it.

I put my eye to the crack. A rumpus[16] arose in the darkness. Two bright eyes shone, and out through that hole that was no wider than a string bean came a weasel. He flew right out at me, landed on my shoulder, gave me a lecture that I shall never forget, and vanished under the scant[17] cover of trillium and bloodroot leaves.

He popped up about five feet away and stood on his hind feet to lecture me again. I said, "Scat!" so he darted right to my knee, put his broad furry paws on my pants, and looked me in the face. I shall never forget the fear and wonder that I felt at the bravery of that weasel. He stood his ground and berated[18] me. I could see by the flashing of his eyes and the curl of his lip that he was furious at me for trapping him. He couldn't talk, but I knew what he meant.

Wonder filled me as I realized he was absolutely unafraid. No other animal, and

---

15. **pewees** [pē′wēz′]: small, insect-eating birds.

16. **rumpus** [rum′pəs]: noisy disturbance; uproar.
17. **scant** [skant]: lacking in amount or quantity; scarcely enough.
18. **berated** [bi rāt′id]: scolded.

Detail, *The Trapper's Camp,* Albert Bierstadt, 1861.

I knew quite a few by now, had been so brave in my presence. Screaming, he jumped on me. This surprised and scared me. He leaped from my lap to my head, took a mouthful of hair and wrestled it. My goose bumps rose. I was too frightened to move. A good thing, too, because I guess he figured I was not going to fight back and his scream of anger changed to a purr of peace. Still, I couldn't move.

Presently, down he climbed, as stately as royalty, and off he marched, never looking back. He sank beneath the leaves like a fish beneath the water. Not a stem rippled to mark his way.

And so The Baron and I met for the first time, and it was the beginning of a harassing but wonderful friendship.

Frightful had been watching all this. She was tense with fright. Although young and inexperienced, she knew an enemy when she saw one. I picked her up and whispered into her birdy-smelling neck feathers.

"You wild ones know."

Since I couldn't go home, I decided to spend the day in the marsh down the west side of the mountain. There were a lot of cattails and frogs there.

Frightful balanced on my fist as we walked. She had learned that in the short span of one afternoon and a night. She is a very bright bird.

On our way we scared up a deer. It was a doe. I watched her dart gracefully away, and said to Frightful, "That's what I want. I need a door for my house, tethers for you, and a blanket for me. How am I going to get a deer?"

This was not the first time I had said this. The forest was full of deer, and I already had drawn plans on a piece of birch bark for deadfalls, pit traps, and snares. None seemed workable.

The day passed. In the early evening we stole home, tree by tree, to find that the warden had gone. I cleaned up my front yard, scattered needles over the bare spots, and started a small fire with very dry wood that would not smoke much. No more wardens for me. I liked my tree, and although I could live somewhere else, I certainly did not want to.

Once home, I immediately started to work again. I had a device I wanted to try, and put some hickory sticks in a tin can and set it to boiling while I fixed dinner. Before going to bed, I noted this on a piece of birch bark:

"This night I am making salt. I know that people in the early days got along without it, but I think some of these wild foods would taste better with some flavoring. I understand that hickory sticks, boiled dry, leave a salty residue.[19] I am trying it."

In the morning I added:

"It is quite true. The can is dry, and thick with a black substance. It is very salty, and I tried it on frogs' legs for breakfast. It is just what I have needed."

And so I went into salt production for

several days, and chipped out a niche[20] inside the tree in which to store it.

"*June 19*

"I finished my bed today. The ash slats work very well, and are quite springy and comfortable. The bed just fits in the right-hand side of the tree. I have hemlock boughs on it now, but hope to have deer hide soon. I am making a figure-four trap as tall as me with a log on it that I can barely lift. It doesn't look workable. I wish there was another way of getting a deer.

"*June 20*

"I decided today to dig a pit to trap a deer, so I am whittling a shovel out of a board I found in the stream this morning. That stream is very useful. It has given me tin cans for pots, and now an oaken board for a shovel.

"Frightful will hop from the stump to my fist. She still can't fly. Her wing feathers are only about an inch long. I think she likes me."

How a Door Came to Me

One morning before the wood pewees were up, I was smoking a mess of fish I had caught in the stream. When I caught more than I could eat, I would bone them, put them on a rack of sticks, and slowly smoke them until they dried out. This is the best way to preserve extra food. However, if you try it, remember to use a hard wood—hickory is the best. I tried pine on the first batch, and ruined them with black tarry smoke. Well, it was very silent—then came a scream. I jumped

---

19. **residue** [rez′ə dōō′]: substance remaining at the end of a process of separation, such as when moisture is removed by heating.

20. **niche** [nich]: recess or hollow.

Lake with Dead Trees (Catskill), Thomas Cole, 1825.

into my tree. Presently I had enough nerve to look out.

"Baron Weasel!" I said in astonishment. I was sure it was the same weasel I had met in the trap. He was on the boulder in front of the hemlock, batting the ferns with his front feet and rearing and staring at me.

"Now, you stay right there," I said. Of course, he flipped and came off the rock like a jet stream. He was at the door before I could stop him, and loping around my feet like a bouncing ball.

"You look glad all over, Baron. I hope all that frisking means joy," I said. He took my pants leg in his teeth, tugged it, and then rippled softly back to the boulder. He went down a small hole. He popped up again, bit a fern near by, and ran around the boulder. I crept out to look for him—no weasel. I poked a stick in the hole at the base of the rock trying to provoke him. I felt a little jumpy, so that when a shot rang out through the woods I leaped a foot in the air and dove into my hole. A cricket chirped, a catbird

My Side of the Mountain 545

scratched the leaves. I waited. One enormous minute later a dark form ran onto the meadow. It stumbled and fell.

I had the impression that it was a deer. Without waiting to consider what I might be running toward, I burst to the edge of the meadow.

No one was in sight, I ran into the grass. There lay a dead deer! With all my strength I dragged the heavy animal into the woods. I then hurried to my tree, gathered up the hemlock boughs on my bed, rushed back and threw them over the carcass. I stuck a few ferns in them so they would look as if they were growing there and ran back to camp, breathless.

Hurriedly I put out the fire, covered it with dirt, hid my smoking rack in the spring, grabbed Frightful and got in my tree.

Someone was poaching,[21] and he might be along in a minute to collect his prize. The shot had come from the side of the mountain, and I figured I had about four minutes to clean up before the poacher arrived.

Then when I was hidden and ready, Frightful started her cry of hunger. I had not fed her yet this morning. Oh, how was I going to explain to her the awful need to be quiet? How did a mother falcon warn her young of danger? I took her in my hands and stroked her stomach. She fought me and then she lay still in my hand, her feet up, her eyes bright. She stiffened and drooped. I kept on stroking her. She was hypnotized, I would stop for a few moments, she would lie still, then pop to her feet. I was sure this wasn't what her mother did to keep her quiet, but it worked.

Bushes cracked, leaves scuttled, and a man with a rifle came into the meadow. I could just see his head and shoulders. He looked around and banged toward the hemlock forest. I crawled up on my bed and stroked the hungry Frightful.

I couldn't see the man from my bed, but I could hear him.

I heard him come to the tree. I could see his boots. He stopped by the ashes of the fire; and then went on. I could see my heart lift my sweater. I was terrified.

I stayed on the bed all morning, telling the fierce little bundle of feathers in my hand that there was deer meat in store for her if she would just wait with me.

Way down the other side of the mountain, I heard another shot. I sure hoped that deer dropped on the poacher's toes and that he would now go home.

At noon I went to my prize. Frightful sat beside me as I skinned and quartered it. She ate deer until she was misshapen.[22]

I didn't make any notes as to how long it took me to do all the work that was required to get the deer ready for smoking and the hide scraped and ready for tanning, but it was many, many days.

However, when I sat down to a venison steak, that was a meal! All it was, was venison. I wrote this on a piece of birch bark. "I think I grew an inch on venison!" Frightful and I went to the meadow when the meal was done, and flopped in the grass. The stars came up, the ground smelled sweet, and I closed my eyes. I heard, "*Pip, pop, pop, pop.*"

---

21. **poaching** [pōch′ing]: hunting or fishing illegally.

22. **misshapen** [mis shā′pən]: twisted or bent out of the usual or natural shape.

"Who's making that noise?" I said sleepily to Frightful. She ruffled her feathers.

I listened. "*Pop, pip.*" I rolled over and stuck my face in the grass. Something gleamed beneath me, and in the fading light I could see an earthworm coming out of its hole.

Nearby another one arose and there was a *pop*. Little bubbles of air snapped as these voiceless animals of the earth came to the surface. That got me to smiling. I was glad to know this about earthworms. I don't know why, but this seemed like one of the nicest things I had learned in the woods—that earthworms, lowly, confined to the darkness of the earth, could make just a little stir in the world.

IN WHICH
Frightful Learns Her ABC's

Free time was spent scraping the fur off the deer hide to get it ready for tanning. This much I knew: in order to tan hide, it has to be steeped[23] in tannic acid.[24] There is tannic acid in the woods in oak trees, but it took me several weeks to figure out how to get it. You need a lot of oak chips in water. Water and oak give off tannic acid. My problem was not oak or water but getting a vessel big enough to put the deer hide in.

Coming home from the stream one night I had an inspiration.

It had showered the day before, and as Frightful and I passed an old stump, I noticed that it had collected the rain. "A stump, an oak stump, would be perfect," I said right out loud to that pretty bird.

So I felled an oak over by the gorge, burned a hole in it, carried water to it, and put my deerskin in it. I let it steep, oh, maybe five days before I took it out and dried it. It dried stiff as a board, and I had to chew, rub, jump on it, and twist it to get it soft. When this was done, however, I had my door. I hung it on pegs inside my entrance, and because it was bigger than it had to be, I would cut off pieces now and then when I needed them. I cut off two thin strips to make jesses, or leg straps, for Frightful. All good falcons wear jesses and leashes so they can be tethered for their training.

I smoked the meat I couldn't eat and stored it. I used everything I could on that animal. I even used one of its bones for a spearhead. I was tired of catching frogs by the jump-and-miss system. I made two sharp points, and strapped them to the end of a long stick, one on each side, to make a kind of fork. It worked beautifully. Frogs were one of my favorite meals, and I found I could fix them many ways; however, I got to like frog soup fixed in this way: "Clean, skin, and boil until tender. Add wild onions, also water lily buds and wild carrots. Thicken with acorn flour. Serve in turtle shell."

By now my two pairs of pants were threadbare[25] and my three sweaters were frayed. I dreamed of a deerskin suit, and watched my herd with clothes in mind.

The deer for my suit did not come easily. I rigged up a figure-four trap under

---

23. **steeped** [stēpt]: soaked in liquid.
24. **tannic** [tan′ik] **acid**: yellowish or brownish mixture of chemical compounds found in the bark and wood of many trees.

25. **threadbare** [thred′bâr′]: having the finish worn off so as to expose the threads of the fabric; shabby.

the log, and baited it with elderberries rolled into a ball. That just mushed up and didn't work. Then I remembered that deer like salt. I made a ball of hickory salt with turtle fat to hold it together.

Every evening Frightful and I, sometimes accompanied by The Baron Weasel, would go to the edge of the meadow and look toward the aspen grove to see if the great log had fallen. One night we saw three deer standing around it quietly, reaching toward the smell of salt. At that moment, The Baron jumped at my pants leg, but got my ankle with an awful nip. I guess I had grown some; my pants and socks did not meet anymore. I screamed, and the deer fled.

I chased The Baron home. I had the uneasy feeling that he was laughing as he darted, flipped, buckled, and disappeared.

The Baron was hard to understand. What did he want from me? Occasionally I left him bites of turtle or venison, and although he smelled the offerings, he never ate them. The catbird would get them. Most animals stick around if you feed them. But The Baron did not eat anything. Yet he seemed to like me. Gradually it occurred to me that he didn't have a mate or a family. Could he be a lonely bachelor, taking up with odd company for lack of an ordinary life? Well, whatever, The Baron liked me for what I was, and I appreciated that. He was a personable[26] little fellow.

Every day I worked to train Frightful. It was a long process. I would put her on her stump with a long leash and step back a few feet with some meat in my hand. Then I would whistle. The whistle was supposed eventually to mean food to her. So I would whistle, show her the meat, and after many false flaps she would finally fly to my hand. I would pet her and feed her. She could fly fairly well, so now I made sure that she never ate unless she flew to my fist.

One day at breakfast I whistled for Frightful. I had no food, she wasn't even hungry, but she came to me anyway. I was thrilled. She had learned a whistle meant "come."

I looked into her steely eyes that morning and thought I saw a gentle recognition. She puffed up her feathers as she sat on my hand. I call this a "feather word." It means she is content.

Now each day I stepped farther and farther away from Frightful to make her fly greater and greater distances. One day she few a good fifty feet, and we packed up and went gathering seeds, bark, and tubers to celebrate.

I used my oldest sweater for gathering things. It was not very convenient, and each time I filled it I mentally designed bigger and better pockets on my deer-hide suit-to-be.

The summer was wonderful. There was food in abundance[27] and I gathered it most of the morning, and stored it away in the afternoon. I could now see that my niches were not going to be big enough for the amount of food I would need for the winter, so I began burning out another tree. When the hickory nuts, walnuts and acorns appeared, I was going to need a bin. You'd be surprised what a

---

26. **personable** [pur′sə nə bəl]: having a pleasing or attractive appearance and manner.

27. **abundance** [ə bun′dəns]: plentiful or overflowing supply.

pile of nuts it takes to make one turtle shell full of nut meats—and not a snapping-turtle[28] shell either, just a box-turtle[29] shell!

With the easy living of the summer also came a threat. Hikers and vacationers were in the woods, and more than once I pulled inside my tree, closed my deer-flap door, and hid while bouncing noisy people crossed the meadow on their way to the gorge. Apparently the gorge was a sight for those who wanted a four-mile hike up the mountain.

One morning I heard a group arriving. I whistled for Frightful. She came promptly. We dove into the tree. It was dark inside the tree with the flap closed, and I realized that I needed a candle. I planned a lamp of a turtle shell with a deer-hide wick, and as I was cutting off a piece of hide, I heard a shrill scream.

The voices of the hikers became louder. I wondered if one of them had fallen into the gorge. Then I said to Frightful, "That was no cry of a human, pretty bird. I'll bet you a rabbit for dinner that our deer trap worked. And here we are stored in a tree like a nut and unable to claim our prize."

We waited and waited until I couldn't be patient any more, and I was about to put my head out the door when a man's voice said, "Look at these trees!"

A woman spoke. "Harold, they're huge. How old do you think they are?"

"Three hundred years old, maybe four hundred," said Harold.

They tramped around, actually sat on The Baron's boulder, and were apparently

Rabbit

going to have lunch, when things began to happen out there and I almost gave myself away with hysterics.

"Harold, what's the matter with that weasel? It's running all over this rock." A scream! A scuttering and scraping of boots on the rocks.

"He's mad!" That was the woman.

"Watch it, Grace, he's coming at your feet." They ran.

By this time I had my hand over my mouth to keep back the laughter. I snorted and choked, but they never heard me. They were in the meadow—run right out of the forest by that fiery Baron Weasel.

I still laugh when I think of it.

It was not until dark that Frightful and I got to the deer, and a beauty it was.

The rest of June was spent smoking it, tanning it, and finally, starting on my deerskin suit. I made a bone needle, cut

---

28. **snapping-turtle**: large American freshwater turtle.
29. **box-turtle**: small North American land turtle.

out the pants by ripping up one pair of old city pants for a pattern. I saved my city pants and burned them bit by bit to make charred cloth for the flint and steel.

"Frightful," I said while sewing one afternoon. She was preening her now silver-gray, black, and white feathers. "There is no end to this. We need another deer. I can't make a blouse."

We didn't get another deer until fall, so with the scraps I made big square pockets for food gathering. One hung in front of me, and the other down my back. They were joined by straps. This device worked beautifully.

Sometime in July I finished my pants. They fit well, and were the best-looking pants I had ever seen. I was terribly proud of them.

With pockets and good tough pants I was willing to pack home many more new foods to try. Daisies, the bark of a poplar tree that I saw a squirrel eating, and puffballs. They are mushrooms, the only ones I felt were safe to eat, and even at that, I kept waiting to die the first night I ate them. I didn't, so I enjoyed them from that night on. They were wonderful. Mushrooms are dangerous and I would not suggest that one eat them from the forest. The mushroom expert at the Botanical Gardens told me that. He said even he didn't eat wild ones.

The inner bark of the poplar tree tasted like wheat kernels, and so I dried as much as I could and powdered it into flour. It was tedious work, and in August when the acorns were ready, I found that they made better flour and were much easier to handle.

I would bake the acorns in the fire, and grind them between stones. This was tedious work, too, but now that I had a home and smoked venison and did not have to hunt food every minute, I could do things like make flour. I would simply add spring water to the flour and bake this on a piece of tin. When done, I had the best pancakes ever. They were flat and hard, like I imagined Indian bread to be. I liked them, and would carry the leftovers in my pockets for lunch.

One fine August day I took Frightful to the meadow. I had been training her to the lure. That is, I now tied her meat on a piece of wood, covered with hide and feathers. I would throw it in the air and she would swoop out of the sky and catch it. She was absolutely free during these maneuvers, and would fly high into the air and hover over me like a leaf. I made sure she was very hungry before I turned her loose. I wanted her back.

After a few tries she never missed the lure. Such marksmanship thrilled me. Bird and lure would drop to the earth, I would run over, grab her jesses, and we would sit on the big boulder in the meadow while she ate. Those were nice evenings. The finest was the night I wrote this:

"Frightful caught her first prey. She is now a trained falcon. It was only a sparrow, but we are on our way. It happened unexpectedly. Frightful was climbing into the sky, circling and waiting for the lure, when I stepped forward and scared a sparrow.

"The sparrow flew across the meadow. Out of the sky came a black streak—I've never seen anything drop so fast. With a great backwatering of wings, Frightful broke her fall, and at the same time seized the sparrow. I took it away from her and gave her the lure. That sounds

Study of Wood Interior, Asher B. Durand, c. 1850.

mean, but if she gets in the habit of eating what she catches, she will go wild."

IN WHICH
I Find a Real Live Man

One of the gasping joys of summer was my daily bath in the spring. It was cold water, I never stayed in long, but it woke me up and started me into the day with a vengeance.[30]

I would tether Frightful to a hemlock bough above me and splash her from time to time. She would suck in her chest,

look startled, and then shake. While I bathed and washed, she preened. Huddled down in the water between the ferns and moss, I scrubbed myself with the bark of the slippery elm. It gets soapy when you rub it.

The frogs would hop out and let me in, and the woodthrush would come to the edge of the pool to see what was happening. We were a gay gathering—me shouting, Frightful preening, the woodthrush cocking its pretty head. Occasionally The Baron Weasel would pop up and glance furtively[31] at us. He didn't care for

---

30. **with a vengeance**: with great force or passion.

31. **furtively** [fur′tiv lē]: secretly.

water. How he stayed glossy and clean was a mystery to me, until he came to the boulder beside our bath pool one day, wet with the dew from the ferns. He licked himself until he was polished.

One morning there was a rustle in the leaves above. Instantly, Frightful had it located. I had learned to look where Frightful looked when there were disturbances in the forest. She always saw life before I could focus my eyes. She was peering into the hemlock above us. Finally I too saw it. A young raccoon. It was chittering and now that all eyes were upon it, began coming down the tree.

And so Frightful and I met Jessie Coon James, the bandit of the Gribley farm.

He came headfirst down to our private bath, a scrabbly, skinny young raccoon. He must have been from a late litter, for he was not very big, and certainly not well fed. Whatever had been Jessie C. James's past, it was awful. Perhaps he was an orphan, perhaps he had been thrown out of his home by his mother, as his eyes were somewhat crossed and looked a little peculiar. In any event he had come to us for help, I thought, and so Frightful and I led him home and fed him.

In about a week he fattened up. His crumply hair smoothed out, and with a little ear scratching and back rubbing, Jessie C. James became a devoted friend. He also became useful. He slept somewhere in the dark tops of the hemlocks all day long, unless he saw us start for the stream. Then, tree by tree, limb by limb, Jessie followed us. At the stream he was the most useful mussel digger that any boy could have. Jessie could find mussels where three men could not. He would start to eat them, and if he ate

them, he got full and wouldn't dig anymore, so I took them away from him until he found me all I wanted. Then I let him have some.

Mussels are good. Here are a few notes on how to fix them.

"Scrub mussels in spring water. Dump them into boiling water with salt. Boil five minutes. Remove and cool in the juice. Take out meat. Eat by dipping in acorn paste flavored with a smudge of garlic, and green apples."

Frightful took care of the small game supply, and now that she was an expert hunter, we had rabbit stew, pheasant[32] potpie, and an occasional sparrow, which I generously gave to Frightful. As fast as we removed the rabbits and pheasants new ones replaced them.

Beverages during the hot summer became my chore, largely because no one else wanted them. I found some sassafras trees at the edge of the road one day, dug up a good supply of roots, peeled and dried them. Sassafras tea is about as good as anything you want to drink. Pennyroyal makes another good drink. I dried great bunches of this, and hung them from the roof of the tree room together with the leaves of winterberry. All these fragrant plants I also used in cooking to give a new taste to some not-so-good foods.

The room in the tree smelled of smoke and mint. It was the best-smelling tree in the Catskill Mountains.

Life was leisurely. I was warm, well fed.

---

32. **pheasant** [fez'ənt]: long-tailed, brightly colored bird.

One day while I was down the mountain, I returned home by way of the old farmhouse site to check the apple crop. They were summer apples, and were about ready to be picked. I had gathered a pouchful and had sat down under the tree to eat a few and think about how I would dry them for use in the winter when Frightful dug her talons into my shoulder so hard I winced.

"Be gentle, bird!" I said to her.

I got her talons out and put her on a log, where I watched her with some alarm. She was as alert as a high tension wire,[33] her head cocked so that her ears, just membranes under her feathers, were pointed east. She evidently heard a sound that pained her. She opened her beak. Whatever it was, I could hear nothing, though I strained my ears, cupped them, and wished she would speak.

Frightful was my ears as well as my eyes. She could hear things long before I. When she grew tense, I listened or looked. She was scared this time. She turned round and round on the log, looked up in the tree for a perch, lifted her wings to fly, and then stood still and listened.

Then I heard it. A police siren sounded far down the road. The sound grew louder and louder, and I grew afraid. Then I said, "No, Frightful, if they are after me there won't be a siren. They'll just slip up on me quietly."

No sooner had I said this than the siren wound down, and apparently stopped on the road at the foot of the mountain. I got up to run to my tree, but had not gotten past the walnut before the patrol cars started up and screamed away.

---

33. **high tension wire:** wire carrying a large amount of electricity.

We started home although it was not late in the afternoon. However, it was hot, and thunderheads were building up. I decided to take a swim in the spring and work on the moccasins I had cut out several days ago.

With the squad car still on my mind, we slipped quietly into the hemlock forest. Once again Frightful almost sent me through the crown of the forest by digging her talons into my shoulder. I looked at her. She was staring at our home. I looked, too. Then I stopped, for I could make out the form of a man stretched between the sleeping house and the store tree.

Softly, tree by tree, Frightful and I approached him. The man was asleep. I could have left and camped in the gorge again, but my enormous desire to see another human being overcame my fear of being discovered.

We stood above the man. He did not move, so Frightful lost interest in my fellow being. She tried to hop to her stump and preen. I grabbed her leash however, as I wanted to think before awakening him. Frightful flapped. I held her wings to her body as her flapping was noisy to me. Apparently not so to the man. The man did not stir. It is hard to realize that the rustle of a falcon's wings is not much of a noise to a man from the city, because by now, one beat of her wings and I would awaken from a sound sleep as if a shot had gone off. The stranger slept on. I realized how long I'd been in the mountains.

Right at that moment, as I looked at his unshaven face, his close-cropped hair, and his torn clothes, I thought of the police siren, and put two and two together.

"An outlaw!" I said to myself. "Wow!" I

had to think what to do with an outlaw before I awoke him.

Would he be troublesome? Would he be mean? Should I go live in the gorge until he moved on? How I wanted to hear his voice, to tell him about The Baron and Jessie C. James, to say words out loud. I really did not want to hide from him; besides, he might be hungry, I thought. Finally I spoke.

"Hi!" I said. I was delighted to see him roll over, open his eyes, and look up. He seemed startled, so I reassured him. "It's all right, they've gone. If you don't tell on me I won't tell on you." When he heard this, he sat up and seemed to relax.

"Oh," he said. Then he leaned against the tree and added, "Thanks." He evidently was thinking this over, for he propped his head on his elbow and studied me closely.

"You're a sight for sore eyes," he said, and smiled. He had a nice smile—in fact, he looked nice and not like an outlaw at all. His eyes were very blue and, although tired, they did not look scared or hunted.

However, I talked quickly before he could get up and run away.

"I don't know anything about you, and I don't want to. You don't know anything about me, and don't want to, but you may stay here if you like. No one is going to find you here. Would you like some supper?" It was still early, but he looked hungry.

"Do you have some?"

"Yes, venison or rabbit?"

"Well . . . venison." His eyebrows puckered in question marks. I went to work.

He arose, turned around and around, and looked at his surroundings. He whistled softly when I kindled a spark with the flint and steel. I was now quite quick at this, and had a tidy fire blazing in a very few minutes. I was so used to myself doing this that it had not occurred to me that it would be interesting to a stranger.

"Desdemondia!" he said. I judged this to be some underworld phrase. At this moment Frightful, who had been sitting quietly on her stump, began to preen. The outlaw jumped back, then saw she was tied and said, "And who is this ferocious-looking character?"

"That is Frightful; don't be afraid. She's quite wonderful and gentle. She would be glad to catch you a rabbit for supper if you would prefer that to venison."

"Am I dreaming?" said the man. "I go to sleep by a campfire that looked like it was built by a boy scout, and I awaken in the middle of the eighteenth century."

I crawled into the store tree to get the smoked venison and some cattail tubers. When I came out again, he was speechless.

"My storehouse," I explained.

"I see," he answered. From that moment on he did not talk much. He just watched me. I was so busy cooking the best meal that I could possibly get together that I didn't say much either. Later I wrote down that menu, as it was excellent.

"Brown puffballs in deer fat with a little wild garlic, fill pot with water, put venison in, boil. Wrap tubers in leaves and stick in coals. Cut up apples and boil in can with dogtooth violet bulbs. Raspberries to finish meal."

When the meal was ready, I served it to the man in my nicest turtle shell. I had to whittle him a fork out of the crotch of a twig, as Jessie Coon James had gone off with the others. He ate and

Kauterskill Gap, Catskill Mountains, John Frederick Kensett (1855–1858).

ate and ate, and when he was done he said, "May I call you Thoreau?"[34]

"That will do nicely," I said. Then I paused—just to let him know that I knew a little bit about him too. I smiled and said, "I will call you Bando."

His eyebrows went up, he cocked his

34. **Thoreau** [thə rō′]: Henry David Thoreau (1817–1862), American writer, philosopher, and naturalist, whose classic book *Walden* (1854) describes the two years he spent living alone in the woods near Concord, Massachusetts.

head, shrugged his shoulders and answered, "That's close enough."

With this he sat and thought. I felt I had offended him, so I spoke. "I will be glad to help. I will teach you how to live off the land. It is very easy. No one need find you."

His eyebrows gathered together again. This was characteristic of Bando when he was concerned, and so I was sorry I had mentioned his past. After all, outlaw or no outlaw, he was an adult, and I still felt unsure of myself around adults. I changed the subject.

"Let's get some sleep," I said.

"Where do you sleep?" he asked. All this time sitting and talking with me, and he had not seen the entrance to my tree. I was pleased. Then I beckoned, walked a few feet to the left, pushed back the deer-hide door, and showed Bando my secret.

"Thoreau," he said. "You are quite wonderful." He went in. I lit the turtle candle for him, he explored, tried the bed, came out and shook his head until I thought it would roll off.

We didn't say much more that night. I let him sleep on my bed. His feet hung off, but he was comfortable, he said. I stretched out by the fire. The ground was dry, the night warm, and I could sleep on anything now.

I got up early and had breakfast ready when Bando came stumbling out of the tree. We ate crayfish, and he really honestly seemed to like them. It takes a little time to acquire a taste for wild foods, so Bando surprised me the way he liked the menu. Of course he was hungry, and that helped.

That day we didn't talk much, just went over the mountain collecting foods. I wanted to dig up the tubers of the Solomon's seal from a big garden of them on the other side of the gorge. We fished, we swam a little, and I told him I hoped to make a raft pretty soon, so I could float into deeper water and perhaps catch bigger fish.

When Bando heard this, he took my ax and immediately began to cut young trees for this purpose. I watched him and said, "You must have lived on a farm or something."

At that moment a bird sang.

"The wood pewee," said Bando, stopping his work. He stepped into the woods, seeking it. Now I was astonished.

"How would you know about a wood pewee in your business?" I grew bold enough to ask.

"And just what do you think my business is?" he said as I followed him.

"Well, you're not a minister."

"Right!"

"And you're not a doctor or a lawyer."

"Correct."

"You're not a businessman or a sailor."

"No, I am not."

"Nor do you dig ditches."

"I do not."

"Well . . ."

"Guess."

Suddenly I wanted to know for sure. So I said it.

"You are a murderer or a thief or a racketeer;[35] and you are hiding out."

Bando stopped looking for the pewee. He turned and stared at me. At first I was frightened. A bandit might do anything. But he wasn't mad, he was laughing. He had a good deep laugh and it kept coming out of him. I smiled, then grinned and laughed with him.

"What's funny, Bando?" I asked.

"I like that," he finally said. "I like that a lot." The tickle deep inside him kept him chuckling. I had no more to say, so I ground my heel in the dirt while I waited for him to get over the fun and explain it all to me.

"Thoreau, my friend, I am just a college English teacher lost in the Catskills. I came out to hike around the woods, got completely lost yesterday, found your fire

---

35. **racketeer**: [rak′ə tēr′]: one engaged in a dishonest or illegal scheme or activity for getting money.

and fell asleep beside it. I was hoping the scoutmaster and his troop would be back for supper and help me home."

"Oh, no." My comment. Then I laughed. "You see, Bando, before I found you, I heard squad cars screaming up the road. Occasionally you read about bandits that hide out in the forest, and I was just so sure that you were someone they were looking for."

We gave up the pewee and went back to the raft-making, talking very fast now, and laughing a lot. He was fun. Then something sad occurred to me.

"Well, if you're not a bandit, you will have to go home very soon, and there is no point in teaching you how to live on fish and bark and plants."

"I can stay a little while," he said. "This is summer vacation. I must admit I had not planned to eat crayfish on my vacation, but I am rather getting to like it.

"Maybe I can stay until your school opens," he went on. "That's after Labor Day, isn't it?"

I was very still, thinking how to answer that.

Bando sensed this. Then he turned to me with a big grin.

"You really mean you are going to try to winter it out here?"

"I think I can."

"Well!" He sat down, rubbed his forehead in his hands, and looked at me. "Thoreau, I have led a varied life—dishwasher, sax[36] player, teacher. To me it has been an interesting life. Just now it seems very dull." He sat awhile with his head down, then looked up at the mountains and the rocks and trees. I heard him sigh.

"Let's go fish. We can finish this another day."

That is how I came to know Bando. We became very good friends in the week or ten days that he stayed with me, and he helped me a lot. We spent several days gathering white oak acorns and groundnuts, harvesting the blueberry crop and smoking fish.

We flew Frightful every day just for the pleasure of lying on our backs in the meadow and watching her mastery of the sky. I had lots of meat, so what she caught those days was all hers. It was a pleasant time, warm, with occasional thundershowers, some of which we stayed out in. We talked about books. He did know a lot of books, and could quote exciting things from them.

One day Bando went to town and came back with five pounds of sugar.

"I want to make blueberry jam," he announced. "All those excellent berries and no jam."

He worked two days at this. He knew how to make jam. He'd watched his pa make it in Mississippi, but we got stuck on what to put it in.

I wrote this one night:

"*August 29*

"The raft is almost done. Bando has promised to stay until we can sail out into the deep fishing holes.

"Bando and I found some clay along the stream bank. It was as slick as ice. Bando thought it would make good pottery. He shaped some jars and lids. They look good—not Wedgwood,[37] he said, but

---

36. **sax**: saxophone, a musical instrument.

37. **Wedgwood** [wej′wood′]: type of clay pottery with a blue or green background and white, raised ornament.

containers. We dried them on the rock in the meadow, and later Bando made a clay oven and baked them in it. He thinks they might hold the blueberry jam he has been making.

"Bando got the fire hot by blowing on it with some homemade bellows[38] that he fashioned from one of my skins that he tied together like a balloon. A reed is the nozzle.

"*August 30*

"It was a terribly hot day for Bando to be firing[39] clay jars, but he stuck with it. They look jam-worthy, as he says, and he filled three of them tonight. The jam is good, the pots remind me of crude flower pots without the hole in the bottom. Some of the lids don't fit. Bando says he will go home and read more about pottery making so that he can do a better job next time.

"We like the jam. We eat it on hard acorn pancakes.

"Later. Bando met The Baron Weasel today for the first time. I don't know where The Baron has been this past week, but suddenly he appeared on the rock, and nearly jumped down Bando's shirt collar. Bando said he liked The Baron best when he was in his hole.

"*September 3*

"Bando taught me how to make willow whistles today. He and I went to the stream and cut two fat twigs about eight inches long. He slipped the bark on them. That means he pulled the wood out of the

bark, leaving a tube. He made a mouthpiece at one end, cut a hole beneath it, and used the wood to slide up and down like a trombone.

"We played music until the moon came up. Bando could even play jazz on the willow whistles. They are wonderful instruments, sounding much like the wind in the top of the hemlocks. Sad tunes are best suited to willow whistles. When we played 'The Young Voyageur' tears came to our eyes, it was so sad."

There were no more notes for many days. Bando had left me saying: "Good-by, I'll see you at Christmas." I was so lonely that I kept sewing on my moccasins to keep myself busy. I sewed every free minute for four days, and when they were finished, I began a glove to protect my hand from Frightful's sharp talons.

One day when I was thinking very hard about being alone, Frightful gave her gentle call of love and contentment. I looked up.

"Bird," I said. "I had almost forgotten how we used to talk." She made tiny movements with her beak and fluffed her feathers. This was a language I had forgotten since Bando came. It meant she was glad to see me and hear me, that she was well fed, and content. I picked her up and squeaked into her neck feathers. She moved her beak, turned her bright head, and bit my nose very gently.

Jessie Coon James came down from the trees for the first time in ten days. He finished my fish dinner. Then just before dusk, The Baron came up on his boulder and scratched and cleaned and played with a fern leaf.

I had the feeling we were all back together again.

---

38. **bellows**: device for producing an air current to make a fire burn faster.
39. **firing**: exposing to the action of fire in order to bake.

READER'S RESPONSE

Do you think that Sam will be able to overcome his loneliness? Why or why not?

STUDY QUESTIONS

Recalling
1. Who comes looking for Sam at his camp?
2. Why does Sam name his hawk Frightful?
3. Name three ways in which Sam's new animal friends help him.
4. List at least five foods that Sam adds to his diet.
5. Who is Bando? Name three things that he and Sam do together.

Interpreting
6. Why does Sam fear discovery?
7. Compare and contrast Sam's life on the mountain with average home life.
8. In what ways has Sam's life improved since his first days on the mountain?

Extending
9. What words would you use to describe Sam's life style? If you were in Sam's place, what would you like or dislike most about this life style?

COMPOSITION

Writing a Character Sketch
Write a character sketch of Sam. **Prewriting:** Make notes on his thoughts, words, feelings, actions, and appearance. **Writing:** Begin by describing Sam's appearance. Then identify three outstanding character traits. Give examples of his actions, words, thoughts, and feelings to explain each character trait. **Revising:** Review your writing to be sure that you have expressed your ideas clearly and logically. Then review for effective word choice and organization. Make sure that your final copy is free of errors in grammar, spelling, and punctuation. *For help with this assignment, see Lesson 3 in the Writing About Literature Handbook at the back of this book.*

Retelling an Incident from a Novel
Write about Sam's raid on the falcon's nest as if Frightful were telling the story. Make Frightful the first-person narrator, and describe her thoughts and feelings instead of Sam's. Be sure to show how Frightful feels about Sam once she gets to know him.

CHALLENGE

Research and Oral Report
On several occasions Bando calls Sam Thoreau. Find information on the American writer Henry David Thoreau that explains why Bando equates Sam with Thoreau. You may check a general encyclopedia or a biographical reference work such as the *Dictionary of American Biography* or *Webster's Biographical Dictionary.* These reference works are in most libraries. Present your findings to the class in a brief oral report.

Detail, *Study of Wood Interior,* Asher B. Durand, c. 1850.

Northern Brook Trout

IN WHICH
The Autumn Provides Food and Loneliness

September blazed a trail into the mountains. First she burned the grasses. The grasses seeded and were harvested by the mice and the winds.

Then she sent the squirrels and chipmunks running boldly through the forest, collecting and hiding nuts.

Then she frosted the aspen leaves and left them sunshine yellow.

Then she gathered the birds together in flocks, and the mountaintop was full of songs and twitterings and flashing wings. The birds were ready to move to the south.

And I, Sam Gribley, felt just wonderful, just wonderful.

I pushed the raft down the stream and gathered arrow-leaf bulbs, cattail tubers, bulrush roots, and the nutlike tubers of the sedges.

And then the crop of crickets appeared and Frightful hopped all over the meadow snagging them in her great talons and eating them. I tried them, because I had heard they are good. I think it was another species of cricket that was meant. I think the field cricket would taste excellent if you were starving. I was not starving, so I preferred to listen to them. I abandoned the crickets and went back to the goodness of the earth.

I smoked fish and rabbit, dug wild onions by the pouchful, and raced September for her crop.

"October 15

"Today The Baron Weasel looked moldy. I couldn't get near enough to see what was the matter with him, but it occurs to me that he might be changing his summer fur for his white winter mantle. If he is, it is an itchy process. He scratches a lot."

Seeing The Baron changing his mantle for winter awoke the first fears in me. I wrote that note on a little birch bark, curled up on my bed, and shivered.

The snow and the cold and the long lifeless months are ahead, I thought. The wind was blowing hard and cool across the mountain. I lit my candle, took out the rabbit and squirrel hides I had been saving, and began rubbing and kneading them to softness.

The Baron was getting a new suit for winter. I must have one too. Some fur underwear, some mittens, fur-lined socks.

Frightful, who was sitting on the foot

post of the bed, yawned, fluffed, and thrust her head into the slate gray feathers of her back. She slept. I worked for several hours.

I must say here that I was beginning to wonder if I should not go home for the winter and come back again in the spring. Everything in the forest was getting prepared for the harsh months. Jessie Coon James was as fat as a barrel. He came down the tree slowly, his fat falling in a roll over his shoulders. The squirrels were working and storing food. They were building leaf nests. The skunks had burrows and plugged themselves in at dawn with bunches of leaves. No drafts could reach them.

As I thought of the skunks and all the animals preparing themselves against the winter, I realized suddenly that my tree would be as cold as the air if I did not somehow find a way to heat it.

"NOTES:

"Today I rafted out into the deep pools of the creek to fish. It was a lazy sort of autumn day, the sky clear, the leaves beginning to brighten, the air warm. I stretched out on my back because the fish weren't biting, and hummed.

"My line jerked and I sat up to pull, but was too late. However, I was not too late to notice that I had drifted into the bank—the very bank where Bando had dug the clay for the jam pots.

"At that moment I knew what I was going to do. I was going to build a fireplace of clay, even fashion a little chimney of clay. It would be small, but enough to warm the tree during the long winter.

"Next Day

"I dragged the clay up the mountain to my tree in my second best pair of city pants. I tied the bottoms of the legs, stuffed them full, and as I looked down on my strange cargo, I thought of scarecrows and Halloween. I thought of the gang dumping ashcans on Third Avenue[1] and soaping up the windows. Suddenly I was terribly lonely. The air smelled of leaves and the cool wind from the stream hugged me. The warblers in the trees above me seemed gay and glad about their trip south. I stopped halfway up the mountain and dropped my head. I was lonely and on the verge[2] of tears. Suddenly there was a flash, a pricking sensation on my leg, and I looked down in time to see The Baron leap from my pants to the cover of fern.

"He scared the loneliness right out of me. I ran after him and chased him up the mountain, losing him from time to time in the ferns and crowfeet. We stormed into camp an awful sight, The Baron bouncing and screaming ahead of me, and me dragging that half scarecrow of clay.

"Frightful took one look and flew to the end of her leash. She doesn't like The Baron, and watches him—well, like a hawk. I don't like to leave her alone. End notes. Must make fireplace."

It took three days to get the fireplace worked out so that it didn't smoke me out of the tree like a bee. It was an enormous problem. In the first place, the chimney sagged because the clay was too heavy to hold itself up, so I had to get some dry grasses to work into it so it could hold its own weight.

---

1. **Third Avenue**: in New York City, long street that runs through Manhattan and the Bronx.
2. **on the verge** [vurj]: on the edge, or brink.

I whittled out one of the old knotholes to let the smoke out, and built the chimney down from this. Of course when the clay dried, it pulled away from the tree, and all the smoke poured back in on me.

So I tried sealing the leak with pine pitch,[3] and that worked all right, but then the funnel[4] over the fire bed cracked, and I had to put wooden props under that.

The wooden props burned, and I could see that this wasn't going to work either; so I went down the mountain to the site of the old Gribley farmhouse and looked around for iron spikes or some sort of metal.

I took the wooden shovel that I had carved from the board and dug around what I thought must have been the back door or possibly the woodhouse.

I found a hinge, old handmade nails that would come in handy, and finally, treasure of treasures, the axle of an old wagon. It was much too big. I had no hacksaw to cut it into smaller pieces, and I was not strong enough to heat it and hammer it apart. Besides, I didn't have anything but a small wooden mallet I had made.

I carried my trophies home and sat down before my tree to fix dinner and feed Frightful. The evening was cooling down for a frost. I looked at Frightful's warm feathers. I didn't even have a deer hide for a blanket. I had used the two I had for a door and a pair of pants. I wished that I might grow feathers.

I tossed Frightful off my fist and she flashed through the trees and out over the meadow. She went with a determination strange to her. "She is going to leave," I cried. "I have never seen her fly so wildly." I pushed the smoked fish aside and ran to the meadow. I whistled and whistled and whistled until my mouth was dry and no more whistle came.

I ran onto the big boulder. I could not see her. Wildly I waved the lure. I licked my lips and whistled again. The sun was a cold steely color as it dipped below the mountain. The air was now brisk, and Frightful was gone. I was sure that she had suddenly taken off on the migration; my heart was sore and pounding. I had enough food, I was sure. Frightful was not absolutely necessary for my survival; but I was now so fond of her. She was more than a bird. I knew I must have her back to talk to and play with if I was going to make it through the winter.

I whistled. Then I heard a cry in the grasses up near the white birches.

In the gathering darkness I saw movement. I think I flew to the spot. And there she was; she had caught herself a bird. I rolled into the grass beside her and clutched her jesses. She didn't intend to leave, but I was going to make sure that she didn't. I grabbed so swiftly that my hand hit a rock and I bruised my knuckles.

The rock was flat and narrow and long; it was the answer to my fireplace. I picked up Frightful in one hand and the stone in the other; and I laughed at the cold steely sun as it slipped out of sight, because I knew I was going to be warm. This flat stone was what I needed to hold up the funnel and finish my fireplace.

And that's what I did with it. I broke it into two pieces, set one on each side

---

3. **pitch**: resin, a sticky substance secreted by certain trees.
4. **funnel**: tube or shaft, here used to carry smoke away.

Detail, *Near the Village, October, 1892,* George Inness (1825–1894).

under the funnel, lit the fire, closed the flap of the door and listened to the wind bring the first frost to the mountain. I was warm.

Then I noticed something dreadful. Frightful was sitting on the bedpost, her head under her wings. She was toppling. She jerked her head out of her feathers. Her eyes looked glassy. She is sick, I said. I picked her up and stroked her, and we both might have died there if I had not opened the tent flap to get her some water. The cold night air revived her. "Air," I said. "The fireplace used up all the oxygen. I've got to ventilate[5] this place."

We sat out in the cold for a long time because I was more than a little afraid of what our end might have been.

I put out the fire, took the door down and wrapped up in it. Frightful and I slept with the good frost nipping our faces.

---

5. **ventilate**: [vent′əl āt′]: admit air into, especially fresh air.

"NOTES:

"I cut out several more knotholes to let air in and out of the tree room. I tried it today. I have Frightful on my fist watching her. It's been about two hours and she hasn't fainted and I haven't gone numb. I can still write and see clearly.

"Test: Frightful's healthy face."

IN WHICH
We All Learn About Halloween

"*October 28*

"I have been up and down the mountain every day for a week, watching to see if walnuts and hickory nuts are ripe. Today I found the squirrels all over the trees, harvesting them furiously, and so I have decided that ripe or not, I must gather them. It's me or the squirrels.

"I tethered Frightful in the hickory tree while I went to the walnut tree and filled pouches. Frightful protected the hickory nuts. She keeps the squirrels so busy scolding her that they don't have time to take the nuts. They are quite terrified by her. It is a good scheme. I shout and bang the tree and keep them away while I gather.

"I have never seen so many squirrels. They hang from the slender branches, they bounce through the limbs, they seem to come from the whole forest. They must pass messages along to each other—messages that tell what kind of nuts and where the trees are."

A few days later, my storehouse rolling with nuts, I began the race for apples. Entering this race were squirrels, raccoons, and a fat old skunk who looked as if he could eat not another bite. He was ready to sleep his autumn meal off, and I

resented him because he did not need my apples. However, I did not toy with him.

I gathered what apples I could, cut some in slices, and dried them on the boulder in the sun. Some I put in the storeroom tree to eat right away. They were a little wormy, but it was wonderful to eat an apple again.

Then one night this was all done, the crop was gathered. I sat down to make a few notes when The Baron came sprinting into sight.

He actually bounced up and licked the edges of my turtle-shell bowl, stormed Frightful, and came to my feet.

"Baron Weasel," I said. "It is nearing Halloween. Are you playing tricks or treats?" I handed him the remains of my turtle soup dinner, and, fascinated, watched him devour it.

"NOTES:

"The Baron chews with his back molars, and chews with a ferocity[6] I have not seen in him before. His eyes gleam, the lips curl back from his white pointed teeth, and he frowns like an angry man. If I move toward him, a rumble starts in his chest that keeps me back. He flashes glances at me. It is indeed strange to be looked in the eye by this fearless wild animal. There is something human about his beady glance. Perhaps because that glance tells me something. It tells me he knows who I am and that he does not want me to come any closer."

The Baron Weasel departed after his feast. Frightful, who was drawn up as

---

6. **ferocity** [fə ros'ə tē]: state or quality of being ferocious; fierceness.

skinny as a stick, relaxed and fluffed her feathers, and then I said to her, "See, he got his treats. No tricks." Then something occurred to me. I reached inside the door and pulled out my calendar stick. I counted 28, 29, 30, 31.

"Frightful, that old weasel knows. It is Halloween. Let's have a Halloween party."

Swiftly I made piles of cracked nuts, smoked rabbit, and crayfish. I even added two of my apples. This food was an invitation to the squirrels, foxes, raccoons, opossums, even the birds that lived around me to come have a party.

When Frightful is tethered to her stump, some of the animals and birds will only come close enough to scream at her. So bird and I went inside the tree, propped open the flap, and waited.

Not much happened that night. I learned that it takes a little time for the woodland messages to get around. But they do. Before the party I had been very careful about leaving food out because I needed every mouthful. I took the precaution of rolling a stone in front of my store tree. The harvest moon rose. Frightful and I went to sleep.

At dawn, we abandoned the party. I left the treats out, however. Since it was a snappy gold-colored day, we went off to get some more rabbit skins to finish my winter underwear.

We had lunch along the creek—stewed mussels and wild potatoes. We didn't get back until dusk because I discovered some wild rice in an ox bow[7] of the stream. There was no more than a handful.

Home that night, everything seemed peaceful enough. A few nuts were gone, to the squirrels, I thought. I baked a fish in leaves, and ate a small, precious amount of wild rice. It was marvelous! As I settled down to scrape the rabbit skins of the day, my neighbor the skunk marched right into the campground and set to work on the smoked rabbit. I made some Halloween notes:

"The moon is coming up behind the aspens. It is as big as a pumpkin and as orange. The winds are cool, the stars are like electric light bulbs. I am just inside the doorway, with my turtle-shell lamp burning so that I can see to write this.

"Something is moving beyond the second hemlock. Frightful is very alert, as if there are things all around us. Halloween was over at midnight last night, but for us it is just beginning. That's how I feel, anyhow, but it just may be my imagination.

"I wish Frightful would stop pulling her feathers in and drawing herself up like a spring. I keep thinking that she feels things.

"Here comes Jessie C. James. He will want the venison.

"He didn't get the venison. There was a snarl, and a big raccoon I've never seen walked past him, growling and looking ferocious. Jessie C. stood motionless—I might say, scared stiff. He held his head at an angle and let the big fellow eat. If Jessie so much as rolled his eyes that old coon would sputter at him."

It grew dark, and I couldn't see much. An eerie yelp behind the boulder announced that the red fox of the meadow was nearing. He gave me goose bumps. He stayed just beyond my store tree, weaving back and forth on silent feet. Every

---

7. **ox bow**: U-shaped bend in a river or other body of water.

now and then he would cry—a wavery owllike cry. I wrote some more.

"The light from my turtle lamp casts leaping shadows. To the beechnuts has come a small gray animal. I can't make out what—now, I see it. It's a flying squirrel. That surprises me, I've never seen a flying squirrel around here, but of course I haven't been up much after sunset."

When it grew too dark to see, I lit a fire, hoping it would not end the party. It did not, and the more I watched, the more I realized that all these animals were familiar with my camp. A white-footed mouse walked over my woodpile as if it were his.

I put out the candle and fell asleep when the fire turned to coals. Much later I was awakened by screaming. I lifted my head and looked into the moonlit forest. A few guests, still lingering at the party, saw me move, and dashed bashfully into the ground cover. One was big and slender. I thought perhaps a mink. As I slowly came awake, I realized that screaming was coming from behind me. Something was in my house. I jumped up and shouted, and two raccoons skittered under my feet. I reached for my candle, slipped on hundreds of nuts, and fell. When I finally got a light and looked about me, I was dismayed to see what a mess my guests had made of my tree house. They had found the cache[8] of acorns and beechnuts and had tossed them all over my bed and floor. The party was getting rough.

I chased the raccoons into the night and stumbled over a third animal and was struck by a wet stinging spray. It was skunk! I was drenched. As I got used to the indignity[9] and the smell, I saw the raccoons cavort[10] around my fireplace and dodge past me. They were back in my tree before I could stop them.

A bat winged in from the darkness and circled the tallow candle. It was Halloween and the goblins were at work. I thought of all the ashcans I had knocked over on the streets of New York. It seemed utterly humorless.

Having invited all these neighbors, I was now faced with the problem of getting rid of them. The raccoons were feeling so much at home that they snatched up beechnuts, bits of dried fish and venison and tossed them playfully into the air. They were too full to eat any more, but were having a marvelous time making toys out of my hard-won winter food supply.

I herded the raccoons out of the tree and laced the door. I was breathing "relief" when I turned my head to the left, for I sensed someone watching me. There in the moonlight, his big ears erect on his head, sat the red fox. He was smiling—I know he was. I shouted, "Stop laughing!" and he vanished like a magician's handkerchief.

All this had awakened Frightful, who was flopping in the dark in the tree. I reached in around the deer flap to stroke her back to calmness. She grabbed me so hard I yelled—and the visitors moved to the edge of my camp at my cry.

8. **cache** [kash]: hidden provisions or treasure.

9. **indignity** [in dig′nə tē]: act or circumstance that lowers or interferes with one's worth, dignity, or status.
10. **cavort** [kə vôrt′]: run and jump around playfully; frisk.

Smelling to the sky, bleeding in the hand, and robbed of part of my hard-won food, I threw wood on the fire and sent an enormous shaft of light into the night. Then I shouted. The skunk moved farther away. The raccoons galloped off a few feet and galloped back. I snarled at them. They went to the edge of the darkness and stared at me. I had learned something that night from that very raccoon bossing Jessie C. James—to animals, might is right. I was biggest and I was oldest, and I was going to tell them so. I growled and snarled and hissed and snorted. It worked. They understood and moved away. Some looked back and their eyes glowed. The red eyes chilled me. Never had there been a more real Halloween night. I looked up, expecting to see a witch. The last bat of the season darted in the moonlight. I dove on my bed, and tied the door. There are no more notes about Halloween.

Raccoon

IN WHICH
I Find Out What to Do with Hunters

That party had a moral ending. Don't feed wild animals! I picked up and counted my walnuts and hickory nuts. I was glad to discover there was more mess than loss. I decided that I would not only live until spring but that I still had more nuts than all the squirrels on Gribley's (including flying squirrels).

In early November I was awakened one morning by a shot from a rifle. The hunting season had begun! I had forgotten all about that. To hide from a swarm of hunters was truly going to be a trick. They would be behind every tree and on every hill and dale.[11] They would be shooting at everything that moved, and here was I in deerskin pants and dirty brown sweater, looking like a deer.

I decided, like the animals, to stay holed up the first day of the season. I whittled a fork and finished my rabbit-skin winter underwear. I cracked a lot of walnuts.

The second day of the hunting season I stuck my head out of my door and decided my yard was messy. I picked it up so that it looked like a forest floor.

The third day of the hunting season some men came in and camped by the gorge. I tried to steal down the other side of the mountain to the north stream, found another camp of hunters there, and went back to my tree.

---

11. **dale**: valley.

By the end of the week both Frightful and I were in need of exercise. Gunshots were still snapping around the mountain. I decided to go see Miss Turner at the library. About an hour later I wrote this:

"I got as far as the edge of the hemlock grove when a shot went off practically at my elbow. I didn't have Frightful's jesses in my hand and she took off at the blast. I climbed a tree. There was a hunter so close to me he could have bitten me, but apparently he was busy watching his deer. I was able to get up into the high branches without being seen. First, I looked around for Frightful. I could see her nowhere. I wanted to whistle for her but didn't think I should. I sat still and looked and wondered if she'd go home.

"I watched the hunter track his deer. The deer was still running. From where I was I could see it plainly, going toward the old Gribley farm site. Quietly I climbed higher and watched. Then of all things, it jumped the stone fence and fell dead.

"I thought I would stay in the tree until the hunter quartered his kill and dragged it out to the road. Ah, then, it occurred to me that he wasn't even going to find that deer. He was going off at an angle, and from what I could see, the deer had dropped in a big bank of dry ferns and would be hard to find.

"It got to be nerve-racking at this point. I could see my new jacket lying in the ferns, and the hunter looking for it. I closed my eyes and mentally steered him to the left.

"Then, good old Frightful! She had winged down the mountain and was sitting in a sapling maple not far from the deer. She saw the man and screamed. He looked in her direction; heaven knows what he thought she was, but he turned and started toward her. She rustled her wings, climbed into the sky, and disappeared over my head. I did want to whistle to her, but feared for my deer, myself, and her.

"I hung in the tree and waited about a half an hour. Finally the man gave up his hunt. His friends called, and he went on down the mountain. I went down the tree.

"In the dry ferns lay a nice young buck. I covered it carefully with some of the stones from the fence, and more ferns, and rushed home. I whistled, and down from the top of my own hemlock came Frightful. I got a piece of birch bark to write all this on so I wouldn't get too anxious and go for the deer too soon.

"We will wait until dark to go get our dinner and my new jacket. I am beginning to think I'll have all the deer hide and venison I can use. There must be other lost game on this mountain."

I got the deer after dark, and I was quite right. Before the season was over I got two more deer in the same way. However, with the first deer to work on, the rest of the season passed quickly. I had lots of scraping and preparing to do. My complaint was that I did not dare light a fire and cook that wonderful meat. I was afraid of being spotted. I ate smoked venison, nut meats, and hawthorn berries. Hawthorn berries taste a little bit like apples. They are smaller and drier than apples. They also have big seeds in them. The hawthorn bush is easy to tell because it has big red shiny thorns on it.

Each day the shooting lessened as the hunters left the hills and went home. As they cleared out, Frightful and I were freer and freer to roam.

The air temperature now was cold enough to preserve the venison, so I didn't smoke the last two deer, and about two weeks after I heard the first alarming shot, I cut off a beautiful steak, built a bright fire, and when the embers[12] were glowing, I had myself a real dinner. I soaked some dried puffballs in water, and when they were big and moist, I fried them with wild onions and skimpy old wild carrots and stuffed myself until I felt kindly toward all men. I wrote this:

"November 26

"Hunters are excellent friends if used correctly. Don't let them see you; but follow them closely. Preferably use the tops of trees for this purpose, for hunters don't look up. They look down and to the right and left and straight ahead. So if you stay in the trees, you can not only see what they shoot, but where it falls, and if you are extremely careful, you can sometimes get to it before they do and hide it. That's how I got my third deer."

I had a little more trouble tanning these hides because the water in my oak stump kept freezing at night. It was getting cold. I began wearing my rabbit-fur underwear most of the morning. It was still too warm at noon to keep it on, but it felt good at night. I slept in it until I got my blanket made. I did not scrape the deer hair off my blanket. I liked it on. Because I had grown, one deerskin wouldn't cover me. I sewed part of another one to it.

---

12. **embers**: the remains of a fire that burn and smoke with little or no flame.

The third hide I made into a jacket. I just cut a rectangle with a hole in it for my head and sewed on straight wide sleeves. I put enormous pockets all over it, using every scrap I had, including the pouches I had made last summer. It looked like a cross between a Russian military blouse and a carpenter's apron, but it was warm, roomy and, I thought, handsome.

IN WHICH
Trouble Begins

I stood in my doorway the twenty-third of November dressed from head to toe in deerskins. I was lined with rabbit fur. I had mittens and squirrel-lined moccasins. I was quite excited by my wardrobe.

I whistled and Frightful came to my fist. She eyed me with her silky black eyes and pecked at my suit.

"Frightful," I said, "this is not food. It is my new suit. Please don't eat it." She peeped softly, fluffed her feathers, and looked gently toward the meadow.

"You are beautiful, too, Frightful," I said, and I touched the slate gray feathers of her back. Very gently I stroked the jet black ones that came down from her eyes. Those beautiful marks gave her much of her superb dignity. In a sense she had also come into a new suit. Her plumage had changed during the autumn, and she was breathtaking.

I walked to the spring and we looked in. I saw us quite clearly, as there were no longer any frogs to plop in the water and break the mirror with circles and ripples.

"Frightful," I said as I turned and twisted and looked. "We would be quite handsome if it were not for my hair. I need another haircut."

I did the best job I was able to do with a penknife. I made a mental note to make a hat to cover the stray ends.

Then I did something which took me by surprise. I smelled the clean air of November, turned once more to see how the back of my suit looked, and walked down the mountain. I stepped over the stream on the stones. I walked to the road.

Before I could talk myself out of it, I was on my way to town.

As I walked down the road, I kept pretending I was going to the library; but it was Sunday, and I knew the library was closed.

I tethered Frightful just outside town on a stump. I didn't want to attract any attention. Kicking stones as I went, and whistling, I walked to the main intersection of town as if I came every Sunday.

I saw the drugstore and began to walk faster, for I was beginning to sense that I was not exactly what everybody saw every day. Eyes were upon me longer than they needed to be.

By the time I got to the drugstore, I was running. I slipped in and went to the magazine stand. I picked up a comic book and began to read.

Footsteps came toward me. Below the bottom pictures I saw a pair of pants and saddle shoes. One shoe went *tap, tap.* The feet did a kind of hop step, and I watched them walk to the other side of me. *Tap, tap, tap,* again; a hop step and the shoes and pants circled me. Then came the voice. "Well, if it isn't Daniel Boone!"[13]

---

13. **Daniel Boone**: American frontiersman (1734–1820).

I looked into a face about the age of my own—but a little more puppyish—I thought. It had about the same coloring—brown eyes, brown hair—a bigger nose than mine, and more ears, but a very assured face. I said, "Well?" I grinned, because it had been a long time since I had seen a young man my age.

The young man didn't answer, he simply took my sleeve between his fingers and examined it closely. "Did you chew it yourself?" he asked.

I looked at the spot he was examining and said, "Well, no, I pounded it on a rock there, but I did have to chew it a bit around the neck. It stuck me."

We looked at each other then. I wanted to say something, but didn't know where to begin. He picked at my sleeve again.

"My kid brother has one that looks more real than that thing. Whataya got that on for anyway?"

I looked at his clothes. He had on a nice pair of gray slacks, a white shirt opened at the neck, and a leather jacket. As I looked at these things, I found my voice.

"Well, I'd rip anything like you have on all to pieces in about a week."

He didn't answer; he walked around me again.

"Where did you say you came from?"

"I didn't say, but I come from a farm up the way."

"Whatja say your name was?"

"Well, you called me Daniel Boone."

"Daniel Boone, eh?" He walked around me once more, and then peered at me.

"You're from New York. I can tell the accent." He leaned against the cosmetic counter. "Come on, now, tell me, is this what the kids are wearing in New York now? Is this gang stuff?"

The Coming Storm, George Inness, 1878.

"I am hardly a member of a gang," I said. "Are you?"

"Out here? Naw, we bowl." The conversation went to bowling for a while, then he looked at his watch.

"I gotta go. You sure are a sight, Boone. Whatja doing anyway, playing cowboys and Indians?"

"Come on up to the Gribley farm and I'll show you what I'm doing. I'm doing research. Who knows when we're all going to be blown to bits and need to know how to smoke venison."

"Gee, you New York guys can sure double talk. What does that mean, burn a block down?"

"No, it means smoke venison," I said. I

took a piece out of my pocket and gave it to him. He smelled it and handed it back.

"Man," he said, "whataya do, eat it?"

"I sure do," I answered.

"I don't know whether to send you home to play with my kid brother or call the cops." He shrugged his shoulders and repeated that he had to go. As he left, he called back, "The Gribley farm?"

"Yes. Come on up if you can find it."

I browsed[14] through the magazines until the clerk got anxious to sell me something and then I wandered out. Most of

---

14. **browsed** [brouzd]: glanced through—as a book, a store, or merchandise—or looked at casually.

the people were in church. I wandered around the town and back to the road.

It was nice to see people again. At the outskirts of town a little boy came bursting out of a house with his shoes off, and his mother came bursting out after him. I caught the little fellow by the arm and I held him until his mother picked him up and took him back. As she went up the steps, she stopped and looked at me. She stepped toward the door, and then walked back a few steps and looked at me again. I began to feel conspicuous and took the road to my mountain.

I passed the little old strawberry lady's house. I almost went in, and then something told me to go home.

I found Frightful, untied her, stroked her creamy breast feathers, and spoke to her. "Frightful, I made a friend today. Do you think that is what I had in mind all the time?" The bird whispered.

I was feeling sad as we kicked up the leaves and started home through the forest. On the other hand, I was glad I had met Mr. Jacket, as I called him. I never asked his name. I had liked him although we hadn't even had a fight. All the best friends I had, I always fought, then got to like them after the wounds healed.

The afternoon darkened. The nuthatches that had been clinking around the trees were silent. The chickadees had vanished. A single crow called from the edge of the road. There were no insects singing, there were no catbirds, or orioles, or vireos, or robins.

"Frightful," I said. "It is winter. It is winter and I have forgotten to do a terribly important thing—stack up a big woodpile." The stupidity of this sent Mr. Jacket right out of my mind, and I bolted down the valley to my mountain. Frightful

flapped to keep her balance. As I crossed the stones to my mountain trail, I said to that bird, "Sometimes I wonder if I will make it to spring."

IN WHICH
I Pile Up Wood and Go On with Winter

Now I am almost to that snowstorm. The morning after I had the awful thought about the wood, I got up early. I was glad to hear the nuthatches and chickadees. They gave me the feeling that I still had time to chop. They were bright, busy, and totally unworried about storms. I shouldered my ax and went out.

I had used most of the wood around the hemlock house, so I crossed to the top of the gorge. First I took all the dry limbs off the trees and hauled them home. Then I chopped down dead trees. With wood all around me, I got in my tree and put my arm out. I made an x in the needles. Where the x lay, I began stacking wood. I wanted to be able to reach my wood from the tree when the snow was deep. I piled a big stack at this point. I reached out the other side of the door and made another x. I piled wood here. Then I stepped around my piles and had a fine idea. I decided that if I used up one pile, I could tunnel through the snow to the next and the next. I made many woodpiles leading out into the forest.

I watched the sky. It was as blue as summer, but ice was building up along the waterfall at the gorge. I knew winter was coming, although each day the sun would rise in a bright sky and the days would follow cloudless. I piled more wood.

This is when I realized that I was scared. I kept cutting wood and piling it like a nervous child biting his nails.

It was almost with relief that I saw the storm arrive.

Now I am back where I began. I won't tell it again, I shall go on now with my relief and the fun and wonderfulness of living on a mountaintop in winter.

The Baron Weasel loved the snow, and was up and about in it every day before Frightful and I had had our breakfast. Professor Bando's jam was my standby[15] on those cold mornings. I would eat mounds of it on my hard acorn pancakes, which I improved by adding hickory nuts. With these as a bracer for the day, Frightful and I would stamp out into the snow and reel down the mountain. She would fly above my head as I slid and plunged and rolled to the creek.

The creek was frozen. I would slide out onto it and break a little hole and ice fish.[16] The sun would glance off the white snow, the birds would fly through the trees, and I would come home with a fresh meal from the valley. I found there were still plants under the snow, and I would dig down and get teaberry leaves and wintergreen. I got this idea from the deer, who found a lot to eat under the snow. I tried some of the mosses that they liked, but decided moss was for the deer.

Around four o'clock we would all wander home. The nuthatches, the chickadees, the cardinals, Frightful, and me. And now came the nicest part of wonderful days. I would stop in the meadow and throw Frightful off my fist. She would wind into the sky and wait above me as I kicked the snow-bent grasses. A rabbit would pop up, or sometimes a pheasant. Out of the sky, from a pinpoint of a thing, would dive my beautiful falcon. And, oh, she was beautiful when she made a strike—all power and beauty. On the ground she would cover her quarry. Her perfect feathers would stand up on her body and her wings would arch over the food. She never touched it until I came and picked her up. I would go home and feed her, then crawl into my tree room, light a little fire on my hearth, and Frightful and I would begin the winter evening.

I had lots of time to cook and try mixing different plants with different meats to make things taste better—and I must say I originated some excellent meals.

When dinner was done, the fire would blaze on; Frightful would sit on the foot post of the bed and preen and wipe her beak and shake. Just the fact that she was alive was a warming thing to know.

I would look at her and wonder what made a bird a bird and a boy a boy. The forest would become silent. I would know that The Baron Weasel was about, but I would not hear him.

Then I would get a piece of birch bark and write, or I would make new things out of deer hide, like a hood for Frightful, and finally I would take off my suit and my moccasins and crawl into my bed under the sweet-smelling deerskin. The fire would burn itself out and I would be asleep.

Those were nights of the very best sort.

One night I read some of my old notes about how to pile wood so I could get to

---

15. **standby**: favorite or reliable choice.
16. **ice fish**: catch fish through a hole in the ice.

it under the snow, and I laughed until Frightful awoke. I hadn't made a single tunnel. I walked on the snow to get wood like The Baron Weasel went for food or the deer went for moss.

IN WHICH
I Learn About Birds and People

Frightful and I settled down to living in snow. We went to bed early, slept late, ate the mountain harvest, and explored the country alone. Oh, the deer walked with us, the foxes followed in our footsteps, the winter birds flew over our heads, but mostly we were alone in the white wilderness. It was nice. It was very, very nice. My deerskin rabbit-lined suit was so warm that even when my breath froze in my nostrils, my body was snug and comfortable. Frightful fluffed on the coldest days, but a good flight into the air around the mountain would warm her, and she would come back to my fist with a thump and a flip. This was her signal of good spirits.

I did not become lonely. Many times during the summer I had thought of the "long winter months ahead" with some fear. I had read so much about the loneliness of the farmer, the trapper, the woodsman during the bleakness of winter that I had come to believe it. The winter was as exciting as the summer—maybe more so. The birds were magnificent and almost tame. They talked to each other, warned each other, fought for food, for kingship, and for the right to make the most noise. Sometimes I would sit in my doorway, which became an entrance to be-

hold—a portico[17] of pure white snow, adorned with snowmen—and watch them with endless interest. They reminded me of Third Avenue, and I gave them the names that seemed to fit.

There was Mr. Bracket. He lived on the first floor of our apartment house, and no one could sit on his step or even make a noise near his door without being chased. Mr. Bracket, the chickadee, spent most of his time chasing the young chickadees through the woods. Only his mate could share his favorite perches and feeding places.

Then there were Mrs. O'Brien, Mrs. Callaway, and Mrs. Federio. On Third Avenue they would all go off to the market together first thing in the morning, talking and pushing and stopping to lecture to children in gutters and streets. Mrs. Federio always followed Mrs. O'Brien, and Mrs. O'Brien always followed Mrs. Callaway in talking and pushing and even in buying an apple. And there they were again in my hemlock; three busy chickadees. They would flit and rush around and click and fly from one eating spot to another. They were noisy, scolding and busily following each other. All the other chickadees followed them, and they made way only for Mr. Bracket.

The chickadees, like the people on Third Avenue, had their favorite routes to and from the best food supplies. They each had their own resting perches and each had a little shelter in a tree cavity to which they would fly when the day was over. They would chatter and call good

---

17. **portico** [pôr'ti kō']: roofed structure, usually attached to a building, supported by columns, and open on at least one side.

Winter, Close of Day, George Inness, 1886.

night and make a big fuss before they parted; and then the forest would be as quiet as the apartment house on Third Avenue when all the kids were off the streets and all the parents had said their last words to each other and everyone had gone to their own little hole.

Sometimes when the wind howled and the snows blew, the chickadees would be out for only a few hours. Even Mr. Bracket, who had been elected by the chickadees to test whether or not it was too stormy for good hunting, would appear for a few hours and disappear. Some-

times I would find him just sitting quietly on a limb next to the bole[18] of a tree, all fluffed up and doing nothing. There was no one who more enjoyed doing nothing on a bad day than Mr. Bracket of Third Avenue.

Frightful, the two Mr. Brackets, and I shared this feeling. When the ice and sleet and snow drove down through the hemlocks, we all holed up.

I looked at my calendar pole one day,

_____

18. **bole** [bōl]: trunk.

and realized that it was almost Christmas. Bando will come, I thought. I'll have to prepare a feast and make a present for him. I took stock of the frozen venison and decided that there were enough steaks for us to eat nothing but venison for a month. I scooped under the snow for tea-berry plants to boil down and pour over snowballs for dessert.

I checked my cache of wild onions to see if I had enough to make onion soup, and set aside some large firm groundnuts for mashed potatoes. There were still piles of dogtooth violet bulbs and Solomon's seal roots and a few dried apples. I cracked walnuts, hickory nuts, and beech-nuts, then began a pair of deer-hide moc-casins to be lined with rabbit fur for Bando's present. I finished these before Christmas, so I started a hat of the same materials.

Two days before Christmas I began to wonder if Bando would come. He had for-gotten, I was sure—or he was busy, I said. Or he thought that I was no longer here and decided not to tramp out through the snows to find out. On Christ-mas Eve Bando still had not arrived, and I began to plan for a very small Christmas with Frightful.

About four-thirty Christmas Eve I hung a small red cluster of teaberries on the deerskin door. I went in my tree room for a snack of beechnuts when I heard a faint "halloooo" from far down the moun-tain. I snuffed out my tallow candle, jumped into my coat and moccasins, and plunged out into the snow. Again a "halloooo" floated over the quiet snow. I took a bearing on the sound and bounced down the hill to meet Bando. I ran into him just as he turned up the valley to fol-low the stream bed. I was so glad to see

him that I hugged him and pounded him on the back.

"Never thought I'd make it," he said. "I walked all the way from the entrance of the State Park; pretty good, eh?" He smiled and slapped his tired legs. Then he grabbed my arm, and with three quick pinches, tested the meat on me.

"You've been living well," he said. He looked closely at my face. "But you're gonna need a shave in a year or two." I thanked him and we sprang up the mountain, cut across through the gorge and home.

"How's the Frightful?" he asked as soon as we were inside and the light was lit.

I whistled. She jumped to my fist. He got bold and stroked her. "And the jam?" he asked.

"Excellent, except the crocks are absor-bent and are sopping up all the juice."

"Well, I brought you some more sugar; we'll try next year. Merry Christmas, Thoreau!" he shouted, and looked about the room.

"I see you have been busy. A blanket, new clothes, and an ingenious fireplace—with a real chimney—and say, you have silverware!" He picked up the forks I had carved.

We ate smoked fish for dinner with boiled dogtooth violet bulbs. Walnuts dipped in jam were dessert. Bando was pleased with his jam.

When we were done, Bando stretched out on my bed. He propped his feet up and lit his pipe.

"And now, I have something to show you," he said. He reached in his coat pocket and took out a newspaper clipping. It was from a New York paper, and it read:

I looked at Bando and leaned over to read the headline myself.

"Have you been talking?" I asked.

"Me? Don't be ridiculous. You have had several visitors other than me."

"The fire warden—the old lady!" I cried out.

"Now, Thoreau, this could only be a rumor. Just because it is in print, doesn't mean it's true. Before you get excited, sit still and listen." He read:

"'Residents of Delhi, in the Catskill Mountains, report that a wild boy, who lives off deer and nuts, is hiding out in the mountains.

"'Several hunters stated that this boy stole deer from them during their hunting season.'"

"I did not!" I shouted. "I only took the ones they had wounded and couldn't find."

"Well, that's what they told their wives when they came home without their deer. Anyway, listen to this:

"'This wild boy has been seen from time to time by Catskill residents, some of whom believe he is crazy!'"

"Well, that's a terrible thing to say!"

"Just awful," he stated. "Any normal red-blooded American boy wants to live in a tree house and trap his own food. They just don't do it, that's all."

"Read on," I said.

"'Officials say that there is no evidence of any boy living alone in the mountains, and add that all abandoned houses and sheds are routinely checked for just such events. Nevertheless, the residents are sure that such a boy exists!' End story."

"That's a lot of nonsense!" I leaned back against the bedstead[19] and smiled.

"Ho, ho, don't think that ends it," Bando said, and reached in his pocket for another clipping. "This one is dated December fifth, the other was November twenty-third. Shall I read?"

"Yes."

"'Mrs. Thomas Fielder, ninety-seven, resident of Delhi, N.Y., told this reporter that she met a wild boy on Bitter Mountain last June while gathering her annual strawberry jelly supply.

"'She said the boy was brown-haired, dusty, and wandering aimlessly around the mountains. However, she added, he seemed to be in good flesh and happy.

"'The old woman, a resident of the mountain resort town for ninety-seven years, called this office to report her observation. Local residents report that Mrs. Fielder is a fine old member of the community, who only occasionally sees imaginary things.'"

Bando roared. I must say I was sweating, for I really did not expect this turn of events.

"And now," went on Bando, "and now the queen of the New York papers. This story was buried on page nineteen. No sensationalism[20] for this paper.

---

19. **bedstead** [bed′sted′]: frame supporting the springs and mattress of a bed.

20. **sensationalism**: [sen sā′shən əl iz′əm]: the practice or effect of presenting news that arouses interest or excitement in order to stimulate an audience.

"'A young boy of seventeen or eighteen, who left home with a group of boy scouts, is reported to be still scouting in that area, according to the fire warden of the Catskill Mountains.

"'Evidence of someone living in the forest—a fireplace, soup bones, and cracked nuts—was reported by Warden Jim Handy, who spent the night in the wilderness looking for the lad. Jim stated that the young man had apparently left the area, as there was no evidence of his camp upon a second trip—'"

"What second trip?" I asked.

Bando puffed his pipe, looked at me wistfully and said, "Are you ready to listen?"

"Sure," I answered.

"Well, here's the rest of it. '. . . there was no trace of his camp on a second trip, and the warden believes that the young man returned to his home at the end of the summer.'

"You know, Thoreau, I could scarcely drag myself away from the newspapers to come up here. You make a marvelous story."

I said, "Put more wood on the fire, it is Christmas. No one will be searching these mountains until May Day."[21]

Bando asked for the willow whistles. I got them for him, and after running the scale several times, he said, "Let us serenade the ingenuity of the American newspaperman. Then let us serenade the conservationists[22] who have protected the American wilderness, so that a boy can still be alone in this world of millions of people."

I thought that was suitable, and we played "Holy Night." We tried "The Twelve Days of Christmas," but the whistles were too stiff and Bando too tired.

"Thoreau, my body needs rest. Let's give up," he said after two bad starts. I banked[23] the fire and blew out the candle and slept in my clothes.

It was Christmas when we awoke. Breakfast was light—acorn pancakes, jam, and sassafras tea. Bando went for a walk, I lit the fire in the fireplace and spent the morning creating a feast from the wilderness.

I gave Bando his presents when he returned. He liked them. He was really pleased; I could tell by his eyebrows. They went up and down and in and out. Furthermore, I know he liked the presents because he wore them.

The onion soup was about to be served when I heard a voice shouting in the distance, "I know you are there! I know you are there! Where are you?"

"*Dad!*" I screamed, and dove right through the door onto my stomach. I all but fell down the mountain shouting, "Dad! Dad! Where are you?" I found him resting in a snowdrift, looking at the cardinal pair that lived near the stream. He was smiling, stretched out on his back, not in exhaustion, but in joy.

"Merry Christmas!" he whooped. I ran toward him. He jumped to his feet, tackled me, thumped my chest, and rubbed snow in my face.

Then he stood up, lifted me from the

---

21. **May Day**: spring festival traditionally celebrated on May 1.
22. **conservationists** [kon' sər vā' shə nists]: people who work to protect and care for natural resources, such as forests, rivers, and wildlife.

23. **banked**: covered a fire with ashes or earth so that it will burn slowly.

snow by the pockets on my coat, and held me off the ground so that we were eye to eye. He sure smiled. He threw me down in the snow again and wrestled with me for a few minutes. Our formal greeting done, we strode up the mountain.

"Well, son," he began. "I've been reading about you in the papers and I could no longer resist the temptation to visit you. I still can't believe you did it."

His arm went around me. He looked real good, and I was overjoyed to see him.

"How did you find me?" I asked eagerly.

"I went to Mrs. Fielder, and she told me which mountain. At the stream I found your raft and ice-fishing holes. Then I looked for trails and footsteps. When I thought I was getting warm, I hollered."

"Am I that easy to find?"

"You didn't have to answer, and I'd probably have frozen in the snow." He was pleased and not angry at me at all. He said again, "I just didn't think you'd do it. I was sure you'd be back the next day. When you weren't, I bet on the next week; then the next month. How's it going?"

"Oh, it's a wonderful life, Dad!"

When we walked into the tree, Bando was putting the final touches on the venison steak.

"Dad, this is my friend, Professor Bando; he's a teacher. He got lost one day last summer and stumbled onto my camp. He liked it so well that he came back for Christmas. Bando, meet my father."

Bando turned the steak on the spit, rose, and shook my father's hand.

"I am pleased to meet the man who sired[24] this boy," he said grandly. I could

Peregrine Falcon

see that they liked each other and that it was going to be a splendid Christmas. Dad stretched out on the bed and looked around.

"I thought maybe you'd pick a cave," he said. "The papers reported that they were looking for you in old sheds and houses, but I knew better than that. However, I never would have thought of the inside of a tree. What a beauty! Very clever, son, very, very clever. This is a comfortable bed."

He noticed my food caches, stood and peered into them. "Got enough to last until spring?"

"I think so," I said. "If I don't keep getting hungry visitors all the time." I winked at him.

---

24. **sired** [sīrd]: was the male parent of; fathered.

"Well, I would wear out my welcome by a year if I could, but I have to get back to work soon after Christmas."

"How's Mom and all the rest?" I asked as I took down the turtle-shell plates and set them on the floor.

"She's marvelous. How she manages to feed and clothe those eight youngsters on what I bring her, I don't know; but she does it. She sends her love, and says that she hopes you are eating well-balanced meals."

The onion soup was simmering and ready. I gave Dad his.

"First course," I said.

He breathed deeply of the odor and downed it boiling hot.

"Son, this is better onion soup than the chef at the Waldorf[25] can make."

Bando sipped his, and I put mine in the snow to cool.

"Your mother will stop worrying about your diet when she hears of this."

Bando rinsed Dad's soup bowl in the snow, and with great ceremony and elegance—he could really be elegant when the occasion arose—poured him a turtle shell of sassafras tea. Quoting a passage from one of Dickens's food-eating scenes, he carved the blackened steak. It was pink and juicy inside. Cooked to perfection. We were all proud of it. Dad had to finish his tea before he could eat. I was short on bowls. Then I filled his shell. A mound of sort of fluffy mashed cattail tubers, mushrooms, and dogtooth violet bulbs, smothered in gravy thickened with acorn powder. Each plate had a pile of soaked and stewed honey locust beans—

mixed with hickory nuts. The beans are so hard it took three days to soak them.

It was a glorious feast. Everyone was impressed, including me. When we were done, Bando went down to the stream and cut some old dried and hollow reeds. He came back and carefully made us each a flute with the tip of his penknife. He said the willow whistles were too old for such an occasion. We all played Christmas carols until dark. Bando wanted to try some complicated jazz tunes, but the late hour, the small fire dancing and throwing heat, and the snow insulating us from the winds made us all so sleepy that we were not capable of more than a last slow rendition[26] of taps[27] before we put ourselves on and under skins and blew out the light.

Before anyone was awake the next morning, I heard Frightful call hungrily. I had put her outside to sleep, as we were very crowded. I went out to find her. Her Christmas dinner had been a big piece of venison, but the night air had enlarged her appetite. I called her to my fist and we went into the meadow to rustle up breakfast for the guests. She was about to go after a rabbit, but I thought that wasn't proper fare for a post-Christmas breakfast, so we went to the stream. Frightful caught herself a pheasant while I kicked a hole in the ice and did a little ice fishing. I caught about six trout and whistled Frightful to my hand. We returned to the hemlock. Dad and Bando

---

25. **the Waldorf**: the Waldorf-Astoria, an elegant New York City hotel.

26. **rendition** [ren dish'ən]: performance of an artistic, dramatic, or musical composition.
27. **taps**: military signal regularly played at the end of the day, usually on a bugle, to indicate that all lights must be turned off; also sounded at military funerals and memorial services.

were still asleep, with their feet in each other's faces, but both looking very content.

I built the fire and was cooking the fish and making pancakes when Dad shot out of bed.

"Wild boy!" he shouted. "What a sanguine[28] smell. What a purposeful fire. Breakfast in a tree. Son, I toil from sunup to sundown, and never have I lived so well!"

I served him. He choked a bit on the acorn pancakes—they are a little flat and hard—but Bando got out some of his blueberry jam and smothered the pancakes with an enormous portion. Dad went through the motions of eating this. The fish, however, he enjoyed, and he asked for more. We drank sassafras tea, sweetened with some of the sugar Bando had brought me, rubbed our turtle shells clean in the snow, and went out into the forest.

Dad had not met Frightful. When she winged down out of the hemlock, he ducked and flattened out in the snow shouting, "Blast off."

He was very cool toward Frightful until he learned that she was the best provider[29] we had ever had in our family, and then he continually praised her beauty and admired her talents. He even tried to pet her, but Frightful was not to be won. She snagged him with her talons.

They stayed away from each other for the rest of Dad's visit, although Dad never ceased to admire her from a safe distance.

Bando had to leave two or three days after Christmas. He had some papers to grade, and he started off reluctantly one morning, looking very unhappy about the way of life he had chosen. He shook hands all around and then turned to me and said, "I'll save all the newspaper clippings for you, and if the reporters start getting too hot on your trail, I'll call the New York papers and give them a bum steer."[30] I could see he rather liked the idea, and departed a little happier.

Dad lingered on for a few more days, ice fishing, setting my traps and snares, and husking walnuts. He whittled some cooking spoons and forks.

On New Year's Day he announced that he must go.

"I told your mother I would only stay for Christmas. It's a good thing she knows me or she might be worried."

"She won't send the police out to look for you?" I asked hurriedly. "Could she think you never found me?"

"Oh, I told her I'd call her Christmas night if I didn't." He poked around for another hour or two, trying to decide just how to leave. Finally he started down the mountain. He had hardly gone a hundred feet before he was back.

"I've decided to leave by another route. Somebody might backtrack[31] me and find you. And that would be too bad." He came over to me and put his hand on my shoulder. "You've done very well, Sam." He grinned and walked off toward the gorge.

I watched him bound from rock to rock. He waved from the top of a large rock and leaped into the air. That was the last I saw of Dad for a long time.

---

28. **sanguine** [sang′gwin]: cheerful; here, pleasant.
29. **provider**: family member whose work or wages provide the family's means of support.
30. **bum steer**: tip-off, or hint, that sends someone who is searching for something in the wrong direction.
31. **backtrack**: trace or pursue.

READER'S RESPONSE

Do you agree with Sam's father that Sam has "done very well"? Explain.

STUDY QUESTIONS

Recalling
1. List three ways in which the animals on the mountain prepare for cold weather.
2. What preparations does Sam make for winter?
3. Whom does Sam meet when he goes to town?
4. What does Bando bring for Sam?
5. Who helps Sam's father find him?

Interpreting
6. Until the first snowstorm (described in the first chapter), what are Sam's feelings about winter on the mountain? Do his feelings change after the snowstorm?
7. What are Sam's reactions to living by himself on the mountain?
8. Why does Sam go to town?
9. Earlier in the novel Sam says, "You know, those first days, I just never planned right." Do you think Sam has learned to plan right? Give at least two examples that support your answer.

Extending
10. What do you think Sam's biggest challenge has been since coming to the mountain?

READING AND LITERARY FOCUS

Conflict

Like a story a novel has **conflict,** or struggle, between two opposing forces. Conflict can be external or internal. An **external conflict** takes place between a character and some outside force. That force may be another person, as when two characters compete in a game. The opposing force may also be nature, as when a character tries to stem the rush of floodwaters. In addition, the opposing force may be society or some other institution, as when a character protests an unjust law. Finally, a character may challenge fate, or circumstances that cannot be changed. For example, a character might try to conquer a fatal illness.

An **internal conflict** takes place within a character's mind. For example, a character may feel conflicting emotions: He or she may feel happy about playing in an important basketball game but be worried about not scoring enough baskets.

A novel usually has both external and internal conflicts. Because of a novel's length, it can contain more conflicts than a short story.

Thinking About Conflict
1. Sam has to decide whether to go home for the winter and then return in the spring. Is this conflict external or internal? Why?
2. What conflict does Sam face when he builds his fireplace? Is the conflict external or internal? Why?

VOCABULARY

Synonyms

A **synonym** is a word that has the same or nearly the same meaning as another word. For example, *easy* and *simple* are synonyms. The italicized words below are from *My Side of the Mountain.* Choose the word that is *nearest* the meaning of each italicized word *as the word is used in the novel.* Write the number of each item and the letter of your choice on a separate sheet of paper.

1. take a *precaution*
   - (a) request
   - (b) safeguard
   - (c) problem
   - (d) reason
2. *abandoned* the party
   - (a) went to
   - (b) hosted
   - (c) left
   - (d) studied
3. *routinely* checked
   - (a) thoughtfully
   - (b) easily
   - (c) briefly
   - (d) regularly
4. could not resist the *temptation*
   - (a) attraction
   - (b) explanation
   - (c) project
   - (d) attempt
5. *complicated* jazz tunes
   - (a) simple
   - (b) happy
   - (c) involved
   - (d) long

We all had our little "patch" in the wilderness. We all fought to return there.

● ●

Chickadee

IN WHICH
I Have a Good Look at Winter and Find Spring in the Snow

With Christmas over, the winter became serious. The snows deepened, the wind blew, the temperatures dropped until the air snapped and talked. Never had humanity seemed so far away as it did in those cold still months of January, February, and March. I wandered the snowy crags, listening to the language of the birds by day and to the noises of the weather by night. The wind howled, the snow avalanched, and the air creaked.

I slept, ate, played my reed whistle, and talked to Frightful.

To be relaxed, warm, and part of the winter wilderness is an unforgettable experience. I was in excellent condition. Not a cold, not a sniffle, not a moment of fatigue. I enjoyed the feeling that I could eat, sleep and be warm, and outwit the storms that blasted the mountains and the subzero temperatures that numbed them.

It snowed on. I plowed through drifts and stamped paths until eventually it occurred to me that I had all the materials to make snowshoes for easier traveling.

Here are the snowshoe notes:

"I made slats out of ash saplings, whittling them thin enough to bow. I soaked them in water to make them bend more easily, looped the two ends together, and wound them with hide.

"With my penknife I made holes an inch apart all around the loop.

"I strung deer hide crisscross through the loops. I made a loop of hide to hold my toe and straps to tie the shoes on.

"When I first walked in these shoes, I tripped on my toes and fell, but by the end of the first day I could walk from the tree to the gorge in half the time."

I lived close to the weather. It is surprising how you watch it when you live in it. Not a cloud passed unnoticed, not a wind blew untested. I knew the moods of the storms, where they came from, their shapes and colors. When the sun shone, I took Frightful to the meadow and we slid down the mountain on my snapping-turtle-shell sled. She really didn't care much for this.

When the winds changed and the air smelled like snow, I would stay in my tree, because I had gotten lost in a blizzard one afternoon and had had to hole up in a rock ledge until I could see where

My Side of the Mountain   583

I was going. That day the winds were so strong I could not push against them, so I crawled under the ledge; for hours I wondered if I would be able to dig out when the storm blew on. Fortunately I only had to push through about a foot of snow. However, that taught me to stay home when the air said "snow." Not that I was afraid of being caught far from home in a storm, for I could find food and shelter and make a fire anywhere, but I had become as attached to my hemlock house as a brooding[1] bird to her nest. Caught out in the storms and weather, I had an urgent desire to return to my tree, even as The Baron Weasel returned to his den, and the deer to their copse.[2] We all had our little "patch" in the wilderness. We all fought to return there.

I usually came home at night with the nuthatch that roosted in a nearby sapling. I knew I was late if I tapped the tree and he came out. Sometimes when the weather was icy and miserable, I would hear him high in the tree near the edge of the meadow, yanking and yanking and flicking his tail, and then I would see him wing to bed early. I considered him a pretty good barometer,[3] and if he went to his tree early, I went to mine early too. When you don't have a newspaper or radio to give you weather bulletins, watch the birds and animals. They can tell when a storm is coming. I called the nuthatch "Barometer," and when he holed up, I holed up, lit my light, and sat by my fire

whittling or learning new tunes on my reed whistle. I was now really into the teeth of winter, and quite fascinated by its activity. There is no such thing as a "still winter night." Not only are many animals running around in the creaking cold, but the trees cry out and limbs snap and fall, and the wind gets caught in a ravine and screams until it dies. One noisy night I put this down:

"There is somebody in my bedroom. I can hear small exchanges of greetings and little feet moving up the wall. By the time I get to my light all is quiet.

"Next Day
"There was something in my room last night, a small tunnel leads out from my door into the snow. It is a marvelous tunnel, neatly packed, and it goes from a dried fern to a clump of moss. Then it turns and disappears. I would say mouse.

"That Night
"I kept an ember glowing and got a light fast before the visitor could get to the door. It *was* a mouse—a perfect little white-footed deer mouse with enormous black eyes and tidy white feet. Caught in the act of intruding,[4] he decided not to retreat, but came toward me a few steps. I handed him a nut meat. He took it in his fragile paws, stuffed it in his cheek, flipped, and went out his secret tunnel. No doubt the tunnel leads right over to my store tree, and this fellow is having a fat winter."

There were no raccoons or skunks about in the snow, but the mice, the

---

1. **brooding**: that hatches eggs and cares for newly hatched young.
2. **copse** [kops]: thicket or grove of small trees or bushes.
3. **barometer** [bə rom′ə tər]: instrument for measuring the pressure put forth by the weight of the earth's atmosphere and indicating the probability of rain.

4. **intruding** [in trōōd′ing]: entering without welcome.

weasels, the mink, the foxes, the shrews, the cottontail rabbits were all busier than Coney Island[5] in July. Their tracks were all over the mountain, and their activities ranged from catching each other to hauling various materials back to their dens and burrows for more insulation.

By day the birds were a-wing. They got up late, after I did, and would call to each other before hunting. I would stir up my fire and think about how much food it must take to keep one little bird alive in that fierce cold. They must eat and eat and eat, I thought.

Once, however, I came upon a male cardinal sitting in a hawthorn bush. It was a miserable day, gray, damp, and somewhere around the zero mark. The cardinal wasn't doing anything at all—just sitting on a twig, all fluffed up to keep himself warm. Now there's a wise bird, I said to myself. He is conserving his energy, none of this flying around looking for food and wasting effort. As I watched him, he shifted his feet twice, standing on one and pulling the other up into his warm feathers. I had often wondered why birds' feet didn't freeze, and there was my answer. He even sat down on both of them and let his warm feathers cover them like socks.

"January 8

"I took Frightful out today. We went over to the meadow to catch a rabbit for her; as we passed one of the hemlocks near the edge of the grove, she pulled her feathers to her body and looked alarmed. I tried to find out what had frightened her, but saw nothing.

"On the way back we passed the same tree and I noticed an owl pellet cast in the snow. I looked up. There were lots of limbs and darkness, but I could not see the owl. I walked around the tree; Frightful stared at one spot until I thought her head would swivel off. I looked, and there it was, looking like a broken limb—a great horned owl. I must say I was excited to have such a neighbor. I hit the tree with a stick and he flew off. Those great wings—they must have been five feet across—beat the wind, but there was no sound. The owl steered down the mountain through the tree limbs, and somewhere not far away he vanished in the needles and limbs.

"It is really very special to have a horned owl. I guess I feel this way because he is such a wilderness bird. He needs lots of forest and big trees, and so his presence means that the Gribley farm is a beautiful place indeed."

One week the weather gave a little to the sun, and snow melted and limbs dumped their loads and popped up into the air. I thought I'd try to make an igloo. I was cutting big blocks of snow and putting them in a circle. Frightful was dozing with her face in the sun, and the tree sparrows were raiding the hemlock cones. I worked and hummed, and did not notice the gray sheet of cloud that was sneaking up the mountain from the northwest. It covered the sun suddenly. I realized the air was damp enough to wring. I could stay as warm as a bug if I didn't get wet, so I looked at the drab mess in the sky, whistled for Frightful, and started back to the tree. We holed up

---

5. **Coney Island**: area of Brooklyn, in New York City, famous for its beach, boardwalk, and amusement park.

just as Barometer was yanking his way home, and it was none too soon. It drizzled, it misted, it sprinkled, and finally it froze. The deer-hide door grew stiff with ice as darkness came, and it rattled like a piece of tin when the wind hit it.

I made a fire, the tree room warmed, and I puttered around with a concoction I call possum sop.[6] A meal of frozen possum stewed with lichens, snakeweed, and lousewort. It is a different sort of dish. Of course what I really like about it are the names of all the plants with the name possum. I fooled for an hour or so brewing this dish, adding this and that, when I heard the mouse in his tunnel. I realized he was making an awful fuss, and decided it was because he was trying to gnaw through ice to get in. I decided to help him. Frightful was on her post, and I wanted to see the mouse's face when he found he was in a den with a falcon. I pushed the deerskin door. It wouldn't budge. I kicked it. It gave a little, cracking like china, and I realized that I was going to be iced in if I didn't keep that door open.

I finally got it open. There must have been an inch and a half of ice on it. The mouse, needless to say, was gone. I ate my supper and reminded myself to awaken and open the door off and on during the night. I put more wood on the fire, as it was damp in spite of the flames, and went to bed in my underwear and suit.

I awoke twice and kicked open the door. Then I fell into a sound sleep that lasted hours beyond my usual rising time. I overslept, I discovered, because I was in a block of ice, and none of the morning sounds of the forest penetrated my glass house to awaken me. The first thing I did was try to open the door; I chipped and kicked and managed to get my head out to see what had happened. I was sealed in. Now, I have seen ice storms, and I know they can be shiny and glassy and treacherous, but this was something else. There were sheets of ice binding the aspens to earth and cementing the tops of the hemlocks in arches. It was inches thick! Frightful winged out of the door and flew to a limb, where she tried to perch. She slipped, dropped to the ground, and skidded on her wings and undercoverts[7] to a low spot where she finally stopped. She tried to get to her feet, slipped, lost her balance, and spread her wings. She finally flapped into the air and hovered there until she could locate a decent perch. She found one close against the bole of the hemlock. It was ice free.

I laughed at her, and then I came out and took a step. I landed with an explosion on my seat. The jolt splintered the ice and sent glass-covered limbs clattering to earth like a shopful of shattering crystal. As I sat there, and I didn't dare to move because I might get hurt, I heard an enormous explosion. It was followed by splintering and clattering and smashing. A maple at the edge of the meadow had literally blown up. I feared now for my trees—the ice was too heavy to bear. While down, I chipped the deer flap clean, and sort of swam back into my tree, listening to trees exploding all over the mountain. It was a fearful and dreadful

---

6. **sop**: piece of food soaked or dipped in a liquid.

7. **undercoverts** [un′ dər kuv′ ərts]: small feathers on the underside of a bird's wings or tail.

February, John Henry Twachtman (1853–1902).

sound. I lit a fire, ate smoked fish and dried apples, and went out again. I must say I toyed with the idea of making ice skates. However, I saw the iron wagon axle iced against a tree, and crawled to it. I de-iced it with the butt of my ax, and used it for a cane. I would stab it into the ground and inch along. I fell a couple of times but not as hard as that first time.

Frightful saw me start off through the woods, for I had to see this winter display, and she winged to my shoulder, glad for a good perch. At the meadow I looked hopefully for the sun, but it didn't have a chance. The sky was as thick as Indiana bean soup. Out in the open I watched one tree after another splinter and break under the ice, and the glass sparks that shot into the air and the thunder that the ice made as it shattered were something to remember.

At noon not a drip had fallen, the ice was as tight as it had been at dawn. I heard no nuthatches, the chickadees called once, but were silent again. There was an explosion near my spring. A hemlock had gone. Frightful and I crept back to the tree. I decided that if my house was going to shatter, I would just as soon be in it.

Inside, I threw sticks to Frightful and she caught them in her talons. This is a game we play when we are tense and bored. Night came and the ice still lay in sheets. We slept to the occasional boom of breaking trees, although the explosions were not as frequent. Apparently the most rotted and oldest trees had collapsed first. The rest were more resilient,[8] and unless a wind came up, I figured the damage was over.

At midnight a wind came up. It awakened me, for the screech of the iced limbs rubbing each other and the snapping of the ice were like the sounds from a madhouse.[9] I listened, decided there was nothing I could do, buried my head under the deer hide, and went back to sleep.

Around six or seven I heard Barometer, the nuthatch. He yanked as he went food hunting through the hemlock grove. I jumped up and looked out. The sun had come through, and the forest sparkled and shone in cruel splendor.

That day I heard the *drip, drip* begin, and by evening some of the trees had dumped their loads and were slowly lifting themselves to their feet, so to speak. The aspens and birch trees, however, were still bent like Indian bows.

Three days later, the forest arose, the ice melted, and for about a day or so we had warm, glorious weather.

The mountain was a mess. Broken trees, fallen limbs were everywhere. I felt badly about the ruins until I thought that this had been happening to the mountain for thousands of years and the trees were still there, as were the animals and birds. The birds were starved, and many had died. I found their cold little bodies under bushes and one stiff chickadee in a cavity. Its foot was drawn into its feathers, its feathers were fluffed.

Frightful ate old frozen muskrat during those days. We couldn't kick up a rabbit or even a mouse. They were in the snow under the ice, waiting it out. I suppose the mice went right on tunneling to the grasses and the mosses and had no trouble staying alive, but I did wonder how The Baron Weasel was doing. I needn't have. Here are some notes about him.

"I should not have worried about The Baron Weasel; he appeared after the ice storm, looking sleek and pleased with himself. I think he dined royally on the many dying animals and birds. In any event, he was full of pep and ran up the hemlock to chase Frightful off her perch. That Baron! It's a good thing I don't have to tie Frightful much anymore, or he would certainly try to kill her. He still attacks me, more for the fun of being sent sprawling out into the snow than for food, for he hasn't put his teeth in my trousers for months."

January was a fierce month. After the ice storm came more snow. The mountaintop was never free of it, the gorge was blocked; only on the warmest days could I hear, deep under the ice, the trickle of water seeping over the falls. I still had food, but it was getting low. All the fresh-frozen venison was gone, and most of the bulbs and tubers. I longed for just a simple dandelion green.

Toward the end of January I began to

---

8. **resilient** [ri zil′yənt]: capable of springing back to the original size, shape, or position after being bent, compressed, or stretched.

9. **madhouse**: formerly, a hospital for the mentally ill.

feel tired, and my elbows and knees were a little stiff. This worried me. I figured it was due to some vitamin I wasn't getting, but I couldn't remember which vitamin it was or even where I would find it if I could remember it.

One morning my nose bled. It frightened me a bit, and I wondered if I shouldn't hike to the library and reread the material on vitamins. It didn't last long, however, so I figured it wasn't too serious. I decided I would live until the greens came to the land, for I was of the opinion that since I had had nothing green for months, that was probably the trouble.

On that same day Frightful caught a rabbit in the meadow. As I cleaned it, the liver suddenly looked so tempting that I could hardly wait to prepare it. For the next week, I craved liver and ate all I could get. The tiredness ended, the bones stopped aching and I had no more nosebleeds. Hunger is a funny thing. It has a kind of intelligence all its own. I ate liver almost every day until the first plants emerged, and I never had any more trouble. I have looked up vitamins since. I am not surprised to find that liver is rich in vitamin C. So are citrus fruits and green vegetables, the foods I lacked. Wild plants like sorrel and dock are rich in this vitamin. Even if I had known this at that time, it would have done me no good, for they were but roots in the earth. As it turned out, liver was the only available source of vitamin C—and on liver I stuffed, without knowing why.

So much for my health. I wonder now why I didn't have more trouble than I did, except that my mother worked in a children's hospital during the war, helping to prepare food, and she was conscious of

what made up a balanced meal. We heard a lot about it as kids, so I was not unaware that my winter diet was off balance.

After that experience, I noticed things in the forest that I hadn't paid any attention to before. A squirrel had stripped the bark off a sapling at the foot of the meadow, leaving it gleaming white. I pondered when I saw it, wondering if he had lacked a vitamin or two and had sought them in the bark. I must admit I tried a little of the bark myself, but decided that even if it was loaded with vitamins, I preferred liver.

I also noticed that the birds would sit in the sun when it favored our mountain with its light, and I, being awfully vitamin minded at the time, wondered if they were gathering vitamin D. To be on the safe side, in view of this, I sat in the sun too when it was out. So did Frightful.

My notes piled up during these months, and my journal of birch bark became a storage problem. I finally took it out of my tree and cached it under a rock ledge nearby. The mice made nests in it, but it held up even when it got wet. That's one thing about using the products of the forest. They are usually weatherproof. This is important when the weather is as near to you as your skin and as much a part of your life as eating.

I was writing more about the animals now and less about myself, which proves I was feeling pretty safe. Here is an interesting entry.

"February 6
"The deer have pressed in all around me. They are hungry. Apparently they stamp out yards in the valleys where they feed during the dawn and dusk, but many of them climb back to the hemlock grove

to hide and sleep for the day. They manage the deep snows so effortlessly on those slender hooves. If I were to know that a million years from today my children's children's children were to live as I am living in these mountains, I should marry me a wife with slender feet and begin immediately to breed a race with hooves, that the Catskill children of the future might run through the snows and meadows and marshes as easily as the deer."

I got to worrying about the deer, and for many days I climbed trees and cut down tender limbs for them. At first only two came, then five, and soon I had a ring of large-eyed white-tailed deer waiting at my tree at twilight for me to come out and chop off limbs. I was astonished to see this herd grow, and wondered what signals they used to inform each other of my services. Did they smell fatter? Look more contented? Somehow they were able to tell their friends that there was a free lunch on my side of the mountain, and more and more arrived.

One evening there were so many deer that I decided to chop limbs on the other side of the meadow. They were cutting up the snow and tearing up the ground around my tree with their pawing.

Three nights later they all disappeared. Not one deer came for limbs. I looked down the valley, and in the dim light could see the open earth on the land below. The deer could forage again. Spring was coming to the land! My heart beat faster. I think I was trembling. The valley also blurred. The only thing that can do that is tears, so I guess I was crying.

That night the great horned owls boomed out across the land. My notes read:

"February 10

"I think the great horned owls have eggs! The mountain is white, the wind blows, the snow is hard packed, but spring is beginning in their hollow maple. I will climb it tomorrow.

"February 12

"Yes, yes, yes, yes. It is spring in the maple. Two great horned owl eggs lie in the cold snow-rimmed cavity in the broken top of the tree. They were warm to my touch. Eggs in the snow. Now isn't that wonderful? I didn't stay long, for it is bitter weather and I wanted the female to return immediately. I climbed down, and as I ran off toward my tree I saw her drift on those muffled wings of the owl through the limbs and branches as she went back to her work. I crawled through the tunnel of ice that leads to my tree now, the wind beating at my back. I spent the evening whittling and thinking about the owl high in the forest with the first new life of the spring."

And so with the disappearance of the deer, the hoot of the owl, the cold land began to create new life. Spring is terribly exciting when you are living right in it.

I was hungry for green vegetables, and that night as I went off to sleep, I thought of the pokeweeds, the dandelions, the spring beauties that would soon be pressing up from the earth.

MORE ABOUT
The Spring in the Winter and the Beginning of My Story's End

The owl had broken the spell of winter. From that time on, things began to happen that you'd have to see to believe. Insects appeared while the snow was on the ground. Birds built nests, raccoons mated, foxes called to each other, seeking again their lifelong mates. At the end of February, the sap began to run in the maple trees. I tapped[10] some trees and boiled the sap to syrup. It takes an awful lot of sap to make one cup of syrup, I discovered—thirty-two cups, to be exact.

All this and I was still in my winter fur-lined underwear. One or two birds returned, the ferns by the protected spring unrolled—very slowly, but they did. Then the activity gathered momentum,[11] and before I was aware of the change, there were the skunk cabbages poking their funny blooms above the snow in the marsh. I picked some and cooked them, but they aren't any good. A skunk cabbage is a skunk cabbage.

From my meadow I could see the valleys turning green. My mountain was still snow-capped, so I walked into the valleys almost every day to scout them for edible plants. Frightful rode down with me on my shoulder. She knew even better than I that the season had changed, and she watched the sky like radar. No life traveled that sky world unnoticed by Frightful. I thought she wanted to be free and seek a mate, but I could not let her. I still de-

Great Horned Owl

pended upon her talents and company. Furthermore, she was different, and if I did let her go, she probably would have been killed by another female, for Frightful had no territory other than the hemlock patch, and her hunting instincts had been trained for man. She was a captive, not a wild bird, and that is almost another kind of bird.

One day I was in the valley digging tubers and collecting the tiny new dandelion shoots when Frightful saw another duck hawk and flew from my shoulder like a bolt, pulling the leash from my hand as she went.

"Frightful!" I called. "You can't leave me now!" I whistled, held out a piece of meat, and hoped she would not get her leash caught in a treetop. She hovered above my head, looked at the falcon and then at my hand, folded her wings, and dropped to my fist.

---

10. **tapped**: pierced in order to draw liquid.
11. **momentum** [mō men′təm]: motion resulting from speed or force.

"I saw that!" a voice said. I spun around to see a young man about my own age, shivering at the edge of the woods.

"You're the wild boy, aren't you?"

I was so astonished to see a human being in all this cold thawing silence that I just stood and looked at him. When I gathered my wits I replied. "No, I'm just a citizen."

"Aw, gee," he said with disappointment. Then he gave in to the cold and shivered until the twigs around him rattled. He stepped forward.

"Well, anyway, I'm Matt Spell. I work after school on the Poughkeepsie[12] *New Yorker*, a newspaper. I read all the stories about the wild boy who lives in the Catskills, and I thought that if I found him and got a good story, I might get to be a reporter. Have you ever run across him? Is there such a boy?"

"Aw, it's all nonsense," I said as I gathered some dry wood and piled it near the edge of the woods. I lit it swiftly, hoping he would not notice the flint and steel. He was so cold and so glad to see the flames that he said nothing.

I rolled a log up to the fire for him and shoved it against a tree that was blocked from the raw biting wind by a stand of hawthorns. He crouched over the flames for a long time, then practically burned the soles off his shoes warming his feet. He was that miserable.

"Why didn't you dress warmer for this kind of a trip?" I asked. "You'll die up here in this damp cold."

"I think I am dying," he said, sitting so close to the fire, he almost smothered it. He was nice looking, about thirteen or fourteen, I would have said. He had a good bold face, blue eyes, hair about the color of my stream in the thaw. Although he was big, he looked like the kind of fellow who didn't know his own strength. I liked Matt.

"I've still got a sandwich," he said. "Want half?"

"No, thanks," I said. "I brought my lunch." Frightful had been sitting on my shoulder through all this, but now the smoke was bothering her and she hopped to a higher perch. I still had her on the leash.

"There was a bird on your shoulder," Matt said. "He had nice eyes. Do you know him?"

"I'm sort of an amateur falconer," I replied. "I come up here to train my bird. It's a she—Frightful is her name."

"Does she catch anything?"

"Now and then. How hungry are you?" I asked as his second bite finished the sandwich.

"I'm starved; but don't share your lunch. I have some money, just tell me which road takes you toward Delhi."

I stood up and whistled to Frightful. She flew down. I undid her leash from her jesses. I stroked her head for a moment; then threw her into the air and walked out into the field, kicking the brush as I went.

I had noticed a lot of rabbit tracks earlier, and followed them over the muddy earth as best I could. I kicked up a rabbit and with a twist Frightful dropped out of the sky and took it.

Roast rabbit is marvelous under any conditions, but when you're cold and hungry it is superb. Matt enjoyed every bite. I

---

12. **Poughkeepsie** [pə kip′sē]: city in southeastern New York.

worked on a small portion to be sociable, for I was not especially hungry. I dared not offer him the walnuts in my pocket, for too much had been written about that boy living off nuts.

"My whole circulatory system[13] thanks you," Matt said. He meant it, for his hands and feet were now warm, and the blue color had left his lips and was replaced by a good warm red.

"By the way, what's your name?"

"Sam. Sam Gribley," I said.

"Sam, if I could borrow a coat from you, I think I could make it to the bus station without freezing to death. I sure didn't think it would be so much colder in the mountains. I could mail it back to you."

"Well," I hesitated, "my house is pretty far from here. I live on the Gribley farm and just come down here now and then to hunt with the falcon; but maybe we could find an old horse blanket or something in one of the deserted barns around here."

"Aw, never mind, Sam. I'll run to keep warm. Have you any ideas about this wild boy—seen anyone that you think the stories might be referring to?"

"Let's start toward the road," I said as I stamped out the fire. I wound him through the forest until I was dizzy and he was lost, then headed for the road. At the edge of the woods I said, "Matt, I have seen that boy."

Matt Spell stopped.

"Gee, Sam, tell me about him." I could hear paper rattle, and saw that Matt's cold

hands were not too stiff to write in his notebook.

We walked down the road a bit and then I said, "Well, he ran away from home one day and never went back."

"Where does he live? What does he wear?"

We sat down on a stone along the edge of the road. It was behind a pine tree, and out of the ripping wind.

"He lives west of here in a cave. He wears a bearskin coat, has long hair—all matted and full of burrs—and according to him he fishes for a living."

"You've talked to him?" he asked brightly.

"Oh, yes, I talk to him."

"Oh, this is great!" He wrote furiously. "What color are his eyes?"

"I think they are bluish gray, with a little brown in them."

"His hair?"

"Darkish—I couldn't really tell under all those coon tails."

"Coon tails? Do you suppose he killed them himself?"

"No. It looked more like one of those hats you get with cereal box tops."

"Well, I won't say anything about it then; just, coon-tail hat."

"Yeah, coon-tail hat's enough," I agreed. "And I think his shoes are just newspapers tied around his feet. That's good insulation, you know."

"Yeah?" Matt wrote that down.

"Did he say why he ran away?"

"I never asked him. Why does any boy run away?"

Matt put down his pencil and thought. "Well, I ran away once because I thought how sorry everybody would be when I was gone. How they'd cry and wish they'd been nicer to me." He laughed.

---

13. **circulatory system**: in animals, the network of tissues that transports blood throughout the body.

Then I said, "I ran away once because . . . well, because I wanted to do something else."

"That's a good reason," said Matt. "Do you suppose that's why . . . by the way, what is his name?"

"I never asked him," I said truthfully.

"What do you suppose he really eats and lives on?" asked Matt.

"Fish, roots, berries, nuts, rabbits. There's a lot of food around the woods if you look for it, I guess."

"Roots? Roots wouldn't be good."

"Well, carrots are roots."

"By golly, they are; and so are potatoes, sort of. Fish?" pondered Matt, "I suppose there are lots of fish around here."

"The streams are full of them."

"You've really seen him, huh? He really is in these mountains?"

"Sure, I've seen him," I said. Finally I stood up.

"I gotta get home. I go the other way. You just follow this road to the town, and I think you can get a bus from there."

"Now, wait," he said. "Let me read it back to you to check the details."

"Sure."

Matt stood up, blew on his hands and read: "The wild boy of the Catskills does exist. He has dark brown hair, black eyes, and wears a handsome deerskin suit that he apparently made himself. He is ruddy and in excellent health and is able to build a fire with flint and steel as fast as a man can light a match.

"His actual dwelling is a secret, but his means of support is a beautiful falcon. The falcon flies off the boy's fist, and kills rabbits and pheasants when the boy needs food. He only takes what he needs. The boy's name is not known, but he ran away from home and never went back."

"No, Matt, no," I begged.

I was about to wrestle it out with him when he said furtively, "I'll make a deal with you. Let me spend my spring vacation with you and I won't print a word of it. I'll write only what you've told me."

I looked at him and decided that it might be nice to have him. I said, "I'll meet you outside town any day you say, providing you let me blindfold you and lead you to my home and providing you promise not to have a lot of photographers hiding in the woods. Do you know what would happen if you told on me?"

"Sure, the newsreels[14] would roll up, the TV cameras would arrive, reporters would hang in the trees, and you'd be famous."

"Yes, and back in New York City."

"I'll write what you said and not even your mother will recognize you."

"Make it some other town, and it's a deal," I said. "You might say I am working for Civil Defense[15] doing research by learning to live off the land. Tell them not to be afraid, that crayfish are delicious and caves are warm."

Matt liked that. He sat down again. "Tell me some of the plants and animals you eat so that they will know what to do. We can make this informative."

I sat down, and listed some of the better wild plants and the more easily obtainable mammals and fish. I gave him a few good recipes and told him that I didn't recommend anyone trying to live off the land unless they liked oysters and spinach.

Matt liked that. He wrote and wrote.

---

14. **newsreels**: short films about current events, formerly shown in movie theaters.
15. **Civil Defense**: organized plan for defense to be carried out by citizens in case of an enemy attack.

Finally he said, "My hands are cold. I'd better go. But I'll see you on April twelfth at three-thirty outside of town. Okay? And just to prove that I'm a man of my word, I'll bring you a copy of what I write."

"Well, you better not give me away. I have a scout in civilization who follows all these stories."

We shook hands and he departed at a brisk pace.

I returned to my patch on the mountain, talking to myself all the way. I talk to myself a lot, but everyone does. The human being, even in the midst of people, spends nine-tenths of his time alone with the private voices of his own head. Living alone on a mountain is not much different, except that your speaking voice gets rusty. I talked inside my head all the way home, thinking up schemes, holding conversations with Bando and Dad and Matt Spell. I worded the article for Matt after discussing it with Bando, and made it sound very convincing without giving myself up. I kind of wanted to write it down and send it to Matt, but I didn't.

I entered my tree, tied Frightful to the bedpost, and there was Jessie Coon James. It had been months since I'd seen him. He was curled up on my bed, asleep. A turtle shell that had been full of cracked walnuts was empty beside him. He awoke, jumped to the floor, and walked slowly between my legs and out the door. I had the feeling Jessie was hoping I had departed for good and that he could have my den. He was a comfort-loving creature. I was bigger and my hands were freer than his, so he conceded[16] me the den. I watched him climb

over The Baron's rock and shinny up a hemlock. He moved heavily into the limbs, and it occurred to me that Jessie was a she-Jessie, not a he-Jessie.

I cooked supper, and then sat down by my little fire and called a forum.[17] It is very sociable inside my head, and I have perfected the art of getting a lot of people arguing together in silence or in a forum, as I prefer to call it. I can get four people all talking at once, and a fifth can be present, but generally I can't get him to talk. Usually these forums discuss such things as a storm and whether or not it is coming, how to make a spring suit, and how to enlarge my house without destroying the life in the tree. Tonight, however, they discussed what to do about Matt Spell. Dad kept telling me to go right down to the city and make sure he published nothing, not even a made-up story. Bando said, no, it's all right, he still doesn't know where you live; and then Matt walked into the conversation and said that he wanted to spend his spring vacation with me, and that he promised not to do anything untoward.[18] Matt kept using "untoward"—I don't know where he got that expression, but he liked it and kept using it—that's how I knew Matt was speaking; everything was "untoward."

That night I fell asleep with all these people discussing the probability of my being found and hauled back to the city. Suddenly Frightful broke into the conversation. She said, "Don't let that Matt come up here. He eats too much." That

---

16. **conceded** [kən sēd′id]: granted or yielded, as a right or privilege.

17. **forum** [fôr′əm]: meeting for discussion of issues or questions of public interest.
18. **untoward** [un tôrd′]: not appropriate or proper for the time or place.

was the first time that Frightful had ever talked in a forum. I was delighted, for I was always sure that she had more to say than a few cries. She had not missed Matt's appetite.

The forum dissolved in a good humor, everyone being delighted with Frightful. I lifted my head to look at her. She had her beak in the feathers of her back, sound asleep.

She spoke in my head, however, and said, "You really want to be found, or you would not have told Matt all you did."

"I like you better when you don't talk," I said, pulled the deer hide over me, and fell into a deep sleep.

IN WHICH
I Cooperate with the Ending

By the middle of March I could have told you it was spring without looking. Jessie did not come around anymore, she was fishing the rewarding waters of the open stream, she was returning to a tree hollow full of babies. The Baron Weasel did not come by. There were salamanders and frogs to keep him busy. The chickadees sang alone, not in a winter group, and the skunks and minks and foxes found food more abundant in the forest than at my tree house. The circumstances that had brought us all together in the winter were no more. There was food on the land and the snow was slipping away.

By April I was no longer living off my storehouse. There were bulbs, tubers, and greens to be had. Meals were varied once more. There were frogs' legs, eggs, and turtle soup on my table.

I took my baths in the spring again rather than in the turtle shell with warmed-over snow. I plunged regularly into the ice water of the spring—shouting as my breath was grabbed from my lungs. I scrubbed, ran for my tree, and dried myself before the fire, shouting as I stepped into my clothes. Then I would sing. I made up a lot of nice songs after my bath, one of which I taught to a man who was hiking along the top of the gorge one day.

He said his name was Aaron, and he was quiet and tall. I found him sitting on the edge of the cliff, looking across the valley. He was humming little tunes. He had a sad smile that never went away. I knew I would not have to hide from him just by looking at him, so I walked up and sat down beside him. I taught him my "cold water song."

I learned he wrote songs and that he was from New York. He had come to the Catskills for the Passover[19] festivities and had wandered off for the day. He was about to go back when I sat down and said, "I heard you humming."

"Yes," he said. "I hum a good deal. Can you hum?"

"Yes," I replied, "I can hum. I hum a good deal, too, and even sing, especially when I get out of the spring in the morning. Then I really sing aloud."

"Let's hear you sing aloud."

So I said, feeling very relaxed with the sun shining on my head, "All right, I'll sing you my cold water song."

"I like that," Aaron said. "Sing it again." So I did.

"Let me suggest a few changes." He changed a few words to fit the tune and

---

19. **Passover**: Jewish holiday observed in spring, recalling the Exodus, when Moses led the Hebrews from Egypt.

Rocky Gorge, George Hetzel, 1869.

the tune to fit the words, and then we both sang it.

"Mind if I use the hum hum hum dee dee part?" he asked presently.

"You can use it all," I said. "Tunes are free up here. I got that from the red-eyed vireo."

He sat up and said, "What other songs are sung up here?"

I whistled him the "hi-chickadee" song of the black-capped Mr. Bracket; and the waterfall song of the wood thrush. He took out a card, lined it with five lines, and wrote in little marks. I stretched back in the sun and hummed the song of the brown thrasher and of Barometer, the nuthatch. Then I boomed out the song of the great horned owl and stopped.

"That's enough, isn't it?" I asked.

"I guess so." He lay back and stretched, looked into the leaves, and said, "If I do something with this, I'll come back and play it to you. I'll bring my portable organ."

"Fine," I said.

Then, after a drowsy pause, he said, "Will you be around these parts this summer?"

"I'll be around," I said. Aaron fell asleep, and I rolled over in the sun. I liked him. He hadn't asked me one personal question. Oddly enough, I wasn't sure whether that made me glad or not. Then I thought of the words Frightful had spoken in my head. "You want to be found," and I began to wonder. I had sought out a human being. This would not have happened a year ago.

I fell asleep. When I awoke, Aaron was gone and Frightful was circling me. She saw me stir, swooped in, and sat on a rock beside me. I said, "Hi," but did not get up, just lay still listening to the birds, the snips and sputs of insects moving in the dry leaves, and the air stirring the newly leafing trees. Nothing went on in my head. It was comfortably blank. I knew the pleasures of the lizard on the log who knows where his next meal is coming from. I also knew his boredom. After an hour I did have a thought. Aaron had said that he was up in the Catskills for Passover. Then it must also be near Easter, and Matt would be coming soon. I had not counted notches in weeks.

A cool shadow crossed my face and I arose, whistled for Frightful to come to my hand, and wandered slowly home, stuffing my pockets with spring beauty bulbs as I went.

Several days later I met Matt on Route 27 at three-thirty. I tied his handkerchief around his eyes and led him, stumbling and tripping, up the mountain. I went almost directly home. I guess I didn't much care if he remembered how to get there or not. When I took off the blindfold, he looked around.

"Where are we? Where's your house?" I sat down and motioned him to sit. He did so with great willingness—in fact, he flopped.

"What do you sleep on, the ground?"

I pointed to the deerskin flaps moving in the wind in the hemlock.

"Whatdaya do, live in a tree?"

"Yep."

Matt bounced to his feet and we went in. I propped the door open so that the light streamed in, and he shouted with joy. I lit the tallow candle and we went over everything, and each invention he viewed with a shout.

While I prepared trout baked in wild grape leaves, Matt sat on the bed and told me the world news in brief. I listened with care to the trouble in Europe, the trouble in the Far East, the trouble in the South, and the trouble in America. Also to a few sensational murders, some ball scores, and his report card.

"It all proves my point," I said sagely.[20] "People live too close together."

"Is that why you are here?"

"Well, not exactly. The main reason is that I don't like to be dependent, particularly on electricity, rails, steam, oil, coal, machines, and all those things that can go wrong."

"Well, is that why you are up here?"

"Well, not exactly. Some men climbed Mount Everest[21] because it was there. Here is a wilderness."

"Is that why?"

"Aw, come on, Matt. See that falcon? Hear those white-throated sparrows? Smell that skunk? Well, the falcon takes the sky, the white-throated sparrow takes the low bushes, the skunk takes the earth, you take the newspaper office, I take the woods."

"Don't you get lonely?"

"Lonely? I've hardly had a quiet moment since arriving. Stop being a reporter and let's eat. Besides, there are people in the city who are lonelier than I."

"Okay. Let's eat. This is good, darned good; in fact, the best meal I've ever eaten." He ate and stopped asking questions.

We spent the next week fishing, hunting, trapping, gathering greens and bulbs. Matt talked less and less, slept, hiked, and pondered. He also ate well, and kept Frightful very busy. He made himself a pair of moccasins out of deer hide, and a hat that I can't even describe. We didn't have a mirror so he never knew how it looked, but I can say this: when I happened to meet him as we came fishing along a stream bed, I was always startled. I never did get used to that hat.

Toward the end of the week, who should we find sleeping in my bed after returning from a fishing trip, but Bando! Spring vacation, he said. That night we played our reed whistles for Matt, by an outdoor fire. It was that warm. Matt and Bando also decided to make a guest house out of one of the other trees. I said "Yes, let's" because I felt that way, although I knew what it meant.

A guest house meant I was no longer a runaway. I was no longer hiding in the wilderness. I was living in the woods like anyone else lives in a house. People drop by, neighbors come for dinner, there are three meals to get, the shopping to do, the cleaning to accomplish. I felt exactly as I felt when I was home. The only difference was that I was a little harder to visit out here, but not too hard. There sat Matt and Bando.

We all burned and dug out another hemlock. I worked with them, wondering what was happening to me. Why didn't I cry "No"? What made me happily build a city in the forest—because that is what we were doing.

When the tree was done, Bando had discovered that the sap was running in willow trees and the limbs were just right for slide whistles. He spent the evening making us trombones. We played them together. That word *together*. Maybe that was the answer to the city.

Matt said rather uncomfortably just

20. **sagely** [sāj′lē]: wisely.
21. **Mount Everest** [ev′ər ist]: highest mountain in the world, located in the Himalayas, in central Asia.

before bedtime, "There may be some photographers in these hills."

"Matt!" I hardly protested. "What did you write?"

It was Bando who pulled out the article.

He read it, a few follow-ups, and comments from many other papers. Then he leaned back against his leaning tree, as it had come to be, and puffed silently on his pipe.

"Let's face it, Thoreau; you can't live in America today and be quietly different. If you are going to be different, you are going to stand out, and people are going to hear about you; and in your case, if they hear about you, they will remove you to the city or move to you and you won't be different anymore." A pause.

"Did the owls nest, Thoreau?"

I told him about the owls and how the young played around the hemlock, and then we went to bed a little sad—all of us. Time was running out.

Matt had to return to school, and Bando stayed on to help burn out another tree for another guest house. We chopped off the blackened wood, made one bed, and started the second before he had to return to his teaching.

I wasn't alone long. Mr. Jacket found me.

I was out on the raft trying to catch an enormous snapping turtle. It would take my line, but when I got its head above water, it would eye me with those cold ancient eyes and let go. Frightful was nearby. I was making a noose to throw over the turtle's head the next time it surfaced when Frightful lit on my shoulder with a thud and a hard grip. She was drawn up and tense, which in her language said "people," so I wasn't surprised

to hear a voice call from across the stream, "Hi, Daniel Boone. What are you doing?" There stood Mr. Jacket.

"I am trying to get this whale of a snapper," I said in such an ordinary voice that it was dull.

I went on with the noose making, and he called to me, "Hit it with a club."

I still couldn't catch the old tiger, so I rafted to shore and got Mr. Jacket. About an hour later we had the turtle, had cleaned it, and I knew that Mr. Jacket was Tom Sidler.

"Come on up to the house," I said, and he came on up to the house, and it was just like after school on Third Avenue. He wanted to see everything, of course, and he did think it unusual, but he got over it in a hurry and settled down to helping me prepare the meat for turtle soup.

He dug the onions for it while I got it boiling in a tin can. Turtle is as tough as rock and has to be boiled for hours before it gets tender. We flavored the soup with hickory salt, and cut a lot of Solomon's seal tubers into it. Tom said it was too thin, and I thickened it with mashed up nuts—I had run out of acorn flour. I tried some orris root in it—pretty fair.

"Wanta stay and eat it and spend the night?" I asked him somewhere along the way. He said, "Sure," but added that he had better go home and tell his mother. It took him about two hours to get back and the turtle was still tough, so we went out to the meadow to fly Frightful. She caught her own meal, we tied her to her perch, and climbed in the gorge until almost dark. We ate turtle soup. Tom slept in the guest tree.

I lay awake wondering what had happened. Everything seemed so everyday.

Moonlight, Ralph Albert Blakelock, c. 1890.

I liked Tom and he liked me, and he came up often, almost every weekend. He told me about his bowling team and some of his friends, and I began to feel I knew a lot of people in the town below the mountain. This made my wilderness small. When Tom left one weekend I wrote this down:

"Tom said that he and Reed went into an empty house, and when they heard the real estate man come in, they slid down the laundry chute to the basement and crawled out the basement window. He said a water main broke and flooded the school grounds and all the kids took off their shoes and played baseball in it."

I drew a line through all this and then I wrote:

"I haven't seen The Baron Weasel. I think he has deserted his den by the boulder. A catbird is nesting nearby. Apparently it has learned that Frightful is tied some of the time, because it comes right up to the fireplace for scraps when the leash is snapped."

I drew a line through this too, and

filled up the rest of the piece of bark with a drawing of Frightful.

I went to the library the next day and took out four books.

Aaron came back. He came right to the hemlock forest and called. I didn't ask him how he knew I was there. He stayed a week, mostly puttering around with the willow whistles. He never asked what I was doing on the mountain. It was as if he already knew. As if he had talked to someone, or read something, and there was nothing more to question. I had the feeling that I was an old story somewhere beyond the foot of the mountain. I didn't care.

Bando got a car and he came up more often. He never mentioned any more newspaper stories, and I never asked him. I just said to him one day, "I seem to have an address now."

He said, "You do."

I said, "Is it Broadway and Forty-second Street?"[22]

He said, "Almost." His eyebrows knitted and he looked at me sadly.

"It's all right, Bando. Maybe you'd better bring me a shirt and some blue jeans when you come next time. I was thinking, if they haven't sold that house in town, maybe Tom and I could slide down the laundry chute."

Bando slowly turned a willow whistle over in his hands. He didn't play it.

IN WHICH
The City Comes to Me

The warblers arrived, the trees turned summer green, and June burst over the mountain. It smelled good, tasted good, and was gentle to the eyes.

I was stretched out on the big rock in the meadow one morning. Frightful was jabbing at some insect in the grass below me when suddenly a flashbulb exploded and a man appeared.

"Wild boy!" he said, and took another picture. "What are you doing, eating nuts?"

I sat up. My heart was heavy. It was so heavy that I posed for him holding Frightful on my fist. I refused to take him to my tree, however, and he finally left. Two other photographers came, and a reporter. I talked a little. When they left, I rolled over on my stomach and wondered if I could get in touch with the Department of Interior[23] and find out more about the public lands in the West. My next thought was the baseball game in the flooded school yard.

Four days passed, and I talked to many reporters and photographers. At noon of the fifth day a voice called from the glen: "I know you are there!"

"*Dad!*" I shouted, and once again burst down the mountainside to see my father.

As I ran toward him, I heard sounds that stopped me. The sound of branches and twigs breaking, of the flowers being crushed. Hordes were coming. For a long moment I stood wondering whether to meet Dad or run forever. I was self-sufficient,[24] I could travel the world over, never needing a penny, never asking anything of anyone. I could cross to Asia in

---

22. **Broadway and Forty-second Street**: a crowded intersection in New York City.

23. **Department of Interior**: U.S. government division in charge of managing the nation's natural resources.
24. **self-sufficient**: independent; able to live without needing any help from anyone else.

a canoe via the Bering Strait.[25] I could raft to an island. I could go around the world on the fruits of the land. I started to run. I got as far as the gorge and turned back. I wanted to see Dad.

I walked down the mountain to greet him and to face the people he had brought from the city to photograph me, interview me, and bring me home. I walked slowly, knowing that it was all over. I could hear the voices of the other people. They filled my silent mountain.

Then I jumped in the air and laughed for joy. I recognized my four-year-old brother's pleasure song. The family! Dad had brought the family! Every one of them. I ran, twisting and turning through the trees like a Cooper's hawk, and occasionally riding a free fifty feet downhill on an aspen sapling.

"*Dad! Mom!*" I shouted as I came upon them along the streambed, carefully picking their way through raspberry bushes. Dad gave me a resounding slap and Mother hugged me until she cried.

John jumped on me. Jim threw me into the rushes. Mary sat on me. Alice put leaves in my hair. Hank pulled Jim off. Joan pulled me to my feet, and Jake bit my ankle. That cute little baby sister toddled away from me and cried.

"Wow! All of New York!" I said. "This is a great day for the Katerskills."[26]

I led them proudly up the mountain, thinking about dinner and what I had that would go around. I knew how Mother felt when we brought in friends for dinner.

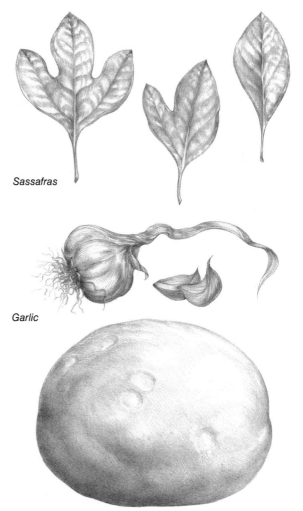

Sassafras

Garlic

Puffball Mushroom

As we approached the hemlock grove, I noticed that Dad was carrying a pack. He explained it as food for the first few days, or until I could teach John, Jim, Hank, and Jake how to live off the land. I winked at him.

"But, Dad, a Gribley is not for the land."

"What do you mean?" he shouted. "The Gribleys have had land for three generations. We pioneer, we open the land." He was almost singing.

---

25. **Bering Strait**: narrow channel connecting the Arctic Ocean with the Bering Sea, between Siberia and Alaska.
26. **Katerskills**: early spelling of Catskills.

"And then we go to sea," I said.

"Things have changed. Child labor laws; you can't take children to sea."

I should have glowed over such a confession from Dad had I not been making furious plans as we climbed; food, beds, chores. Dad, however, had had since Christmas to outplan me. He strung up hammocks for everyone all through the forest, and you never heard a happier bunch of kids. The singing and shouting and giggling sent the birds and wildlife deeper into the shadows. Even little Nina had a hammock, and though she was only a toddler, she cooed and giggled all by herself as she rocked between two aspens near the meadow. We ate Mother's fried chicken. Chicken is good, it tastes like chicken.

I shall never forget that evening.

And I shall never forget what Dad said, "Son, when I told your mother where you were, she said, 'Well, if he doesn't want to come home, then we will bring home to him.' And that's why we are all here."

I was stunned. I was beginning to realize that this was not an overnight camping trip, but a permanent arrangement. Mother saw my expression and said, "When you are of age, you can go wherever you please. Until then, I still have to take care of you, according to all the law I can find." She put her arm around me, and we rocked ever so slightly. "Besides, I am not a Gribley. I am a Stuart, and the Stuarts loved the land." She looked at the mountain and the meadow and the gorge, and I felt her feet squeeze into the earth and take root.

The next day I took John, Jim, and Hank out into the mountain meadows with Frightful to see if we could not round up enough food to feed this city of people. We did pretty well.

When we came back, there was Dad with four four-by-fours,[27] erected at the edge of my meadow, and a pile of wood that would have covered a barn.

"Gosh, Dad," I cried, "what on earth are you doing?"

"We are going to have a house," he said.

I was stunned and hurt.

"A house! You'll spoil everything!" I protested. "Can't we all live in trees and hammocks?"

"No. Your mother said that she was going to give you a decent home, and in her way of looking at it, that means a roof and doors. She got awfully mad at those newspaper stories inferring that she had not done her duty."

"But she did." I was almost at the point of tears. "She's a swell mother. What other boy has a mother who would let him do what I did?"

"I know. I know. But a woman lives among her neighbors. Your mother took all those editorials personally, as if they were Mr. Bracket and Mrs. O'Brien speaking. The nation became her neighbors, and no one, not even—" He hesitated. A catbird meowed. "Not even that catbird is going to think that she neglected you."

I was about to protest in a loud strong voice when Mother's arm slipped around my shoulder.

"That's how it is until you are eighteen, Sam," she said. And that ended it.

---

27. **four-by-fours**: wooden posts or bars measuring four inches by four inches in cross section.

READER'S RESPONSE

Does Sam lose his freedom and independence when his family arrives?

STUDY QUESTIONS

Recalling

1. Where does Sam get his weather forecasts? Whom does he call Barometer?
2. What keeps Sam from feeling bad about the ruins of the ice storm?
3. When does Sam notice the first sign of spring? What is his reaction to the coming of spring?
4. What does Sam imagine that Frightful tells him about Matt Spell?
5. What does Bando tell Sam about being different?
6. According to Sam's father, what did Sam's mother say when he told her where Sam was?

Interpreting

7. Why is Sam excited to see signs of spring?
8. Do you think that Sam is different from Aaron, Bando, and Matt? If so, in what ways?
9. What do you think Sam has learned about independence?

Extending

10. Do you think Sam is happy that his family has come to live with him? Why or why not?

READING AND LITERARY FOCUS

The Total Effect

A novelist uses plot, setting, characterization, and a narrator to develop **themes,** or general ideas about life. The **plot,** or sequence of events, must capture the interest of the reader. The **setting** is the time and place in which the action of the novel takes place. Descriptions of the setting often add to the overall mood of the work. **Characterization** refers to the personality of a character. It also refers to the method an author uses to reveal this personality to

the reader. Sometimes one of the characters of the work is also the narrator. The **narrator** is the person who tells the story. Sometimes the narrator is a third-person storyteller who is not involved in the action.

Unlike a short story a novel is long enough to have several themes that present the novelist's views. All the elements of a novel work together to create a **total effect**—its impact on the reader.

Thinking About Plot

1. Identify an important internal conflict in Sam's story. Then identify an important external conflict. Which of these conflicts is easier for Sam to resolve? Why?

Thinking About Setting

2. There are many descriptions of the weather in *My Side of the Mountain*. Why are these descriptions important in the novel?

Thinking About Character

3. Name three of Sam's personality traits. Give examples of Sam's actions to illustrate each trait.
4. List four characters who affect Sam's life in the Catskills. Briefly describe the influence of each one.
5. Give at least two examples of ways in which you think Sam changes during the year he spends living by himself.

Thinking About Narrator

6. Who is the narrator of *My Side of the Mountain*?
7. Tell how the story would be different if it were told by a different narrator.

Thinking About Theme

8. Consider how Sam sticks to his plan of living on his great-grandfather's farm even when he encounters problems. What theme do you think the author is suggesting about making plans and setting goals?
9. Think about what Sam does when he needs information in order to find the old Gribley farm and wants to know more about falcons. What theme about knowledge do you think the author is suggesting?

My Side of the Mountain 605

10. Consider how Sam uses plants and animals to meet his needs. What theme about nature does this suggest?

COMPOSITION

Writing a Book Review

Write a book review of *My Side of the Mountain*. **Prewriting:** Collect information about the author and the work. Make notes on the setting, characters, and plot. Think about your overall opinion of the book. **Writing:** First present some general information on the book and its author. Then describe the setting of the story and the main characters. Next summarize the plot. Conclude by giving your opinion of *My Side of the Mountain* backed by examples from the book. **Revising:** Review your writing to be sure that you have expressed your ideas clearly and logically. Then review for effective word choice and organization. Make sure that your final copy is free of errors in grammar, spelling, and punctuation.

Writing a Diary Entry

Pretend that you are Sam. Write a diary entry that he might have written while building the new house on the Gribley land. Try to capture the reactions that Sam would have been likely to have.

CHALLENGE

Illustration

Draw a picture of Sam's home. Look at the descriptions of his tree house, and consider where it is in relation to the stream and other landmarks. Make a short list of what you want to include in your illustration. Then draw a picture, and indicate where the landmarks are located, making sure to identify them. Compare your picture with someone else's.

Detail, *Rocky Gorge*, George Hetzel, 1869.

Thinking Skills: Representing

DEFINITION

Representing is a way of picturing data, or information. Diagrams, graphs, maps, charts, and other images can help you organize data and think about what they mean. The following steps tell how to picture information using one form of representing—overlapping circles.

STEPS

1. **Identify the subjects you will think about.**
   Write the subjects in overlapping circles like the ones on this page.

2. **Identify individual features or qualities of the subjects.**
   Write the features that apply only to the first subject in one circle. Write the features that apply only to the second subject in the other circle. Write the features shared by both subjects in the area where the circles overlap.

3. **Based on some or all of the features, make a statement about the subjects.**
   What do the overlapping circles tell you about the subjects? What features belong only to one subject? What features are shared?

EXAMPLE

Imagine that you are asked to write about meat-eating animals and plant-eating animals. The topic is so broad that you need to organize the information about it. You decide to use overlapping circles to think about the many different aspects of the subject.

1. **Identify the subjects you will think about.** You

write *meat-eating* in one circle and *plant-eating* in the other circle.

2. **Identify individual features or qualities of the subject.** You write the names of meat-eating animals in one circle and the names of plant-eating animals in the other circle. You write the names of any animals that eat *both* meat and plants in the area where the circles overlap.

3. **Based on some or all of the features, make a statement about the subjects.** You write, "While most animals are either meat-eating or plant-eating, some animals eat both meat and plants."

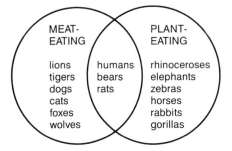

ACTIVITY

Follow the three steps of representing to make overlapping circles for Sam's experiences in *My Side of the Mountain*. Write *positive experiences* in one circle, and list experiences that Sam found good, comforting, or delightful. Write *negative experiences* in the other circle, and list experiences that Sam found bad, frightening, or harmful. In the area where the circles overlap, list experiences that were *both* positive and negative, that had a good side and a bad side. Make a statement about what Sam learned from these experiences.

The Novel

My Side of the Mountain is a novel about the different sides of independence—fear and self-confidence, discipline and freedom. It is a novel about nature and human nature and the relationship between them. Survival, in this novel, is shown to be much more than merely learning to live *in* nature. Survival becomes a matter of learning to live *with* nature.

1. **Survival Skills** Survival skills are often a combination of practicality, knowledge, and imagination. As a group identify an environment in which it would be extremely difficult for a person to survive alone—for example, a vast desert or an arctic wilderness. Brainstorm to list the kinds of threats to life that would have to be faced in that environment.

   Each member of the group should then use the library to research the particular skills necessary for surviving in the environment you chose. Books about exploring and handbooks for camping and wilderness survival may be a good source. Your library may also have videotapes that teach particular skills. Each member of the group should choose one survival skill and have it approved by your teacher. Demonstrate the skill, using whatever props, costumes, pictures, and diagrams are necessary to make your presentation clear.

2. **Collage and Display** As the world becomes more and more industrialized, preserving the environment becomes more and more vital. As a group create a collage and display illustrating environmental protection in your part of the world. Choose one particular aspect of the environment, such as the air, water, or animal life.

   Use your library as a resource. Also consider getting information from the United States Environmental Protection Agency or from local environmental groups or companies. You may want to organize your display to show what is being done now to save the environment or to show what still needs to be done to ensure a healthy environment.

Collaborative Learning:
Across the Curriculum

The Novel

1. **Literature and Health and Nutrition: Oral Report** Nutrition is vital not only to human survival but also to one's well-being. In *My Side of the Mountain*, Sam becomes painfully aware that he is suffering from a vitamin deficiency. He makes some changes in his diet, and the results are a dramatic improvement in his health.

   As a group research and report on the basic vitamins and minerals that are necessary for a healthy human being. Identify the daily amounts of each vitamin and mineral that are necessary. Identify the best food sources of these vitamins and minerals as well as the foods that should be avoided.

2. **Literature and Social Studies: Biography and Illustration** History is filled with stories of people who have survived under extraordinary circumstances. Think of the struggles of the early explorers—Christopher Columbus, for example. Or think of the Pilgrims who survived their first winter in America and celebrated the first Thanksgiving.

   Work together as a group to write and illustrate a short biography of a famous survivor. Review and discuss well-known figures from history and current events. Choose one, and divide the task of research so that each member of the group has approximately equal responsibility. Narrate the events clearly so that your reader always knows what is happening. Illustrate the events with drawings, paintings, or photographs.

STUDENT'S RESOURCES

WRITING ABOUT LITERATURE HANDBOOK   612

READING AND LITERARY TERMS HANDBOOK   626

REVISING AND EDITING CHECKLIST

The lessons in this handbook have been planned to help you to think and write clearly about literature. When you think clearly about literature, you will be able to write clearly about literature.

The lessons show you that writing is a process with several steps. For each essay assignment the lessons suggest prewriting steps to follow. The lessons will also suggest steps for you to follow as you go from paragraph to paragraph. In addition, each lesson will remind you to revise and edit your first draft.

When you have finished the first draft, it is important that you review your work.

1. Read your writing aloud. Your ear has been responding to words longer than you have been writing.

2. Use the following checklist to revise, edit, and proofread your written work. Prepare a final version.

I. Organization
   a. Have you turned the assignment question into a thesis statement?
   b. Does each following paragraph have a topic sentence and supporting details?
   c. Does the final paragraph restate the thesis statement and perhaps add additional insights and comments?

II. Content
   a. Does the essay as a whole answer the question asked in the assignment?
   b. Is each idea satisfactorily developed with supporting details from the selection itself?

III. Grammar, Usage, Mechanics
   a. Have you used complete sentences?
   b. Have you used correct punctuation, capitalization, and spelling?

IV. Word Choice, Style
   a. Have you used appropriate words?
   b. Have you avoided wordiness?
   c. Have you varied sentence length?

WRITING ABOUT LITERATURE HANDBOOK

LESSON 1:   Writing About Plot

The **plot** of a story is the sequence of events or actions that occurs within the course of that story. The plot usually hinges on a conflict, or struggle, that the story's main character must face.

■ CONCEPTS TO REMEMBER

A plot is made up of several stages:

1. **Beginning of a story:** Here we learn about the characters, the setting, and the situation in which the main character finds himself or herself.
2. **Conflict:** As the story progresses, we find out about the conflict that the main character faces.
3. **Climax:** At the point of highest interest, or the climax, of the story, we form a good idea of how the story will end. After the climax we see how the conflict is settled. We learn what takes place as a result of settling the conflict.

■ TYPICAL ESSAY QUESTION

When you are asked to write about the plot of a story, you will often have to answer a question like the following one:

Analyze the plot by discussing its major parts. First identify the conflict, and discuss who or what is engaged in a struggle. Explain what problems make it difficult for the main character to resolve the conflict. Tell how the story concludes.

■ PREWRITING

Break down the assignment into its various parts. Draw a chart with space in which to make notes about each part of the assignment. A sample chart appears at the top of the opposite page. Then think about each part of the assignment. Use the following guidelines and questions as aids to your thinking and note making.

1. Identify the conflict in the story, and clarify for yourself who or what is involved in the conflict. Ask yourself questions such as the following:

   a. Is the conflict between two people? If so, is the conflict about another person? About a place? About a possession? About an event?
   b. Is the conflict between a person and something in nature, such as an animal or an environment?
   c. Is the conflict between a person and society? What is the problem?
   d. Is the conflict within a person's mind?

2. Examine the story closely to figure out why the main character has trouble settling the conflict. Ask yourself questions such as the following:

   a. Is the main character physically unable to settle the conflict? Is he or she too far away or too weak or handicapped in some way?
   b. Is the main character too confused to settle the conflict? Is he or she lacking some important information that is necessary to settle the conflict?

3. Make sure you understand exactly what happens at the end of the story. Ask yourself the following questions:

   a. Does the main character settle the conflict for himself or herself? If so, does the character use intelligence or physical strength or something else to settle the conflict?
   b. Does another character come to the rescue and settle the conflict?
   c. Is the character satisfied with the solution?

SAMPLE CHART: ANALYZING PLOT	
SELECTION: "The Boy with Yellow Eyes"	
PART OF ESSAY QUESTION	**NOTES FOR ANSWER**
1. WHAT IS THE CONFLICT? WHO OR WHAT IS INVOLVED IN THE CONFLICT?	The conflict between Norman and Willie—arguing about the value of knowledge vs. physical activity. Other conflict between the two boys and the spy.
2. WHAT PROBLEMS MAKE IT DIFFICULT FOR THE MAIN CHARACTER(S) TO SETTLE THE CONFLICT?	Conflict between the boys is settled by Norman's story-telling skills. The conflict with the spy is settled when Norman alerts Willie to what the spy is doing and both overcome the man's superior strength.
3. HOW DOES THE STORY CONCLUDE?	Norman and Willie become heroes. Later Willlie adopts Norman's values, and as adults they exchange lists of books every year.

■ WRITING PARAGRAPH BY PARAGRAPH

You may be able to answer the essay question in a single paragraph, or you may take more space to develop your answer. Refer to the chart with the notes you made in response to the questions suggested under Prewriting. Then convert your notes to sentences and paragraphs, following the steps listed here. (If your answer is just one paragraph long, think of these steps as applying to each sentence rather than to each paragraph.)

1. In your introductory paragraph write a thesis statement, putting the central idea of the essay question into your own words. You may follow the thesis statement with one or more sentences telling how your essay will proceed.

Example of Thesis Statement

In the plot of "The Boy with Yellow Eyes," Gloria Gonzalez shows us how two boys, with totally conflicting values, overcome their differences and join forces when faced with an unusual and dangerous situation.

2. In each of the middle paragraphs present a topic sentence based on your chart notes. Each topic sentence should answer one of the questions on the chart. After each topic sentence offer supporting details.

Example of Topic Sentence and Supporting Detail

Although the two boys have always been at odds with one another, Willie listens to and is impressed by Norman's retelling of *Dracula.* As a result, although he has no idea what the tapping noises mean, he accepts Norman's explanation of them without making fun of him.

3. In your concluding paragraph restate your thesis statement, using different words from those in your introductory paragraph. If you wish to include an additional comment about the plot, you may state whether you found the conclusion satisfactory.

■ REVISING AND EDITING

See the Revising and Editing Checklist on page 611 for detailed reminders about improving your writing.

■ ASSIGNMENTS

1. Use the chart given in this lesson and ideas of your own to analyze the plot of Gloria Gonzalez's "The Boy with Yellow Eyes" (page 7).

2. Select "The Landlady" (page 15), "May I Have Your Autograph?" (page 25), or another story you have read in this book and write a composition about plot in which you analyze the plot by discussing its major parts.

Writing About Literature Handbook **613**

LESSON 2:   *Answering an Essay Question*

Writing is a process with several steps. When you follow these steps, any writing assignment becomes more manageable and seems easier. As a result your finished product will be thoughtful, informative, well organized, and polished. This lesson will teach you a step-by-step method to use when you are asked to analyze and write about a piece of literature.

■ PREWRITING

Before you begin to write, think carefully about the writing assignment, and organize your thoughts. To do so, follow these steps:

1. Read the essay question, copying down important words that tell you what is expected in your answer. Notice the key words that are underlined in the following example. Notice also that there often is a main question followed by a request for details, or further explanation.

Example of Essay Question
Write a short essay in which you tell whether or not you liked a particular work of literature. Then explain your response by answering the following questions: (a) Did the selection hold your attention? (b) Was the outcome of the selection satisfying? (c) Did you care about what happened to the main character? Support your opinions with examples.

main question

request for further information

2. Make a chart on which to jot down ideas in note form. The chart below helped a writer develop and organize ideas for the assignment given in Prewriting 1. The chart is based on "Miss Hinch" (page 55).

■ WRITING PARAGRAPH BY PARAGRAPH

After you have put your thoughts down as notes on a chart or an outline, you may follow these steps to present them in carefully constructed paragraphs:

1. Restate the question as a statement. This sentence will be your thesis statement, a clear statement of your central idea. You may follow the thesis statement with one or more sentences telling how your answer will proceed.

Example of Thesis Statement
"Miss Hinch" by Henry Sydnor Harrison is a particularly exciting, absorbing story that holds a reader's attention throughout, provides a shocking conclusion, and presents two characters whose daring and unpredictable behavior leave a reader breathless.

2. Begin each of the middle paragraphs of your answer with a topic sentence, which states the main idea, purpose, or plan for the paragraph. Each sentence that follows the topic sentence should support it. The supporting sentences can be examples, quotations, or incidents taken from the selection.

Example of Topic Sentence and Supporting Example for Second Paragraph
The story captures the reader's attention instantly. With the first sentence Harrison arouses reader interest: "In the bright light of the entrance to the . . . subway, two strangers came almost face to face."

3. Write a concluding paragraph. Begin it with the idea expressed in your thesis statement, but use different words.

Example of Topic Sentence in Concluding Paragraph
From its beginning to its end, Harrison's

SAMPLE CHART: NOTES FOR ANSWERING AN ESSAY QUESTION		
QUESTION	**ANSWER**	**EXAMPLES**
a. DID THE SELECTION HOLD YOUR ATTENTION?	I wondered where Miss Hinch was and if she would be caught.	The man and woman in the subway, themselves mysterious figures, seem to be obsessed with the case.
	I learned about the art of acting and disguise and about the power of persistence.	Miss Hinch could be anyone, as could Miss Dark, who was set not to break her record.
b. WAS THE OUTCOME OF THE SELECTION SATISFYING?	The outcome was more shocking than satisfying. I was glad Miss Hinch was caught but sorry Miss Dark died bringing her to justice.	Miss Hinch is a coldblooded murderer who kills again to avoid capture. Though Miss Dark dies tragically, her record for snaring killers remains unbroken.
c. DID YOU CARE ABOUT WHAT HAPPENED TO THE MAIN CHARACTER?	I wanted Miss Hinch to be caught, though I was amazed at her boldness and cunning.	It takes a freak accident to catch the clever Miss Hinch, but justice is done.

"Miss Hinch" interests the reader with its exciting action and its unpredictable and daring main characters.

You may round out this paragraph by adding other thoughts about your reaction to the story. For example, who else do you think would enjoy the story?

■ WRITING A ONE-PARAGRAPH ANSWER

If your answer is limited to one paragraph, begin with a strong topic sentence that restates the question in the essay assignment. Each of your following sentences should develop one aspect of the topic sentence. You must give evidence to support your topic sentence.

■ REVISING AND EDITING

See the Revising and Editing Checklist on page 611 for detailed reminders about improving your writing.

■ ASSIGNMENTS

1. Finish the answer to the question presented in this lesson about "Miss Hinch."
2. Do an assignment called "Answering an Essay Question" on pages 239 and 352. Be sure to use examples to support your opinions.

LESSON 3:   *Writing a Character Sketch*

A **character** is a person or animal presented in a work of literature. An author may use several techniques to make a character seem real. For example, an author may (1) describe the character's physical appearance, (2) present the character's speech, actions, thoughts, feelings, and motivations, and (3) illustrate reactions of other people or animals to the character. As a reader you can show your understanding of a character by writing a character sketch.

■ CONCEPTS TO REMEMBER

1. A **character sketch** is a short written portrait of a character from literature or real life. In this lesson we will use the term *character sketch* to refer to writing about characters from literature only. The character sketch zooms in on just a few incidents, scenes, or encounters in order to illustrate those qualities.
2. A character in literature has outstanding traits. *Trait* is simply another word for "quality" or "characteristic." *Outstanding* in this usage simply means "most important."

■ TYPICAL ESSAY QUESTION

When you are asked to analyze a character in a piece of literature, you may be asked to examine that character's personality and patterns of behavior. A typical assignment follows:

Choose a character, and discuss the character's outstanding traits.

■ PREWRITING

1. Think about which character from a particular selection interests you the most. When you have decided on that character, review the selection, asking yourself the following questions:

   a. Who is the character? What is his or her name, age, job, or role?

   b. What does the character look like?
   c. How does the character speak? How does the character act? Which words or actions in particular illustrate what the character is like?
   d. Does the character have any unusual or noteworthy habits?
   e. What details can you mention to illustrate the character's thoughts and feelings?
   f. What motivates, or drives, this character to act the way he or she acts?
   g. Does the character remain the same from the beginning to the end of the literary selection, or does the character change? If the character changes, tell how.
   h. How do other characters in the selection respond to the character about whom you are writing?

2. To help you organize your ideas about the character's outstanding traits, record the answers to the preceding questions on a chart such as the one on the opposite page.

■ WRITING PARAGRAPH BY PARAGRAPH

If your answer is just one paragraph long, think of the following steps as applying to each sentence rather than to each paragraph.

1. Begin your introductory paragraph with a thesis statement in which you identify the character, the work in which the character appears, and the character's outstanding traits.

Example of Introductory Paragraph

   In *Watership Down* the author Richard Adams shows several of Hazel's outstanding traits: his sensitivity, sense of responsibility, decisiveness, ability to lead, and awareness of his own limitations. Adams allows us to see Hazel's traits by providing details about his appearance, his speech and actions, his

CHARACTER TRAIT CHART

SELECTION: *Watership Down*

CHARACTER: Hazel

OUTSTANDING TRAITS: sensitivity; sense of responsibility; decisiveness; ability to lead; and awareness of his own limitations

DETAILS USED TO REVEAL OUTSTANDING TRAITS

PHYSICAL APPEARANCE	SPEECH AND ACTIONS	THOUGHTS AND FEELINGS
" . . . he had not the harassed look of most 'outskirters. . . .'" "He looked as though he knew how to take care of himself." " . . . a shrewd and buoyant air about him . . ."	*Speech:* He comforts Fiver: " . . . let me look after you. . . ." "If I ever get into the Owsla, I'll treat outskirters with a bit of decency." "Fiver and I will be leaving the warren tonight." To the threatening Owsla captain he says, "Go, or you will be killed." *Actions:* " . . . He led the way . . ." "He decided to go straight in the wood . . . and to trust the rest would follow."	*Thoughts:* " . . . he did . . . think that Fiver was likely to know better than himself." "I'm not going to let Bigwig run everything. . . ." "What would happen to a rabbit that left the shelter . . . of the . . . tree?" *Feelings:* "He did not want to believe Fiver, and he was afraid not to." "It was warm praise and it cheered him."
MOTIVATIONS OR GOALS	**CHANGES IN CHARACTER**	**OTHERS' REACTIONS TO CHARACTER**
to save Fiver, himself, and others who wish to join them from the nameless danger that terrifies his brother	from absolute self-confidence to an awareness of his own limitations: "Yes, the time's come now, all right." "Hazel felt at a loss." "He felt close to despair."	Other rabbits respect Hazel: "If you are [going to leave the warren] I'll come . . ." "Well done," whispered Dandelion. "Running our risks for us, are you . . ."

thoughts and feelings, his motivations, and the reactions of others to Hazel. The changes in Hazel also tell us something of the kind of individual Hazel is.

2. In each of the paragraphs that follow, present a topic sentence in which you identify one outstanding trait of the character. For the remaining sentences of the paragraph, provide details from the chart that support your topic sentence.

3. In the concluding paragraph restate your thesis using different words. You may end your character sketch by commenting in general on the character and indicating whether you were

impressed or otherwise affected by the character.

■ REVISING AND EDITING

See the Revising and Editing Checklist on page 611 for detailed reminders about improving your writing.

■ ASSIGNMENTS

1. Use the chart for Richard Adams' *Watership Down* (page 107) to write about Hazel's outstanding traits. Tell what these traits are and how they are revealed.

2. Complete an assignment called "Writing a Character Sketch" on pages 194, 266, or 559.

LESSON 4:   *Writing a Story*

A **short story** is a brief work of prose fiction. Important elements in any short story include plot, character, and setting. In order to plan and write an effective story, you must consider each of these elements.

■ CONCEPTS TO REMEMBER

1. **Plot** is the sequence of events, or what happens in a story. Each event causes or leads to the next. At the center of a plot is a problem, or conflict, that the main character faces. For example, this problem may be a personal goal, a competition with another person, or a struggle against hardship. The story builds toward its point of highest interest, the climax. The character solves the problem and learns something about himself or herself.

2. A **character** is an individual in a story. Most stories have only one or two major characters. They should have believable personality or character traits and clear motivations for their actions.

3. The **setting** is the time and place in which a story happens. Details of setting can give a story mood, or atmosphere. For example, a story may be gloomy or cheerful.

■ TYPICAL ASSIGNMENT

When asked to write a story, you will often be given an assignment like this one:

Write a short story that has a logical sequence of events. Describe your characters and setting clearly.

■ PREWRITING

1. To find an idea for your story, try to think of an interesting problem, an unusual person, or a colorful place. Most people write best when they write about things they know. Perhaps your hobbies and interests—for example, baseball or dancing—can inspire you. You may also want to page through a magazine or travel book. Some action, face, or location may give you an idea. Keep in mind that a story can be about very common, everyday occurrences—such as a school election. List some different ideas on a chart like the one that follows.

2. From your chart choose the problem, character, and setting for your story. Ask yourself the following questions: In what ways will your character react to the problem? How will the problem be solved?

3. Try to imagine how your characters look, sound, and act. Then fill in a chart like the one called "Characters" above. You may not use all this information in the actual story, but the chart will help you to picture the characters as believable people. The sample chart contains information about characters that one writer has in mind for a story.

4. Picture your setting. Then fill in a chart like the one called "Setting" above. You may not actually use all this information in your story, but the details will help you to picture the setting. The sample chart contains information about the setting that one writer is planning for a story. Imagine the place and time of the story as well as the weather and other details.

5. Write an outline to help organize your thoughts. In the outline that follows, the sections printed in boldface type are the steps that every story outline should include. The sections in italics are examples from the two charts on this page.

STORY OUTLINE

I. **Beginning**
   A. **Introduce the main character.** *Janet is twelve.*
   B. **Describe the setting.** *It is a rainy week, the first week of school in the suburban middle school.*

POSSIBLE IDEAS FOR A STORY		
PROBLEMS	**CHARACTERS**	**SETTINGS**
lost ticket	sports fan	World Series
limited oxygen supply	deep-sea diver	underwater colony
stolen deed to gold mine	prospector	Old West
desire to be human	robot	computer store
strange messages in lunch bag	newspaper writer	school classroom
school election	students	school cafeteria
engine failure	stunt pilot	over a mountain range
lost in a wilderness	camper	mountain forest
escape from a sea creature	swimmer	lake
school play auditions	shy adolescent	school auditorium
drought	farmer	farm in summer
noises in the attic	baby sitter	neighbor's house

C. Begin the plot. *Janet is running for class president.*

II. Middle

A. Introduce the character's problem. *Janet finds that some of her campaign posters have been destroyed.*

B. Introduce minor characters. *Steven is Janet's opponent. He tells Janet that he will make sure that she loses.*

C. Build toward the point of highest interest, or climax. *On election day Steven wins by a vote of 34–32. Janet tells others that Steven obviously voted twice because the class has only sixty-five students.*

III. Ending

A. Reach the point of highest interest. *Alice, Janet's friend, admits that she cast the extra vote to help Janet win.*

B. Wind down the action. *Janet apologizes to Steven.*

C. Give the final solution. *Janet vows not to jump to conclusions.*

6. When you have completed your outline, recite your plot aloud. Be sure that your plot builds in interest to a climax and then tells how the problem was finally solved.

7. Plan to use dialogue, or conversation between characters. Dialogue makes your story more realistic and more exciting. Remember the following points when you write dialogue.

a. All words spoken by characters must be surrounded by quotation marks. A direct quotation can come at the beginning or the end of a sentence.

b. A direct quotation begins with a capital letter. If a quotation is interrupted, the second part begins with a small letter.

c. A direct quotation is set off from the rest of a sentence by commas. If a direct quotation is interrupted, commas are placed before and after the interruption. The comma before a direct quotation falls outside the quotation marks. The comma—or any punctuation—after a direct quotation falls inside the quotation marks.

Examples

● She smiled and thought, "I think I am going to win this one!"

● "No, I am the best person for the job," corrected Steven.

● "Jan," he said with a laugh, "I'm going to make sure that you lose this election."

d. Dialogue is less formal than other kinds of writing. To make your characters sound natural, you may use short sentences and contractions in dialogue.

CHARACTERS								
CHARACTER	**PHYSICAL TRAITS**					**PERSONALITY OR CHARACTER TRAITS**		
	AGE	**HEIGHT, WEIGHT**	**HAIR**	**DRESS**	**FEATURES**	**PERSONALITY**	**SPEECH**	**BEHAVIOR**
Janet	12	5 feet, 2 inches; 95 pounds	brown, long, worn up	skirts and sweaters	freckles, glasses	enthusiastic, optimistic, hardworking	clear, careful	nice to others, jumps to conclusions
Steven	11	5 feet, 6 inches; 115 pounds	blond, very short	jeans	sloped shoulders	acts tough, determined	not talkative	serious, sometimes abrupt

e. In a conversation between characters, start a new paragraph each time the speaker changes.

f. Be careful not to use the word *said* too often. Use other, livelier verbs, such as *whispered, yelled, mumbled, snapped,* and *confessed.*

8. When you have completed your outline, choose a title for your story. The title may refer to an important event, object, character, or setting in the story.

■ WRITING PARAGRAPH BY PARAGRAPH

1. Following your outline, begin your first paragraph by describing your main character and your setting. The first paragraph should also introduce the plot with one important action. You may wish to have your main character speak.

Example

Janet pinned up her hair and put on her glasses in order to look official. Now that she was running for president of the sixth grade, she planned to work hard and look the part. Later, as she walked down the halls of the Valley Middle School, she looked at her bright campaign posters on the gray walls. She smiled and thought, "I think I am going to win this one!"

2. In the next paragraph introduce the character's problem. Describe the problem in detail, and include the character's reaction. Describe minor characters who are involved in the problem.

Example

As she rounded the corner of the math room, Janet spotted two of her posters on the floor. Someone had torn them up. Janet scooped up the colorful scraps of paper. As she walked away with the pieces, she passed Steven, her opponent.

"Jan," he said with a laugh, "I'm going to make sure that you lose this election."

3. In the paragraph or paragraphs that follow, build suspense as the story moves toward the point of highest interest, the climax, and the character tries to solve his or her problem. Be sure that your character acts according to the information in your chart for characters.

4. In the final paragraph or two, present the climax. Be sure that the solution to the character's problem is believable. End by showing what the character learned from the problem.

■ REVISING AND EDITING

Once you have finished the first draft, you must take time to polish it into an improved second draft. Read your story aloud. Use the following checklist to revise, proofread, and edit your writing.

I. Content
   A. Does your title point to something important

SETTING			
HISTORICAL PERIOD, YEAR, SEASON, TIME OF DAY	LOCATION (CITY, COUNTRY, INDOORS, OUTDOORS)	WEATHER	OTHER DETAILS
present day, beginning of school year, during school time	a suburban middle school	rainy	gray hallways decorated with bright campaign posters

in the story and grab the reader's interest?

B. Have you included details that describe your characters and setting?

C. Do you present the main character's problem clearly? Does each event of the plot grow logically from what happened before?

D. Is your climax a clear solution to the problem? Does your plot end soon after the climax? Do you show the main character's reaction to the climax?

E. Do you use dialogue to make the story more interesting and realistic?

II. Style

A. Have you cut out unnecessary details?

B. Have you used colorful adjectives and verbs wherever possible?

C. Does your dialogue sound real?

D. Do you use both long and short sentences for variety?

III. Grammar, Usage, Mechanics

A. Is each sentence complete (no fragments, no run-ons)?

B. Are all words spelled correctly? If you are

not sure of the spelling of a word, have you consulted a dictionary?

C. Have you punctuated and capitalized your sentences correctly? In dialogue, have you used quotation marks and capital letters correctly?

D. Do you begin a new paragraph whenever the subject, time, or place changes or whenever the speaker in a dialogue changes?

■ ASSIGNMENTS

1. Complete the story begun in this lesson by using the charts. You may follow the outline to the end of the story, or you may create your own ending if you wish. Give the story a title. Be sure that your plot develops as a logical sequence of events. In addition, use vivid details of character and setting.

2. Do an assignment called "Writing a Story" (page 14 or 352). Your plot should be a logical sequence of events. Describe your characters and setting clearly.

LESSON 5: *Writing About Poetry*

Reading or listening to a poem is a rich experience. A poem not only involves your mind but also excites your senses and stirs your emotions. The full power of a poem does not come only from its word-by-word meaning. Rather, a poem's power grows out of the special techniques that a poet uses to bring an idea to life. When you analyze a poem, you should consider how these poetic techniques add up to produce the poem's overall impact, or total effect.

■ CONCEPTS TO REMEMBER

1. The **total effect** of a poem is the overall impact that it has on the reader or listener. The total effect of a poem is made up of its meaning, its sound, its images, and its figures of speech.

2. **Sound devices:** Many sound devices contribute to the poem's effect. These devices include

   Alliteration: the repeating of consonant sounds, usually at the beginnings of words
   Rhythm: the pattern created by arranging stressed and unstressed syllables
   Rhyme: the repeating at regular intervals of similar or identical sounds

3. **Images:** The poet also relies on images, or mental pictures created with words, which appeal to one or more of the senses—sight, hearing, taste, smell, touch.

4. **Figures of speech:** The poet uses language that stretches words beyond their usual meanings. The most common figures of speech are

   Simile: A simile is a stated comparison between two otherwise unlike things. The comparison uses the word *like* or *as*.
   Metaphor: A metaphor is an implied comparison between two things. The comparison does not use the word *like* or *as*.
   Personification: Personification is a figure of speech in which the poet gives human qualities to an animal, object, or idea.

■ TYPICAL ESSAY QUESTION

When you are asked to write about poetry, you may find yourself answering an assignment such as the following:

Write about the total effect of a poem. First describe the poem's overall impact on you. Explain the poem's meaning. Then give examples of the sounds, imagery, and figures of speech that help to create the poem's impact.

■ PREWRITING

1. Read the poem out loud. Then reread it silently, thinking about its **meaning**, or the central idea or emotion behind the poem. If it will help you, paraphrase the poem, restating it in your own words. If you still have difficulty grasping the poem's meaning, ask yourself these questions:

   a. Does the poem spotlight a person, place, thing, idea, or feeling?
   b. What emotion do you feel when you read the poem?

2. Read the poem again, asking yourself the following questions about the techniques:

   a. **Sound:** What is the rhythm of the poem? Is it regular or irregular? Fast or slow? Gentle or driving? Does the poet use alliteration? Rhyme? How do these techniques add to the poem's meaning, emotion, and music?
   b. **Imagery:** What images does the poet use? Which seem most vivid? To which senses does each image appeal? What do these images add to the meaning and emotion of the poem?
   c. **Figures of Speech:** What examples of simile, metaphor, and personification can you find? What do these figures of speech contribute to the poem?

3. After you have thought about the meaning of the

TOTAL EFFECT OF A POEM

SELECTION: "Life Doesn't Frighten Me"

MEANING	SOUND	IMAGERY
Paraphrase: The speaker claims that in his or her world of reality and the imagination nothing is frightening. Only in dreams the speaker admits feeling fear. Yet the speaker's constant denial of fear shows how frightened he or she really is and that his or her escape may exist only in dreams. *Emotion:* terror, bravado, loneliness	*Rhythm:* regular *Alliteration:* "Mean old Mother Goose"; "Lions on the loose"; "Panthers in the park" *Rhyme:* frequent end rhyme: "wall / hall," "Goose / loose," "fun / run," "park / dark"	*Images of Sight:* "Shadows on the wall"; "Big ghosts in a cloud"; "Lions on the loose"; "Dragons breathing flame" *Images of sound:* "Noises down the hall"; "Bad dogs barking loud" *Images of motion:* "Boys all pull my hair"; "I can walk the ocean floor"

poem and have looked carefully at the techniques used in the poem, prepare a chart that will help you see how the techniques contribute to the meaning and how the poem as a whole affects you. One reader of "Life Doesn't Frighten Me" (page 290) prepared the chart above. A similar chart for another poem might also include a column headed FIGURES OF SPEECH.

■ WRITING PARAGRAPH BY PARAGRAPH

If your answer is just one paragraph, think of the following steps as applying to each sentence rather than to each paragraph.

1. Begin your introductory paragraph with a thesis statement, which should restate the major points made in the assignment. In other words, the thesis statement should refer briefly to the poem's impact on you, its meaning, and those techniques that the poet uses to create the poem's impact. The introductory paragraph can also include other general thoughts about the poem before you go on to discuss the specifics.

Example of Thesis Statement

In "Life Doesn't Frighten Me" Maya Angelou uses sound and imagery to remind us that all of us, each in our own way, have had to fight fears, both actual and imagined.

2. In each of the following paragraphs, focus on one technique. Supply examples of each technique.
3. In the concluding paragraph restate your thesis, using different words.

■ REVISING AND EDITING

See the Revising and Editing Checklist on page 611 for detailed reminders about improving your writing.

■ ASSIGNMENTS

1. Use the chart in this lesson to finish writing about the total effect of Maya Angelou's "Life Doesn't Frighten Me" (page 290).
2. Choose another poem from this book, and write about its total effect. Explain which techniques contribute to that effect. Use specific examples to support your views.

LESSON 6: *Writing About Nonfiction*

Nonfiction is factual prose writing. It provides true accounts of real people in real situations. Autobiographies, biographies, diaries, journals, essays, and magazine and newspaper articles are all examples of this kind of writing. Whether a piece of nonfiction is only a few paragraphs or as long as a book, you can analyze it using the same approach. First identify its central idea, and then discuss the various techniques that the author uses to communicate that idea.

■ TYPICAL ESSAY QUESTION

When you are asked to write about a piece of nonfiction, you are often asked to do an assignment such as the following:

A piece of nonfiction always has a central idea. To convey the central idea the author may use various techniques. For example, the author may provide facts, describe details, and give examples. What is the central idea in this piece of nonfiction? Mention the general techniques that the author uses to convey this idea, and give specific instances of each technique.

■ PREWRITING

1. Think about the central idea of the selection. If you have difficulty determining what the central idea is, ask yourself the following:

   a. What, if anything, does the title suggest about the author's opinion of the subject discussed in the selection?
   b. What opinion about life is suggested by the experiences that the author relates?
   c. What opinion about people in general is suggested by the experiences that the author relates?
   d. What ideas about the world in general are suggested by the details of setting?

2. Once you have determined the central idea of the selection, prepare a chart in which to record specific instances of the techniques that the author uses to convey that idea. After reading "Roanoke: The Lost Colony" (page 47), you might prepare the chart that appears in this lesson.

■ WRITING PARAGRAPH BY PARAGRAPH

If your answer is just one paragraph long, think of the following steps as applying to each sentence rather than to each paragraph.

1. Begin your introductory paragraph with a thesis statement that (1) indicates the central idea of the selection and (2) indicates in general terms which techniques the author uses to convey that central idea.

   Example of Thesis Statement
   In "Roanoke: The Lost Colony" Dan Lacy uses facts, descriptive details, and examples to show that the English settlers of Roanoke Island are remembered for their courage and the mystery of their fate.

   The rest of the introductory paragraph may say more about the central idea itself.

2. In each of the following paragraphs, show how the author uses one particular technique to communicate the selection's central idea. Following the topic sentence, give specific occurrences of that technique within the selection.

3. In the concluding paragraph restate your thesis statement from your introductory paragraph, using different words. This is also the place where you can tell whether you think the author supported the central idea as well as possible.

■ REVISING AND EDITING

See the Revising and Editing Checklist on page

ANALYZING NONFICTION

SELECTION: "Roanoke: The Lost Colony"

CENTRAL IDEA: The Roanoke Island settlers live on in our hearts, remembered both for their courage and for the sad and touching mystery of their disappearance.

FACTS	DESCRIPTIVE DETAILS	EXAMPLES
" . . . a large group of soldiers . . . sent to the island to build a fort . . . used up their supplies and returned to England . . ." "More than a dozen men had been left . . . to hold the island . . ."	When the settlers landed in 1587 to found their colony, all they found was "one bare skeleton" and a destroyed fort.	*Examples of unsuccessful attempts to solve mystery:* Because the captain of the little fleet refused to bring his damaged ships back to the stormy Outer Banks, John White was unable to return to Roanoke. He never saw his daughter and her child or any of the other settlers again.
" . . . colonists set out to make new . . . homes. Before end of August 1587, two . . . children of English parents . . . were born in America. Governor John White left for England to get 'more supplies.'"	"The gate hung open" and the huts were empty. "Pumpkins grew on the dirt floor and vines twined through the windows. . . . Books, papers, and pieces of armor were scattered about . . ."	Twenty years later, the English who settled Jamestown sent out explorers to discover what happened to the Lost Colony. "But . . . no survivors . . . were ever found."
"Not until 1590 did White . . . get back to Roanoke Island." "The settlers were gone, leaving nothing . . ."	"On a tree was carved the full word CROATOAN."	
White planned to leave next day for Croatan. "But a severe . . . storm left the . . . ships [of his fleet] unable to sail to the village." "John White never got back to Roanoke."	"The captain of the . . . fleet . . . was not willing to bring his damaged ships back to the stormy Outer Banks." " . . . no white man ever saw the settlers again."	
"Nobody knows what happened to them." "Twenty years later the English settled Jamestown in Virginia and [tried] to learn the fate of the lost colonists."	There were rumors that Powhatan had wiped out the colony. Other rumors said that some settlers had survived and were living among the Indians. " . . . no . . . survivors, if there were any, were ever found."	

611 for detailed reminders about improving your writing.

■ ASSIGNMENTS

1. Using the chart provided in this lesson for "Roanoke: The Lost Colony," discuss Lacy's central idea, and explain how he conveys that idea.

2. Choose "Bats" (page 415) or another selection you have read in this book and write a composition about nonfiction. Discuss the author's central idea and the techniques used to convey that idea.

READING AND LITERARY TERMS HANDBOOK

ALLITERATION *The repetition of consonant sounds, most often at the beginning of words.* For example, the title and first line of "Sarah Cynthia Sylvia Stout Would Not Take the Garbage Out" (page 353) repeat the sound of *s*.

   Sarah Cynthia Sylvia Stout

See page 355.
See also REPETITION.

ATMOSPHERE *The mood, or feeling, of a work of literature.* A vivid description of a story's setting creates an atmosphere that runs through the story. For example, the vivid descriptions of the cold weather in "The Cold Wave" (page 377) help the reader understand the challenges and dangers of winter.

See page 342.
See also DESCRIPTION,
SETTING.

AUDIENCE *The type of reader for whom a literary work is intended.* For example, Isaac Asimov probably wrote "Sarah Tops" (page 3) for an audience of readers who enjoy mystery and suspense.

See page 434.
See also PURPOSE.

AUTOBIOGRAPHY *The story of a person's life written by that person.* In the selection from *Homesick* (page 113), Jean Fritz writes about her life in China.

See page 125.
See also BIOGRAPHY,
NONFICTION.

BIOGRAPHY *The story of a person's life written by someone other than that person.*

See also
AUTOBIOGRAPHY,
NONFICTION.

CAUSE AND EFFECT *A relationship between events in which one event — the cause — is the reason that another event — the effect — takes place.* When the hay is cut in "The Exposed Nest" (page 374), the bird's nest is exposed. Cutting hay is the cause, and the exposed nest is the effect.

See page 233.
See also MOTIVATION.

CHARACTER *A person or animal in a story, novel, or play.* Each character has certain qualities, or **character traits,** that the reader discovers as the work unfolds. **Major characters** are the more important characters in a work, and **minor characters** are the less important characters. For example, in "President Cleveland, Where Are You?" (page 344), Jerry is a major character, while his friend Roger is a minor character.

See pages 106, 413, 467.
See also CONFLICT,
MOTIVATION.

CHARACTERIZATION *The personality of a character and the method by which an author reveals that personality to the reader.* For example, in "The Rescue of the Perishing" (page 245), Saroyan writes, "The angrier his father got with people, the kinder he became with his family," a direct statement about the father's personality. A character's personality also may be revealed indirectly, through the character's own words and actions. For instance, in the same story when his father offers to replace the stolen bike, the boy replies, "I liked my bike because I'd bought it with money I'd earned myself." These words reveal the boy's independence.

See page 266.
See also INFERENCE, MOTIVATION.

CHRONOLOGICAL ORDER *The time order in which events naturally happen.* In a literary work that follows chronological order, the event that takes place first is described first and so on until the last event. For instance, "The Water of Life" (page 201) is told in chronological order.

See page 206.
See also FLASHBACK.

CLIMAX *The point of the reader's highest interest and greatest emotional involvement in a story, novel, or play.* For example, the climax in "The Boy with Yellow Eyes" (page 7) occurs when Norman and Willie capture the stranger.

See page 14.
See also PLOT.

COMPARISON AND CONTRAST *A similarity (comparison) or difference (contrast) between two or more items.* For instance, in "The Jacket" (page 464) the contrast between the black leather biker's jacket with silver studs that the narrator wants and the green vinyl jacket that he gets helps the reader understand the frustration and disappointment that he feels.

CONFLICT *In the plot of a story, novel, or play, the struggle between two or more opposing forces.* An **external conflict** occurs when a character struggles against an outside force, such as nature, fate, or another person. For example, in "Watership Down" (page 81) there are external conflicts as the group of rabbits faces Threarah's men, the lendri, the dog, and a difficult river crossing. An **internal conflict** takes place within a character's mind. There is internal conflict within each of the rabbits'

minds as they struggle with the decision to leave the safety of the warren.

See pages 107, 321, 467, 582.
See also PLOT.

DESCRIPTION *The type of writing that creates a clear picture of something—a person, animal, object, place, or event.* Description is used in both fiction and nonfiction. For example, in "The Medicine Bag" (page 498) the descriptive writing used by the author when Martin's grandfather arrives creates a vivid picture of the event.

See page 385.
See also DETAILS, ESSAY, NARRATION, PERSUASION.

DETAILS *Particular features used to make descriptive writing more precise and lifelike.* For instance, in "The Green Mamba" (page 366) Roald Dahl helps the reader to see the snake-man with these details: "His eyes were pale blue, deep-set in a face round and dark and wrinkled as a walnut. Above the eyes, the eyebrows were thick and startlingly white, but the hair on his head was almost black. In spite of the thick leather boots, he moved like a leopard, with soft slow cat-like strides."

See pages 78, 420.
See also DESCRIPTION.

DIALOGUE *Conversation between characters in a literary work.* Dialogue can advance the plot or reveal the personalities of the characters. In drama dialogue is the most important method by which the author provides information about the characters.

See page 170.
See also DRAMA.

DRAMA *The form of literature that presents a story to be performed for an audience.* The written script of a drama contains **dialogue**—the speeches of the characters—and **stage directions**—the writer's descriptions of settings, characters, and actions. For example, the story of *The Phantom Tollbooth* (page 132) was first written as a novel, but in this book it is presented as drama so that the story may be performed.

See page 170.

ESSAY *A short piece of nonfiction that can deal with any subject.* An essay uses facts, examples, and reasons to express an idea or opinion. "Three Days to See" (page 299) is an essay that expresses Helen Keller's ideas and opinions about the sense of sight.

See page 309.
See also DESCRIPTION,
NARRATION,
PERSUASION.

FABLE *A brief folk tale told to teach a moral, or lesson.* Often the characters in fables are animals.

See also FOLK
LITERATURE, FOLK TALE,
MYTH.

FICTION *A prose narrative work of the imagination, including novels and short stories.*

See page 289.
See also NOVEL, SHORT
STORY.

FIGURATIVE LANGUAGE *Imaginative language used for descriptive effect and not meant to be taken as the literal truth.* Instances of figurative language are called **figures of speech.** For example, Nancy Wood uses figurative language in "Who Will Teach Me?" (page 356) when she describes time:

The years are clouds.

See also FIGURE OF
SPEECH, METAPHOR,
PERSONIFICATION,
SIMILE.

FIGURE OF SPEECH *A kind of figurative language.* **Similes** and **metaphors** are among the most

common figures of speech. For instance, in *My Side of the Mountain* (page 560), Jean Craighead George uses similes to describe the autumn sky at night when she writes, "'The moon is coming up behind the aspens. It is as big *as* a pumpkin and *as* orange. The winds are cool, the stars are *like* electric light bulbs.'"

See also FIGURATIVE
LANGUAGE, METAPHOR,
PERSONIFICATION,
SIMILE.

FLASHBACK *In a narrative, a scene or incident that breaks the normal time order of the plot to show an event that happened earlier.* For instance, after Kenny chooses his colt in "My Friend Flicka" (page 252), there is a flashback to the year before, when the colt was born. From this flashback the reader learns that Kenny loves the colt from the first time he sees her and why he names her Flicka.

See page 535.
See also
CHRONOLOGICAL
ORDER.

FOLK HERO *The central character in a folk tale.* Folk heroes have special traits, such as great strength or cleverness, that are much admired in their culture. In "The Wise Old Woman" (page 190) the farmer's mother is a folk hero.

See page 194.
See also FOLK
LITERATURE, FOLK TALE,
HERO.

FOLK LITERATURE *The collection of beliefs, customs, and traditions of a people.* Folk tales, myths, legends, and fables are part of folk literature. The selections found in "Myths, Tales, and Fabulous Beasts" are examples of folk literature.

See page 189.
See also FABLE,
FOLK TALE, LEGEND,
MYTH.

FOLK TALE *An old story that originally was told orally, or by word of mouth.* Folk tales are part of **folk literature**. In modern times a folk tale may be retold by a professional writer. For example, "Why the Tortoise's Shell Is Not Smooth" (page 186) is a folk tale retold by the contemporary author Chinua Achebe.

> See page 194.
> See also FABLE,
> FOLK HERO,
> FOLK LITERATURE,
> MYTH.

HERO *The central character of a work of literature.* A hero may be either male or female. In myths and folk tales heroes often have superhuman abilities. In most modern works heroes are more like ordinary people. In "The Rescue of the Perishing" (page 245), the boy is the hero of the story.

> See page 251.
> See also FOLK HERO.

IMAGE *A picture or likeness that is created with words.* Images are most often visual, but they may appeal to any of the five senses (sight, hearing, touch, taste, and smell). In "The Horned Toad" (page 506) Gerald Haslam uses a visual image, describing the vacant lot as resembling his father's head, "bare in the middle but full of growth around the edges."

> See also IMAGERY.

IMAGERY *Language that appeals to the senses.* Imagery is the combination or collection of images in a work of literature. For example, in "April Rain Song" (page 485) Langston Hughes appeals to the senses of touch and sound as well as sight to describe rain.

> See page 488.
> See also IMAGE.

INFERENCE *A conclusion that can be drawn from the available information.* For instance, in "Ta-Na-E-Ka" (page 269) when Mary returns, the reader learns about the state of her cousin Roger: "His eyes were red and swollen. He'd lost weight. His feet were an unsightly mass of blood and blisters." From this information we can infer that Roger underwent the ritual as he was trained to do.

> See page 112.
> See also
> CHARACTERIZATION,
> MOTIVATION.

LEGEND *A story that has some basis in history and is handed down from the past.* Most legends were originally passed down orally. The characters and actions are often exaggerated. "A Narrow Escape" (page 207) is a legend that is set in twelfth-century England and includes actual historical figures from that time.

> See page 217.
> See also FOLK
> LITERATURE.

LYRIC POEM *A poem that expresses a personal thought or emotion.* Most lyric poems are short and present vivid images of a particular thing. For example, "Life Doesn't Frighten Me" (page 290) is a lyric poem containing descriptions of what frightens the narrator.

> See page 292.
> See also NARRATIVE
> POEM.

MAIN IDEA *A sentence or group of sentences that sums up the author's message.* The main idea is the central idea of a work of literature. Details are used to illustrate and develop the main idea. For example, the main idea of "Earthquake: The Story of an Eyewitness" (page 327) is that San Francisco was struck by an earthquake and fires quickly followed. Jack London uses many details to describe how this happened.

> See page 420.
> See also TOPIC
> SENTENCE.

METAPHOR *A figure of speech that compares or equates two basically different things.* For example, in "Who Will Teach Me?" (page 356) Nancy Wood uses a metaphor in lines 6–7:

The years are clouds which
Cover my ancestors.

> See page 357.
> See also FIGURATIVE
> LANGUAGE, SIMILE.

MOTIVATION *A feeling, idea, or goal that causes a character to act in a certain way.* For instance, in *My Side of the Mountain* (page 536), when Sam finds a man asleep in his camp whom he fears may be an outlaw, he wakes him, talks to him, and helps him because of his desire for human companionship. This desire is Sam's motivation to communicate with the man.

> See page 477.
> See also CHARACTER,
> INFERENCE.

MYSTERY *A work of literature in which something is secret, hidden, or unknown.* For example, in "Sarah Tops" (page 3) the meaning of the words *Sarah Tops* is unknown throughout most of the story.

> See pages 32, 51.
> See also SUSPENSE.

MYTH *An ancient, anonymous story that conveys the beliefs and ideals of a culture and usually involves gods and goddesses.* Myths often provide examples of the way in which humans should behave. **Mythology** refers to the collection of myths of a particular people. "Pegasus and Bellerophon" (page 181) is an example of a Greek myth.

> See page 180.
> See also FOLK HERO,
> FOLK LITERATURE,
> FOLK TALE.

NARRATION *The type of writing that tells a story.* A narrative work may be either fiction or nonfiction.

Types of narrative writing include **autobiographies, biographies, narrative essays, short stories, novels,** and **narrative poems.**

> See page 407, 463.
> See also DESCRIPTION,
> ESSAY, PERSUASION.

NARRATIVE POEM *A poem that tells a story.* The events are often told in chronological sequence. Narrative poems usually include setting, characters, action, and conflict. "freddie the rat perishes" (page 310) is an example of a narrative poem.

> See page 313.
> See also LYRIC POEM.

NARRATOR *In a short story or novel, the person who tells the story.* A **first-person narrator** is a character in the work who tells the story as he or she experiences it. For example, Martin is a first-person narrator in "The Medicine Bag" (page 498), as he tells the story from his point of view. A **third-person narrator** is an outside observer—not a character in the story—who describes the thoughts and experiences of the characters. "The Landlady" (page 15) is written in the third person.

> See page 463.

NONFICTION *Factual prose writing.* Nonfiction always tells about incidents that really happened and people who really lived. Nonfiction includes **autobiography, biography,** and **essays.**

> See pages 51, 289.
> See also
> AUTOBIOGRAPHY,
> BIOGRAPHY, ESSAY.

NOVEL *A long work of prose fiction that tells a story.* Jean Craighead George's *My Side of the Mountain* (page 519) is a novel.

> See page 516.
> See also FICTION,
> PROSE, SHORT STORY.

OPINION *A statement expressing an individual's personal belief.* An opinion in not a **fact,** which is a statement that can be proved true. For example, in "The Game" (page 478) at the end of the first half, the narrator says, "They were beating us by seven points," a statement that can be proved true. After the second half starts and the narrator and Turk are put into the game, he says, "I know I'm not the best basketball player in the world, although I'm not bad, and I know Turk is worse than me," a statement that expresses the narrator's personal belief, or opinion.

> See also PERSUASION.

ORAL TRADITION *The handing down of songs, poems, legends, and folk tales from generation to generation by word of mouth.* The poem "Song for the Sun That Disappeared Behind the Rain Clouds" (page 79) is part of the oral tradition of the Hottentot people of Africa.

> See page 189.
> See also FOLK
> LITERATURE, FOLK TALE,
> LEGEND, MYTH.

PERSONIFICATION *A figure of speech in which an animal, object, or idea is given the characteristics of a human being.* For instance, in "Mi Madre" (page 296) the poet gives human qualities to the desert by describing it as she would her mother.

> See page 298.
> See also FIGURATIVE
> LANGUAGE, FIGURE OF
> SPEECH.

PERSUASION *The type of writing in which an author attempts to make the reader accept an opinion or take action of some kind.* For example, "Three Days to See" (page 299) is a persuasive essay in which Helen Keller expresses her opinions in order to persuade the reader to appreciate the sense of sight.

> See page 309.
> See also DESCRIPTION,
> ESSAY, NARRATION.

PLOT *The sequence of events in a short story, novel, or play.* A plot has a **conflict,** or struggle between opposing forces. The **climax** of a plot is the point of the reader's highest interest.

> See page 14, 225.
> See also CLIMAX,
> CONFLICT.

POETRY *Imaginative writing in which language, images, sound, and rhythm combine to create a special emotional effect.* Poetry is usually arranged in lines. Many poems have a regular **rhythm,** or pattern of beats, and some have **rhyme,** or repetition of sounds. Types of poetry include **narrative poetry** and **lyric poetry.**

> See pages 32, 292, 313.
> See also LYRIC POEM,
> NARRATIVE POEM.

PREDICTING OUTCOMES *Use of an author's clues to anticipate what will happen next in a story.* Predicting outcomes is a type of **inference.** For instance, when the man in "Miss Hinch" (page 55) leaves the restaurant to buy a newspaper, the reader can predict that the old woman will take the opportunity to leave as well.

> See page 67.
> See also INFERENCE,
> SUSPENSE.

PROSE *The kind of writing that is used in short stories, novels, works of nonfiction, journalism, and so forth.* Prose is distinguished from **poetry.** Unlike poetry, prose is usually written in lines that run from margin to margin across a page. Prose is also divided into sentences and paragraphs and is more like everyday speech than poetry.

> See also POETRY.

PURPOSE *The author's intention or goal in writing a particular work.* A writer's purpose may be to inform, entertain, or persuade the reader or to express an idea. For example, Russell Freedman's purpose in writing "A Cow Herder on Horseback" (page 284) is to inform readers about the factual details of a cowboy's life.

See page 434.
See also AUDIENCE, NONFICTION.

REPETITION *The repeated use of sounds, words, phrases, or lines.* Repetition emphasizes important items and helps unify a poem or other work of literature. For example, in "Arithmetic" (page 399) *double it, bigger,* and *higher* are repeated in the sixth line to emphasize how numbers increase when they are multiplied.

See also ALLITERATION, RHYME.

RHYME *The repetition of the same or similar sounds in words that appear near each other in a poem.* The most common type of rhymes are **end rhymes,** which occur at the ends of lines. **Perfect rhymes** are words that sound exactly alike except for the first consonant sound—for example, *go, low,* and *toe.* Lines 3 and 4 of "The Microscope" (page 396) contain end rhymes that are also perfect rhymes:

The waiting townsfolk fumed and *fussed*
As Anton's dry goods gathered *dust.*

See page 398.
See also REPETITION.

RHYTHM *The pattern of beats made by stressed and unstressed syllables in the lines of a poem.* A poem's rhythm usually reflects its meaning. For instance, a fast rhythm fits a poem of action, while a slower rhythm is appropriate in a poem that expresses a calm feeling. Rhythm may be regular and follow a repeated pattern, or it may be irregular. The first two lines of "The Bat" (page 421) follow a regular rhythm of alternating unstressed and stressed syllables:

By day / the bat / is cous / in to / the mouse.
He likes / the at / tic of / an ag / ing house.

See page 422.

SETTING *The time and place in which a work of literature takes place.* For example, the setting of "Earthquake: The Story of an Eyewitness" (page 327) is San Francisco after the earthquake of 1906.

See page 78.
See also ATMOSPHERE, DESCRIPTION.

SHORT STORY *A brief account of fictional events written in prose.* Most stories have one or more **characters**—people or animals—and take place in a particular time and place, or **setting.** The **plot** is the sequence of events in the story.

See page 6.
See also CHARACTER, FICTION, NARRATOR, PLOT, SETTING.

SIMILE *A figure of speech that uses the words* like *or* as *to compare two seemingly unlike things directly.* For example, in "freddy the rat perishes" (page 310), Don Marquis uses a simile to compare the tarantula to a match:

i am
so hot if you scratch me i will light
like a match.

See page 335.
See also FIGURATIVE LANGUAGE, METAPHOR.

STAGE DIRECTIONS *In drama, the writer's instructions for performing the work as well as descriptions of sets, characters, and actions.* For example, in *The Phantom Tollbooth* (page 132) before Scene One begins, there is a description of the scene and instructions: *"Lights up on the* CLOCK, *a huge alarm clock."* Often the writer gives short instructions for how a character should act; these are printed in parentheses following the character's name:

"DODECAHEDRON. [*Glaring from his upset face.*]"

See also DRAMA.

STAGING *The acting, costumes, sets, lighting, sound effects, and other special effects that bring a play to life.*

> See also DRAMA.

SUSPENSE *The reader's interest in the outcome of a work of literature.* For example, in "Miss Hinch" (page 55) the reader is eager to learn who the characters really are.

> See page 24.
> See also CLIMAX,
> PREDICTING OUTCOMES.

THEME *The central idea of a literary work, usually expressed as a generalization about life.* A **stated theme** is one that the author expresses directly in the work. For example, in "The Wise Old Woman" (page 190) Yoshiko Uchida states the theme of the folk tale in this sentence: "At last he realized how much wisdom and knowledge old people possess." An **implied theme** is one that is not stated directly in the work but is suggested by the work's other elements. For instance, in the selection from *Homesick* (page 113), the outcome of the conflict with which Jean Fritz struggles suggests the story's theme: "We can be proud of our nationality in a quiet manner."

> See pages 170, 275,
> 365, 447.

TITLE *The name of a work of literature.* The title sometimes refers to an important character or event or provides a clue to the main idea. For example, finding a way "To Build a Fire" (page 276) becomes Tom Vincent's goal in the story with that title.

TOPIC SENTENCE *A sentence that expresses the main idea of a paragraph.* The topic sentence usually appears very early in the paragraph, and the rest of the paragraph develops the idea stated in that sentence. For example, the fifth paragraph of "The Life and Death of a Western Gladiator" (page 441) describes the characteristics of the snake that allow it to survive. The first sentence of the paragraph states this topic: "He had certain qualifications that fitted him to be a competitive creature of this world and equipped him for its warfare."

> See also MAIN IDEA.

TOTAL EFFECT *The overall impact that a work of literature has on the reader.* All of the literary elements that a writer uses—**plot, character, setting,** and **theme**—work together to create the total effect.

> See pages, 513, 605.
> See also CHARACTER,
> PLOT, SETTING, THEME.

WORD CHOICE *The selection of words in a literary work to convey meaning, suggest the author's attitude, and create images.* For instance, in "Twister" (page 334) words like *ripped, tossed,* and *banged* help the reader understand the power of a tornado.

> See page 333.

GLOSSARY

The following Glossary lists words that are from the selections but may be unfamiliar to you. Many of the words have several different meanings. However, they are defined here only as they are used in the selections. Some words may be familiar to you in other contexts but may have unusual meanings in this text.

Each Glossary entry contains a pronunciation, a part of speech, and a definition. Some words are used in more than one way in the textbook and therefore have more than one definition. Occasionally a word has more than one part of speech. Related words are often combined in one entry: The main form (for example, the adjective *absurd*) is defined, and another form (for example, the noun *absurdity*) is listed after the main definition. Adverbs ending in *-ly* are usually listed after the definition of the adjective form.

Some unusual words or meanings of words are labeled ARCHAIC (old-fashioned). Other special usage labels include INFORMAL, CHIEFLY BRITISH, and so on.

The following abbreviations are used in this Glossary:

n.	noun	*adv.*	adverb
v.	verb	*conj.*	conjunction
adj.	adjective	*n. pl.*	plural noun

A key to pronunciations may be found in the lower right-hand corner of each right-hand page of the Glossary.

A

abide [ə bīd′] *v.* to put up with. —**abide by** to comply with; go along with.

absentminded [ab′sənt mīn′did] *adj.* lost in thought. —**absentmindedly,** *adv.*

absurd [ab surd′, ab zurd′] *adj.* ridiculous; contrary to reason and common sense. —**absurdity,** *n.*

abundance [ə bun′dəns] *n.* plentiful or overflowing supply; number or amount that is more than enough.

accelerate [ak sel′ə rāt′] *v.* to increase the speed of; cause to move faster.

access [ak′ses] *n.* way of entering or approaching.

accountant [ə kount′ənt] *n.* one who has charge of business and financial records.

accumulate [ə kū′myə lāt′] *v.* to grow in size, quantity, or number; increase gradually.

accusation [ak′yə zā′shən] *n.* charge of wrongdoing.

accuse [ə kūz′] *v.* fo find at fault or in error; blame; charge.

acidy [as′i dē] *adj.* sharp, biting, or sour in nature.

acknowledge [ak nol′ij] *v.* **1.** to admit the truth or fact of; confess. **2.** to express recognition of; take notice of.

acquainted [ə kwān′tid] *adj.* familiar (with someone or something).

acquire [ə kwīr′] *v.* **1.** to gain or get. **2.** to come to have.

acute [ə kūt′] *adj.* sharp; sensitive; intense.

adolescent [ad′əl es′ənt] *adj.* youthful; immature.

admonish [ad mon′ish] *v.* to advise strongly.

advantageous [ad′vən tā′jəs] *adj.* favorable; beneficial. —**advantageously,** *adv.*

affect [ə fekt′] *v.* to influence the emotions of; move.

afoot [ə foot′] *adv., adj.* **1.** on foot. **2.** astir.

agent [ā′jənt] *n.* person who has the power or authority to represent or act for another.

aggression [ə gresh′ən] *n.* practice of making violent attacks. —**aggressive** [ə gres′iv] *adj.*

agile [aj′əl] *adj.* able to move or think quickly and easily.

agitation [aj′ə tā′shən] *n.* state of being emotionally upset, shaken, or disturbed. —**agitated** [aj′ə tāt′id] *adj.*

agonize [ag′ə nīz′] *v.* to feel great pain; suffer greatly.

aimless [ām′lis] *adj.* without purpose or direction. —**aimlessly,** *adv.*

albatross [al′bə trôs′, al′bə tros′] *n.* web-footed sea bird having a long, hooked beak and able to fly for long periods of time.

allot [ə lot′] *v.* to distribute or divide into portions.

ally [ə lī′] *v.* to unite for a common purpose.

aloof [ə lōōf′] *adv.* at a distance; apart.

altar [ôl′tər] *n.* raised structure where sacrifices are made or gifts are given to a god.

amber [am′bər] *adj.* yellowish-orange or yellowish-brown color.

amid [ə mid′] *prep.* in the middle of; surrounded by.

amidst [ə midst′] *prep.* in the middle of; surrounded by.

ample [am′pəl] *adj.* more than enough.

anticipate [an tis′ə pāt′] *v.* **1.** to look forward to; expect. **2.** to take care of ahead of time; consider in advance.

anticipation [an tis′ə pā′shən] *n.* feeling of looking forward to something; expectation.

anxiety [ang zī′ə tē] *n.* feeling of fearful uneasiness; worry.

apparatus [ap′ə rat′əs, ap′ə rā′təs] *n.* machine, equipment, device, or appliance for a particular purpose.

applicant [ap′li kənt] *n.* person who asks or applies (for something).

appreciate [ə prē′shē āt′] *v.* **1.** to recognize the worth or quality of; value. **2.** to be grateful for. **3.** to be keenly sensitive to. —**appreciative** [ə prē′shə tiv] *adj.* —**appreciatively,** *adv.*

appreciation [ə prē′shē ā′shən] *n.* **1.** act of recognizing the quality or worth of. **2.** gratitude. **3.** sensitive understanding.

apprehension [ap′ri hen′shən] *n.* fear of what may happen.

arc [ärk] *v.* to move in a curved line.

armor [är′mər] *n.* defensive or protective covering for the body, usually made of metal.

arrogant [ar′ə gənt] *adj.* overly proud; conceited.

ascend [ə send′] *v.* to move upward physically; rise.

ashen [ash′ən] *adj.* pale.

aspect [as′pekt] *n.* appearance.

aspen [as′pən] *n.* a poplar tree found in the Northern Hemisphere, having small, rounded, papery leaves.

assimilate [ə sim′ə lāt′] *v.* to take in and include in one's own thinking.

assortment [ə sôrt′mənt] *n.* varied collection.

assumption [ə sump′shən] *n.* something taken for granted.

assurance [ə shoor′əns] *n.* freedom from doubt; certainty.

attentive [ə ten′tiv] *adj.* paying attention; quick to notice. —**attentiveness,** *n.*

attire [ə tīr′] *v.* to clothe; dress.

audible [ô′də bəl] *adj.* loud enough to be heard.

auditory [ô′də tôr′ē] *adj.* relating to the sense organs and hearing.

auspicious [ôs pish′əs] *adj.* promising; favorable; showing signs of success.

authentic [ô′then′tik] *adj.* genuine; real.

autograph [ô′tə graf′] *n.* one's personal signature.

avert [ə vurt′] *v.* to turn away or aside.

avid [av′id] *adj.* eager; enthusiastic.

B

baboon [ba boon′] *n.* African monkey that has a long, doglike muzzle, cheek pouches that store food, front and back legs of almost equal length, and a short tail.

bade [bad, bād] *v.* past tense of **bid.**

banish [ban′ish] *v.* **1.** to send away. **2.** to force to leave a country or land.

bank [bangk] *n.* rising ground bordering a body of water.

bankrupt [bangk′rupt′, bangk′rəpt] *v.* to use up completely, especially funds.

barometer [bə rom′ə tər] *n.* instrument for measuring the pressure put forth by the weight of the earth's atmosphere, used in weather forecasting.

baron [bar′ən] *n.* **1.** man of noble birth or rank. **2.** a businessman of great wealth and influence.

barracks [bar′əks] *n. pl.* set of buildings for housing soldiers or other military personnel.

barrier [bar′ē ər] *n.* something that blocks the way.

basin [bā′sin] *n.* container that is usually round with a wide, flat bottom and sloping sides; shallow bowl.

bayonet [bā′ə nit, bā′ə net′] *n.* large knife or dagger that can be attached to the end of a rifle and used for stabbing.

beacon [bē′kən] *n.* guiding or warning signal, especially a light or fire.

bear [bâr] *v.* **1.** to give birth to. **2.** to bring forth; produce.

befall [bi fôl′] *v.* to happen to.

beseech [bi sēch′] *v.* to beg; plead with. —**beseeching,** *adj.* —**beseechingly,** *adv.*

bewilder [bi wil′dər] *v.* to confuse completely.

bewilderment [bi wil′dər mənt] *n.* state of complete confusion.

bewitching [bi wich′ing] *adj.* fascinating; enchanting; charming. —**bewitchingly,** *adv.*

bid [bid] *v.* **1.** to tell (someone) what to do; command; order. **2.** to say; wish.

bide [bīd] *v.* to wait. —**bide one's time** to wait patiently for a good opportunity.

bleak [blēk] *adj.* **1.** dreary; cheerless; depressing. **2.** bare; open; empty.

blissful [blis′fəl] *adj.* full of supreme happiness or joy. —**blissfully,** *adv.*

bluff [bluf] *v.* to discourage or frighten without really meaning what one does.

blunt [blunt] *adj.* straight to the point in both speech and manner; outspoken. —**bluntness,** *n.*

bobwhite [bob′hwīt′, bob′wīt′] *n.* American bird of the eastern and central United States having reddish-brown feathers with streaks of white, brown, and tan.

boisterous [bois′tə rəs, bois′trəs] *adj.* noisy and lively.

boredom [bôr′dəm] *n.* the state or condition of weariness or restlessness because something is dull or uninteresting.

borne [bôrn] *v.* past participle of **bear.**

bout [bout] *n.* contest of strength or skill.

bribe [brīb] **1.** *n.* money or gifts given in order to persuade someone to do something. **2.** *v.* to give money or gifts in order to persuade someone to do something.

brood [brood] *n.* **1.** all of the children in one family. **2.** a group of the same kind or breed.

browse [brouz] *v.* **1.** to glance through or look at casually or leisurely. **2.** to feed, as on leaves or twigs.

brusque [brusk] *adj.* rude in manner or speech; abrupt. —**brusquely,** *adv.*

buck [buk] *n.* adult male animal, as of the deer, antelope, or rabbit.

bunt [bunt] *v.* to strike or push with the head; butt.

buoyant [boi′ənt, boo′yənt] *adj.* cheerful; lighthearted.

burrow [bur′ō] *n.* hole or tunnel dug in the ground, as by a rabbit or fox, for safety or a place to live.

C

cache [kash] *n.* provisions or treasure hidden or stored in a hiding place.

calculate [kal′kyə lāt′] *v.* to determine by reasoning.

calculation [kal′kyə lā′shən] *n.* careful planning.

camouflage [kam′ə fläzh′] **1.** *n.* any disguise that serves to hide by blending in with the background. **2.** *v.* to disguise something in order to hide it.

caper [kā′pər] *v.* to leap or jump about in a playful manner.

carcass [kär′kəs] *n.* the dead body of an animal.

carp [kärp] *n.* freshwater fish.

carriage [kar′ij] *n.* manner of carrying and holding the head and body.

cask [kask] *n.* large, wooden barrel, usually used to hold liquids.

catastrophe [kə tas′trə fē′] *n.* great and sudden disaster or misfortune.

cattail [kat′tāl′] *n.* tall marsh plant having long, narrow leaves and flowers clustered in spikes that turn velvety brown.

ceremony [ser′ə mō′nē] *n.* established act that is performed in a set way on or for some particular occasion. —**ceremonial** [ser′ə mō′nē əl] *adj.*

chagrin [shə grin′] *v.* to embarrass; annoy greatly.

champ [champ] *v.* to crush and chew vigorously and noisily.

chaotic [kā ot′ik] *adj.* utter confusion and disaster.

characteristic [kar′ik tə ris′tik] *n.* quality or feature that is typical of or essential to a person or thing.

characterize [kar′ik tə rīz′] *v.* to describe the qualities or features of (a person or thing).

chemistry [kem′is trē] *n.* science dealing with the composition and properties of substances and their changes.

cherish [cher′ish] *v.* to care for tenderly; hold dear.

chrysanthemum [krə san′thə məm] *n.* plant with large, globe-shaped, and often very brightly colored flower heads.

cinders [sin′dərz] *n. pl.* ashes.

circuit [sur′kit] *n.* **1.** act of going around; circular motion. **2.** route over which a person or group makes repeated journeys at certain times.

---

at; āpe; cär; end; mē; it; īce; hot; ōld; fôrk; wood; fool; oil; out; up; ūse; turn; ə in ago, taken, pencil, lemon, circus; bat; chin; dear; five; game; hit; hw in white; joke; kit; lid; man; not; singer; pail; ride; sat; shoe; tag; thin; this; very; wet; yes; zoo; zh in treasure; KH in loch, German ach; N in French bon; œ in French feu, German schön

civilized [siv'ə līzd'] *adj.* advanced beyond what is crude and simple; refined.

clamber [klam'bər, klam'ər] *v.* to climb awkwardly.

clamor [klam'ər] *n.* loud, noisy outcry; uproar.

cobble [kob'əl] *n.* a rounded stone, used in paving streets.

colleague [kol'ēg] *n.* fellow member of a profession or worker.

collective [kə lek'tiv] *adj.* **1.** united. **2.** representing a whole group. —**collectively,** *adv.*

colt [kōlt] *n.* male horse under four years old.

commend [kə mend'] *v.* to express admiration for; praise.

commotion [kə mō'shən] *n.* noisy disturbance, excitement, or disorder.

companionship [kəm pan'yən ship'] *n.* friendship; fellowship.

compassion [kəm pash'ən] *n.* sorrow for another's suffering, combined with a desire to help. —**compassionate,** *adj.*

compel [kəm pel'] *v.* to force; command.

compensate [kom'pən sāt'] *v.* to make equal return or payment to; make up for.

competition [kom'pə tish'ən] *n.* trial or match for determining relative skill or ability; contest with another or others. —**competitive** [kəm pet'ə tiv'] *adj.*

competitor [kəm pet'ə tər] *n.* one who is involved in a competition.

complex [kəm pleks', kom'pleks] *adj.* difficult to understand or analyze; complicated.

compound [kom'pound'] *n.* enclosed area.

comprehend [käm'pri hend'] *v.* to understand.

compulsion [kəm pul'shən] *n.* driving force; an urge that cannot be resisted.

compulsory [kəm pul'sər ē] *adj.* that must be done; required.

comrade [kom'rad, kom'rəd] *n.* companion; associate; friend.

concede [kən sēd'] *v.* to grant or give (what is asked), as a right or privilege.

concoction [kon kok'shən, kən kok'shən] *n.* mixture of several ingredients.

condescend [kon'di send'] *v.* to act as if one is coming down to the level of someone lower than oneself; make oneself seem superior.

confines [kon'fīnz] *n. pl.* limit; boundary; border.

conflict [kon'flikt] *n.* **1.** clash; opposition; disagreement. **2.** emotional struggle of opposite desires within a person.

confront [kən frunt'] *v.* to bring face to face with; put before.

congeal [kən jēl'] *v.* to change from a fluid to a solid state; solidify.

congenial [kən jēn'yəl, kən jēn'ē əl] *adj.* agreeable; pleasant; friendly.

congregate [kong'grə gāt'] *v.* to bring or come together in a crowd.

conscience [kon'shəns] *n.* mental or emotional sense that makes one do what is right and recognize the difference between right and wrong.

consequence [kon'sə kwens', kon'sə kwəns] *n.* **1.** What results from an earlier action; effect. **2.** social distinction, as in rank or position; importance in society.

conservationist [kon'sər vā'shə nist] *n.* person who works for the protection and care of natural resources, such as forests, rivers, and wildlife.

considerable [kən sid'ər ə bəl] *adj.* great in amount or extent. —**considerably** [kən sid'ər ə blē] *adv.*

consideration [kən sid'ə rā'shən] *n.* careful thought.

consistent [kən sis'tənt] *adj.* showing no change; not varying. —**consistently,** *adv.*

conspicuous [kən spik'ū əs] *adj.* attracting attention; easily seen.

conspiracy [kən spir'ə sē] *n.* secret plan by several people to perform some evil or illegal act.

constitution [kon'stə tōō'shən, kon'stə tū'shən] *n.* physical makeup or structure of the human body, especially in regard to strength or ability to resist disease.

construct [kən strukt'] *v.* to put together; build.

contemplation [kon'təm plā'shən] *n.* act of thinking about something long and thoroughly.

contempt [kən tempt'] *n.* the feeling that a person, act, or thing is low or worthless.

contend [kən tend'] *v.* **1.** to fight; compete. **2.** to deal (with something). —**contender,** *n.*

contraption [kən trap'shən] *n.* INFORMAL. mechanical device, especially when being criticized.

contrivance [kən trī'vəns] *n.* invention; mechanical device.

contrive [kən trīv'] *v.* to plan in a clever way; invent.

convincing [kən vin'sing] *adj.* able to be believed. —**convincingly,** *adv.*

coon [kōōn] *n.* INFORMAL. raccoon.

corpse [kôrps] *n.* dead body, especially human.

corral [kə ral'] *n.* area that is fenced in for cattle, horses, or other livestock.

correlation [kôr'ə lā'shən, kor'ə lā'shən] *n.* relationship of or connection of one thing with another.

correspondence [kôr'ə spon'dəns, kor'ə spon'dəns] *n.* communication through the writing of letters.

cosset [kos'it] *v.* to treat as a pet; treat very tenderly; pamper.

countenance [koun'tə nəns] *n.* facial expression; look.

covet [kuv'it] *v.* to want eagerly or excessively to own or have something.

cower [kou'ər] *v.* to crouch, cringe, or tremble, as in fear.

coyote [kī ō'tē, kī'ōt] *n.* wolflike mammal that is found mainly in the prairies of central and western North America, known for its howling at night.

crag [krag] *n.* steep, rugged, or projecting rock or cliff.

cranny [kran'ē] *n.* small, narrow opening; crack.

crave [krāv] *v.* to long for; eagerly desire.

crossbeam [krôs'bēm'] *n.* any large beam that is placed across another.

crosswise [krôs'wīz'] *adv.* so as to be crossed; across.

culvert [kul'vərt] *n.* any structure that provides for the free flow of water under such passages as roads, sidewalks, and railroads.

curdle [kurd'əl] *v.* to thicken, especially in regard to sour milk.

D

dagger [dag'ər] *n.* small swordlike weapon, having a pointed blade.

dainty [dān'tē] *adj.* graceful; delicate. —**daintily** [dān'ti lē] *adv.*

dame [dām] *n.* elderly woman.

darn [därn] *v.* to mend (a tear or hole in clothing) by sewing.

dauntless [dônt'lis] *adj.* fearless; courageous. —**dauntlessly,** *adv.*

deceitful [di sēt'fəl] *adj.* lying; dishonest. —**deceitfulness,** *n.*

decipher [di sī'fər] v. to make out the meaning of (something difficult to read or understand).

decisive [di sī'siv] adj. showing determination; firm. —**decisively**, adv.

decline [di klīn'] n. decrease, as in amount.

decree [di krē'] **1.** v. to issue an official decision or order. **2.** n. official decision or order.

deem [dēm] v. to think; believe; judge.

defensive [di fen'siv] adj. protective; guarding against attack. —**defensively**, adv.

deficiency [di fish'ən sē] n. lack of something essential or important.

deformed [di fôrmd'] adj. badly shaped, especially in body or limbs.

deft [deft] adj. skillful, especially in movement of the hands. —**deftly**, adv.

defy [di fī'] v. to resist openly or strongly. —**defiance**, n.

dehydrate [dē hī'drāt] v. to lose water; become dry. —**dehydration** [dē'hī drā'shən] n.

dejected [di jek'tid] adj. low in spirits; depressed. —**dejectedly**, adv.

dejection [di jek'shən] n. sadness; depression.

delectable [di lek'tə bəl] adj. highly pleasing to the taste; delicious.

delicacy [del'i kə sē] n. uncommon or choice food.

delirium [di lēr'ē əm] n. wild excitement or emotion.

deplorable [di plôr'ə bəl] adj. miserable; terrible.

depot [dē'pō] n. railroad or bus station.

deranged [di rānjd'] adj. mentally disordered; insane; crazy.

derive [di rīv'] v. to get or obtain from a source or origin.

derrick [der'ik] n. structure built over an oil well that supports the drilling machinery.

descendant [di sen'dənt] n. one who is the offspring of a particular ancestor or group of ancestors.

desist [di zist', di sist'] v. to stop.

desolate [des'ə lit] adj. deserted.

desolation [des'ə lā'shən] n. condition of being deserted.

detached [di tacht'] adj. not emotionally involved; unconcerned.

detachment [di tach'mənt] n. state of not being emotionally involved; lack of concern.

detect [di tekt'] v. to notice; discover; find out.

detonate [det'ən āt'] v. to explode or cause to explode suddenly and with a loud noise. —**detonation** [det'ə nā'shən] n.

devastate [dev'əs tāt'] v. to destroy; ruin.

diagonal [di ag'ən əl] adj. running at a slant from corner to corner. —**diagonally**, adv.

dialect [dī'ə lekt'] n. form of a language spoken in a specific area or by a specific group of people that differs enough from the standard form of the language to be a distinct variety but not enough to be a separate language.

digestion [di jes'chən, dī jes'chən] n. process by which food is broken down into simple parts so that it can be used by the body. —**digestive** [di jes'tiv] adj.

dilemma [di lem'ə] n. difficult choice.

diligence [dil'ə jəns] n. constant attention to one's work or duty. —**diligent** [dil'ə jənt] adj. —**diligently**, adv.

discern [di surn', di zurn'] v. to be or become aware of through the senses; recognize.

disconcert [dis'kən surt'] v. to throw into disorder or confusion.

disconsolate [dis kon'sə lit] adj. without cheer, hope, or comfort. —**disconsolately**, adv.

discordant [dis kôrd'ənt] adj. not in agreement or harmony; clashing; sharply differing.

disdain [dis dān'] v. to consider unworthy or beneath oneself; look down on. —**disdainful**, adj. —**disdainfully**, adv.

disenchant [dis'in chant'] v. to free from a spell. —**disenchantment**, n.

dishonor [dis on'ər] n. shame; disgrace. —**dishonorable**, adj.

disinfectant [dis'in fek'tənt] n. substance used to destroy harmful germs.

disinterested [dis in'tris tid, dis in'tər is tid] adj. uninterested; indifferent. —**disinterestedly**, adv.

dislodge [dis loj'] v. to move or force out of a place or position.

dismal [diz'məl] adj. dreary; miserable; cheerless.

dismissal [dis mis'əl] n. the act of sending away.

dispense [dis pens'] v. to give out; distribute.

distinction [dis tingk'shən] n. act of making or noting a difference.

disuse [dis yōoz'] v. to use no longer; stop using.

divert [di vurt', dī vurt'] v. to draw (the mind or attention) to another direction.

divine [di vīn'] adj. having superhuman qualities; supremely excellent.

documentary [dok'yə men'tər ē, dok'yə men'trē] adj. presenting material that is based on fact, not made up or created.

doe [dō] n. adult female animal, as of the deer, antelope, or rabbit.

domestic [də mes'tik] adj. of animals living with or near human beings and cared for by them; tame; gentle.

domesticate [də mes'tə kāt'] v. to train an animal to live with human beings; tame.

dominant [dom'ə nənt] adj. most powerful or numerous; leading. —**dominance** [dom'ə nəns] n.

dominate [dom'ə nāt'] v. **1.** to rule over; govern. **2.** to occupy a towering position over (the surroundings).

doom [dōom] n. something that cannot be escaped, especially something unfavorable; destiny.

dormant [dôr'mənt] adj. inactive; quiet; still.

dote [dōt] v. to give extreme affection or love.

drone [drōn] **1.** n. dull, continuous buzzing or humming sound. **2.** v. to talk in a dull, unchanging, or unvaried tone.

dry [drī] adj. lacking warmth or emotion; cold. —**dryly**, adv.

dry goods [drī gōodz] n. fabrics and related items, such as thread, ribbon, or lace, as distinguished from other merchandise, such as hardware or groceries.

dumbfound [dum'found', dum'found'] v. to surprise greatly and make unable to speak; amaze.

dutiful [dōo'ti fəl, dū'ti fəl] adj. obedient; respectful. —**dutifully**, adv.

dwelling [dwel'ing] n. place of residence; house.

---

at; āpe; cär; end; mē; it; īce; hot; ōld; fôrk; wood; fōol; oil; out; up; ūse; turn; ə in ago, taken, pencil, lemon, circus; bat; chin; dear; five; game; hit; hw in white; joke; kit; lid; man; not; singer; pail; ride; sat; shoe; tag; thin; this; very; wet; yes; zoo; zh in treasure; KH in loch, German ach; N in French bon; œ in French feu, German schön

dwindle [dwind′əl] *v.* to become gradually smaller or less; shrink.

dynamic [dī nam′ik] *adj.* showing great energy; forceful.

dynamite [dī′nə mīt′] *n.* **1.** a powerful explosive. **2.** one who has explosive or powerful qualities.

E

ecology [ē kol′ə jē] *n.* relationship of living things to their environment and to one another.

economy [i kon′ə mē] *n.* system of managing the production, distribution, and consumption of wealth, goods, and services.

ecstatic [ek stat′ik] *adj.* overwhelmed with joy; greatly delighted. —**ecstatically**, *adv.*

effective [i fek′tiv] *adj.* producing or capable of producing a desired result.

efficient [i fish′ənt] *adj.* able to produce the effect wanted without waste of time or energy. —**efficiency** [i fish′ən sē] *n.*

elate [i lāt′] *v.* to make joyful; excite.

element [el′ə mənt] *n.* any of the four substances—earth, water, air, and fire—once believed to make up the universe.

elk [elk] *n.* large, mooselike deer found in northern Europe or Asia.

eloquent [el′ə kwənt] *adj.* using expressive, effective, and vivid language, especially in public speaking. —**eloquence** [el′ə kwəns] *n.*

elude [i lood′] *v.* to avoid or escape; slip away from.

embark [em bärk′] *v.* to set out, as on an adventure or course of action.

embed [em bed′] *v.* to stick (something) into an enclosing or surrounding object or substance.

embers [em′bərz] *n. pl.* the remains of fires that burn and smoke with little or no flame.

emboss [em bôs′, em bos′] *v.* to decorate with designs or prints that are raised above the surface.

emigration [em′ə grā′shən] *n.* the act of moving from one place or country to live in another.

eminence [em′ə nəns] *n.* a very high place or thing.

empire [em′pīr] *n.* union of countries or territories ruled or controlled by the government of one country.

employ [em ploi′] *v.* to use the services of (someone) for wages, salary, or other compensation; hire.

employee [em ploi′ē, em′ploi ē′] *n.* one who works for another person or business for wages or salary.

employer [em ploi′ər] *n.* person or business that uses the services of one or more other persons for wages, salary, or other compensation; boss.

endure [en door′, en dyoor′] *v.* to put up with; tolerate.

engage [en gāj′] *v.* **1.** to attract and hold (one's attention or interest); involve. **2.** to enter into and fight.

ensue [en soo′] *v.* to occur as a consequence; come afterward; follow.

envious [en′vē əs] *adj.* **1.** feeling dislike or desire because another has what one wants; jealous. **2.** longing; wishful. —**enviously**, *adv.*

envision [en vizh′ən] *v.* to picture in one's mind; imagine.

equate [i kwāt′] *v.* to treat or represent as equal or comparable.

escort [es′kôrt] *n.* person who goes along with another as a courtesy or honor or to protect, especially a male who accompanies a female to a party.

essence [es′əns] *n.* quality or feature that makes a thing what it is; necessary part.

essential [i sen′shəl] *adj.* **1.** necessary for the existence of something. **2.** belonging or basic to something by its very nature.

estate [es tāt′] *n.* large piece of land, usually owned by one person.

examination [ig zam′ə nā′shən] *n.* test.

exertion [ig zər′shən] *n.* vigorous use of energy; strenuous effort.

exile [eg′zīl, ek′sīl] *n.* state of being forced to live away from home and country.

exotic [ig zot′ik] *adj.* strangely beautiful or pleasant; highly unusual.

expanse [iks pans′] *n.* wide, unbroken area.

exploit [eks′ploit, iks ploit′] *n.* notable, heroic deed.

exterminate [iks tur′mə nāt′] *v.* to destroy (living things); wipe out. —**extermination** [iks tur′mə nā′shən] *n.*

extinguish [iks ting′gwish] *v.* to put out; quench.

extremity [iks trem′ə tē] *n.* extreme condition, especially of danger.

exultation [eg′zul tā′shən, ek′sul tā′shən] *n.* extreme joy or delight.

F

faculty [fak′əl tē] *n.* one of the natural powers of the mind or body.

falcon [fal′kən, fôl′kən, fô′kən] *n.* hawklike bird having a short, hooked bill, pointed wings, and gray or brown feathers, usually with white markings.

famine [fam′in] *n.* extreme shortage or lack of food.

famish [fam′ish] *v.* to be extremely hungry; starve.

fanatical [fə nat′i kəl] *adj.* overly and unreasonably devoted to a cause or belief.

fashion [fash′ən] *v.* to give form to; shape; mold.

fawn [fôn] *n.* deer less than one year old.

feeble [fē′bəl] *adj.* weak. —**feebly** [fē′blē] *adv.*

feline [fē′līn] *adj.* of or relating to cats or the cat family.

feminine [fem′ə nin] *adj.* characteristic of or relating to a female.

fend [fend] *v.* **1.** to provide for oneself. **2.** to keep away; ward off.

ferocity [fə ros′ə tē] *n.* state or quality of being savage, cruel, or fierce.

fertile [furt′əl] *adj.* producing or able to produce many crops, plants, or vegetation.

fertilize [furt′əl īz′] *v.* to make fertile; make productive.

fervent [fur′vənt] *adj.* showing deep feeling or great emotion; enthusiastic. —**fervently**, *adv.*

fidget [fij′it] *v.* to be nervous or uneasy; move about restlessly. —**fidgety**, *adj.*

flabbergast [flab′ər gast′] *v.* INFORMAL. to astonish; put in a state of confusion.

flagging [flag′ing] *adj.* weakening; tiring.

flail [flāl] *v.* to toss or thrash about.

flank [flangk] **1.** *n.* part between the ribs and the hip on either side of an animal or human being. **2.** *v.* to be located at the side of.

flannel [flan′əl] *n.* soft cotton fabric.

flask [flask] *n.* small, flattened, bottle-shaped container made to be carried in the pocket.

flats [flats] *n. pl.* unbroken, level ground.

flaw [flô] *n.* broken or weak spot; crack.

fleck [flek] *v.* to mark with small particles; spot.

flinch [flinch] *v.* to draw back or away, as from something painful or unpleasant; shrink.

flint [flint] *n.* a hard, dull-gray mineral that produces sparks when struck against steel.

flounder [floun′dər] *v.* to move with stumbling motions; struggle clumsily.

flourish [flur′ish] *v.* to grow or develop strongly or successfully; thrive.

fluster [flus′tər] *v.* to cause to be embarrassed or at a loss; confuse.

fodder [fod′ər] *n.* coarse food for livestock (cattle, horses, or sheep), such as various grasses or straw.

foliage [fō′lē ij] *n.* growth of leaves on a tree or other plants.

folly [fol′ē] *n.* lack of good sense or understanding; foolishness.

forage [fôr′ij, for′ij] *v.* to hunt or search about for food.

forcible [fôr′sə bəl] *adj.* having strength; powerful. —**forcibly**, *adv.*

forelock [fôr′lok′] *n.* lock or cluster of hair growing just above the forehead.

foremost [fôr′mōst′] *adv.* before any other or anything else.

foreshadow [fôr shad′ō] *v.* to show or indicate beforehand.

foresight [fôr′sīt′] *n.* care or thought for the future.

forester [fôr′is tər, for′is tər] *n.* one who practices or has been trained in forestry, the science that deals with the management and care of forests.

foretell [fôr tel′] *v.* to tell about beforehand; predict.

foretold [fôr tōld′] *v.* past tense of **foretell.**

forlorn [fôr lôrn′] *adj.* hopeless; miserable; very unhappy.

formidable [fôr′mi də bəl] *adj.* **1.** arousing fear or dread because of size or power. **2.** causing admiration or wonder; very impressive.

found [found] *v.* to set up or establish.

fracture [frak′chər] *v.* to break; split; crack.

fray [frā] *n.* noisy fight or disturbance.

frigid [frij′id] *adj.* extremely cold.

frock [frok] *n.* woman's or girl's dress.

frond [frond] *n.* leaflike part of certain plants.

fruitful [frōōt′fəl] *adj.* producing results; profitable.

fruitless [frōōt′lis] *adj.* producing no effect or result; useless. —**fruitlessly**, *adv.*

full-fledged [fool′flejd′] *adj.* having full rank or status.

fund [fund] *n.* sum of money set aside for a specific purpose.

fundamental [fun′də men′təl] *n.* anything that serves as the basis of a thing or system; basic or essential part.

funnel [fun′əl] *n.* tube that carries away smoke or provides fresh air.

furtive [fur′tiv] *adj.* done or acting in a secret manner. —**furtively**, *adv.*

fuse [fūz] *v.* to blend or unite.

futile [fū′til, fū′tīl] *adj.* not having an effect; useless. —**futilely**, *adv.*

G

gadget [gaj′it] *n.* small mechanical device.

gaiety [gā′ə tē] *n.* merrymaking; cheerful liveliness.

gait [gāt] *n.* way of walking or running.

gallant [gal′ənt] *adj.* brave; noble; high-spirited.

galvanize [gal′və nīz′] *v.* to cover (metal, especially iron or steel) with a protective coating of zinc.

garb [gärb] *n.* clothing, especially a particular style of dressing.

garland [gär′lənd] **1.** *n.* wreath of flowers, leaves, vine, or similar materials, usually worn around the head for decoration. **2.** *v.* to decorate with one or more garlands.

garment [gär′mənt] *n.* article or piece of clothing.

garter [gär′tər] *n.* band or strap, usually elastic, worn to hold up a stocking or a sock.

gawk [gôk] *v.* stare stupidly.

gazette [gə zet′] *n.* newspaper.

generosity [jen′ə ros′ə tē] *n.* willingness to give or share freely.

genial [jēn′yəl, jē′nē əl] *adj.* pleasant and cheerful; friendly. —**genially**, *adv.*

glade [glād] *n.* open space in a wood or forest.

glaze [glāz] *v.* to become glassy.

glimmer [glim′ər] **1.** *n.* dim, flickering light. **2.** *v.* to shine with a dim sparkle.

glower [glou′ər] *v.* to look at angrily or threateningly.

goad [gōd] *v.* to urge on; stir to action.

goner [gô′nər, gon′ər] *n.* one who or something that is dying, ruined, lost, or beyond help or recovery.

gouge [gouj] *v.* to dig or tear out; poke out.

graduate [graj′ōō āt′] *v.* to arrange or place in a series of steps, stages, or degrees.

granite [gran′it] *n.* hard, lasting rock made of feldspar, quartz, and other, darker minerals, often used for buildings.

grievous [grē′vəs] *adj.* of a very serious nature; dangerous.

grimace [grim′is, gri mās′] *v.* to twist or distort the face, as in expressing pain or displeasure.

grind [grīnd] *v.* to wear down, smooth, or sharpen by rubbing one object against another.

gristle [gris′əl] *n.* tough connective tissue in meat. —**gristly**, *adj.*

grudge [gruj] **1.** *n.* strong feeling of ill will or anger that is held for a long time. **2.** *v.* to give or allow with resentment. —**grudging**, *adj.* —**grudgingly**, *adv.*

guile [gīl] *n.* skill in deception; slyness.

guileless [gīl′lis] *adj.* honest; sincere.

gully [gul′ē] *n.* ditch cut in the earth by running water.

gut [gut] *v.* to destroy the inside of.

guzzle [guz′əl] *v.* to drink (or eat) greedily.

H

habitation [hab′ə tā′shən] *n.* place where people live; settlement.

haggard [hag′ərd] *adj.* worn and thin from being tired or from suffering in some way.

harass [har′əs, hə ras′] *v.* to bother or annoy constantly.

hasten [hā′sən] *v.* to cause to move or act quickly; speed up.

---

at; āpe; cär; end; mē; it; īce; hot; ōld; fôrk; wood; fōol; oil; out; up; ūse; turn; ə in ago, taken, pencil, lemon, circus; bat; chin; dear; five; game; hit; hw in white; joke; kit; lid; man; not; singer; pail; ride; sat; shoe; tag; thin; this; very; wet; yes; zoo; zh in treasure; KH in loch, German ach; N in French bon; œ in French feu, German schön

hasty [hās'tē] *adj.* hurried; quick.

haughty [hô'tē] *adj.* having or showing excessive pride in oneself and looking down on others. —**haughtily** [hô'ti lē] *adv.*

haven [hā'vən] *n.* place of safety or shelter.

havoc [hav'ək] *n.* general destruction; ruin.

hazel [hā'zəl] *adj.* yellowish-brown color.

hazy [hā'zē] *adj.* not clear; not easily understood. —**hazily** [hā'zi lē] *adv.*

heave [hēv] *n.* act of rising and falling in a continuously flowing pattern.

heedless [hēd'lis] *adj.* not paying attention; careless. —**heedlessly,** *adv.*

heifer [hef'ər] *n.* young cow that has not given birth.

hemlock [hem'lok'] *n.* a tall evergreen tree of the pine family, found in North America and Asia.

herald [her'əld] *n.* one who proclaims or announces; messenger.

heritage [her'ə tij] *n.* what is handed down from previous generations or from the past; tradition.

hesitate [hez'ə tāt'] *v.* to wait or stop a moment; pause briefly. —**hesitating,** *adj.* —**hesitatingly,** *adv.*

hesitation [hez'ə tā'shən] *n.* delay in action because one cannot decide or is unsure. —**hesitant** [hez'ə tənt] *adj.* —**hesitantly,** *adv.*

hilarious [hi lār'ē əs, hī lār'ē əs] *adj.* very funny. —**hilariously,** *adv.*

hinder [hin'dər] *v.* to hold back.

hindsight [hīnd'sīt'] *n.* the understanding of an event and its effects after it is over.

hoard [hôrd] *n.* group of items that have been stored up and often hidden, especially for future use.

hoax [hōks] *n.* trick or deception.

horde [hôrd] *n.* large group or crowd moving or doing something together.

horrendous [hô ren'dəs, ho ren'dəs] *adj.* horrible; dreadful; frightful.

horrify [hôr'ə fī', hor'ə fī'] *v.* to shock greatly; cause terror.

hospitable [hos'pi tə bəl, hos pit'ə bəl] *adj.* offering a friendly and generous welcome to guests or strangers.

hospitality [hos'pə tal'ə tē] *n.* generous treatment of guests and strangers.

hostility [hos til'ə tē] *n.* state of being an enemy; feeling of extreme hatred.

hubbub [hub'ub] *n.* loud confused noise, as of many voices or sounds.

humanity [hū man'ə tē, ū man'ə tē] *n.* all human beings taken together.

hurl [hurl] *v.* to throw with force.

hysteria [his ter'ē ə, his tēr'ē ə] *n.* extreme terror, anger, grief, or other strong emotion. —**hysterical** [his ter'i kəl] *adj.*

ideally [ī dē'ə le, ī dēl'ē] *adv.* perfectly or in the best possible way.

idle [īd'əl] **1.** *adj.* not engaged in any work or activity; inactive. **2.** *v.* to move aimlessly or without care. —**idly** [īd'lē] *adv.*

illuminate [i loo'mə nāt'] *v.* to give light to; light up.

imminent [im'ə nənt] *adj.* about to happen, in regard to something bad; threatening.

immortal [i môrt'əl] *n.* a being that does not die, such as a god in Greek mythology.

impel [im pel'] *v.* to drive or urge to some action.

impending [im pen'ding] *adj.* about to happen, in regard to something bad; threatening.

implement [im'plə mənt] *n.* tool; instrument.

implore [im plôr'] *v.* to beg; plead with; ask earnestly. —**imploring,** *adj.* —**imploringly,** *adv.*

improvise [im'prə vīz'] *v.* to make up and say on the spur of the moment and without preparation.

impulse [im'puls] *n.* **1.** force that causes one to act without thinking or planning. **2.** sudden force that causes motion.

impulsive [im pul'siv] *adj.* tending to act without thinking or planning.

incense [in'sens] *n.* a substance producing a pleasant odor when burned.

incessant [in ses'ənt] *adj.* never stopping; constant. —**incessantly,** *adv.*

incidentally [in'sə dent'lē, in'sə dent'əl ē] *adv.* by the way.

incite [in sīt'] *v.* to cause by urging or arousing; do something to bring about.

inclined [in klīnd'] *adj.* having a tendency toward some quality or condition.

incomprehensible [in'käm pri hen'sə bəl] *adj.* unable to be understood.

inconsiderate [in'kən sid'ər it] *adj.* showing a lack of care for others and their feelings; thoughtless. —**inconsiderateness,** *n.*

incredible [in kred'ə bəl] *adj.* seemingly impossible; hard to believe. —**incredibly** [in kred'ə blē] *adv.*

incredulous [in krej'ə ləs] *adj.* not willing to believe something; doubting.

indestructible [in'di struk'tə bəl] *adj.* unable to be destroyed; lasting. —**indestructibility** [in'də struk'tə bil'ə tē] *n.*

indifferent [in dif'ər ənt, in dif'rənt] *adj.* **1.** having or showing a lack of feeling, concern, or care. **2.** not having a preference one way or another. —**indifference** [in dif'ər əns] *n.*

individualize [in'də vij'oo ə līz'] *v.* to consider separately.

induce [in doos', in dūs'] *v.* to lead by influence; motivate; persuade.

industry [in'dəs trē] *n.* a particular branch of business, trade, or manufacture. —**industrial** [in dus'trē əl] *adj.*

ineffectual [in'i fek'choo əl] *adj.* not getting the desired result; producing no effect.

infrared [in'frə red] *adj.* relating to energy waves just beyond the red end of the visible spectrum of light.

ingenuity [in'jə noo'ə tē, in'jə nū'ə te] *n.* cleverness; originality.

ingratitude [in grat'ə tood', in grat'ə tūd'] *n.* lack of appreciation; ungratefulness.

inhabitant [in hab'ət ənt] *n.* person or animal that lives in a place.

inherit [in her'it] *v.* to receive from an ancestor, predecessor, or previous era.

inheritance [in her'ət əns] *n.* anything that is received from an ancestor, predecessor, or previous era; something that is or may be inherited.

inimitable [in im'ə tə bəl] *adj.* unable to be imitated; unique.

initiate [i nish'ē āt'] *v.* to introduce or begin.

inject [in jekt'] *v.* to force (fluid) through the skin into a muscle, vein, or other organ.

injection [in jek'shən] *n.* introduction of some factor into a situation.

inlet [in′let′] *n.* narrow channel of water between islands.

innermost [in′ər mōst′] *adj.* farthest from the outside; most inward.

inscription [in skrip′shən] *n.* message written on something when it is presented or given to someone.

insignificant [in′sig nif′ə kənt] *adj.* having little meaning or importance.

insistent [in sis′tənt] *adj.* being positive and firm, as in repeating a statement. —**insistently,** *adv.*

instantaneous [in′stən tā′nē əs] *adj.* occurring at once or without delay.

instinctive [in stingk′tiv] *adj.* arising from a natural, unlearned tendency to behave in a certain way. — **instinctively,** *adv.*

intact [in takt′] *adj.* complete or not tampered with.

intent [ɪn tent′] *n.* intention; aim; purpose. —**intentness,** *n.*

interact [in′tə rakt′] *v.* to act on or influence each other. —**interaction** [in′tə rak′shən] *n.*

intersperse [in′tər spurs′] *v.* to scatter at certain points between or among other things.

intervene [in′tər vēn′] *v.* to be or lie between.

intimate [*v.*, in′tə māt′; *adj.*, in′tə mit] **1.** *v.* to hint; suggest. **2.** *adj.* having a close personal connection.

intimidate [in tim′ə dāt′] *v.* to make timid or fearful.

intoxicate [in tok′sə kāt′] *v.* to excite greatly; delight.

intrude [in trood′] *v.* to enter or come in without welcome or permission. —**intruder,** *n.*

intuitive [in too′ə tiv, in tū′ə tiv] *adj.* possessing the ability to learn or know something without conscious or deliberate reasoning.

inventory [in′vən tôr′ē] *n.* detailed list of articles in stock at a given time.

invincible [in vin′sə bəl] *adj.* unable to be overcome or defeated. —**invincibility** [in vin′sə bil′ə tē] *n.*

involuntary [in vol′ən ter′ē] *adj.* happening without choice or control. —**involuntarily** [in vol′ən ter′i lē] *adv.*

irrepressible [ir′i pres′ə bəl] *adj.* cannot be held back.

irrigate [ir′ə gāt′] *v.* to supply (land) with water by means of channels, streams, or pipes. —**irrigation** [ir′ə gā′shən] *n.*

irritable [ir′ə tə bəl] *adj.* easily excited to impatience or anger; easily annoyed.

isolate [ī′sə lāt′, is′ə lāt′] *v.* to place or set apart; separate from others. —**isolation** [ī′sə lā′shən] *n.*

J

jack rabbit [jak rab′it] *n.* a North American hare having very long ears and long, powerful back legs.

jaded [jā′did] *adj.* worn-out; tired.

jalopy [jə lop′ē] *n.* old or broken-down automobile.

jaunt [jônt, jänt] *n.* short trip, especially one taken for pleasure.

jest [jest] *v.* to speak or act in a joking or playful manner.

jigsaw puzzle [jig′sô′ puz′əl] *n.* puzzle consisting of irregularly shaped cardboard or wood pieces that can be fitted together to form a picture.

jubilant [jōō′bə lənt] *adj.* joyful; in high spirits.

K

keel [kēl] *n.* **1.** main timber or steel piece that extends the whole length of the bottom of a boat or ship. **2.** any structure or part that looks like a ship's keel.

kin [kin] *n.* one's whole family; relatives.

kindred [kin′drid] *adj.* like; similar.

kinfolk [kin′fōk′] *n. pl.* one's whole family; relatives.

knave [nāv] *n.* dishonest or disloyal man.

knoll [nōl] *n.* small, rounded hill or mound.

L

laborer [lā′bər ər] *n.* worker, especially one who performs work with the hands.

laden [lād′ən] *adj.* loaded with things.

lair [lâr] *n.* home or resting place, especially of a wild animal.

lanky [lang′kē] *adj.* ungracefully tall and thin.

lapse [laps] *v.* to slip or fall into a former condition.

larder [lär′dər] *n.* place where food is kept; pantry.

lavender [lav′ən dər] *n.* pale reddish-purple color.

lavish [lav′ish] *adj.* **1.** given or done excessively or generously. **2.** showy; overly done. —**lavishly,** *adv.*

layoff [lā′ôf′] *n.* act of firing a large number of workers.

leisure [lē′zhər, lezh′ər] *n.* freedom from the demands of work or duty.

leisurely [lē′zhər lē, lezh′ər lē] *adv.* in an unhurried or relaxed manner.

lest [lest] *conj.* in order to prevent the possibility that; for fear that.

lethargy [leth′ər jē] *n.* state of being inactive or dull; lack of energy.

levitate [lev′ə tāt′] *v.* to rise or float in the air. —**levitation** [lev′ə tə′shən] *n.*

liberal [lib′ə rəl, lib′rəl] *adj.* plentiful; generous; more than enough.

lichen [lī′kən] *n.* a nonflowering plant that grows on tree trunks, rocks, or the ground.

light-headed [līt′hed′id] *adj.* dizzy or mentally confused.

listless [list′lis] *adj.* without energy; showing little interest.

literally [lit′ər ə lē, lit′rə lē] *adv.* without exaggeration; actually; really.

loaf [lōf] *v.* to spend time doing nothing.

loam [lōm] *n.* soil that is a mixture of clay, sand, and other matter that has been carried and deposited by water.

loathing [lō′thing] *n.* extreme disgust or hate.

locomotion [lo′kə mō′shən] *n.* act of moving from place to place.

lodging [loj′ing] *n.* temporary place to stay, as for the night.

loiter [loi′tər] *v.* to hang around without a purpose or without anything to do.

lollop [läl′əp] *v.* to move in a clumsy or relaxed way.

lounge [lounj] **1.** *v.* to lean or sit lazily or in a relaxed manner. **2.** *n.* a room, as in a hotel, filled with comfortable furniture for relaxing. —**lounger,** *n.*

lull [lul] *v.* to lead into a quiet or calm condition.

lunge [lunj] *v.* to move forward suddenly.

lure [loor] *v.* to attract powerfully.

lurid [loor′id] *adj.* shining with a reddish glow or fiery glare.

---

at; āpe; cär; end; mē; it; īce; hot; ōld; fôrk; wood; fōōl; oil; out; up; ūse; turn; ə in ago, taken, pencil, lemon, circus; bat; chin; dear; five; game; hit; hw in white; joke; kit; lid; man; not; singer; pail; ride; sat; shoe; tag; thin; this; very; wet; yes; zoo; zh in treasure; KH in loch, German ach; N in French bon; œ in French feu, German schön

M

magnitude [mag′nə too͞d′, mag′nə tūd′] *n.* greatness of size or extent.

maiden [mād′ən] *n.* girl or young unmarried woman.

majestic [mə jes′tik] *adj.* very grand, dignified, or noble. —**majestically,** *adv.*

malicious [mə lish′əs] *adj.* desiring to cause harm or injury to another; intentionally harmful.

malignant [mə lig′nənt] *adj.* very harmful; tending to become worse and cause death.

mangle [mang′gəl] *v.* to disfigure or mutilate, as by tearing or crushing; bruise badly.

mango [mang′gō] *n.* **1.** yellowish-red, oval, edible fruit having a sweet, spicy taste. **2.** tropical evergreen tree bearing this fruit.

manicure [man′ə kyoor′] *v.* to trim evenly, closely, or elaborately.

manila [mə nil′ə] *adj.* made of Manila hemp, a fiber.

manipulate [mə nip′yə lāt′] *v.* to manage or work with the hands, especially with skill; handle.

marina [mə rē′nə] *n.* dock where supplies, repairs, and other services are available for small boats.

mariner [mar′ə nər] *n.* sailor.

marshal [mär′shəl] *n.* officer who carries out orders and performs other duties similar to those of a sheriff.

massage [mə säzh′] *v.* to rub parts of the body, especially to relax muscles or ease pain.

massive [mas′iv] *adj.* marked by great size or extremely large, as in scope, scale, degree, or intensity.

mast [mast] *n.* long pole of wood set upright in a sailing boat or ship to support the sails and rigging.

materialize [mə tēr′ēə līz′] *v.* to appear (in physical form).

meager [mē′gər] *adj.* small in amount or quantity.

melancholy [mel′ən kol′ē] *adj.* gloomy; sad.

membrane [mem′brān] *n.* thin layer of tissue that acts as a lining or covering for an organ or body part.

mesh [mesh] *n.* **1.** knit or knotted fabric made of an open network of threads with evenly spaced, small holes. **2.** interconnected web.

midriff [mid′rif] *n.* area of the body below the chest and above the waist; middle part of the body.

migrant [mi′grənt] *n.* one who moves seasonally or periodically from one region or climate to another.

migration [mi grā′shən] *n.* the movement of large groups of animals from one region to another that occurs at regular periods, such as seasons.

mildew [mil′doo͞′, mil′dū′] *v.* to be affected with nongreen plants that appear as discolored areas on leather or other materials.

misshapen [mis shā′pən] *adj.* twisted or bent out of the usual form or shape.

modification [mod′ə fi kā′shən] *n.* small change; adjustment.

momentous [mō men′təs] *adj.* of great importance.

monarch [mon′ərk] *n.* **1.** one like a king or queen in rank, dignity, or importance. **2.** king or queen having limited powers.

monotone [mon′ə tōn′] *n.* single, unvaried tone in speaking.

monotonous [mə not′ən əs] *adj.* **1.** displaying a lack of change or sameness in tone or sound. **2.** tiresome or uninteresting because of a lack of change or variety.

moor [moor] *v.* to put, fasten firmly, or anchor (a ship or other craft) in place.

morsel [môr′səl] *n.* small bite or portion, as of food.

mottled [mot′əld] *adj.* spotted or streaked with color.

multitude [mul′tə tood′, mul′tə tūd′] *n.* a large number of people or things.

mundane [mun dān′, mun′dān] *adj.* common; ordinary.

mutilate [mūt′əl āt′] *v.* to injure seriously and horribly by cutting, tearing, or breaking off some part; deform.

mutiny [mū′tə nē] *n.* forcible or open rebellion against authority.

mutual [mū′choo əl] *adj.* possessed or shared in common.

muzzle [muz′əl] *n.* projecting part of the head of an animal, including the mouth, nose, and jaws; snout.

myriad [mir′ē əd] *adj.* of an indefinitely large number; countless.

N

nestle [nes′əl] *v.* to be situated in a snug or sheltered place.

niche [nich] *n.* part in a wall that is hollowed out or indented from the rest.

nigh [nī] *adv.* practically; almost.

nonchalant [non′shə länt′, non′chə länt′] *adj.* showing a lack of interest or enthusiasm. —**nonchalantly,** *adv.*

nonetheless [nun′the les′, nun′the les′] *adv.* nevertheless; however.

notation [nō tā′shən] *n.* system of signs or symbols used to represent values, quantities, or other facts or information.

nuisance [noo͞′səns, nū′səns] *n.* one who annoys or offends.

O

oasis [ō ā′sis, ō′ə sis] *n.* any place or thing that gives relief from dullness or sameness.

obsess [əb ses′] *v.* to occupy or trouble the mind greatly, especially as a fixed idea; preoccupy.

obstacle [ob′stə kəl] *n.* one who or that which opposes, stands in the way, or blocks progress.

ogre [ō′gər] *n.* fearsome giant or monster.

ominous [om′ə nəs] *adj.* suggesting future evil; threatening.

opposition [op′ə zish′ən] *n.* state of being against someone or something.

oppressive [ə pres′iv] *adj.* **1.** very uncomfortable; causing physical or mental exhaustion. **2.** causing a feeling of pressure or distress; weighing heavily upon one.

ornate [ôr nāt′] *adj.* overly or heavily decorated or designed.

oust [oust] *v.* to force or drive out.

outskirts [out′skurts′] *n. pl.* regions or sections at the edge of a specified area.

P

pageant [paj′ənt] *n.* elaborate presentation, parade, procession, or exhibition.

pall (pôl] *n.* a dark, gloomy covering.

palsied [pôl′zēd] *adj.* powerless, as if paralyzed; helpless.

panic [pan′ik] *n.* sudden, overpowering fear. —**panicky,** *adj.*

panorama [pan′ə ram′ə, pan′ə rä′mə] *n.* complete or unbroken view of an area in every direction.

panther [pan′thər] *n.* large wild animal of the cat family, especially one having a solid black coat.

paralysis [pə ral′ə sis] *n.* loss of the power of motion or sensation in any part of the body.

paralyze [par′ə līz′] *v.* to make helpless, powerless, or ineffective.

parchment [pärch′mənt] *n.* material made from the skin of sheep or goats for use in writing.

partridge [pär′trij] *n.* game bird found mainly in regions of Europe, Asia, and Africa, having feathers patterned with gray, brown, and white markings.

patrol [pə trōl′] *v.* to go through or around (an area or place) for the purpose of guarding or inspecting. —**patroller,** *n.*

patron [pā′trən] *n.* customer.

pedestal [ped′əst əl] *n.* base or supporting structure, especially for a statue.

pedigree [ped′ə grē′] *n.* pure breed. —**pedigreed,** *adj.*

pellet [pel′it] *n.* small ball, as of food, medicine, or paper.

peppercorn [pep′ər kôrn′] *n.* dried fruit of the black pepper, used as a spice, either whole or ground.

perchance [pər chans′] *adv.* by chance; possibly; perhaps.

peremptory [pə remp′tər ē] *adj.* not permitting argument or delay; commanding.

peril [per′əl] *n.* **1.** chance or risk of injury, loss, or destruction; danger. **2.** something that may cause injury or damage.

perpendicular [pur′pən dik′yə lər] *adj.* upright; vertical.

perpetual [pər pech′ōō əl] *adj.* lasting forever or a very long time that seems forever. —**perpetually,** *adv.*

perplex [pər pleks′] *v.* to fill with uncertainty; confuse.

perplexity [pər plek′sə tē] *n.* confusion.

pervasive [pər vā′siv] *adj.* able to or tending to spread through every part.

perverse [pər vurs′] *adj.* willfully tending to go against what is expected or required. —**perversely,** *adv.*

pessimistic [pes′ə mis′tik] *adj.* expecting the worst.

pestilence [pes′tə ləns] *n.* easily and rapidly spreading disease.

petroleum [pi trō′lē əm] *n.* thick, sticky, flammable liquid used to make products such as gasoline.

petty [pet′ē] *adj.* of little importance.

philosophy [fə los′ə fē] *n.* the study of the basic purpose and nature of humanity, the universe, and life itself. —**philosophical,** *adj.*

pile [pīl] *n.* **1.** large building. **2.** raised cut or uncut soft loops that form the surface of a fabric or carpet.

pillar [pil′ər] *n.* long, upright structure, usually of stone, wood, or metal, that serves as a support for a building or stands alone as a monument; column.

placard [plak′ärd, plak′ərd] *n.* **1.** large, usually printed paper or cardboard sign; poster. **2.** small sign or notice.

plague [plāg] *v.* to trouble or annoy greatly.

plight [plīt] *n.* unfortunate or dangerous situation.

plot [plot] *n.* small piece of ground or land.

plow [plou] *v.* to break and turn up the surface of (soil) with a farm tool, usually drawn by animals or a tractor.

plumage [plōō′mij] *n.* entire coat of feathers of a bird.

plumed [plōōmd] *adj.* adorned with feathers.

poach [pōch] *v.* to hunt or fish illegally, as on another's property.

poignant [poin′yənt] *adj.* bringing out emotions, especially sadness; touching.

polliwog [pol′ē wog′] *n.* early form or stage of a frog or toad, having external gills, an egg-shaped body, and a slender tail; tadpole.

pommel [pum′əl, pom′əl] *n.* upward-projecting front part of a saddle, with a horn that is used for gripping or holding a lariat.

ponder [pän′dər] *v.* to consider; think over in a careful way.

ponderous [pon′dər əs] *adj.* **1.** extremely heavy. **2.** clumsy, slow, or difficult. —**ponderously,** *adv.*

poplar [pop′lər] *n.* any of a small group of fast-growing trees of the willow family, having pale bark and wide leaves.

portal [pôrt′əl] *n.* large doorway, gate, or entrance.

porter [pôr′tər] *n.* one who is hired to carry things, such as luggage, for another, especially a man who is hired to carry luggage at a railroad station or in a hotel.

posthole [pōst′hōl′] *n.* a hole in the ground that holds a fence post.

pout [pout] *v.* to be gloomy, sad, or resentful.

precautionary [pri kô′shə ner′ē] *adj.* advising or using caution or care beforehand.

precede [pri sēd′] *v.* to come before or ahead of.

precipitous [pri sip′ə təs] *adj.* very steep. —**precipitously,** *adv.*

predator [pred′ə tər] *n.* animal that lives by hunting and killing other animals for food.

preside [pri zīd′] *v.* to have authority, direction, or control (over).

prestige [pres tēzh′, pres tēj′, pres′tij] *n.* influence or authority based on success, reputation, or achievements.

presumable [pri zōō′mə bəl] *adj.* likely; probable. —**presumably,** [pri zōō′mə blē] *adv.*

prevail [pri vāl′] *v.* **1.** to be effective; succeed. **2.** to be the most usual; exist most widely.

primarily [pri mer′ə lē] *adv.* chiefly; most importantly.

primary [prī′mer′ē, prī′mər ē] *adj.* **1.** first or greatest in importance. **2.** original.

probe [prōb] *v.* to investigate, examine, or explore completely.

proceeding [prə sē′ding] *n.* action or course of action.

proclamation [prok′lə mā′shən] *n.* that which is officially announced.

profound [prə found′] *adj.* far-reaching; extensive.

promenade [prom′ə nād′, prom′ə näd′] *n.* place or area for leisurely walking.

proposal [prə pō′zəl] *n.* something put forward for consideration, such as a plan or course of action.

propose [prə pōz′] *v.* to make an offer of marriage.

proprietor [prə prī′ə tər] *n.* owner.

prospect [pros′pekt] *v.* to search or explore, especially for valuable material.

prospective [prə spek′tiv] *adj.* probable or expected; future.

prosper [pros′pər] *v.* to succeed; have wealth or good fortune. —**prosperous,** *adj.*

protein [prō′tēn, prō′tē in] *n.* any of a large group of compounds containing carbon, nitrogen, hydrogen, and oxygen and present in all living cells.

---

at; āpe; cär; end; mē; it; īce; hot; ōld; fôrk; wood; fōōl; oil; out; up; ūse; turn; ə in ago, taken, pencil, lemon, circus; bat; chin; dear; five; game; hit; hw in white; joke; kit; lid; man; not; singer; pail; ride; sat; shoe; tag; thin; <u>th</u>is; very; wet; yes; zoo; zh in treasure; ᴋʜ in loch, German ach; ɴ in French bon; œ in French feu, German schön

proverb [prov'ərb] *n.* short saying expressing popular wisdom.

provide [prə vīd'] *v.* to fit out with what is needed or desired. —**provider,** *n.*

proximity [prok sim'ə tē] *n.* nearness; closeness.

prudent [prōōd'ənt] *adj.* having good judgment; wise.

pudgy [puj'ē] *adj.* fat.

pulsation [pul sā'shən] *n.* single beat or vibration.

punctual [pungk'chōō əl] *adj.* acting or happening at the correct or appointed time. —**punctuality** [pungk'chōō al'ə tē] *n.*

purify [pyoor'ə fī'] *v.* to make or become totally pure or clean.

Q

quagmire [kwag'mīr', kwog'mīr'] *n.* soft, muddy ground.

quail [kwāl] *n.* game bird having gray or brown feathers that are usually speckled with white.

qualification [kwol'ə fi kā'shən] *n.* any ability or accomplishment that makes someone or something suitable for a certain privilege, position, or other function.

quest [kwest] *n.* search or pursuit made in order to achieve a goal.

R

ragamuffin [rag'ə muf'in] *n.* ragged, dirty, unkempt person.

ragged [rag'id] *adj.* rough or uneven.

ramshackle [ram'shak'əl] *adj.* likely to fall down; rickety.

rank [rangk] *adj.* having a strong, rotten smell.

ravine [rə vēn'] *n.* deep, narrow valley.

ravishing [rav'i shing] *adj.* causing much joy; delightful.

realm [relm] *n.* kingdom.

rebellious [ri bel'yəs] *adj.* refusing to obey; resisting authority and control.

receptive [ri sep'tiv] *adj.* able or willing to receive or meet.

recollect [rek'ə lekt'] *v.* to remember.

recount [ri kount'] *v.* to tell in detail, especially a story.

reed [rēd] *n.* tall grass having long, narrow leaves and slender, hollow stems, growing mainly around wet areas.

reek [rēk] *v.* to give off a very strong odor or smell.

refugee [ref'ū jē', ref'ū jē'] *n.* one who leaves home because of danger and seeks safety in another place.

regulate [reg'yə lāt'] *v.* to control according to a rule or system.

regulation [reg'yə lā'shən] *n.* order intended to control behavior or procedure.

reign [rān] *v.* to hold or exercise the power of a ruler.

rejoin [rē join'] *v.* to come together again.

relapse [*n.,* rē'laps'; *v.,* ri laps', rē'laps'] **1.** *n.* act of falling back into an earlier and worse condition. **2.** *v.* to slip or fall back into a former condition.

relative [rel'ə tiv] *adj.* resulting from or determined by comparison. —**relatively,** *adv.*

relent [ri lent'] *v.* to become softer or gentler in attitude; give in.

relentless [ri lent'lis] *adj.* not easing or lessening, as in intensity.

relish [rel'ish] *n.* pleasure; enjoyment.

reluctance [ri luk'təns] *n.* unwillingness.

remainder [ri mān'dər] *n.* what is left; remaining part.

remote [ri mōt'] *adj.* not near; far away or off.

render [ren'dər] *v.* to cause to be or become; make.

reproach [ri prōch'] *v.* to blame for a fault or wrongdoing.

reproduce [rē'prə dōōs', rē'prə dūs'] *v.* to create others of the same kind, especially living creatures.

reservation [rez'ər vā'shən] *n.* land set aside by the U.S. government for an Indian tribe or group to live on.

residence [rez'ə dəns] *n.* place where one makes one's home permanently or for a long period of time. —**residential** [rez'ə den'shəl] *adj.*

respite [res'pit] *n.* short period of rest or relief, especially from work or unpleasantness.

revelation [rev'ə lā'shən] *n.* the recognition of new information, especially when it is striking.

reverberate [ri vur'bə rāt'] *v.* to send back the sound of; resound.

reverie [rev'ər ē] *n.* daydream.

ridge [rij] *n.* long and narrow elevation of land.

rigamarole [rig'ə mə rōl'] *n.* foolish rambling talk; nonsense.

rigid [rij'id] *adj.* not bending; stiff.

rind [rīnd] *n.* firm outer covering or skin.

riotous [rī'ə təs] *adj.* disorderly; noisy.

ritual [rich'ōō əl] *n.* formal set of acts performed on a special occasion.

rivalry [rī'vəl rē] *n.* the act of attempting to get someone or something that another person wants; competition.

rivet [riv'it] *v.* to fasten or hold (attention) firmly.

rude [rōōd] *adj.* roughly made or formed.

ruinous [rōō'i nəs] *adj.* bringing or tending to bring destruction; disastrous.

rummage [rum'ij] *v.* to search thoroughly and haphazardly.

runner [run'ər] *n.* one of the long narrow parts on which a sled glides.

ruthless [rōōth'lis] *adj.* without mercy or pity. —**ruthlessly,** *adv.*

S

sac [sak] *n.* pouch or pouchlike part in a plant or animal that often contains a liquid.

sacred [sā'krid] *adj.* regarded with respect similar to the kind shown to holy things.

sage [sāj] *n.* pleasant-smelling leaves of a small plant of the mint family that are usually used for flavoring but may be used for healing.

sassafras [sas'ə fras'] *n.* a small tree found in North America and Asia, whose roots have a bark that is used as a flavoring.

satchel [sach'əl] *n.* small bag, sometimes having a shoulder strap.

saunter [sôn'tər, sän'tər] *v.* to walk in a leisurely, relaxed way; stroll.

savor [sā'vər] *v.* to take great delight or pleasure in.

scorch [skôrch] *v.* **1.** to damage the surface of by burning. **2.** SLANG. to travel at high speed.

scores [skôrz] *n. pl.* uncertain large number; very many.

scoundrel [skoun'drəl] *n.* dishonest person.

scraggy [skrag'ē] *adj.* having a rough, ragged appearance.

scythe [sīth] *n.* a hand tool consisting of a long, curved blade attached at an angle to a long, bent handle.

sear [sēr] *v.* to burn the surface of; scorch.

security [si kyoor'ə tē] *n.* protection from danger.

sedate [si dāt′] *adj.* quiet; calm.

seethe [sēth] *v.* to be in continuous motion or activity.

segment [seg′mənt] *n.* section; part.

semicircle [sem′ē sur′kəl] *n.* half a circle or something in the form of half a circle.

sentry [sen′trē] *n.* person or animal that is stationed to keep watch and alert others of danger.

serene [sə rēn′] *adj.* peaceful; calm.

serial [sēr′ē əl] *n.* long story broken up into parts, usually with the end of each part leading into the next.

shaft [shaft] *n.* **1.** ray; beam. **2.** a harsh, critical remark.

sharecropper [shār′krop′ər] *n.* person who farms land for the owner in return for part of the crops.

sheer [shēr] *adj.* straight up or down; extremely steep.

shoal [shōl] *n.* large group.

shrewd [shrood] *adj.* clever in practical matters.

shun [shun] *v.* to keep away from; avoid.

shutter [shut′ər] *v.* to close in order to provide protection or privacy.

sidewise [sīd′wīz′] *adv.* toward one side; sideways.

sidle [sīd′əl] *v.* to move sideways, especially in a sneaky manner.

significant [sig nif′ i kənt] *adj.* expressing a meaning; full of meaning.

silhouette [sil′oo et′] *v.* to cause to appear as a dark image outlined against a lighter background.

simulate [sim′yə lāt′] *v.* to have or take on the appearance of; imitate.

simultaneous [sī′məl tā′ne əs, sim′əl tā′ne əs] *adj.* existing or happening at the same time. —**simultaneously,** *adv.*

sinister [sin′is tər] *adj.* threatening or suggesting evil.

situated [sich′oo ā′tid] *adj.* located.

skeptical [skep′ti kəl] *adj.* showing doubt or suspicion; questioning; disbelieving. —**skeptically,** *adv.*

skewer [skū′ər] *v.* to fasten or pierce with a long, pointed piece of wood or metal.

skirmish [skur′mish] *n.* **1.** minor conflict between small forces. **2.** any brief or minor conflict.

sleet [slēt] *n.* rain that is frozen or partially frozen.

slog [slog] *v.* to move slowly or with great effort.

sluggish [slug′ish] *adj.* lacking in energy or alertness.

smite [smīt] *v.* to strike hard.

smolder [smōl′dər] *v.* to burn and smoke with little or no flame.

smote [smōt] *v.* past tense of **smite.**

sodden [sod′ən] *adj.* filled with water; soaked through.

solace [sol′is] *n.* relief from sorrow or disappointment; comfort.

solitude [sol′ə tood′, sol′ə tūd′] *n.* the state or quality of being alone or remote from others.

soothing [soo′thing] *adj.* calming; quieting. —**soothingly,** *adv.*

sound [sound] *n.* long, narrow passage of water between larger bodies of water or between the mainland and an island.

souvenir [soo′və nēr′, soo′və nēr′] *n.* thing serving as a reminder of a person, place, or event.

sow [sō] *v.* to spread or scatter (seed) over the ground for growth.

spacious [spā′shəs] *adj.* great in size or extent; not limited.

span [span] *v.* to extend over or across.

sparse [spärs] *adj.* thinly spread; not crowded.

speculation [spek′yə lā′shən] *n.* act of thinking casually and coming to a guess.

spew [spū] *v.* to cast up, throw out, or eject.

spire [spīr] *n.* tall, pointed structure on the top of a tower.

spirit [spir′it] *v.* to carry off secretly or quickly.

spiritual [spir′i choo əl] *adj.* relating to the moral or religious aspect of a person.

splay [splā] **1.** *adj.* spread or spreading out. **2.** *v.* to spread out; extend.

spoils [spoilz] *n. pl.* goods or property taken by force, especially in a fight.

spokesman [spōks′mən] *n.* one who speaks for another or others.

sporadic [spə rad′ik] *adj.* scattered; occasional.

sprout [sprout] *v.* to begin to grow.

spurn [spurn] *v.* to reject with hate.

squad [skwod] *n.* small group of persons organized for a specific purpose.

stash [stash] *v.* INFORMAL. to store or hide for safekeeping or future use.

static [stat′ik] **1.** *n.* interference on electrical equipment that may be heard as crackling or hissing sounds. **2.** *adj.* showing no movement.

stature [statch′ər] *n.* height of a body, especially a person in a normal standing position.

stead [sted] *n.* place or position usually or previously occupied by another and filled by a replacement.

steed [stēd] *n.* horse, especially a high-spirited riding horse.

stifle [stī′fəl] *v.* to hold back or cut off; muffle.

stoat [stōt] *n.* weasel, whose fur is brown in the summer and white with a black-tipped tail in the winter.

stoical [stō′i kəl] *adj.* unaffected by pain or pleasure.

stout [stout] *adj.* **1.** brave; courageous. **2.** physically strong.

stout-hearted [stout′här′tid] *adj.* brave; courageous.

strapping [strap′ing] *adj.* strong and solidly built.

strenuous [stren′ū əs] *adj.* requiring great effort or energy.

strew [stroo] *v.* to throw about at random; scatter.

strife [strīf] *n.* disagreement; conflict; struggle.

strive [strīv] *v.* to try hard; make an effort.

stymie [stī′mē] *v.* to bring to or keep at a standstill; block.

subconscious [sub kon′shəs, sub kon′chəs] *adj.* that exists in a person's mind but that the person is not aware of.

subordinate [sə bôr′də nit] *adj.* having less importance; minor.

subscription [səb skrip′shən] *n.* right to receive a newspaper, magazine, or similar material for a certain period of time in return for a set payment.

subside [səb sīd′] *v.* to decrease in volume or activity.

substantial [səb stan′shəl] *adj.* great or large in amount.

subtle [sut′əl] *adj.* having a faint, delicate quality, so as to be nearly not noticed. —**subtlety,** *n.*

suburb [sub′urb] *n.* area close to or on the outer edges of a city.

---

at; āpe; cär; end; mē; it; īce; hot; ōld; fôrk; wood; fool; oil; out; up; ūse; turn; ə in ago, taken, pencil, lemon, circus; bat; chin; dear; five; game; hit; hw in white; joke; kit; lid; man; not; singer; pail; ride; sat; shoe; tag; thin; this; very; wet; yes; zoo; zh in treasure; KH in loch, German ach; N in French bon; œ in French feu, German schön

succession [sək sesh′ən] *n.* group of people or things following one after another in time or place; sequence.

sufficient [sə fish′ənt] *adj.* as much as is needed; enough. —**sufficiently,** *adv.*

suitor [sōō′tər] *n.* a man who seeks the love and affection of a woman, with the intent to marry.

sullen [sul′ən] *adj.* **1.** gloomy; saddening. **2.** withdrawn; sulky. —**sullenly,** *adv.*

summary [sum′ər ē] *n.* brief statement containing the main points.

summit [sum′it] *adj.* at the highest level, especially involving official leaders or heads of government.

superficial [sōō′pər fish′əl] *adj.* lacking depth or thoroughness; shallow.

superintend [sōō′prin tend′, sōō′pər in tend′] *v.* to direct or control the work or operation of.

supple [sup′əl] *adj.* able to move quickly and lightly.

surmount [sər mount′] *v.* to climb up or get over physically.

surplus [sur′plus′, sur′pləs] *n.* amount or quantity over and above what is used or needed; excess.

symmetry [sim′ə trē] *n.* properly proportioned shape, structure, or arrangement of parts; beauty or harmony of form.

sympathetic [sim′pə thet′ik] *adj.* marked by understanding and sharing of the feelings of another.

T

tactile [tak′til, tak′tīl] *adj.* relating to touch.

tantalize [tant′əl īz′] *v.* to tempt by seeming to promise something that is withdrawn or is impossible to get; tease.

tarantula [tə ran′chə lə] *n.* hairy spider found mainly in tropical and semitropical areas.

taunt [tônt, tänt] *v.* to tease with insults.

taut [tôt] *adj.* tightly stretched; not loose.

tavern [tav′ərn] *n.* public place providing food, drink, and lodging, especially for travelers.

tawny [tô′nē] *adj.* brownish-yellow color.

tedious [tē′dē əs, tē′jəs] *adj.* long and tiring; boring.

teem [tēm] *v.* to be at or as if at the point of overflowing; pour out.

telepathy [tə lep′ə thē] *n.* communication of one mind with another mind by means other than ordinary speaking, writing, or gesturing. —**telepathic** [tel′ə path′ik] *adj.*

tenement [ten′ə mənt] *n.* a building that is divided into rooms or sets of rooms and occupied by separate tenants.

terminal [tur′mə nəl] *adj.* relating to or in the final state of a deadly disease.

terrain [tə rān′, te rān′] *n.* region or area of land, especially with regard to its natural features.

terrier [ter′ē ər] *n.* a lively, rugged, usually small dog with a coat that ranges from smooth and short to wiry and fairly long.

testimony [tes′tə mō′nē] *n.* formal statement of something that happened, especially by a witness.

tether [teth′ər] **1.** *n.* rope, chain, or other material used to fasten an animal so that it is confined within certain limits. **2.** *v.* to fasten an animal with a rope, chain, or other material so that it is confined within certain limits.

theoretical [thē′ə ret′i kəl] *adj.* not based on fact or experience; derived from an unproved idea. —**theoretically** [thē′ə ret′i klē] *adv.*

thicket [thik′it] *n.* a growth of small trees or shrubs that are closely packed together.

thong [thông, thong] *n.* narrow strip of leather used to fasten or hold something.

threadbare [thred′bār′] *adj.* worn; shabby.

threshold [thresh′old, thresh′hōld′] *n.* entrance.

throng [thrông, throng] *n.* large number of things crowded together.

tipi [tē′pē′] *n.* cone-shaped tent, usually made of animal skins, used by North American Indians.

toil [toil] *n.* very hard work or effort.

token [tō′kən] *n.* sign; symbol.

tolerance [tol′ər əns] *n.* the power or ability to endure or put up with.

tolerant [tol′ər ənt] *adj.* able or inclined to endure or put up with.

toll [tol] *n.* total damage that has been done.

tortilla [tôr tē′yə] *n.* thin, round, unleavened bread made from water and cornmeal and baked on a griddle.

toxic [tok′sik] *adj.* poisonous.

tract [trakt] *n.* continuous area of land.

traitor [trā′tər] *n.* **1.** person who betrays one's country. **2.** one who betrays any trust or is unfaithful.

trance [trans] *n.* dazed or stunned state; stupor.

transfix [trans fiks′] *v.* **1.** to pierce through with or as if with a sharpened instrument. **2.** to make motionless, as from awe.

transform [trans fôrm′] *v.* to change or alter in shape, form, condition, or appearance. —**transformation** [trans′fər mā′shən] *n.*

transfusion [trans fū′zhən] *n.* the act of transferring a fluid (especially blood) into the body of an individual from a container or another individual.

treacherous [trech′ər əs] *adj.* not to be trusted; not faithful; disloyal.

treachery [trech′ər ē] *n.* willful betrayal.

treason [trē′zən] *n.* betrayal of one's country or any trust.

treaty [trē′tē] *n.* formal agreement, especially between nations, signed and approved by each party.

tremulous [trem′yə ləs] *adj.* shaking; trembling.

trench [trench] *n.* long, narrow ditch.

trifle [trī′fəl] *n.* **1.** something of little or no value or importance. **2.** small amount; bit.

trivial [triv′ē əl] *adj.* having little or no importance.

trough [trôf] *n.* long, deep, narrow container, used especially to hold water.

tundra [tun′drə, toon′drə] *n.* very large, treeless plain in the arctic regions, having a layer of permanently frozen soil several layers beneath the surface.

turf [turf] *n.* grassy area.

typhoid [tī′foid] *n.* infectious, sometimes fatal fever.

U

unconscious [un kon′shəs, un kon′chəs] *adj.* **1.** not physically or mentally awake for a period of time. **2.** not deliberately realized, done, or planned; not intentional. —**unconsciously,** *adv.*

uncordial [un kôr′jəl] *adj.* not friendly. —**uncordially,** *adv.*

undaunted [un dôn′tid, un dän′tid] *adj.* not frightened; fearless; very brave.

undisputed [un dis pūt′id] *adj.* not challenged or questioned.

uneasy [un ē′zē] *adj.* lacking comfort or ease of mind; disturbed; worried. —**unease,** *n.*

unobtrusive [un′əb trōō′siv] *adj.* that does not cause notice or disturbance; not easily seen. —**unobtrusively,** *adv.*

unpretentious [un′pri ten′shəs] *adj.* not showy; simple.

unseemly [un sēm′lē] *adj.* not proper.

upholstery [up hōl′stər ē, up hōl′strē] *n.* material used in fitting (furniture) for coverings, padding, etc.

V

vacate [vā′kāt] *v.* to leave empty.

vague [vāg] *adj.* **1.** not exact or clear. **2.** hazy; dim.

valiant [val′yənt] *adj.* brave; courageous. —**valiantly,** *adv.*

vantage [van′tij] *n.* position or situation that gives one a clear and full view or understanding.

vapor [vā′pər] *n.* visible or cloudy matter floating in the air, as mist or smoke.

vault [vôlt] *n.* compartment or room used as a cellar or storeroom.

veer [vēr] *v.* to change the direction or course of; shift; turn.

vendor [ven′dər] *n.* one who sells goods or merchandise.

venison [ven′ə sən, ven′ə zən] *n.* flesh of a deer, used for food.

venom [ven′əm] *n.* poisonous substance of some animals that is usually put into the body of a victim by a bite or sting.

venture [ven′chər] **1.** *n.* attempt to do something, especially involving risk or danger. **2.** *v.* to express or say something at the risk of criticism, objection, or the like.

veranda [və ran′da] *n.* open porch, usually with a roof.

verdict [vur′dikt] *n.* decision; conclusion; judgment.

verge [vurj] *n.* edge or margin of something; brink.

vertical [vur′ti kəl] *adj.* upright; straight up and down.

vestige [ves′tij] *n.* trace or sign of something that once existed but no longer exists.

veteran [vet′ər ən, vet′rən] *n.* one who has had a great deal of service or experience, as in an occupation, office, or position.

vineyard [vin′yərd] *n.* area used to grow grapes.

virtually [vur′chōō ə lē] *adv.* practically; in effect.

virulent [vir′yə lənt, vir′ə lənt] *adj.* very poisonous or harmful.

vista [vis′tə] *n.* overall mental view of a series of events.

vulnerable [vul′nər ə bəl] *adj.* able to be physically wounded or hurt.

W

wad [wod] *n.* small, compact lump of any soft material.

waft [waft, wäft] *v.* to carry or float lightly and gently through the air or over water.

wager [wā′jər] *v.* to pledge or risk (money or some other set thing) in a bet.

warbler [wôr′blər] *n.* a small songbird often having brightly colored feathers with red, blue, or yellow markings.

warrant [wôr′ənt, wor′ənt] *v.* to provide proper grounds or reasons for; justify.

warren [wôr′ən, wor′ən] *n.* a place or limited area in which rabbits live and breed.

wary [wār′ē] *adj.* always on the alert; watchful; careful. —**warily** [wār′ə lē] *adv.*

waver [wā′vər] *v.* to move unsteadily from side to side; sway.

wean [wēn] *v.* to get (a child or young animal) used to food other than the mother's milk.

welfare [wel′fār′] *n.* aid or help given to those in need.

wharf [hwôrf, wôrf] *n.* structure built along a shore where boats can be tied up and passengers and cargo are loaded and unloaded; dock.

wheedle [hwēd′əl, wēd′əl] *v.* to persuade by flattery or nice words.

whet [hwet, wet] *v.* to make sensitive; stimulate.

winsome [win′səm] *adj.* attractive or pleasing; charming.

wiry [wīr′ē] *adj.* lean and strong.

wisp [wisp] *n.* small or slight bit.

wither [with′ər] *v.* to dry up or shrivel, as from heat or loss of moisture.

wrangler [rang′glər] *n.* in the western United States, one who herds or tends horses or other livestock; cowboy.

wreathe [rēth] *v.* to cover completely.

wreckage [rek′ij] *n.* the remains of something that has been damaged or destroyed.

wrench [rench] **1.** *n.* a tool having fixed or movable jaws, used for gripping and turning a nut, bolt, or pipe. **2.** *v.* to injure or strain by twisting or turning suddenly or violently.

wretched [rech′id] *adj.* very unhappy; deeply distressed. —**wretchedly,** *adv.*

writhe [rīth] *v.* to twist; turn; squirm.

wrought [rôt] *v.* past tense of **work,** to create.

wry [rī] *adj.* humorous in an unusual or unexpected way. —**wryly,** *adv.*

Y

yam [yam] *n.* sweet potato.

yearling [yēr′ling] *n.* animal that is one year old or in its second year.

yield [yēld] *v.* **1.** to produce or give forth by a natural process. **2.** to give up to a superior power; surrender.

---

at; āpe; cär; end; mē; it; īce; hot; ōld; fôrk; wood; fōōl; oil; out; up; ūse; turn; ə in ago, taken, pencil, lemon, circus; bat; chin; dear; five; game; hit; hw in white; joke; kit; lid; man; not; singer; pail; ride; sat; shoe; tag; thin; this; very; wet; yes; zoo; zh in treasure; ᴋʜ in loch, German ach; ɴ in French bon; œ in French feu, German schön

INDEX OF TITLES BY GENRE

INDEX OF SKILLS

Page numbers in boldface italics indicate entries in the Writing About Literature Handbook. Page numbers in italics indicate entries in the Handbook of Reading and Literary Terms.

continued from page iv

Farrar, Straus & Giroux, Inc.
ROALD DAHL: "The Green Mamba" from *Going Solo*. Copyright © 1986 by Roald Dahl.
ELIZABETH BORTON DE TREVINO: Excerpt from *El Güero*. Copyright © by Elizabeth Borton de Trevino.
ISAAC BASHEVIS SINGER: "The Fools of Chelm and the Stupid Carp" from *Naftali the Storyteller and His Horse, Sus and Other Stories*. Copyright © 1976 by Isaac Bashevis Singer.
All are reprinted by permission of Farrar, Straus & Giroux, Inc.

Estate of Charles G. Finney
CHARLES G. FINNEY: "The Life and Death of a Western Gladiator" is reprinted by permission of the Estate of Charles G. Finney.

Angel Flores
ANGEL FLORES: "The Stub-Book" from *Spanish Stories, Cuentos Españoles*. Edited by Angel Flores, copyright owner, Palenville, N.Y. 12463. Reprinted by permission of Angel Flores.

Samuel French, Inc.
SUSAN NANUS AND NORTON JUSTER: *The Phantom Tollbooth*. Copyright © 1977 by Susan Nanus and Norton Juster. Reprinted by permission of Samuel French, Inc. *Caution:* Professionals and amateurs are hereby warned that *The Phantom Tollbooth*, being fully protected under the copyright laws of the United States of America, the British Commonwealth countries, including Canada, and the other countries of the Copyright Union, is subject to a royalty. All rights, including professional, amateur, motion picture, recitation, public reading, radio, television and cablevision broadcasting, and the rights of translation into foreign languages, are strictly reserved. Amateurs may produce this play upon payment of a royalty of $35.00 for the first performance and $25.00 for each additional performance, payable one week before the play is to be given, to Samuel French, Inc. at 45 West 25th Street, New York, N.Y. 10036, or at 7623 Sunset Blvd., Hollywood, Calif. 90046, or if in Canada, to Samuel French (Canada) Ltd., 80 Richmond Street East, Toronto M5C 1P1.

Herbert Goldstone
HERBERT GOLDSTONE: "Virtuoso" from *The Magazine of Fantasy and Science Fiction*. © 1953 by Mercury Press, Inc. © renewed 1980. Reprinted by permission of the publisher and the author.

Harcourt Brace Jovanovich, Inc.
ITALO CALVINO: "Bellinda and the Monster" from *Italian Folktales*. Copyright © 1956 by Giulio Einaudi editore, s.p.a., English translation copyright © 1980 by Harcourt Brace Jovanovich, Inc.
T. S. ELIOT: "Macavity: The Mystery Cat" from *Old Possum's Book of Practical Cats*. Copyright 1939 by T. S. Eliot and renewed 1967 by Valerie Eliot.
CARL SANDBURG: "Arithmetic" from *The Complete Poems of Carl Sandburg*. Copyright 1950 and renewed 1978 by Carl Sandburg.
All are reprinted by permission of Harcourt Brace Jovanovich, Inc.

Harper & Row, Publishers, Inc.
M. E. KERR: "Where Are You Now, William Shakespeare?" from *Me Me Me Me Me*. Copyright © 1983 by M. E. Kerr.
SHEL SILVERSTEIN: "Sarah Cynthia Sylvia Stout Would Not Take the Garbage Out" from *Where the Sidewalk Ends* by Shel Silverstein. Copyright © 1974 by Evil Eye Music, Inc. Both are reprinted by permission of Harper & Row, Publishers, Inc.

Henry Sydnor Harrison
HENRY SYDNOR HARRISON: "Miss Hinch."

Gerald Haslam
GERALD HASLAM: "The Horned Toad." Copyright © 1983 by Gerald Haslam. Reprinted by permission of the author.

John Hawkins & Associates, Inc.
MARY O'HARA: "My Friend Flicka" was originally published in *Story Magazine*. Copyright © 1941 by Mary O'Hara. Reprinted by permission of John Hawkins & Associates, Inc.

William Heinemann Ltd. Publishers
CHINUA ACHEBE: "Why the Tortoise's Shell Is Not Smooth" from *Things Fall Apart*. Reprinted by permission of the publishers.

Henry Holt and Company, Inc.
ROBERT FROST: "The Exposed Nest" from *The Poetry of Robert Frost* edited by Edward Connery Lathem. Copyright 1916, © 1969 by Holt, Rinehart and Winston, copyright 1944 by Robert Frost. Reprinted by permission of Henry Holt and Company, Inc.

Houghton Mifflin Company
RUSSELL FREEDMAN: Excerpts from *Cowboys of the Wild West*. Copyright © 1985 by Russell Freedman.
JANE VAN LAWICK-GOODALL: "The Chimps Come to Camp" from *In the Shadow of Man*. Copyright © 1971 by Hugo and Jane van Lawick-Goodall.
REED WHITTEMORE: "Science Fiction" from *The Mother's Breast and the Father's House*. Copyright © 1974 by Reed Whittemore.
All are reprinted by permission of Houghton Mifflin Company.

Francisco Jiménez
FRANCISCO JIMÉNEZ: "The Circuit" from *The Arizona Quarterly*, Autumn 1973. Reprinted by permission of the author.

Dan Lacy
DAN LACY: "The Lost Colony" from *The Colony of North Carolina*. Copyright © 1975 by Franklin Watts, Inc. Reprinted by permission of the author.

Lescher & Lescher, Ltd.
JUDITH VIORST: "The Southpaw" from *Free to Be . . . You and Me*. Copyright © 1974 by Judith Viorst. Reprinted by permission of Lescher & Lescher, Ltd.

Sterling Lord Literistic, Inc.
AMIRI BARAKA: "Song Form" from *Black Magic: 1961–1967*. Copyright © 1969 by Amiri Baraka. Reprinted by permission of Sterling Lord Literistic, Inc.

Macmillan Publishing Company
RICHARD ADAMS: Excerpt from *Watership Down*. Copyright © 1972 by Richard Adams.
RICHARD BACH: Excerpt from *Jonathan Livingston Seagull*. Copyright © 1970 by Richard D. Bach and Leslie Parrish-Bach.
Both are reprinted by permission of Macmillan Publishing Company.
MARGARET EVANS PRICE: "Pegasus and Bellerophon" from *Myths and Enchantment Tales*. Copyright © 1960 by Rand McNally & Company. Reprinted by permission of Checkerboard Press, a Division of Macmillan, Inc.
CYNTHIA RYLANT: "Papa's Parrot" from *Every Living Thing*. Copyright © 1985 by Cynthia Rylant. Reprinted by permission of Bradbury Press, an Affiliate of Macmillan, Inc.

Minnesota Historical Society Press
LOIS PHILLIPS HUDSON: "The Cold Wave" from *Reapers of the Dust* (reprint edition, St. Paul: Minnesota Historical Society Press, 1984). Reprinted with permission.

New Directions Publishing Corporation
FEDERICO GARCÍA LORCA: "Conch Shell" from *The Cricket Sings.* Copyright © 1980 by the Estate of Federico García Lorca and Will Kirkland. Reprinted by permission of New Directions Publishing Corporation.

New Yorker Magazine
DIANE ACKERMAN: "Bats" is excerpted from "Bats," which appeared in *The New Yorker,* February 28, 1988. Reprinted by permission of the author.

Robert Nye
ROBERT NYE: "Beowulf" from *Beowulf: A New Telling.* Copyright © 1968 by Robert Nye. Reprinted by permission of the author.

Harold Ober Associates Incorporated
JAMES HERRIOT: "The Christmas Cat" from *All Things Wise and Wonderful.* Copyright © 1976, 1977 by James Herriot.
RUSSELL HOBAN: "Jigsaw Puzzle" from *Allsorts 3.* Copyright © 1970 by Russell Hoban.
LANGSTON HUGHES: "Juke Box Love Song" from *Selected Poems.* Copyright 1951 by Langston Hughes. Copyright renewed 1979 by George Houston Bass.
All are reprinted by permission of Harold Ober Associates Incorporated.

Murray Pollinger Ltd.
ROALD DAHL: "The Green Mamba" from *Going Solo.* Copyright © 1986 by Roald Dahl. Reprinted by permission of Murray Pollinger Ltd.

The Putnam Publishing Group
JEAN FRITZ: Chapter 1 from *Homesick* by Jean Fritz. Text copyright © 1982 by Jean Fritz. Reprinted by permission of G. P. Putnam's Sons.

Random House, Inc.
MAYA ANGELOU: "Life Doesn't Frighten Me" from *And Still I Rise.* Copyright © 1978 by Maya Angelou.
ROBERT CORMIER: "President Cleveland, Where Are You?" from *Eight Plus One.* Copyright © 1980 by Robert Cormier. Reprinted by permission of Pantheon, a Division of Random House, Inc.
ROALD DAHL: "The Landlady" from *Kiss Kiss.* Copyright © 1959 by Roald Dahl. Reprinted by permission of Alfred A. Knopf, Inc.
LANGSTON HUGHES: "April Rain Song" from *The Dream Keeper and Other Poems.* Copyright 1932 by Alfred A. Knopf, Inc. and renewed 1960 by Langston Hughes. Reprinted by permission of Alfred A. Knopf, Inc.
ROBERT NEWTON PECK: Excerpt from *A Path of Hunters.* Copyright © 1973 by Robert Newton Peck. Reprinted by permission of Alfred A. Knopf, Inc.
JOHN UPDIKE: "January" and "September" from *A Child's Calendar.* Copyright © 1965 by John Updike. Reprinted by permission of Alfred A. Knopf, Inc.
Maya Angelou selection is reprinted by permission of Random House, Inc.

Marian Reiner
EVE MERRIAM: "How to Eat a Poem" from *A Sky Full of Poems* by Eve Merriam. Copyright © 1964, 1970, 1973 by Eve Merriam. All Rights Reserved. Reprinted by permission of Marian Reiner for the author.

The Richmond Organization
JOHN A. LOMAX AND ALAN LOMAX: Excerpt from *I Am Fur from My Sweetheart* collected, adapted and arranged by John A. Lomax and Alan Lomax. TRO-© Copyright 1938 (renewed) Ludlow Music, Inc., New York, N.Y. Used by permission.

St. Martin's Press
JAMES HERRIOT: "The Christmas Cat" from *All Things Wise and Wonderful.* Copyright © 1976, 1977 by James Herriot. Reprinted by permission of St. Martin's Press.

William Saroyan Foundation
WILLIAM SAROYAN: *The Rescue of the Perishing.* Copyright by the William Saroyan Foundation and used with their permission.

Scholastic Inc.
JIM MURPHY: *The Last Dinosaur.* Text Copyright © 1988 by Jim Murphy.
MARY WHITEBIRD: "Ta-Na-E-Ka" from *Voice,* December 1973. Copyright © Scholastic Inc.
Both are reprinted by permission of Scholastic Inc.

Marjorie Weinman Sharmat
MARJORIE WEINMAN SHARMAT: *May I Have Your Autograph?* Copyright © 1984 by Marjorie Sharmat. Used by permission of the author.

Simon and Schuster
LEO TOLSTOY: "The Jump" from *Twenty-two Russian Tales for Young Children.* Selected and translated by Miriam Morton. © 1969.
Used by permission of the publisher, Simon and Schuster, New York, New York 10020.

Virginia Driving Hawk Sneve
VIRGINIA DRIVING HAWK SNEVE: "The Medicine Bag" from *Boy's Life,* March 1975. Reprinted by permission of Virginia Driving Hawk Sneve.

The Society of Authors
WALTER DE LA MARE: "Summer Evening" is used by permission of The Literary Trustees of Walter de la Mare and The Society of Authors as their representative.

The Estate of May Swenson
MAY SWENSON: "Southbound on the Freeway" from *To Mix with Time.* Copyright © 1963 by May Swenson. This appeared originally in *The New Yorker,* February 16, 1963. Reprinted by permission.

Third Woman Press
SANDRA CISNEROS: "Twister Hits Houston" from *My Wicked, Wicked Ways.* Copyright © 1987. Published by Third Woman Press and reprinted with their permission.

Yoshiko Uchida
YOSHIKO UCHIDA: "The Wise Old Woman" from *The Sea of Gold and Other Tales from Japan.* © 1965 by Yoshiko Uchida. Reprinted by permission of the author.

Viking Penguin Inc.
PURA BELPRÉ: "The Stone Dog" from *Once in Puerto Rico.* Copyright © 1983 by Pura Belpré. Published by Warne.
DORIS GATES: "Pygmalion" from *Two Queens of Heaven.* Copyright © 1974 by Doris Gates.
WALTER DEAN MYERS: "The Game" from *Fast Sam, Cool Clyde, and Stuff.* Copyright © by Walter Dean Myers.
All are reprinted by Viking Penguin Inc. a division of Penguin USA.

George Weidenfeld & Nicolson Limited
JANE VAN LAWICK-GOODALL: "The Chimps Come to Camp" from *In the Shadow of Man.* Published by George Weidenfeld & Nicolson Limited and used with their permission.

CREDITS

Illustrations

Hunt, Robert, 338–339.
Preston, Heather, xii, 54, 521, 531, 536, 541, 549, 560, 567, 579, 583, 591, 603.
Taber, Ed, 133, 135, 141, 145, 147, 157, 163, 170.

Paintings, Photographs, Prints, Drawings, Sculpture

ADDISON GALLERY OF AMERICAN ART, Phillips Academy, Andover, Massachusetts, Gift of Edward W. Root, **11; 451;** Gift of Stephen C. Clark, **497;** Gift of Mrs. Frederic Durand, **551, 559.**
Anonymous, Greek Bronze, **183.**
ALBERTINA, Graphische Sammlung, Vienna/Bridgeman Art Library, London, **87, 101.**
ALBRIGHT-KNOX ART GALLERY, Buffalo, New York; Room of Contemporary Art Fund, 1940, 70–71; Gift of Seymour H. Knox, 1959, **400;** Albert H. Tracy Fund, 1900, **571.**
ALLEN MEMORIAL ART MUSEUM, Oberlin College, Oberlin, Ohio, Gift of Charles F. Olney, 1904, **545.**
AMON CARTER MUSEUM, Fort Worth, Texas, **285.**
ANSCHUTZ COLLECTION, The, Courtesy of, **287.**
AP/WIDE WORLD PHOTOS, **353, 498.**
ART INSTITUTE OF CHICAGO, The, © 1990, Friends of American Art Collection, 1942.51, **59;** © 1990; Restricted gift of Charles C. Haffner II, 1987.169, **375;** © 1988, Joseph Winterbotham Collection, 1959.1, **359,** All Rights Reserved.
ARTE PUBLICO PRESS, Courtesy of University of Houston, **296.**
ASHMOLEAN MUSEUM, Oxford, **93.**
Aurness, Craig ©/WEST LIGHT, **461.**
Azel, Jose ©/WOODFIN CAMP, **vi, 109** (bottom).

BBC Broadcasting House ©, London, **207, 401.**
Beebe, Morton/THE IMAGE BANK WEST, **356.**
BETTMANN ARCHIVES, **245, 276, 294, 299, 310, 327, 374, 397, 398, 399, 468, 483** (middle).
Boltin, Lee/LEE BOLTIN PHOTOGRAPHY, **187.**
Blank, Alan/BRUCE COLEMAN, INC., **443.**
Boehm, Christopher/NORTHERN KENTUCKY UNIVERSITY, **425, 427, 429, 431.**
Brandenburg, Jim/BRUCE COLEMAN, INC., **211.**
Breese, Penelope, **423.**
BRIGHAM YOUNG UNIVERSITY MUSEUM OF FINE ARTS, Courtesy of, **75.**
BRITISH MUSEUM/Michael Holford, **49.**
Bruchac, Carol, **267.**
BUFFALO BILL HISTORICAL CENTER, Cody, Wyoming, **77.**
Burri, Rene ©/MAGNUM PHOTOS, INC., **501.**

Cabrera, Elba, **237.**
CARNEGIE MUSEUM OF ART, The, Pittsburgh, Patrons Art Fund, 1954, **13.**
Cavagnaro, David/DAVID CAVAGNARO PHOTOGRAPHY, **267.**
CHASE MANHATTAN BANK COLLECTION, The, **291.**
CINCINNATI ART MUSEUM, Gift of Emilie L. Heine in memory of Mr. and Mrs. John Hauck, **563.**
Cleary, Manon, in the artist's collection, **311, 312.**
CLEVELAND MUSEUM OF ART, The, The Charles W. Harkness Gift, 27.388, **575.**
CORCORAN GALLERY OF ART, The, In the Collection of; William A. Clark Collection, **601.**

DALLAS MUSEUM OF ART, Bequest of Joel T. Howard, **529.**
Davey, Peter, BRUCE COLEMAN, INC., **79.**
Degginger, Edward R./BRUCE COLEMAN, INC., **34, 334.**
DETROIT INSTITUTE OF ARTS, The, Bequest of Robert H. Tannahill, **31;** Founders Society Purchase with funds from the Gerald W. Chamberlin Foundation, Inc., Mr. and Mrs. Charles M. Endicott, Mrs. Howard P. Stoddard, and Mr. and Mrs. Stanford C. Stoddard, **193;** Gift of Dr. D. T. Burton, Dr.

M. E. Fowler, Dr. J. B. Greene, and Mr. J. J. White, **295;** Founders Society Purchase, General membership and Donations Fund, **x, 393.**
Dunne, Robert L./BRUCE COLEMAN, INC., **33.**

Elani, John/HOLIDAY HOUSE, INC., **284.**

FARRAR, STRAUSS & GIROUX, **73.**
FINE ART PHOTOGRAPHIC LIBRARY LIMITED, **17, 37;** Courtesy of Marble Hill Gallery, **39.**
Fischer, Curt/CURT FISCHER PHOTOGRAPHY, **477.**
Fusco, Paul ©/MAGNUM PHOTOS, INC., **363.**

GEORGIA O'KEEFFE ESTATE, Courtesy of, **4, 297.**
GUGGENHEIM MUSEUM, Solomon R., Collection, New York, **199.**
Guzmán, Rubén, **334.**

Haas, C. Ernst/ERNST HAAS PHOTOGRAPHY, **257, 469.**
HARPER & ROW PUBLISHERS, CO., **358.**
HARVARD UNIVERSITY ART MUSEUMS, Courtesy of the Fogg Art Museum, HARVARD UNIVERSITY, Cambridge, Massachusetts, Bequest of Grenville L. Winthrop, **236.**
Harvey, David Alan ©/WOODFIN CAMP, **225, 383.**
Hirst-Smith, Peter/© PUFFIN BOOKS, **81.**
Holford, Michael, **viii, 317, 319.**
HONOLULU ACADEMY OF ARTS, The James A. Michener Collection, **242–243.**
Hrynewych, Bohdan/STOCK, BOSTON, **239.**

IBM CORPORATION Collection, Armonk, New York, **487.**

KENNEDY GALLERIES, Inc., New York; Photograph courtesy of, private collection, **273;** Courtesy of, **516–517.**
Krementz, Jill, © 1990, **3, 113, 196, 226, 290, 391, 396, 458, 471, 483** (top), **489, 518.**

Lessing, Eric/MAGNUM PHOTOS, **231.**
LIBRARY OF CONGRESS, **117, 329, 331.**
Long, Stephen, **186.**

MACMILLAN PUBLISHING CO., **454.**
MARTIN, Joseph/Scala/Art Resource, **303.**
MARY EVANS PICTURE LIBRARY, London, **121, 483.**
MAS, Barcelona, **33.**
Matsumura, Glenn/SANTA CLARA UNIVERSITY, Courtesy of, **360.**
McGoon, James F., **415.**
McKenna, Rollie, **52, 421.**
Menzel, Peter ©/PETER MENZEL PHOTOGRAPHY, **411.**
METROPOLITAN MUSEUM OF ART, The, Arthur H. Hearn Fund, 1958, **24;** Huntley Bequest, 1958–1959 (58.11.6a–d), **183.**
Migdale, Lawrence ©/STOCK, BOSTON, **482.**
Morrill, Dan/© DAN MORRILL PHOTOGRAPHY, **43, 179, 263, 379.**
MUSEE CLUNY, Paris, Scala/Art Resource, **174–175.**
MUSEUM OF FINE ARTS, BOSTON, The, Bequest of Martha C. Karolik for the Karolik Collection of American Paintings, 1815–1865, 1948, **403;** Juliana Cheney Edwards Collection, **486;** Charles Henry Hayden Fund, **587.**
MUSEUM OF MODERN ART, The, New York, Collection; Acquired through the Lillie P. Bliss Bequest, **xiv–1, 200.**
MUSKEGON MUSEUM OF ART, Courtesy of, Muskegon, Michigan, **324–325.**

NATIONAL GALLERY OF ART, Washington, D.C.; Gift of Helen Farr Sloan, **61;** Widener Collection, **229;** Andrew W. Mellon Collection, **233;** Gift of the Morris and Gwendolyn Cafritz Foundation, **388–389;** Courtesy Gwynne Garbisch McDevitt. Gift of Edgar William and Bernice Chrysler Garbisch, **xi, 452;** Gift of the Avalon Foundation, **484;** Gift of Mr. and Mrs. Irwin Strasburger, **438–439.**
Nees, John ©/ANIMALS ANIMALS, **369.**
NORTH CAROLINA MUSEUM OF ART, Raleigh, North Carolina, Purchased with funds from the State of North Carolina, **465.**

OLDHAM ART GALLERY, Lancashire/The Bridgeman Art Library, **41.**

ORANGERIE, Paris, Giraudon/Art Resource, **235.**

PENGUIN BOOKS ©, **234.**
Place, Charles C./IMAGE BANK, **298.**
PUFFIN BOOKS ©, **15, 35, 366.**

RANDOM HOUSE, INC. **344, 448.**
Rawlings, Walter/ROBERT HARDING ASSOCIATES, London, England, **503.**
REYNOLDA HOUSE, Museum of American Art, Winston-Salem, North Carolina, **525.**
ROCKWELL, Mr. and Mrs. Thomas, In the collection of, **ix, 351.**
Rogers, Martin ©/WOODFIN CAMP, **247.**
Ross, Bill ©/WOODFIN CAMP, **111.**
Running, John ©/STOCK, BOSTON, **357,** JOHN RUNNING PHOTOGRAPHY, **509.**
Sapieha, Nicholas/STOCK, BOSTON, **481.**
SCHMED III, Courtesy of Mr. and Mrs. Paul, Boston, Massachusetts, **555.**
SCHOLASTIC, INC., **344, 478.**
Silbert, Layle, **31, 111, 496.**
Snow, Mary, **377.**
SONOMA STATE UNIVERSITY, Courtesy of, **506.**
Soto, Carolyn, **464.**
STARY-SHEETS FINE ART GALLERIES, Irvine, California, **491, 494.**
STEDELIJK MUSEUM, Amsterdam, **127.**
Stock, Dennis ©/MAGNUM PHOTOS, INC., **105, 457.**
Storms, Deborah/MACMILLAN PUBLICATION CO., **190.**
Strode, William ©/WOODFIN CAMP, **27.**
Sund, Harald/MAGNUM PHOTOS, INC., **282,** HARALD SUND PHOTOGRAPHY, **470.**

TATE GALLERY, London/Art Resource, New York, **vii, 203.**
TOLEDO MUSEUM OF ART, The, Toledo, Ohio, Museum Purchase Fund, **307;** Gift of Florence Scott Libbey, **485;** Gift of Edward Drummond Libbey, **533.**
TOP AGENCE PHOTOGRAPHIQUE, **249.**
Tuttle, Merlin D. ©/BAT CONSERVATION INTERNATIONAL, **417, 419, 421, 422.**

UNIVERSITY OF NEW MEXICO PRESS, Courtesy of, **356.**

WESTMORELAND MUSEUM OF ART, Collection of, Director's Discretionary Fund, Greensburg, Pennsylvania, 80.33, **597, 606.**
WHITNEY MUSEUM OF AMERICAN ART, Collection of; Gift of Gertrude Vanderbilt Whitney, 31.691, **63;** Josephine N. Hopper Bequest, 70.1114, **110;** Purchase, with funds from Gertrude Vanderbilt Whitney, 31.426, **455.**
WICHITA ART MUSEUM, Wichita, Kansas, Courtesy of; The Roland P. Murdock Collection, **279.**
Winburn, Jr., Jay Te, **25.**
Wolinsky, Cary/STOCK, BOSTON, **381.**
Wood, Merrell/THE IMAGE BANK WEST, **29.**
Woolfitt, Adam ©/WOODFIN CAMP, **44.**
WORCESTER ART MUSEUM, Worcester, Massachusetts, **238.**
Wright, J./BRUCE COLEMAN, INC., **80.**

YALE UNIVERSITY ART GALLERY, Whitney Collections of Sporting Art Fund, given in memory of Harry Payne Whitney by Francis P. Garvan, **543.**
YORK CITY ART GALLERY/The Bridgeman Art Library, London, **21.**

Zahm, Gary R./BRUCE COLEMAN, INC., **335.**

INDEX OF FINE ART

INDEX OF AUTHORS AND TITLES

E. Dickinson   William Faulkner   Tom Wolfe

Gerard M. Hopkins S.J.   Mark Twain   Rudyard Kipling

Gwendolyn Brooks   Randall Jarrell   Joseph Conrad

Stephen Spender   R.M. Rilke   C Brontë   Virginia Woolf

John Keats   Arthur Conan Doyle   Sidney

Robert Burns   A Bradstreet   William Shakespeare

A Lincoln   Henry W. Longfellow

James Joyce   Fredk Douglass   W Blake   P.B. Shelley

Wallace Stevens   Phillis Wheatley

C Brontë   James   F Scott Fitzgerald